# FRENCH POP

## from Music Hall to Yé-Yé

## Gareth Jones

**MUSIC MENTOR BOOKS**

York, England

British Library Cataloguing-in-Publication Data
A catalogue record for this book is available from the British Library.

**ISBN-13: 978-1-7399667-0-6**

Published worldwide by Music Mentor Books *(Proprietor: G.R. Groom-White)*
69 Station Road, Upper Poppleton, York YO26 6PZ, North Yorkshire, England.
*Telephone:* +44 (0)1904 330308    *Email:* music.mentor@ntlworld.com

Cover by It's Great To Be Rich, York.

Printed and bound in Great Britain by Inc Dot Design & Print, York.

*For my father, who taught me that
good music could be found anywhere.*

# Author's Note and Acknowledgements

So why a book on French pop? I have been asked this question more times than I remember, and have never been able to give a satisfactory answer, although it was comforting to find a band of like-minded enthusiasts bonding together via the Internet, making me feel less alone in my fascination with what many consider to be a backwater of popular music. Contemporary interest is largely focused on the end of the French pop industry which looks to the UK and the US for its inspiration (the rock or *yé-yé* scene), and my original intention was to write a book focusing on those styles of music, with the sixties as the decade of choice. However, I soon realised that it would be both difficult and misleading to tell this story without reference to the traditional forms of French pop and *chanson* which competed with rock and *yé-yé* in the marketplace of the period. To take but one example: given his huge influence both on his contemporaries in France and on British and American songwriters, it seemed wrong to omit the great *chansonnier* Jacques Brel from the book altogether, yet to include him would necessitate giving some detail about the musical environment he inhabited – a completely different world from that populated by the leading *yé-yé* stars.

I therefore decided to widen the book's remit to take in developments within French music hall, the *chanson* and the easy listening market in addition to the pop market, and to go back in time to explore the roots of all that was to follow. As a result, the earliest chapters of the book stretch back to the dawn of the French recording industry, although the bulk of this volume concerns itself with the fifties and the early sixties, largely because of the growth in popularity of recorded music in this period, but also because the changes that took place in these (and later) years were far more rapid than the musical evolutions of the first half of the twentieth century.

I also faced the question as to whether to limit the book to French performers, which would again mean leaving out Jacques Brel (and thus leave a great hole in the heart of certain chapters), or whether to include performers from the other francophone countries. To ensure that the book accurately reflects what was happening in France during these years, I took the decision to include those performers from Belgium and Switzerland who either recorded in French or aimed their releases, at least in part, at a French audience. French Canada proved a more difficult question, but, as the Québécois music market operated pretty much independently of France, I took the decision to include only those artists who travelled to France for some or all of their careers, and those French performers who chose to relocate to Quebec. Similarly, foreign performers who released records in French are also excluded, with the exception of those who based themselves in France whilst doing so.

All of this meant that the book would either be too short to do the subject justice, or too long to function as a worthwhile project. The inevitable choice was to split it into several distinct entities, with this first volume covering the grand days of music hall, the birth pangs of the country's rock'n'roll industry and finally the initial *yé-yé* explosion; the second will cover the glorious golden age of *yé-yé*, while subsequent volumes will take the story on through progressive and hard rock, seventies' pop, modern *chanson*, glam rock, punk, new wave and disco. I draw the line somewhere in the early eighties, when the internationalisation of pop music made the French scene less distinctive and, to my ears at least, less interesting.

Throughout, I have opted for a narrative history that allows the tale to unfold as it did at the time, structuring the chapters so as to make it possible for readers to omit sections that fall outside their areas of interest. It is of necessity a history of *recorded* music, for, while many French music hall performers (particularly those who wrote their own *chansons*) had a tendency to perform new songs for months or years before they got around to recording them – which sometimes meant that other singers managed to get them onto the market first – it is mainly through records, CDs and mp3s that we can access the music today, and so it is recordings, rather than live performances, that have come to dominate this story.

My aim was to tell the history of French pop in the fifties, sixties and seventies: the good, the bad, the dull, the brilliant, the strange, the simple, the plain, the unremittingly tedious and the mind-shatteringly amazing, and to do so within a cultural and historical framework that non-French readers could understand. It may be that I have not succeeded in this aim. If not, then I hope that the results are enjoyable on their own merits.

While some knowledge of French will inevitably be helpful, it is by no means essential in order to access the information contained within these pages. In those rare instances where a translation is desired, readers will be able to easily access one of the various free translators available online.

Similarly, while a great many French artists performed under pseudonyms, I have generally not noted their real names, in part for reasons of space. Nowadays, these too can easily be found online if required.

Although I had heard the likes of Édith Piaf and Charles Trenet as a child, my interest was properly sparked a few years later when I first stumbled across the names of Johnny Hallyday and Les Chats Sauvages in a rock history magazine, although the impossibility of hearing the records in Australia at the time meant that I soon moved on to other things. Arriving in France for the first time in 1989, that interest was reawakened when I heard Johnny Hallyday and Françoise Hardy on a jukebox in a café, and flared up again a year or two later when I first heard Scott Walker's wonderful interpretations of the songs of Jacques Brel. Shortly afterward, out of curiosity I picked up a few records while on a weekend trip to France. These included albums by Brel,

Hallyday, Dalida and France Gall – a strange cross-section that suggested to me that there was something worth investigating on the other side of the Channel. Subsequent trips to Paris from my home in London always involved further record buying, and by the end of the nineties I was hooked. Three thousand or so purchases later, I am now taking the opportunity to share some of my discoveries with the world.

This first volume contains my account of the development of French pop in the twenty years or so following the Second World War, from the music hall stages of Paris to the pages of *Salut les copains*. The facts in the story are as correct as my research allows them to be. Any errors or omissions are unintentional, and will be corrected in future editions – all correspondence will be gladly received. As for the opinions expressed about the music under discussion, these are my own, and, as with all opinions, may be accepted or challenged as the reader sees fit.

A publication of this length can never be the work of one man alone, and there are many who have helped me to reach the end of the journey; I am sure that they all know who they are. Some are unknown, even to me: namely the bloggers, website contributors and YouTube aficionados who have opened the contents of their record collections and shared their knowledge of the music with the world. Indeed, the vast increase in information on the Web is one reason why it has taken me so long to finish – every time I thought that I was done, I found yet more to include, until finally I had to call a halt.

Among those who can be named, let me first thank Marc Liozon and Jacques Leblanc and their respective teams at *Club des Années 60* and *Jukebox* magazines, whose research provided the bedrock of knowledge from which I began my journey (and both of whom helped me to acquire back issues of their peerless magazines to set me on my way). Thanks also to Jacques Barsamian and François Jouffa, whose seminal early research gave me a framework on which to hang the latter half of the book, and to Thierry Liesenfeld, whose monumental history of early French rock'n'roll forced me to reassess my approach to this part of the story. In particular, I would like to thank Belgian rock'n'roll fanatic Christian Nauwelaers, whose tireless proofreading helped eliminate many errors of fact, and Terry Kay, whose eye for grammar, syntax and other literary detail helped to make the book tighter, more focused and ultimately more readable. I am also grateful to Jean-Louis Rancurel and Michel Rigot for allowing me to include their wonderful photographs.

Let me also thank Chrystalla Orphanides, who over dinner one night in Brighton first gave me the idea for the book, and Damian Gelle, for convincing me that leaving Virgin Megastores to write the first draft was the right thing to do. Thanks also to Nigel Turner, Stephen Powis, Annette Gately, Sheila Payne and David Grantham at the Royal Free Hospital for allowing me to be flexible enough with my working week to give me time to do the actual writing, and to my teachers Anne Jacobs, Helen Collins, Laurence Pons, Sylvie Pons and Magali Falco for giving me the linguistic skill to enable me to work my way through a mountain of French literature and music. Thanks too to my delightful cat, the late Mr Cato Fur, whose attempts to help me with the typing were always well intentioned, even if his spelling was often dubious.

Above all though, thanks go to two individuals, without whom I would never have written anything at all. Thanks then to my editor, George Groom-White, for believing in the project and for having the patience to wait until I finished it. Secondly, and most importantly, thanks to my partner Pascale, who, despite not liking the music much, has read through several drafts, corrected my dodgy French, disabused me of some of my more foolhardy notions and, most importantly, given me the space to get the thing written. Thanks for putting up with me while I struggled to get it done. It is finished now, Pascale, so before the literary urge strikes again, let's go and see what the birds in the garden are up to. There is always time enough for that.

*Gareth Jones*
*frenchpopbook@gmail.com*
*October 2021*

# Contents

# Preface

In late 1959, struggling French rock'n'roll singer Richard Anthony recorded the song 'Nouvelle vague'. Adapted from a little-known American tune by the Coasters, 'Three Cool Cats', the recording exceeded all expectations by becoming a hit, its cheeky references to the better-known *nouvelle vague* (new wave) revolution in French cinema chiming with a sea change in attitudes amongst French teenagers. In its own humble way, the song generated a revolution (at 45 r.p.m.) of its own, marking a turning point in the evolution of French popular song by kick-starting a national boom in teenage pop music which, after many years of neglect, is now coming to be recognised across the globe as a rich and rewarding body of work. The story of this transition from music hall to rock'n'roll, roughly from the dawn of the fifties to the early sixties, forms the core subject matter of this book.

In musical terms, the story of the Anglo-American 1950s is generally held to be synonymous with the story of rock'n'roll, with the first half of the decade often glossed over as being of little merit. However, following the resurgence of interest in the Great American Songbook over the past three decades, pop historians are now inclined to place Elvis Presley within the continuum of American popular music, rather than considering him a starting point for a 'Year Zero' approach to musical history (in reality, Presley represented both a continuation of the past and the dawn of a new day). This view of the fifties as a turning point in popular music nevertheless makes some sense, as the US and UK pop charts that respectively closed the decade with Frankie Avalon's 'Why' and Emile Ford & The Checkmates' 'What Do You Want To Make Those Eyes At Me For' were immeasurably different from those topped by Gene Autry's 'Rudolph The Red-Nosed Reindeer' and the Ink Spots' 'You're Breaking My Heart' a decade earlier. Although neither Avalon nor Ford was truly reflective of the changes that had been wrought in the intervening ten years, they nevertheless provided testament to the triumph of youth over experience as the teenage record buyer came to dominate the market for singles. The following five years would see this trend continue, climaxing in the phenomenal international success of the Beatles.

France was slower to catch on to the rock'n'roll sounds that swept the globe during the final years of the fifties, and as a result the 'rock era' began much later there than it did elsewhere. Hitherto dominated by traditional music hall artists and the accordions of the *bals-musette*,[1] the fifties opened with the queen of the *chanteuses réalistes*, Édith Piaf, standing centre stage, while the

---

[1] The *musette* was a sensual, polka-styled, accordion-driven form of dance music that first became popular in Paris in the 1880s. The venues in which it was performed were known as *bals-musette*.

French *chansons* of the day differed little in essence from those performed over the preceding fifty years, though the influence of jazz and the tango could be discerned beneath the accordion swirls and orchestration. The subsequent development of French pop into something completely different was the result of a post-war collision between the music hall and *chanson* traditions and the newer, harsher sounds emanating from the other side of the Atlantic. Just as American pop – white and black – would become the dominant musical form across the Western world, so too in France this highly popular manifestation of American cultural imperialism would eventually cast its magic spell, in the process throwing down a challenge to the old musical order.

It is therefore possible to paint the story of French pop in the same colours as those used elsewhere, with the final tableau showing the young Johnny Hallyday ruthlessly elbowing aside aging *chansonniers* like Maurice Chevalier to command the battleground like a victorious general, but in truth the story is more complicated than that – and far more interesting. While the American pop music that gave way to rock'n'roll is often (sometimes rightly) criticised as mass-produced, vacuous and ready for the knacker's yard to which rock'n'roll would shortly consign it – an analysis that completely fails to account for Frank Sinatra's magnificent run of albums for Capitol Records – French pop in the fifties was a far more creative place, with a generation of songsmiths breathing fresh life into that most traditional of musical forms, *la chanson française*. Singers like Édith Piaf and Juliette Gréco, and songwriters like Jacques Brel, Charles Aznavour and Georges Brassens built on the foundations of French *chanson* to create something that was both contemporary *and* grounded in tradition, and which was much admired abroad by those seeking a more poetic alternative to the moribund predictability of Mitch Miller's Columbia Records stable in the US.

While it is true that France underwent its own Miller-like convulsion during the exotica[2] boom of the mid-fifties, the developments in the *chanson* not only took this most home-grown of art forms to new heights, but also served as a buffer against the growing internationalisation of pop music (and culture more generally) that followed the arrival of the American forces in Europe during and after the Second World War. And if the country did crumble in the end, undergoing its own rock'n'roll revolution as the fifties turned into the sixties, this was as much a demographic as a musical change, and the traditional French approach to music-making continued to enjoy wide popularity right up to the end of the period covered by this volume, and indeed beyond. While in one sense it tells the story of the replacement of traditional music hall and *chanson* by rock'n'roll and the home-grown variant that came to be known as *yé-yé*, there are rather more currents running underneath than at first meet the eye.

---

[2] The term 'exotica' is popularly used to refer to the musical genre inspired by US orchestra leader Martin Denny in the 1950s. Sometimes described as 'tropical jazz', it attempts to evoke images of far-flung tropical islands and jungle paradises through the use of lush strings, bird calls, Afro-Cuban rhythms, unusual instrumentation and sound effects. In this book however, 'exotica' is used in its more general sense (something unusual, mysterious or exciting from other countries) to describe songs emanating from glamorous locations like Italy or South America, for which the French had a particular predilection in the mid-to-late 1950s.

After years of international ridicule, *yé-yé* is at last coming to be recognised not as a watered-down, bastardised version of rock'n'roll (although it could at times be guilty of being exactly that), but as a vibrant, enjoyable musical form in its own right, giving a distinctively French spin to what might otherwise have been a routine copy of British or American popular music. In part, the reason for this distinctiveness lies in the French language, and in a French fondness for girl singers that far outstrips that found in the US or UK (or, at least, it did during the sixties), but credit should also be given to the country's own musical heritage, against which its rock'n'roll and *yé-yé* singers had to struggle before eventually succeeding in making their marks.

Although *yé-yé* is finally beginning to register on global pop consciousness thanks to the Internet, networks of record collectors, specialist music magazines and the efforts of the reissue industry, *chanson* now seems lost from view, though a visit to any music store with a selection of French CDs in the 'World Music' section will probably throw up more *chanson* than it does *yé-yé* (or, indeed, contemporary French pop). Yet, at the time, it was *chanson* far more than *yé-yé* that inspired audiences across the world, with Brel and Aznavour selling out concerts at Carnegie Hall in New York and the Royal Albert Hall in London, while Johnny Hallyday and Sylvie Vartan came no closer to international stardom than recording sessions in the States and a joint appearance in the UK at the 1965 *Royal Command Performance*.[3] In part, this international preference for *chanson* over *yé-yé* was generational (it wasn't teenagers who snapped up albums by Juliette Gréco and Yves Montand, but their older siblings and parents), however it also reflected a widely held belief amongst British and American teenagers that the only good pop music came from the US (or later, during the years of the British Invasion, the UK).

Thus, ignored by British and American listeners, French pop was free to make its own way in the world, concentrating its efforts on the domestic market and responding only fitfully to the prevailing breezes blowing across international pop. When, by the late fifties, the winds had become strong enough to bring about a generational shift within French pop, this by no means spelled the death of more traditional sounds, and *chanson* and *yé-yé* continued to develop side by side almost to the end of the sixties, when a rather more violent change swept across the country, transforming everything in its path.

Moving on from *chanson* to jazz, novelty songs and thence to rock'n'roll, French pop echoed the same changes as those familiar to music fans in the UK and the US, but with the names of French stars like Claude François and Françoise Hardy supplanting those of British and American heroes. While at times these performers seemed to be merely recycling the ideas of their cross-Channel and transatlantic cousins, at their best they served up a rewarding blend of Anglo-American pop and French sophistication, giving the country a rich pop heritage that, until now, has largely been ignored in the wider international pop market.

This volume draws to a close as 1963 gives way to 1964, shortly before

---

[3]  At least, if one defines international stardom in Anglo-American terms. Vartan was and remains a star in Japan, and both singers enjoyed wide acceptance across Europe and South America.

the Beatles first arrived on French soil – largely because their impact in France was as seismic as it was everywhere else, and also because the flowering of the *yé-yé* generation that followed their arrival deserves a book all of its own – in the shape of Volume 2.

# A BRIEF HISTORY OF THE FRENCH RECORDING INDUSTRY

It can be argued that the global recording industry had its origins in France, where in 1857 the bookseller and printer Édouard-Léon Scott de Martinville received a patent for the earliest known sound recording device, the phonautograph. Unfortunately, his invention could only capture pictorial representations of sound waves, but not the actual sound itself. French inventor Charles Cros subsequently developed a proper recording device, shortly after Thomas Edison's American breakthrough in 1877. And so it was not France but the US, where the first commercially-released 'records' appeared in the 1880s, that would lead the way in establishing a recording industry. In the early decades of the twentieth century, shellac discs replaced wax cylinders as the preferred format, disc speeds were standardised at 78 r.p.m., electrical recording techniques led to greatly improved sound, and the record business began to grow at a phenomenal rate. Despite the ravages of the Great Depression and the Second World War, by the early fifties it had supplanted sheet music as the primary medium for sales of music.

The first French record company of note, Pathé, was up and running before the end of the nineteenth century, competing with the early American market leaders Victor, Edison and Columbia. By the start of the thirties, it had been joined in the marketplace by branches of other European labels including Polydor, Deutsche Grammophon and EMI (via their Odéon subsidiary), and a huge range of records, both international releases and home-grown recordings, could be purchased from Parisian stores like the Galeries Lafayette and Printemps.

As the industry's fortunes fluctuated over the years, there was some weeding out of early companies, with some going to the wall and others being bought out by larger players. A degree of to-ing and fro-ing across the Atlantic occasionally led to confusing outcomes, such as the existence of both an American and a British 'Columbia' label: the former went on to become part of CBS and largely vanished from French shores until the sixties, while the latter formed part of the EMI empire and was a major player in France.

Up until the end of the 1940s, the only format on sale in France was the two-sided 78 r.p.m. disc.[4] This would change following US Columbia's launch of the 33⅓ r.p.m. long-playing record (LP) in 1948 and RCA's introduction of the 45 r.p.m. single the following year. Both formats made their way into the French market in the early fifties, in the standard international sizes of 10 inches (25 cm) for LPs and 7 inches (17 cm) for 45s.

The turning point, however, came in 1953, when the 7-inch extended-play album was conceived. Offering double the playing time of singles, the four-track EP found immediate favour both with French record buyers and the French

---

[4] Referred to in this book, for convenience, as a 'single', even though that term is rather more modern.

record industry, and by the mid-fifties the 'Super 45', as it came to be dubbed, had virtually supplanted the single. This was in marked contrast to most other countries,[5] where the two-track 45 r.p.m. single remained the dominant format until the late sixties, while EPs were mostly regarded as a vehicle for recycling recent hits or a selection of an artist's work.

Additionally, while most of the world transitioned from 10-inch to longer 12-inch LPs by the early sixties, French record companies continued to use the smaller format until 1964-65, though some major artists also saw their work released on 12-inch. In part, this decision came down to cost, but it also reflected the prices that the home market could afford. Just as EPs offered better value for money than singles, 10-inch LPs were more affordable than 12-inchers, and so French record stores of the time were awash with 7-inch EPs and 10-inch LPs.

French EPs and LPs were generally untitled or self-titled, although they sometimes carried numbers indicating their position in a performer's discography. In the media, they were often referred to by the title of the opening track, or sometimes by the title of the set's best-known song. To add to the confusion, 10-inch and 12-inch LPs were sometimes issued under the same title. This lack of consistency led to different charts sometimes listing the same record under different titles.[6] To avoid repeating this confusion here, I usually refer to a particular album by its number, or else by the title by which it is generally known today.

For the purposes of this volume, I have regarded the 78 r.p.m. record as the standard format in France until around 1954-55, and the EP thereafter. Unless otherwise specified, the recordings discussed were issued on these formats. Where a song was initially or only released on LP, then this is noted in the text. Readers should assume this refers to a 10-inch LP unless otherwise stated.

The key industry players in the story outlined in these pages are a mixture of French and international companies: US giants like RCA (later RCA Victor) and Mercury, European labels like Polydor, Philips, Fontana, Decca (UK), Columbia (UK) and La Voix de son Maître (His Master's Voice), and an assortment of domestic labels ranging from majors like Pathé (later part of EMI) and Vogue through decent-sized independents like Ducretet-Thomson, Barclay, Festival and Disc AZ, to tiny fly-by-night outfits and vanity pressers that often offered provincial singers and groups their only chance of making a record. Some labels (like Barclay) proved better than others (like Vogue) at adapting to the changes that marked out these years, and the choice of one label over another often directly affected the fortunes of the singer or group concerned.

A list of the principal labels whose releases are covered in this volume, as well as the main artists who recorded for each, appears on the following pages.

---

[5]  Spain being a notable exception.
[6]  This problem has persisted into the modern age, with CD reissues of albums often appearing under multiple titles.

### Barclay

*Major independent run by bandleader Eddie Barclay.*

Frank Alamo, Charles Aznavour *(from 1960)*, Jacques Brel *(from 1962)*, Eddie Constantine, Dalida, Jean Ferrat *(from 1963)*, Léo Ferré *(from 1961)*, Danyel Gérard *(until 1960)*, Gillian Hills, Les Chaussettes Noires, Eddy Mitchell, Moustache *(from 1958)*, Henri Salvador *(1958-60)*, Vince Taylor.

### Bel-Air

*Subsidiary of Barclay.*

Les Champions, Les Pirates, Dany Logan, Rika Zaraï.

### Columbia

*French division of EMI's Columbia label.*

Richard Anthony, Lucienne Boyer, Maurice Chevalier *(1920s)*, Annie Cordy, François Deguelt, Fréhel *(1930s)*, Christian Garros, Les Compagnons de la Chanson *(until 1962)*, Édith Piaf *(from 1946)*, Tino Rossi, Charles Trenet.

### Daems

*Small independent based in Paris.*

Johnny et les Cascadeurs, Les Daems Boys.

### Decca

*French division of British Decca.*

Maurice Chevalier *(1940s)*, Jean Ferrat *(until 1963)*, Nancy Holloway, Frankie Jordan, Les Pingouins, Sophie, Pierre Vassiliu.

### Disc AZ

*Independent label affiliated to radio station Europe No. 1.*

Danyel Gérard *(from 1963)*.

### Ducretet–Thomson
*Independent label affiliated to radio and TV set manufacturer.*

Michèle Arnaud *(until 1960)*, Charles Aznavour *(until 1960)*, Claude Piron.

### Festival
*French independent label affiliated to Radio Luxembourg.*

Marie Laforêt, Les Surfs, Les Vautours, Johnny Taylor et les Strangers, André Verchuren.

### Fontana
*Subsidiary of Philips.*

Lucky Blondo, Claude François *(until 1963)*, Francis Lemarque, Les Trois Ménestrels, Nana Mouskouri.

### Golf Drouot
*Subsidiary of Barclay, active 1963-66.*

Les Aiglons, Les Jumelles, Ron et Mel.

### JBP
*Small independent based in Lyon.*

Les Gones/Gun's Rock, Les Korrigans.

### La Voix de son Maître
*French division of EMI's His Master's Voice label.*

Adamo *(from 1963)*, Gilbert Bécaud, André Dassary *(until 1955)*, Gloria Lasso, Luis Mariano, Jean-Claude Pascal, Jean Sablon.

### Le Chant du Monde
*Independent label funded by the French Communist Party.*

Léo Ferré *(until 1956)*.

### Mercury
*French division of US Mercury.*

Vic Laurens, Les Gam's.

### Mouloudji
*Independent label founded in 1964 by the singer Mouloudji.*

Mouloudji.

### Odéon
*French subsidiary of British EMI. In the mid-sixties, the French catalogue was sold to the American label CBS, but the Odéon marque was retained by EMI and reserved henceforth for British artists, including the Beatles.*

Billy Bridge, Léo Ferré *(1956-61)*, Fréhel *(1920s)*, Yves Montand *(until 1958)*, Patrice et Mario, Berthe Sylva.

### Pacific
*Small independent based in Paris.*

The Allegrettes, Long Chris *(until 1962)*.

### Palette
*Belgian independent operating in France, the UK and elsewhere.*

The Cousins, Les Waikiki's.

### Pathé

*A former French independent and pioneer of recording, by the 1950s Pathé was a French division of British EMI.*

Adamo *(1962-63)*, Michèle Arnaud, Bourvil, Aristide Bruant, André Claveau, Lucienne Delyle, Georges Guétary, Jacques Hélian *(until 1956)*, Yvette Horner, Les Chats Sauvages, Enrico Macias, Mistinguett, Marie-Josée Neuville, Line Renaud, Dick Rivers, Ray Ventura et ses Collégiens *(until 1945)*.

### Philips

*Dutch label highly active across Europe, part of the Philips electronics empire.*

Brigitte Bardot, Guy Béart, Georges Brassens *(from 1956)*, Jacques Brel *(until 1962)*, Philippe Clay, Sacha Distel *(1959-62)*, Claude François *(from 1963)*, Jacqueline François, Serge Gainsbourg, France Gall, Juliette Gréco, Johnny Hallyday *(from 1961)*, Zizi Jeanmaire, Les Frères Jacques, Les Parisiennes, Les Quatre Barbus, Les Swingle Singers, Long Chris *(from 1962)*, Yves Montand *(from 1958)*, Dario Moreno, Mouloudji *(until 1961)*, Magali Noël, Claude Nougaro *(from 1962)*, Patachou, Henri Salvador *(until 1958)*, Catherine Sauvage, Sheila, Sœur Sourire (The Singing Nun), Boris Vian, Rocky Volcano.

### Polydor

*West German label highly active across Europe. Operated as a subsidiary of Philips in France from the early 1950s and was eventually acquired by Philips in 1962.*

Adamo *(1961)*, Marcel Amont, Georges Brassens *(until 1956)*, Maria Candido, Colette Deréal, Fréhel *(1930s)*, Danyel Gérard *(1961-62)*, Jocelyne, Les Compagnons de la Chanson *(from 1962)*, Édith Piaf *(until 1945)*, Ray Ventura et ses Collégiens *(1946-55)*, John William.

### Président

*Small independent based in Paris.*

Les Schtroumpfs, Claude Nougaro *(1950s)*.

## RCA / RCA Victor
*French division of American RCA / RCA Victor.*

Alain Barrière, Sacha Distel *(from 1962)*, Sylvie Vartan.

## RGM
*Small independent based in Paris.*

Francis Linel.

## Ricordi
*Italian label active in France.*

Danny Boy et ses Pénitents.

## Rigolo
*Independent label run by singer/entertainer Henri Salvador.*

Audrey Arno, Les Bretell's, Jacky Moulière, Henri Salvador *(from 1964)*, Tiny Yong.

## Salvador
*Independent label run by singer/entertainer Henri Salvador. Superseded by Rigolo (above) in 1964.*

Audrey Arno, Les Bretell's, Jacky Moulière, Henri Salvador *(1961-64)*, Tiny Yong.

## Soder
*Small independent based in Lyon.*

Les Gadgets *(1963)*.

## Teppaz
*Independent label affiliated to the famous Lyon-based gramophone manufacturer.*

Tonia Bern, Castel et Casti, Phily Form, Les Gadgets *(1962)*.

### Trianon
*Small Paris-based independent later acquired by Pathé/EMI.*

Jacques Hélian *(from 1957)*.

### Twist
*Short-lived Decca affiliate.*

Larry Gréco, Michel Laurent, Eddie Vartan et son Orchestre.

### Véga
*Small independent based in Paris.*

André Dassary *(from 1955)*, Moustache *(until 1957)*, Georges Ulmer.

### Versailles
*Independent label co-founded by Bruno Coquatrix and bandleader Ray Ventura, principally for the distribution of American jazz and rhythm & blues recordings in France.*

Sacha Distel *(until 1958)*, Mac-Kac, Ray Ventura et ses Collégiens *(from 1956)*.

### Vogue
*Major French label.*

Petula Clark, El Toro et les Cyclones, Johnny Hallyday *(until 1961)*, Françoise Hardy, Mouloudji *(1961-64)*, Les Copains, Les Fantômes, Pierre Perret, Colette Renard.

# THE FRENCH CHARTS

The first publication to produce any kind of pop music chart in France was the popular newspaper *Le Figaro*, which began publishing a monthly list of best-selling sheet music titled *La Bourse des chansons* in September 1955. The chart ranked all known recordings of a song together, without taking into account which version was driving the sales. A month later, they were joined by another monthly publication, *Music-Hall*, which listed the best-selling records and the most-requested selections on jukeboxes amalgamated into one chart. Both charts were published monthly, although they were not always published during the summer holidays. With the former based on sheet music sales and the latter on record sales and jukebox requests, there was sometimes a wide divergence between the two – a trend which became more apparent as the decade progressed and the emerging youth market began to set the agenda for record sales.

The *Music-Hall* chart ceased in the summer of 1959, leaving France once again without a published chart for record sales. *La Bourse des chansons* lasted into the sixties, by which time it had been picked up by the magazine *La Discographie Française* but by then sales of sheet music were far less reflective either of record sales or the general popularity of songs across the country – a situation highlighted by the fact that only two real rock'n'roll records topped that chart during the first two years of the French rock'n'roll explosion[7]. The sheet music chart was discontinued at the end of 1961 and was subsequently replaced in *La Discographie Française* by a sales chart, which ran into 1963 before disappearing.

In 1961, a new journal appeared on the magazine racks in Paris. *Disco revue* had a strong bias toward rock'n'roll, but, being run on a shoestring, it was beset by difficulties and only appeared sporadically – fortnightly, monthly, or sometimes at more random intervals. From its inception, the magazine featured a hit parade of best-selling records, although this was compiled from a very small (albeit regionally widespread) sample of shops and tended to list only the lead track of each EP, leaving

---

[7] Les Chaussettes Noires' 'Daniela' in September 1961, and the covers of 'Let's Twist Again' ('Viens danser le twist') by Richard Anthony and Johnny Hallyday at the end of that year.

other 'hits' on the record unrecognised. Confusingly, this sometimes led to the lead track being changed during a record's chart run. Later on, the chart was augmented by a readers' poll of their favourite songs, which in 1964 replaced the sales chart altogether.

It was the arrival of the monthly *Salut les copains* (launched in 1962 as a spin-off from the radio show of the same name) which first provided the new teenage music with a chart that truly reflected its popularity, based on votes by readers. Initially, it was compiled by song title, with French and foreign versions ranked together, however this system was

soon scrapped and replaced by two separate charts, one listing the top 50 songs by French artists, the other listing the top 15 foreign titles.[8] Shortly afterwards, the magazine ceased to aggregate multiple versions, allowing readers to express a clear preference for a particular version of a song. The drawback was that there was no guide as to how the songs on the French chart compared in popularity with those on the other, so there was/is no way of acertaining whether, for example, Elvis Presley or Johnny Hallyday had the overall No. 1.

There were other problems with this chart as well, as it reflected the popularity of individual *songs*, rather than records. With EPs featuring four songs apiece, it was common for really popular artists to appear in two, three or even four places with different tracks from the same disc. A split in preference between various songs could result in a record being ranked lower than its sales justified,[9] while the fact that the latest Johnny Hallyday or Claude François EP occupied up to four positions in the Top 50 prevented other artists and records from entering the chart at all. Further anomalies occurred when readers voted for LP tracks, or (occasionally) for an acetate or an import which had been played on the show ahead of release.

---

[8] This may seem a strangely nationalistic bias, but it reflected fairly accurately the division of record sales in the country at the time.

[9] The same problem afflicted many early charts as they switched from sheet music to record sales. The *Billboard* charts in the US split sales this way until late 1969.

LE HIT PARADE DE SALUT LES COPAINS

Emission diffusée tous les jours à 17 h sur Europe 1 (1647 m G.O.) par Daniel Filipacchi.

La liste « Vedettes » est obtenue par le classement des artistes qui ont été le plus souvent demandés sous leur nom, quel que soit le titre de chanson indiqué par les auditeurs. La liste « Chansons » est obtenue par le classement des titres qui ont été le plus souvent demandés, quelle que soit l'interprétation dans laquelle les auditeurs souhaitaient l'entendre.

**Classement des chansons pour la période du 15 décembre 1962 au 15 janvier 1963**

1 - ELLE EST TERRIBLE (—)
JOHNNY HALLYDAY

2 - L'IDOLE DES JEUNES (4)
(Teen age idol)
1) JOHNNY HALLYDAY
2) RICKY NELSON

3 - BELLES ! BELLES ! BEL-
LES ! (—)
CLAUDE FRANÇOIS

4 - LA BAGARRE (—)
JOHNNY HALLYDAY

5 - PAS CETTE CHANSON (3)
(Don't play that song)
1) JOHNNY HALLYDAY
2) BEN E. KING

6 - LOIN (—)
RICHARD ANTHONY

7 - TELSTAR (—)
1) LES SPOTNICKS
2) LES TORNADOES

8 - OUBLIE-MOI (—)
LES CHAUSSETTES NOIRES

9 - VENUS EN BLUE-JEANS (—)
1) CLAUDE FRANÇOIS
2) LES CHAMPIONS

10 - C'EST A L'AMOUR
AUQUEL JE PENSE (—)
FRANÇOISE HARDY

11 - DANSONS (12)
(Let's dance)
1) SYLVIE VARTAN
2) CHRIS MONTEZ

12 - DERNIERS BAISERS (—)
(Sealed with a kiss)
LES CHATS SAUVAGES

13 - TOUS LES GARÇONS ET
LES FILLES (5)
FRANÇOISE HARDY

14 - SHEILA (7)
1) LUCKY BLONDO
2) TOMMY ROE

15 - TOUS MES COPAINS (—)
SYLVIE VARTAN

**Classement des vedettes pour la période du 15 décembre 1962 au 15 janvier 1963**

1 - JOHNNY HALLYDAY (1)
1) ELLE EST TERRIBLE
2) L'IDOLE DES JEUNES
3) LA BAGARRE
4) PAS CETTE CHANSON
5) COMME L'ETE DERNIER
ETC.

2 - CLAUDE FRANÇOIS (—)
1) BELLES ! BELLES ! BELLES !
2) VENUS EN BLUE-JEANS
3) MOI JE PENSE ENCORE A TOI
4) HEY POTATOES
(EXCLUSIVEMENT)

3 - CHAUSSETTES NOIRES (3)
1) OUBLIE-MOI
2) PARCE QUE TU SAIS
3) TOI QUAND TU ME QUITTES
4) JE REVIENDRAI BIENTOT
5) ÇA NE PEUT PLUS DURER
COMME ÇA
ETC.

4 - RICHARD ANTHONY (2)
1) LOIN
2) J'ENTENDS SIFFLER LE TRAIN
3) J'AI PLEURER SOUS LA
PLUIE
4) HEY BABY JE DANSE
5) L'INCENDIE
ETC.

5 - SYLVIE VARTAN (5)
1) DANSONS
2) TOUS MES COPAINS
3) M'AMUSER
4) LE LOCO MOTION
5) MOI JE PENSE ENCORE A TOI
ETC.

6 - FRANÇOISE HARDY (8)
1) C'EST A L'AMOUR AUQUEL JE
PENSE
2) TOUS LES GARÇONS ET LES
FILLES
3) TON MEILLEUR AMI
4) J'AI JETE MON CŒUR
ETC.

7 - DICK RIVERS (—)
1) ON A JUSTE L'AGE
2) AU CŒUR DE LA NUIT
3) BABY JOHN
4) VOULEZ-VOUS DANSER
ETC.

8 - RAY CHARLES (—)
1) WHAT'D I SAY
2) YOU ARE MY SUNSHINE
3) I CAN'T STOP LOVING YOU
4) GEORGIA ON MY MIND
5) I GOT A WOMAN
ETC.

9 - ELVIS PRESLEY

10) SHE'S NOT YOU
2) GIRLS ! GIRLS ! GIRLS !
3) RETURN TO SENDER
4) GOOD LUCK CHARM
5) NIGHT RIDER
ETC.

10 - PETULA CLARK
1) CŒUR BLESSE
2) CHARIOT
3) L'ENFANT DO
4) VILAINE FILLE, MAUVAIS
GARÇON
5) LE TRAIN DE NUIT
ETC.

11 - LUCKY BLONDO
1) SHEILA
2) MULTIPLICATION
3) ISABELLE
4) AVEC TOI
5) DIS-MOI OUI
ETC.

12 - CHATS SAUVAGES (8)
1) DERNIERS BAISERS
2) SHERRY
3) TOUT LE MONDE TWISTE
ETC.

Figuraient dans la liste précé-
dente : Little Eva, Claude Nougaro.

*  Les chiffres entre parenthèses indiquent les classements précédents.

Worse still, because the chart was compiled solely from the preferences of listeners to a particular radio show and readers of a particular magazine, songs that were popular elsewhere but were not played on radio station Europe No. 1's *Salut les copains* programme failed to even register. The still vast adult market was not represented at all, and major artists like Jacques Brel were arbitrarily deprived of a placing by virtue of the age of their fans. Nevertheless, for much of the sixties, this chart was generally accepted by the pop audience as being the nearest thing to an 'official' French national chart.

It was, however, not the only chart to enjoy a widespread following. Rival radio stations such as Radio Andorra, Radio Monte-Carlo and Radio Luxembourg all compiled charts of their own, each reflecting the playlists favoured by the station's owners, disc jockeys and listeners. Some of these persisted with the split between French and foreign recordings, while others did not, giving a very disjointed picture of what was actually popular at any given moment. Other magazines (e.g. *Bonjour les amis*; *Top réalités jeunesse*) also published charts, further clouding the issue, although to most of the teenage audience it was *Salut les copains* that would remain the yardstick for popularity until 1968.

The difficulties in gauging the popularity of adult-oriented sounds was partly addressed by the radio station France Inter, which ran a nightly listing of hits largely ignored by the *yé-yé* market. Less obsessed by the 'new and now' of popular taste, this was a slower-moving chart, reflecting the slower sales patterns of the more traditional show-business recordings, but still giving an indication of the relative popularity of each song or artist at a given point. These records sold steadily over a period of time, often ultimately outselling the *yé-yé* smashes that grabbed the headlines in *Salut les copains*. There was, of course, no way to compare this chart with the *yé-yé* one to ascertain the relative popularity of each type of music.

For the period covered by this volume, therefore, there is no truly comprehensive guide to the French hit parade. As regards the early sixties, the listings in *Disco revue* are probably the most reliable and have been republished in the now-defunct collectors' magazine *Jukebox*, while those in *Le Figaro*, *Music-Hall* and *Salut les copains* were republished in the (now sadly defunct) monthly *Platine* (although the latter only saw fit to publish the French-language listings; happily, the full listings are now available online via a fan's blog site). Although none of these surveys is perfect, I have to a large extent used them as a means to distinguish hits from flops, at least in the youth market.

In the absence of any definitive charts from which to work, I am indebted to four further sources of information, all of more recent origin and all seeking to bring retrospective to the French hit parade.

Starting in the nineties, *Jukebox* attempted to retrospectively combine the various pop charts of the sixties on a monthly basis into an all-encompassing Top 50 including both French and foreign songs to give a balanced view of musical tastes among the young over the years, though this chart does not reflect the popularity of the more adult-oriented artists.

More useful in this regard is the website **www.infodisc.fr**, which offers what the site's creator, Dominique Durand, describes as a 'synthesis' of all the French charts published since the fifties. It is a useful guide to the relative popularity of all styles of music during the fifties and sixties (and beyond), although, as with all such syntheses, its accuracy is open to question.

The same caveat applies to a useful book by Daniel Lesueur entitled *Hit Parades*, in which the author attempts to weigh up the various charts on a monthly basis and combine them into an all-encompassing Top 30. Though not without its faults (and it is interesting that Lesueur includes some titles which do not appear on Durand's website at all), this is as good a guide as has been made available to us in the shops. A summary of Lesueur's charts was republished in Yannick Suiveng's *Dictionnaire des Tubes en France*, which is the first real attempt at producing a French equivalent to the *Guinness Book of British Hit Singles*. I am also grateful to both Lesueur and Durand for the introductions with which they prefaced their works, in which they provide a detailed discussion of all the charts they have used. I have incorporated much of this information into my own summary above.

Lastly, there is Fabrice Ferment, who has worked through several decades' worth of actual sales returns as reported by record companies to create a series of weekly retrospective charts for the sixties and beyond. This survey, which can be found online at **http://top.france.free.fr**, is probably the most accurate representation of the country's best-selling releases during this period, although, as with the publications listed above, one needs to remember both that this is not a chart that was available to fans at the time and that sales figures are not the only way to judge a song's or a record's popularity.

Details of the publications and websites mentioned above can be found in the *Recommended Reading* section.

# Chapter I

## PLAISIR D'AMOUR
### French pop at the start of the twentieth century

*While the French pop music of the second half of the twentieth century and beyond owes much to the sounds and styles that emanated from across the Atlantic, its roots lie closer to home in the traditional folk songs sung in rural and urban society over the preceding centuries. France, like much of continental Europe, has a rich tradition of troubadours: wandering minstrels who captured the times in song and journeyed from place to place, teaching the words and the tunes to locals, who in turn would sing them at village gatherings or urban festivities. The origins of most of these works are lost in the mists of time and many have no known author, forming a part of the great international mass of music credited to those famous tunesmiths Trad. and Anon. or, in this case, to their French cousin, Folklore.*

*The oldest French song to which both a lyricist and a composer can be attributed with any certainty is 'Plaisir d'amour', a poem by Jean-Pierre Claris de Florian which was set to music by Jean-Paul Martini sometime between 1750 and 1780.[10] 'Plaisir d'amour' was also one of the first songs to skip quickly across the regional boundaries that kept France culturally divided for centuries, being sung around the country from north to south and from east to west, beginning a trend toward a national style of folk balladry.*

### Café-concert

This process was greatly boosted during the second half of the eighteenth century by the evolution in the major cities of a new type of establishment, the *café-concert* (colloquially *caf' conc'*) – a café where songs were performed by professional or semi-professional singers. This new form of entertainment grew rapidly in popularity over the course of the nineteenth century as citizens of the country's major cities, especially Paris, flocked to enjoy the performances of singers like Thérésa and Paulus, arguably the first pop stars the country had ever known. With the redevelopment of Paris during the reign of Napoléon III (1852-70), these establishments and shows flourished, and by the end of the century they formed the centre of much of the capital's social life.

---

[10] Fittingly perhaps for the foundation stone of what would become a multi-million-euro industry, 'Plaisir d'amour' has become an international standard, recorded among others by Joan Baez and Marianne Faithfull, while the melody formed the basis for Elvis Presley's 'Can't Help Falling In Love'.

In their wake, many smaller cabarets sprang up, with those clustered about Montmartre (including such internationally famous haunts as Le Lapin Agile and Le Chat Noir) becoming the home of what later became known as *la chanson française*. The cabarets were not, in essence, that much different from the *caf' conc'* venues, although they tended to be less ostentatious affairs and featured a musical approach somewhat at odds with the Establishment. While the *caf' conc'* movement gave rise to what would become the mass-market 'pop' audience, the cabarets became home to the first musical underground – although it would be many years before this distinction was clearly realised.

## Music hall

*Harry Fragson.*

Just as opera and classical music had their magnificent halls, so popular song increasingly demanded larger venues to accommodate the crowds wishing to hear the leading singers of the day. As in Victorian Britain, this need was met by the music halls, of which the most famous was the Olympia Theatre in Paris. This hallowed establishment opened in 1893, although bizarrely the headliner on opening night was not a singer, but Le Pétomane, a startlingly original performer who entertained audiences by producing a variety of sounds from the opposite end of his anatomy. With this unusual distraction out of the way, the hall settled into a long career presenting revues in the manner of the early Broadway theatres, with the leading singers of the day as the stars of the show.

As the calendar moved on into the twentieth century, names like Mistinguett and Harry Fragson were seen listed at the top of the bill with increasing regularity. Fragson was unusual, not only for claiming to have been born in the UK rather than in France,[11] but also because he accompanied himself on the piano instead of roaming the stage like most of his contemporaries. This idiosyncratic approach allowed him to make a name for himself with another innovation: the incorporation of a strange rhythm of American origin known as ragtime. This unusual sound soon gained him a loyal audience, though his unconventional musical approach did not endear itself to the mainstream. Mistinguett, on the other hand, was the ultimate embodiment of the show-business establishment. An expressive, glamorous long-legged dancer with a

---

[11] Although his father was British, Fragson was actually Belgian, his English accent affected rather than real. He did, however, begin and end his career in the UK, where he is best remembered as the creator of the music hall favourite 'Hello, Hello, Who's Your Lady Friend?'.

vocal talent to match, she typified the revues that would dominate the opening decades of the century and was by 1911 the main star at the world-famous Folies-Bergère.

Once recording technology became established in France, these singers, already secure in their domination of the music halls, duly became the first stars of the French record industry. Fragson's successes included 'Reviens, veux-tu' and 'Si tu veux... Marguerite', while Mistinguett enjoyed two decades' worth of popular smashes like 'J'en ai marre' and 'Folies-Bergère', the latter name-checking the Parisian nightspot where she could still be seen as the twenties began to swing.

*Mistinguett.*

## Operetta

Many of the leading lights of the early music hall circuit were singers who crossed over from the more rigorously demanding world of classical music. The emergence of Jacques Offenbach[12] in the middle of the nineteenth century as one of the country's most popular composers brought his chosen form of composition to the fore. Operetta or 'light opera' was derived from the great operas of the past, but was less serious and offered a more uplifting sense of theatre. The first successful show of this type was probably Hervé's now little-known *Don Quichotte et Sancho Pança* in 1848, but it was Offenbach who transformed the genre into mass entertainment with popular productions like *Orphée aux enfers*,[13] *La belle Hélène* and *La vie parisienne*.

Operetta quickly caught on with the French upper classes and soon established itself as a popular musical form in its own right. Unlike the American style of musical theatre which was to develop during the early twentieth century as a blend of dialogue, action and song, operetta relied almost entirely on the libretto to sustain the storyline and thus needed strong singers for the main roles, rather than character actors with some singing ability. Many of the performers became singing stars in their own right, and those willing to abandon their dedication to 'art' were easily able to make the transition to *caf' conc'* and subsequently to music hall.

By the 1900s, French popular song was developing along two distinct, though interlinked lines, the continued success of operettas providing the country with a polished, structured form of popular art and the music halls (which were slowly crippling the old *caf' conc'* establishments) providing a more lowbrow, yet equally stylised form of entertainment. Both styles continued to evolve, with stars frequently crossing between genres to create

---

[12] Offenbach was born in Cologne, Germany, but spent most of his career in Paris.
[13] *Orpheus In The Underworld.*

popular hits that would endure for decades. In Marseilles, composer Vincent Scotto moved on from writing popular songs to create a run of operettas that were far funnier than those of the preceding century, inventing a form of French musical comedy that proved massively popular for over fifty years.[14]

**Early music hall stars**

Scotto's songs also proved very popular with rising music hall stars like Georgel (who recorded the first version of his soon-to-be-a-standard 'Sous les ponts de Paris' in 1913) and Félix Mayol (who turned 'Elle vendait des p'tits gateaux' into a hit in the same year). Mayol was an example of what the French call a *chanteur de charme* – a smooth, suave figure with a genial smile and a warm, open personality, an image perfectly reflected in the ballads and comic novelties which comprised the bulk of his repertoire.

The music hall milieu was also open to talents with rather more dubious musical credentials, but the humorous song (best exemplified by the works of the comic Bach, whose 1909 effort, 'La soupe et l'bœuf', was an early classic of the genre) nonetheless occupied a place of some importance in an industry largely given over to providing a diversion from the travails of everyday life. Like several other comedians of the era, Bach specialised in barrack-room humour, best evidenced by 1913's 'Avec Bidasse', a heart-warming tale of camaraderie between an army conscript and his pal.[15]

The outbreak of war in 1914 did little to change the musical entertainment on offer in France, although it did lead to an increase in the popularity of stirring, martial songs at a time when the country was fighting for its very existence. Among the most enduring were Bach's rousing 1914 offering, 'Quand Madelon',[16] although three years later the mood had turned distinctly bleaker, reflected through such nostalgic songs as Jean Flor's 'Tu l'reverras, Paname' and Georgel's 'L'assommoir'. However, there was little, aside from the lyrical content, to distinguish these hits from those earlier in the century, with piano and accordion continuing to provide the usual musical backdrop to catchy, somewhat melodramatic songs of love, sorrow and regret.

**The 1920s**

In the years following the war, a wish to forget the horrors of the recent past saw an upsurge in popularity for all forms of diversion. Georgel's 'Aux Halles', referencing the famous market in Paris, was a typical period piece celebrating the return to normality, but the newly developed technology of cinema was fast beginning to eat into the audience for music hall entertainers. Nevertheless, the twenties were to prove a fertile ground for performers such as the singer/songwriter Georgius, who had begun his career during the war, penning the popular 'Les archers du roi' in 1916 before racking up a string of hits with humorous outings like 'La plus bath des javas', 'Sur un air de

---

[14] Scotto would also go on to score such cinematic gems as Marcel Pagnol's *La femme du boulanger* (1938), but it was the hit songs from his operettas that remain his claim to fame.
[15] The song was later successfully revived by Fernandel as 'Avec l'ami Bidasse' on his 1957 LP, *Les succès du comique troupier.*
[16] Bach first sang this on stage in 1914. It was adopted by the French army as a marching song throughout the war, though he did not get around to recording it himself until 1919.

shimmy' and 'Le fils-père'.

The traditional sounds of the accordion also remained extremely popular – often to the point where singers became unnecessary, as with the *guinguette*[17] style of dance music featured on the likes of Michel Peguri's 1923 recording, 'Mignonette', and Émile Vacher's catchy 'Reine de musette' four years later.

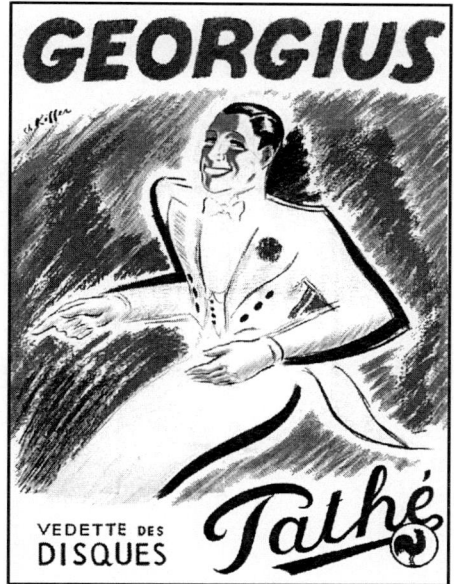

GEORGIUS

VEDETTE DES DISQUES *Pathé*

In the aftermath of the worst war in living memory, the early 1920s were a time both of nostalgia for a lost innocence (reflected in hits like Montéhus' 'La butte rouge'[18]) and of dreams for a better future (typified by Adolphe Bérard's romantic 'L'amour au clair de lune'), both themes converging in a long series of songs celebrating the country's vibrant capital that would culminate later in the decade with the likes of Georgel's rather over-earnest 'Tout autour de Paris' and Louis Charco's 'Le petit bal boisse'.

While the music halls enjoyed a commercial boom in the wake of the war, operetta likewise continued to draw city-dwellers to packed houses. As happened on Broadway, the songs from the shows quickly found a life of their own as popular hits in music halls like the Moulin Rouge and on a new invention called radio that was beginning to find its way into French homes.

Some of these would travel the world – most notably Mistinguett's 1920 smash, 'Mon homme', which became a US triumph two years later for Fanny Brice as 'My Man'.[19] Mistinguett dominated the decade with such immortal hits as 'J'suis nature' (1926) and 'Gosse de Paris' (1929), but generally speaking her repertoire was too rooted in French musical tradition to find an international audience, and songs like her risqué 1927 Moulin Rouge show-stopper, 'Il m'a vue nue', remained unique to France.

## Maurice Chevalier

The same cannot be said for another of the era's musical giants. Having started out as a comic, Maurice Chevalier abandoned his original peasant-like stage persona for a dandyish figure and slogged his way up the bill in the most demanding halls in the country. After years supporting superstars like Mistinguett, he found success as a star of operetta, enjoying a huge success

---

[17] These were popular drinking establishments, usually with a restaurant and dancing. The lively accordion style which accompanied the latter also came to be known as *guinguette*.

[18] A description of a battle that would later be taken up as an anthem by the French Left.

[19] Now best known to English-speaking audiences in the version by Barbra Streisand, who played Fanny Brice in the musical *Funny Girl*, both on Broadway and in Hollywood. Streisand actually recorded 'My Man' twice: initially for a 1965 single, and again in 1968 for the soundtrack of the film.

*Maurice Chevalier in 'The Love Parade' with Jeanette MacDonald.*

with *Dédé*. The show netted him his first popular hit, 'Dans la vie faut pas s'en faire',[20] in 1921, followed three years later by the classic 'Valentine'. These were among the first in a long string of hits, all of them selling largely thanks to his gregarious delivery. Smooth, charming and sophisticated, Chevalier cut a stylish path through the theatres and music halls of the day and was a perfect representative to the world of the suave, urbane Frenchman of the inter-war years.

Moving on from his domestic success, Chevalier conquered London in the revue *White Birds*, then crossed the Atlantic to take on the American market, where he enjoyed a smash in 1929 with 'Louise'. He went on to establish himself on stage, screen and radio, enjoying further stateside hits like 'My Love Parade'[21] and the standard, 'You Brought A New Kind Of Love To Me' (both in 1930), while continuing to rack up hits at home with more traditional fare.

In many ways, he was the archetypal music hall performer, delivering often-banal songs in a highly personalised way that enabled him to transcend the mundane nature of his material. In other ways, though, Chevalier was different, even though American audiences regarded him as the defining model of Frenchness for generations. While most of his contemporaries stuck firmly to their native tongue, Chevalier was perfectly happy to sing in English, hamming up his French accent to the hilt. He seldom, if ever, appeared without his trademark straw hat and was perfectly content to be considered a figure of amusement. His overseas success can ultimately be chalked up to the novelty value he offered to American audiences, although it was also true that he was receptive to the new musical ideas on offer in the US, offering a bridge across the Atlantic between the New World sounds of Broadway and the more traditional French popular music that he had left behind him in Paris.

---

[20] This song was so popular that it became a standard and was still widely known and performed in the seventies.
[21] From the 1929 film, *The Love Parade*, in which he starred opposite Jeanette MacDonald.

# Chapter 2

## J'AI L'CAFARD

### The *chanson* tradition in French music (1880-1940)

*While Chevalier, Mistinguett and the other stars of music hall provided entertainment for the masses, those seeking a more serious diversion turned instead to the cafés and basement clubs of Paris's more bohemian quarters: in Montparnasse, in Montmartre, and above all in Saint-Germain-des-Prés. Largely hidden from view, a small group of literary, political and musical free thinkers had been kicking off a quiet revolution, intent upon wreaking their own series of changes upon the* chanson.

### Chanson réaliste

In French, the word *chanson* simply means 'song', and its current Anglo-American usage to describe a *certain kind* of song is therefore somewhat inaccurate. Nonetheless, the term – in its international sense – serves a useful function in identifying a particular strand of traditional French popular music known to the French as *la chanson réaliste*.[22] The style was brought to life by performers sometimes termed *chansonniers*, who observed the society in which they lived through portrayals of real daily life, rather than the idealised world favoured by the more escapist music hall singers. While some of the *chanteurs réalistes* used the same clichés as their light-hearted contemporaries, relying on the passion of the performance to inject a note of realism into the song, others tended toward the sarcastic and the satirical while giving vent to a more poetic flair. Both approaches were rooted deep in French cultural history. The first mention of the term *réaliste* in a musical context appeared in the nineteenth century, while the more poetic colours of the *chansonniers'* palette date back to fifteenth-century 'bad boy' writers like François Rabelais and the poet François Villon. However, the distinction between the two styles was never clear-cut, and singers and writers often slipped back and forth between them as the mood demanded.

During the mid-nineteenth century there was an abundance of raw material from which to fashion songs, with political matters high on the agenda and a scale of turbulence to rival that of the Revolutionary Wars.

---

[22] The term *chanson réaliste* (a song with a focus on real life) had its counterpart in the *chanson fantaisiste* (a song designed purely for entertainment, often comic in intent and delivery). While the first of these terms is used and understood across the world, the latter has never caught on internationally. Essentially, *chanson fantaisiste* can be seen as the forerunner of pop music, and *chanson réaliste* (or *chanson* to anglophone audiences) as the forerunner of more serious musical forms.

However, as things settled down following the death rites of the Paris Commune in 1871, more everyday issues began to seep into the works of singers and the *chanson réaliste* slowly made its way into the world via the small cabarets that dotted the streets of Montmartre. The new breed of singers soon attracted a sizeable following, and in the early years of the twentieth century many made the jump to large music halls, beginning a slow process of incorporation into the mainstream.

## Aristide Bruant

The founding father of the *chanson réaliste* was Aristide Bruant, whose poetic and satirical approach appealed to an educated audience well versed in the French literary tradition. Bruant was a long-haired singer-poet with a penchant for red scarves, black capes and extravagant hats – an image that was as distinctive as it was outrageous, and which has been preserved for eternity in posters by Toulouse-Lautrec. Bruant took François Villon's ballads and reworked his ideas for a new generation, lambasting the French bourgeoisie through his songs, calling them pigs, camels or far worse as they flocked to his recitals to be entertained.[23]

Commencing in 1885, Bruant's performances brought the worlds of poetry and song back together, reviving an old tradition that would bear rich fruit in the following century. Many of his earliest works went unrecorded by him,[24] but songs such as 'Mad'moiselle écoutez-moi donc' and 'Dans la rue' would become classics, much covered by others in the succeeding half-century. His commentaries on the different *quartiers* of Paris in particular became standards, with 'À La Villette' providing Arletty with a hit in the thirties, and the likes of 'À Montparnasse' and 'À Batignolles' regularly resurfacing whenever a singer sought to pull together an anthology of Parisian song. A fatalist rather than a socialist, Bruant was more comfortable delivering the resigned acceptance of 'L'impôt sur les revenus' than the rabble-rousing sentiments of 'Les canuts', and was even content to dip into the well of romance for 'Rue Saint-Vincent'. Nevertheless, whatever he sang or wrote was always informed by a sense of realism far removed from the dreamy fantasies of his more optimistic contemporaries. A huge influence on

---

[23] As one of the first performers anywhere to actively bait his audience rather than pander to it, Bruant was the spiritual ancestor of the punk movement of the 1970s, although musically he adhered to highly traditional forms.

[24] Indeed, some pre-date the existence of proper recording techniques.

French *chanson* as it developed in the twentieth century, Bruant was nevertheless a rare male performer in a genre largely dominated by women.

## Fréhel and Damia

A child of the streets, Fréhel slogged her way to prominence with a sizeable hit in 1927 with 'J'ai l'cafard', although she never achieved the widespread following enjoyed by Maurice Chevalier or Mistinguett. Successes like 'Sur les bords de la Riviera' and 'Rien ne vaut l'accordéon' were indicative of the traditional nature of her repertoire but despite the often-banal material, such as 1928's already-stereotypical 'À Paris la nuit', she put her heart and soul into every performance. She continued to draw crowds right through the following decade, with further classics such as 1933's 'La zone', 1936's 'Tel qu'il est', and end-of-the-decade readings of the dance songs 'La der des der'[25] and 'La java bleue' (the latter composed by

*Fréhel.*

Vincent Scotto) continuing to up the ante for singers across the country. Fréhel brought a dose of realism to the often vacuous world of 1920s music hall, and along with singers like Damia and Berthe Sylva was able to reach a large audience, albeit only really hitting home when she (and they) turned to overly sentimental material.

Damia sang everything as if it were recorded amidst tragedy, adopting the pose of a *grande dame* of opera to put across material like 'D'une prison', a jaw-dropping performance adapted from a poem by Paul Verlaine. Singing everything from Kurt Weill to Fred Astaire's classic 'Night And Day' ('Tout le jour, toute la nuit') to the waltz-time 'La guinguette a fermé ses volets' and 'Le grand frisé' in the same powerful manner, she was an absolutely riveting performer. Indeed, from the Great War until the mid-thirties, she was arguably the most important exponent of the *chanson réaliste*. Even so, despite picking up hits with the likes of 'Les goélands' and a version of Fréhel's 'J'ai l'cafard', Damia never enjoyed a smash as big as 'Les roses blanches', which had launched the recording career of her long-time rival, Berthe Sylva.

## Berthe Sylva and Rina Ketty

Sentimental and more than a little contrived, 'Les roses blanches' was one of the biggest hits of the twenties and established the tear-soaked Berthe Sylva as a major star in 1925. She remained a significant presence for years, enjoying a major hit in 1931 with 'Du gris', but it was 'Les roses blanches' that sealed her

---

[25] Although the title derives from the French description of the Great War, *La guerre des guerres* [the war of wars], Fréhel's song does not reference this event.

immortality.[26] For two decades, she cranked out a stream of hits that redefined the *chanteuse réaliste*'s art: 'Fleur de musette', 'Monte-Carlo', the hilariously melodramatic 'La prière des petits gueux', 'On n'a pas tous les jours vingt ans' and an irresistible 1935 revival of the turn-of-the-century music hall hit 'Frou-frou'. With her already large fan base swelled to enormous proportions by her radio broadcasts, by the middle of the thirties Sylva was causing stampedes among audiences clamouring to hear her perform, the reports of seat-slashing and damage to theatres eerily foreshadowing events that were to unfold again some two decades later.

Italian-born Rina Ketty began in the small cabarets of Montmartre with a similarly uncontentious repertoire.

*Les Chansons de Léon Raiter*

# Les Roses Blanches

*CHANSON SENTIMENTALE DE*
CH. L. POTHIER et LEON RAITER

créée par

### Berthe SYLVA et Jane MATHÉA

*Demandez chez votre Marchand de Musique*
LES PLUS GRANDS SUCCÈS ENREGISTRÉS PAR
**BERTHE SYLVA**
*Petit Pierre, On n'a pas tous les jours vingt ans,*
*Grisante Folie, La Prière des Petits Gueux,*
*Petite Fleur, Tango d'Adieu, Souvenir,*
*Comme une Poupée, Ne quittez jamais votre enfant.*

Les Éditions Sylvain RAITER, 17, rue de l'Echiquier – PARIS (X⁰)
ORGERET, dépositaire, 24, rue Palais-Grillet – LYON

After early recordings like 'Tout s'efface' had tumbled into the reject tray, she broke through in 1938 with 'Rien que mon cœur' and the Mexican-tinged 'Sombreros et mantilles'. Later that year, she hit the jackpot with the ballad 'J'attendrai' (adapted from Carlo Buti's Italian classic 'Tornerai', inspired by a Puccini aria). In 1939, she earned another hit with 'Mon cœur soupire' (this time an adaptation of an air from Mozart's *Le nozze di Figaro*[27]), establishing herself at the forefront of the country's recording industry.

## Songs with substance

Other *chansonniers* were considerably more abrasive. During the twenties, French society was rocked by the attacks launched upon it by one known simply as Rip, whose protest songs pointed the finger at the much-despised Third Republic, the creaking administration that was leading France down the road to ruin. He made a commercial breakthrough in the following decade when singer/actress Jeanne Aubert appeared in the revue *Sur la commode*, finding widespread success with his eponymous theme song.

Aubert had started out in music hall, working alongside Mistinguett before scoring a major hit in 1925 with 'Si par hasard tu vois ma tante'. Success in London and on Broadway was followed by a shift to motion pictures and then a return to France. Both Rip and Aubert took delight in exposing the flaws of society to ridicule, offending many in what was still a deeply conservative country, while gaining a following among the intellectuals who frequented the cabarets and bars of Paris between the wars.

---

[26] 'Les roses blanches' would still be voted the country's favourite song as late as the 1990s!

[27] Known in English as *The Marriage of Figaro*.

Jeanne Aubert.

The thirties produced any number of songwriters following in the footsteps of Bruant and Rip – among them singers and writers like Gabriello and Raymond Souplex, who continued to create a literate alternative to the superficial pleasantries on offer in the music halls and opera houses.

Gabriello was a man of many talents, acting on stage and screen, and writing more than three thousand songs in a career that ran to several decades. His 1936 hit, 'Un bouquet de lilas blanc', marked a career highpoint, though his songs were usually better received when sung by others.

Souplex wrote lyrics in a variety of styles, playing it straight in 1936 on the lovely waltz 'Les beaux jours' and hamming it up in 1937 on the comic sketch 'La Hurlette et Carmen', which he recorded with actress Jane Sourza. A prolific writer of both songs and sketches, he was also a popular live performer, but enjoyed his biggest commercial success when writing for others, most notably Maurice Chevalier's 1937 hit, 'L'amour est passé près de vous', from the revue *Paris en joie*.

## Nice and Paris in the *chanson*

Down on the Côte d'Azur, the Continent's elite continued to take their holidays in the sun. By now, the tradition of spending long months on the Riviera was well established[28] and it soon began to find itself reflected in the repertoires of the singers of the day. The musical trend had actually begun in the late twenties, with the annual *Carnaval de Nice* even having its own theme songs, such as Alibert's 'Tralala' (1928), Max Réjean's 'Ah! Ah!' (1929),

---

[28] It began in the nineteenth century, but probably reached a peak (for the elite, anyway) in the period between the wars.

Gesky's 'Carnaval y a bon' (1930) and Alibert's 'Pi...ouit' (1931).

The *Carnaval* continued with further official theme songs throughout the thirties, but the new decade also brought forth other paeans to the Mediterranean coast including Dierdy's 'Nice, la jolie', Les Frères Peguri's accordion workout, 'À Juan-les-Pins', Prior's 'Entre Marseille et Toulon', Jean Lumière's 'Une nuit à Monte-Carlo' and Robert Burnier's smoothly crooned 'Partir pour la Côte d'Azur' (the latter two sourced from contemporary films). Despite the popularity of such escapist fare, few of them survived the passage of time to become standards – in marked contrast to the flow of Parisian tributes that ran right on into the thirties, thanks to such popular tunes as Germaine Béria's 'Dans les musettes de Paris', Georgius' 'Encore Paris', Marjal's 1931 revival of Georgel's 'Sous les ponts de Paris'[29] and Albert Préjean's 1939 favourite, 'Dédé de Montmartre'. Henri Garat's 'En parlant un peu de Paris' tapped the same sentiment, but hitched its lyrics to a vaguely jazz-band feel, as did Perchicot on 'Quand on revoit la tour Eiffel'. However, it was Maray's 'C'est notre Montmartre' – a typical *musette* – that better typified mainstream French pop as the Wall Street stock market crash began to reverberate around the world.

## The Great Depression and the 1930s

Neither the Great Depression,[30] nor his lengthy absences abroad could diminish the popularity of Maurice Chevalier. After returning home from the US, he racked up further smashes with music hall offerings like 1935's 'Prosper' and 1936's 'Ma pomme' and 'Le chapeau de Zozo'. The biggest name in the land, he drew immense crowds wherever he appeared, and aimed for the largest possible audience with his 1938 classic, 'Ah! Si vous connaissiez ma poule', by including affectionate nods toward international stars like Greta Garbo and Marlene Dietrich. By the time of his infectious 1939 smashes, 'Ça c'est passé un dimanche' and 'Ça fait d'excellents français', he was at the peak of his career.

*Maurice Chevalier.*

One of Chevalier's biggest mid-thirties hits was the superb 'Quand un vicomte', composed by rising singer/actress Mireille and lyricist Jean Nohain. The multi-talented Mireille had previously worked with Noël Coward and on Broadway, but returned to France in 1932 after her 'Couchés dans le foin' became a smash for music hall

---

[29] The song was revived again in 1955, with English lyrics, as 'Under The Bridges Of Paris', and went on to chart in the UK for both Eartha Kitt and Dean Martin.

[30] 1929-39.

Lucienne Boyer.

duo Pills et Tabet. Although her songs were often better known in the hands of others, she managed a string of hits of her own, typified by 1933's 'Papa n'a pas voulu' and 1938's 'Le temps qu'une hirondelle', and went on to become a star of stage, screen and radio.

Radio was now providing music hall stars with a new way to reach a large audience, helping to launch the career of Lys Gauty, whose biggest success came in 1931 with 'Le chaland qui passe' (a cover of Vittorio de Sica's Italian hit, 'Parlami d'amore Mariù').[31] Gauty enjoyed a second smash a couple of years later with the moving 'À Paris, dans chaque faubourg', beginning a run of hits that also took in her 1933 triumph, 'C'est le plaisir que j'aime', and 1938's sentimental 'Le bonheur est entré dans mon cœur' and 'Une femme, un accordéon, un caboulot'.

Suzy Solidor guaranteed herself an audience by virtue of running her own cabaret, La Vie Parisienne. With her androgynous looks, the openly lesbian Solidor was a totemic figure in thirties' France, painted by both Pablo Picasso and Tamara de Lempicka. The 1934 ode to sapphism, 'Ouvre', is her best-remembered recording today, but at the time it was overshadowed by the likes of 'Escale' and 'Johnny Palmer'. Both were decent sellers in the middle of a decade that saw her keeping her career in shape right up to 1939's 'La java au clair de lune' and 'J'écrirai', the latter giving her deep tones the opportunity to shine through a hackneyed arrangement and to stamp her authority on a rather ordinary song.

Showcasing a more sedate sound, Lucienne Boyer's attractive recording of 'Parlez-moi d'amour' established the five-year-old ballad as a standard in 1931. Boyer was one of the many rising stars at the time, having debuted in 1926 with Vincent Scotto's 'Tu me demandes si je t'aime' and the piano-pounding 'Youp et youp'. After a nine-month booking on Broadway, where her dynamic style caused a sensation, Boyer returned to France in 1928, where favourites like the heavily orchestrated 'Dans la fumée' (1930), the waltz-tempo 'Si petite' (1932) and the Scotto-penned 'Sans toi' (1932) established her as one of the biggest stars of the thirties. By the middle of the decade she was at the top of her game, racking up hits with 'Un amour comme le nôtre' and 'Venez donc chez moi'. While regularly touring both North and South America, she did, however, return home frequently for film and stage work, and to marry singer Jacques Pills (of Pills et Tabet) in 1939.

---

[31] Gauty's hit was was famously and inappropriately interpolated into the soundtrack of Jean Vigo's 1934 cinematic masterpiece, *L'Atalante*.

## Guinguette, *musette* and the accordion tradition

While such popular singers attracted large followings, there also remained a huge national affection for the country's accordion tradition, and the sounds of the *bal-musette* continued to find favour on the airwaves, on record and anywhere that live music was played. Many traditional singers and musicians could be found treading the boards of the country's music halls on a regular basis, delivering their individual interpretations of the hits of the day.

The best known of them also appeared on record. So it was that Jean Lumière used his high-pitched vocal cords to good effect on the 1933 hit, 'Vous, qu'avez vous fait de mon amour', Albert Préjean embraced the traditional sounds of 'Une java' in 1936, and Robert Burnier crooned his way through 'La java du cinéma' a year later.

Rubbing shoulders with them were Les Frères Peguri, who wrapped their accordions around 'Les nocturnes' and 'Enivrante', Joseph Colombo, whose 1937 recording, 'Germaine', typified the sounds of thirties' Paris, while Adolphe Deprince's 'Edelweiss' (1938) reminded listeners of the instrument's potential for the dance floor. The thirties were the highpoint of popularity for the traditional *guinguettes*, with records and radio carrying the sounds across the country.

## Comic *chanson*

The thirties were also a rich time for the actor, singer and comedian Fernandel, one of the funniest performers on the music hall circuit. His facial expressions, emphatic delivery and precise gestures combined with a powerful sense of humour to deliver a run of hilarious music hall knockabouts typified by the 1935 dance-song parody 'Javanons', 1937's 'Ignace' and 1938's 'Félicie aussi'.

Comic songs remained popular throughout the decade – perhaps because they distracted audiences from the harsh economic realities of the day – with records like Charpini et Brancato's mock-operatic 'Duetto' and Dranem's deliberately stupid 'Le trou de mon quai' competing in the music halls with Audrée Turey's lament, 'Mon anisette' and the more upbeat 'Parler pointu'. Ploughing a similar furrow, comic stalwart Ouvrard unleashed the classic 'Je n'suis pas bien portant' in

*Fernandel.*

1932 – a song that would travel the decades to re-emerge with each new generation of comics, although in his case this marked the end, rather than the beginning, of a long career on the boards.

## Operetta in the 1930s

For those who preferred something more highbrow, *L'Opéra de quat' sous* (a French adaptation of Kurt Weill's immensely successful *Die Dreigroschenoper*[32]) was staged by the Théâtre Montparnasse in 1930. Weill's work was taken up across the spectrum of French music hall, resulting in recordings like Lys Gauty's 'Complainte de la Seine' and a heart-rending performance of 'La fiancée du pirate' by Florelle, one of the many new singers tilting at Mistinguett's crown (not that the latter had any intention of abdicating, adding 1933's 'C'est vrai' to her list of triumphs).

Operetta remained immensely popular too, with many singing stars of the thirties not only appearing in the productions, but often enjoying success with the leading tunes on record as well. While the shows themselves are now long forgotten, hits such Pauline Carton and René Koval's rapid-fire duet, 'Sous les palétuviers', and Arletty's sophisticated 'Ah! Le joli jeu', both from 1934, remained favourites for years.

## Tino Rossi

The decade's biggest new star was Tino Rossi, a Corsican singer who came to prominence interpreting the songs of Vincent Scotto, his high-pitched crooning generating hits with the likes of 'Ô Corse, île d'amour'. He rocketed to stardom in 1934 with 'Adieu Hawaï', a French variant on the relaxed vocal style that was generating gold across the Atlantic for Bing Crosby. The record shifted half a million copies – an incredible total for the time. One of the most versatile singers ever to grace a recording studio, Rossi turned his hand to any song or style that caught his ear, mixing waltzes, ballads and jazz in a repertoire that, whether it was the nineteenth-century Communard standard 'Le temps des cerises', Raymond Souplex's dreamy 'Les beaux jours' or Schubert's 'Ave Maria', always bore his unmistakable stamp. His main

*Tino Rossi.*

speciality was songs evoking his Corsican heritage, and outings like 'Vieni, vieni' (with a chorus redolent of the British Boy Scout song, 'Ging Gang Goolie') and the catchy 'Chanson pour Nina' were massive hits that firmly established him at the heart of French show business.

In 1936, cinema came calling and Rossi's appearance in *Marinella* pushed him further up the stairway to the stars, netting him strong sales for

---

[32] Known to English-speaking audiences as *The Threepenny Opera*.

the swayathon 'Tchi-tchi'[33] and the rhythmic theme tune. The same year saw him chalking up further hits with the slow dance-floor favourites 'Laissez-moi vous aimer' and 'Tant qu'il y aura des étoiles'. He also enjoyed great success in 1938 with 'Paris, voici Paris' and a cover of Rina Ketty's 'J'attendrai', and in 1939 with 'De Nice à Monte-Carlo' and 'Carioca' (a version of Fred Astaire's 'The Carioca'). By the close of the decade, Rossi was a star of stage, screen and radio whose popularity extended far beyond the boundaries of France.

## Cinema and theatre

Cinema also made a star of Danielle Darrieux, who was equally at home in drama or musical comedy. In addition to a successful screen career that would take her to Hollywood at the end of the thirties, she cut a run of hit records, mainly drawn from her films. These included a jazz-tinged duet with actor Pierre Mingand, 'On ne voit ça qu'à Paris' from *La crise est finie* (1934), 'Le bonheur, c'est un rien' from *Mademoiselle Mozart* (1936) and 'Le premier rendez-vous' and 'Chanson d'espoir' from *Premier rendez-vous* (1941).

Georges Milton was a stage and film actor who enjoyed recording success with 'C'est pour mon papa' in 1930 and 'C'est pa... pa... parisien' a year later. A favourite on radio, he discovered that airplay could generate huge audiences for provincial tours, but renown in the halls and cabarets (or in Milton's case, on the screen) usually remained a prerequisite for securing a record contract.

While Milton went from stage to screen, character actor Jean Gabin made the journey in the opposite direction, duetting with Mistinguett on the accordion-soaked 'La java de Doudoune' in 1928. While never abandoning

---

[33] One of his biggest sellers, this is another hit which endured for decades.

himself to a singing career, his 1933 recording of 'La môme caoutchouc', the 1934 *guinguette* 'Viens, Fifine' and 1936's 'Quand on se promène au bord de l'eau' were sufficient to make him a star on record as well, despite a vocal style that offered little in the way of originality.[34]

## Saint-Germain-des-Prés

*Yvonne George.*

There were others, however, who shied away from such commercial considerations and sought to carry on the Bruant tradition in small clubs and cabarets away from the bright lights of the music halls. Infused with the political ideals of the era, enthused by Kurt Weill's groundbreaking celebrations of the underworld, and almost hidden from view on the Left Bank of the Seine, the habitués of Saint-Germain-des-Prés sought to present a different view of the world in a poetic vernacular far removed from the jollity and sentimentality of the biggest stars.

Among them was Brussels-born Yvonne George, who was whistled off stage at the Olympia Theatre in Paris in 1920 before achieving moderate success a few years later with 'Pars'. A muse for the poet Jacques Prévert, who sought to create for her a repertoire in her own image, her material was frequently rejected by her record company, although she did manage to get the Érik Satie-penned 'Je te veux' onto the market later in the decade. She eventually opted for a less contentious repertoire, enjoying hits with revivals of old folk songs ('Les cloches de Nantes'), parodies ('Impressions de dancing') and songs more akin to the work of the *chanteuses réalistes* ('Le petit bossu'), and returning to the Olympia Theatre in triumph. Sadly, her moment of glory was cut short by her tragically early death in 1930.

While George was heading out for stardom, back in Saint-Germain-des-Prés songwriter Jean Tranchant was creating a distinctive repertoire that in many ways summed up the ethos of the *quartier* during the thirties. Although he only recorded occasionally, demonstrating a more-than-acceptable vocal talent on 1938's 'Minuit à Paris', his real contribution was crafting a series of songs for a range of underground talents, each as remarkable as the other. There was very little sweetness and light in his compositions, which tended toward a more bittersweet, if not downright sour, form of nostalgia, epitomised by the 1933 hit he provided for Lucienne Boyer, 'Moi j'crache dans l'eau' (though the song was given a more striking treatment by Germaine Lix). The same year saw the appearance of 'La ballade du cordonnier', rich in irony and

---

[34] And, if one wanted to be less than charitable, little in the way of musicality either.

brought to the ears of the public both by the underrated Pierre Doriaan and the better-known Lys Gauty.[35] Tranchant's status as a rising star was sealed when German cabaret legend Marlene Dietrich chose his 'Assez' for her first French-language recording, sharing the marketplace with a version by Germaine Sablon. However, Tranchant's greatest collaborations came when he teamed up with the equally breathtaking Marianne Oswald.

Born of mixed French and German parentage, Oswald had a strange, androgynous appeal and a singing style that was both frightening and utterly compelling – not unlike that of Marlene Dietrich, but far less conventional. Her dissection of the sarcastic 'Complainte de Kesoubah' would have sounded threatening in the *sixties*; released in 1933, it was nothing short of shocking. A brace of *chansons parlées* or spoken-word songs gifted by Jean Cocteau, 'Anna la bonne' and 'La dame de Monte-Carlo', did little to hasten a move into the mainstream. A further Cocteau effort, 'Mes sœurs, n'aimez pas les marins', was followed by 1934's 'Le jeu de massacre', which sounded positively conventional by comparison – until the macabre lyrics sank in. After sweetening the sound on her 1936 recording, 'Toute seule', Oswald returned to form the following year with 'La grasse matinée', the latest in a long line of striking, powerful and utterly original performances which understandably failed to take her out of the shadows.

These last two songs were both written by Jacques Prévert, whose savage lyrics also provided the appeal in Gilles et Julien's otherwise sweetly sung 'Familiale'. A conventional performing duo, they had recorded another in the long list of songs about the capital, 'Fleur de Paris', back in 1932, but the more challenging 'Familiale' ranks as their greatest achievement.

Prévert would go on to further triumphs as a songwriter, but his thirties' work continued to lag behind that of Tranchant, who found his final great collaborator in 1934 when Nane Cholet recorded a heavily orchestrated arrangement of his caustic 'J'ai pas la gueule qui plaît aux riches' and the aggressive 'La courroie'. Like Oswald, Cholet proved too far removed from what was expected of a *chanteuse* to be commercially successful.

---

[35] Gauty also covered Tranchant's 'Le piano mécanique' and 'J'aime tes grands yeux' before turning her attention to Jacques Prévert and his songwriting partner, Joseph Kosma, for the unforgettable 'Deux escargots qui vont à l'enterrement d'une feuille morte'.

## Marie Dubas and Lucienne Delyle

*Marie Dubas.*

Although the practitioners of the nascent Left Bank *chanson* often struggled to be heard in the wider marketplace, their approach soon found echoes in the work of the next generation of *chanteuses réalistes*. No one combined the two styles more successfully than Marie Dubas, who emerged in the late twenties with the sweet 'Quand je danse avec lui' and enjoyed major popularity in 1932 with 'Le doux caboulot'. Starting out as an actress, Dubas had graduated to operetta and then to music hall, leading in the 1932 revue *Sex Appeal Paris 32* at the Casino de Paris. With a style that made Berthe Sylva look positively restrained, she rewrote the rule book for French *chanson* and enjoyed a long run of hits, peaking in 1936 with a pair of absolute gems, 'Le fanion de la légion' and 'Mon légionnaire'. With a striking, high-pitched voice and a dynamism that demanded listeners pay attention, Dubas dominated the final years of the decade, mellowing enough to score with the more sentimental and amusing 'La java du crochet' in 1939.

Toward the end of the thirties, she was joined on the boards by Lucienne Delyle, an orphan whose troubled upbringing found full expression in her work. Delyle's style, melancholy and nostalgic rather than emotional, stood in stark contrast to Dubas' strident approach, and it took some time for her to find the same level of success. Her moment finally came in 1939, when she made her move into the spotlight with the excellent 'Elle fréquentait la rue Pigalle', 'Dans mon cœur' and the latest tribute to the capital, 'Sur les quais du vieux Paris', a major hit as storm clouds began to gather over Europe.

## Édith Piaf

While Dubas and Delyle took the *chanson* in new directions, away from the limelight another singer was honing a style that would lift her to prominence at the close of the decade. Édith Piaf was born in Paris but raised in a brothel in Normandy after being abandoned by her mother. Reclaimed by her entertainer father, the pair travelled across the country, performing in the streets for a living. At the age of fifteen, she was discovered by nightclub owner Louis Leplée, who booked her into Le Gerny's in 1935. The diminutive singer[36] was a major sensation, pouring her whole being into the songs and forcing an indifferent crowd to listen.

Piaf not only wore her heart on her sleeve when she sang, she practically

---

[36] Piaf stood at only 147 cm, or 4 feet 10 inches.

handed it around the audience, inviting examination and demanding a response. Emotional, unrestrained and dynamic in a way that had rarely been seen on a European stage, she has been called the first European blues singer, and while she had little in common with the music of Black America, her passionate performances made her more than deserving of that title. Success at Le Gerny's led to bookings at other cabarets and a recording deal with Polydor. By 1936, she was on her way to becoming the most talked-about singer in Paris.

Issued in 1936, Piaf's early recordings gave little hint of what was to follow, although her distinctive warbling style was already in evidence. She gave a good account

*Édith Piaf.*

of herself on her first release, the conventional piano ballad 'L'étranger' and the accordion-backed 'Les mômes de la cloche', while her second, 'Mon apéro', also had its moments. As her style developed, however, Piaf's heart-stopping vocal pyrotechnics moved to centre stage and the piano-dominated 'Reste' gave her the chance to inject some drama into the proceedings. 'J'suis mordue', the swirling 'Les hiboux' and the *guinguette*-flavoured 'Fais-moi valser' were equally impressive, and with the music now serving mainly as a backdrop to her voice, Piaf began to stamp her authority over the songs – albeit in a way that only hinted at the vocal power she projected in live performance.

Looking to make her mark with stronger material, Piaf recorded a version of Marie Dubas' hit, 'Mon légionnaire', in 1937. A tribute to her most obvious musical influence, Piaf's recording also revealed that she had already far surpassed Dubas as a *chanteuse réaliste*. From then on she could do no wrong, whether singing her heart out on 'Entre Saint-Ouen et Clignancourt', tugging on the heartstrings of her listeners on 'Un jeune homme chantait', or, as her success grew, dabbling in more elaborate arrangements like the heavily orchestrated 'Paris-Méditerranée'. She followed these up with 'C'est lui que mon cœur a choisi' (1938) and the unusual 'Je n'en connais pas la fin' (1939), the latter of which was still on the airwaves as the thirties drew to a close.

Piaf, Delyle and Dubas represented a creative high watermark for the *chanson réaliste*, taking the traditional French *chanson* into uncharted waters. By the end of the decade, though, this most French of musical forms was under increasing threat from a strange new music that had begun to make its way across the Atlantic.

# Chapter 3

## JE SUIS SWING
### The arrival of jazz (1920-40)

*Jazz first crossed the Atlantic during the Great War, with black American servicemen forming military bands that quickly diversified from marches into a repertoire more in keeping with their own musical tastes. The best known was the Hellfighters Band,[37] who undertook a tour of French cities during the early months of 1918, bringing their strange rhythms to an audience who had no idea of what they were hearing. Following the Treaty of Versailles in June 1919, things were rather slow to take off, despite the presence of Louis Mitchell's Jazz Kings in Paris for the best part of a decade. Hardly a 'hot' jazz band (in the parlance of the times), Mitchell's ensemble was nonetheless a significant bridge between the Old World and the New, serving as a support system for other visiting players, including, in 1919, Sidney Bechet. Although many of its leading luminaries toured Europe in the early twenties, jazz found it difficult to gain a foothold in France until an American performer appeared in the right place and at the right time to spark a musical revolution.*

### Joséphine Baker and other American influences

Joséphine Baker was a black singer from St. Louis who first appeared in Paris in 1925 as part of the *Revue nègre*. With an erotically charged act that scandalised as many as it delighted, the show was an instant hit, transforming her into a star and prompting her to permanently quit the US for France,[38] where she remained a major concert attraction throughout the next two decades. Drawing her early repertoire almost entirely from contemporary American sources, Baker introduced the sounds of black America via songs like Ethel Waters' 'Dinah' to an initially uncomprehending audience who had principally come to see her outrageous costumes – including one apparently made entirely from bananas.

By 1927, she had begun to include French tunes in her performances and, while she wasn't the greatest of singers, her style, broad smile and personality came across well. She quickly became a major recording star off the back of 1930's 'Dis-moi Joséphine' and 'La petite Tonkinoise', a charming revival of a pre-war hit by comic singer Polin composed by Vincent Scotto, who went on to pen the slow ballad 'J'ai deux amours' for her the same year. By this time, her work as a musical ambassador was complete, as, dotted

---

[37] Drawn from the ranks of the 369th Infantry Regiment.
[38] It is likely that the racism she encountered back home also played a part in her decision.

*Joséphine Baker.*

around the country, the beginnings of a home-grown form of jazz began to take shape.

Baker's arrival in France coincided with that of the American label Columbia, whose shift from mechanical to electrical recording in 1925 led to a huge improvement in the sound quality of French records. The change in technology made it possible to hear the instrumentation behind the singer with greater clarity, creating a market for inventive orchestration. Together with the boom in radio broadcasts, this provided fertile ground for the stars of both music hall and operetta, and gave the newly emerging jazz musicians the opportunity to expand their operations into the recording industry.

Baker's success also led to the first significant attempts to adapt American hits into French for the domestic audience, Saint-Granier's 1928 reworking of Gene Austin's 'Ramona' proving so popular that it sparked the first campaign to put a stop to the practice. Other singers[39] also tried their luck with covers of US hits over the years, though this would not become a major trend until the fifties. Nevertheless, it marked the first step toward a gradual Americanisation of French popular music and was thus regarded by culturally minded Frenchmen and women as a threat to the country's musical heritage.[40] Other threats would soon follow.

---

[39] Including Baker, who in 1937 recorded an excellent version of the Ray Noble–Hal Kemp hit, 'I've Got You Under My Skin' released as 'Vous faites partie de moi'.

[40] In the fifties and sixties, this same fear led to the creation of song festivals designed to promote French compositions, and in the nineties to a 40% quota being imposed on radio to guarantee that a certain amount of French material was heard over the airwaves.

## The tango

The tango hit France like a thunderbolt following Carlos Gardel's arrival from Argentina for a series of concerts in 1931. Crowds in Paris went wild for the new, sensual dance, and within weeks of his first appearances the singer had sold over 100,000 records – a phenomenal number for the time. The popularity of the tango presented a threat to the more traditional forms of French dance music such as the waltz, and small-time bands struggled to accommodate the new sound into the traditional *bals-musette*, with accordions rolling over the top of strident South American rhythms. Their performances paled when compared to the real thing, however, and the good-looking baritone quickly became one of the French record industry's biggest stars.

Curiously, Gardel was actually French, having been born in Toulouse in 1890, though he was raised in South

*Carlos Gardel.*

America and held both Uruguayan and Argentinian citizenship. Inspired by the dramatic, emotional approach of his native land's music hall stars, his melancholy, yearning tangos were perfect for the dark days of the thirties and he was an immediate sensation, revolutionising the music and rapidly emerging as the biggest name in South American pop. After conquering France, he moved on to the US, where his matinée-idol charms took him to Hollywood for ten films, most notably the 1934 box office smash, *Tango On Broadway*.

Gardel's premature death in an air crash in 1935 did little to reduce his popularity, and his funeral in Buenos Aires attracted crowds that would not be rivalled until the days of Eva Péron. The tango remained popular in Europe for years after his death, reflected in the songs of Tino Rossi ('Tango de Marilou'), Fernandel ('Ne me dis plus «tu»'), Alibert ('Le plus beau tango du monde') and countless others, until it eventually outstayed its welcome.

Jazz, though, was proving harder to dislodge.

## French jazz: Ventura, Salvador and Le Hot Club de France

The jazz bands that sprang up in thirties' France did not find the going easy, although instrumental outfits and dance bands enjoyed considerable prominence, thanks to the continuing popularity in the provinces of the *musette*. Among its more successful early exponents were Ray Ventura et ses Collégiens, a big band whose style sat somewhere between the sweet music of Paul Whiteman and the swing of Benny Goodman. Tempering his work with large doses of humour, Ventura quickly became the biggest attraction in the country, introducing jazz to an audience who came to dance and to be entertained by such confections as 'La légende du roi Marc' and 'Les chemises de l'archiduchesse'. His band enjoyed regular work, chalking up dozens of hits including the amusing 'Ça vaut mieux que d'attraper la scarlatine' and 'Tout va très bien, madame la marquise', touring abroad to huge acclaim, and ending the decade with a classic in 'La complainte des caleçons'.

While working on the Mediterranean coast, Ventura discovered guitarist Henri Salvador, a Guyanese expatriate who had ventured across to France and made a name for himself as an old-school showman. Permanently dressed all in white and never failing to please his audiences with his talents as a singer, guitarist and humorist, Salvador would play alongside Ventura during the dark days of the war before achieving success on his own in rather different circumstances.

While Ventura may have watered down his jazz for mass consumption, and others like accordionist Jean Vaissarde (on 'Déception') or Fred Adison (on his 1938 hit, 'Le swingalero') peddled an odd hybrid between jazz and *musette*, many sought to bring real jazz to prominence in France. Among them was Hugues Panassié, a jazz fan who in 1932 established Le Hot Club de France as a venue for the music, initially simply for the playing of records. However, it was not long before live music began to be featured, initially by visiting American musicians, then shortly afterward by their French emulators – among them two giants who towered above the rest of their compatriots for originality.

## Django Reinhardt and Stéphane Grappelli

Belgian-born Gypsy guitarist Django Reinhardt had been schooled in the ways of the *musette* and had already acquired a reputation within his own community as a supremely gifted technician. In 1928, disaster struck when his caravan caught fire and he was badly burned. The damage was particularly acute on his left hand, causing him to lose the use of his fourth and fifth fingers, and he feared that he might never play again. Determined to overcome this setback, he developed a completely new and revolutionary technique largely dictated by his disability. Having refined his unique picking style over several years, he joined forces with violinist Stéphane Grappelli in 1934 to form Le Quintette du Hot Club de France.

Temperamentally, the pair were an odd match, Reinhardt's ramshackle approach to performing contrasting sharply with the more organised manner of his Paris-born comrade-in-arms: where Reinhardt was unreliable, Grappelli was precise and punctual. Despite this difference in attitude, they were united

*Le Quintette du Hot Club de France.*

by a love of the music created by Eddie Lang and Joe Venuti, and began to play small-group jazz in the style of the American duo, although before long they were adding something of their own into the mix. While both were passionate jazz fans, Reinhardt also demonstrated tremendous loyalty to his Gypsy roots, fusing the playing style of his forefathers with American jazz, while Grappelli's distinctive violin improvisations gave the band a flavour of its own, thus gifting the world the first distinctively *French* style of jazz.

The blend of Reinhardt's and Grappelli's differing approaches lay at the heart of their success and they were soon recognised, at home and abroad, as being among the most creative talents in contemporary jazz. Commencing with their 1934 covers of the Original Dixieland Jazz Band's 'Tiger Rag' and Bing Crosby's recent revival of Ethel Waters' twenties' hit, 'Dinah', the Quintette recorded some of the best jazz ever laid down in a studio – on either side of the Atlantic. For the next five years, they turned out a steady stream of recordings, mixing versions of American jazz standards like Fats Waller's 'Ain't Misbehavin' ', Paul Whiteman's 'Limehouse Blues', Ben Bernie's 'Sweet Georgia Brown' and Bing Crosby's 'Shine' with original compositions like 'Black And White', 'Minor Swing', and Reinhardt's breath-taking improvisation, 'Nuages', which became something of a standard itself.

Although the ensemble also backed vocalists from time to time, their instrumental

abilities alone were sufficient to gain them a wide audience, and they even managed to score a sizeable US hit in 1937 with their reworking of the old Henry Burr & Albert Campbell hit, 'After You've Gone'. By then, Reinhardt's reputation as the world's leading jazz guitarist was secure, and the late thirties saw him cutting loose on the records that remain his greatest legacy – among them 'Billets doux' and a revival of Gus Arnheim's 'Them There Eyes' (both 1937), and the following year's 'Montmartre'.

## Jean Sablon and Léo Marjane

Despite their success as an instrumental unit, it was the Quintette's work with singer Jean Sablon[41] that did most to bring the sounds of jazz and swing into the French mainstream. Sablon had started out in operetta before graduating to music hall as opening act for Mistinguett. This in turn led to recording success, beginning in 1932 with the ballad 'Puisque vous partez en voyage' and 'Ce petit chemin' a year later, just two of several duets he cut with Mireille. Her support gave his career a huge boost and further hits were quick to follow, among them a cover of Lucienne Boyer's 'Venez donc chez moi'. Sablon's genial personality and charming manner made him a big hit with the female audience, but he was less interested in the sounds of music

*Jean Sablon.*

hall than in those being made across the Atlantic by Bing Crosby.

The first of the crooners to make an impact on the record market, Crosby had a huge influence on Sablon and his light, jazzy style was to totally transform not only Sablon's own recordings, but in time the whole spectrum of French pop. Teaming up with a few like-minded souls, Sablon cut some of the finest vocal jazz records yet released in France, helping to introduce the joys of swing to an initially baffled audience who came to his shows expecting ballads from the charmer *par excellence*. His early efforts were impressive, if commercially unviable, but sides like 1932's 'Béguin-beguine' and 1933's 'Je suis sex appeal' slowly found an audience. By 1934, when Sablon teamed up with Reinhardt and Grappelli, he was well on his way to becoming a major star, racking up steady sales with the children's novelty 'Prenez garde au grand méchant loup' (adapted from the Three Little Pigs' 'Who's Afraid Of The Big Bad Wolf' from the classic Walt Disney short) and the more serious 'Rendez-vous sous la pluie'.

Not content with these innovations, Sablon went further in 1936 and

---

[41] Son of the successful songwriter Charles Sablon. Jean Sablon's sister, Germaine Sablon, also enjoyed success on record, most notably in 1933 with the sweetly orchestrated 'Assez'.

became the first French performer to take to the stage with a microphone – a move that drew disdainful reviews and accusations that his voice was too weak for him to sing in public without it. The innovation enabled him to croon quietly and still reach the back rows, but the point was completely lost on critics for whom 'live' performance precluded any form of electronic gimmickry.

Disgusted by what he saw as an unappreciative, unimaginative audience, Sablon took off for the US, where his singing style met with immediate success and the critical acclaim denied him at home. Despite his overseas popularity, he returned to France at regular intervals, determined to establish his new singing style on home turf. He gradually won over his old audience, making his mark as the leading crooner in the country with the superb 'Je tir' ma révérence'. Toward

*Léo Marjane.*

the end of the decade, he recorded a version of the traditional folk song 'Sur le pont d'Avignon' in a jazzy style, a release which proved the perfect vehicle for establishing jazz and swing as viable forms of entertainment in a hitherto suspicious country.

Sablon's closest female counterpart was Léo Marjane, a young singer who shot to stardom in 1938 with 'En septembre sous la pluie' (a superb reading of Guy Lombardo's 'September In The Rain') and Artie Shaw's arrangement of Xavier Cugat's 'Begin The Beguine'. From this promising beginning, she established herself as the country's most popular jazz *chanteuse*, with a repertoire that ranged from Shep Fields' 'In The Chapel In The Moonlight' ('La chapelle au clair de lune') to Judy Garland's 'Over The Rainbow' ('L'arc-en-ciel'), occasionally drifting into schmaltz, but generally keeping her recordings at the highest standard possible. Although she lacked Garland's 'little girl lost' charm, Marjane had a voice to die for and by the close of the decade was firmly established as one of the country's biggest concert draws.

### Charles Trenet

Perhaps the greatest of the pre-war jazz aficionados who sought to do something new with French pop was Charles Trenet, a colourful, flamboyant individual possessed of a charming voice and a knack for composing jolly melodies around lyrics that evoked pure joy. He began his career in 1933, performing and writing songs in conjunction with Swiss pianist Johnny Hess, another jazz devotee. Recording as Charles et Johnny, the duo scored hits in 1934 with 'Sur le Yang-Tsé-Kiang' and 'L'école buissonnière (Une chanson

*Charles Trenet.*

quand on était petits)', and in 1936 with the infectious 'Tout est au duc'. Kicking along to highly accessible jazz rhythms, their songs had an ever greater impact in the repertoires of others – most importantly that of Jean Sablon, who recorded their moving 'Vous qui passez sans me voir'.

The partnership ended abruptly in October 1936, when Trenet was called up for miltary service. Hess continued as a solo act, enjoying a hit in 1938 with the effervescent 'Je suis swing', though he generally preferred to concentrate on running his own cabaret and writing tunes for others.

Upon his discharge from the army in December 1937, Trenet resumed his career by penning 'Y'a d'la joie', a major hit for Maurice Chevalier in 1938 (and later one of Trenet's own best-loved recordings), and cutting a string of hits in his own right. His run began with the jolly 'Je chante' and 'La polka du roi', and also took in a tribute to Paris, 'Ménilmontant', but most notable of all was 'Boum!!..', a joyful, uplifting recording that became another timeless classic. Replete with corny lyrics, farmyard sounds and gibberish syllables, it encapsulated Trenet's musical vision in one near-perfect piece of pop nonsense, establishing as the court jester of French music hall. Small wonder that he was nicknamed *'Le fou chantant'*.

By the close of the decade, Trenet's songs were all over the airwaves, driving patrons onto dance floors and sung in every music hall across France. And, with 'Boum!!..' being covered by a number of British dance bands, he was even starting to make inroads into the international market.

Trenet's achievements in bringing jazz into the French mainstream cannot be understated, but what is often overlooked (at least, by foreign audiences captivated by his seductive melodies) is just how well he succeeded in marrying the new rhythms to the rich literary tradition of French *chanson*. A musical ultra-modernist with a startlingly deft way with the French language, Trenet elevated the *chanson* to a higher plane.

# Chapter 4

## DOUCE FRANCE
### War and liberation (1940-50)

*The opening months of the war did not bring about any significant changes on the French musical landscape, which saw Charles Trenet riding high with his latest release, 'Le soleil et la lune', although Lucienne Boyer's 'Mon p'tit kaki (Lettre de femme)' had at least some connection with the reality that was about to unfold. As in the UK, most people believed it would be a short, spectacular affair that would cause little disruption, despite still-recent memories of the last great conflagration. Accordingly, the first songs to surface which expressly referenced war were optimistic, jingoistic efforts such as Ray Ventura's jazz-tinged hit, 'On ira pendre notre linge sur la ligne Siegfried', an appropriation of Flanagan & Allen's '(We're Gonna Hang Out) The Washing On The Siegfried Line'. For the stars of music hall too, it was very much 'business as usual', with Joséphine Baker titillating audiences with 'Mon cœur est un oiseau des îles', Alibert celebrating 'Ma belle Marseillaise' in the company of Mireille Ponsard, and the newly prominent Agnès Capri reviving Yvonne George's 'Je te veux' alongside a reading of Jacques Prévert's 'Quand tu dors'. On 10 May 1940, the day that the war came to France with a vengeance, Jacques Pills was safely esconced in a recording studio laying down the gently nostalgic 'Dans un coin de mon pays', blissfully unaware that in another corner of the country Stukas were already laying waste to the landscape.*

### A musical exodus

By the end of the year, with half of France under German occupation and the other half suffering under the Vichy regime, such joyful airs were no longer appropriate. The disaster had come so quickly that musicians and singers everywhere were caught on the hop; some were out of the country and would have to remain so for the duration. Stéphane Grappelli saw out the war in London, braving the Blitz and bringing his unique style of jazz violin to bear on a new group of musicians for whom he would become an inspirational figure. Ray Ventura and Jean Sablon were also abroad and chose to remain on the other side of the Atlantic. Both did, however, get their records released back home, where their rival renditions of 'Insensiblement' enjoyed good airplay until being ordered off the air following the Vichy regime's realisation that the song had been written by Jewish songwriter Paul Misraki.

Another Jew, Marie Dubas, found her career curtailed and had little option but to flee to Switzerland, leaving Édith Piaf (who always acknowledged

Dubas as her role model) to establish herself as the embodiment of French sentiment. The result was that Piaf's 1936 recording of 'Mon légionnaire', a staple of her wartime shows, is now considered a timeless classic of the pre-war years, while Dubas' original recording has largely been forgotten.

## The Occupation

Joséphine Baker and Django Reinhardt both elected to stay in France – a brave move for a black singer (who put herself further at risk by working for the Resistance) and a man of Gypsy extraction, both of whom might easily have wound up in a concentration camp. Ditto the homosexual Charles Trenet. All three remained active throughout the Occupation, providing audiences with a much-needed escape from the grim nature of their day-to-day existence.

While Baker focused on live performances in both occupied and neutral parts of the Continent, Reinhardt linked up with saxophonist Alix Combelle and clarinet maestro Hubert Rostaing for a variation on his old Quintette sound, sparkling across such jazz workouts as 'Les yeux noirs' and 'Swing 42', and breathing new life into old chestnuts like Louis Armstrong's 'All Of Me'. Trenet likewise continued to record during this dark period in the country's history, setting the words of poet Paul Verlaine to a jazz accompaniment on 'Verlaine', teaming up with comic songwriter Francis Blanche for the wonderful 'Débit de l'eau, débit de lait', and crafting the beautiful, melancholy 'Que reste-t-il de nos amours?' and the heartfelt 'Douce France' for a country wrapped in grief and pain.[42]

This nostalgic tinge in Trenet's songs found a reflection in the work of many of his contemporaries, among them Mistinguett, whose 1942 recording 'La tour Eiffel est toujours là' gave a new meaning to the endless stream of tributes to the capital. Other notable 'Paris songs' of the period included Maurice Chevalier's 'La marche de Ménilmontant' in 1943 and the lovely 'La fête à Neuneu' a year later, and Damia's 1944 outings 'Ma rue' and 'On danse à La Villette'. Danielle Darrieux meanwhile came over all romantic on 'Les fleurs sont des mots d'amour', while newcomer Lina Margy focused on the great French winemaking tradition with 'Ah! Le petit vin blanc'.

Perfectly in tune with the troubled times of the Occupation, Lucienne Delyle rose to become a major star, scoring hits with the desperately sad 'Prière à Zumba' and the memorable 'Mon amant de Saint-Jean' as the country suffered under the jackboots of the Third Reich and the organised thuggery of the Vichy regime. By 1944, when

---

[42] Like Bach's 'Quand Madelon' in the previous war, Trenet's 'Douce France' became a popular hit on the back of live performances well before he got around to recording it. The first version to be released on disc was by Roland Gerbeau, in 1944.

she recorded her interpretation of Trenet's 'Que reste-t-il de nos amours?',[43] she was at the peak of her career.

Others responded in different ways. Toeing the party line, André Dassary recorded the strident 'Maréchal nous voilà', a tribute to Marshall Philippe Pétain, hero of the Great War and now head of state of the Vichy regime, that served as an alternative national anthem for the remaining years of the regime's existence.

With English titles suddenly taboo, some musicians simply pretended that they were French songs. This resulted firstly in the release of unacknowledged cover versions such as Ray Ventura's 'Dans l'ambience' (a recrafting of Glenn Miller's 'In The Mood'), and secondly in the creation of fake labels to disguise American recordings like Louis Armstrong's 'St. Louis Blues', which was repackaged as 'La tristesse de Saint-Louis'.

The artists who stayed behind in France lived a difficult existence, often being forced to perform for their hated German masters. Édith Piaf used the opportunities this presented to provide undercover assistance to the growing Resistance movement. Delighting in offending the Germans, Piaf openly flouted Nazi orders by dating a Jewish pianist and used concerts in POW camps to enable prisoners to escape, almost daring the Gestapo to take her away. Although her recording career slowed down during the Occupation, she continued to craft a repertoire purpose-built to describe her life and those of the people around her. She tipped her hat to her fellow countrymen with the delightful 'L'accordéoniste' and lamented the absence of loved ones on 'Où sont-ils mes petits copains?', then took her first significant steps toward the sound of American jazz with 1941's upbeat 'J'ai dansé avec l'amour' and her 1943 hit, 'C'était une histoire d'amour'.

## Jazz and the *zazou* resistance

The Occupation had an impact on French *chanson* in other ways too. The fact that their German overlords had made plain their distaste for American culture meant that, for French adolescents, listening to jazz or any other form of American-inspired music became a way of rebelling against the Nazis. The French, like their counterparts in the Netherlands, Belgium and elsewhere, reacted like a bull to a red rag and home-grown jazz became a boom industry. Georgius and Fred Adison enjoyed hits with 'Mon heure de swing' and 'Le swing à l'école' respectively, while Django Reinhardt covered the absent Stéphane Grappelli's parts on 1942's 'Blues en mineur' and shone as brightly as ever on the following year's 'Manoir de mes rêves'. Fresh from their work with Reinhardt, clarinettist Hubert Rostaing and saxophonist Alix Combelle found their popularity on the increase, while Lucienne Delyle's trumpeter

---

[43] Going head to head with an achingly moving reading by Lucienne Boyer.

husband, Aimé Barelli,[44] began his long career in Noël Chiboust's band, cutting the impressive 'Noël's blues'[45] in 1940. Similarly, female jazz singer Léo Marjane was a hugely popular during the war years with songs like the melancholy 'Seule ce soir', a Charles Trenet-penned lament for couples separated by the war.

It is deeply ironic that the Nazis' desire to stamp out what they saw as an alien culture creeping across Europe served only to increase the appeal of jazz within France and other European countries, leading to a huge boom in popularity that had seemed unlikely only five years earlier. Cut off as they were from the latest developments across the Atlantic, French players inevitably started to look backwards in their search for something new, often turning to records that hadn't sold well when originally released. Their quest led them to the sounds of New Orleans, a journey which culminated in the establishment in 1942 of one of the world's first traditional jazz revival bands, Claude Abadie et son Orchestre, led by clarinettist Abadie and trumpeter Boris Vian.[46]

However, it was not trad jazz that was the music of the moment, and most French bands brave enough to defy the authorities stuck to the big band sound that had developed during the thirties. The young fans who followed the bands, pejoratively nicknamed *les petits swings* by the Vichy regime, delighted in dressing provocatively, not realising the danger they were putting themselves in. By the winter of 1941, they had mutated into a youth cult known as *les zazous*. With the entry of the US into the war that December, the anti-American thrust of the regime became much stronger. Openly attacked in the street by local thugs and fascists, the *zazous* took their lives into their hands just by going out of the house, but the success of the 1942 film *Mademoiselle Swing* proved that the appeal of jazz and swing as a form of passive resistance ran far deeper than adolescents with a passion for odd hairstyles and clothing.

The Allied landing in Algeria at the end of 1942 effectively put paid to the quasi-independent Vichy government and saw the Nazi occupation extended to the whole country, leading to increased repression that effectively stamped out the *zazou* rebellion. What it failed to do was kill off either the growing

---

[44] A disciple of American jazz trumpeter/bandleader Bunny Berigan.
[45] Which also featured Django Reinhardt on guitar.
[46] Although the band recorded during the war, nothing was released until many years later.

French obsession with jazz (among others, Ray Ventura continued on his merry way with the 1943 hit 'Tiens, tiens, tiens'); nor could it prevent the survival of the *guinguette* as a defiantly French form of music, as evidenced by the success of Émile Vacher's 'Reine d'amour', Henri Garat's 'Avoir un bon copain' and Adolphe Deprince's liberty-loving 'Le retour des guinguettes'.

The use of music as a means of passive resistance continued throughout 1943 and 1944 as the repression deepened and tightened, with deportations, forced labour and the worst excesses of the Holocaust intensifying as the Nazi military machine started falling apart at the seams. As the prospect of liberation began to seem ever more likely, old and new stars alike set out their stalls with a richly varied palette of sounds and songs. The newcomers ranged from music hall entertainer Georges Guétary ('Robin des bois') to Patrice et Mario (who offered the faraway fantasy 'Avec son ukulélé'[47]), while older favourites like Jacques Pills and André Dassary found success with the engaging 'Symphonie' and the exotic-sounding Basque favourite 'Ramuntcho' respectively.

**Liberation**

The liberation of France in 1944 and the end of the war the following year brought a mixture of emotions for the citizens of France. Despair and desolation at the destruction that had been wrought during the conflict and under the German occupation were mixed with joy at the prospect of peace, freedom and reconstruction of the country. Harried and tormented both by the war and the subsequent process of dealing with alleged 'collaborators', France was in urgent need of some diversion. The stars of music hall were quick to oblige, with Maurice Chevalier carrying on as if little had changed, taking to the airwaves in celebration with 'Quai de Bercy' and selling record numbers of seats for his Paris shows.

Tino Rossi celebrated the first year after the Liberation with 'Besame mucho' (a hit rendition of the Mexican tune recently taken to the top of the US charts by Jimmy Dorsey) and cleaned up with the saccharine 'Petit Papa Noël', a Yuletide smash that sold in the millions and now represents Christmas to the French in the way that Bing Crosby's 'White Christmas' does to the Americans. Already the biggest star in the French panoply, Rossi became a phenomenon after the war, almost everything he recorded leaping out of the record racks. As each year unfolded, so a new series of hits poured forth, running from his 1946 offerings, 'J'ai deux chansons' and 'Sérénade à la brise', via his 1948 smash, 'Midinettes de Paris', to the end-of-the-decade 'Ma guitare et mon cœur' (a cover of Alan Dale's 'My Guitar'), his rich tenor sitting comfortably on the airwaves regardless of the competition.

Lucienne Delyle also carried on where she had left off with the defiantly old-fashioned 'Un air d'accordéon' and a run of more joyful pop hits best exemplified by 1946's 'Le moulin de la Galette' and a version of the much-covered 'Les amants du dimanche', before triumphing at the end of the decade with yet another addition to the 'Paris song' corpus, 'Les quais de la Seine'.

For those who had spent the war years abroad, things were less straightforward. Marie Dubas was one of many who returned home to find that

---

[47] A Jacques Pills composition which placed the instrument not in the music hall milieu of British entertainer George Formby, but in its spiritual homeland of Hawaii.

she had been overtaken in popularity by rivals who had remained in the country: although she successfully reclaimed her audience at the ABC Theatre in 1945, she discovered that Édith Piaf had meanwhile ascended the ladder of French show business and effectively stolen her crown.

Jean Sablon returned from his overseas exile to a frosty reception from audiences who resented his having avoided the tribulations they had suffered. It took years of eating humble pie on the music hall circuit before he succeeded in re-establishing himself in his homeland.

Also struggling in the new world was Rina Ketty, whose style seemed to have gone out of fashion overnight. Despite some good recordings like 1946's 'J'écoute sur la route', she never regained her previous position, eventually giving up altogether and relocating to Quebec in the fifties, where she found the audience that had eluded her back in France.

Léo Marjane, Suzy Solidor and Charles Trenet fared even worse, being accused of collaboration for entertaining German troops. Marjane attempted to plead myopia, claiming she had no idea who was in the audience, but the court disagreed, plunging her career into a tailspin. Solidor was also convicted and her career never truly recovered. Trenet, on the other hand, bravely fought his case and defended himself well. Despite widespread criticism, he escaped with a minor reprimand. Thereafter, he resumed his career, enjoying major hits like 'France dimanche', the delightful 'Revoir Paris' and the timeless 'La mer', an absolute pearl of French *chanson*, borne along by a gentle melody line that perfectly evokes the seaside scenario described by the lyric. Picked up by Benny Goodman in 1948, it was given an English lyric by Jack Lawrence and duly became an international standard as 'Beyond The Sea'.[48]

## The triumph of Édith Piaf

Towering above the whole edifice was Édith Piaf, who emerged from the war with a great deal of credit for her Nazi-baiting antics and continued her rise to the top with a repertoire of sentimental and heartfelt songs, delivered in her trademark warble with all the passion she could muster. Firmly established as the leading attraction in the country, she scored a major hit in 1946 with the song that best typifies the immediate post-war era and will forever be linked with her. 'La vie en rose' was an attempt to see the world through rose-tinted glasses at a time when all around was poverty, deprivation and destruction.

1946 also saw Piaf record the smash hit 'Les trois cloches' in conjunction with the nine-man vocal group, Les Compagnons de la Chanson. An overly

---

[48] The song is eternally associated with Trenet in France, although (as with 'Douce France'), it was Roland Gerbeau's 1945 recording that hit the market first. Bobby Darin's 1960 hit recording remains the best-known English-language version.

sentimental recording packed with pathos, it became an international smash and was subsequently reworked in English (by Les Compagnons de la Chanson, as well as a host of others) to become a folk standard under the title 'The Three Bells'. She made further recordings with the Compagnons (among them the harrowing 'Dans les prisons de Nantes' and a revival of the anti-war folk song 'Le roi a fait battre tambour') before they set forth on their own career, as well as blazing her own trail with 'Adieu mon cœur' and the uncharacteristically optimistic 'C'est merveilleux'.

Further classics such as 1946's 'Un refrain courait dans la rue', 1947's 'Un homme comme les autres' and 1948's 'Il a chanté' confirmed Piaf's unrivalled position in France. In 1947, she outdid all the competition by taking her show to the US, where she was acclaimed as a phenomenon – so much so, that for the next decade she would spend as much time there as in her native land. To cater to this new market, she began to record occasional sessions in English, but it is noteworthy that, like Jean Sablon a decade earlier, she made her name with a repertoire sung almost entirely in French. The gap left by her lengthy absences from the French stage was quickly filled by new generation of singers, each with their own style to offer, although none came close to matching the emotional intensity of a Piaf recital.

## Post-war stars

Having ridden to success on Piaf's apron strings, Les Compagnons de la Chanson established themselves as a major attraction in their own right with a repertoire ranging from old folk songs like 'Perrine était servante' to more contemporary compositions by Charles Trenet ('L'ours') and Piaf herself ('Les yeux de ma mère'). The hits came quickly, 1947's 'C'est pour ça' being followed two years later by a cover of Trenet's 'Mes jeunes années' and 'Les cavaliers du ciel' (adapted from Vaughn Monroe's 'Riders In The Sky (A Cowboy Legend)' – one of the first signs of their willingness to rework foreign songs). 1950 bought them a major smash with 'Le galérien' as they effortlessly staked a claim to be the leading vocal group in the land.

With a hilarious stage act based around a 'Norman peasant' persona, the singer and comedian Bourvil was an instant hit in a country looking for light relief. He began his run of hits in 1946 with the stylised 'Les crayons' and scored with the comic song 'À bicyclette' a year later, before making a move into films. This generated further hits including amusing efforts like 1950's 'La tactique du gendarme', while the knockabout 'Le pêcheur' reinforced his ever-smiling music-hall-clown image in the minds of listeners forever. Though he could be described as a kind of French counterpart to Britain's George Formby, Bourvil was a better actor and had a way with a romantic ballad that Formby could never have emulated. Although he occasionally deviated to

*Bourvil.*

foreign sources, such as his 1949 retread of Arthur Godfrey's 'Too Fat Polka' ('La dondon dodue'), his delivery and sense of the ridiculous were undeniably and inescapably French, and he became one of the country's biggest box office stars, scoring another hit in 1950 with the jaunty 'En revenant d'la revue'.

Jostling for space as a new generation made their advance, the remainder of the old guard continued to make their presence felt. Lina Margy scored a major hit in 1948 with the nostalgic 'Voulez-vous danser, Grand-Mère?', while Arletty triumphed two years later with the gently romantic, if overstylised 'Deux sous d'violettes'. Less well known than Margy or Arletty, Pierre Dudan had struggled through the war in the small cabarets of Montmartre, but made a splash in 1946 with the excellent 'On prend l'café au lait au lit' and then co-wrote[49] the much-covered 'Clopin-clopant', but never found the same commercially-rewarding recipe again.

'Clopin-clopant' was also one half of a double-sided hit for Henri Salvador, who split from Ray Ventura for a solo career that brought him instant success in 1948. The flip was a gentle Antillean folk song called 'Maladie d'amour',[50] which, like the same year's 'Le portrait de tante Caroline', showcased his gentle guitar-picking and smooth vocal style perfectly. The ultimate all-round entertainer, Salvador never quite abandoned his commitment to jazz, returning to his first love at regular intervals, as evidenced by 1950's 'C'est le be-bop'. However, thanks to hits like 1948's 'Chanson surréaliste' and its insane flipside, 'Salvador s'amuse' (on which he simply laughed for three minutes), he established a niche for himself as the new clown

*Henri Salvador.*

---

[49] With Bruno Coquatrix.
[50] British and American audiences will be more familiar with the English-language version, 'Melodie d'amour', recorded in 1957 by the Ames Brothers.

prince of French pop. It was a role he would be slow to give up, despite a string of successes that put his musical talents to rather better use – such as the endearing (and enduring) Latin-flavoured lullaby 'Le loup, la biche et le chevalier', which graced the airwaves as 1950 turned into 1951.

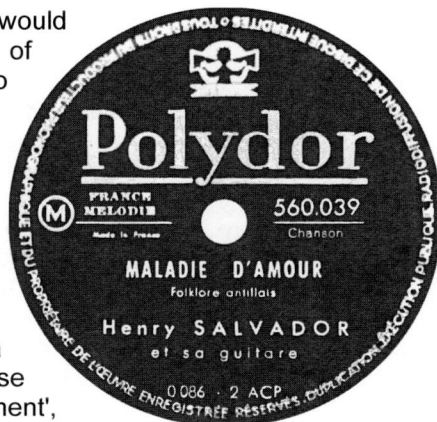

Having also previously served time as a member of the Ventura band, André Dassary put his vocals to good use in operetta while picking up a number of popular hits along way. These included three 1947 smashes ('Éperdument', the dreamily romantic 'Enchantement d'un beau soir d'été' and the similarly seasonal 'Tant que le printemps'), and the inevitable 'Paris' the following year. One of a number of post-war hits to continue the great 'Paris song' tradition, this sat comfortably on the airwaves alongside Joséphine Baker's twee 'Paris, Paris' and a more impressive big band-styled effort from crooner Georges Ulmer, 'Nuits de Paris'.

## Music hall's new generation

*Jacqueline François.*

Born in Denmark, Ulmer was a talented singer/songwriter who had risen to fame in 1946 with 'Pigalle', a tribute to the nightspots of the famous Parisian *quartier*, its wonderfully evocative lyric set to a swirling melody that became a classic of the post-war *chanson*. He followed this breakthrough with tributes to other cities, notably 'Les rues de Copenhague' and 'Casablanca', and had firmly established himself at the heart of the French music hall milieu as the decade drew to a close.

Joining him among the bright hopes of the new generation was Jacqueline François, who had begun her career as a *chanteuse réaliste* in the aftermath of the war with the moderately successful 'Ce n'était pas original', a title which summed up her approach perfectly. Seeing the error of her ways, she redefined herself as a charming champion of the music hall, hitting the heights in 1948 with the joyous 'C'est le printemps' (adapted from 'It Might As Well Be Spring' from the 1945 film, *State Fair*) and 1950's sweet 'Trois fois merci', which rapidly became her signature tune.

The latter song was originally recorded by Renée Lebas, who, despite having started her career before the war, had to wait until the Liberation to find fame. She scored in 1945 with the syrupy 'Insensiblement', and again a few months later with the rather better 'Où est-tu mon amour?'.

Actress Suzy Delair landed a big hit in 1946 with the jolly 'Avec son tra-la-la'. Both Delair and Lebas went on to enjoy moderately fruitful singing careers, although neither reached the same heights as François, and both were swiftly overtaken in 1948 by the newly emerged Line Renaud, who headed straight to the top off the back of her smash hit ballad, 'Ma cabane au Canada'.

Yvette Giraud made a splash in 1946 with the sentimental 'Mademoiselle Hortensia' before falling under the spell of American show tunes. Three years later, she had a massive hit with 'Ma guêpière et mes longs jupons' (Dinah Shore's 'Buttons And Bows') – the springboard to an international career that saw her elevated to superstar status in Japan.

Crooner Georges Guétary built on his wartime success with a run of smooth hits, ranging from the harmonious 'À Honolulu' to the unashamedly transatlantic 'Quand un cow-boy', peaking in 1946 with 'Comme une étoile', 'Le p'tit bal du samedi soir' and the nostalgic 'La valse des regrets'. Ever ambitious, he crossed the Channel in 1947 to appear in the West End musical *Bless The Bride*. After slipping back home in 1948 for the smash hit, 'Boléro', he returned to London as the prelude to an assault on the American market at the end of the decade.

Also rising in popularity, smooth vocal duo Patrice et Mario shook off wartime shackles to flirt with a variety of international sounds including 'Les trois caballeros' (a cover of Bing Crosby & The Andrews Sisters' 1945 hit, 'The Three

Caballeros'), 'Viva la samba' and 'La rumba des cigales'. Occasionally they got it wrong (as on the curious 1947 hybrid, 'Tango hawaïen'), but when they were on form (as on their 1948 hit, 'Le village brésilien'), they delivered an imaginative blend of French music hall and exotic sounds. They also took care to include a few home-grown items in their repertoire, though their take on 'Les trois cloches' could not compete against Édith Piaf's original. Rather better suited to their talents, 'La rumba de la pluie' gave them another hit in 1948 and they rolled on into the fifties, ranging across the globe to seek out 'Les trappeurs de l'Alaska' and 'Montagnes d'Italie' without ever breaking a sweat.

The tango also enjoyed a revival in the post-war years, although by now it was less of a novelty and more a part of the music hall mainstream. Released in 1946, Armand Mestral's 'Jalousie' took the pop marketplace by storm, wowing listeners the world over when an English adaptation ('Jealousy') performed by Frankie Laine became a global smash.

## Yves Montand

Yves Montand started out as a singer of mock-cowboy songs like 'Dans les plaines du Far-West' – an early sign of the growing Americanisation of French pop in the aftermath of the war – but a meeting (and brief love affair) with Édith Piaf put an end to his Wild West fantasies. Taking the handsome young singer under her wing, she put him on the road to success by getting him to change his repertoire and his image, and working with him on his stagecraft.

Intially, the results were disappointing. Released in 1945 and 1946, Montand's first recordings sold poorly. These included 'Matilda' (a bizarre adaptation of the Australian folk song, 'Waltzing Matilda'), though the music hall-friendly 'Luna Park' and 'Battling Joe' better defined his early style. Similarly, his first film, *Les Portes de la nuit* (1946), was a box office disaster.

However, things took a turn for the better in 1947, when Piaf wrote the wonderful 'Mais, qu'est-ce que j'ai?' for him, allowing his real personality to shine through on record for the first time. Coupled with the equally strong 'Ma gosse, ma p'tite môme' (written by long-time Piaf collaborator Marguerite Monnot), the song established Montand as a contender. In 1948, he scored his first major hit, 'C'est si bon', a jazzy shuffle that established his smooth, sophisticated approach and went on to become an international standard.[51]

The song won Montand an across-the-board following, catapulting him to the forefront of the industry. A string of hits quickly followed, including his interpretation of 'Clopin-clopant', a jazzy reading of the Mireille-penned 'Parce que ça me donne du courage', and a quality performance of Jacques Prévert and Joseph Kosma's 'Les enfants qui s'aiment', which allowed him to focus on weightier matters. He turned to Prévert and Kosma again in 1949 for the carnival sounds of 'Et la fête continue' and the poetic recitation 'Barbara', but it was his definitive reading of their 'Les feuilles mortes' that same year that did most to establish the song – and Montand himself – as one of the shining lights of *la chanson française*.

---

[51] As evidenced by hit versions from Eartha Kitt and Louis Armstrong.

## Jazz, swing and big bands

*Jacques Hélian.*

Montand may have abandoned his cowboy fantasies in exchange for success on stage, record and screen, but others proved more circumspect in giving up the music they loved. The post-war years saw a joyous outpouring of jazz bands from across the country, and if jazz never quite supplanted music hall and *chanson* as the French music of choice, it was nevertheless the hip music lover's badge of pride.

Many musicians were content to recreate the sounds they heard on American records, but some were more inventive. In 1946, Django Reinhardt reunited with Stéphane Grappelli for a stunning reinvention of their pre-war hit, 'Nuages'. Later that year, Reinhardt toured the US with Duke Ellington's orchestra, switching to electric guitar[52] to make himself heard and, after a shaky start, proved himself to be equally adept as on the acoustic. After returning to France, he recorded the remarkable 'Mélodie au crépuscule' with a new quintet, followed by a string of moody, sometimes sentimental pieces with a host of emerging French talent – among them further collaborations with Hubert Rostaing, including a rousing take on Benny Goodman's 'Topsy' and the delightful 'Danse norvégienne' (adapted from one of Grieg's *Norwegian Dances*).

Ray Ventura returned to France after the war and picked up where he had left off, starring in a pair of unmemorable, formulaic films in 1950 and 1951[53] and picking up hits with such light-hearted offerings as 'Maria de Bahia' and 'À la mi-août'. Increasingly drawn to the business side of the industry, he discovered that he had lost a considerable amount of ground to newcomer Jacques Hélian, whose combination of Paul Whiteman's 'sweet music' style and the hits of the day proved to be commercial gold.

Like Whiteman, Hélian featured top-flight musicians in his band but kept them on a tight leash, playing a strictly arranged easy listening variation on jazz that proved perfect for the years following the war. Though lacking in any real jazz improvisation, they were easily the biggest dance band in the country for the best part of a decade, racking up hits almost at will with the likes of 'Les jeunes filles de bonne famille' (1947), the exotic rumba, 'Au Chili'

---

[52] A Gibson ES-300, reputedly provided by the promoter from the William Morris Agency.
[53] The similarity of the titles – *Nous irons à Paris* and *Nous irons à Monte-Carlo* – is indicative of the lack of imagination that went into the making of them, although Ventura's band contributed some excellent performances.

(1949) and the Latin-tinged 'Monsieur le consul à Curityba' (1950), as well as backing Bourvil on his 1949 Glenn Miller-style swing effort, 'D'où viens-tu?'.

The success of the band also put the spotlight on Hélian's leading vocalists, the female duo Les Sœurs Étienne. They enjoyed a hit of their own in 1949 with 'Qui sait, qui sait, qui sait' (a richly orchestrated cover of Osvaldo Farrés' 'Quizàs, quizàs, quizàs'[54]) and another in 1950 with a pretty take on Dinah Shore's 'It's So Nice To Have A Man Around The House' ('Avoir un homme sous son toit').

## The trad jazz revival

The burgeoning jazz scene in France was also given a boost when American clarinettist Mezz Mezzrow set up home in Paris in 1948, followed shortly afterward by Sidney Bechet. Both were hugely influential even before their arrival, but the chance to hear two masters at work was like manna from heaven to the Parisian jazz community, who were drawn to their concerts like moths to the proverbial flame.

The flame burned particularly deep inside Claude Luter, a reed player who had made his name at the 1948 *Nice Jazz Festival*[55] with a style based on the traditional sounds of New Orleans, as exemplified by his 1947 revival of the Original Dixieland Jazz Band's 'Tiger Rag'. Another musician bitten by the same bug was pianist Claude Bolling, whose records spanned a wider spectrum than Luter's, from the slow, rolling rhythms of his 1948 take on the spiritual 'Nobody Knows The Trouble I've Seen' (a hit for Marion Anderson back in 1925) to a more uptempo stroll through Duke Ellington's 'Doin' The Voom-Voom' in 1949. Both Bolling and Luter were good enough to impress visiting American musicians and both would establish themselves, alongside British exponents like Ken Colyer and Chris Barber, as pillars of the European trad jazz revival.

## Édith Piaf and the *chanson* tradition

Jazz was steadily growing in popularity, but not even its biggest stars could hold a candle to the woman who had, by the end of the forties, established herself as the undisputed queen of French music hall. It was Édith Piaf who best characterised the French national psyche at this difficult yet optimistic time in the country's history, as, wracked with emotion, she extracted every ounce of pathos from the lyrics, leaving audiences mystified as to how so much power could be hidden away in such a tiny body. From the lush orchestration of her 1947 smash, 'J'm'en fous pas mal', to the brash, strident sounds of the 1949 hit, 'Bal dans ma rue', Piaf was impossible to ignore as her dynamic stage performances made her a legend on both sides of the Atlantic. Whether waltzing across the airwaves with 'L'orgue des amoureux' or baring her soul on 'Pour moi tout' seule' (both released in 1949), her recordings were both modern and international, yet defiantly French – a dichotomy that explained how she was able to take an unremarkable film

---

[54] Better known to anglophone audiences through Gordon Jenkins' much-covered adaptation, 'Perhaps, Perhaps, Perhaps'.

[55] This was the first staging of what became an annual event. The *Nice Jazz Festival* is still one of the major dates in the international jazz calendar today.

*Édith Piaf.*

theme like 'Paris'[56] and sell it to audiences all over the world.

Her compatriots may have been struggling with the aftermath of the war, but through it all Piaf found hope for the future. This optimism shone through in her songs, making the unspeakable heartbreak of her 1950 smash, 'Hymne à l'amour' (written following the tragic death of her lover, boxing champion Marcel Cerdan) all the more unbearable.[57] On this supreme example of the *chanteuse réaliste*'s art, Piaf wore both her own pain and the suffering of her country on her sleeve for all to see.

Piaf may have expressed the feelings of her audience in her songs, but, for all her earnest realism, neither she nor any of the other leading stars of the time did so in terms that would have been recognisable outside the world of popular song. Powerful vocal performances notwithstanding, musically and lyrically there was little to differentiate her work from that of countless other performers, even if her songwriting collaborators (many of whom owed their own careers to their discovery by, and the patronage of *la môme* Piaf) were able to capture her rough-and-tumble street-urchin origins to perfection in the words they gave her to sing.

It was another Piaf discovery who would find a way to bring the *chanson* into contact with the earthy reality of life in the second half of the twentieth century, a writer who would pen several of her greatest songs, and who would, alongside a host of other singers and writers of his generation, go on to kick-start a revolution in the way songs were sung and heard in France. It is in the work of Charles Aznavour, and in the smoke-filled back rooms of the country's concert halls and cabarets, that the story of modern French pop truly begins.

---

[56] From the now long-forgotten *L'Homme aux mains d'argile* (1949).

[57] One of the finest torch songs ever written, this survived a mangled translation into English as 'If You Love Me (Really Love Me)' to become a major transatlantic hit for both Kay Starr and Vera Lynn, although no singer ever came close to matching Piaf's performance.

# Chapter 5

## MOI, J'AIME LE MUSIC-HALL
### A return to normality (1948-59)

*Born to Armenian parents who had escaped the 1915 Ottoman massacre and settled in France, Charles Aznavour was an unlikely candidate to lead a musical revolution. Small of stature, slight of frame, and possessing neither classical good looks nor a powerful singing voice, he seemed at first glance to have little to offer. The thing that distinguished Aznavour from his contemporaries was a unique musical vision inspired by the jazz rhythms of Charles Trenet: like Frank Sinatra, with whom he would later be compared, he sang with genuine swing, and once he made his belated commercial breakthrough, he turned the world of French pop on its head.*

*Roche et Aznavour.*

### Aznavour, Bécaud, and the younger generation

Aznavour's career began quietly in 1942, when he formed a performing duo and songwriting partnership with pianist Pierre Roche. At first, they struggled to make headway, but after Georges Ulmer turned their composition 'J'ai bu' into a decent-sized hit in 1946, people began to take notice. Very soon, they found themselves in demand as songwriters, providing material for bandleader Jacques Hélian (the swinging 'Départ express'), tango specialist Marie-José ('Il me reste encore mon cœur'), Lisette Jambel ('Premier verre de champagne'), crooner Jean-Louis Tristan ('Sosthène'), Tohama ('Il y avait trois jeunes garçons') and the great Lucienne Delyle, who enjoyed a major hit in 1949 with 'C'est un gars'. Ironically, Roche et Aznavour's own recordings (1948-50) met with no success whatsoever, though the jazzy shuffle 'Voyez! C'est le printemps', on which Aznavour signalled his future direction, deserved a better reception.

Roche et Aznavour got their biggest break when they met Édith Piaf, who booked them as support act on her tours across France and the US in 1947-48. Piaf also gave Aznavour tips on stage presentation and encouraged him to develop his own style. Her vocal accompanists on tour, Les Compagnons de la Chanson, were likewise rapid converts, covering the duo's 'Je n'ai qu'un sou' and 'Cinq filles à marier' among their early recordings. The pair subsequently went to Canada for a year and a half, during which time they were offered a 40-week residency at the Au Faisan Doré cabaret in Montreal. The extended sojourn in Quebec also led to a break-up of the act: Pierre Roche fell in love with a local *chanteuse*, Aglaé, and decided to remain in Canada,[58] forcing Aznavour to strike out on his own.

Although his early recordings, such as the 1951 piano-led finger-snapper, 'Poker', went nowhere, and his live performances received catcalls from crowds and vicious reviews from critics, he persevered. He was by this time also developing a distinctive style of writing and his services were much in demand, both for his adaptations of recent American hits like Tony Bennett's 'Because Of You' (a hit for Éliane Embrun as 'Sans ton amour') and Phil Harris's 'The Thing' (covered by Les Compagnons de la Chanson as 'L'objet'), and for increasingly sophisticated original compositions like 'Ay! Je l'aime' (which was given a dramatic reading by Maria Vincent in 1953). Édith Piaf also recorded a number of his songs, including the taboo-shattering 'Une enfant' and his adaptation of Frankie Laine's 'Jezebel',[59] before he finally found his own audience in 1954 with the moving ballad 'Viens au creux de mon épaule'.

What made Aznavour different from the rest of his generation was his direct, honest, almost confrontational approach to the songwriter's art. While performers such as Yves Montand and even Piaf were content to rely on lyrical clichés, Aznavour wrote it and sang it as he saw it, laying bare the tragedy of 'Une enfant' without recourse to sentimentality, and casually recounting the deflowering of a young woman

---

[58] Roche and Aglaé relocated to Paris during the fifties, when Aglaé enjoyed a short run of popular hits that led to her co-starring alongside Tino Rossi in the 1955 operetta *Méditerranée*. The couple returned to Quebec in 1963.

[59] A typically powerful performance that obliterated a rival version by Paul Péri.

in 'Il y avait trois jeunes garçons' in a way that was startling to audiences accustomed to the treacly offerings of the likes of Tino Rossi. More importantly, he sang in the language of the street rather than the theatre or poetry book, which gave his songs an earthy realism far removed from the usual sounds of the hit parade.

Musically too, he stood one step apart from the crowd, his tunes clipping along to polished, American-inspired rhythms or wallowing in the melancholy minor keys of blues-tinged jazz, representing a more modern sound for a post-war age. The honesty of 'Je t'aime comme ça' and the bittersweet regret of 'Le palais de nos chimères' (both released in 1955 and wrapped in modern arrangements) provided fresh insight into the possibilities of popular song, dispensing with the pathos-laden approach of Piaf in favour of a gritty realism that redefined the concept of a *chanteur réaliste*. While his biggest early hits were plain-speaking love songs like 'Sur ma vie', his forthright approach to sex on outings like 'Une enfant' found a willing audience among the young. Stifled by the conservatism of the post-war world, French youth responded to Aznavour's directness with alacrity, flocking to his shows and buying his records in ever-increasing quantities.

Like many cultural revolutions, Aznavour's was slow to get underway, and in the event he was beaten to the top by his friend, Gilbert Bécaud. A classically-trained pianist, Bécaud had likewise put in time working with Édith Piaf before striking out on his own. Though more dynamic on stage than Aznavour, he lacked the latter's gift with words, relying on outside help for lyrics to go with his readily accessible melodies. Indeed, one of his earliest collaborators was Aznavour himself, with whom he penned several songs including 'Donne-moi', 'Je veux te dire adieu' (both of which Bécaud recorded during his early flurry of hits) and 'Viens', a hit in 1952 for Jacques Pills. 'Je veux te dire adieu' was also recorded, in a more old-fashioned arrangement, by the fast-fading Marjane,[60] shortly before she threw in the towel and retired to raise horses.

Bécaud approached his songs from the same perspective as his friend and rival, eschewing the French equivalent of rhyming 'moon' with 'June' in favour of a more pertinent approach. His first single, 'Les croix', released in 1953, asked some rather pointed questions of organised religion in light of the events which had recently convulsed the Continent, finding a ready response from a generation only too willing to question the certainties of the past. Replete with American references, the contagious pop melody of the flip, 'Mes mains', showed him to be musically forward-looking as well, and the song deservedly became a smash in its own right. Subsequent releases generated hits like 'Quand tu danses' and 'C'était mon copain',[61] which placed Bécaud within the music hall rather than the jazz tradition, although the bright rhythms of songs like 'Ah! Dites-moi pourquoi je l'aime' were light years from the traditional piano-based style generally favoured in the French music industry, clearly pointing the way to a new style of popular music.

---

[60] Léo Marjane had dropped her first name after the war, but the rebranding did little to revive her fortunes.

[61] 'C'était mon copain' was also covered in 'smooth harmony' style by Les Compagnons de la Chanson.

*Gilbert Bécaud.*

Just how far ahead of the game Bécaud was became clear in 1954, when he was booked as support act for Lucienne Delyle (at that time riding high with a hit cover of Hank Williams' 'Jambalaya') at the reopening of the Olympia Theatre.[62] Bécaud blew Delyle offstage, totally inhabiting his songs and stealing the show with a dynamic act that marked the triumph of youth over experience. Both at this show and a second run of dates in 1955, he whipped his young audience into a frenzy with his incredible showmanship, topped by the unheard-of spectacle of playing the piano with his feet.[63] His performance sparked a riot that saw the theatre's seats reduced to rubble in a clear precursor to the rock'n'roll riots of the coming years. The excitement was captured on a superb live album, *Le tour de chant de Gilbert Bécaud à l'Olympia*, where he worked his magic on an audibly excited crowd, storming his way through hits like 'La ballade des baladins' and 'Laissez faire, laissez dire'.

Neither Aznavour nor Bécaud could remotely be described as a rock'n'roll singer, but in their appeal to the younger generation they filled the same void as Bill Haley (and subsequently Elvis Presley) in the US. Their direct approach and personal style of performing made them teen idols before the hour, standing in stark contrast to old-fashioned music hall singers like Dany Dauberson.[64] Perhaps the best comparison is to Johnnie Ray, who inspired similar scenes of fan frenzy in the early fifties in the US and the UK. In time, Bécaud, like Ray, would temper his wild exuberance, although he never abandoned his commitment to lyrical realism, or to the dramatic potential of his material. The less dynamic Aznavour never lost his preference for the direct approach either, but as more threatening singers appeared, he too found himself adopted by the mainstream without having adjusted his style in any way. This two-pronged assault on the French music hall milieu challenged the status quo in a way not seen since before the war, yet Aznavour and Bécaud were both swiftly absorbed into the heart of the French show-business establishment.

---

[62] Former songwriter Bruno Coquatrix had taken over the building, which had been used as a cinema since 1929, and established it as the most prestigious live venue in France.

[63] Nobody outside of the southern USA – and precious few inside – had even heard of Little Richard or Jerry Lee Lewis at the time, let alone seen them perform.

[64] Who nevertheless recorded Aznavour's 'Bal du faubourg' in 1950.

## Francis Lemarque and the Communist *chanson*

In this they were more successful than Francis Lemarque, whose overt Communist sympathies made him something of an outsider at a time when the French media were dominated by the conservative state. Lemarque had started his career before the war, but only really began to make headway after Yves Montand recorded his 'Ma douce vallée' and 'À Paris' in 1948. It would have been easy to mistake the latter for the latest in the endless series of tributes to the capital, but the detailed lyric and Montand's delivery combined to paint an altogether different picture of modern life, subtly changing his image from the American-loving crooner of his debut into a more challenging, politicised animal. The change was completed in 1952, when he recorded Lemarque's defiantly pacifist 'Quand un soldat'.

The transformation did little damage to Montand's commercial standing. As the new decade opened and *chansons* from the likes of Aristide Bruant (the gentle 'Rue Saint-Vincent') and adaptations from poets such as Guillaume Apollinaire ('Saltimbanques') gave way to the Mireille-penned character sketch 'Une demoiselle sur une balançoire' and the accordion favourite 'Rue Lepic', Montand was the country's top live draw, breaking attendance records for his one-man shows in Paris – a series of performances combining songs with poetry that set the standard for all his subsequent shows. However he would return to Lemarque for material in 1953 and 1954, recording his celebrations of the life of the industrial working classes: 'Les routiers',[65] the sensitive love song, 'Toi, tu n'ressembles à personne', and the more typical commentary, 'La ballade de Paris'.

Montand's patronage proved invaluable to Lemarque, who had launched his recording career in 1949 with an accordion-laden but equally vibrant version of 'À Paris'. He proved popular with audiences and record buyers, scoring a hit in 1950 with the upbeat 'Bal, petit bal',[66] and another in 1951 with the gently orchestrated 'Patins à roulettes'.[67] He had a major hit in 1955 with the musical fable 'La grenouille', and even made international inroads by proxy, hitting the US and UK Top 10s in 1954, when the Gaylords and Petula Clark covered his pretty children's song, 'Le petit cordonnier', for their respective markets as 'The Little Shoemaker'.

Back in France, Lemarque enjoyed respectable sales with his 1955 hit, 'Mon copain d'Pékin', an ode to brotherhood infused with a poppy orchestration to better get his message across. Equally typical was 'John

---

[65] Which Lemarque would himself record in 1956.

[66] Although its impact was rather more muted than it might have been, as the song was also covered by Montand.

[67] This song is sometimes known by its alternate title, 'Bois de Boulogne'.

Black', whose jazzy backing helped to sweeten the anti-racist lyrics that drove the song. However, it was only in 1957 that Lemarque hit a commercial peak with the sweet-and-easy 'L'air de Paris' and the smash hit 'Marjolaine', a relatively innocuous but highly infectious slice of music hall pop that was quickly covered by a host of others.[68]

## Male stars of the 1950s

Trailing along behind Montand, the remaining survivors of the post-war reconstruction jockeyed for position in a market gearing up for a new golden age of music hall. In commercial terms, the form horse remained Tino Rossi, who bestrode the landscape like a giant with a string of hits including 'Belle, ma belle' (1950), 'Joli mois de mai' (1951), 'J'ai gardé ta photo' (1952), 'Mouettes sur Sorrente' (1953) and a deliberately 'olde worlde' harpsichord-backed revival of the centuries-old ballad 'Plaisir d'amour' (1954). The following year, he returned to the stage in the custom-made operetta *Méditerranée*, generating further hits with the sweetly crooned, if stereotypical title song and the similarly structured (even down to the massed vocal choruses) 'Ajaccio'. Meanwhile, the stripped-back 'Complainte corse' offered a less glitzy example of his still-exquisite, if slightly dated, way with a melody.

Irrespective of the musical settings, it was Rossi's voice that sold the records, and, in the middle of the fifties, twenty years after his debut, he still ranked among the biggest-selling artists in the French recording industry. With a repertoire anchored in his beloved Mediterranean, he bombarded the airwaves and concert halls with sentimental classics like 'Catari, Catari' (1955), 'Tango mediterranée' (1956), 'Mandoline amoureuse' (a smash in 1957) and 'Naples au baiser de feu' (1957)[69], with occasional nods to outside sources like 'Cindy' (Eddie Fisher's 'Cindy, Oh Cindy') along the way. While he offered nothing new, his old-fashioned, unashamed sentimentality guaranteed him a loyal audience.

Also at home in the world of operetta, André Dassary impressed the critics with his performances in *La toison d'or* in 1954, but never forgot his roots in the Basque region of France. He cut a series of best-sellers in the early fifties, each recalling his homeland, the likes of 'Beth ceü de Pau' and 'Vent du sud' making him as much a hero to the Basques as Tino Rossi was to the Corsicans. Like Rossi, he also possessed a wider appeal, shifting over a million records by 1952, with 'Paris at night'[70] and 'La strada' finding their way into thousands of homes.

Although he didn't sell quite as many records, former rugby player-turned-operetta star Henri Génès broke through via 1948's *4 jours à Paris*, in which he introduced the much-covered 'La samba brésilienne', the first of a string of hits running into the fifties. Among his classic performances were an impressive reworking of Bourvil's 1950 smash, 'La tactique du gendarme', the outstanding comic performance 'Hector', and the tango 'Tantina de Burgos', on which he displayed both his sense of humour and a charm that was utterly

---

[68] Including good versions by Yvette Giraud, François Deguelt and André Claveau.
[69] From the operetta of the same name, itself inspired by the 1937 film in which Rossi had starred.
[70] Sung in French, despite the English title.

unexpected from someone of his imposing physique.

Like Dassary and Génès, Luis Mariano was part of the new generation of operetta stars who prospered after the war. A refugee from Franco's Spain who had moved to France before hostilities began, Mariano started out singing Spanish-tinged novelties like 'Une nuit à Grenade' before finding success in the mid-forties with 'La belle de Cadix'. Further hits followed, many with Spanish or Latin themes, including a 1949 take on Osvadlo Farrés' 'Quizàs, quizàs, quizàs' ('Qui sait, qui sait, qui sait'). However, it was the 1952 operetta *Le chanteur de Mexico* that made him a star, spinning off hits with 'Mexico', 'Maria Cristina'[71] and the pretty 'Rossignol'. Mariano enjoyed his biggest success in 1953 with 'L'amour est un bouquet de violettes' (from the 1952 film *Violetas impériales*), and continued cranking out the hits throughout the fifties – among them a seductive revival of Lucienne Boyer's 'Mon cœur est un violon' which typified his approach as the suave Mediterranean crooner. By 1955, he was the biggest star in the country, selling over half a million records in that year alone.

Egyptian-born Greek Georges Guétary had a similar background to Mariano, and by the dawn of the fifties already had several hits under his belt. Having established himself on both sides of the Channel, he spent the early part of the new decade conquering the American market (most notably via a starring role opposite Gene Kelly in the classic 1951 MGM musical, *An American in Paris*), although he was capable in a number of fields, singing and dancing through operettas, and recording ballads and novelty songs for record release. Back home in France, his performances in light opera gifted him a hit in 1952 with the big production number 'La route fleurie', his romantic 'Latin lover' personality selling the song to an appreciative audience. A duet with Bourvil on the amusing 'C'est la vie de bohême' in the same year established him as a pillar of the mighty Pathé label, and he went on to record hit after hit, scoring in 1955 with 'C'est vous, c'est vous' and the following year with 'Le berger mexicain' to cement his place in the heart of French show business.

*Georges Guétary.*

---

[71] When issued on LP, this song was subtitled 'Marie Cristina (...veut toujours commander)'.

## The lure of Hollywood

Maurice Chevalier also took advantage of the end of hostilities to cross the Atlantic – in his case to resume, rather than begin, a stateside career. If the international hits now lay in the past, back home he could still set cash registers ringing with records like the enjoyable tribute to his fellow citizens, 'Les parigots'. He had to endure a three-year ban in the US, imposed at the height of the McCarthy era on account of his support for the French Communist Party, but remained undeterred, returning in 1954 and undertaking a full tour of the country a year later.

Chevalier restarted his Hollywood film career in 1957, starring in *Love In The Afternoon*.[72] In 1958, he made a memorable appearance in the MGM musical *Gigi* alongside Louis Jourdan, Hermione Gingold and the young Leslie Caron, a rising talent among the French acting community. Although Caron had enjoyed a US pop hit in 1953 with 'Hi-Lili, Hi-Lo',[73] she never reached the same elevated position as Chevalier, who remained a much-loved figure around the world. The movie introduced him to a new audience, thanks to the immortal 'Thank Heaven For Little Girls' – a song that perfectly reflected the more innocent times of its creation – and his deliberately stumbling, but effortlessly endearing duet with Gingold, 'I Remember It Well'.

Also succumbing once again to the lure of the Yankee dollar, Danielle Darrieux left the Swiss sanctuary to which she had retreated during the war to star alongside Jane Powell in the 1951 MGM musical *Rich, Young and Pretty*, the first of a short run of films that culminated in a controversial 1955 adaptation of D.H. Lawrence's *Lady Chatterley's Lover*. By the middle of the decade, Darrieux had tired of the studio system and returned home to France, where she revived her dormant singing career, getting things underway with 1955's 'Tout au bout de la semaine'.

---

[72] Co-starring Audrey Hepburn and Gary Cooper.
[73] A duet with Mel Ferrer from the film *Lili*, for which she had also received an Oscar nomination. The song immediately resurfaced in French as 'Ma Lili, hello' and was covered by Jacques Hélian and a host of others.

## Treading the boards

Bourvil, on the other hand, opted to remain a star of French cinema rather than trying his luck in America and continued a parallel recording career that allowed him to display his comic skills on a wide variety of music hall favourites. Among the many hits he enjoyed during the first half of the fifties were the very silly 'À Joinville-le-Pont' and the equally popular 'Les haricots'. Even so, for all his musical endeavours, it was as a much-loved comic figure on both screen and stage that he enjoyed his most enduring popularity. His massively successful 1950 live recording of the comic sketch 'Causerie anti-alcoolique', in which a very 'drunk' Bourvil delivers a barely comprehensible diatribe on the evils of the demon drink, perfectly summed up his unique appeal.

Of more serious intent was André Claveau, whose career began during the war. A classically trained baritone, he was a crooner in the style of Jean Sablon, and with the latter struggling to regain his pre-war popularity, Claveau soon found an audience for his romantic ballads. A recording artist since the end of the forties, he peaked in 1950 with the classic 'Cerisier rose et pommier blanc', a sway-along favourite that became an international standard five years later in the hands of both Pérez Prado and Eddie Calvert as the trumpet instrumental 'Cherry Pink And Apple Blossom White'.

Further hits followed as Claveau established himself as the swoon idol of the hour with smooth ballads like 'Domino' and 'Deux petits chaussons' (a cover of the Charlie Chaplin-composed Frank Chacksfield hit, 'Terry's Theme From "Limelight" '), best-sellers in 1951 and 1952 respectively. The latter marked a rare excursion into foreign material, but the following year's 'Tango des jours heureux' saw him firmly back on French territory, even if the musical inspiration exhibited more than a hint of Argentinian influence. More typical was the 1952 hit 'Gigi', a slice of pop balladry dedicated to the French author Colette,[74] and further lightweight offerings such as 'Vous, vous, vous' and 1954's mock-*musette* 'Bals de France' (though the intrusive strings made it seem more like a Hollywood take on France than the real thing), which kept him at the forefront of the recording industry. Claveau continued to ply his trade throughout the fifties, scoring a major smash in 1956 with 'Viens valser

---

[74] Colette's novella of the same name had been adapted into a successful Broadway play (with Audrey Hepburn in the starring role) before being made into the Hollywood musical featuring Maurice Chevalier referred to earlier.

avec Papa' (a nauseating duet with a young Catherine Hiegel,[75] adapted from Eddie Albert's 'Come Pretty Little Girl'), followed by a succession of covers of other people's hits, most notably Gilbert Bécaud's 'Marie, Marie' (1959).

Better known as an screen actor, Robert Lamoureux scored a hit in 1950 with the comical 'Papa, Maman, la bonne et moi'. Further novelties followed, including the cautionary tale of 'La voiture d'occasion', but despite his cinematic appeal he was unable to sustain a successful recording career.

John William hailed from the French colony now known as Côte d'Ivoire [Ivory Coast], but moved to France as a child. Deported by the Nazis in 1944 for his activities in the Resistance, he sang to his fellow concentration camp inmates to keep up their spirits and in doing so discovered that he possessed a magnificent voice. After being freed, he found work performing at a Paris cinema as a support act to the films before progressing to cabaret. He began his recording career in 1952 with a hit interpretation of 'Si toi aussi tu m'abandonnes', the theme from the popular western *High Noon* (1952).[76] With his baritone voice and commanding presence, William established himself as a domestic equivalent of Paul Robeson, emphasising his roots with the song 'Je suis un nègre' and carving out a distinctive niche for himself in the heart of music hall.

A gifted comic who sang in an operatic tenor, the rotund Dario Moreno would have been a natural for operetta, but it was cinema that gave him his first break. Having established himself on the silver screen, he branched out into the music industry with 'Istamboul' (an enjoyable reworking of the Four Lads' 1953 US hit, 'Istanbul (Not Constantinople)') before scoring a hit in 1955 with a smooth cover of 'C'est magnifique' (Lilo's classic Cole Porter song from the musical *Can-Can*), sharing sales with Luis Mariano and Lucienne Delyle. It was to be the first of a lengthy run of similar light-hearted hits. Ever-smiling and never taking himself seriously, Moreno was the perfect star for the years of post-war recovery. The quasi-operatic style he brought to bear on favourites like 'Un ange comme ça', the Latin-tinged 'Mé qué... mé qué' and his 1954 remake of Jacques Pills' 'Viens'[77] was perfect ear candy for those looking for bright and uplifting popular music.

Despite the bitter feelings still lingering after the recent war, French audiences eagerly adopted German-born Félix Marten as one of their own, gifting him a substantial hit with the old-school jazz arrangement of 'La Marie

[75] The daughter of Pathé A&R man Pierre Hiegel, the ten-year-old would go on to a long career as an actress.
[76] Or *Le train sifflera trois fois*, as it was known in France.
[77] 'Mé qué... mé qué' and 'Viens' were penned by Charles Aznavour and Gilbert Bécaud, both of whom also recorded the former, albeit in rather different styles.

*Marcel Amont.*

Vison'[78] in 1955. A handsome singer with all the good looks of a pre-war film star, Marten followed this breakthrough with a second smash, 'Le briquet', before diversifying into the world of acting with equal success.

François Deguelt began his career in the cabarets of the Left Bank. With his attractive smile and a suave crooning voice, he became known as *'Le saltimbanque du charme'*,[79] but although he dressed his songs in contemporary sounds, he remained a romantic at heart. His early releases were mainly ballads delivered in a light Crosbyesque style, although 'Dimanche matin' owed its origins to a Breton folk song, which allowed it to sit somewhat adrift from the mainstream. Far more typical were his 1957 hits, 'Les âmes fières'[80] and 'Moisson (La terre est basse)', which were also covered by a host of other singers including both Yves Montand and Les Compagnons de la Chanson. However, his penchant for recording songs that were also available in other versions[81] diminished his own appeal, and, for all his obvious talent, he never quite reached the level of the era's leading stars.

Marcel Amont started out as a parodist before breaking through in 1956 with the gentle 'Le pigeon voyageur' and the cod-Spanish nonsense of 'Escamillo', the contrast between the two neatly summing up the dichotomy in his approach. Peddling light entertainment pure and simple, he rode the charts with efforts like his 1957 hits 'Allez à la pêche' and 'Julie', both easy-on-the-ear pop songs with no aspiration to be anything else. While he did make occasional stabs at a more substantial repertoire, such as the Aznavour-penned 'Aïe mon cœur',[82] it was the more traditional sounds of songs like 'Barcarolle auvergnate' that confirmed his potential mass appeal, even if he was yet to scale the heights of his leading contemporaries.

## Female stars of the 1950s

Black American gospel trio the Peters Sisters had worked back home with Duke Ellington and Cab Calloway before setting up base in France after the

---

[78] Covered rather more impressively by Yves Montand as 'La Marie-Vison' the following year.
[79] 'The charming entertainer'. This was also the title of one of his EPs.
[80] Adapted from the theme tune to the 1956 film *The Proud Ones*, this had to compete with a rival version from old-school crooner André Dassary.
[81] This was probably down to record company insistence. Well into the mid-sixties, rival firms would rush to cover each other's hits in an attempt to cash in on their popularity.
[82] Which brought him into competition with veteran André Claveau, who also covered Amont's 'Sophie'.

war, appearing at the Folies-Bergère and in the 1949 film, *Nous irons à Paris*. Popular on both sides of the Rhine, they made their continental recording debut the same year with 'Un joli slow', the success of which precipitated an abandoning of their jazz and gospel roots in favour of music hall fluff that kept them in work throughout the fifties.

Having already found her audience in the previous decade, Yvette Giraud soared high at the start of fifties with the seductive rhythms of 'Avril au Portugal', adapted from fado queen Amália Rodrigues' 'Coïmbra'.[83] She kept the hits flowing throughout the early years of the decade, enjoying her greatest glory with 'Un p'tit peu d'argent' in 1955.

*Lucienne Delyle.*

Lucienne Delyle's continued reliance on her considerable vocal prowess and sweet musical backings did her no harm as she enjoyed further commercial triumphs in 1950 with the low-key jazz balladry of 'Monte-Carlo' and a lush revival of Georgel's already much-covered 'Sous les ponts de Paris'. She filled the next few years with a diverse mixture of jazz, *chanson réaliste*, tango, *musette* and romantic balladry, touching all bases without truly establishing herself as mistress of any particular style, before scoring again in 1953 with the uptempo 'La valse des orgueilleux'.

Equally popular was Mick Micheyl, a superb entertainer who burst into view

in 1950 with the charming 'Marchand de poésie' before crafting 'Un gamin de Paris', a timeless slice of Parisian pop that was swiftly covered, albeit less impressively, by Yves Montand.[84] None of her other recordings caught the imagination in quite the same way, but she remained a fixture on the concert hall circuit with the likes of 'Ma maman' and 'Cano... canoë', though it was as a revue leader rather than a singer that she truly shone.

Zizi Jeanmaire was one of the hottest live draws in Paris, combining song and dance to create a spectacle

---

[83] The *fado* is a traditional Portuguese form of popular song that shares the power and passion of French *chanson*. It was Giraud's rendition that led to its being reworked into English as 'April In Portugal', a global smash by Les Baxter & His Orchestra.

[84] As 'Le gamin de Paris'.

unrivalled at the time. The title song from her 1950 revue *La croqueuse de diamant* gave her a hit that year, establishing her as a star. The song was a perfect marriage of late-night jazzy rhythms and French music hall savvy, and subsequent releases mined the same seam to perfection, each of them crafted specifically with a nightclub performance in mind. The nearest thing the fifties could offer to the glory days of Mistinguett, it was entirely logical that Jeanmaire chose to revive the classic tunes of her great predecessor, releasing top-class reworkings of 'La java' and 'Ça c'est Paris'. Further hits flowed during the early years of the decade, her understated performance of 'Paris – Bohême' and the dramatic 'Je suis la femme' helping to keep her in the public eye. Increasingly marginalised once the emphasis switched from theatre seats to record sales, she endured as a popular star for many years on the back of her incredible live energy.[85]

The same commitment to live entertainment underpinned the career of Line Renaud, who enjoyed a succession of hits in the early fifties including the string-swept 'Étoile des neiges' (based on Franz Winkler's German hit 'Fliege mit mir in die Heimat'[86]) and 'Ma petite folie' (Guy Mitchell's 'My Truly, Truly Fair'). However, Renaud really came to life on the concert stage, where her ease with American swing styles set her apart from her fellow performers. Having made her name as the opening act for Yves Montand, she soon became a star in her own right and in 1951 travelled to London, where she became one of the few French stars to successfully export her popularity to British cabaret and record-buying audiences.

Appearances in films such as *Ils sont dans les vignes* (1952) and *La route du bonheur* (1953) were followed by further hits like the same year's classic 'Mademoiselle from Armentières' and the 1953 sway-along smash, 'Printemps d'Alsace'. One of the brightest French stars of the fifties, she mixed original songs such as 'Tire, tire l'aiguille'[87] and the 1953 ballad 'Je ne sais pas' with material drawn from overseas sources, such as her excellent 1954 remake of Les Paul & Mary Ford's 'Vaya Con Dios'.[88] Among her greatest triumphs was

---

[85] Jeanmaire retained sufficient popularity and international recognition over the years to find herself name-checked at the end of the following decade on UK singer Peter Sarstedt's 1969 hit, 'Where Do You Go To (My Lovely)'.

[86] Though it is more likely the inspiration came from Perry Como's English-language version, 'Forever And Ever' – as can be clearly heard on a smoochy interpretation by André Claveau.

[87] The song was also given a sprightlier reading by Henri Génès (as 'Tire l'aiguillle') which placed greater emphasis on its mock-Arabic sound. On some of Renaud's releases, the song is subtitled 'Tire, tire l'aiguille (Laï, laï, laï)'.

[88] Which was also given a cheesier makeover by Luis Mariano as 'Que Dieu pense à toi'.

1953's 'Moulin Rouge', a gentle ballad that toured the world as 'The Song From Moulin Rouge (Where Is Your Heart)', topping the US and UK charts for Percy Faith and Mantovani[89] respectively.

The following year, Renaud broke attendance records at the selfsame Moulin Rouge over a four-month season during which she was spotted by an impressed Bob Hope. He invited her to join him in the US, where she appeared on five television shows, wowed audiences at New York nightclubs and recorded a marvellous comic duet with Dean Martin, 'Relax-Ay-Voo', which introduced her to a large American audience and even resulted in a minor hit in the UK.[90] However, Renaud never forgot her fans back home and made regular return trips to Paris throughout her golden decade, continuing to rack up hits with 'J'ai vu maman embrasser le Père Noël' (an adaptation of Jimmy Boyd's 'I Saw Mommy Kissing Santa Claus'), 'Mambo bacan', the jazzy 'Casino de Paris', an enjoyable cover of Louis Prima's classic 'Buona Sera', and 'Quand ', the stirring theme song from the 1955 film, *La Madelon*.

Swiss singer Lys Assia made fewer ripples in the French marketplace but was more successful internationally, scoring around the world with the contrived but undeniably catchy 'O mein Papa' in 1954. Like much of her repertoire, this was sung in German.[91] She had already topped the UK sheet music chart three years earlier with the enjoyable 'Mademoiselle de Paris', and her light-hearted style brought her hits on both sides of the Channel with the novel 'Ba-loom ba-la' (a cover of Nilla Pizzi's Italian hit, 'Papaveri e papere') and the sugary 'Téléphonez-moi, chéri'.

'Mademoiselle de Paris' was also a hit for Jacqueline François, who recorded it in the same year as Assia. Originally a classy interpreter of American songs like Nat 'King' Cole's 'Nature Boy' ('Étrange garçon'), she had risen rapidly to become one of the biggest stars of the early fifties, shifting over a million records by 1953 thanks to best-sellers like 'J'ai peur de l'automne' (1950) and 'Le manège aux souvenirs' (1953). In 1955, she carved her name into the history books with 'Les lavandières du Portugal'[92] – the first record to reach No. 1 on the newly-created national hit parade.[93] It was the biggest of the countless hits she recorded during the decade, which included the understated ballad 'Est-ce ma faute?' and a dramatic interpretation of Charles Aznavour's 'On ne sait jamais', though most of them were jolly music

---

[89] Mantovani's version carried the amended title 'The Song From The Moulin Rouge'.
[90] Although it wasn't placed in the *New Musical Express* record chart, it peaked at No. 21 in the sheet music chart.
[91] She also recorded it in French as 'Oh! Mon Papa', as did Tino Rossi.
[92] Also recorded by a host of other singers including Yvette Giraud, the song was later reworked into a US hit for Joe 'Fingers' Carr (aka Lou Busch) as 'Portuguese Washerwoman'.
[93] *La Bourse des chansons*, first published in *Le Figaro* in September 1955.

hall knockabouts little different from those enjoyed by audiences before the war. A consummate performer, François was perfectly at home in front of an international audience, and, like Lys Assia, was quick to spread her wings beyond the borders of her homeland when the opportunity arose.

Belgian singer Annie Cordy came up the hard way, treading the boards in her native country for several years before heading south to sing at the Moulin Rouge. She eventually made her name in operetta while recording bright, upbeat material like the middle-

of-the-road swayer 'Le bal des voyous' and the lightly orchestrated pop nonsense of 'Les trois bandits de Napoli', which became her first hit in early 1953. She enjoyed further successes with rhythmic dance band material like 'Bonbons – caramels', mock-western novelties like 'La fille du cov-bois', jazzy pop workouts like 'Fleur de papillon' and covers of Charles Aznavour's 'La bagarre' and 'Et bâiller et dormir'. By the middle of the fifties she was one of the biggest stars on the music hall circuit.

A light opera star during the forties, Georgette Plana looked backwards for inspiration to relaunch herself with a jazzy repertoire that went right back to the twenties. Offering a viable alternative to the more traditional music hall sounds available elsewhere, she enjoyed a run of best-selling EPs and albums, landing the biggest hit of her career in 1956 with a version of the much-recorded 'Java'.

Anny Gould enjoyed a major hit in 1955 with 'Monsieur mon passé', although her rather dated style had an oddly jarring effect when she tackled Aznavour's 'Sur ma vie'. Conversely, Guylaine Guy,[94] demonstrated a more modern feel on the same singer's 'Ça' in 1955. Guy's stock-in-trade was a Doris Day-like approach, and she picked up her first hit in 1954 with 'Rien qu'une chanson', and another in 1956 with a version of Charles Trenet's 'Où sont-ils donc?', leading to a run of successes to the end of the decade.

Colette Renard made her name on the stage in 1956 in the timeless *Irma la douce*[95] and brought a refreshingly vibrant approach to her material, as may be heard on her hit EP of songs from the musical,[96] among them 'Avec les anges', 'Ah! Dis donc' and the immortal

---

[94] The Canadian was discovered by Charles Trenet when he toured over there and followed him back to Paris to try her luck in the French market.

[95] Later a Broadway hit, then a Hollywood film starring Shirley MacLaine and Jack Lemmon.

[96] Co-written by Alexandre Breffort and Édith Piaf's regular collaborator, Marguerite Monnot.

theme song. Despite a penchant for the music of Édith Piaf, Renard found fame with a less strident style, scoring hits with the likes of 'Sa casquette' (1957) and the amusing 'Mon homme est un guignol' (1959). While she may have been as dependent on outside writers as most of the upper echelons of French music hall, she injected some real personality into the proceedings, carving out a market niche for her jolly, upbeat recordings.

Mathé Altéry debuted in 1953 with the theme from *Les belles de nuit*, and subsequently made a career dubbing French vocals onto such Hollywood musicals as *Seven Brides For Seven Brothers*[97] for home consumption. A doll-like singer whose appeal rested as much on her image as on her singing voice, she was a popular variety star, releasing a long series of albums such as the retrospective *13 valses de la Belle Époque*, which wrapped up a baker's dozen of classic oldies from the golden age of music hall. She enjoyed a long and moderately successful career that reached its zenith when she represented France at the first *Eurovision Song Contest* with 'Le temps perdu' in 1956.

### Eurovision

Now a venerable institution in the world of light entertainment, the *Eurovision Song Contest* was the brainchild of Frenchman Marcel Baison, who, inspired by the success of the annual *San Remo Song Festival* which had started in 1952, sought to bring the nations of Europe together through the newly available power of television. It began inauspiciously in a Swiss theatre as a contest between seven nations, each of which was represented by one or more of their leading entertainers. The winner was Switzerland's Lys Assia with the sorrowful 'Refrain', which duly demonstrated the commercial power of *Eurovision* by becoming a hit across much of Europe.[98]

Assia was already a major star, but the early years of the song contest

*Lys Assia.*

also gave valuable exposure to the less prominent purveyors of French music hall. Among those to follow in Assia's and Altéry's footsteps were female balladeer Paule Desjardins (who came second in 1957 with the French entry, 'La belle amour') and Danièle Dupré (who finished fourth for Luxembourg that same year with 'Amours mortes (Tant de peine)').

Belgium's Fud Leclerc virtually made a career out of the competition,

---

[97] Titled *Les sept femmes de Barbe-Rousse* in France.
[98] No ranked list of the entries was announced that year, so it is not known where Mathé Altéry's French entry finished on the night.

appearing four times between 1956 and 1962 without ever carrying off the prize. His best placing was fifth with 'Ma petite chatte' in 1958, while his biggest claim to fame came in 1962, when 'Ton nom' was one of four songs to be awarded *nul points* – the first year in which any song was so poorly rated.[99] Despite the exposure he gained by his appearances in the contest, Leclerc never established himself outside of his national borders.

By 1959, the contest had grown so much in stature that pre-war singer Jacques Pills sought to use it to relaunch a career that had stalled a few years earlier, when the overly dramatic 'Le grisbi' began a fall from favour. However, his 'Mon ami Pierrot'[100] (the first ever entry for Monaco) fared badly on the night, picking up only one point and finishing last.

## The giants of the 1950s

The *Eurovision* entrants were all popular but none of them enjoyed anything like the audience devotion inspired by Édith Piaf, who dominated the early fifties, scoring hits at home and abroad with ease. A pair of American albums, *Édith Piaf Sings* (1949) and *Édith Piaf Sings Again* (1951), were steady sellers, the latter featuring her latest French hits, 'Il y avait' and 'Il fait bon t'aimer', both examples of her patent vocal style. The era also witnessed her first English-language recordings, including adaptations of her hits 'Hymne à l'amour' ('Hymn To Love'), 'Les trois cloches' ('The Three Bells') and 'La vie en rose',[101] as well as a reading of Yves Montand's 'Les feuilles mortes' ('Autumn Leaves'), but these lacked the power and passion she exuded when singing in her own language. Seeking fresh pastures, Piaf starred in the operetta *La p'tite Lili* for a seven-month run on the Parisian stage in 1951, but the restrictive nature of the material left her struggling to impose her personality on the songs, only the rapid-fire 'Rien de rien' and the sweeter 'Du matin jusqu'au soir' bearing comparison with her forties' hits.

Despite her onstage triumphs, the year marked a turning point for Piaf after two serious car accidents left her in poor physical shape, dependent on morphine to dull the pain. Added to her increasing alcohol consumption, the drug had a hugely detrimental effect on her health. The following year, she married Jacques Pills, but the relationship didn't last. It did, however, produce the superb 'Je t'ai dans la peau', an exercise in restraint for the queen of the power vocal, written for her by Pills and Gilbert Bécaud. The next two years resulted in some of her greatest recordings, among them Charles Aznavour's lovely 'Plus bleu que tes yeux', the brash, waltz-tempo 'Padam... Padam'[102] and the sound effect-laden 'Télégramme'. However, by late 1953 her lifestyle had caught up with her, and following some disastrous live shows she all but disappeared from view in order to deal with her addictions.

---

[99] Although another Belgian singer, Solange Berry, had come close when representing Luxembourg in 1958 with 'Un grand amour'. She finished joint last with only one point.

[100] Inspired by the nineteenth-century folk song 'Au clair de la lune', Pills' song reworked the lyrics and sentiments into a more contemporary narrative. Four years later, the original tune was reworked by UK folk-pop outfit the Springfields as 'Say I Won't Be There'. 'Au clair de la lune' thus gave birth to two very different songs during a four-year period.

[101] So well known already that it had no need of an English title.

[102] The punctuation in this title appears to be highly mobile, appearing on some record sleeves after the second word rather than the first, and disappearing altogether from others.

While Piaf offered the ultimate in torch-song melodrama, Charles Trenet provided the antithesis with his bright, optimistic, joyful tunes of good times gone by and others still to come. He crowned his career in 1951 with 'L'âme des poètes (Longtemps, longtemps)'[103] and spent much of his time on the road, enchanting audiences across the globe. His occasional returns to the studio saw him add to his collection of classic tunes the wonderful 'Valse des amours passés', 'Le cœur de Paris' and the South American fantasy 'Printemps à Rio' (all 1952) and the charming 'En avril à Paris' (1954). Meanwhile his classic work also found a new audience in the hands of bandleader Jacques Hélian,[104] whose 1954 LP *Charles Trenet et Jacques Hélian vous invitent à danser* recast a dozen or so of Trenet's old hits in dance-floor-friendly arrangements.

Having shaken off the shadows of the war, Trenet epitomised French music hall in the fifties, both at home and abroad. While the decade witnessed a gradual slowing-down of record sales for the great entertainer, the hits were far from over. The surreal motoring saga 'À la porte du garage' raised his standard high in 1955, while a year later the nostalgic 'La maison du poète' tugged effortlessly at the heartstrings. His classic tunes were now largely behind him but he still had a few aces up his sleeve, like his 1955 smash, 'Moi, j'aime le music-hall', on which he name-checked most of the big stars of the day, and 1957's 'Le jardin extraordinaire', an exquisite melody married to one of his greatest flights of lyrical fancy.

Despite his ongoing popularity, by the middle of the 1950s Trenet was effectively yesterday's man. Piaf was able to ride the changes by turning to up-and-coming writers like Aznavour and Bécaud for material, but Trenet was left to his own devices, remarkable though they were. He had risen to the top before the war, while Piaf had peaked in its aftermath, and, though firmly rooted in the past, she represented the future direction of French pop far more effectively. Trenet's fusion of poetry and jazz had been innovative in its day, but by the mid-fifties he had been overtaken by Charles Aznavour, whose modern style and feel for swinging rhythms were more in keeping with the new decade, while the veteran's joyful lyrics seemed at odds with the reality of life in the failing Fourth Republic. Having been in the right place at the right time to see the country through the war and the reconstruction that followed, Trenet seemed unable to turn his pen to describe the world as it now was, continuing to blend nostalgia and romance into a still-attractive but somewhat backward-looking repertoire. Instead, the challenge would be taken up by a new generation of singer-poets who set about revolutionising the art of the *chansonnier*, fusing the sounds and ideas of Aznavour and Bécaud with the poetic approach of the past to take the *chanson* to a new and higher level.

---

[103] Subsequently adapted into English as 'At Last, At Last', under which title it became a hit for Tony Martin.

[104] Then at the peak of his popularity as an orchestra leader and the second-biggest recording act in the country after Tino Rossi.

# Chapter 6

## JE SUIS COMME JE SUIS
### Existentialism and a new type of *chanson* (1950-58)

*The traditional mix of poetry and song which lies at the heart of the* chanson *had tended to be overlooked in the aftermath of the war in favour of the escapism provided by the music hall entertainers. Away from the spotlights, however, a new breed of songwriters began to emerge, rubbing shoulders with the likes of Charles Aznavour and Gilbert Bécaud on the fringes of the music industry. The new* chansonniers *were not so much successors to the musical revolution launched by the new idols of French youth, but contemporaries, strumming away at their guitars or plunking away at the piano, scratching out their lyrics on paper and attempting to give voice to their ideas. Their natural home was not the glittery stages of the music halls, but the dimly lit cabarets that dotted the bohemian quarters of Paris, where they assembled repertoires of highly literate compositions. Picking up where the pre-war singer-poets of Saint-Germain-des-Prés had left off, they crafted songs that were as pointed and forceful as those of Aznavour, but delivered in language that could be read as well as sung.*

### Félix Leclerc and the troubadour tradition

Somewhat surprisingly, the key figure in this redevelopment of a long-established form was an outsider: Québécois songwriter Félix Leclerc. Having grown up in Canada, where he was exposed to both French *chanson* and the folk songs of the great American troubadour Woody Guthrie, Leclerc crossed

the Atlantic to bring a new musical vision to the French marketplace: that of a modern-day *chansonnier*, plying his art while hunched over his guitar.

Arriving in Paris in 1950, the Canadian took the cabaret circuit by storm. His first release, the acoustic ballad 'Moi, mes souliers', established a style that would serve him well for many years: gentle strumming augmented by light orchestration. Later that year, he scored a major hit with 'Le p'tit bonheur', a catchy tune reminiscent of Paul Dukas' classical favourite, 'The Sorcerer's Apprentice'.

89

Both of these recordings appeared on his first album, *Félix Leclerc chante ses derniers succès*, a distinctive set of songs of which 'Bozo', 'Train du nord' and the sprightly 'Le roi heureux' were the highlights.

Leclerc represented the simple man: unsophisticated, close to nature, and a world away from romantics like Tino Rossi who packed the country's music halls with adoring fans. The slow 'Notre sentier' (1951) and the rhythmic 'Chanson du pharmacien' (1954) were steady sellers, and his second album, *Félix Leclerc chante* (1957), was every bit as strong as its predecessor. The LP presented the singer's world view through incisive analyses like 'Le roi et le laboureur' and 'Ce matin-là', while 'Le Québécois' planted his heart firmly on his sleeve. Leclerc never achieved the recognition of the stars of music hall or operetta, but he built a sizeable fan base among the intelligentsia. His approach also proved to be an attractive model for other singers to follow.

### The existentialists of Saint-Germain-des-Prés

Leclerc's arrival was less a revolution than a confirmation that the denizens of Paris's bohemian *quartiers* were already on the right track. The Latin Quarter and the streets around the Boulevard Saint-Germain had long been the preserve of poets, philosophers and students from the nearby Sorbonne. In the immediate post-war era, the area became home to a new movement that took form in the cellars and cafés of Saint-Germain-des-Prés. There, at the Café de Flore, the writers and philosophers Jean-Paul Sartre, Simone de Beauvoir and Albert Camus had come together during the Occupation and began to evolve the philosophy that came to be known as existentialism. Although Camus soon quarrelled with his colleagues and disavowed the movement, he personified the romantic hero at its heart and joined Sartre as a role model for those attracted to the new creed.

Among those who set out their stall with the existentialists was Juliette Gréco, a wayward teenager who came to personify the movement in the popular press. Having developed a rebellious streak to counter her strict upbringing, Gréco had early aspirations to become a dancer, but these were curtailed by the outbreak of war. During the Nazi occupation, her mother's activities in the Resistance led to her being arrested and deported. Gréco was also arrested, but was released after a few months and left to walk the eight miles back to Paris, where she joined the Comédie-Française theatre company and fell in with the rapidly-growing bohemian crowd in and around Saint-Germain-des-Prés. The free-spirited teenager was promptly adopted by the era's movers and shakers, and by 1947 was a fixture at Le Tabou, one of the existentialists' regular late-night haunts.

With pale, white skin that contrasted vividly with her all-black attire, she created a fashion for outsiders that would last through successive waves of beatniks, punks, goths and slackers to remain the definitive uniform for disaffected youth even seventy years later. When the press first revealed existentialism to the world in 1947 in a series of articles presenting this new philosophical creed as a home-grown alternative to the American beat generation, it was Gréco's striking image that provided much of the photographic accompaniment.

As the public face of the movement, it was perhaps inevitable that she would find her way into the world of cinema, debuting in Jean Cocteau's *Orphée* in 1949. Next, she tried her hand as a singer, with *chansons* written for her by fellow habitués of the scene: Jean-Paul Sartre's 'La rue des blancs-manteaux' and Joseph Kosma's 'Si tu t'imagines'. Although none of her early record releases found much of an audience outside Paris, further songs emanating from Kosma's writing partnership with poet Jacques Prévert, such as 'La belle vie' and 'À la belle étoile', made the case for her interpretive skills. Her heartfelt 1951 reading of their 'Je suis comme je suis' not only staked a claim as the public manifesto of the existentialist credo, but also served as a personal calling card for the rest of her career.

*Juliette Gréco.*

Strikingly beautiful, and gifted with a strong voice, a distinctive public image and a dynamic stage presence, Gréco was a perfect shop window for the intellectuals of the Left Bank cafés and had all the necessary credentials to take the movement out of the shadows and onto the main stage. After mixing further originals like Kosma's 'Amours perdues' with versions of songs already doing the rounds in the hands of Yves Montand ('Les feuilles mortes') and Édith Piaf ('Sous le ciel de Paris'), she took a quantum leap forward with a stunning reading of Charles Aznavour's controversial 'Je hais les dimanches'.[105]

By 1952, Gréco was a rapidly rising star in the constellation of French *chanson*, but she had greater ambitions and now turned her attention to the art-song world of Kurt Weill, cutting magnificent renditions of his 'La chanson de Barbara' and 'La fiancée du pirate' before crossing the Atlantic to garner rave reviews in the United States for her performances in the revue *April In Paris*.[106]

At the same time that Gréco was breathing new life into an old tradition, two rather different performers were making steps in the same direction.

Philippe Clay broke through in 1953 with the Aznavour composition 'Le noyé assassiné', a sparkling excursion with Spanish overtones that set him on his way to a career that would see him alternating quality *chansons* with more commercial material like Aznavour's dramatic 'Ah!' and the twenties'

---

[105] Recorded after Piaf had rejected it, it was promptly covered by the diminutive titan of French *chanson* after Gréco turned it into a major smash.

[106] The show's title was borrowed from the Great American Songbook standard that had originally appeared in the 1932 Broadway musical, *Walk A Little Faster*.

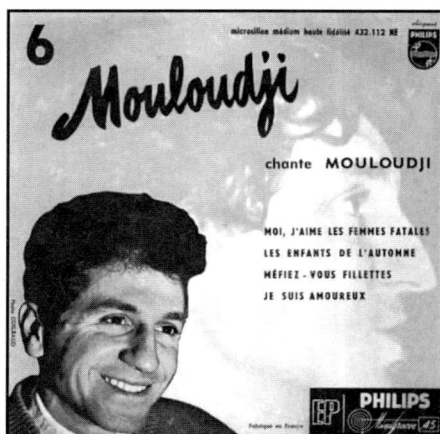

throwback 'Le danseur de Charleston', though it was 1955's 'Les voyous' and the jazz-tinged 'Qu'est-ce que j'en ai à foutre' – yet another Aznavour song – that best illustrated his appeal. 1956's 'C'est une chanson' was less effective, but his forceful personality enabled him to overcome a less-than-photogenic appearance to establish himself as a respected interpreter of quality contemporary *chanson*.

Mouloudji, on the other hand, opted for a sweeter style with delicate orchestrations, launching his recording career in 1950 with a cover of Gréco's 'Si tu t'imagines' before finding his feet with the old-fashioned *guinguette* sounds of 'Rue de Lappe' and netting his first real success in 1951 with the lyrically striking 'La complainte des infidèles'. Less abrasive than Gréco or Clay, his pretty 'Tu te moques' was another triumph, the tune providing a perfect setting for his gently crooned vocal, though his revival of the pre-war classic 'Les petits pavés', also released that year, was a better example of his art.

Having built a fan base for his thoughtful, literate mix of old and new material, Mouloudji hit the jackpot in 1952 with the huge-selling ballad 'Comme un p'tit coquelicot'. Despite the popularity of the song, however, he never succeeded in establishing himself in the mainstream of French show business – in part at least because he suffered censorship for his criticisms of both the French government and the hypocrisy he perceived at the heart of French morality. His record sales suffered accordingly, except when he strayed from the *chanson* to cover pop hits like Al Hibbler's 'Unchained Melody' ('Les enchaínés'), though he often found himself battling against rival cover versions. Nonetheless, he also plotted his own course to some extent with 1957's 'Moi, j'aime les femmes fatales' and demonstrated his ongoing commitment to quality *chansons* with his 1959 revival of Marianne Oswald's 1936 hit, 'La dame de Monte-Carlo' (rebaptised for the occasion as 'Le joueur de Monte-Carlo'), enabling him to retain a loyal following among concert-goers and the self-proclaimed intellectuals in French society.

## Léo Ferré and the political *chanson*

Operating further from the centre of the music business, Monaco-born Léo Ferré had been raised in Italy before heading for France in the 1930s to study politics. A classically-trained musician with a flair for orchestration, he moved to Paris after the war to try to establish himself on the cabaret circuits in Montmartre and along the Left Bank of the Seine. Although blessed with a gift for melody and a talent for crafting poetic lyrics in the grand tradition of the *chanson*, he was not a great singer and his early performances met with little enthusiasm. Fiercely political and leaning very much to the Left, he scandalised audiences in 1948 with 'Mon général', a vicious diatribe against the staunchly anti-Communist Charles de Gaulle that was deemed too controversial for record release.[107]

Although a number of singers ventured to record his songs,[108] Ferré made little commercial headway until 1948, when Édith Piaf recorded 'Les amants de Paris', after which other artists began to cover his work in increasing numbers. His own early waxings for the independent Chant du Monde label in 1950[109] met with negligible success, despite including such gems as 'La chanson du scaphandrier' and the piano-heavy 'L'Île Saint-Louis', as well as such future staples of the *chanson* circuit as 'La vie d'artiste' and 'Monsieur William'.

Among those queuing to record his songs were vocal group Les Frères Jacques, a visually striking quartet kitted out in colourful tunics, matching capes and top hats. Sarcastic and satirical, they were a popular live attraction and had been cult favourites since 1949, when 'L'entrecôte', their distorted variation on the American barbershop quartet sound, had made them into unlikely stars. Equally adept at reviving genuine oldies like Aristide Bruant's 'Rue Saint-Vincent' (reworked as 'Rose blanche') or delivering new songs created to sound like old ones, they were lyrically daring to the point of being foolhardy. Indeed, so caustic was their repertoire that it was surprising they got any airplay at all. As it was, they were among the most-censored acts of all time, being struck off the airwaves for a less-than-deferential attitude toward Charles de Gaulle (the wickedly satirical 'Général à vendre') and the police ('La gavotte des bâtons blancs'); for obscenity ('Son nombril'); for scatological humour (the otherwise pretty 'Petite fable sans morgue (La complainte des petits cabinets)'[110]); and even for the use of an unsavoury pun in a character's name (Ducon) in the 1950 recording, 'Quelqu'un'.

Despite their many battles with the censors, Les Frères Jacques managed some decent commercial triumphs, turning the more offbeat creations of Jacques Prévert & Joseph Kosma into vocal group classics and picking up moderate hits with the likes of the jolly 'Inventaire'. Lyrics aside, the latter sounded positively ordinary compared to the wacky 'La pêche à la baleine', a stage-performance-in-song that was also given a less impressive

---

[107] Ferré would not attempt a recording until 1961, but even that remained unreleased until 1989. However, a live version did appear on record in 1963 (see page 359).

[108] Among them Yves Montand, who enjoyed steady sales with the anti-fascist 'Le flamenco de Paris'.

[109] Later compiled into the 10-inch LP *Chansons de Léo Ferré* (1954).

[110] A forerunner in a way to UK beat group Dave Dee, Dozy, Beaky, Mick & Tich's 1967 music hall knockabout, 'Loos Of England'.

(and more old-fashioned) reading by pre-war singer Agnès Capri. Other notable hits included the somewhat sweeter 'Barbara' (1949),[111] 'La queue du chat' (1953), the simple but effective 'La Saint-Médard' (1953), 'La truite', a vocal adaptation of Schubert's 'Piano Quintet in A major' aka 'The Trout Quintet' (a smash in 1954) and 'La Marie-Joseph' (1956), on which their vocal blend and love of ridicule combined to perfection. Sadly, although their arrangement of Ferré's 'Monsieur William' was equally good, it proved commercially unsuccessful.

Also working the same circuit was an older quartet, Les Compagnons de la Route,[112] founded in 1939, who specialised in the traditional arts of folk songs and sea shanties. Sundered during the war, they reassembled in its aftermath, grew a set of facial hair and resurfaced as Les Quatre Barbus. Their initial approach was typified by their 1948 single, 'Y avait dix marins', but when this proved to be an artistic straightjacket, they threw it overboard and adopted a new style, often specialising in reworkings of classical themes as humorous vocal group recordings.

Thus reborn, they kicked off their new career in 1949 with 'La pince à linge' (adapted from Beethoven's *Fifth Symphony*), complete with lyrics by comedian Francis Blanche. This was the first of many classical adaptations to appear during the first half of the fifties, including 'Fantaisie pédagogique' (a barking-mad recitation of the alphabet based on themes by Mozart) and 'Ouverture du Barbier de Séville' (an equally madcap romp through the overture to Rossini's *Il barbiere di Siviglia* [*The Barber of Seville*]). They continued to amuse with the 1956 hit, 'Le Maennerchor de Steffisbourg',[113] which married their operatic vocals to a typically surreal lyric. Their sense of humour was also to the fore on the same year's 'Dans la marine suisse', while the bizarre 'L'homme de Cro-Magnon' was the highlight of their 1958 EP, *Feu de camp*, which purported to be a collection of Boy Scout campfire songs, but was in fact a rather racier affair. Utterly unique, they operated in a universe far removed from the gritty day-to-day realities voiced by Les Frères Jacques or *chansonniers* like Léo Ferré.

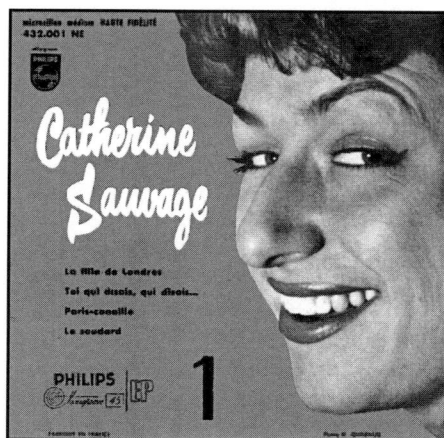

Ferré's biggest break came in 1952, when he began to make regular appearances alongside another fringe singer, Catherine Sauvage. She had started out as an actress before switching to singing, and had already established a reputation as an uncompromising artiste. Her powerful performances soon won her both a recording contract and critical acclaim for her startling reading of Ferré's as yet unrecorded 'L'homme'. This sat amidst a run of similar recordings, starting with a 1953 take on his

---

[111] The same song that was a hit for Yves Montand (see page 67)
[112] Sometimes styled as Quatuor Vocal des Compagnons de la Route.
[113] Some releases style this as 'Le Männerchor de Steffisburg'.

'Paris-canaille', a far catchier offering than usual which duly became a major hit, followed by another successful collaboration, 'Le piano du pauvre', in 1954. These proved to be the opening salvoes in a career that established her not only as Ferré's leading interpreter, but as a significant recording star in her own right. Taking the *chanson* out of the Left Bank ghetto and onto the stages of the leading music halls, Sauvage was responsible for such classics as 1954's odd collision of jazz and *chanson*, 'Mets deux thunes dans l'bastringue', and further offerings from the Ferré songbook in 'Graine d'ananar' and 'Le temps du plastique'.

## Georges Brassens and Jacques Brel

Despite Ferré's growing commercial appeal, the most important of the *chansonniers* to emerge in the early fifties didn't care much for his style of orchestral sweetening and instead developed a sound closer to that of Félix Leclerc. Georges Brassens took the guitar-and-vocal approach of the troubadours and married it to a rhythmic sensibility that had clear links to the jazz-influenced songs of Aznavour and Trenet. However, as with all the *chansonniers*, he never allowed the tune or the arrangement to get in the way of the words. Like Ferré, Brassens had strong political views and was an ardent supporter of the anarchists. He initially worked as a writer for political magazines before deciding in 1951 to focus on writing songs.[114] A warm, avuncular figure who seldom appeared without his pipe, his public image belied the politically charged and sometimes graphically explicit nature of his compositions, and early releases such as 'Le gorille' (an attack on the death penalty) suffered at the hands of the censors. Lyrically, his work took the poetry of the earlier *chansonniers* and elevated it to a higher level, mixing rich wordplay with the slang expressions of the countryside, and balancing his political ideals with a deep love of humankind.

Hated by the Right, Brassens found an audience across the rest of French society – especially among the young, who were drawn to his simple tunes and accessible lyrics. Two albums, *Georges Brassens chante les chansons poètiques (...et souvent gaillardes)* and *Georges Brassens No. 2*, issued in 1952 and 1953 respectively, rounded up material that had first

---

[114] Brassens had been dabbling with songwriting since the war, but only began to take it seriously at the start of the fifties. Many of his later triumphs were originally drafted during the 1940s, although his habit of reworking lyrics over many years meant that some would not surface in their final form for over a decade.

appeared on 78s, giving a second chance to 'Le petit cheval' and the hard-hitting 'Le fossoyeur' on the former, and to the jolly 'Bancs publics' and his musical interpretation of a poem by Louis Aragon, 'Il n'y a pas d'amour heureux', on the latter.

Songs like 'La mauvaise réputation', which raised the banner for individualism, and the delightfully folksy 'La chasse aux papillons' swiftly established themselves as best-sellers across the country. Equally popular with listeners was the musical parable 'La cane de Jeanne', while 'Le mauvais sujet repenti' (on the LP *Georges Brassens No. 3*, released in 1954) continued his probing examination of French society. Fusing jazz, politics and poetry with the folk tradition, he created a sensation in the music industry and sent record companies scurrying to find other singers in the same vein.

Brassens had first been brought to the public's attention through his appearances at Les Trois Baudets, a cabaret run by Jacques Canetti. A visionary figure who provided early support for many of the *chansonniers* of the fifties, including Mouloudji and Catherine Sauvage, Canetti was an important power broker in the industry. In the aftermath of Brassens' commercial break-through, his interest was piqued by a 78 r.p.m. disc he received from the Belgian branch of the Philips record label. It featured two songs, although neither the accordion-laden top deck, 'La foire', nor the rudimentary flip, 'Il y a', were anything outstanding, and the record had struggled to shift even two hundred copies north of the border. Even so, Canetti felt the singer had potential and summoned Jacques Brel to Paris for a trial.

Gawky and totally lacking in stage presence, Brel was hardly typical star material,[115] but as it turned out, he wrote songs in a strong and original manner, and Canetti offered to record a debut album by the newcomer. Released in 1954, the nine-track LP *Jacques Brel et ses chansons* contained a few worthwhile moments, most notably the melancholy 'Sur la place' and the striking imagery of 'Le diable (Ça va)'. However, while elaborate orchestration had served to add colour to Léo Ferré's recordings, Brel seemed out of his depth in the the same surroundings, swamped in a morass of strings on an ultimately disappointing collection. His fortunes were transformed by the intervention of Juliette Gréco, whose dynamic cover of 'Le Diable'[116] served to keep his career afloat.

---

[115] Then again, neither were Philippe Clay or Charles Aznavour.
[116] In her case styled 'Ça va (Le diable)'.

## Poetry and the *chanson*

Although they are often mentioned in the same breath today, Brel, Brassens and Ferré were in essence very different from one another, each having a different approach to their art. Of the three, Ferré took the most trouble over his arrangements, often scoring for orchestra, but sometimes stripping things down to the bare minimum, as on the organ-dominated 'La fortune' (1956). However, 1955's 'La rue' was more typical: an ornate offering combining a catchy melody, complex orchestration and a decent vocal performance with a lyric that was an exemplary essay in the descriptive art. On the same EP, the uptempo 'Vise la réclame' and the banjo-toting 'Monsieur mon passé' offered further fine examples of his talents as a wordsmith, composer and arranger.

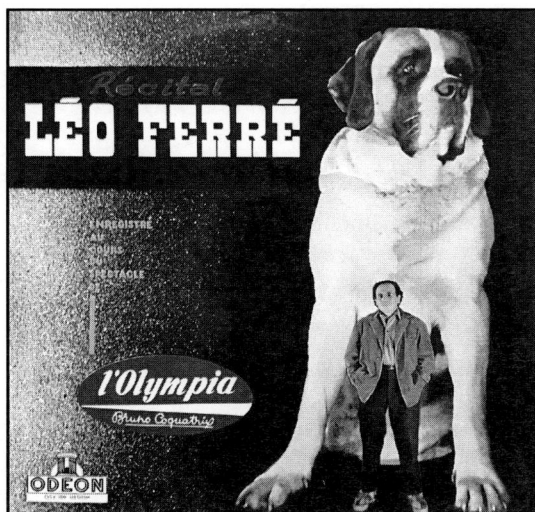

These stood in complete contrast to Georges Brassens, who was content to simply scratch away at his guitar, providing rudimentary support to his ever-eloquent lyrics.[117] Despite this, Brassens also enjoyed greater commercial success, each of his albums outselling its predecessor. They abounded in consummate examples of the *chansonnier*'s art, such as his hard-hitting adaptation of a poem by Francis Jammes, 'La prière', a damning indictment of religion that confirmed the singer's reputation as a champion of outsiders everywhere. One of the highlights of the soberly titled *Georges Brassens No. 3*, it overshadowed other classic *chansons* on the album, such as 'Les sabots d'Hélène', 'La première fille (qu'on a pris dans les bras)', and the elaborate anarchist metaphor 'La mauvaise herbe', though it was 'Chanson pour l'Auvergnat', a heartfelt ode to a 'good Samaritan' figure, which predominated and gifted him a major hit in 1954.

While Brassens ascended the ladder of show business, Ferré survived mainly thanks to covers of his songs by other artists. In the wake of Catherine Sauvage's success with his material, he made a triumphant appearance at the Olympia Theatre in 1955 which resulted in the live album *Récital Léo Ferré*,[118] featuring renditions of 'Paris-canaille', 'L'homme', 'Graine d'ananar' and 'Le piano du pauvre' alongside powerful readings of 'Monsieur William' and 'Mon p'tit voyou'. This was the first fruit of a new and better deal with the

---

[117] Interestingly, with a few exceptions, Brassens actually wrote his songs on the piano and then transposed them for the guitar. As a result, his music contains complex chord changes and harmonic structures unusual in guitar-based *chanson*.

[118] The full title, as listed on the front cover, is *Récital Léo Ferré enregistré au cours du spectacle de l'Olympia Bruno Coquatrix*.

Odéon label that was to reveal an increasingly interesting repertoire. Despite the inclusion of the incisive 'Le temps du plastique' and two future classics in 'Le guinche' and 'Pauvre Rutebeuf',[119] sales of his 1956 set, *8 chansons nouvelles*, were only moderate but critics were in little doubt that a major talent had arrived.

'Pauvre Rutebeuf' was an adaptation by Ferré from various pieces by the thirteenth-century poet Rutebeuf into a coherent work which he then set to music, confirming the link between himself and the country's poetic tradition – a link which Ferré also made in reverse when the same album's 'L'amour' was included in a book of contemporary French verse. This was followed in 1956 by the publication of *Poètes, vos papiers!*, a collection of seventy poems and lyrics, further reinforcing his standing as a wordsmith *par excellence*.

Catherine Sauvage remained Ferré's leading interpreter, adding versions of 'Java partout' and 'Le temps du tango' to the long list of his works in her repertoire. So strong was this link, that in 1958 she released a third EP[120] dedicated to his work, offering forthright readings of such jewels as 'La sisique' and 'Comm' dans la haute'.[121] Her next EP offered another four of Ferré's wares, and, while she dabbled in other material along the way (including a version of Charles Trenet's 'Où sont-ils donc?' in 1956), in the public's mind Sauvage remained inextricably linked with Ferré.

# LÉO FERRÉ

Ph. A. Bonnet

## 8
## chansons nouvelles

LE GUINCHE
LA FORTUNE
MA VIEILLE BRANCHE
T'EN AS
LA GRANDE VIE
LE TEMPS DU PLASTIQUE
PAUVRE RUTEBEUF
L'AMOUR

I
disque
microsillon
33 T. OS. 1126

*Ces titres figurent également en deux disques 45 T. longue durée (7 MOE. 2.041 et 2.042).*

## EN EXCLUSIVITÉ
sur disques

# ODÉON

Meanwhile, Ferré's own popularity slowly continued to increase, and the late fifties saw a run of EPs that boosted his commercial standing with such standouts as 'Le pont Mirabeau' and 'Java partout', culminating in his first significant hit with 'Le temps du tango' in 1958. This was also the highlight of his next album, *Encore... du Léo Ferré*, issued the same year. His best set to date, it contained instant classics like 'Mon camarade' and the anti-racist

---

[119]  Both quickly covered by Catherine Sauvage.
[120]  The first, containing her version of 'Pauvre Rutebeuf', had appeared two years earlier.
[121]  Ferré's versions were listed as 'La zizique' and 'Comme dans la haute' on his EP sleeves.

'Dieu est nègre'. Commercial considerations were acknowledged with 'Le jazz-band', although this diversion was out of keeping with his real musical inclinations.

Those preferences had been made clear in his bid for artistic glory with the oratorio *La chanson du mal-aimé*, which he recorded in 1957, nearly three years after it was first performed in Monte Carlo. The same year saw the release of the album *Les fleurs du mal*, on which he placed the words of poet Charles Baudelaire in contemporary musical settings, as exemplified by the stripped-down backing on 'Le serpent qui danse'. The mournful tone that Ferré often brought to bear on his material was also to the fore on 'Les hiboux' and 'La vie antérieure'. He did, however, come to life on the exquisite 'À celle qui est trop gaie', on which the low-key jazz backing provided exactly the right amount of colour to lift the song off the floor, showing just how skilful an interpreter he had become. The album confirmed Ferré's critical standing, yet this most poetic of *chansonniers* remained a peripheral figure, reliant for much of his income on the many recordings of his songs made by other, more popular singers.

Brel, meanwhile, continued to battle unsympathetic arrangements on his second LP, 1956's *Jacques Brel 2*, which revealed a rapid maturing of his songwriting style. The album kicked off with the gentle love song 'Quand on n'a que l'amour', a beautiful ballad that celebrated love itself as much as it did a lover. His first classic, it easily overshadowed the rest of the album, which, despite intrusive orchestration that marred songs such as 'L'air de la bêtise' and 'Qu'avons-nous fait, bonnes gens?', included two further highlights in the heartbreak of 'J'en appelle' and the folksy 'La bourrée du célibataire', which celebrated drunken optimism in a highly amusing manner.

Despite the leap in quality, the album was a commercial failure, although regular radio play for 'Quand on n'a que l'amour' helped the song become Brel's first hit in 1957. A series of concerts with Philippe Clay drew attention to his much-improved stage performances, and thereafter his star went into the ascendant as the outclassed Clay's began to fall to earth. Brel's sales may have lagged a long way behind those of the decade's leading artists, but 1958's *Jacques Brel No. 3* saw him carving out his own territory with the delightful 'Au printemps', the character sketch 'Le colonel', and the mildly over-elaborate 'La lumière jaillira', one of several collaborations with his pianist, François Rauber. Like Brassens and Ferré, Brel was pushing the boundaries of what passed for popular song, and over the coming years the three of them would rewrite the rule book for the *chanson*, dominating the music halls as their songs rapidly became standards, both in their own renditions and in the hands of interpreters such as Juliette Gréco.

## Juliette Gréco and Patachou

Gréco was by now as much a touchstone for the new generation of songwriters as Édith Piaf, and her adoption of Brel was no different from her support for Brassens and Ferré. In many cases, she planted her flag on material that was already known, although her readings of Ferré's 'Le guinche' and Brassens' 'Chanson pour l'Auvergnat' were given startling new arrangements in keeping with her usual musical style. She performed a similar favour for Gilbert Bécaud, though his 'Les croix' was, like Brassens' opus, in little need of a boost, as it was flying out of record shops under its own steam. Gréco generally preferred poetic lyrics she could get her teeth into, such as the Raymond Queneau-penned 'Chanson de Gervaise', and so the works of Brel, Brassens and Ferré were a logical fit. Indeed, all three songwriters were well represented in a live concert captured for posterity on the 1955 album *Juliette Gréco à l'Olympia*, which featured Ferré's 'La rue', Brassens' 'Chanson pour l'Auvergnat' and Brel's 'Le Diable (Ça va)', alongside a delightful interpretation of Charles Trenet's 'Coin de rue'.

Taken together with the work of Charles Aznavour and Gilbert Bécaud, the songs of the new *chansonniers* showed French *chanson* to be in good health as the fifties unfolded. Not only were the likes of Brel, Ferré and Brassens bringing a new sense of literature to songwriting, but the up-to-date rhythms of Aznavour and Bécaud pointed the way toward a future where French popular song would have more in common with the sounds emanating from across the Atlantic. As a result, the *chanson* underwent a major transformation and enjoyed a massive uplift in popularity within the space of a few short years. This change did not occur in isolation, however, but against a backdrop of growing creativity across the cultural spectrum. As existing music hall stars like Trenet hit their creative peaks, newer stars began to emerge from the shadows to bring the work of the *chansonniers* into the mainstream.

Patachou had started out singing the songs of Georges Brassens in her Montmartre cabaret, Chez Patachou. Indeed, she had helped to get the avuncular songwriter established in the first place, recording a rare duet with him (the jazzy 'Maman... Papa...') in 1953. This was one of several Brassens songs with which she set out her stall as a recording artist, among them 'La prière', the amusing 'Le bricoleur'[122] and an excellent reading of 'Brave Margot'. The release of the LP *Patachou chante Brassens* in 1954 ensured the link remained strong, with the singer pumping new blood into the likes of 'La chasse aux papillons' and 'Bancs publics.'[123]

Capable of handling a far broader range of material, Patachou also delivered a superb revival of Mistinguett's twenties' classic, 'Mon homme', and endorsed the work of both Léo Ferré ('Le piano du pauvre') and Charles Aznavour ('Plus bleu que tes yeux' and 'Parce que'). Although the latter's

---

[122] A song Brassens never recorded himself.
[123] Originally released on 78, Patachou's version was titled 'Les amoureux du banc public'.

commercial success rendered her 1955 version of 'Viens au creux de mon épaule' superfluous, she continued recording his songs long after he had become a star, including a reading of 'Sur ma vie' on a 1956 EP that also included a cover of Francis Lemarque's 'Paris se regarde'. By this time, her repertoire had diversified to take in jazzman Michel Legrand's carousel-like 'Allume tes lampions' alongside further interpretations of songs by Ferré ('Le temps du plastique') and Aznavour ('Vivre avec toi'). 1956's 'La bague à Jules' retained the feel of her early material, but a 1957 EP dedicated to the songs of rising star Guy Béart[124] (among them 'Le quidam', 'Bal chez Temporel' and 'Poste restante') showed that she also had her finger firmly on the pulse of the contemporary *chanson*.

Patachou.

## New *chansonniers*

Béart had also written songs for Zizi Jeanmaire ('Je suis la femme', 'Qu'on est bien' and 'Il y a plus d'un an'), some of which he also recorded himself, enjoying moderate airplay with 'Bal chez Temporel' in 1957. His understated arrangements may have been a little too easy on the ear, but 'Chandernagor' prompted several cover versions, including a superb reading by Juliette Gréco.[125] 'Qu'on est bien' and the rapid-fire 'Le quidam' were likewise welcome additions to the French airwaves, setting him up for the smash that was to catapult him to stardom in 1958: the pretty film theme, 'L'eau vive'. The record overshadowed the remainder of his repertoire, despite such worthy efforts as 'Moitié toi, moitié moi' and the jazz-tinged 'L'oxygène'.

Another artist to benefit from Gréco's assistance was a strange-looking piano player (the ever-sympathetic press described him as 'even uglier than Philippe Clay') who was earning his keep providing accompaniment for singers while writing songs on the side. Serge Gainsbourg, a former painter with an ear for melody and a talent for crafting strange and disturbing lyrics suffused with linguistic games, was an anomaly even on the Left Bank cabaret circuit. Cynical, world-weary and seemingly permanently hungover, he was a shy, nervy performer who preferred to hide away from the spotlights. His compositions were grounded in the same contemporary jazz style as those of Charles Aznavour, but lyrically they seemed to come from somewhere else altogether: a darker, gloomier world populated by misfits and outsiders, whom Gainsbourg seemed fated to join. However, with Gréco

---

[124] Father of actress Emmanuelle Béart.
[125] It was also covered by Philippe Clay in 1959.

singing his praises and covering his songs,[126] the reluctant performer soon found himself with a record deal of his own.

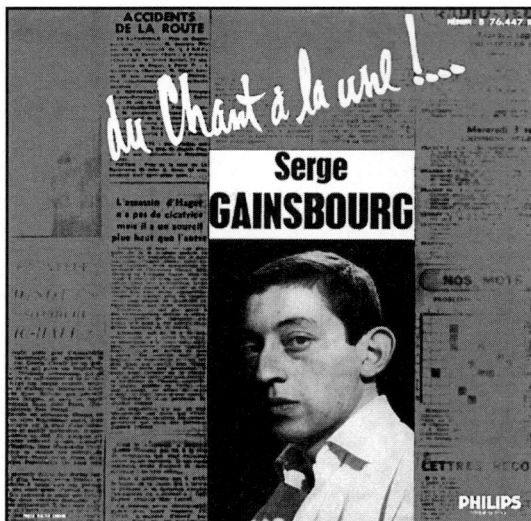

His 1958 debut album, *Du chant à la une!...* won plaudits for its inventive mixture of jazz and *chanson* on the likes of 'Du jazz dans le ravin' and 'Ce mortel ennui', but his rich wordplay, softly crooned vocals and dark sense of humour proved too offbeat for mass consumption. Critically acclaimed for the sardonic 'Le poinçonneur des Lilas',[127] the album was a commercial failure, although Gainsbourg proved a popular choice for singers unable to write their own material.

Hugues Aufray began his career with a debut EP that included two Gainsbourg tunes in the shape of the otherwise unavailable 'Mes petites odalisques' (a near-amoral offering guaranteed to be struck from the airwaves) and a pleasant version of 'Le poinçonneur des Lilas'. From this less than auspicious beginning, he moved on to cover Kurt Weill's 'Mackie Messer' as 'La complainte de Mackie' in a rather more sedate manner than Bobby Darin displayed on his version ('Mack The Knife'). Aufray's second release brought no more commercial success than its predecessor, leading him to rethink his approach to recording.

## Charles Aznavour and his disciples

Charles Aznavour meanwhile went from strength to strength as the decade progressed, recording a string of hits that were as startling in their diversity as in their lyrical thrust. While the organ on 'Moi j'fais mon rond' offered a sound still unusual in French pop, the rapid-fire rhythm and optimistic, humanist lyrics of 'Terre nouvelle' were a perfect fit for the 'Brave New World' sentiments starting to surface as Europe moved on from the horrors of the war that had ended a decade earlier. By the time he came to record his third album, *Charles Aznavour chante Charles Aznavour 3* in 1956,[128] he was in fine form, turning out a defiantly modern set of songs ranging from the lyrically daring evocation of post-carnal repose, 'Après l'amour', to the joyous celebration of 'J'aime Paris au mois de mai'.

As much a master of the big band sound of fifties' easy listening as Frank Sinatra, Aznavour used swinging musical settings to paint a picture both

---

[126] Gréco performed the unusual 'Il était une oie' (which Gainsbourg himself never recorded) on an EP dedicated to his work, highlighted by the sensual and ambiguous 'L'amour à la papa'.

[127] Quickly covered in trademark fashion by Les Frères Jacques.

[128] The previous two volumes were compilations of his early hits.

*Michèle Arnaud.*

grittier and more realistic than the romantic portraits conjured up on the American's contemporary albums for Capitol, getting straight to the point on 'Vivre avec toi', announcing his intentions of matrimony in the most direct way possible on 'Prends garde', and sidling around the dance floor crooning what can only be described as a modern hymn on 'Le chemin de l'éternité'. Along the way, he revisited his already bulging back catalogue, reclaiming 'Une enfant' from Édith Piaf in an effective though less dramatic rendition, and reworking Georges Ulmer's 'J'ai bu' in his own inimitable style, even as a host of other singers descended on his compositions.

Leading the flock was the Michèle Arnaud,[129] who rendered the songs of Aznavour, Brassens and Ferré in a style that was more showbiz than *chanson*, although her reading of the latter's 'La vie d'artiste' was not without its charms. Arnaud had an appealing public image and built a sizeable following for her warm, polished interpretations. As the decade progressed, her covers of Mouloudji's 'Un jour tu verras' and Aznavour's 'Sa jeunesse' established her as a light-hearted rival to the still-dominant Piaf. In 1956, she was chosen to represent Luxembourg at the *Eurovision Song Contest*, but failed to carry off the top prize despite impressing with the lyrical 'Les amants de minuit'.

Among the lesser-known singers hitching a ride on Aznavour's train was sweet-voiced Claude Goaty, whose understated 1957 reading of 'Si je n'avais plus' should have given her a follow-up hit to her previous year's smash, 'Le bidon', but didn't. Another was Aznavour's own sister, Aïda, whose string-swept version of 'Sarah' that same year argued for a decent talent that failed to flower. However, her marriage to songwriter Georges Garvarentz provided her brother with access to an able songwriting partner whenever he needed one.

With hits like the gently rhythmic 'Monsieur le consul à Curityba', actor and singer Francis Linel established himself as a master of light entertainment, his pleasant recordings finding favour with an undemanding audience. Drawn to Aznavour's more modern style, he recorded perfunctory versions of 'Ça' and 'Je cherche mon amour' in the early fifties, but his unadventurous approach added little that was not already better delivered by others. His slick take on 'L'amour a fait de moi' was exactly the kind of high-class fluff that might otherwise have been heard on the soundtrack of an

---

[129] Serge Gainsbourg's employer, insofar as he provided piano accompaniment for her live performances. She recorded six of Gainsbourg's songs before the decade was out, including excellent readings of 'Douze belles dans la peau' and the provocative 'La femme des uns sous le corps des autres' in 1958, and a sparkling cover of 'Il était une oie' in 1959.

MGM musical (and none the worse for that), but his versions of 'On ne sait jamais' and 'J'aime Paris au mois de mai' paled in comparison to those laid down by Aznavour himself.

Jean-Claude Pascal was more substantial, debuting with a version of Aznavour's 'Je voudrais' in 1955. However, despite possessing a pleasant voice, he was simply not a dynamic performer, and although he found an audience among those looking for something soothing, he offered little in the way of creativity.

In similar vein, Jean Bertola cut a routine version of Aznavour's 'Viens au creux de mon épaule', but the recording was swamped by a celestial choir and bizarre keyboard sounds, denying his admittedly decent voice space to breathe. The same criticisms could also be made of the rest of his repertoire, his version of the much-recorded 'Gelsomina' being left in the dust by a far stronger interpretation by the still-buoyant Lucienne Delyle.

## Left Bank *chanson*

Back in Saint-Germain-des-Prés, singers like Delyle were of little relevance to audiences seeking something more cerebral than mere entertainment. Juliette Gréco was their high priestess, though she had no shortage of temple assistants, among them Germaine Montero, a veteran of the Spanish Civil War who had cut 'Et puis après' (the original, less strident version of Gréco's 'Je suis comme je suis') back in 1948. While never attaining the wider popularity enjoyed by Gréco, she made some interesting, if unusual recordings in the early fifties, including a 1952 adaptation of a poem by Pierre Mac Orlan, 'La fille de Londres',[130] a delightfully old-fashioned ditty dedicated to schoolchildren titled 'Airs pour les enfants pas sages', and a 1954 romp through Léo Ferré's 'Paris-canaille' that got lost in the shuffle of competing versions. Despite her considerable vocal ability, she always seemed to be chasing the times and never made the jump from her Left Bank fan base to wider popularity.

Cora Vaucaire cut the original version of the classic 'Les feuilles mortes' well before either Yves Montand or Gréco got it down on tape,[131] but despite a moving vocal performance, her version had struggled to get out of the starting gates. She mixed classical tunes by Érik Satie with traditional folk songs and the poetry of Jacques Prévert to create a repertoire entirely in her own image, dipping into surreal humour on a revival of Lys Gauty's 'Deux escargots qui vont à l'enterrement d'une feuille morte.'[132]

---

[130] Later covered with greater commercial success by Catherine Sauvage.
[131] Although Montand did sing it first, in the 1946 film *Les portes de la nuit.*
[132] Vaucaire used the amended title 'Deux escargots s'en vont à l'enterrement'. It was also covered by Les Frères Jacques, who styled their version '2 escargots s'en vont à l'enterrement'.

By 1950, she was running a subterranean club and using it to promote other rising stars, even though she never reached the top of the ladder herself. Her best recording of the period was the gentle 1953 ballad 'Frédé', but her closest brush with real fame came in 1954, when she appeared in Jean Renoir's film, *French Cancan*, singing the excellent 'La complainte de la Butte', a delightful, swirling slice of bittersweet tenderness that deservedly became a hit.[133]

Even further back in the shadows, sweet-voiced Claire Leclerc showed great promise in 1950 with her interpretations of two tunes originally featured in the 1942 film, *Les visiteurs du soir*, both of them pseudo-medieval ballads that were actually the work of Jacques Prévert and Maurice Thiriet. 'Démons et merveilles'[134] was the more distinctive of the two, although 'Le tendre et dangereux visage de l'amour' offered a less-than-rosy picture of love that was more in keeping with the mood of her public. Sadly, neither song found a wider audience, and with health problems dogging her every move, Leclerc soon beat a retreat from the stage.

Fate was no kinder to veteran Agnès Capri, whose 1952 recording, 'Loin du bal', sounded positively quaint when set against the more modern offerings of Gréco or Catherine Sauvage, whose assertive outlook she could never hope to match.

Stéphane Golmann at least abandoned the trappings of forties' music hall for his 1952 offering, 'La Marie-Joseph', although it was not enough to lift him out of the cellar clubs that were his natural habitat.

Jean-Claude Darnal's rather bland and inoffensive musical approach concealed the strident anti-militarist sentiments behind his 1954 hit, 'Le soudard', but the limitations of his style left him struggling to survive as a singer. Fortunately, he soon found gainful employment writing songs for others.

Rather more successful was newcomer René-Louis Lafforgue, whose 1954 release, 'Le marchand de saisons', featured a stripped-down accompaniment not a million miles from Georges Brassens, although Lafforgue's smooth vocal lacked the latter's character. Another refugee from Franco's Spain, there was little in his repertoire to suggest an Iberian influence and he racked up a series of moderate hits during the fifties, starting in 1953 with 'Le poseur de rails' and peaking in 1957 with the chart-topping 'Julie la Rousse', a joyous, uplifting piece of infectious pop that overshadowed everything else he ever wrote.

---

[133] And was rapidly covered by both Mouloudji and Patachou.
[134] Also recorded by Cora Vaucaire.

## Piaf, Delyle and Montand

Despite the success of newcomers like Lafforgue, it was the established stars who made the biggest waves during the mid-fifties. Édith Piaf overcame her battles with ill health to return to the top in late 1954 with the jaunty 'La goualante du pauvre Jean',[135] fighting off a rival version by Yves Montand to reassert her authority over the music hall milieu. Even so, it was not a vintage year for her, with only the martial 'Le «ça ira»' and the powerful 'Sœur Anne' passing muster compared to her earlier hits. The slow ballad 'Heureuse' was a decent enough song, but it was swamped by an overpowering organ that robbed it of its life, while the more worthy 'Johnny, tu n'es pas un ange' was, unusually for Piaf, a cover of an American tune (Les Paul & Mary Ford's 'Johnny (Is The Boy For Me)') which had to compete for space with a strong alternative rendition by Catherine Sauvage.

The following year, Piaf got back to business with a clutch of dramatic singles (most notably the excellent 'Avec ce soleil') and a magnificent live album recorded at the Olympia, *Récital*[136], containing a selection of superb songs including Gilbert Bécaud's mini-drama, 'Légende', the more traditional 'Enfin le printemps', and the show-stopping 'Miséricorde'. The long-player provided proof of what everyone had always known: it was only on stage that she truly came to life. Two more live albums, *Le tour de chant d'Édith Piaf à l'Olympia No. 2* and *Édith Piaf à l'Olympia No. 3*, followed in 1956 and 1958, to similar commercial and critical success.

Even though her body was wracked by drug and alcohol abuse, and her private life continually stretched to breaking point, Piaf's spirit remained indomitable, and her series of stunning live recordings proved beyond all doubt that she remained unrivalled as the country's leading emotional singer. Never quite as comfortable in the studio, she nevertheless turned out a string of near-perfect stories-in-song, most notably the vivid depiction of streetwalkers in 1957's 'C'est à Hambourg' and the atmospheric 'Les neiges de Finlande' the following year. Piaf's occasional reliance on foreign material, such as her 1955 version of Gogi Grant's much-covered 'Suddenly There's A Valley' ('Soudain une vallée'), could not diminish the essential Frenchness of her repertoire and the accordion was never far away, as could be heard on 1958's exquisite 'Tant qu'il y aura des jours'.

---

[135] This song sometimes appears on records as 'La goualante *de* pauvre Jean'. It is known to English-speaking audiences as 'The Poor People Of Paris'.

[136] Also released as *Le tour de chant d'Édith Piaf*.

Lucienne Delyle picked up more hits in 1955 with a cover of Lilo's 'I Love Paris' (from the Cole Porter musical *Can-Can*), the big band-backed slice of sleazy jazz that was 'Le rififi', and 'Un ange comme ça', a near-perfect combination of her still-impressive vocal prowess and the tasteful orchestration of Aimé Barelli. The following year, she scored again with the infectious 'Java', 'Fleur de mon cœur' and 'Je me sens si bien'.

Yves Montand was also on a winning streak, mixing new material like the 1953 piano ballad 'Car je t'aime' with revivals of revolutionary songs such as 'Le temps des cerises' and 'Le chant de la libération', both of which served to accentuate his strong political leanings. In between times, he displayed his abilities as a character actor on 'Donne-moi des sous' and emphasised his place in the world of *la chanson* with a strange, organ-dominated revival of Aristide Bruant's 'Les canuts'. While his film work prevented him from recording as often as fans might have liked, it also won him an international audience and his records sold all over the world as he, like Maurice Chevalier before him, came to typify the popular image of the suave, sophisticated Frenchman abroad.

## Gilbert Bécaud and friends

la ville
il fait des bonds... le pierrot qui danse
le jour ou la pluie viendra

7 EGI 296

11

*GILBERTBECAUD*

Gilbert Bécaud meanwhile went from strength to strength, closing 1955 with the enjoyable 'Le marchand de ballons' and topping the charts in 1956 with his bullfighting commentary, 'La corrida'. The lovely 'Je t'ai ouvert les yeux' and 'C'est ça qu'on appelle aimer' marked out the path to a less frenetic style that reached out across the generations, while the lengthy 'Le pianiste de Varsovie' (a heartfelt tribute to Frédéric Chopin, complete with classical piano touches) was a triumph on stages across the country, as well as showcasing for the first time in a studio setting just how much drama he could pack into a performance. Bécaud showed no sign of slowing down as he continued into 1957 with the jolly 'Les marchés de Provence' and hit a new peak in 1958 with 'Le jour où la pluie viendra', 'Il fait des bonds... le pierrot qui danse', the jazzy 'C'est merveilleux, l'amour' and the movie theme 'Croquemitoufle'.

Lost in the shuffle was the 1955 ballad 'Je t'appartiens'. A subdued effort written by Bécaud and lyricist Pierre Delanoë, it was given an almost throwaway arrangement but proved strong enough to overcome its lowly origins. Picked up for US consumption by Jill Corey in 1957 as 'Let It Be Me', it was subsequently covered by the Everly Brothers in 1960 and turned into a standard.

Others too, were increasingly drawn to Bécaud's material, among them a new vocal act called Les Trois Ménestrels.[137] A gifted harmony outfit attracted

---

[137] Usually styled 'Les 3 Ménestrels' on their record sleeves, though not on their debut release.

to the theatrical style of groups like Les Frères Jacques, this mixed-gender trio were a neat fit in 1956 for 'Ballade de Davy Crockett' (a cover of Fess Parker's 'Ballad Of Davy Crockett'), proving their worth again two years later with 'Quadrille au village' ('The Farmer And The Cowman' from the Broadway musical *Oklahoma!*). Pitched somewhere between a folk group and a music hall act, they made a name for themselves with highly visual live performances, but their records were equally strong – none more so than a 1958 EP housing four of Bécaud's recent hits, of which the highlight was their pretty reworking of 'Le mur'. By the end of the decade, they had found their style, and releases like 1959's 'L'homme du monde' and the following year's 'Les képis' and 'Les rois fainéants' saw them mapping out a unique blend of the musical and visual arts far beyond the energetic entertainment provided by Bécaud.

Les Compagnons de la Chanson were another group that dabbled in the Bécaud songbook, teaming up with the maestro himself for the good-natured 'Alors, raconte...' in 1956. Mixing adaptations of recent American hits like 'Chanson à ma bien-aimée' ('The Whiffenpoof Song') and 'Un amour pleurait' (Johnnie Ray's 'The Little White Cloud That Cried') with home-grown offerings like 1952's 'Elle chante', they were the kings of the harmony ballad and far and away the most popular vocal outfit in the country. By the middle of the decade, they had broken out of this artistic straightjacket with a run of more uptempo hits, among them 1954's 'La java du Diable' from the pen of Charles Trenet. A singing compendium of the decade's pop hits, the Compagnons were as much at home with Brassens' 'Chanson pour l'Auvergnat' as they were with Bing Crosby & Grace Kelly's hit from *High Society*, 'True Love' ('Premier matin'), processing it all through the mix and always emerging with something true to their own image.

The traditional sounds offered by many of the stars of music hall reflected the state of affairs that had persisted since the start of the century, with only the jazzy rhythms of Gilbert Bécaud and Charles Aznavour showing any overt signs of foreign influence. Over the course of the 1950s, however, an increasing number of French singers had had hits with songs of foreign origin. To a certain extent, Les Compagnons de la Chanson became standard-bearers in this regard, with arrangements of popular tunes like Frankie Laine's 'Cry Of The Wild Goose' ('Légende indienne') and 'I Believe' ('Je crois en toi'), and Nat 'King' Cole's 'Mona Lisa'. Such reworkings were hardly a new trend, having begun in the twenties, but their increasing popularity served notice that, the fresh artistic triumphs of the leading *chansonniers* notwithstanding, the new pop audience could not be taken for granted.

# Chapter 7

## AMOUR, CASTAGNETTES ET TANGO
### The exotica boom (1954-58)

*As the fifties drew on, audiences across the globe began to search for something different to entertain them: new rhythms for dancing and fresh musical styles to replace the old sounds dating back to before the war. In the US, this desire for change was accelerated by the economic pressures that had resulted in the collapse of the big bands, and by a series of musicians' union strikes that inadvertently led to the rise in prominence of the singer over the band. This, in turn, had transferred power from bandleaders into the hands of record companies. While this in itself was not necessarily a bad thing and resulted in an outpouring of classic hits by the likes of Frank Sinatra, Bing Crosby, Dinah Shore and Perry Como, it also resulted in an early-fifties craze for inane novelty records, fed to a seemingly insatiable market by producer Mitch Miller and his stable of singers. This was followed by a brief craze for the mambo, and then by the rock'n'roll explosion which engulfed the entire country by the end of the decade.*

### American songs and French hits
In France, where mainstream audiences had barely begun to digest jazz, rock'n'roll was as yet too extreme for domestic consumption, but the same thirst for novelty drove listeners away from the *chanteurs réalistes* toward a less intense, more joyful form of music. Initially, this saw a number of pop songs crossing the Atlantic, such as Leroy Anderson's 'Blue Tango' (adapted as 'Tango bleu' in 1952 by both Line Renaud and Tino Rossi) and Patti Page's 'The Doggie In The Window' (which, reworked in French as 'Le chien dans la vitrine', became a hit for Line Renaud in 1953). Les Compagnons de la Chanson continued their ransacking of the American songbook in 1954 with the phony folk outing, 'Trop beau pour être vrai' (Dean Martin's 'Hey Brother Pour The Wine'), while in 1956, Luis Mariano and André Dassary both opted for covers of the Four Aces' 'Love Is A Many-Splendored Thing' ('La plus belle chose au monde'). Such hits served to bring the American and French markets closer together, but compared to the musical riches on offer from the emerging generation of *chansonniers*, most of the foreign covers lacked originality and excitement.

A far more enticing development was the international success in 1955 of German-based Italian singer[138] Caterina Valente's 'Malagueña', a hit across much of Europe that turned the French audience's taste for the occasional Spanish or Latin American-styled song into a full-blown craze.

Initially, the challenge was taken up both by bandleaders like Jacques Hélian, who cut the perfunctory 'Lolo... Lola' (adapted from Bob London's 'Lola'[139]), and by music hall stars: André Claveau adopted a South American theme for 'Prière péruvienne', while Line Renaud and Dario Moreno cut rival versions of the Rosemary Clooney/Dean Martin hit, 'Mambo Italiano', Renaud singing it with her customary swing and Moreno playing it rather more tongue-in-cheek.

The popularity of the mambo was also reflected in Henri Salvador's typically amusing take on Perry Como's 'Papa Loves Mambo' which left the American crooner's tame version in the starting blocks, and in an equally enjoyable version by Dario Moreno. In turn, the success of the mambo brought about a revival of the tango, with Line Renaud's silly 'Tango de l'éléphant' (adapted from the Commanders' 'The Elephants Tango') spawning a rash of further tango hits, most notably George Guétary's 'Tango mandoline' and Gloria Lasso's intriguingly titled 'Amour, castagnettes et tango'.

## The queens of exotica

Lasso, the first new star of the fad for exotica[140], was a Spanish singer with a fiery temper and a stormy love life who had made a minor ripple in 1955 with 'Quand je danse dans tes bras', a cover of Portuguese fado queen Amália Rodrigues' atypically upbeat 'Uma casa portuguesa'. Lasso exploded onto the French pop scene later that year with 'Toi, mon démon', a richly orchestrated affair emphasising her considerable vocal ability and highlighting the Latin-tinged rhythm section. Equally adept at ballads like 'Bonne chance', she was more popular when she turned on the exotic charm, as on the tango-friendly 'Dolores', or her 1956 revival of a thirties' fado by José Galhardo, 'Lisboa antiga'.[141] Already a star in her native land, she brought a breath of fresh air to the French music hall circuit and was soon amongst the biggest

---

[138] As it happens, Valente was actually born in Paris, but although she had hits in France, virtually her entire career was played out abroad.

[139] An early composition by soon-to-be-hot songsmiths Jerry Leiber and Mike Stoller.

[140] See footnote 2 (page 14).

[141] American bandleader Nelson Riddle took the song to the top of the US charts as 'Lisbon Antigua' in the same year.

names in the country.

Despite the title, Lasso's rendition of 'Amour, castagnettes et tango' was actually a string-washed cover of Archie Bleyer's 'Hernando's Hideaway' that emphasised the tango over the castanets, raising the stakes in the torch song marketplace. In 1956, she enjoyed massive hits with 'L'étranger au paradis' (aka 'Stranger In Paradise', Tony Bennett's 1955 UK chart-topper from the musical *Kismet*),[142] a cover of Caterina Valente's 'Malagueña', and the trite 'Mandolino', which upped the tempo and varied the sonic palette to take in the sounds of contemporary Italy. Perfect fodder for the glossy magazines that were coming to dominate newsstands across the country, Lasso packed a powerful vocal punch and delivered her songs with a spark and passion markedly different from Édith Piaf's, but no less enthralling. Her 1956 hit, 'Le torrent' (adapted from Italian singer Tullio Pane's 'Torrente') was a rhythmic, if slightly over-the-top slice of musical drama typical of her style, and for two years she reigned supreme as the country's most glamorous diva.

MARIA CANDIDO
20 866 Méd.
TU ME DONNES (COME PRIMA)
SI TU VAS A RIO
NE ME DIS JAMAIS ADIEU
DONNE DU RHUM A TON HOMME

Lasso's success soon brought forth a rash of imitators, as artists like Maria Candido took to the new sounds and styles like ducks to water. Candido had started out in operetta before scoring a hit in 1952 with the lilting 'Je-te-le-le' and making an early attempt at exotica a year later with 'Jamaïca', but it was the Italian ballad 'La jolie barcarolle' (Luciano Virgili's 'Terra straniera') and then the Spanish-styled 'Granada' that established her as a star in 1956. Despite her talent, however, Candido always lingered in Lasso's shadow, lacking the media-attractive personality needed to keep her on the front pages. Although her version of 'Le torrent' failed to match the power of her rival's, she racked up a string of best-sellers over the decade – among them the dramatic 'Jardins d'Andalousie' (adapted from the great Cuban bandleader Ernesto Lecuona's 'Andalucia'[143]) and 1958's Cuban-flavoured 'Donne du rhum à ton homme', but, despite a real feel for the material, she never truly established herself as a serious challenger to the far more proficient Lasso.

The ultimate superstar of the fad for overseas sounds was Dalida, an Egyptian-born Italian who made her way to Paris in 1954 and first came to the public's attention with an appearance on the radio show *Les numéros 1 de demain*, broadcast on Europe No. 1. Sponsored by station supremo Lucien Morisse, her paramour, and label boss Eddie Barclay, she was launched onto the record market in 1956. Her first two EPs, which included a worthy adaptation of Amália Rodrigues' fado classic 'Barco negro' ('Madone') and a decent cover of Lasso's 'Le torrent', failed to garner much attention. At the

---

[142] Having fought off strong versions by Dario Moreno and Luis Mariano.
[143] Though the most likely inspiration was Caterina Valente's recent revival under the English title adopted back in 1940 by Jimmy Dorsey, 'The Breeze And I'.

start of 1957, however, her third, 'Bambino', exploded across the airwaves to top the hit parade, launching the dynamic singer with the strange accent as a major star. The song was adapted from Italian star Marino Marini's 'Guaglione', a mambo-styled tune subsequently made famous in the US by Pérez Prado.[144] The record was perfect for the pop market, being issued shortly after Brigitte Bardot made her famous appearance dancing the mambo in Roger Vadim's *Et Dieu... créa la femme* (1956). As sensual a performer in her own way as the celebrated screen goddess, Dalida became a major star, swiftly overtaking Gloria Lasso (whose version of 'Bambino' was swamped by hers) to become the hottest singer in the country.

During 1957, Dalida consolidated her position with three further EPs, although none of them matched the success of 'Bambino'. The gentle 'La plus belle du monde' (a treacly effort adapted from Marino Marini's 'La più bella del mondo') provided her with a further hit, and 'Tu n'as pas très bon caractère' (a cover of Renato Carosone's 'Scapricciatiello') gave her a second chart-topper before the year was out, leaving the hapless Maria Candido's version trailing in her wake. With her appeal relying largely on her exotic accent, Egyptian background and tempestuous love life, Dalida combined exotica with Italian-styled pop on the inescapably catchy 'Calypso italiano' (adapted from Lou Monte's American hit of the same name[145]), steadily pulling away from her contemporaries to establish herself as a viable rival to Édith Piaf for the throne of the reigning queen of French pop.

Dalida actually recorded a more varied range of material than a list of her biggest hits might suggest. Charles Aznavour's 'Ay! Mourir pour toi' and Jacques Brel's 'Quand on n'a que l'amour' figured among her early efforts, and she enjoyed a major hit in 1958 with Gilbert Bécaud's 'Le jour où la pluie viendra'. Generally, however, her hits tended to be of foreign origin, many of them dreamy Italian romantic ballads that swayed like a palm tree on a summer's day – an approach that paid dividends, as 1958's 'Come prima' and the following year's 'Ciao, ciao bambina' attested.[146] Italy was also the source of the enjoyable nonsense of 'Du moment qu'on s'aime' (Teddy Reno's 'Piccolissima serenata'[147]), while Argentinian bandleader Juan d'Arienzo was the source of the sweet ballad 'Buenas noches, mi amor'.[148] Searching far and

---

[144] Prado's 1958 recording was later used to great effect in a popular commercial for Guinness screened on British TV during the 1990s.

[145] Although not listed in the *Billboard* charts, Monte's recording made the Top 50 in the rival *Music Vendor* publication.

[146] Hits by Tony Dallara and Domenico Modugno respectively, the latter under the title 'Piove'.

[147] Quickly covered by both Gloria Lasso and Dario Moreno.

[148] This much-recorded number also generated hit versions by André Claveau, Maria Candido and Henri Salvador.

wide across the spectrum of international pop, Dalida's eclectic approach resulted in more success with 1959's 'Dansons mon amour' (adapted from the Jewish folk song 'Hava Nagila') and the jazzy vocal group sound of 'Ce serait dommage' (Jack Segal's 'Impatient Lover'). It was, however, Italian ballads that delivered her greatest triumphs, with 'C'est ça l'amore' (Nicola Arigliano's 'I Sing "Ammore" ') and Peppino di Capri's 'Luna caprese' keeping her at the top through to the end of the decade.

The inexorable rise of Dalida continued to overshadow Gloria Lasso, who found her sales starting to dip as Dalida's soared. Her record company's insistence on having her cover the same material as her rival – 1958's 'Gondolier', for instance – made comparisons unavoidable.[149] Still, for now the hits continued, her 1957 cover of Joe Reisman's 'Armen's Theme' ('Amour perdu') being followed by the Latin drama 'Bahia' and the 1958 smash 'Je t'aimerai, t'aimerai'. The same year saw her tackling Perry Como's 'Magic Moments' ('Tout ça') in a rinky-dink arrangement that was not one of her biggest sellers, but her waltz through 'Bouquet d'Amsterdam' (Ernst Bader's 'Die Tulpen aus Amsterdam') was better, if less successful than the English version, 'Tulips From Amsterdam', by UK crooner Max Bygraves. Equally comfortable with a romantic ballad, in 1959 she turned her attention to the nascent Rat Pack, covering Dean Martin's 'Return To Me' ('Bonjour, chéri') and Frank Sinatra's 'All The Way' ('À jamais') in richly orchestrated fashion, but was unable to overtake her now unstoppable rival.

Maria Candido likewise struggled to escape from Dalida's shadow, and despite a pleasingly clear vocal style that generated hits with 1957's 'Le bateau de Tahiti' and 'Le petit tango', her pretty renditions of the likes of 'Gondolier'[150] lacked the emotional punch delivered by her rivals. Despite this, the French fondness for the exotic ensured all three singers a large degree of airplay, at least until the market began to shift in 1958.

## The floodgates open

Dalida's huge success turned the trickle of foreign-born hits into a torrent, with Latin America proving a rich source of material for French singers looking for easy hits. Gloria Lasso had already scored a major hit in 1956 with 'Deux petits arbres' (Chucho Martínez Gil's mariachi favourite, 'Dos arbolitos'), but

---

[149] This was of course standard practice in the music industry into the early sixties, driven as much by the desire of music publishers to maximise the earning potential of a song as it was by record companies' eagerness to eat into the sales of the competition. Accordingly, some of the decade's biggest hits ended up on the market in a dozen or more versions.

[150] Her version was mysteriously retitled 'Le gondolier', although that's not what she sang on the record.

the Latin-styled 'Histoire d'un amour' was a hit in 1957 for André Claveau, Gloria Lasso *and* Dalida. Even Édith Piaf, who under normal circumstances was disinclined to record novelties, reached out across the Atlantic for a Peruvian waltz by Susana Rinaldi, 'Amor de mis amores', and turned it into one of the biggest hits of her career: 1958's 'La foule'.

Always at home with foreign sounds, Henri Génès, who had in 1955 cut the amusing (for the times) mock-Arab tango 'Sidi bel Abbès', took a break from what was becoming a flourishing cinematic career to cut the 1956 singalong smash 'Le facteur de Santa-Cruz'. He followed this up in 1957 with the rather too obvious 'Les mecs de Mexico', by which time music was less important to him as a creative outlet than it once had been.

Jacqueline François picked up two smashes from the same 1956 EP with the curious 'Chiens perdus sans collier' and 'Samba fantastique' (a cover of Jorge Goulart's 'Samba fantastico'). However, she was more at home with jazz, as evidenced by 'Lola (La légende du pays aux oiseaux)' – a decent reading of George Shearing's 'Lullaby Of Birdland', or traditional *chanson*, exemplified by her interpretation of Mouloudji's 'Un jour tu verras'. Though her sweet, melodic style gradually fell into disfavour as the decade progressed, she managed to pick up another hit in 1956 duetting with Henri Decker on 'Main dans la main' (a lush reworking of Tony Martin's 'Walk Hand In Hand') before turning to domestic sources for a version of Francis Lemarque's 'L'air de Paris' the following year. However, when her 1958 take on 'Gondolier'[151] went nowhere, it became clear that she was going to struggle against the divas of exotica, and her cover of Domenico Modugno's 'Nel blu dipinto di blu'[152] ('Dans le bleu du ciel bleu') was left standing by Dalida's massively successful interpretation.

By the end of the decade, her star was fading, despite quality recordings like the theme from Jacques Tati's 1958 film *Mon oncle* and 'La vie mondaine', a strong cover of 'The Lady Is A Tramp', the Mitzi Green classic recently revived by Frank Sinatra. Even material from heavyweights like Henri Salvador ('Pour une femme'), Charles Aznavour ('Tant que l'on s'aimera') and Gilbert Bécaud ('Le mur') was not enough to restore her to glory, although she remained a popular attraction on stage and on television.

Patrice et Mario had rarely dabbled in anything *but* exotica, so for them the new craze was heaven-sent. They happily sailed on into the middle of the decade, cruising from South America ('Marie-Brésil') via Italy ('La fête à Capri') to the islands of the Caribbean ('La petite Martiniquaise'), then heading back to Italy for a cover of Renato Rascel's 'Arrivederci Roma'. However, their decision to go head-to-head with Dalida on a cover of 'Bambino' proved less successful, exposing their now-dated appeal when set against the queen of exotica. They repeated the error any number of times, cutting weak-kneed versions of her 'Tu n'as pas très bon caractère' and 'Gondolier' to moderate success, although the string-swept 'Trinidad' offered rather more in the way of originality.

Bourvil had been another early proponent of exotica with his oriental-sounding 1953 recording, 'Nous n'irons pas à Calcutta', although on that occasion the idea was played strictly for laughs. Tino Rossi travelled even

---

[151] François' version bore the same title as Candido's: 'Le gondolier'.
[152] Covered in the US by Dean Martin as 'Volare'.

further afield for his 1958 hit, 'Le bateau de Tahiti', while Dario Moreno, who had enjoyed an early break in 1954 with 'L'air du Brésilien',[153] drew on Brazilian sources for 'Quand elle danse' (Mercedes Valdés' 'Me voy pa'l pueblo') and the carnival sounds of 'Si tu vas à Rio' (Joel de Almeida's 'Madureira chorou').

André Dassary sailed through the second half of the fifties with a run of big-selling releases that mixed covers of 'Bambino' and other records that were turning into gold for Dalida with exotica like 1957's 'Le plus beau de tous les tangos du monde' and revivals of turn-of-the-century hits like Harry Fragson's 'Reviens!' and the much-covered 'Frou-frou'. Although his sales declined as the decade neared its end, his bright take on the Jewish

*André Dassary.*

folk song 'Hava Nagila' ('Dansons mon amour') compared favourably to the hit version by Dalida. However, exotica was but one weapon in his musical armoury and he retained a loyal following thanks to releases like the 1958 EP *Marches et chants républicains*, which included a heartfelt interpretation of 'La Marseillaise', and a run of religious and festive recordings that were steady sellers every time the Christmas trees came out.

François Degeult likewise went for an exotic sound on the jaunty 'Têtes de mort' and a cover of Domenico Modugno's pop-swayer 'Le puparu' ('Le bonhomme aux marionettes'), though he lacked Modugno's vocal swagger. Elsewhere, Claude Robin made his name with the 1955 hit 'Ave Maria no morro' (a Brazilian song first recorded by O Trio de Ouro in 1942), following up with the offbeat 'African tango' and 'Tango des Pyrennées'.

Marcel Amont was more creative, giving Charles Aznavour's 'Sur la table' a mambo-flavoured makeover in 1956. After slipping into cliché the following year on 'Pantuflas mambo cha cha cha', he had the good taste to include Charles Trenet's contribution to the exotica craze, 'Cha cha boum', on his 1958 *Marcel Amont à l'Olympia* album.

Not all these songs were necessarily covers of overseas hits, but in all cases the inspiration came from beyond the borders of France, thus marking a clear break with the insular, closed-shop world of traditional French music hall. The emphasis was firmly on exotic sounds – not only in music, but also in accents. Dalida (Italian) and Gloria Lasso (Spanish) were the tip of an iceberg that subsequently gouged a huge hole in the side of the French pop industry. Alongside these two great rivals emerged a host of foreign singers, who, for a variety of reasons, chose to base themselves in France.

---

[153] Strictly speaking, this was operetta rather than exotica, based as it was on Offenbach's classic, *La vie parisienne*.

One of the first was Eddie Constantine, an American vocalist discovered by Édith Piaf at the start of the fifties. After making his name alongside his *patronne* in the operetta *La p'tite Lili*, duetting with her on the inconsequential 'Si, si, si', he racked up a series of hits, his heavily-accented vocals providing much of the appeal. His specialities were American or American-styled novelty songs sung in French. He hit the jackpot in 1953 with a gentle clip-clop rendition of the Charles Aznavour-penned 'Et bâiller et dormir', fighting off a stiff challenge from a more traditional treatment by crooner Jean Bretonnière, while at the same time anticipating the *faux*-country recordings that would bring international success to Dean Martin a decade later. The jauty 'L'enfant de la balle' followed a more mainstream path marked out with

L'HOMME et L'ENFANT 70009
Mon ami réveille-toi ★ Je suis un sentimental
Laisse-moi rêver de toi (Make yourself comfortable)

TANIA ET EDDIE CONSTANTINE
Accompagnés par Wal-Berg et son Orchestre

Barclay DISQUES

further successes like the smoothly crooned 'Les trottoirs' and the big band bash of 'Ça bardait'. Constantine enjoyed his biggest hit in 1955 with the saccharine 'L'homme et l'enfant', a duet with his daughter Tania that would be reworked in the US a couple of years later as 'Little Child' by Eddie Albert & Sondra Lee.[154] In 1956, he scored with a duet with Juliette Gréco, 'Je prends les choses du bon côté', and also made a bid for Yuletide glory with a cover of Tino Rossi's already unavoidable 'Petit Papa Noël' for the same year's Christmas market.

Despite a fondness for songwriters like Léo Ferré ('Les amoureux du Havre') and Aznavour ('Je t'aime comme ça' and 'Deux pour aimer', the latter recorded as a big band duet with Paulette Rollin), it was Constantine's American cool that underpinned his appeal – especially to the young. Ever eclectic, he covered both Perry Como's 'Hot Diggity' ('Hop digui-di') and the pacifist ode 'Quand les hommes vivront d'amour'[155] on the same 1956 EP, the difference between them glossed over by his sympathetic croon. A year later, he took on Les Compagnons de la Chanson with a version of Como's 'Round And Round' ('Ronde, ronde'[156]) and transitioned to country music to score a major smash in 1957 with 'Cigarettes, whisky et p'tites pépées' (a revival of Red Ingle & The Natural Seven's 'Cigareets, Whuskey, And Wild, Wild Women'), battling for airplay against a more restrained rendition by Annie Cordy.[157]

One of the most versatile singers ever to grace a music hall stage, Cordy followed up with the amusing hoedown 'La petite rouquine du vieux Brooklin', but she was too eclectic to stay in one place for long and the exotica boom gave her a perfect opportunity to switch gears whenever the fancy took her.

---

[154] Also a minor US hit for Cab & Lael Calloway, Danny & Dena Kaye, and Gisele MacKenzie & Billy Quinn.

[155] This song later became a virtual anthem in Quebec, although this had nothing to do with Constantine's recording.

[156] Les Compagnons titled their version 'Ronde, ronde, ronde'.

[157] There was also a less successful version by Philippe Clay.

She proved to be a mistress of all styles, moving with ease between the big band jazz of 1955's 'Oh! Bessie' to the mambo-flecked 'La petite Martiniquaise', to the New Orleans-flavoured 'La clarinette' – one of four tracks on the EP *Jazz-party chez Annie Cordy*, where she also showed off her jazz chops on the smoky 'Sammy'. Thereafter, she headed south for a reworking of Henri Génès' tango, 'Tantina de Burgos', drifted up to Scandinavia for 'Viens à la gare' (Thory Bernhards' 'Ann-Caroline'[158]), then crossed the Atlantic again for 'Tout ce que veut Lola' (Gwen Verdon's 'Whatever Lola Wants'[159]).

As comfortable with comic material as with straight pop songs, Cordy hit with 'La p'tite sonnette', 'Les caballeros' and the children's favourite, 'Le petit pélican', although more in keeping with the times were straightforward mambos like 'Oranges, tabac, café' and 'Faut pas t'énerver comme ça'. As the prevailing wind changed, so did she, scoring one of the biggest hits of 1957 with 'Coquelicots polka' (a cover of Scottish accordion star Jimmy Shand's 'Bluebell Polka') before diving back into the exotica of Renato Carosone's 'Toréro' and Teddy Reno's 'Chella llà' ('Oh! La, la'[160]). One of the brightest stars in the music hall pantheon, she kept busy for much of the year, appearing in the operetta *Tête de linotte*, for which she recorded a soundtrack album combining exotica such as 'Le rythme des tropiques' and 'La samba d'Ali Baba' with sweeter offerings like the lovely ballad 'T'es mon terr'neuve', on which she duetted with co-star René Marquay.

The original queen of exotica was, of course, Joséphine Baker. Her moment may have passed, but she could still leave them clamouring for more wherever she performed and she continued to record throughout the fifties, scoring an early exotica hit in 1950 with 'Chiquita madame'. Her approach may have been dated and her repertoire given over to lightweight material, but she could turn it on whenever she chose to do so, as demonstrated by her 1957 revival of Charles Trenet's 'Revoir Paris'. Far more exotic were the same year's 'Bahiana' and 1958's 'Olele, olela', while her 1959 effort, 'Moi' (adapted from Domenico Modugno's 'Io') revealed a willingness to tap Italian sources. The records may have failed to sell, but the blame did not lie with Baker, and

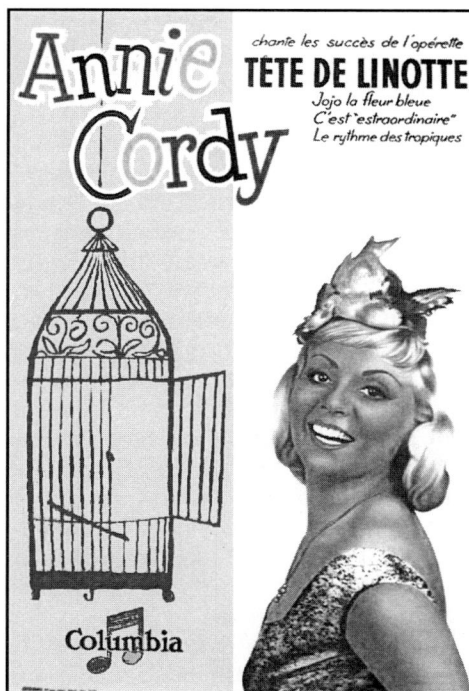

---

[158] Although the inspiration was most likely Anne Shelton's English-language hit cover, 'Lay Down Your Arms'.

[159] From the 1955 Broadway musical *Damn Yankees*.

[160] Also covered, more spectacularly, by Dalida.

she continued to make triumphant stage appearances at will – the epitome of the all-singing, all-dancing showgirl.

The same showgirl appeal lay at the heart of the Kessler Sisters, identical blonde twins from Germany who were regular fixtures at the Lido nightclub in Paris, where their leggy appearance and Andrews Sisters-style harmonies made them a popular live attraction among the great and good of French society. International cabaret stars with hit records in West Germany and Italy, their first French EP only appeared in 1959, when the self-referential 'Deux jeunes filles blondes' surprisingly failed to give them the chart success they deserved. A follow-up offering the clichéd 'À Monte-Carlo' fared equally badly, offering little of the emotional substance of Piaf or Dalida.

## Transatlantic breezes

As the decade progressed and the Latin winds began to abate, singers turned their attention once again to North America – a path that would eventually lead them to rock'n'roll. The most obvious target was Doris Day's 1956 smash, 'Whatever Will Be, Will Be', transformed into 'Que sera, sera' and on the market by no fewer than *twelve* different French singers, among them François Deguelt, Georges Guétary and Luis Mariano – the latter two ideal for the exotica boom, with accents from Greece and Spain respectively.

Among the female interpreters were Jacqueline François, Line Renaud and Michèle Arnaud, who put one foot in the exotica camp while keeping the other in the world of the *chansonniers*. Although she was known primarily as an interpreter of quality *chanson*, Arnaud also dabbled in lighter material, and the exotica boom gave her the opportunity to mix a cover of Domenico Modugno's 'La cicoria' ('Les fleurs et l'amour')[161] into her usual diet of songs, although it was the likes of Léo Ferré's 'En amour' that cemented her commercial appeal".

As the owner of her own Montmartre nightspot, Patachou pretty much had free reign with her material, but, like Arnaud, was not above having a flutter at an obvious hit. However, her 1956 cover of Rosemary Clooney/Sammy Davis Jr.'s 'Hey There' ('Eh Ben!')[162] was not indicative of her usual style, which was better represented by the pre-war classic 'Les voyous' and Léo Ferré's 'Nous les filles', both of which were far more in keeping with her role as a *chanteuse réaliste*.

The search for new rhythms to captivate French audiences led to a brief flirtation with calypso music in 1957 and 1958 (mirroring the style's huge American popularity in the hands of Harry Belafonte), with Les Compagnons

---

[161] Albeit with a lyric from *chansonnier* Francis Lemarque.
[162] Also covered by Dalida.

de la Chanson's version of Belafonte's 'Banana Boat (Day O)'[163] leading the way. The late fifties were hugely successful years for the veteran outfit, who were easily the most popular vocal ensemble in the land. Their distinctive sound hinged on massed harmonies and well-conceived counterpoint arrangements, and they built their success on near-acappella covers of Charles Aznavour's 'Sur ma vie', Gilbert Bécaud's 'Je t'appartiens' and a host of other favourites. They also appropriated Perry Como's 'Catch A Falling Star' ('Garde ça pour toi') for the home market while pursuing the exotica craze wherever it led. In 1958, they scored with the Italian-styled ballad 'Gondolier', Latin-tinged pop ('Si tu vas à Rio') and cod-Spanish Gypsy music ('Les Gitans'), sharing their hits with versions by other stars of the day and preserving their place in the hearts of the public.

Also hanging on to the exotica baton, Henri Salvador issued a run of records in the style of his birthplace, 1957's 'Eh! Mama!' relying as much on his humorous vocal asides as on the Caribbean percussion flourishes that were all the rage at the time. The following year, he cut a version of Harry Belafonte's 'Island In The Sun' ('Une île au soleil'), achieving greater sales with his calypso-tinged balladry than he had done with his more lyrical efforts, while a revival of his ever-popular 'Maladie d'amour' provided him with a big hit in 1958.[164] Almost as successful was the West Indian-styled ballad 'Dans mon île', while the calypso 'Mathilda' saw him sprinkling his trademark silly voices over a lovely arrangement. Perfect easy listening for a summer's day, they showed a more sensitive side of the great entertainer, although he was too much of a maverick to stick with one style for long.

Calypso also provided easy pickings for Annie Cordy ('Calypso romana'), and for John William, who turned in high-quality renditions of 'Day-O' and 'Une île au soleil' as a diversion from his usual fare of film themes and cowboy songs. Although not one of the biggest sellers during the exotica boom, William maintained a presence in the market with western-themed offerings like 1958's 'Banjo Bill de l'Arizona', while his version of Nat 'King' Cole's 'Hajji Baba' ('Hadji baba') offered a variation on the usual foreign themes dominating the French airwaves. It was, however, his interpretation of the Paul Robeson classic, 'Ol' Man River', that established his credentials,[165] and his recordings of black American

---

[163] A reworking of a traditional folk song known originally as 'Daydah Light (Banana Loaders' Song)', it is best known in Europe as 'The Banana Boat Song', under which title it was recorded by Shirley Bassey. The French version was also a hit for Dario Moreno, and was covered by many other artists.

[164] Reissued by Philips as Salvador jumped ship to Barclay. The reissue was prompted by the 1957 American hit cover by the Ames Brothers.

[165] Though it had to share space with a showboating version from Eddie Constantine. William's version was listed on the record sleeve as 'Old Man River'.

spirituals likewise proved highly popular, if something of a sideshow outside the mainstream of French show business.

With a similar background in gospel and jazz, the Peters Sisters were well placed to ride the changes, shimmying their way through a 1958 revival of Charles Trenet's 'Vous qui passez sans me voir' and jumping onto the exotica bandwagon with 'Rumbadi bumbadi cha cha cha'.

Meanwhile, the American charts continued to be plundered for novelties like 'Je vais revoir ma blonde' (Mitch Miller's 'The Yellow Rose Of Texas'), which produced a smash hit for both Eddie Constantine and Dario Moreno. Already popular thanks to his stage and screen appearances, Moreno also enjoyed impressive record sales with lightweight fluff like the brassy mambo 'Le marchand de bonheur'[166] and invested in Mexican gold for the demented 'Coucouroucoucou' (Tomás Méndez's classic 'Cucurrucucu paloma'[167]), He gave Tete Montoliu's Spanish tango 'Eso es el amor' the same jovial spin for another major hit, this time sharing the airwaves with a rival version by Les Chakachas.

Fronted by Cuban-born singer Kari Kenton, Les Chakachas were a group of jazz musicians from Belgium who were perfectly placed to cash in on the exotica boom. They followed up their breakthrough hit with danceable novelties like 'Ay! Mulata' and 'Guapacha', trading on their Cuban connections for all they were worth, and hammering home the dominance of the exotic as the fifties ticked on toward the sixties.

## Cross-Channel currents

When they could find no American records to fit the bill, singers could always look to the UK for inspiration. Dalida's 1957 success 'Le ranch de Maria' actually originated in Italy (Gino Latilla's 'Casetta in Canadà') but sounded like the work of Britain's Alma Cogan, while her 1958 smash, 'Gondolier', was lifted from a UK hit by Petula Clark ('With All My Heart'[168]). When Dalida also swooped on her follow-up cover of the Shepherd Sisters' 'Alone (Why Must I Be Alone)',[169] adapting it as 'Je pars', Clark's record label, Pye Nixa, decided that enough was enough and set about launching her as a singer in France.

Initially reluctant, Clark changed her mind after falling in love with her French A&R man, Claude Wolff, and subsequently threw herself into her new

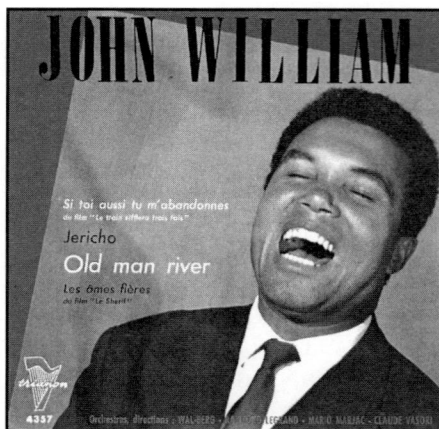

---

[166] A much-recorded song, this was all over the airwaves in a multitude of versions by everyone from Les Compagnons de la Chanson to André Dassary and Georges Guétary, although nobody gave it the same *joie de vivre* as the ever-smiling Moreno.

[167] Introduced to American audiences by Harry Belafonte.

[168] Clark's hit was itself a cover, having originally been recorded in the US by Jodie Sands.

[169] Clark's version was simply titled 'Alone'.

career. Her repertoire had, in fact, already overlapped into the world of French pop on more than one occasion. Indeed, she had enjoyed UK hits in 1954 and 1955 with covers of Francis Lemarque's 'Le petit cordonnier' ('The Little Shoemaker') and Gilbert Bécaud's 'Mes mains' ('With Your Love') respectively[170] – but even so she found the going in France difficult. After several false starts trying to find the right style, including an insipid duet with Claude Robin ('Allô mon cœur') and the jazzy 'Java pour Petula', she clicked in 1959 with a version of the rhythmic 'Guitare et tambourin' (Robert P. Marcucci's 'Holiday In Naples'), her English accent proving as charming and exotic to the French as the assorted Italian, Spanish and other accents that had preceded her.

## Mediterranean sounds

Jean-Paul Mauric offered a different approach to the world of exotica, adding a smooth, suave sophistication to proceedings. After his 1958 debut release misfired, he established himself with covers of Italian singer Tony Dallara's (and Dalida's) 'Come prima'[171] and Pérez Prado's 'Patricia'. These set him up for a short career turning out variations on the hits of the day, including other classics of the era such as Dalida's 'Ciao, ciao bambina' (with gender change) and 'Luna caprese', though he never managed to move out of the shadow of other, rather better performers.

At the height of the exotica boom, most of the established music hall stars dipped at least a toe into the water. Georges Guétary covered most of Dalida's hits (notably 'Bambino' and 'Le ranch de Maria' in 1957, and 'Ciao, ciao bambina' in 1959) in his own charming style. At the same time, he continued to croon sweet nothings on the likes of 1956's 'En courant le monde', establishing himself on television as a French equivalent of Perry Como and enjoying his last major success with 'Papa aime Maman' in 1960.

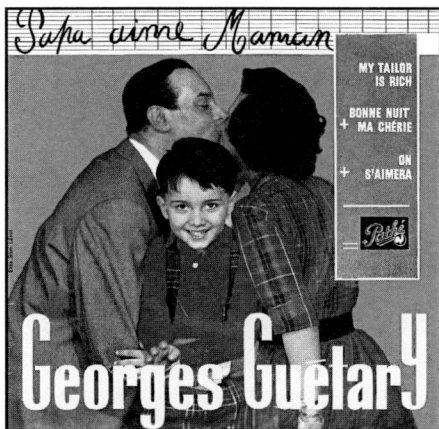

Luis Mariano also churned out versions of anything that looked like a hit to huge commercial reward throughout the decade, finding success in 1957 with 'Canastos' (an inconsequential duet with Gloria Lasso that was as catchy as the common cold, though far more appealing) and the much-recorded 'Gelsomina' (written by Nino Rota for Federico Fellini's 1954 movie masterpiece, *La Strada*). His hit-making streak continued in 1958 with 'Chanson de Lima', and he continued to mine the exotica vein for all it was worth with 'Argentina sérénade'

---

[170] Although it did not make the singles chart, Clark's 'With Your Love' was one of five versions that helped push it to No. 3 on the UK sheet music chart.

[171] Mauric's version carried the subtitle 'Come prima (Tu me donnes)', and a number of other versions released that year did the same. Some even reversed the titles: 'Tu me donnes (Come prima)'. The French record industry was nothing if not inconsistent.

and a cover of Lou Monte's 'Calypso Italiano'.

The same approach was adopted by bandleader Bob Azzam, who brought a sense of fun to everything he did. Italian ballads, Latin dance novelties, even watered-down rock'n'roll – you name it, he recorded it, and from 1958 onwards he enjoyed a string of major hits across Europe with dance-floor reworkings of Italian pop gems like Mina's 'Tintarella di luna' and Peppino di Capri's (and Dalida's) 'Luna caprese'.

## A change in the wind

Of course, not every record sold in France during the early fifties had overseas roots; nor would it be true to say that the fad for exotica carried all before it. Nevertheless, while the early fifties had seen the airwaves cluttered with such future classics of French pop as Les Compagnons de la Chanson's version of 'Moulin Rouge',[172] Édith Piaf's 'Notre-Dame de Paris' and 'Bravo pour le clown!', Tino Rossi's 'Si jamais' and 'Ce beau dimanche là', and Line Renaud's 'Je veux', by the middle of the decade French songwriters were increasingly having to share the market with their international counterparts.

Neither could all the imports be classed as exotica. Ballads were as popular as ever, Tino Rossi scoring in 1955 with a cover of David Whitfield's 'Cara Mia' and repeating the feat a year later with a version of Renato Rascel's much-covered 'Arrivederci Roma', but the wind was turning away from traditional music hall styles as the public demanded something new and fresh.

The phenomenal success of the exotica boom was one of the greatest upheavals in the history of French pop, compelling record companies to look outside the country for mass-market hits. While the continued popularity of Édith Piaf and the growing sales enjoyed by the leading *chansonniers* indicated that the market for home-grown songs was as healthy as it had ever been, it was equally clear that the public thirst for entertainment was not going to be quenched by merely rehashing the same ingredients over and over. Aznavour, Bécaud and *chansonniers* like Jacques Brel had shown what could be done within the strictures of traditional French pop, but it was their earthy lyrics and dynamic stage performances, not the tightly structured musical arrangements, that attracted young fans to their concerts. While those who had suffered during the war were happy to escape into the fantasy world of Dalida, Gloria Lasso *et al*, the younger generation wanted the substance offered by the *chansonniers*, but they also sought excitement in their music. Back across the Atlantic, the answer would explode like a thunderbolt with the arrival of rock'n'roll in 1955, but in France, where the exotica boom was by that time firmly entrenched, the music industry was poorly placed to bring about a similar revolution. Instead, those looking for music that offered more than novelty value found it within the jazz community along the Left Bank of the Seine, where in dimly lit, smoky rooms the roots of a new style had long been coming together.

---

[172] The song also featured in the repertoires of Tino Rossi, Georges Guétary, Line Renaud and André Claveau.

# Chapter 8

## À SAINT-GERMAIN-DES-PRÉS
### Post-war jazz (1945-58)

*When the Latin Quarter was exposed in the press as the seedbed of the existentialist movement, it had much the same impact on the area as the coverage of San Francisco's Haight-Ashbury district would have on the hippy neighbourhood two decades later: it focused attention on the activities of the quarter's bohemian elements and sought to commodify them for public consumption. While the Parisians did not go quite as far as organising bus tours (as would happen in San Francisco), the area nevertheless became a national – and later an international – magnet for disaffected elements of society, as well as for tourists looking for some form of alternative to mainstream culture. Both could be seen loitering at night in the hope of catching a glimpse of Jean-Paul Sartre, or maybe witnessing a recital by Juliette Gréco in her natural setting. The overwhelming and frequently inaccurate coverage by the popular press painted the area as a threat to public morals, a hotbed of radicalism and much more besides, completely overlooking the spirit that existed at its heart. This constant misrepresentation, and the floods of weekend beatniks, prompted a written response by one of the area's leading cultural lights, jazz trumpeter Boris Vian.*

### Manuel de Saint-Germain-des-Prés

Part history, part geographical guide, Vian's *Manuel de Saint-Germain-des-Prés* was a heartfelt, witty description of the district and its habitués, tracing the evolution of the famous cellar clubs in some detail and debunking the more ludicrous myths that had gained currency in the previous few years. Scheduled for publication in 1951, its release was cancelled when the publisher went broke,[173] leaving it to serve as a precious time capsule, capturing the peculiarities of the district in loving detail shortly before the commercial exploitation that followed in the wake of Juliette Gréco's success.

Naturally, Gréco was included in the book, in the anthology of personalities, alongside a host of other famous and not-so-famous names, including philosophers and writers (Jean-Paul Sartre, Albert Camus), singers (Mouloudji, Les Frères Jacques), musicians (Claude Luter, Michel de Villers) and the locals who owned the clubs, worked in the stores, or simply hung out at night. Ironically, although she represented the public face of the *quartier*, Gréco's rise to popularity meant she would soon depart to pursue a stellar career.

---

[173] It was finally published in 1974 and has since been translated into English (see page 469).

## American jazz in Paris

Gréco's departure left less of a hole than might have been expected, as the music of choice at existentialist gatherings was not French *chanson,* but jazz – preferably American, and preferably by black musicians. Miles Davis, who passed through the capital in 1947, was considered to be a major talent despite (or perhaps because of) his relative lack of commercial success, and Gréco was only one of many Parisians who took the opportunity to hang out with the great trumpeter. When American musicians were not available, the local musicians who had been *in situ* since before the war were ready and willing to step in. The result was that the Left Bank of the Seine became the hub of a thriving jazz community broad enough to take in everything from the commercial sounds favoured by dance bands, to the traditional sounds of New Orleans favoured by the revivalists, to the more esoteric bebop styles then evolving in New York.

France, of course, had had a jazz underground since the 1930s – one which had briefly risen to prominence during the Occupation before being submerged by the resurgence of music hall since the end of the war. By then, however, jazz had taken a strong hold on the French imagination, influencing much of contemporary pop,[174] and, despite being overshadowed by more traditional *chanson* and *variétés,*[175] it enjoyed a strong following around the country. By the mid-fifties, more than half of the jazz records released in the US were also available in France – a phenomenal statistic given the huge disparity in population between the two countries. The immense popularity of jazz in France was doubtless one of the factors that led Sidney Bechet and Mezz Mezzrow to follow in the footsteps of Joséphine Baker and settle there at the end of the forties.[176]

Clarinet legend Bechet had first visited France in the 1920s, playing some of the same shows as Baker. When he returned in the late forties to appear at the *Paris Jazz Fair*, he decided to stay. After enjoying a million-selling smash in 1950 with 'Les oignons', he quickly established himself not only within the jazz fraternity, but also in the wider market, becoming an all-round entertainer popular enough to rival Maurice Chevalier. In addition to jazzy workouts like 1952's 'Dans les rues d'Antibes', he recorded several crossover hits, of which the most famous were 'Le marchand de poissons' and 'Petite fleur' (both also 1952).

Thanks to the British trad jazz boom, both songs enjoyed a further lease of life at the close of the decade: 'Le marchand de poissons' was covered as 'The Fish Man' by Ian Menzies & His Clyde Valley Stompers for a 1960 UK hit, while 'Petite fleur' provided Chris Barber's Jazz Band with a global smash in 1959. Barber also turned to Bechet for a follow-up, enjoying another UK hit with 'Lonesome' ('Si tu vois ma mère') that same year, but the accolades came too late. Barber's recordings were still clambering up the charts as Bechet was laid to rest in his adopted home of Antibes.

Barber's success with 'Petite fleur' prompted a successful reissue in

---

[174] As evidenced by the styles of Charles Trenet and Charles Aznavour.
[175] As the music generally performed in music halls was known. The term correlates roughly to the Anglo-American expression 'popular song'.
[176] Racism in the US was doubtless another.

France of Bechet's original version, as well as several covers including a decent performance by fellow jazzman Georges Jouvin and more hackneyed renditions by accordionist Aimable and orchestra leader Franck Pourcel. Several months later, in December 1959, a vocal version with a lyric by Fernand Bonifay appeared and went on to become a hit for Mouloudji, Annie Cordy, Henri Salvador and a host of others.

Clarinettist/saxophonist Milton 'Mezz' Mezzrow made less of an impact on the wider French public, although he was just as influential within the jazz community, thanks to rough-and-ready recordings like 1951's 'If I Could Be With You'. Mezzrow's 1953 revival of Louis Armstrong's 'West End Blues' proved to be his best-ever recording and established him as one of the giants of the traditional jazz movement then sweeping the Continent. The same year saw him playing with visiting American star Lionel Hampton on the superb *Hamp in Paris* album, and he continued in a similar vein for many years, often forming mixed-race bands and always staying true to the spirit of New Orleans that drove him.

Bechet and Mezzrow both provided employment for French musicians, giving a helping hand to the likes of clarinettist Claude Luter, who played with both of them at various times during the early fifties. Luter, who had been leading his own band and cutting primitive but engaging revivals of standards like the Original Dixieland Jazz Band's 'Tiger Rag' for some years, soaked up the experience and went on to run France's biggest and best trad jazz band. They cut a series of superb records,[177] both originals and revivals, for the Vogue label during the fifties, among them the studiedly old-time 'Rag de dent' in 1951.

Saxophonist Michel de Villers was less visible, although he did serve time in the more mainstream orchestra of Géo Daly, appearing on the latter's 1953 'sweet music' take on Duke Ellington's 'I Got It Bad (And That Ain't Good)'.

Pianist Claude Bolling was less prescriptive in his choice of repertoire, cutting a series of albums dedicated to the works of jazz masters like Ellington (*Claude Bolling joue Duke Ellington*) and Django Reinhardt (*Nuages*) while continuing to frequent the cellar clubs

---

[177] Including another version of 'Petite fleur'

of Saint-Germain-des-Prés. Significantly, Bolling did not feature in Vian's book, perhaps because his commercial approach sat less well with the 'purist' view gaining currency at the time. Although both Luter and Bolling enjoyed significant sales and long careers, it is doubtful that either was accorded the same level of respect by their Parisian audiences as their American contemporaries.

Following in the footsteps of Bechet and Mezzrow came singer/trumpeter Taps Miller[178] and saxophonist James Moody. Miller cut a fine single, 'Ferme la bouche', for the Belgian Ronnex label in 1953 – one of the earliest European recordings of small-group rhythm & blues. Moody however, took a completely different musical approach. Initially inspired by Count Basie, he radically changed his style after the war, after working alongside bebop pioneer Dizzy Gillespie for two years before moving to Paris in 1948. There, he found a natural home in Saint-Germain-des-Prés, where his 'Boptet' of French and visiting American musicians laid down a series of cool grooves in 1950, most notably the languorous beauty that was 'Real Cool'. In 1952, he cut the first version of his classic, 'Moody's Mood For Love' (an improvisation based on 'I'm In The Mood For Love'). It became a sizeable jazz hit, prompting him to return to the US to pursue a successful career, leaving behind an audience thirsting for new variations on the jazz of old.

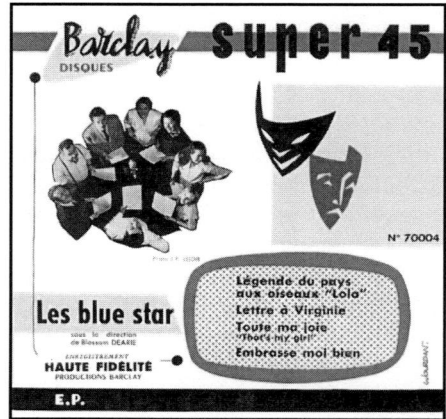

American singer Blossom Dearie moved to Paris in 1952, where she formed Les Blue Stars, an eight-piece unit comprising four male singers/instrumentalists and four female singers. With complex vocal arrangements, the ensemble enjoyed instant success with their rendition of George Shearing's 'Lullaby of Birdland' ('Légende du pays aux oiseaux (Lola)'). Featuring the talents of rising jazz stars such as vocalist Christiane Legrand, her brother, arranger Michel Legrand, and American arranger Lamar Ward Swingle, Les Blue Stars were an international sensation, offering a totally fresh approach to jazz singing. Although Dearie was subsequently lured back to the States in 1956 by a contract with Verve, she was unable to take the group with her, leaving them behind in France to enjoy further hits with less startling renditions of the hits of the day.

Jane Morgan also crossed the Atlantic after the war and became such a popular live draw on the Continent that she decided to set up base in Paris, although for the most part she continued to sing and record in English. Despite enjoying success in the US in 1956 with 'Two Different Worlds' and 'Fascination', she became so identified with her new home that, on return trips to the States, she was often billed as *The American Girl from France*.

---

[178] From Buck Clayton's band.

Morgan enjoyed a number of international hits during the decade, many of them drawn from the repertoire of her French contemporaries. The most notable of these was a cover of Gilbert Bécaud's 'Le jour où la pluie viendra' which (adapted into English as 'The Day The Rains Came') topped the UK charts in early 1959,[179] prompting her to raid the Bécaud songbook again for the follow-up, 'If I Could Only Live My Life Again' ('Si je pouvais revivre un jour ma vie'). The following year, a number of her French favourites were compiled for the Canadian market on the album, *Jane Morgan chante pour ses amis canadiens*, introducing audiences to such sweet novelties as 'Fais-toi belle'. By then her popularity in France was in decline and she began spending increasing periods of time back in the States, leaving the French audience to seek out home-grown jazz artists to support.

### Django Reinhardt and his successors

Within the French jazz community, Django Reinhardt remained the biggest name. Despite an unreliability that saw him skipping shows in favour of taking walks on the beach or in the country, he nevertheless continued to make fine recordings in the post-war years, among them a reworking of his old standard, 'Belleville'. A 1949 reunion with Stéphane Grappelli resulted in a charming arrangement of Charles Trenet's 'La mer', along with two further classics in 'Daphne' and the sublime 'Djangology', the latter reconfirming his status as the country's first guitar hero. While Reinhardt remained at home, Grappelli increasingly chose to ply his trade overseas, recording with a host of top-flight American and British performers, although he took time out to cut the impressive *Improvisations* album in Paris in 1956.

With his unique approach to the instrument already being widely imitated by a host of amateur musicians, Reinhardt entered the fifties in fine style, laying down masterful interpretations of material as diverse as Leo Reisman's 'Stormy Weather', Roger Wolfe Kahn's 1920s hit, 'Crazy Rhythm', and the Kurt Weill-penned Walter Huston favourite, 'September Song'. At the same time, he continued to compose his own equally sublime tunes, adding 1952's 'Flèche d'or' and the following year's 'Deccaphonie' to his already impressive stack of recordings. Ready and willing to confront the changes in popular music head on, he was well placed to ride out the storm that would soon appear on the horizon, but his premature death from a brain haemorrhage in 1953 robbed France of its most distinctive contributor to international jazz.

Stepping up to fill the gap came former Reinhardt sideman Marcel Bianchi and two acolytes of bandleader Ray Ventura, Henri Salvador and Ventura's

---

[179] Her French version of the song was on the flip side.

nephew, Sacha Distel, who was voted best amateur jazz guitarist in France in 1953.

Bianchi had been an early convert to the electric guitar, earning his keep as a much-in-demand sessionman. He was also a fan of boogie-woogie, cutting a number of engaging tunes during the early fifties including sprightly toe-tappers like 'Foogy boogie' and the whimsical 'Cocotte boogie' before settling in to play guitar in Jacques Hélian's orchestra.

Distel meanwhile won wide admiration within the jazz community for his fluid solos and regularly sat in with American visitors like Louis Armstrong and Stan Getz, at the same time attracting a great deal of female attention for his matinée-idol looks and piercing blue eyes. Records such as 'Bag's groove' and 'Scotch hop' made ripples in the jazz scene, but vocal recordings such as 1957's gentle 'Tout bas' (adapted from the 1944 Guy Lombardo hit, 'Speak Low') and a 1958 revival of Lucienne Boyer's 'Un amour comme le nôtre' suggested that, if he chose, he might have a future in the market niche left vacant by the faded Jean Sablon.

While Distel concentrated on jazz, Henri Salvador dabbled in a variety of styles. He enjoyed a big hit in 1953 with the Latin-tinged 'Le petit Indien' but he was nothing if not versatile and his comic talents were well to the fore on outings like the same year's amusing 'Elle me donne'. The dichotomy between these songs neatly summarised the way his career would pan out as he sought to juggle his many talents into a coherent whole. Although he penned much of his own material, as well as writing for the likes of Maurice Chevalier,[180] he was also content to record other people's compositions, such as Léo Ferré's 'Chanson du scaphandrier'[181] in 1951. Like Distel, he also remained a widely admired figure for his abilities on the guitar, even as he carved out a career as an all-round entertainer and the new clown prince of French pop, as was perfectly exemplified on his 1954 parody of American blues, 'Le roi des caves'.

**Big band jazz**

Although Salvador and Distel attracted widespread support for their more modern approach to jazz, France's leading jazzman in the post-war years remained Jacques Hélian, who favoured an old-fashioned big band sound, leading an outfit modelled on those of the Dorsey brothers for a long run of hits. By the start of the fifties, his 'sweet music' style was so popular that he became only the second French artist to sell a million records.[182]

---

[180] Who enjoyed a hit with Salvador's tribute to Mistinguett, 'Fleur de pavé', in 1949.

[181] Salvador's rendition was titled simply 'Le scaphandrier'.

[182] Tino Rossi was the first. The French market was relatively small at the time, so selling a million across a whole discography was an impressive feat; the days where an artist could

PARMI LES DERNIERS GRANDS SUCCES
IL A NEIGE SUR HAWAI
45 t. 62041   E.P. 72060
SUR MA VIE
45 t. 62038   E.P. 72056
JE VAIS REVOIR MA BLONDE
45 t. 62037   33 t. 82046
ARRIVEDERCI ROMA
45 t. 62029   E.P. 72030
CZARDAS TANGO
45 t. 62034   E.P. 72055
et les MUSIQUES DE FILMS
en Super 45 t. E.P. et 33 tours

**eddie barclay**

With mass-audience acceptance as his primary objective, Hélian turned his hand to anything that looked like a hit, resulting in some decidedly non-jazz tunes ending up in his repertoire. However, with a team of crack musicians and a battery of capable singers to call on, Les Paul & Mary Ford's 'Vaya Con Dios', the Four Lads' 'Istanbul (Not Constantinople)' ('Istambul'), Frank Sinatra's 'Love And Marriage' ('Amour, mariage') and Alma Cogan's 'Twenty Tiny Fingers' ('Vingt petits doigts') were all effortlessly transformed into vaguely jazzy French-language pop hits to sit alongside his home-grown material.

Others also found that the best way to supplement their bank balance was by recording jazz arrangements of pop hits – and not always in a particularly appropriate manner. Among the musicians who chose to earn a franc in this way was Jack Diéval, who at least had the good taste to cut a great version of Sinatra's 'Learnin' The Blues' in 1956. Less impressive was the work of trumpeter Jacques Jay, who turned out nonsense like 'Polka des gaziers', a less-than-stellar example of the type of dance-floor pap that passed for jazz in certain parts of the country. Aimé Barelli found easy pickings as bandleader at the casino in Monte Carlo – a well-paid job that made record sales a bonus rather than a necessity – but he too recorded jazzy variations on the pop hits of the day, most notably his 1957 hits 'Mimi la rose' and 'Les âmes fières'.[183]

The same approach paid dividends for Eddie Barclay, whose orchestra was one of many to content itself with churning out covers of everybody else's favourites. However, he was more astute than most and even managed to

___

sell a million copies of a single were still some way into the future. British and American observers tend to think of Édith Piaf as the biggest French star of the time, but these figures demonstrate that Rossi and Hélian were some considerable distance in front of her, at least in commercial terms.

[183] A cover of the theme from the 1956 western *The Proud Ones*, which had been a US hit for composer Lionel Newman, for Nelson Riddle and for LeRoy Holmes. The change in title reflected the French title of the film.

land a hit across the Atlantic when his version of 'The Bandit'[184] climbed into the American Top 20 in 1955. Barclay was savvy enough to realise that the real money was to be made elsewhere, and although he enjoyed a domestic hit in 1956 with a version of 'Java', by the end of the decade he was more heavily occupied with the affairs of his eponymous record label.

Michel Legrand was more original, working hard on his compositions and arrangements, and spending much of his time with American musicians like Dizzy Gillespie and Blossom Dearie. A gifted arranger with a superb ear for melody, he cut a series of well-received LPs and EPs (some under the pseudonym Big Mike) and even succeeded in landing four Top 20 LPs in the *Billboard* albums chart during 1954-56. The first of these, *I Love Paris*, picked up over 200,000 sales stateside – a remarkable achievement for a French jazzman, and one which confirmed his standing in the world of post-war jazz.

### Accordions and harmonicas

Trying to put more of a French spin on things, accordion player Charley Bazin attempted to fuse jazz with the traditional *musette*. This would in due course bring about changes, but at the time the experiment failed to satisfy either jazz audiences or fans of more traditional sounds, leading him to regress to instrumental reworkings of hits like Mouloudji's 'Un jour tu verras'.

The same ploy paid off rather better for another accordionist, Aimable, who was rewarded for his dedication with a steady stream of sales winners. Most notable among these was the catchy 'La Tamise et mon jardin', an infectious tune that was subsequently given an English lyric and turned into a UK chart-topper by Ruby Murray as 'Softly, Softly'. Although not particularly fashionable, he sold thousands of copies of his simple accordion tunes, flying the flag for traditional French popular music in the face of the jazz revolution.

*Aimable.*

Aimable remained a popular attraction through the fifties, though his triumphs were overshadowed by the success of fellow accordionist Yvette Horner, who was seldom absent from the variety shows that dominated French radio, and later television. Covering everything from traditional folk tunes to the hits of the day, Horner enjoyed commercial success with instrumental romps through hits like René-Louis Lafforgue's much-covered 1957 smash, 'Julie la Rousse', and Dalida's 'Histoire d'un amour', selling hundreds of thousands of

---

[184] The theme from the acclaimed 1953 Brazilian film, *O Cangaceiro*.

YVETTE HORNER

EA 166 ⑤

HISTOIRE D'UN AMOUR
PEPITA DE MAJORQUE
ROSE D'OR
LE TOURNIQUET

*Pathé*

records despite remaining utterly peripheral to the main concerns of the music industry.

Sounding a different note was Albert Raisner, who led Trio Raisner, a harmonica group in the style of Jerry Murad's Harmonicats, but focused more on jazz and less on humour. With a repertoire ranging from Louis Armstrong's 'Muskrat Ramble' through the jazz standard 'After You've Gone' to classical tunes like Khachaturian's 'Sabre Dance', Trio Raisner cut across all boundaries to forge an international reputation for Raisner's idiosyncratic take on jazz and blues. As the country's leading exponent of the harmonica, he quickly became a nationally known figure, supplementing his income by playing on sessions for the likes of Charles Trenet and Édith Piaf.

## Jazz on the Left Bank

Entertaining though they were, such records had little to do with the basement clubs on the Left Bank of the Seine that had first nurtured the music. Jazz musicians continued to find the existentialists' haunts an ideal place to set up late at night and have a blow, trying out their skills for an appreciative audience. The connection between the music and the place was made most explicit, at least to the uninitiated, on Jacques Hélian's insufferably glossy-magazine evocation of 'À Saint-Germain-des-Prés', though his smooth approach and kitsch vocal arrangements cut no ice down at Le Tabou. Similarly, while the South American rhythms of Alix Combelle's 1955 effort, 'Mambo en sax', conjured up perfectly the 'existentialist' scenes in the 1957 Audrey Hepburn film, *Funny Face*, attendees at the Bœuf sur le Toit and other bohemian haunts were more likely to have been treated to lengthy improvisations by musicians in search of something new. A perfect example of the sounds that *could* be heard every night was Belgian saxophonist Bobby Jaspar's 1956 album *Modern jazz au Club Saint-Germain*, an in-concert set featuring Sacha Distel and a host of other top Parisian jazz players.

As the fifties unfolded, stages were likely to be shared with *chansonniers* trying out their wares before a largely enthusiastic audience, and many of the leading jazz musicians found themselves called upon to provide musical backings when the singers subsequently made recordings. All in all, it was a vibrant, lively scene and far less cloistered than the trad jazz movement flourishing in the UK at the time. Given the nature of the Left Bank clubs, there was a great deal of cross-pollination between musical styles, and jazzers were able to flit between bebop, *chanson* and more traditional jazz forms at the drop of a beret, creating an environment in which experimentation was encouraged and new sounds and ideas were always welcome.

## Boris Vian, jazz and *chanson*

Nobody symbolised the musical freedom of the era better than trumpeter Boris Vian. Apart from having played with the legendary Django Reinhardt in the late forties, he was also a poet, novelist, translator of foreign literature and scriptwriter for the cinema. He also ran his own jazz club, wrote for the magazine *Jazz hot*, collaborated with Jean-Paul Sartre and Albert Camus on other magazines, led his own jazz band,[185] and somehow still found the time to develop a formidable talent in writing songs. A regular attendee at Left Bank gatherings, Vian was the ultimate multi-talented individual and, unlike many of his contemporaries, had a wide-ranging artistic vision that was always open to new ideas and influences. In 1950, he began a songwriting partnership with Henri Salvador that resulted in hits for the

*Boris Vian.*

latter with 'C'est le be-bop' and 'La vie grise'. These jazzy offerings, along with Salvador's 'Ma chansonette' (a Vian-penned adaptation of Bing & Gary Crosby's 'Sam's Song'), helped establish Vian as one of the leading songwriters in French pop.

In addition to his love of jazz, Vian had a passion for politics and a hatred of war and hypocrisy – feelings he made plain in the songs he wrote later in the decade. Chief among them was his 1954 anti-war classic 'Le déserteur', a melancholy ballad which met with outright hostility when first performed (by Mouloudji) at the time of the Dien Bien Phu disaster that ended French rule in Vietnam. It would be another year before Vian recorded it himself on his first (and only) album, *Chansons 'possibles' et 'impossibles'*, much of which was quickly banned from the airwaves.

Through such songs, and the similarly themed but musically more expansive 'Java des bombes atomiques', Vian established a style that was highly influential on the leading *chansonniers* of the day, even though his own recordings barely made it out of record stores. The smooth 'Je bois' and the exotica-tinged 'Le petit commerce'[186] showed how jazz could be combined with complex, thoughtful lyrics without detracting from either, while the rapid-fire arrangement of his superb homage to popular cinema, 'Cinématographe', was the best example of his ability to marry music (supplied in this instance by pianist Jimmy Walter) and words to perfection. The more acerbic side of Vian's character came to the fore on the magnificent 'On n'est pas là pour se

---

[185] Sadly unrecorded, apart from a few acetates since issued on CD.
[186] Both featuring Claude Bolling's band.

faire engueuler',[187] while the late-night jazz of 'J'suis snob' crept seductively around a lyric dripping with cynicism, self-awareness and derision. Perhaps it was the directness of the delivery, together with the ban on 'Le déserteur', that prevented the album finding the audience it deserved.

Although Vian's recordings met with near-universal indifference, Mouloudji's gentle, almost apologetic 1955 reading of his 'Le déserteur' became a sizeable hit despite a total absence of airplay, thanks to well-received live performances of the song and a decision to surround it with a trio of less contentious Vian *chansons* on the EP[188] including a magnificent, if less elaborate interpretation of 'Cinématographe'.

The record's success helped to boost Vian's notoriety within the music industry, prompting a steady stream of covers from the likes of Philippe Clay (superb versions of 'On n'est pas là pour se faire engueuler' in 1955, and 'Je n'peux pas m'empêcher' two years later), Les Frères Jacques (who cut 'Le tango interminable des perceurs de coffres-forts' for a 1956 EP), Jacqueline François (who turned 'Les gars de Rochechouart' and 'Java mondaine' into acceptable pop vehicles in 1957), Henri Salvador (who featured the amusing calypso 'Y'a rien d'aussi beau' on a 1957 EP amidst a trio of Vian collaborations) and Catherine Sauvage (whose reading of Vian's adaptation of Kurt Weill's 'Alabama Song' graced the record racks in 1958).

During the middle fifties, Vian was everywhere and involved in everything, both actively pushing jazz toward the boundaries, and merging it with *chanson* and literature to create something new and dynamic. In the hands of interpreters like Mouloudji (who cut superb renditions of 'J'suis snob' and 'Valse jaune' in 1955) and Juliette Gréco (who recorded 'Musique mécanique' in 1957), this new style held a strong attraction for younger intellectuals, providing at least a part of the rapidly growing post-war teenage audience with something that spoke to them, rather than to their parents.

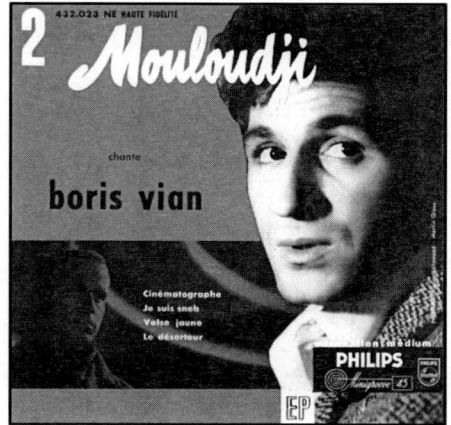

---

[187] Shortened to 'On n'est pas là pour se faire eng...' on the album, for no apparent reason. Philippe Clay's version likewise carried the same self-censored title.
[188] Mouloudji also slightly modified Vian's lyrics, although not enough to get the song onto the airwaves.

With her distinctive look, hit records and free-thinking approach to life, Gréco was the first teen idol of this new generation, but two things conspired to halt the Left Bank revolution in its tracks. One was her increasing involvement with Hollywood,[189] which deprived the movement of its greatest visual asset and its public face at exactly the wrong time. The second was a young man from Tupelo, Mississippi, who was busy shaking his hips on American TV and offering the world a different kind of musical fusion.

---

[189] Embroiled in a passionate affair with Darryl Zanuck, who was then resident in Europe, Gréco never actually left France for the US, but, by spending increasing amounts of time before the cameras, she had less time for recording or performing on stage, and her record sales suffered accordingly.

# Chapter 9

## SALUT LES COPAINS

### A new generation finds its feet (1952-58)

*The rock'n'roll explosion that engulfed the United States and eventually the rest of the world was, in essence, a youth-sponsored affair. Teenage spending power, a phenomenon unheard of before the fifties, provided the record industry in America with an economic shot in the arm that was both welcome and unexpected. While some faint-hearted label managers may have recoiled in horror at the sounds and sights unleashed on the world in the name of rock'n'roll, the more business-minded among them were quick to spot the potentially huge financial rewards for those who delivered the new music to an expectant audience. Starting with Bill Haley and Pat Boone, American record companies began to follow up on the strange reports coming in from around the country: stories of white teenagers listening to black radio stations or hanging out in black record stores. When RCA Victor hit the jackpot in 1956 by luring Elvis Presley away from Sun Records and getting a No. 1 hit with 'Heartbreak Hotel', the trickle of interest became a flood and within months the American charts were swamped with rock'n'roll.*

### Marlon Brando, James Dean and the rise of the teenager

With the advantage of hindsight, it is hard to understand how record companies were so slow in catching on to the need for change. In Hollywood, movie studio heads were well aware of the younger generation's need for idols of their own – brooding outsiders whose sullen inarticulateness reflected the growing teenage population's own mystifying discontent. While suburban America basked in post-war prosperity, their affluent offspring were champing at the bit and looking for ways to escape the straitjacket of the McCarthy years. In many ways the first *bona fide* idol of the new generation, Marlon Brando spoke for a huge subsection of the country's (and, indeed, world's) youth in 1953's *The Wild One*,[190] when, challenged to say what exactly he and his fellow bikers were rebelling against, he memorably answered, 'What ya got?' The fact that the film was a hit not only in the US, but also around the world, suggested that teenagers everywhere felt much the same way.

Even before his early fifties' run of cinematic triumphs, Brando had been considered cooler than cool by the Parisian in-crowd. On a visit to the French capital in 1949, shortly after finishing his Broadway run in *A Streetcar Named Desire*, the actor was seen hanging out with Jean Cocteau and Roger Vadim,

---

[190] Released in France as *L'Équipée sauvage*.

and scaling the wall of Juliette Gréco's apartment on his way to a seduction. His first half-dozen films were all box-office hits in France and made him a hero among French teenagers.[191] By 1955, though, Brando had a rival in *the* archetypal inarticulate youth, James Dean, whose *Rebel Without A Cause*[192] captivated French audiences as much as it did American youth.

It is easy to make a case for Dean as the ultimate embodiment of the bored, disenfranchised teenager, especially as his life seemed to imitate his art. Dean conveyed the hopelessness of the situation, the despair and sheer hell of growing up cocooned in post-war America. He too had international appeal, wooing audiences across the globe in each of the three films he made before his tragic death in a car crash. 'Live fast, die young' became a catchphrase of the era, ultimately spawning the Who's incendiary battle cry *'I hope I die before I get old'* in 'My Generation', and a host of others.[193]

The triumphs of Dean and Brando gave teenagers actors to call their own, contrasting vividly with the mainstream appeal of stars like Rock Hudson. Dean may have been a 'rebel without a cause', but for teenagers he was at the vanguard of a movement that a decade later would find a cause to embrace, with devastating effect. At the time, though, he represented every teenager's desire for freedom and a culture to call their own – something the American music industry was initially slow to provide.

### Bardot, Belmondo and the *nouvelle vague*

Things were no better in France, with the record industry preferring to pursue the exotica boom rather than providing anything tailored for the rapidly growing youth market. Once again, it was cinema that took the lead with a new wave of film directors tearing up the rule books to come up with something new and exciting. Even so, aside from a couple of early efforts by Claude Chabrol, the *nouvelle vague* garnered a slightly older, more intellectual audience, rather than tapping into the desires of the teenagers who flocked to watch Dean, Brando and American films in general.

The most important home-grown star was Brigitte Bardot, whose success in Roger Vadim's *Et Dieu... créa la femme* (1956) provided the country with a new, young sex symbol whose complicated private life showed little respect for traditional morality, turning her both into a pin-up and a role model for the more adventurous. Jeanne Moreau's controversial role in *Les amants* (1958) offered further evidence of a demand for convention-challenging performances in the arts. Significantly, both Bardot and Moreau offered a female counterpart to Brando's on-screen sexuality.[194] However, it was not until late 1959 that France produced a Brando of her own in Jean-Paul Belmondo, the anti-hero star of Jean-Luc Godard's *À bout de souffle*, whose iconic image had a huge influence on the young men who would soon become the country's first rock'n'rollers. The massive success of this

---

[191] Including thirteen-year-old Jean-Philippe Smet – the future Johnny Hallyday – who sat through repeated screenings of the 1954 classic, *On The Waterfront* (retitled *Sur les quais* for French audiences) at his local cinema.

[192] Titled *La fureur de vivre* in France.

[193] Among them Johnny Hallyday's 1967 scream from the heart, 'J'ai crié à la nuit'.

[194] And both would later add hit records to their cinematic laurels.

*Jean-Paul Belmondo.*

revolutionary film confirmed that there was a vast audience waiting to be tapped by a singer who could bring the image of Dean, Brando and Belmondo to life on record. It was this market that would fall at the feet of Elvis Presley and the great rock'n'rollers who followed in his wake.

Presley quickly became America's biggest-selling recording star, carried across the US by ratings-hungry radio, but across the globe things were slower to pick up. In the UK, for instance, where the staid BBC dominated the airwaves, sales were negligible until Radio Luxembourg kicked the Presley phenomenon into life. Over the Channel in France, radio was equally unsupportive, and although Radio Luxembourg broadcast the sounds of the King into the country, as it did in the UK, few teenagers were able to take control of the family radio to listen to the new teenage gospel.

### Rhythm & Blues in France

Even so, for those who knew where to look, there were already small inroads being made in France, if not by rock'n'roll then at least by boogie-woogie and rhythm & blues. Blues guitarist Big Bill Broonzy was a frequent presence in Paris during the first half of the fifties, recording seven sessions there for French release. These included a stripped-down performance of the work song 'Take This Hammer' and 1951's powerful, anti-racist 'Black, Brown And White', perhaps the first pure blues recordings made in France. Broonzy's appearances inspired a generation of French jazz musicians to explore other forms of black American music, though he never enjoyed much

record success in Europe himself. Still, bandleaders began to increase the beat behind their recordings, Eddie Barclay's 'Lucky Boogie' and Jacques Hélian's 'Bing bang blues' (aka Ella Mae Morse's 'The Blacksmith Blues') being just two examples. The trend became even more pronounced after Lionel Hampton's explosive performances in Paris in early 1956.

Already known to jazz fans for his classic 1940 and 1942 recordings of his signature tune, 'Flying Home', Hampton was a regular visitor to France, cutting 'Walking At The Trocadero' with Claude Bolling and 'À la French' with Sacha Distel. His magnificent 1956 live album, *Lionel Hampton à l'Olympia*, brought the big beat to the fore on numbers like 'Rockin' At The Olympia' and the vibraphone-led 'Flying At The Olympia'. It wasn't really rock'n'roll, or even rhythm & blues, but it was exciting enough in its own way, adding fuel to the argument that it was the jazz being developed across the Seine, rather than the driving beat of Presley, that was the right way forward.

This was a reasonable assumption, given that the only live American music on offer in France at the time that even hinted at the sound about to convulse young America were four shows by Johnnie Ray at the Moulin Rouge and a series of performances by the Goofers.

Ray was not a rock'n'roller, although his histrionic performances clearly drew their inspiration from the same sources, and his nightclub appearances in late 1955 were savaged by the press (as had been the reaction to his US debut four years earlier). However, Gilbert Bécaud was one member of the audience who was impressed, while Georges Ulmer would a couple of years later include a version of Ray's 'Cry' in a show dedicated to the development of jazz, rhythm & blues and rock'n'roll captured on the album *À l'Alhambra Maurice Chevalier: Histoires de Rythme*.

The Goofers were a clean-cut white vocal outfit who specialised in covering rhythm & blues hits like the Charms' 'Hearts Of Stone' and Joe Turner's 'Flip, Flop And Fly'[195] in a tame, though far from disgraceful style. Showcased at the Lido nightclub as part of the revue *Jazz Train*, they were the first rock'n'roll outfit of any kind to play on French soil, but they simply weren't *that* good, and in any case were playing in the wrong place at the wrong time to the wrong crowd. They headed back to the States having failed to connect in any way.

---

[195] Exactly the same artists who inspired Elvis Presley.

## Rock'n'roll arrives... on film

Deprived of the opportunity to find an audience either through live performance or radio play, the rock'n'roll revolution failed to take hold in the land of the *chanson*, at least until Hollywood rode to the rescue. It was Glenn Ford's *Blackboard Jungle* (1955) that carried the songs of Bill Haley around the world, lighting the touchpaper for the rock'n'roll explosion in the US, the UK and elsewhere, even though its main focus was the juvenile delinquency depicted on the screen, rather than the music played over the titles. Released in France in late 1955[196] to substantial press coverage, it provoked a somewhat milder response than it had found in the anglophone world. Even so, it was reasonably well received, prompting the independent CIC label to release some Bill Haley records onto the French market, enjoying slow but steady sales that fell some way short of those achieved across the Channel.

By the end of 1956, however, Haley was well known enough to justify a French release of his own cinematic debut, *Rock Around The Clock*, giving French youth their first exposure to real rock'n'roll, albeit in a rather contrived setting. A few months later, he was back on screen in *Don't Knock The Rock*, by which time discerning fans could also revel in the sights and sounds of Chuck Berry, Frankie Lymon & The Teenagers, LaVern Baker and a host of others in the Alan Freed vehicle, *Rock, Rock, Rock*. Two months later, in April 1957, they got the chance to see the greatest of all the fifties' rock'n'roll movies, *The Girl Can't Help It*, and the sight of Gene Vincent, Little Richard and Eddie Cochran in 'gorgeous life-like color by DeLuxe' had a major effect in setting the boules rolling.[197]

Strangely, they were initially denied the opportunity to see Elvis Presley's big screen debut, *Love Me Tender* (1956), which sat on the shelf until 1958 before finally gaining a release. In the event, it was beaten onto the screens by his sophomore effort, *Loving You*, which stunned audiences expecting a John Wayne-style western.[198] French teenagers were, however, initially slow

---

[196] As *Graine de Violence*.

[197] Haley's two films were retitled *Rock and roll* and *Rock cocktail* for French release. *The Girl Can't Help It* went out as *La blonde et moi*. Freed's film retained its original title.

[198] The future Johnny Hallyday was only one of countless teenage moviegoers whose life was transformed by the experience. *Loving You* was retitled *Amour frénétique* for French consumption, while *Love Me Tender* became *Le cavalier du crépuscule*.

to respond to Presley's incendiary performances, and his next two pictures, *Jailhouse Rock* (1957) and *King Creole* (1958), were held off from French release until 1960.[199] Even so, for those who cared to notice, the King's performances did much to give voice to a youth movement struggling to be heard and set in progress a chain of events that would snowball into the French pop explosion of the sixties. The roots of this movement were evident in the success not only of Brando, Dean, Haley and Presley, but also of Belmondo, Bardot and Moreau, yet it would be wider changes within the music business, and in French society as a whole, that would give the subsequent youth market the strength to bulldoze its way to the forefront of the entertainment industry.

## French society in the 1950s

The fifties were characterised by the advent of the 'baby boomers' and nowhere was this incredible demographic change more pronounced than in France. By 1959, some 35% of the population was accounted for by 'children', the vast majority of whom were still at school. Those who had left tended to remain at home, rather than moving out to start their own families, which increased the number of young people in the family home. Households were thus younger – and more fun-oriented – than at any time in recent memory. While respect for the family and for traditional values may have been stronger in France than in Britain, French teenagers were no less interested than their counterparts in going out, having a good time and seeking out their own tastes and leisure activities.

In France, the need for diversion was given added impetus by the escalation of the Algerian War, which had been building in intensity since 1954. The crisis of 1958 which led to the downfall of the Fourth Republic and brought General de Gaulle out of retirement ushered in a period of strict governmental conservatism, throwing the country under a tight yoke and a blanket of consensus. Despite the dull, if worthy authoritarianism that de Gaulle imposed upon the country, a healthy intellectual opposition made its presence felt within French society. Both the existentialist movement of the Left Bank and the Communist Party enjoyed wide support among the young, to whom de Gaulle represented the worst values of the old France. Even so, under his leadership the country weathered the storm and went on to see a marked increase in economic prosperity over the following decade. Government controls prevented a wage explosion such as had occurred in Britain, but standards of living rose steadily throughout the late fifties and early sixties, jobs became easier to obtain, and teenagers found themselves with money to spend and their own ideas of how to spend it. Cinema and records were two obvious targets for the teenage franc, and it was teenage audiences who were largely responsible for both the huge popularity of American films and the commercial success of dynamic singers like Dalida and Eddie Constantine.

---

[199] Titled *Le rock du bagne* and *Bagarres au King Creole* respectively. The latter film actually reached French screens first.

**Records and radio**

The increase in teenage spending power also coincided with the music industry's switch from 78s to EPs and LPs, which greatly boosted the attractiveness of records as a consumer item. While the more expensive LPs appealed mainly to adults and remained largely out of reach for teenagers, EPs soon attracted the attention of youngsters with money to burn.[200]

Teenagers might have been less interested in building up collections of EPs if they'd still had to argue with their parents over what got played on the family record player. This problem was neatly solved by Marcel Teppaz, who in 1952 began the mass-marketing of the lightweight portable record player which bore his name. Like the Dansette in the UK, the Teppaz player gave teenagers the option of listening to records in their bedroom, well away from parental ears. By the end of the decade, enough households owned a Teppaz to allow the marketing of records directly to a teenage audience.

The new formats enabled companies to repackage much of their back catalogue, and the resultant increase in profits allowed them the commercial freedom to take a punt on any new artist who caught the fancy of the head of the A&R department. This freedom ensured that, when rock'n'roll finally hit French shores, record companies were able to try out their own rock'n'rollers without really knowing anything about the style.

For French teenagers in search of their own musical identity, there remained one more stumbling block. Up until the mid-fifties, choice had been stifled by the nature of French radio, which boiled down to the state-run national station, RTF, augmented by the independent Radio Monte-Carlo (broadcasting from the principality of Monaco, outside of French governmental control) and the maverick Radio Luxembourg. Additionally, there was the American Forces Network, while those in the north of the country might have been fortunate enough to pick up broadcasts from Belgium, West Germany, the Netherlands or the UK.[201]

This suffocating blanket was lifted in 1955 with the launch of France's first national commercial station, Europe No. 1[202] – a modern affair which circumvented broadcasting laws by beaming its transmissions from West Germany, though the disc jockeys and station staff worked in Paris (the signals were sent over the border and then back into France in a convoluted, but apparently legal piece of subversiveness). With ratings and advertising revenue the only matters deemed worthy of consideration, the new station focused on a repertoire of hip and happening hits, playing the hottest records of the moment repeatedly throughout the day in the manner of the successful Top 40 stations in the US. It was an instant hit with young and old, and station head Lucien Morisse made an immediate impact on French show business with his campaign to make his lover, Dalida, a star in 1957. From then on, Europe No. 1 became the leading broadcaster in the country, and airplay on the station quickly became essential for a record to become a hit.

---

[200] This led record companies to pay close attention to the cover artwork of their releases, resulting in the delightful sleeve illustrations that today provide a large part of the pleasure in collecting French records from the fifties and sixties.

[201] Not that 'Auntie BBC' offered much of an alternative to RTF.

[202] Later renamed Europe 1.

*Lucien Morisse and Dalida.*

Following its initial commercial success, Europe No. 1 took the initiative to brighten up the airwaves with the launch in 1956 of live-to-air concerts under the banner *Musicorama*. Multi-artist shows that gave fans a chance to see and hear up to a dozen artists on one bill, they offered real value for money, and the broadcasts proved equally popular. The format allowed for an adventurous booking policy, and many new and unknown artists gained their first public exposure on the show, creating a ready-made audience for their next record release, which would duly be played by Europe No. 1. This gave further encouragement to record companies to try their luck with new artists, as a *Musicorama* booking would give them a better-than-average chance of a hit. In any case, recording costs were low, and even if only ten percent of their output found an audience, the company would still make a profit, so there was no harm in experimenting with something new.

### *Salut les copains* radio show
In 1959, Europe No. 1 belatedly responded to the demographic changes taking place and the burgeoning youth market. Noting that increasing numbers of young listeners were writing in with requests, jazz fans Daniel Filipacchi and Frank Ténot pitched the concept of a dedicated youth programme to the station's management board and were given a daily slot to try out their ideas. Commencing at 5.00 p.m., the show took its name from an uptempo, high-energy song by Gilbert Bécaud. 'Salut les copains' was already two years old, but perfect as a theme tune. Featuring a great deal of input from the listeners themselves, the show was a huge hit and *Salut les copains* quickly established itself as essential listening for the home-from-school audience, providing the music industry with a direct line to the hearts and minds of teenage France.

The first artists to benefit from the huge exposure offered by the show were established stars like Charles Aznavour (who virtually ceased recording during 1958-59, sitting out his record deal as company politics took their toll) and Gilbert Bécaud (whose hits that year included the superb 'Ah! Si j'avais des sous').[203] However, listener requests quickly made it clear that, though the audience displayed a fondness for these artists that would be slow to disappear, what they really wanted was something new; something they didn't have to share with their parents.

## The television revolution

The French music industry was equally quick to take advantage of another change in technology: the arrival of television. Here, though, the accent remained firmly on the conventional and the safe. After all, few households had TVs at the end of the fifties and those that did only had one set, which would be watched by all the family. The first French TV variety show was probably *36 Chandelles*, an unimaginative affair that included singers and orchestras among a diet of acrobats, comedians and dancers. This quickly spun off a more music-oriented sister show, *36 Chansons*, but here too the emphasis was firmly on the mainstream. It was therefore predictable that the music favoured by the heads of the television wing of RTF[204] would be that of established stars like Édith Piaf (about to reach a new career peak with the timeless 'Milord') or middle-of-the-road entertainers such as Annie Cordy (who was all over the airwaves in 1958 with the infectious 'Hello, le soleil brille!', adapted from Mitch Miller's 'March From The River Kwai and Colonel Bogey') and Dario Moreno (then in the midst of a hit run which included a top-notch cover of Louis Prima's 'Buona Sera'). Once a new star was established, he or she might be booked on one or other of the mediocre variety shows that dotted the television schedules,[205] but the medium offered little opportunity to record companies looking to break a new star, even if they could find one that might appeal to the growing youth audience.

## Minou Drouet and Marie-Josée Neuville

One option might have been the precocious Minou Drouet, a young Bretonne who came to fame in 1955 as an eight-year-old poet of some distinction. After a handful of recorded recitals, she turned to singing, releasing the enjoyable 'Les spaghettis' and the more impressive 'Bilou' in 1956. Although vastly talented, Drouet was too young to appeal to the teenage crowd, her literate style better suited to fans of *la chanson française*. She simply had too many interests to be constrained by the world of music and, in any case, had school lessons to attend to. Although she remained a media sensation, she never translated her critical acclaim into record success.

---

[203] Oddly, Dalida, who was very much a star among the young, got short shrift from Filipacchi, though she scored massive airplay on the station's other shows, picking up a big hit that year with a slushy cover of Johnny Dorelli's 'Love In Portofino (À San Cristina)'.
[204] At the time, the only TV station in the country.
[205] These tended to be broadcast once a month, rather than weekly, as was/is the norm in other countries.

Seventeen-year-old Marie-Josée Neuville was the nearest the country came to producing a teenage idol of its own in the mid-fifties. She made a splash on Pathé in 1956 with 'Johny boy', a self-penned effort backed by simple acoustic guitar that sat midway between the new-style *chansons* of Georges Brassens and the country-tinged pop beginning to make headway across the Atlantic. Issued on EP with the gentle 'Une guitare, une vie' and the equally accessible 'Gentil camarade', the song was an instant smash, transforming the young singer into an overnight sensation.

Neuville's second EP delivered on the promise of the first, garnering another hit with 'Dix-huit ans' and picking up much airplay for the exquisite 'Le monsieur du métro' and the lovely 'Par derrière ou par devant', as the quickly nicknamed *'Collégienne de la chanson'* rose rapidly and unprecedentedly through the ranks. Sadly, her youthful appeal did not last, and a third EP release in 1957 failed to maintain the pace, despite containing another jewel in the form of 'Dans les trains, dans les gares'. Although Neuville continued to record until the end of the decade, the hits soon became a distant memory as the youth market began to look for harder, flashier sounds.

As the decade progressed, these developments in technology, economic circumstances and the broadcasting industry combined to create the fertile ground from which French pop was to blossom into the distinctive and exciting form that would characterise the sixties. Ready to receive the new music was a teenage audience with a desire for freedom from the cultural norm. Growing economic prosperity meant that many youngsters owned mopeds – some even owned cars – giving them the ability to get away from home to enjoy new cultural pursuits that were almost entirely imported from the US. With their own movie stars, their own fashion sense, and their own cultural reference points, all they needed now was their own music. But before that could happen, the industry had to learn how to cope with the new American sounds increasingly demanded by the teenage audience. Once again, the first steps in this journey into the unknown would be taken in the jazz clubs of Saint-Germain-des-Prés.

# Chapter 10

## GEORGES, VIENS DANSER LE ROCK N' ROLL!

### The early movers and shakers (1954-58)

*As happened in the UK, it was the jazz fraternity who first showed interest in the rock'n'roll storm brewing up across the Atlantic. Always receptive to changes in the American jazz scene, bandleaders of the forties had noted the popularity of so-called 'jump blues' music, with Ray Ventura covering Louis Jordan's 'Caldonia' as early as 1946. However, the early fifties' rhythm & blues boom made little impact in France, and it was only in the mid-fifties that a few musicians began taking steps into the world of small-combo dance music.*

### The trailblazers

First to dip his toes into the water was clarinet player Hubert Rostaing, who traded his instrument for a saxophone to cut a version of Gene & Eunice's 'Ko Ko Mo' under the assumed name 'Earl Cadillac' in 1955, although his record met with little success.

Of the music hall singers, Line Renaud led the way that same year with a jolly rendition of LaVern Baker's big crossover hit, 'Tweedle Dee'. This move was less revolutionary than it might at first appear, as the song had just been emasculated for the white American audience by Georgia Gibbs, which is probably how it came to her attention. Renaud was simply following her current policy of covering US hits for home consumption – a policy that would deliver success for her in 1956 with versions of Al Hibbler's 'Unchained Melody' ('Les enchaînés') and Dean Martin's 'Memories Are Made Of This' ('Les souvenirs sont faits pour ça').

Although the French pop scene of the mid-to-late fifties was dominated by exotica, American hits remained fair game. Perry Como's 'Hot Diggity' and Fess Parker's 'Ballad Of Davy Crockett' were turned into smashes by Annie Cordy as 'Hop digui di' and 'La ballade de Davy Crockett' respectively, while Terry Gilkyson's 'Marianne' wound up on the charts in 1957 in cover versions by a host of performers including Gloria Lasso, Maria Candido, Dario Moreno and Les Compagnons de la Chanson. Nevertheless, 'Tweedle Dee' was a departure of sorts, marking the first time a song that began life on the *Billboard* 'R&B' chart[206] found its way into the French hit parade.

---

[206] It actually hit both the pop and R&B charts in the same week.

## Rock Around The Clock

The first genuine rock'n'roll song to chart in France was 'Rock Around The Clock'[207] by Bill Haley & His Comets, which made the Top 10 in early 1956. This was quickly covered by Les Bingsters[208] as 'Les heures qui sonnent', a rhythmic effort that was as far removed from rock'n'roll as it was possible to get. Those brave enough to flip the record discovered a rather better reworking of the Platters' 'The Great Pretender' ('L'homme qui passe'). The trio subsequently diversified into skiffle with 'Le train du vieux noir', a strange take on Lonnie Donegan's retread of the Leadbelly classic, 'Rock Island Line'.

Hubert Rostaing also had a crack at 'Rock Around The Clock' (as 'Toutes les heures qui sonnent'), this time under his own name, but this lacked even the punch of his previous outing. It was joined in the shops by several other versions, of which the most idiosyncratic was Trio Raisner's harmonica-driven arrangement, and the least inspired a boogie-woogie treatment by Jacques Hélian's orchestra, complete with vibraphone solo.[209] Performed by jazz players for whom musical prowess was of more importance than a rocking rhythm, none of these versions exhibited any feeling for rock'n'roll. In truth, they were more a symptom of the growing tendency of covering US hits for the French market than of any real interest in the rock'n'roll genre.

In the spring of 1956, several other artists tried their hand at the new American sound still scarcely available in France at that time.[210] Trombonist Benny Vasseur had a stab at 'Rock Around The Clock' under the alias 'Benny Rock' – the first of several attempts he would make over a year or so without capturing the spark that was inflaming American youth. Meanwhile, Belgian jazzman Benny Couroyer purloined the name of Benny Rock for some saxophone-led rock'n'roll recorded in West Germany, including (logically) 'Rock around the Rhine', before reinventing himself as Benny Jackson at the end of the year for the wonderfully titled 'Rock 'n' sock', but saw no commercial success.

Playing it strictly for laughs was the oddly named Peb Roc, who featured

---

[207] When the song appeared in the French hit parade in 1956, it was the instrumental version by the MGM Studio Orchestra from the *Blackboard Jungle* film that was listed, not Haley's, although it was the latter that was driving the sales. However its impact in France was minor when compared with the UK, where provincial cinemas screening the film were damaged by over-enthusiastic fans wanting to dance to Haley's theme tune.

[208] An Andrews Sisters-type trio from Belgium famous for such pap as 'Le tango de l'éléphant', adapted from the Commanders' 1955 hit, 'The Elephants Tango'. Line Renaud also tangoed with the elephant, although her version omitted the definite article from the beginning of the title.

[209] Hélian's version was actually the first French recording of the song, which is about the kindest thing that can be said about it.

[210] When rock'n'roll did show up on records, the sleeves tended to describe the tunes as 'foxtrots'.

female vocalists Christiane Legrand and Jeannine Wells on a pair of rock'n'roll parodies penned by Boris Vian, but 'Rock à la niche' and 'Chaperon rock' held little appeal for teenagers searching for the real thing. Roc's EP was completed by yet another version of the Haley hit, plus a big band rendition of Freddie Bell & The Bell Boys' 'Giddy-Up-A Ding Dong' that could have worked as a novelty record, but didn't.

Even less impressive was a soulless excursion through Haley's 'See You Later, Alligator'[211] (retitled 'See you alligator') by the Lido nightclub's bandleader, Jean-Pierre Landreau. As an attempt to give the song an arrangement worthy of the Glenn Miller Orchestra, it was not entirely unsuccessful from an artistic standpoint, but had little to recommend it to fans of rock'n'roll.

Harmony quartet Les Quatre de Paris found more promising pickings in the Chords/Crew-Cuts hit, 'Sh-boom' ('Ça boume'[212]), but neither this, nor their take on Tennessee Ernie Ford's 'Sixteen Tons' ('Seize tonnes') was a hit. However, 1957's 'Daisy (La pin-up des juke-box)' fared better, sitting somewhere between Bill Haley and Louis Jordan. The record's moderate success prompted a swinging cover by crooner Michel Gaillard,[213] demonstrating that vocalists could also take a stab at the new style.

### The first French rockers?

None of the above records really qualified as rock'n'roll. However, in early 1956, a group of jazz musicians got together to do the job properly on a record helmed by drummer Jean-Baptiste Reilles, who masqueraded for the occasion under the name Mac-Kac.[214] A more joyous affair than Landreau's effort, Mac-Kac's version of 'See You Later, Alligator' ('T'es pas tombé sur la tête') was a bouncy and sincere attempt to harness the Haley rhythm to a jazz-based horn section, and a fine waxing in its own right.

---

[211] Although the song was originally recorded by its composer, Bobby Charles, Haley's version was clearly the inspiration.

[212] The title was also used for an earlier jazz treatment by bandleader Alix Combelle.

[213] Released as 'Daisy, la pinup des juke-box'.

[214] A bad pun on the French word for a type of monkey (*macaque*) and arguably the stupidest name ever used by a French rock'n'roll singer.

His EP was also noteworthy for a cover of the Teen Queens' 'Eddie My Love' ('J'en ai assez') and more sedate strolls through 'Et là-bas' and 'Great big bulging eyes' – both written by guitarist Sacha Distel, who thereby earned the credit of having written the country's first original rock'n'roll songs.[215] The disc may have lacked the electric punch of the American originals, but the musicians escaped their roots for long enough to make for an enjoyable experience. It sold moderately, if unspectacularly, among the jazz community, as well as to the nascent, and as yet small, rock'n'roll audience.

Given rock'n'roll's lack of sophistication, it was unsurprising that most French jazz musicians regarded it as a simplistic novelty, rather than an exciting and enduring style in its own right. Few of them had experienced first-hand the audience responses being generated by the likes of Bill Haley, Chuck Berry or Elvis Presley, so it was unsurprising that the first attempts to make rock'n'roll records in France relied heavily on humour for their commercial appeal.

One musician who *had* witnessed the Haley phenomenon in person was Michel Legrand, who had recently returned from a concert tour of the US. Impressed by Haley's success, he got together with Boris Vian to see if they could come up with something original. Bringing in Henri Salvador to front the operation, they concocted a quartet of songs that duly appeared, a month after Mac-Kac's efforts, on an EP issued under the *nom de guerre* 'Henry Cording and his Original Rock and Roll Boys'.

As was often the case with Salvador's collaborations with Vian, humour was the main selling point, with titles like 'Rock and roll-mops' and 'Va t'faire cuire un œuf, man!' testifying to a lack of serious intent. The songs carried the requisite big beat, but the playing was too clinical and the lyrics made fun of the music rather than celebrating it. Even so, driven by strident saxophone and a gutsy rhythm section, 'Rock and roll-mops' was a major step forward, showing that rock'n'roll *could* be made in France, even if the substance fell short of American standards. The bluesier 'Dis-moi qu'tu m'aimes rock' and the driving 'Rock-hoquet' were equally impressive, and, although more of a

parody than a genuine rock'n'roll record, the result was surprisingly effective. Following steady sales, the EP was reissued under Salvador's name and continued to sell for several months to come.

The fun nature of these recordings led to a rash of similar releases over the next few months. Pianist Jack Diéval led his septet through the ridiculous 'Le loufoque du rock' on an EP saved from ignominy by two rather more interesting efforts: a decent rendition of the Willows/Diamonds doo-wop hit, 'Church Bells May Ring'

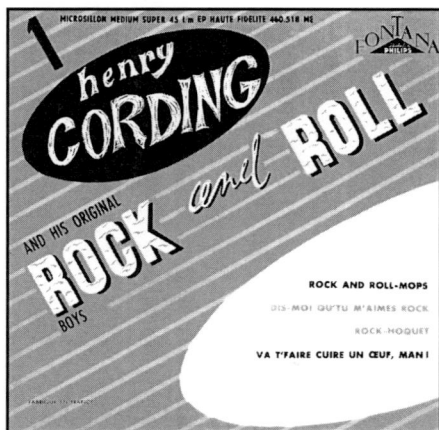

---

[215] Although in truth, the latter didn't rock that much.

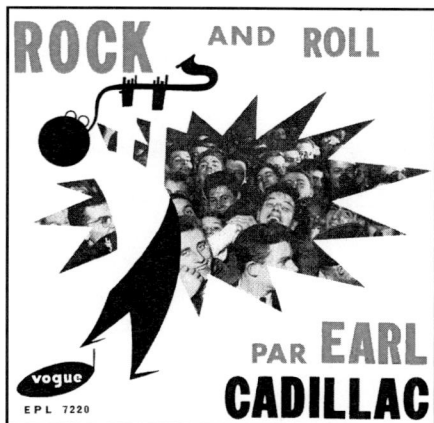

('Bing! Bang! Rock!'), and an almost unrecognisable reworking of Warren Smith's 'Rock 'n' Roll Ruby' ('Vas-y Ruby!'). Hubert Rostaing (as 'Earl Cadillac') had another go with the enjoyable 'Rock Mr. Cadillac' and a cover of Tennessee Ernie Ford's 'Sixteen Tons' ('Seize tonnes'), while Michel Attenoux and Jacques Hélian recorded variations on 'Rock Around The Clock' and 'Sixteen Tons' ('Seize tonnes') respectively.

Adopting yet another moniker, Rostaing cut an EP as 'Dick Rasurell et ses Berlurons', three-quarters of which (including the tasty 'Peppermint rock' and 'Rock around Europe') emanated from the pen of fellow bandleader Jerry Mengo.[216] Rostaing then recorded a whole album under his 'Rasurell' alias, *Interdit aux poids lourds*, offering further instrumental workouts alongside two vocal efforts, of which the amusing 'Roll steak frites' self-consciously recalled Henri Salvador's 'Rock and roll-mops', while the rather better 'Tu m'as laissé tomber' mimicked Bill Haley in all respects except the vocal delivery.

Over the border in Belgium, Dutch-born jazzman Ferry 'Rock' Barendse took a cover of Henri Salvador's 'Rock and roll-mops' into the charts, giving a boost to Belgium's nascent rock'n'roll scene. Barendse's rock'n'roll offerings were compiled for the French market on a four-track EP that allowed listeners to sample both his excellent take on Haley's 'The Saints Rock 'n Roll' ('Qu'elle affaire ce rock 'n' roll') and the ridiculous vocal that marred the otherwise worthy 'T'as l'bonjour d'Alfred'.

These primitive attempts at rock'n'roll were placed in harsh perspective by the July 1956 release of the first French EP by Elvis Presley, a stunning set comprising 'Heartbreak Hotel', 'Mystery Train', 'I Forgot To Remember To Forget' and 'I Was The One'. As yet though, few record buyers were willing to pick up a copy.

It was Presley who inspired the Paris-based British singer/pianist Johnny Hawkins to have a crack at rock'n'roll. His 1956 EP contained a mannered reading of 'Heartbreak Hotel' complete with fine solos on guitar and saxophone, but he was unconvincing as a rock'n'roll singer.

---

[216] Mengo had himself recorded a routine rendition of 'Sixteen Tons' ('Seize tonnes') before taking a punt with a brassy big band rendition of 'Rock around Europe'.

149

In early 1957, Hawkins delivered four instrumental workouts on his *Rock 'n roll session* EP, but, despite titles like 'Rock Kansas roll', they were more jazz than rock'n'roll. Still, the frenzied soloing and boogie-woogie piano on 'Rolling back baby' alone were worth the price of the record, while the polished 'Rock n' Rolls Royce' likewise featured a decent rhythm, though the saxophone solo was too clean to rival the sounds now trickling into France from the US.[217]

## Music hall rock

More commercially successful, if just as unconvincing, was Édith Piaf's only venture into the Leiber & Stoller songbook, 'L'homme à la moto', a cover of the Cheers' 'Black Denim Trousers And Motorcycle Boots'. Although it was a smash hit for her in 1956, Piaf opted not to pursue a new career unearthing R&B hits for a French audience, continuing instead as a stalwart of *la chanson française*.

Later that year, Eddie Constantine included the self-explanatory 'Rock, rock' in his shows at the Olympia Theatre, subsequently recording it for an EP. As an American, he had less difficulty with the rhythm, being familiar with Louis Jordan, if not with the harder-edged sounds of Elvis Presley. The vocal was a tad too sedate, but he was convincing enough to appeal to those teenagers who had already taken the music to their hearts. Constantine stuck with the beat for the following year's 'Le rock du marin' and 'Laisse tomber', but neither suggested he had a future as a rock'n'roller.

Félix Marten made fun of the music, including a rock'n'roll backing on his 'Please barman', on which he simply called out the word *'barman'*[218] – a decision which avoided him having to show how little feel he had for the sound. Georges Guétary displayed a similar lack of empathy and treated Bill Haley's style as the latest exotica fad on the risible 'Georges, viens danser le rock n' roll!', a misplaced attempt at humour that did nothing to endear him to the teenage audience.

Line Renaud proved better at getting to grips with things with 'Mon mari est merveilleux', though a lyric celebrating the perfect husband held little appeal for the young listeners who were presumably its target audience. Also surprisingly listenable was Annie Cordy's 'Qu'est-ce que t'as, mon vieux', a track on her *Jazz-party chez Annie Cordy* EP that saw her edging toward a small-combo sound, although again it was some way from rock'n'roll.

---

[217] Thanks in part to Sacha Distel's astute licensing of the Atlantic Records catalogue for Ray Ventura's Versailles label.

[218] Marten's record was eerily prescient of Splodgenessabounds' eighties' cartoon-punk classic, 'Two Pints Of Lager And A Packet Of Crisps Please'. For all its faults, it was still better than pianist/bandleader Raymond Bernard's instrumental version.

## Boris Vian and Magali Noël

In the closing months of 1956, the desire to try out rock'n'roll reached a peak, with countless musicians fooling around on stage and in the studio. One of the key figures was Boris Vian, who wrote songs for a number of artists and put together the bands that turned his ideas into reality. In October he cut a brace of EPs under the name 'Rock Failair[219] et son Orchestre de P'tits Milliardaires' with trumpeter Jacky Vermont and a gaggle of jazz players. 'Rock and roll sérénade' and 'Rock de Monsieur Failaire' showed that the musicians were beginning to find their feet, but Vermont's vocals were weak and unconvincing. Despite including a passable adaptation of Georgia Gibbs' not-exactly-rocking 'Rock Right' ('Tangage et roulis'), the records flopped.

More impressive was Vian's work with actress Magali Noël, whom he attempted to model into France's first female rocker.[220] Together with Vian, she cut four tracks in a similar style to the Henry Cording release, the sado-masochistic 'Fais-moi mal Johnny!..'[221] in particular being a cut above the usual standard. The backing was still a tad too jazzy, but Noël's breathless delivery gave the song the required edge and her performance was strong enough to be convincing. The remaining cuts wasn't quite of the same calibre, with 'Strip-rock' offering rather less than the title suggested and 'Rock des petits cailloux' coming closer to late-night jazz than rock'n'roll. However, 'Alhambra-rock' kicked along nicely, thanks to a rapid-fire vocal performance underpinned by some decent guitar-work.

Noël's four cuts initially appeared on a Various Artists LP titled *Rock and Roll*, where they shared space with tracks by the bands of Alix Combelle, Michel Legrand and saxophonist Pierre Gossez. Combelle's 'Rock at the Apollo' and 'Rock à gogo' were passable horn-led instrumentals, but Gossez's take on Henri Salvador's 'Dis-moi qu'tu m'aimes rock' was disappointing and devoid of any real excitement. These recordings sounded exactly like what they were: jazzmen cashing in on the popularity of rock'n'roll. Other than Noël's cuts, the only tracks worth the purchase price were those by Legrand, whose explosive version of 'Rock Around The Clock' was the best of the many covers issued in France. Legrand's arrangement slowed down the tune, but gave it a tremendous backbeat, that, if not really rock'n'roll, wasn't exactly jazz either. The album was not a major success, but spin-off EPs by Legrand

---

[219] Another dreadful pun, this time on Nelson Rockefeller.

[220] Noël had earlier recorded 'Le rififi', the theme to Jules Dassin's *Du rififi chez les hommes* (1955). This was released on an EP of film themes – among them a passable reworking of Peggy Lee's 'Johnny Guitar' that demonstrated the attraction – and limitations – of her voice. She got the gig for the Vian session after Juliette Gréco declined to take part.

[221] Its lyrics caused a mini-scandal, six years before the Crystals' similarly themed 'He Hit Me (And It Felt Like A Kiss)' was struck off US airwaves by puritan broadcasters.

(notably *Rock and Roll*, featuring 'Rock Around The Clock' and the thumping 'Riff and rock') and Noël made enough of an impact to keep the fledgling rock'n'roll industry ticking over.

As it turned out, Noël decided against further experiments in the same vein, opting instead for a cover of Jill Corey's 'I Love My Baby' ('Un coup de foudre') and a return to jazz with 'Mon oncle Célestin' on her next EP, *Magali se déchaîne*. She then tickled male fancies with the EP *Sexy songs*, the best of which was Vian's 'Oh! (C'est divin)', though only the lyrical theme and the subtle groove of 'Nous avions vingt ans' had anything remotely to do with rock'n'roll. Noël subsequently returned to acting, appearing in Federico Fellini's cinematic masterpiece, *La dolce vita* (1960).[222]

## The big beat: Rock'n'roll drummers

While Vian kept busy with Failair and Noël, Mac-Kac laid down a second EP offering four slices of joyous abandon in time for the summer of 1956. The toe-tapping 'J'vais m'en j'ter un derrière la cravate' was written by Sacha Distel with drummer François-Alexandre Galepides and offered just the right combination of good-humoured fun, swinging jazz and the tight combo sound of Bill Haley's Comets, while 'Moi, je suis dans l'coup' was a straight lift from Haley's 'The Saints Rock 'n Roll'.

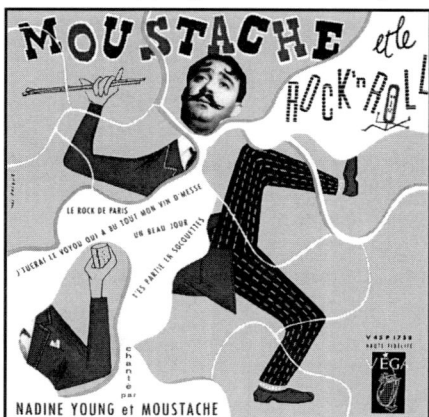

Galepides' own recordings were issued under the pseudonym 'Moustache'. These included a rock'n'roll EP whose highlights were the piano-pounding 'Le rock de Paris', the hilarious 'J'tuerai le voyou qui a bu mon vin de messe', and a song originally gifted to Mac-Kac, 'T'es partie en socquettes'. In October 1956, he joined Mac-Kac on stage during the first ever *Musicorama* broadcast[223] for a joint version of the latter's 'J'ai j'té ma clef dans un tonneau d'goudron'. In 1957, Moustache resurfaced on the soundtrack of the film *Le grand bluff*, resulting in an EP on which he declared himself to be *'King of Saint-Germain-des-Prés'* on a rocking instrumental that sat somewhere in the middle ground currently being staked out in France between jazz and rock'n'roll.

Neither Mac-Kac's nor Moustache's EPs made the charts, but Mac-Kac's sold well enough to warrant the release of a LP in late 1956, *Mac-Kac et son rock and roll*, which included a version of Moustache's 'J'tuerai le voyou qui a bu mon vin de messe'.[224] It was not a big success, but somehow found its

---

[222] Noël would occasionally return to the recording studio over the following two decades, without achieving any real commercial success.

[223] Headlined by Juliette Gréco and Eddie Constantine. The following week, Henri Salvador unleashed a wild version of 'Rock-hoquet', giving the country at large its first exposure to rock'n'roll, or at least its French incarnation.

[224] Mac-Kac's version bore the slightly amended title 'J'tuerai l'voyou qui a bu mon vin de messe'.

way across the Atlantic[225] for a slightly different US release, *Mac-Kac & His French Rock & Roll*. Released late in 1957, this featured liner notes that made rather more of the performer's limited success than was honest.

Hot on the album's heels came a couple of EPs by Mac-Kac's one-time drummer Christian Garros. The first, *Rockin' with Garros*,[226] included a rocked-up *à la* Haley instrumental version of 'Sixteen Tons' ('Seize tonnes'), as well as a decent take on Eddie Fisher's 'Dungaree Doll' ('Tou lou lou te'). The second, *Rock n' roll*, kicked off with a tight remake of Georgia Gibbs' 'Rock Right' that outpointed the original, and followed through with the finger-snapping 'Girl rock', featuring a tasty saxophone solo that was right on the money, while the slicing electric guitar, prominent drums and occasional shouts of *'Crazy!'* on the instrumental 'Crazy rock' saw him moving closer still to the sound that was inspiring teenagers across the world.[227]

### Jazz goes rock

In the shadow of these pioneers, other jazz musicians took to the studio to cut rock'n'roll records of their own. In late 1956, drummer Armand Molinetti stripped a pair of Gilbert Bécaud tunes down to basics and turned them into imitations of rock'n'roll.[228] It was an interesting idea, but neither 'Ça claque' nor 'Ça c'est formidable' carried the emotive punch of Bécaud's own releases.

In early 1957, electric guitar pioneer Marcel Bianchi masqueraded as Johnny Rock 'Guitare' on an instrumental EP enhanced by the wailing saxophone of Pierre Gossez that showcased his Les Paul-like guitar effects in the best possible way on the squealing 'Roule-toi dans l'rock' and the storming guitar-and-saxophone duel, 'Ah! C'que ça rock ici'.[229] A second EP issued more or less contemporaneously offered two more crackers in the swing-rock of 'Rue Saint-Rock' and the stupidly titled 'Le rock fait l'air'. Despite the latter offering one of the most exciting sounds yet to emerge from a French recording studio and a sleeve depicting not Bianchi, but black American bluesman Clarence 'Gatemouth' Brown, the record was not a hit.

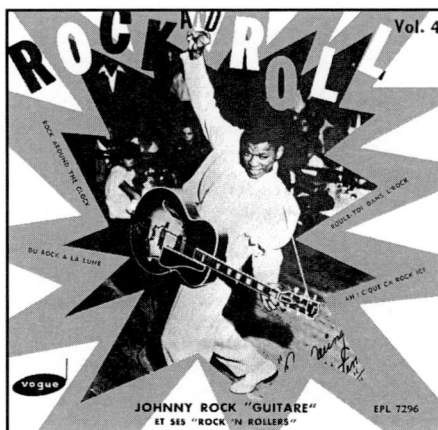

Bianchi's EPs was actually closer to the rhythm & blues style favoured by Hubert Rostaing for his 'Earl Cadillac' alter ego, under which name he had just issued the swinging 'Rock & roll rhapsody'. This shared space in

---

[225] As did Henri Salvador's 'Rock and roll-mops', which appeared on a Columbia 45.

[226] Garros had earlier released the more mundane *Rythmes à votre service* EP, falling back on tunes like 'Cha-cha-cha' and 'Mambo'.

[227] Garros also released a single featuring a cover Bill Haley's 'A.B.C. Boogie', but this lacked the spark of his other offerings. Both this and 'Rock Right' were sung in English, with Nadine Young on vocals and Garros leading the band.

[228] On an EP credited to 'Molinetti's Rocking Quintette'.

[229] Although the inclusion of yet another version of 'Rock Around The Clock' was a disappointment.

the record racks with another EP, this time under Rostaing's own name, featuring two strong slices of jazz-tinged rock'n'roll in 'J'ai perdu la tête' and the scat vocals with Haley-style backing of 'Qu'est-ce que c'est?'. [230]

While Rostaing had by now come out of the closet,[231] nobody was willing to own up to hiding behind the soubriquet of Chou Rave Hageur et ses Hot Dogs, whose late 1956 'Peb rock et broc' featured a meaningless vocal that indicated a lack of seriousness on the part of all concerned. The rhythmic 'Rock aïe' was a worthy effort, but was let down by a vibes solo that was anathema to any real rock'n'roll fan. As for the failed hybrid 'Rock mambo', the less said the better. Whoever the band were, there was no attempt to repeat the experiment – at least, not under the same name.

In the early months of 1957, pianist Raymond Le Sénéchal came up with two enjoyable EPs containing some attractive guitar-work, especially on the swinging 'Roquette 08-69' and 'Laisse tomber',[232] while a third offered the far from restful 'Lullaby blues' and the novel 'Hawaïen rock'. Meanwhile, fellow pianist Michel Ramos disguised himself as 'Virginie Morgan' on his substandard arrangements of Bill Haley's 'The Saints Rock 'n Roll' and Mac-Kac's 'Great big bulging eyes', while Alix Combelle weighed in with the thumping instrumental 'Marche à la rock' – all recordings that saw them inching closer to the real thing.

Saxophonist Michel de Villers and guitarist Jean-Pierre Sasson combined rock'n'roll with music hall on an EP of songs by Charles Trenet that served only to show that past classics such as 'Boum!!..' had nothing whatsoever to do with rock'n'roll.[233] Even Jacques Hélian had a go, resulting in such horror shows as the xylophone-and-sax collision of 'Rock and roll parade'

---

[230] Rostaing's EP came out at the end of 1956. Cadillac's 'Rock & roll rhapsody' appeared in early 1957 on the second of two Cadillac EPs to carry the title *Rock and Roll atomique*. The first, issued in late 1956, contained the jumping 'Rock fort & roll mops'.

[231] This notwithstanding, he returned to his Earl Cadillac *nom de disque* to turn in a sparkling instrumental cover of Henri Salvador's 'Va t'faire cuire un œuf, man!' (Cadillac's version lost the 'man' from the title) and the engaging 'Vis' la poupée'.

[232] Featuring singer Bob Martin.

[233] The song lost the exclamation mark from its title on this EP – testament to the record's lack of excitement.

and the blatant lie of 'C'est le rock and roll'. Meanwhile, Jacques Jay deserved marks for imagination for his *Rock' saltimbanque* EP, a fusion between rock'n'roll and *musette*, featuring covers of three Lonnie Donegan skiffle numbers and a banjo-powered reworking of Little Richard's 'Tutti Frutti' that has to be heard to be believed.

1957 also saw bandleader Eddie Warner record yet another variation on 'Rock Around The Clock',[234] as well as a weak instrumental cover of Haley's 'R.O.C.K.' and a rather better one of his 'Mambo Rock'. His self-penned 'Rock and schnock' was a reasonable stab at an original tune in the Haley mould, although it was spoiled by an arrangement featuring too-lavish soloing from the band.

Somewhat better was the LP *Rock 'n roll* by bandleader Georges Richard. This surprisingly strong set included covers of Bill Haley's 'Rock-A-Beatin' Boogie', Elvis Presley's 'Hound Dog', Tennessee Ernie Ford's 'Sixteen Tons' and similar numbers reworked in a credible forties' jump blues style, but failed to find the audience it deserved.

Out of this mixture of jazz, rhythm & blues and jump band sounds, perceptive musicians and singers began to discover what made rock'n'roll tick. As a result, during 1957, a few half-decent records crept out onto a market that shamefully responded with almost complete indifference. Jean Constantin[235] hid behind the name 'Big César' on an instrumental EP including the plangent 'Métro du rock' and the boogie-woogie workout 'Rock' Amadour'. Elsewhere, Canadian import Guylaine Guy cut impressive takes on 'Bac and roll' and 'Madame Bertrand' for an EP released at the start of 1957.[236] Both songs were also covered in considerable style by Jean-Pierre Cernay on a 1958 EP rounded out with the brassy rock of 'Elle s'était fait couper les cheveux', but, impressive as they were, neither came close to the real thing.

Little-known American immigrant Irène Hilda turned out the minimalist 'Tap... tap... rock and roll', a worthwhile effort that clipped along in a most satisactory manner. Released in early 1957, Hilda's EP also contained the bluesy 'Love me baby', but her lack of commitment to the genre was exposed in 1958 when she included an amusing parody of a *rockeuse* on 'Rien ne vaut l'amour', on the live EP *Irène Hilda à l'Olympia*.[237]

---

[234] Haley's classic had already been done to death, although that wouldn't stop clarinettist Camille Sauvage having another go a few months later. Warner's version, along with the other two tracks mentioned here, appeared on a self-titled LP in May 1957.

[235] Better known as a songwriter for the likes of Édith Piaf.

[236] The latter tune also made it to Guy's second Canadian album, *French Doll*.

[237] In the interest of fairness, she also took a pop at Édith Piaf, Dario Moreno, Charles Aznavour and Italian star Marino Marini on the same record.

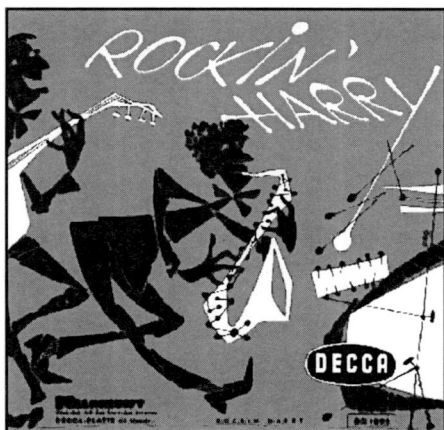

Up in Belgium, Rockin' Harry cut loose on 'Bugle rock',[238] a Haley-styled rearrangement of the classic reveille call, and gave pride of place to the electric guitar on the superb 'Jelly rock' and the perfunctory 'Baby rock'. A second EP, *Rock 'n Roll at the Regina*, was a 'fake-live' recording that placed greater emphasis on vocals on the excellent 'Faut pas m'énerver' and 'Ne fait pas l'idiot, Jo'. The guitar was, however, well represented on 'Funny beat', which featured one of the first genuinely exciting guitar solos to show up on a French (well, Belgian) rock'n'roll recording. This was as far as Harry was prepared to go, although he did provide the backing for the strong 'Ça, c'est du rock 'n roll' by fellow Belgian André Pierre.

Belgian bandleader Francis Bay recorded the superb LP *Meet Francis Bay* late in 1957. This included two of the best examples of the now dated (and never truly commercially successful) big band rock'n'roll that had previously gripped the jazz world, the crash-bang-wallop of 'Rock and roll at four' and the swinging 'Rock, look, listen' more than matching the records of two years earlier for quality and inventiveness.

Back in France, the French Benny Rock upped the ante with his 1957 EP, *Benny Rock... and Roll*, featuring instrumental covers of Louis Jordan's 'I Want You To Be My Baby'[239] and Nervous Norvus's 'Dig' (the latter being the first – and only – successful attempt to play rock'n'roll on an accordion), plus a version of Elvis Presley's 'Love Me Tender' taken at a more swinging tempo than the original. This gave birth to a LP released in the US[240] under the name 'Roland Rock & His Orchestra'. *Rock 'n' Roll à la Française* rounded up capable arrangements of Bill Haley's 'Razzle Dazzle' and 'Two Hound Dogs' and a version of Henri Salvador's 'Va t'faire cuire un œuf, man!' for American consuption, but sales are likely to have been minimal.

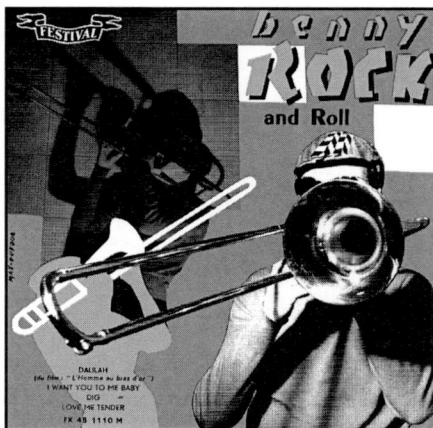

Predictably, most bandleaders added at least one rock'n'roll tune to their repertoire, although the enthusiasm – and quality – varied widely. José Candrino's 'Rock en folie' was folly

---

[238] This predated Johnny & The Hurricanes' 'Reveille Rock' (1959) by a couple of years. He also recorded jazz under his real name, Harry Frékin.
[239] Lillian Briggs' 1955 revival being the likely inspiration.
[240] But not, apparently, in France.

indeed, while Marcel d'Anella's 'Désir-fox' (featured in the 1958 film, *Le souffle du désir*) was more foxtrot than rock'n'roll. The Fontana Club Orchestra (who recorded, as might have been guessed, for the Fontana label) turned Francis Lemarque's 'Seul un homme peut faire ça' into a reasonable boogie, although the more upfront 'Rocking tap' was less impressive. Bandleader Bob Allan reworked the Belgian Benny Rock's 'Rock around the Rhine' and 'Rock boogie' on *Surprise-partie 'Comme ça'*,[241] an album of otherwise mediocre party fodder which suggested that rock'n'roll was at least beginning to be accepted as dance music, if nothing else.

Trumpeter Georges Jouvin blasted out a hot solo on the chunky 'Rock – Rock',[242] while fellow trumpeter Philippe Brun's cover of the Chords' 'Sh-Boom' ('Ça boume') and multi-instrumentalist Noël Chiboust's 'Mister Martin's mop' were both advertised as rock'n'roll, but weren't.[243]

The rough vocals on 'C'est le rock and roll' were no reflection on the big band sound of guitarist Jésus Ramírez, who led one of the better outfits on the French South-West circuit. The song surfaced on an EP released locally by the Toulouse-based Andorra label, which also included the not-at-all-bad 'Rock and roll', although neither number was truly what it claimed to be.

As 1957 ticked on, songwriter Florence Véran[244] had a stab with the pleasant 'Où est donc passé Paul?',[245] operetta star Jean Bretonnière made a decent fist of Dick Williams' 'Rock Hearted Mama' ('Dédée cœur de rock'), and Belgium's Jean Vallin tried to combine the joys of rock'n'roll and pinball machines on 'Tilt and flipper'. Songwriter Pierre Arvay's misleading 'Rock 'n Mars', which surfaced in early 1958, was typical of the misguided nature of most of these efforts.

## Different approaches

Ever since late 1956, when Roger Pierre et Jean-Marc Thibault enjoyed a hit of sorts with their utterly nonsensical 'Le cuirassier de Reichshoffen', music hall performers had tended to favour the comic approach to rock'n'roll. Little more than a comic sketch set to a catchy rock'n'roll rhythm, it was impossible to ignore and deservedly became regarded as a classic over the coming years.[246]

Comedy also underpinned the appeal of vocal duo Castel et Casti,

---

[241] One of a number of such long-players that surfaced in France over the course of the fifties.

[242] Rival versions by Jimmy Hayward and Charles Verstraete ought to have remained buried.

[243] Chiboust's 1957 single, 'Noël rock', came rather closer to the required sound.

[244] Co-writer, with Charles Aznavour, of Juliette Gréco's classic, 'Je hais les dimanches'.

[245] Also picked up by the little-known *chanteuse* Souris, with equal lack of success.

[246] It was rapidly given a makeover by a gang of jazzmen moonlighting as Gino Galieri et ses Rockers before resurfacing in a straight – and enjoyable – cover by orchestra leader Jean-Pierre Cernay a year or so later.

although their 1957 version of the Marty Robbins/Guy Mitchell hit, 'Singing The Blues' ('C'est beau, ça') for Decca was delivered straight. The off-kilter 'Le juke-box est en panne', a 1958 release on Teppaz, was more their style, though far from becoming a rock'n'roll classic.

The novelty angle of Maurice Chevalier's 1957 in-concert recording of 'Rock and roll' was typical of its time, with a humorous lyric that was as amusing as any of Stan Freberg's parodies in the US. The same could be said of Bourvil's 1958 release, 'Et ta sœur', though in his case the rock'n'roll feel was more muted. Comic superstar Sim gave the new music both barrels on 'Le rock coquin' in 1957, though Tartempion's 'Rock... fort... folies!', issued the same year, would have been best left on the shelf.

At least the results were amusing, unlike the bastardised cross between rock'n'roll and *musette* peddled in early 1957 by accordionist Charley Bazin on the comic 'Ah! Les Américains'[247]. Despite ample evidence to demonstrate that the accordion was *not* a rock'n'roll instrument, the country's leading practitioners could not be convinced, resulting in such monstrosities as Raymond Boisserie's 'Rock a pic' and Yvette Horner's 'Rocket rock', as well as her equally bizarre 1958 take on Bill Haley's 'Rock-A-Beatin' Boogie'.[248]

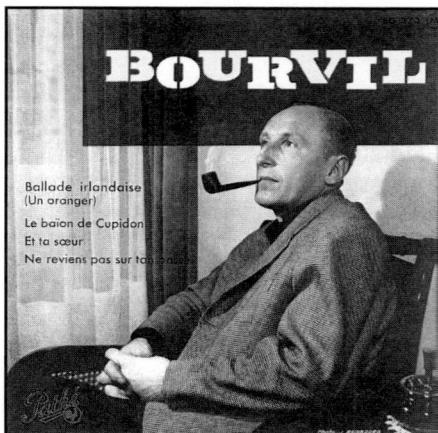

Equally unfathomable was the late 1957 decision by Jean Laporte, band-leader at the Cirque Medrano, to inflict the unbelievably bad 'Rock around the circus' on an undeserving public, who understandably gave both this and Nino Nardini's similarly-themed instrumental Haley rip-off, 'Rock rock circus' (1958), a wide berth.

Only guitarist Sarane Ferret offered anything new, incorporating the style of the late Django Reinhardt

---

[247] This intriguing oddity was covered in 1958 by the splendidly named Arsène Hic et son Orchestre d'Empoisonneurs Diplomés.

[248] Horner's efforts were reserved for album release (on Volumes 2 and 3 of *Yvette Horner joue ses grands succés* respectively). The horror show continued into 1958 with Robert Trabucco's 'Nini la tendre', Jean Gaston's 'Mad'moiselle Rock and Roll' and 'Rock and roll d'amour, reaching a peak of sorts with Jo Privat's 'Rock accordéon'. This generated an unbelievable cover by L'Orchestre Musette de la Rue de Lappe, in which jazz and *musette* were present, but the rock'n'roll promised by the title was hard to spot. It was also recorded by Maurice Vittenet in equally dire fashion.

into a rock'n'roll framework on 1957's 'Le rock ça chauffe',[249] although the performance was marred by a bizarre xylophone solo that had no right to be there. Nevertheless, the fretwork of the guitar master was sufficient to lift the record out of the ranks of the mediocre to represent a worthwhile purchase for those fortunate enough to have heard it.

In late 1957, Swiss multi-instrumentalist Hazy Osterwald led his Sextette through a strong Bill Haley rip-off, 'Solid man', which showed that the band had his sound down pat, though they still managed to sound original. The rather rudimentary follow-up, 'Fais danser Jenny', was a disappointment, but they came up trumps again in 1958 with an on-the-button arrangement of Duane Eddy's 'Rebel Rouser', its emphasis rightly on the guitar. This sold well enough on both sides of the Rhine to prompt the band to lay down a swinging adaptation of Roy Hamilton's 'Don't Let Go' ('Fais-les danser') that captured their variation on rock'n'roll to perfection. Osterwald, always more popular in West Germany than in France, subsequently changed tack and enjoyed a pan-European hit with 'Kriminal-Tango', his Sextette mutating into a dance band in a career that would run for decades.

Despite the fact that few of the French attempts at rock'n'roll had so far found any real commercial success, as 1957 turned into 1958 there was no shortage of singers trying to jump on the musical bandwagon. The results ranged from the worthwhile (songwriter Gaby Verlor's punchy 'Tu n'as pas'[250]), to the passable (Anne Angeli's 'Maman, je veux un homme'), to those of dubious merit (Amy Anahïd's 'Rock, c'est un rock') and to those of no merit whatsoever (Maria Angelica's 'Rock d'enfer'). [251]

## A switch to covers

A change had occurred during 1957, when artists begans switching their attention from comic novelties to cover versions. Raymond Legrand[252] laid down a passable 'L'âge atomique' (the Lancers' 'Rock Around The Island',[253] from the film *The Lieutenant Wore Skirts*) and also a take on Tennessee Ernie Ford's popular 'Sixteen Tons', although neither added anything to the versions already available. Legrand abandoned rock'n'roll as quickly as he had embraced it, but, despite hostility to the music in the French press, audiences

---

[249] Previously recorded by trumpeter Michel Gauthier in a less impressive version.

[250] Originally cut for an EP by Gino Galieri et ses Rockers. Verlor also delivered a brassy take on Guylaine Guy's 'Madame Bertrand'.

[251] Anahïd 's rocker was penned by *chansonnière* Mick Micheyl. Maria-Angelica also cut a very strange version of 'Rock Around The Clock' ('Graine de violence') that is best avoided.

[252] A more-than-capable songwriter, Legrand should have had no need to resort to cover versions.

[253] These included an earlier vocal outing of 'L'âge atomique', cut under Legrand's auspices by his secretary, Colette Renard. Hubert Rostaing also recorded a version in his 'Earl Cadillac' guise.

– especially young audiences – continued to respond with their feet, flocking out onto the floor whenever an enterprising bandleader gave his band a chance to cut loose.

Belgian jazzman Fred Maloni impressed on a 1957 single that paired a bright and bouncy take on Joe Turner's 'Corrine, Corrina' with the brassy 'Eh! Jack'.[254] Sales were poor, but the record proved that Belgium was just as capable as France of turning out decent rock'n'roll-styled records, even if neither had yet found its own Elvis.

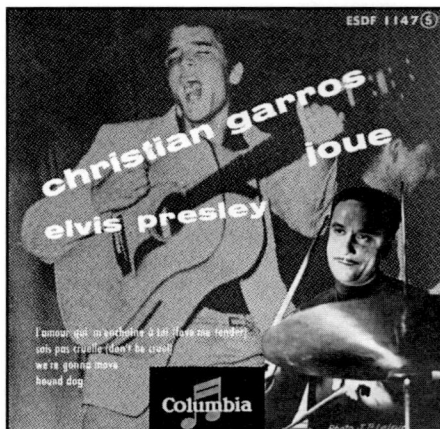

American-in-Paris Benny Waters slummed it in the summer of 1957 with another take on Bill Haley's 'See You Later, Alligator' ('T'es pas tombé sur la tête'). He also laid down an unusual arrangement of Elvis Presley's 'Love Me Tender' that had as much to do with rock'n'roll as Presley's own version did.

More interestingly, Paris-based Dutchman Serge Singer adapted all four tracks from Presley's *Love Me Tender* EP into French for an EP of his own, *Le cavalier du crépuscule*, issued in the spring of 1957. Curiously, the title track was not an interpretation of 'Love Me Tender' as might have been expected (that song was reworked as 'L'amour qui m'enchaîne à toi'), but of 'We're Gonna Move'. Singer also made a decent fist of Presley's country hoedowns 'Poor Boy' and 'Let Me' ('Je veux gagner' and 'Laisse-moi danser'). The record sold poorly, but by showing what could be done, Singer had laid down a marker for the future.[255]

One of the first to grasp the nettle was Christian Garros, who went for broke in the summer of 1957 with the release of an EP featuring four Presley songs: 'Love Me Tender' ('L'amour qui m'enchaîne à toi'), 'Hound Dog', 'We're Gonna Move' and 'Don't Be Cruel' ('Sois pas cruelle'). Columbia also included a large photograph of Elvis on the front of the sleeve, although this was more a marketing ploy than a statement of empathy. Henri Salvador's 'Rock and roll-mops' notwithstanding, Garros' 'Sois pas cruelle' was the first real French rock'n'roll recording to achieve any real recognition (perhaps because, almost alone among the jazzers tinkering with rock'n'roll, Garros had a genuine enthusiasm for the music). It prompted a host of rival versions, of which one of the better attempts was that by Albert Raisner's harmonica outfit,[256] Trio Raisner, though it could hardly be described as rock'n'roll.

Garros' example was also taken up by Georges Ulmer for his laid-back

---

[254] This latter track would be covered in France in 1958 in a weak-kneed version by Jean-Louis Tristan.

[255] It was not long before Yvette Giraud also had a version of 'L'amour qui m'enchaîne à toi' on the market, in a style more in keeping with her usual approach. It has often been reported that Tino Rossi also recorded a cover of 'Love Me Tender' at this time, but the fact that no copies have surfaced makes this seem very unlikely. He may of course have sung it in concert, and he did record it many years later as 'Il faut s'aimer tendrement'.

[256] Released under its original English title.

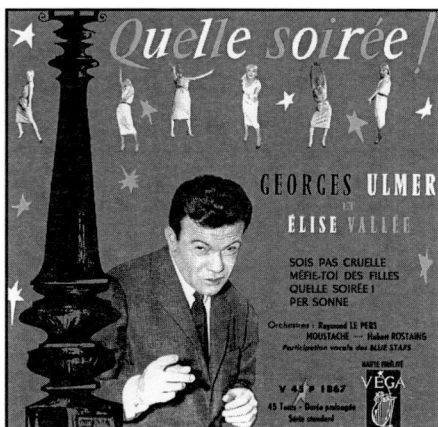

cover of 'Don't Be Cruel' ('Sois pas cruelle'), which became a moderate hit late in 1957 despite failing to hold a candle to Presley's original. Ulmer's success duly focused attention on those songs which had already made the American charts, and while this was no innovation in itself, it gave an added impetus to the cover version industry that was already beginning to dominate French pop.

A rather better attempt on the Presley songbook was laid down in late 1957 by Mississippi-born blues and gospel singer Brother John Sellers, the latest American to settle in Paris. His self-titled set[257] straddled the musical landscape from jazz ('You've Been Gone Five Years') to blues (B.B. King's 'Woke Up This Morning') to rhythm & blues (Joe Turner's 'Morning, Noon And Night'), to the self-penned 'Let's Rock And Roll', while Carl Perkins' 'Blue Suede Shoes'[258] was imaginatively recast as a down-home blues. The album was a remarkable artistic achievement, presenting rock'n'roll in its natural setting alongside jazz and blues, but was roundly ignored by the French record-buying public. Sellers chose not to hang around, decamping soon after to New York.

Nevertheless, the moderate success enjoyed by Garros and Ulmer served to highlight that the way to break rock'n'roll in France was by adapting American hits into French, rather than with original tunes that never quite hit the mark. Once this realisation had dawned, the experimentation of the early years gave way to a more calculated approach.

There were two immediate consequences for the development of rock'n'roll in France. The first was a glut of cover versions in the record racks, among them bandleader Roger Roger's arrangement of 'Love Me Tender' and trumpeter Jimmy Hayward's 'Corrine, Corrine' (an interpretation of Joe Turner's 'Corrine, Corrina'). The other was the second major hit in France by an American rock'n'roll act.[259]

## The Platters in France

The Platters are rarely remembered as one of the major forces in the rock'n'roll revolution that transformed the face of popular music. While the contributions of country & western and rhythm & blues are widely recognised, the vocal group tradition, although hugely popular at the time, is often dismissed as a footnote. Even where doo-wop is recalled with pride, the Platters are rarely offered up as one of the leading lights of the genre, perhaps because so many of their hits were slow ballads drawn from the American popular songbook. Nevertheless, they were a presence on the US

---

[257]  Helmed by saxophonist Guy Lafitte and backed by a host of the country's leading jazz players.
[258]  Best known to European audiences via the version by Elvis Presley.
[259]  After Bill Haley's 'Rock Around The Clock'.

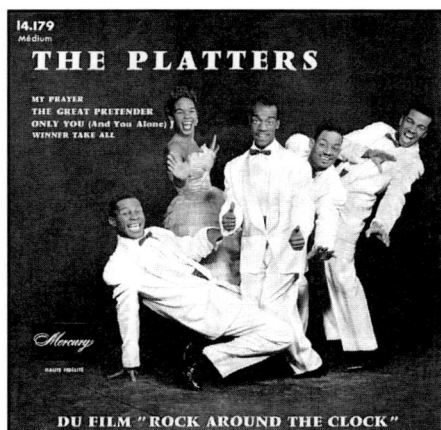

charts even before Elvis Presley made his RCA Victor debut, and thus in the vanguard of the rock'n'roll movement – a position reflected by their inclusion in the 1956 Bill Haley film *Rock Around The Clock* which first introduced them to French audiences.

Although records by Presley and other leading rockers were being released in France at the time, aside from a modest cult following in the major urban centres, there was very little response. The Platters though, were stars. In 1956, an EP containing 'Only You (And You Alone)', 'Winner Takes All', 'The Great Pretender' and their revival of Glenn Miller's 'My Prayer' picked up interest from all age groups, bouncing around just below the charts for much of the year. It broke into the *Music-Hall* listings in the wake of Georges Ulmer's success with 'Sois pas cruelle', and by the end of 1957 'Only You' was climbing toward the top of the French hit parade, spurred along in October by the group's three-week engagement at the Olympia Theatre.

Situated at the 'easy listening' end of the rock'n'roll spectrum, 'Only You' was perfect fodder for a French adaptation, and before the year was out several home-grown covers were in the shops. Luis Mariano's 'Loin de vous' bore little similarity to the original, being given the slick makeover common to most of his recordings, but Anny Gould's rendition picked up so many spins that she was declared 1958's *'Reine des juke-box'* ['*Queen of the Jukeboxes'*].[260] In truth, it was a poor record, with celestial vocal backings replacing the warm tones of the Platters, reducing it to routine pop fodder – but it was a major hit and encouraged a rash of rival versions, most of them insufferably dreadful.[261]

One of the more palatable was that by François Deguelt. A Crosby-esque crooner, Deguelt had hovered on the edges of the big time for much of the decade, but it was 'Loin de vous' that catapulted him into the spotlight. His recording closely copied the arrangement of the original, although it lacked its bluesy edge. Deguelt continued in this direction for a short while, covering the Platters' 'My Prayer' ('Ma prière') the following year, along with supper-club renditions of Presley's 'Loving You' ('Sans amour')

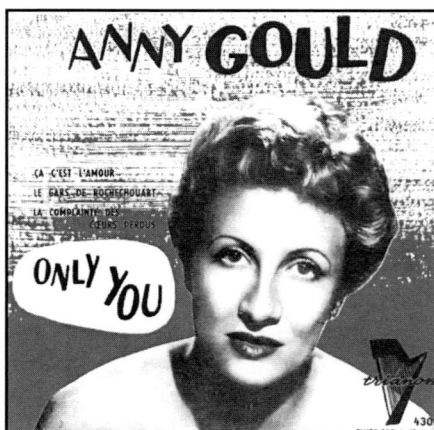

---

[260] Precisely how Gould came by this title is lost in the mists of time, however she was still credited as such in her 2013 obituaries.

[261] None more so than Jo Privat's accordion rendition.

**François Deguelt**

*Exclusivité disques*

**Columbia**

**Ma prière** ( "My Prayer" )
Quand
April love
Sans amour
Super 45 t. ESRF 1166

**Loin de vous** ( "Only you" )
Marjolaine
Un homme dans la foule
Les saisons de l'amour
Super 45 t. ESRF 1128

**PATHÉ MARCONI** (M)

PUBLICIS

and Pat Boone's 'April Love' ('Les amours de jeunesse').

As 1957 turned into 1958, Gould, Deguelt and the Platters continued to face each other down over the airwaves, the American group's success leading to a sell-out tour of the country, a recording session in Paris that produced the hit 'Smoke Gets In Your Eyes'[262] (duly given a treacle-coated, but still quite enjoyable makeover by Deguelt as 'Fumée aux yeux'), and a second run at the Olympia Theatre in August. The first major rock'n'roll stars to tour France, the Platters attracted far more than a teenage audience to their shows, and the general acceptance of these cultivated ambassadors for rock'n'roll did much to counter the reports of riots that were filtering across the Atlantic.

Inevitably, their repertoire was swiftly ransacked by the great and the good of French music hall: Mick Micheyl attempted '(You've Got) The Magic

---

[262] A revival of a much-recorded 1934 hit for, among others, Paul Whiteman.

Touch' ('L'apprivoisée'), Vicky Autier crooned her way through 'My Prayer' ('Ma prière'[263]), François Deguelt and vocal group Les Babs' Boys battled it out with rival versions of 'Twilight Time'[264] ('Les amoureux'), and Jean Bertola took a stab at 'The Great Pretender' ('L'homme qui passe').

Shuffling along in the shadows was a mysterious outfit known as the Allegrettes, who neither appeared in public, nor on their record sleeves. Singing in English, the accents suggested that the vocalists at least were American, and it is likely that they were either US servicemen based in France, or moonlighting jazz musicians with an exceptionally good feel for rock'n'roll. They showed off their credentials with well-crafted covers of the Diamonds' 'The Stroll', the Crescendos' 'Oh Julie' and a gutsy take on the Champs' 'Tequila', while their cover of 'Twilight Time', though not up to the level of the Platters' recording, was a creditable effort worthy of radio play.

With the Platters all over the airwaves, 1958 was the first year that the French began to listen to rock'n'roll in any great number. The success of Elvis Presley's films boosted interest both in his records and rock'n'roll in general, so singers and musicians began to pay closer attention in their search for a hit. However, with the jazz community unable to see beyond the novelty value of Trio Raisner's monstrous 'Rock au Tyrol' or the Donald Duck impressions on 'Donald rock',[265] Raymond Bernard's big-band 'Bac and rock', or trumpeter Fred Gérard's take on Bill Haley's 'Two Hound Dogs', it seemed that nobody really knew how to turn the dream of a home-grown rock'n'roll hit into reality.

## Paul Anka

The catalyst that would eventually break rock'n'roll to the masses turned out not to be Elvis Presley, or even the Platters, but an altogether more restrained performer: the Canadian teen-pop prodigy Paul Anka. When the Véga label issued his 'Diana' on an EP in the spring of 1958, the results surpassed all expectations as the record vaulted up the charts and stayed there for the rest of the year.

Less threatening than Presley, Anka became a massive star in France,[266] a *bona fide* teen idol whose young fans bought his records in droves. His breakthrough hit duly became the next target for the cover version industry, and record stores were swamped with competing adaptations.

---

[263] On an EP that also included a sweet but listenable adaptation of Elvis Presley's 'Loving You' ('Sans amour').

[264] Originally recorded by the Three Suns in 1947, although it was the Platters' version that inspired the French adaptations.

[265] To be fair, Raisner did turn out the surprisingly acceptable 'Voici le rock 'n roll' for the same EP.

[266] And would remain so well into the 1960s.

Among the better attempts[267] was one by Jacques Hélian's former vocalist, Jean-Louis Tristan,[268] though he did far better with the home-grown 'À coup de dents'.

The most popular of the 'Diana' covers was a version by Gloria Lasso, which attempted to replicate the swinging rhythm of the original, but came across more like a novelty foxtrot. It wasn't the instrumental backing that was the problem, so much as Lasso's over-the-top vocal bravado, far removed from Anka's youthful enthusiasm. Ultimately, the tempestuous Lasso proved incapable of coming to terms with rock'n'roll, and neither this, nor her earlier 'Bon voyage' (an almost-martial take on Clyde McPhatter's 'Without Love'), offered anything to compete with the originals. Both were hits anyway, selling strongly despite their flaws to an audience who still needed to hear their pop music in their own language.

## Tequila! – From exotica to rock'n'roll

Dalida also climbed aboard the rock'n'roll train in 1958, reworking the Shepherd Sisters' 'Alone (Why Must I Be Alone)' as 'Je pars' for a sizeable hit which in turn prompted Dario Moreno to record a rival version. Moreno relied on his charisma to carry the song, but Dalida, almost uniquely among the stars of music hall, seemed to have both a feel for the style and the personality to carry it off – factors that explain why she maintained a substantial following even as rock'n'roll began to make headway into the market dominance of the exotica stars. Surprisingly though, she made no further attempts at rock'n'roll that year, concentrating instead on covers of sedate American hits like Eydie Gormé's 'Love Me Forever' ('Dieu seul'), although her version of Robert P. Marcucci's 'Holiday In Naples' ('Guitare et tambourin') was sufficiently rhythmic to confirm that, should she wish to return to rock'n'roll, she had the goods to back up the ambition.

Claude Robin[269] was another to have a go at 'Je pars', unsuccessfully attempting to challenge Dalida in the French marketplace. He also took on Gloria Lasso with a version of Paul Anka's 'Diana' which was pleasant enough, but no more so than his routine stroll through Louis Prima's 'Buona Sera' later in 1958. He also produced a strong vocal reading of the Champs' 'Tequila', although nobody took the opportunity to join him for a drink.

---

[267] The others included versions from vocal group Les Quatre de Paris, jazz trumpeter Georges Jouvin, fellow jazzer Claude Bolling, comic-opera specialist Jean Bretonnière, and even (albeit in a very subdued manner) the *chansonnier* Mouloudji.

[268] Tristan had earlier turned out an unexpectedly worthwhile adaptation of Joe Turner's 'Corrine, Corrina'.

[269] Robin had earlier cut a (now rarer than hen's teeth) rock'n'roll single, 'Rock fan', for the obscure Belgian label, Victory.

Drummer Armand Molinetti likewise covered 'Tequila', as a follow-up to his weak attempt at the Platters' 'Only You' ('Loin de vous'), although the self-penned 'T'en veux un bout quand' better displayed his commitment to the big beat.[270] Bandleader Francis Bay, trombonist Jacques Brienne and violinist Jo Bouillon all recorded their own versions of 'Tequila' in 1958, though the inappropriate orchestral arrangement on the latter suggested that Bouillon really preferred a glass of Beaujolais to a swig of Mexico's finest. Rather better was his delightful 'Stroll-blues',[271] which sounded as if it might have skulked endearingly around the background of a *film noir*, though it came no closer to rock'n'roll than any of the above.

Vocalist Didier Lapeyrère's rendition of 'Tequila' proved to be a better proposition, though no more commercially viable than his earlier half-decent adaptation of the Jive Bombers' 'Bad Boy' ('Sale gosse'). The latter was picked up in the same month by jazz trumpeter Pierre Sellin, but both Lapeyrère and Sellin were beaten to market by Claude Bolling, whose version of 'Bad Boy' was released in early 1958 as a follow-up to his covers of Elvis Presley's 'Loving You' and Julie London's 'Cry Me A River'. Bolling also delivered a jazzy reworking of Bill Justis's 'Raunchy' ('Plus jamais'), which in turn was picked up by Lapeyrère for a vocal version.[272]

Among the more interesting records to emerge during 1958 were whistle- and pipe-blower Alain Michel's take on Elvis Presley's 'Hot Dog', which had to be heard to be believed, and singer/dancer Dora Néri's 'Dans l'enfer', which was hardly infernal, but swung enough to get audiences moving. While neither could truly be classed as a rock'n'roll record, they nevertheless marked out a terrain that was all their own – in contrast to the derivative efforts of bandleaders like Robert Wagner ('Gorets d'amour') and Houdigand ('Pour bien danser le rock'n'roll').

Vocal group Les Six Trognes played it safer with a cover of Guy Mitchell's 'Rock-A-Billy', a song which was nothing of the sort, in either version. More typical of their work was their take on Alma Cogan's 'Funny, Funny, Funny'[273] on the same EP, but neither was likely to get teenagers jiving on the dance floor. This softer approach also resulted in a cover of Pat Boone's 'April Love' by Christian Garros being included on his 1958 EP, *Jazz danse* – the final attempt by the drummer to identify with the sound now sweeping across the world.

---

[270] All three issued in 1958.

[271] On the same EP. The record also contained a depressingly poor version of 'Diana'.

[272] Recorded under the supervision of Boris Vian.

[273] Cogan probably got the song from Zoro Reid, but Les Six Trognes almost certainly got it from Cogan.

Opting for original material, singer Paul Roby[274] worked with jazzman Jimmy Walter and lyricist Claude Nougaro, who crafted him the surprisingly strong 'Coupez-les moi... au rasoir!!' and 'Jour et nuit'. The same EP also offered the excellent 'Les anges', a songwriting collaboration between Nougaro and Henri Salvador,[275] but none of them made any impact on the record-buying public.

Of greater interest to the growing number of rock'n'roll fans was 'Blouse du dentiste', Salvador's return to the sound he had pioneered back in 1956. Another collaboration with Boris Vian, it was far superior to their earlier stabs at the genre. Based around standard blues progressions, the song was a parody, with a lyric detailing a disastrous trip to the dentist delivered over a strident backing by Quincy Jones's band.[276] While the big band might have sounded out of place on an early Elvis Presley recording, the overall effect was not too different from the New Orleans rock'n'roll featured in his 1958 film, *King Creole*. Salvador's humorous vocal ensured the record received a warm reception from adults and teenagers alike.

Although the EP also included a cover of Bill Haley's 'The Saints Rock 'n Roll' ('Oh! Quand les saints'), neither Vian nor Salvador genuinely loved the music, and the remainder was given over to a mix of jazz and comic lyrics, with 'Moi, j'préfère la marche à pied' proving a classic of the genre. Salvador was more interested in the sounds emerging from South America and the Caribbean, showering the same year's 'Mazurka pour ma mie' and 'Ça pince' with Brazilian percussion, although both were actually collaborations with Vian. Once their big-band blues effort had slipped off the airwaves, Vian and Salvador teamed up with Quincy Jones again for the cool 'J'aimerais tellement ça', a marvellous slice of late-fifties' jazz that was far more to the taste of all

---

[274] Not Paul Robi/Roby of the Platters, but a French singer whose real name is lost to history.
[275] Nougaro would also later record it himself.
[276] Jones was resident in Paris at the time, appearing on a host of jazz records.

the parties involved.

While Salvador was charting his own course, his fellow pioneer Moustache also took a second stab at rock'n'roll with 'C'est ça le blues', a slower effort featuring a decent vocal over a too-jazzy arrangement. However, the faster-paced 'J'ai j'té ma clé dans un tonneau d'goudron'[277] was perhaps the best among the many French efforts to tap into the Haley sound. With a powerful beat underpinning a tight guitar line and only a minimal horn section, it was a fine piece of work, and the self-titled LP on which it appeared was the best rock'n'roll album yet to surface in France – not that it had a lot of competition. Though the likes of 'J'ai du Beaujolais' came closer to the jazz that remained Moustache's first love, the infectious 'Vieux frère (Bon anniversaire)' had a tight bass line wandering underneath the big band, and, while the piano that fuelled 'Viens donc bergère' may not have hailed from New Orleans, it was certainly on an ocean liner somewhere offshore. Even so, the album still didn't measure up to the more exciting sounds on offer from Elvis Presley or even Paul Anka, whose 'Diana' was still dominating the airwaves.

## The Kalin Twins

In the autumn of 1958, Anka followed up his hit with another smash, 'You Are My Destiny', but he was beaten to the top of the French charts by another American rock'n'roll act, the Kalin Twins. A Top 5 hit in the US, the catchy 'When' peaked at No. 1 in the UK and this success quickly extended across the Channel. Released in France on a Brunswick EP, the song was an instant hit, easily elbowing aside a weak cover by Les Babs' Boys ('Viens'). The French trio also reworked the Kalins' 'Jumpin' Jack' as 'Ce vieux Jack',[278] but their smooth sound lacked the youthful enthusiasm of the Americans and failed to generate many sales. Dario Moreno's formulaic cover of 'When' ('Viens') proved more popular, although whether it could truly be called rock'n'roll was another question altogether.[279]

That October, the Kalin Twins appeared at the Olympia Theatre, where they sang their big hit[280] over the backing track from their recording, as

---

[277] Originally cut as a parody by Mac-Kac, under the title 'J'ai j'té ma clef dans un tonneau d'goudron'.

[278] As did the unimpressive Rose Mania.

[279] Further late 1958 covers followed from jazz bassist Pierre Michelot (on an EP which also saw him having a flutter at the Platters' 'Twilight Time'), trombonist Jacques Brienne, accordionist Loulou Legrand (who also tackled the Champs' 'Tequila' on the same EP) , bandleader Alain Goraguer and fellow bandleader Jack Baker (who also churned out dull versions of the Platters' 'Twilight Time' and 'My Prayer', as well as a pointless and somewhat belated attempt Bill Haley's 'Rock Around The Clock'.

[280] And nothing else!

caught out as everyone else by their unexpected success. In truth, it was the song, rather than the singers, which drove the sales – a point hammered home when their follow-up, 'Forget Me Not', was quickly forgotten by radio programmers and music buyers alike.[281]

Another artist to have a flutter at 'When' was Belgian singer Tonia Bern, who made her name on UK television before being brought to France by Maurice Chevalier. Her late 1958 version ('Viens') was unremarkable, but a revamp of Perry Como's 'The Girl With The Golden Braids' ('Pour aller danser') had a hidden sting in its tail, with Pierre Arvay's band cutting loose into a wild arrangement of the folk song 'Sur le pont d'Avignon'. Better still was her reworking of Brenda Lee's 'Ring-A-My Phone',[282] but despite her undeniable charm, nobody was interested in giving her a call.[283]

While Bern and Les Babs' Boys covered the dubiously talented Kalin Twins, others sought out the harder-to-find recordings of the Everly Brothers. Digging into the American duo's roots, Marc Taynor adopted a country-ish style for a 1958 take on their 'Bye Bye Love', while retaining something of a boogie-woogie feel.[284] The song also attracted a second cover by singer/ guitarist Henri Breyre, whose upbeat reading (styled 'Bye-Bye Love' on the label) wasn't bad at all, though it wasn't exactly rockabilly. The same EP saw Breyre covering Louis Prima's 'Buona Sera' and bidding for the youth market with yet another version of Paul Anka's 'Diana'.

It was becoming clear that, whether the Establishment liked it or not, rock'n'roll was on its way to

---

[281] But not before both Hazy Osterwald and crooner Jean-Paul Mauric had added it to their repertoires under the title 'Ne m'oublie pas' in 1958 and 1959 respectively.

[282] Although not listed as such on the sleeve, Bern's adaptation of this song was titled 'Quand tu téléphones'.

[283] Married to speed-record holder Donald Campbell, Bern returned to the UK, where she lived quietly until her husband's death in 1967 in the infamous *Bluebird* disaster. After a brief retirement, she resumed work as a cabaret artist.

[284] Taynor had already cut an interesting version of LaVern Baker's 'Tweedle Dee' and an excellent tribute to guitar hero Les Paul (the punningly titled 'Laisse Paul tranquille'), although it was his tilt at the Everlys' songbook that saw him coming out as a fan of rock'n'roll. He later tackled numbers as diverse as Eydie Gormé's 'Love Me Forever' ('Dieu seul') and the Champs' 'Tequila' with little commercial success.

France. As 1958 ended, Paul Anka flew in to Paris for a month of sell-out concerts at the Olympia Theatre, followed by a national tour that took the music deep into the country. Hot on the heels of successful shows by the Platters and Bill Haley, they provided further confirmation that French youth had finally acquired a taste for the music that had already driven the rest of the world's teenagers wild.

ROBERT DORFMANN présente *les nouveaux visages du cinéma français*

Un Film de MARCEL CARNÉ

les tricheurs

Dialogues de JACQUES SIGURD

avec ROLAND ARMONTEL - ROLAND LESAFFRE

This point was doubly emphasised by the success in late 1958 of veteran film-maker Marcel Carné's *Les tricheurs*, the first French picture of the decade to effectively tap into the desires of the teenage audience.[285] With a soundtrack that mixed the cool jazz of Gerry Mulligan with the big beat of Lionel Hampton and the rock'n'roll of the Champs, the movie told the tragic love story of two teenagers (played by Jacques Charrier[286] and the ravishing Pascale Petit) determined to be cool and detached, but ruthlessly manipulated by the film's anti-hero (Laurent Terzieff), climaxing in the death of the heroine in a James Dean-like car crash to the accompaniment of wild jungle drums. While the score contained more jazz than rock'n'roll, the screen was filled with images of jukeboxes, teen hops and even a glimpse inside the largest record shop on the Champs-Elysées (where Charrier could be seen alongside a Fats Domino album). The film also captured the same sense of ennui portrayed by James Dean in *Rebel Without A Cause* and Marlon Brando in *The Wild One*, captivating teenagers like no French film before it. Overnight, young people began to copy the fashions of the leading players, further emphasising their difference from the older generation and boosting the demand for rock'n'roll.

**The great and good start rocking**

Even so, the airwaves and charts remained the province of music hall stars delivering enjoyable, if unexciting, covers of rock'n'roll songs as the record industry struggled to digest the lessons being taught by Paul Anka and the Kalin Twins. Anka's 'You Are My Destiny' was rapidly adapted into French

---

[285] Although dismissed at the time by *nouvelle vague* directors like François Truffaut, it has been retrospectively acclaimed as a classic, and, while not on a level with Carné's 1945 epic, *Les enfants du paradis*, it was nevertheless both an artistic and a commercial triumph.

[286] Who would later marry Brigitte Bardot.

as 'Tu m'étais destinée' and duly recorded by a host of performers.[287] As 1958 turned into 1959, crooners Claude Robin and Serge Lenormand, Swiss guitarist Pierre Cavalli, trumpeter Georges Jouvin and exotica duo Patrice et Mario all covered both Anka's new hit and the Kalin Twins' chart-topper,[288] with Cavalli's sleazy roll around the former proving particularly effective. However, it was Dalida who transformed 'Tu m'étais destiné' into a French smash,[289] providing serious competition for the original version. In reality though, the market was splitting in two, with the adult audience opting for covers and their teenage offspring staying loyal to the American originals.

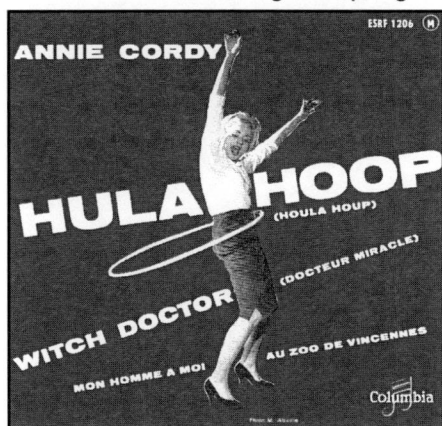

The softer side of rock'n'roll proved proved equally palatable to Annie Cordy, whose 1958 cover of Bobby Helms's 'My Special Angel' ('J'avais rêvé d'un ange'[290]) adopted the heavenly choir of Malcolm Vaughan's UK version, but retained enough piano triplets to remind listeners of the song's origins. Later in the year, Cordy covered the Georgia Gibbs/Teresa Brewer hit, 'The Hula Hoop Song' ('Houla houp'), which, while not rock'n'roll, was certainly a fun record, homing in directly on a new teenage fad that had recently gripped the Western world.[291]

In late 1958, Belgian comic-song specialist Émile Lambert turned out the more rock'n'roll-flavoured 'Le houla-bop' and a cover of Betty Johnson's similarly-themed 'Hoopa Hoola' ('Le houp à houla'[292]), while French old-school crooner Roland Gerbeau took the hoop back to its Hawaiian origins at the start of 1959 for his own hybrid arrangement of 'Hoopa hoola', which found Hawaiian guitars colliding with a light rock rhythm in surprisingly effective fashion.[293]

However, none of the many hula hoop songs enjoyed as much commercial success as Cordy's trailblazer, which was accompanied on EP by her amusing, if hardly rocking, rendition of David Seville's unknown-in-France

---

[287] Among them bandleader Jo Bouillon (1958) and jazz guitarist Marcel Bianchi (1959), the former using the original title.

[288] Patrice et Mario also laid down a surprisingly strong 1959 version of Perry Como's 'Catch A Falling Star' ('Garde ça pour toi').

[289] The slightly amended title reflected the gender of the singer. In this form, it was also a lesser hit for Gloria Lasso.

[290] Cordy's version shared the honours with a rival rendition by Serge Lenormand, though neither was a big hit.

[291] Cordy's celebration in song was reworked for accordion by Émile Prud'homme, for harmonica by Trio Raisner, and for rock-tinged jazz band by Moustache.

[292] With backing by jazz guitarist Harry Frekin (*aka* Rockin' Harry).

[293] Gerbeau also picked up on the latest rock'n'roll offering from Boris Vian, 'Frankenstein', which, in common with much of Vian's output, treated it as a comic novelty rather than a valid musical form. Nowhere near as enjoyable – either as comedy or rock'n'roll – as Vian's work with Henri Salvador, this comic-sketch-in-song was also picked up by Louis Massis, although neither recording made much commercial impact.

'Witch Doctor' ('Docteur miracle'). Both were decent-sized hits as 1958 drew to a close, but as yet, despite countless attempts, the number of commercially successful *genuine* rock'n'roll records made in France could be counted on the fingers of one foot. For all their years of experience, the established French stars who had taken a gamble on rock'n'roll lacked the one thing that Paul Anka, the Kalin Twins and Elvis Presley had in abundance: youth. Slowly but surely, the realisation began to dawn that, if France was going to produce some home-grown rock'n'roll, it would need to be sung by some new, young singers. The search was on for the country's first rock'n'roll idol!

# Chapter II

## ROCK, C'EST UN ROCK
### Rock'n'roll, French style (1958-59)

*By the end of 1958, rock'n'roll had taken a hold across the English-speaking world and a number of European countries, yet France continued to hold the music at arm's length. While Paul Anka, the Kalin Twins and the Platters enjoyed wide followings and respectable sales, raunchier performers like Elvis Presley lagged some way behind when it came to sales figures. In part, this was due to the preference among French listeners for songs sung in their own language – something that seemed to matter less the further north the music went across Europe – but the strength of contemporary French chanson undoubtedly played a part as well, even if younger listeners found the earnest warblings of Édith Piaf et al lacking in excitement. Nevertheless, the year had seen the French starting to listen to rock'n'roll in significant numbers, even if, as with Annie Cordy's take on David Seville's 'Witch Doctor', it was in a watered-down style purveyed by the country's music hall stars. With this particular record though, everything changed: instead of simply seeing off the American competition, Cordy found herself challenged by one of the first serious contenders for French rock'n'roll stardom, Claude Piron.*

### Claude Piron
Claude Piron had kicked off his career in 1958 with a Platters-style rock'n'roll ballad, 'Mon cœur bat', the highlight of an unsuccessful EP also notable for a swinging cover of Castel et Casti's 'Le juke-box est en panne' and a decent stab at Jean-Louis Tristan's 'À coup de dents', though neither made a real case for the singer as France's answer to Elvis. It was Piron's decision to record versions of both 'Witch Doctor' ('Docteur miracle') and the Kalin Twins' 'When' ('Viens') for a follow-up release in November that proved he had the vocal ability to back up his ambition.

More importantly, he was young and had no previous musical baggage to hinder his assault on the hearts and minds of the country's youth. Piron couldn't be accused of jumping onto a commercial bandwagon to prop up a career under threat; in his case, rock'n'roll was to be a launch pad for stardom, not an attempt at prolonging it. Dressed in leather, he looked every inch the rocker he sought to be – even if his record company had to play down the connection with the *blousons noirs*[294] who were causing trouble at the few rock'n'roll dances being held at the time. Musically, the record marked

---

[294]  The French equivalent of Britain's Teddy boys.

Hé ! Youla
VIENS (When)

DOCTEUR MIRACLE

D'OU VIENS-TU
BILLIE BOY

chantés par

CLAUDE PIRON

4 BEST SELLERS

disque 45 tours 460 V 429

DUCRETET THOMSON

a major leap forward, the backing on 'Viens' more than matching that on the original, and Piron's vocal performance on 'Docteur miracle' carrying more punch than Annie Cordy's 'played for laughs' delivery.

'Docteur miracle' was not the first completely satisfying rock'n'roll record cut in France – that honour goes to the largely unheard 'Devil rock', released without success by the unknown and unremembered Max Alan in 1957. Piron's record, however, was the first genuine rock'n'roll effort (rather than watered-down music hall cover) to achieve widespread popularity, selling strongly alongside the more established Cordy and lending credence to Piron's claim to be the country's first rock'n'roll star. By strange coincidence, his only rivals for the title all released their first recordings in the same month as his hit, November 1958 – a date which can therefore be said to mark a turning point in the history of French pop.

## Gabriel Dalar, Danyel Gérard and Richard Anthony

GABRIEL
DALAR
et ses chansons
CHOC !

Super 45 t.
● Docteur Miracle (Witch docteur) - Viens
(When) - Croque-Crâne-Creux (purple
people eater) - Hé ! Youla (Hey ! Eula)
460.602 ME
● Oo - shoo - be - doo - be - N'oublie pas
39 de Fièvre - Arc-en-Ciel
460.607 ME
45 t. simples
● Viens (When) - Hé ! Youla (Hay ! Eula)
261.085 MF
● Croque-Crâne-Creux (purple people eater)
- Docteur Miracle (Witch docteur)
261.088 MF
● 39 de Fièvre (Fever) - Oo-shoo-be-doo-be
261.089 MF

GABRIEL DALAR
champion
d'ALLO CHANSONS
de "FRANCE-SOIR"
10 affals à la minute
(3.512 appels en 64 )
pour entendre son
Sensationnel
"DOCTEUR
MIRACLE"

En exclusivité sur disques

fontana

Swiss singer Gabriel Dalar was a protégé of Boris Vian and his debut EP shared three songs with Claude Piron's second, his take on 'Docteur miracle' winning airplay alongside the versions by Piron and Annie Cordy, and 'Viens' joining the myriad others on the airwaves. His raunchy revamp of Barry Cryer's 'Hey! Eula'[295] ('Hé, Youla!') allowed him to slink spectacularly around a tight and incisive backing on a record that, if not exactly rock'n'roll, wasn't quite jazz or blues either. Equally popular was his 'Croque-crâne-creux', a rollicking cover of Sheb Wooley's 'The Purple People Eater'[296] which tapped the same appeal as 'Docteur miracle'. Dalar was a confident vocalist and a vibrant performer, but the cuts suffered from a cluttered arrangement and lacked the earthiness of the best rock'n'roll records. Nevertheless, his EP was a minor hit, entering the singer in the contest to become the country's leading rock'n'roller.

Danyel Gérard transcended similar musical problems to deliver a gem of an EP that offered, in addition to an excellent, albeit redundant version of the already much-covered 'Viens', the inspired 'D'où reviens-tu Billie Boy?',[297] a variant of an old British folk song known as 'Charming Billy'.[298] This was a cover (with lyrics by Boris Vian) of the obscure Dorothy Collins single 'Where Have You Been Billie Boy' and has often –

---

[295] Also included on Piron's EP, this frequently overlooked tune had started life as a piece of incidental film music by Alex North.

[296] Like David Seville's 'Witch Doctor', Wooley's record had topped the US charts that year, but Dalar and Vian may have picked up on it via the UK version by Barry Cryer, given that both also covered the flip side of Cryer's record, 'Hey! Eula'.

[297] Also recorded, somewhat less impressively, by Piron.

[298] It would be covered in the US under that title by Johnny Preston in 1960.

erroneously – been cited as the first French rock'n'roll record. It wasn't the first, but it *was* a decent slice of rock'n'roll strongly reminiscent of Little Willie John's 'Fever', and it picked up sporadic airplay over the winter months. Sitting alongside the covers was the overlooked 'Tais-toi', a teen ballad in a style close to that of the great American doo-wop groups, suggesting that, although Gérard's singing was perhaps a little too mannered, he had both the vocal and compositional talents to set him apart from the crowd. Dark and moody, he looked even more like a teen idol than Piron or Dalar, and his frenetic performances indicated that he could well win the battle to become the French king of rock'n'roll, assuming he could find the right song to take him into the charts.

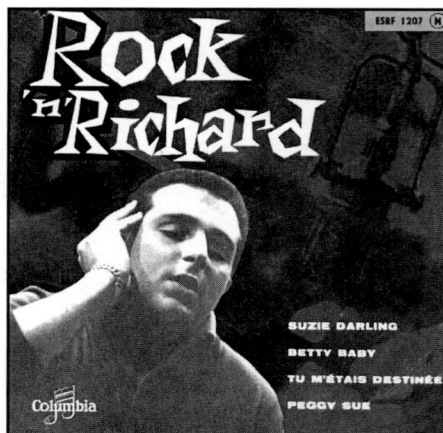

Incredibly, November 1958 also produced a fourth strong challenger for the rock'n'roll crown in the unassuming figure of Richard Anthony. Another young singer with no track record, Anthony had never even performed live, having auditioned for the Columbia label by singing along to a Paul Anka recording. However, his cosmopolitan upbringing in Egypt, Argentina, Britain and France meant that he was more than comfortable with American-styled material. The moody Gérard, the super-cool Dalar and the raunchy Piron all looked more convincing than the cuddly, family-friendly Anthony, but he was more than a match for them in vocal prowess, and his recording debut was suffused with a confidence absent from most of the previous French attempts at rock'n'roll.

For his debut EP, Anthony chose to cover four current American smashes: Paul Anka's 'You Are My Destiny' ('Tu m'étais destinée'), Connie Francis's 'Stupid Cupid' ('Betty, baby'), Robin Luke's 'Susie Darlin'' ('Suzy darling') and Buddy Holly's 'Peggy Sue'. Although his perfomances were spirited, the musical backings left something to be desired and the record flopped. Even so, Anthony and Columbia were both convinced that they were on the right track.

## Building toward success

Although none of the four leading contenders had as yet managed a big hit (Piron came closest with 'Docteur miracle', but he had been overshadowed by Annie Cordy), the record industry was quick to respond to the emergence of new faces bearing fresh material to cover. Gérard's near-hit, 'D'où reviens-tu Billie Boy?' was picked up by both Jean-Louis Tristan[299] and Jean Bretonnière,

---

[299] Released on an EP that also included a version of the film theme 'Toi, le venin', a genuinely exciting big band blues. Tristan also cut 'Rock de l'inauguration', from the same film, one of the better French attempts to work a rock'n'roll rhythm into a motion picture soundtrack. Both titles were also on the market in superb readings by jazzman Michel de Villers.

tea for two
CHA
CHA
CHA

JUST A DREAM
TEARS ON MY PILLOW
NEAR YOU

THE ALLEGRETTES

PACIFIC

but neither version sold particularly well.[300] Of the others, 'Hé, Youla!' was covered by lapsed jazzmen Marcel Bianchi and Jacques Brienne,[301] while Moustache hollered his way through both that one and 'Docteur miracle'. The latter was also tackled both by crooner Roland Gerbeau[302] and pianist Alain Goraguer, although the market really didn't want to know.

The Allegrettes offered a better alternative, cutting excellent versions (in English) of both 'Witch Doctor' and 'When' before introducing French listeners to the hits of Johnny Cash ('Guess Things Happen That Way'), Ricky Nelson ('Poor Little Fool'), Fats Domino ('Whole Lotta Lovin' ') and the Elegants ('Little Star'). However, their instrumental cover of Pérez Prado's mambo hit, 'Patricia', sounded like the work of a completely different group (which, given their anonymous status, it may well have been). They redeemed themselves with excellent reworkings of Jimmy Clanton's 'Just A Dream' and Little Anthony & The Imperials' 'Tears On My Pillow', before getting to the heart of things with a couple of Elvis covers, 'One Night'[303] and 'I Got Stung'. The latter rocked harder than anything else that had yet issued forth from a French recording studio, which made their decision to cover the Chipmunks' 1958 US chart-topper, 'The Chipmunk Song', all the more unfathomable.

Although they were clearly the closest thing to a genuine rock'n'roll group that France had to offer (or at least had musicians and singers within their ranks who could have made such a claim), the Allegrettes' reluctance to perform live did them few favours. None of their records sold particularly well,[304] despite the quality of their lazily grooving cover of Bobby Darin's 'Queen Of The Hop' and their incendiary reworking of Lloyd Price's classic 'Stagger Lee'.

Paul Anka's songbook was full of easy pickings, his lighter touch making it easier to assimilate than Presley's harder-edged material, and 1959 saw one Anka song after another reworked with French lyrics, or given instrumental readings by French jazzmen. 'Crazy Love' was a case in point, covered by singers Jean-Claude Dague and Gil Bernard,[305] and given a bluesy big band treatment by Claude Bolling. Meanwhile Hubert Rostaing bypassed all of his earlier pseudonyms to resurface as 'Joe Kalamazoo' on an EP featuring four of Anka's compositions, including the otherwise overlooked 'Don't Gamble

---

[300] Bretonnière's was titled simply 'Billy boy'. There were also versions by bandleader Raymond Le Pers, vocal duo Pascal et Dominique, and the unremarkable Élise Vallée (in a gender-reversed rewrite titled 'D'où reviens-tu Élisa?').

[301] The latter as 'Eh! Youla'.

[302] Gerbeau also attempted a vocal version of the Champs' 'Tequila'.

[303] The Allegrettes' version was titled 'One nite with you' and followed Presley's sanitised lyric rather than the Smiley Lewis original, 'One Night Of Sin'.

[304] Although their version of 'When' did chart in Italy.

[305] In the latter case as 'Amour insensé'.

With Love' and a tight, saxophone-powered take on 'Midnight'.

Line Renaud continued her occasional dalliances into rock'n'roll in early 1959 with 'Sept cœurs', a song she had originally cut in German as 'Sieben junge Männer', and the purpose-built 'Tilt (Mon cœur a fait tilt...)'.[306] Both were overshadowed by her reading of Sam Cooke's 'Only Sixteen' ('Seize ans'). Exactly the type of mid-tempo rock that Renaud could deliver in her sleep, the results were surprisingly pleasing to the ear.[307]

Flailing around somewhere further back was fading crooner Francis Linel,[308] who attempted to get with the times by taking on Richard Anthony with a rival version of 'Betty, baby'. More impressive than his challenge to Annie Cordy with 'J'avais rêvé d'un ange', it was still a long way from the sound that the four main contenders were edging toward.

Although the sales figures achieved by their first releases were somewhat disappointing, they all had another shot in early 1959, with varying results. Claude Piron came off worst, compelled by his record label, Ducretet–Thomson, to cover Russ Tamblyn's 'Tom Thumb's Tune' ('La chanson de Tom Pouce') from the 1958 Hollywood fantasy-musical, *Tom Thumb*, and a disappointing adaptation of Ruby Murray's 'In My Life' ('Dans la vie'). Only his upbeat cover of Tommy Sands' 'Bigger Than Texas' ('Plus grand') came close to the quality of his previous release. Frustrated at not being allowed to record the type of material he wanted, Piron decamped to Spain for the summer, leaving the field free for the competition.

Gabriel Dalar came up trumps with the sizzling '39 de fièvre', a cover of the Little Willie John/Peggy Lee hit, 'Fever', which deserved to be a smash, but incredibly wasn't.[309] The same EP also included two dynamic originals,

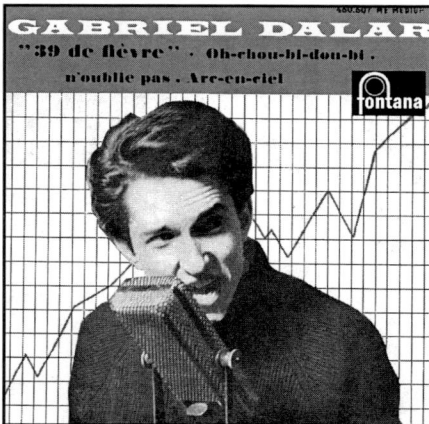

'N'oublie pas' and 'Arc-en-ciel', which showed that Dalar had what it took to go all the way, though a cool cover of Dizzy Gillespie's 'Oo-Shoo-Be-Doo-Be' ('Oh-chou-bi-dou-bi') suggested that he remained a jazz fan at heart. The record enjoyed steady sales, but his career nosedived soon after, when his mentor, Boris Vian, moved on, leaving him stranded. Despite some well-received stage shows in Paris later in the year, he never recorded again.

As Piron and Dalar both exited stage left, Danyel Gérard cut a second EP that held out just as much promise as

---

[306] The former was also recorded by Dora Néri, while the latter was quickly picked up by the country's jazz musicians and resurfaced in big band versions by both Jack Baker (as 'Mon cœur a fait tilt') and Jean Leccia.

[307] Although most fans probably preferred to play her version of Dalida's 'Ciao, ciao bambina' on the other side.

[308] Linel had already cut a pointless rendition of 'Viens' and a rather better cover of Les Quatre de Paris' 'Daisy' titled 'Daisy (La pin-up des juke boxes)'.

[309] This was possibly down to competition by German-based singer Caterina Valente, who cut an inferior version of the song (in French) around the same time.

the first. Its highlight was a cover of the Fraternity Brothers' not-very-rock'n'roll 'Passion Flower' ('Tout l'amour'), but the record also contained strong takes on Marty Robbins' 'She Was Only Seventeen' ('Elle n'avait que dix-sept ans'[310]) and Don Gibson's 'Oh Lonesome Me' ('Ô pauvre amour'), plus a decent teen ballad titled 'Ne lui en veux pas'. The excellent 'Tout l'amour' picked up scattered airplay, although it was blown off the airwaves by a more polished, albeit less exciting version by Dalida. Nevertheless, the EP, and his live performances, made the case for Gérard as a quality rock'n'roller. Sadly though, his bid for stardom was forestalled when he was called up for army service and despatched to Algeria, effectively ruling him out of the running for the next two and a half years.

That left only Richard Anthony to keep the fires burning, but his second EP was less satisfying than his debut. His passable covers of Ricky Nelson's 'Lonesome Town' ('La rue des cœurs perdus') and Tommy Edwards' 'It's All In The Game' ('C'est le jeu') garnered little airplay, while a limp rendition of Cliff Richard's 'Move It' ('Chanson magique') showed how far he had to go to be convincing with uptempo material. The record was a commercial failure, and, with little incentive to go out on the road, Anthony remained hidden from the young audience he was trying to target.

With all four French hopefuls faltering at the second hurdle, British-born newcomer Stephen Bruce attempted to sneak in ahead of them. Falsely billed as American on his record sleeve,[311] he weighed in with 'Celui qui tient le monde dans ses mains' (a cover of Laurie London's gospelly rocker, 'He's Got The Whole World In His Hands', with French lyrics by Boris Vian), though his reading of Ricky Nelson's 'Poor Little Fool' ('Pauvre de moi') was a far better effort. London's hit was also picked up by American expat June Richmond,[312] whose soulful vocal was more in keeping with the lyric, and by Jamaican-born Zack Matalon,[313] who actually got to the song first, but buried it on an EP with several others drawn from the Great American Songbook. At the end of the day, however, Matalon, Richmond and Bruce were nowhere near as convincing as Piron or Gérard, and none of them made even a ripple.

---

[310] With French lyrics by Francis Lemarque, who also recorded it himself.

[311] In fairness, he did have American parents.

[312] A veteran of Jimmy Dorsey's orchestra, the African-American singer had set up home in France in the late forties and was a fixture on the Parisian jazz circuit. She made some superb jazz recordings, most notably 1957's 'C'est chouette', which appeared on an EP alongside her excellent reading of LaVern Baker's 'Tra La La'. She made one more attempt to get with the beat, laying down an unfairly ignored and vastly superior cover of Annette's 'Tall Paul', as well as a surprisingly strong original, 'One, two, three, four times'.

[313] Matalon had previously come no nearer to rock'n'roll than Pat Boone's saccharine ballad, 'April Love' ('Les amours de jeunesse'), although his take on Jimmie Rodgers' revival of the Weavers' 'Kisses Sweeter Than Wine' ('Ses baisers me grisaient'), with lyrics by Boris Vian, had at least exhibited a sense of rhythm.

## The jazz rock experiment fizzles out

The commercial failure of the proto-rockers did not prevent the older generation rushing to cover their wares, although by now those jazzers still in the game had lost their edge and were simply delivering pale reflections of the more creative work that was beginning to emerge. Although Danyel Gérard had come closest to a hit this time around, it was Gabriel Dalar's '39 de fièvre' that best suited the jazz community, and instrumental versions of 'Fever' soon began flooding onto the market. The best of these was a stripped-back arrangement by Le Paris Jazz Trio, although the big band assaults by Georges Jouvin and Aimé Barelli were more typical. Barelli's EP also featured a version of Gérard's 'Tout l'amour' under its original title, 'Passion Flower', which was also given a rather weak-kneed interpretation by Francis Linel, and a somewhat better one by Georges Ulmer.

Even worse were the recordings of bandleader Pierre Spiers, whose trumpet and *pizzicato* string arrangement of Richard Anthony's 'Chanson magique' ('Move It') was at the same time strangely fascinating and unbelievably poor, while his formulaic version of the Platters' 'Smoke Gets In Your Eyes' ('Fumée aux yeux') was little better.

The fast-fading Jacques Hélian[314] had likewise never come to terms with rock'n'roll, and his attempts to remain relevant with versions of the Castel et Casti/Claude Piron near-hit 'Le juke-box est en panne' and the much-covered 'Docteur miracle' were laughably inept, though his take on Dalar's 'Oh-chou-bi-dou-bi'[315] – being jazz to start with – was a much better proposition.

Others having a final fling with rock'n'roll included trombonist Jacques Brienne, whose sleazy 'Stroll-Blues' was perfect for a slow dance, but less so for jiving; Michel Attenoux, whose 1959 take on 'Rock Around The Clock' was three years too late and sounded even more behind the times than that; and Noël Chiboust, whose version of Brenda Lee's 'Dynamite' was considerably less explosive than the title promised. Equally poor was 'Comment ça va', a rare vocal performance by Albert Raisner which left listeners begging him to pick up his harmonica again.

Inevitably, the boogie-woogie of American-in-Paris Hazel Scott was more palatable, with the uptempo 'Viens danser' proving a perfect invitation. Also impressive was the work of fellow American Cootie Williams, who brought his trumpet to Paris for a tour at the start of 1959. After wowing audiences with his combination of jazz and R&B, he took time out to cut the album *Cootie* in a Parisian studio, laying down a set of jazz standards plus a couple of tracks that were an object lesson in how to combine the two musical forms, Joe Turner's 'Hide And Seek' and Lloyd Price's 'Lawdy Miss Clawdy'.

Aptly renamed 'Trumpet Boy', jazz virtuoso Fernand Verstraete rocked out on a mid-1959 cover of the film theme 'Toi, le venin' on an EP which also boasted an excellent instrumental reworking of Frankie Ford's 'Sea Cruise'. Although the trumpet was hardly a standard rock'n'roll instrument, Verstraete's band blew up a storm, making both this and his subsequent take on Wilbert Harrison's 'Kansas City' surprisingly strong examples of the French

---

[314] Whose star had been completely eclipsed as small combos replaced big bands, and who had now fallen so low as to have to seek a new record deal with the independent Trianon label.

[315] Hélian's version dropped the hyphens to become simply 'Oh chou bi dou bi'.

rock-jazz hybrid. That said, neither these, nor his cover of the Fleetwoods' 'Come Softly To Me' ('Tout doux, tout doucement') sounded convincing to the teenage audience at whom the records were aimed.

Perhaps the best attempt of all was by Swiss guitarist Pierre Cavalli, whose incisive playing on a cover of the Platters' 'Twilight Time' and sizzling arrangement of Roy Hamilton's 'Don't Let Go' showed what could be achieved by those who took the music seriously.[316]

## Rocking the music halls

Marcel Amont cut a strong rendition of 'Tout doux, tout doucement' in 1959 and was rewarded with a huge hit, nudging aside a version by Annie Cordy which attempted to impose a Hawaiian guitar onto a song that was better off without one. No more rock'n'roll than his cross-Channel counterpart Frankie Vaughan,[317] Amont then scored an even bigger smash with Johnny Tillotson's 'True True Happiness' ('Bleu, blanc, blond') and continued to dabble in rock'n'roll-tinged pop to the end of the decade, including a lightweight but highly enjoyable version of Lloyd Price's 'I'm Gonna Get Married' ('Oui, je me marie (Johnny)') in 1960.[318]

Rather better was the latest offering from Boris Vian and Henri Salvador, who collaborated on the latter's cool finger-snapper 'Mon ange gardien' in early 1959. Too laid-back for rock'n'roll, the record nevertheless sashayed around with the requisite swagger,[319] and for once the pair appeared to be playing it straight, rather than for laughs. Vian's work with Salvador now comprised his main rock'n'roll outlet, but their collaboration came to an abrupt end when Vian was felled by a heart attack and died before the year was out. He would never see the final triumph of the music he had done so much to popularise.

## Sacha Distel

While Salvador dallied once again at the gateway to rock'n'roll stardom, unwilling to cross the threshold and take the glory that was rightfully his, he was overtaken by fellow jazz guitarist Sacha Distel. Though he had been one of the early champions of rhythm & blues in France,[320] Distel's records offered little in the way of rock'n'roll. However, he possessed the good looks necessary to qualify as a teenage pin-up, and his recent fling with Brigitte Bardot (commemorated on his 1958 release, 'Brigitte') had given him a degree of playboy notoriety.

The turning point came in early 1959, when he left the Versailles label for the more commercially minded Philips organisation and recorded the joyfully ridiculous 'Scoubidou (Pommes et poires)'. A light-hearted knockabout

---

[316] Sadly, Cavalli's sparkling recordings were the exception rather than the rule, with Aimé Barelli's orchestral mangling of Hamilton's classic rocker, issued alongside a syrup-soaked take on Bobby Helms's 'My Special Angel' that lacked even Annie Cordy's pizzazz, proving far more typical of the general approach.
[317] Vaughan enjoyed a Top 10 UK hit in the spring of 1959 with 'Come Softly To Me'.
[318] Amont's success buried a half-decent version by Jean-Louis Tristan, in his case simply titled 'Johnny'.
[319] The swagger went AWOL when the song was covered by crooner Jean-Paul Mauric.
[320] Distel had worked on early rock'n'roll releases by Mac-Kac and Moustache, as well as licensing Atlantic recordings for the Versailles label.

adapted from Peggy Lee's 'Apples, Peaches And Cherries', it possessed the same youthful energy as the early rock'n'roll sounds of Paul Anka and the Kalin Twins, albeit lacking their commitment to the big beat. Issued on an EP alongside the jazzy 'Ce serait dommage' (Jack Segal's 'Impatient Lover'), it was an instant and a massive hit, outselling almost everything else on its way up the charts and prompting the usual flurry of cover versions.

Aimé Barelli's big band arrangement was as dull as it was predictable, but a rather better variation on the theme came from jazz singer Simone Alma.[321] Although Alma effortlesly swung her way around the lyric, her version went largely unheard in the wake of Distel's huge success, and her ultra-cool take on the Little Willie John/Peggy Lee hit, 'Fever', was likewise left unwanted on the shelf. Distel's smash also prompted a wonderful parody by Bourvil, 'Salade de fruits', which became an even bigger hit.[322] Nothing, though, could detract from his sudden and unprecedented success. Out of nowhere, almost without trying, France had finally found its first real teen idol.

A follow-up in the early summer of 1959 generated another couple of hits. Distel's rendition of Don Gibson's 'Oh Lonesome Me' ('Oh! Quelle nuit') muscled both Danyel Gérard's rock'n'roll reading and Annie Cordy's jazzier interpretation out of the way, and inspired a further unnecessary cover by the

underwhelming Jean-Paul Mauric. The EP also contained a finger-snapping rendition of Doris Day's 'Everybody Loves A Lover' ('Dis! O dis!'), but it was the poppier material that hogged the airwaves. By the summer, Distel's face was to be found staring out across the country from countless magazine covers. Teenage girls covered their walls with his picture and record racks groaned under the weight of further covers of 'Oh! Quelle nuit', with Henri Salvador hamming it up, Jean-Louis Tristan smoothing it out, and Pierre Cavalli imbuing it with the same guitar wizardry

---

[321] Alma had earlier cut a superb take on W.C. Handy's 'St. Louis Blues' ('Mon âme pleure').

[322] In an early example of inspired marketing, Pathé released six versions of the song on the same day – by Mathé Altéry, Bourvil, Annie Cordy, Georges Jouvin, Luis Mariano and Franck Pourcel, all in different styles – effectively preventing any other company from muscling in on the action. Cordy's version was the first to catch on, but it was Bourvil's interpretation that became a French pop classic.

as he displayed on a cover of Duane Eddy's 'Rebel Rouser'.

Although Distel was not really a rock'n'roll singer, and never really wanted to be, his success represented a triumph for youth in the world of pop. With Dalar and Gérard out of action, Piron sulking in Spain and Anthony struggling to get his act together, the way was clear for Distel to ride to the top with a smoother, family-friendly sound. Nevertheless, while girls were happy to scream whenever he took to the stage, out on the streets the *blousons noirs* were less impressed.

### Brenda Lee and Elvis Presley

With live rock'n'roll still something of a rarity, France's next jolt of modernity came when Gilbert Bécaud introduced the country to fourteen-year-old Brenda Lee, who opened the show at his concerts at the Olympia Theatre in February and March 1959, winning the affection of audiences for her decidedly raunchy music. Lee's records had already been plundered by the rampant cover version industry, and her extreme youth meant that her presence in the country was brief, though the teenage dynamo more than held her own against Bécaud, highlighting once again the gap that existed between the French music hall take on rock'n'roll and the real thing.

Across the Alps, things were further advanced, and in May Parisian audiences were treated to an explosive performance by Italian rock'n'roll star Little Tony, shortly before rumours began circulating that the King himself, Elvis Presley (then undertaking his military service in West Germany) was on his way to Paris. This turned out to be true, and Presley did indeed take a short break in the French capital in June, hanging out with the Kessler Sisters[323] and the Paris-based American singer Nancy Holloway. He also took in a live performance by Line Renaud, jamming with the French star after the show. Sadly, this turned out to be the extent of his involvement with the country of *la chanson*, although he would return for a further brief visit in early 1960. Instead, French youth continued to survive on a diet of home-grown adaptations, unless they were lucky enough to find a store stocking the American recordings now being issued in France on EPs and LPs in increasing numbers.

### Radio-friendly rock'n'roll

Although real rock'n'roll was becoming easier to find for those who knew what to look for, radio continued to favour French-language recordings over foreign ones – the newly born *Salut les copains* programme being an honourable exception. This gave the comedy duo Armoir et Pari an opportunity to lay down a worthwhile cover of the Gladiolas/Diamonds hit, 'Little Darlin' ' ('Little darling'[324]), while Luis Mariano finally found a rock'n'roll number he could handle, the Big Bopper's 'Chantilly Lace' ('Ma p'tite chérie').[325]

---

[323] Who had just released the big band thump of 'N'y allez pas par quatre chemins' and the superb piano-tinkling boogie-woogie, 'Teenagers blues'.

[324] Also available in a shockingly poor recording by Francis Linel.

[325] Being a comedy record in the first place, it was easier to take than his earlier manglings of Nat 'King' Cole's 'When Rock And Roll Came To Trinidad' ('Escapade à la Trinidad') and Jackie Wilson's 'To Be Loved' ('Quelqu'un que j'aime').

In a similar vein, vocal group Les Chantecler turned out a mundane reading of the popular 'Passion Flower' ('Tout l'amour'), but their old-fashioned approach worked better on their cover of the Paul Anka/Andy Rose hit, 'Just Young' ('Les gosses'). Though this lacked Anka's *joie de vivre*, it was considerably more effective than Francis Linel's attempt to stay hip, 'Des gosses'.

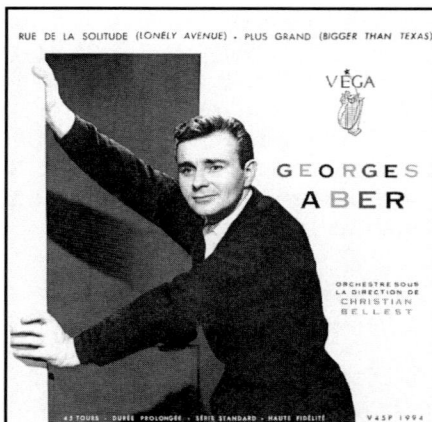

Despite some impressive earlier attempts at rock'n'roll, bandleader and western music enthusiast Marc Taynor completely missed the target with his mangled cover of 'Witch Doctor', but redeemed himself with a superb version of Wilbert Harrison's 'Kansas City'. He reverted to country music with a decent instrumental take on Johnny Horton's 'The Battle Of New Orleans' bizarrely retitled 'La bataille de Waterloo', though it's doubtful that many French listeners would have wanted reminding about their country's legendary military defeat.

Georges Aber did rather better, making a few waves with a well-executed adaptation of Ray Charles's 'Lonely Avenue' ('Rue de la solitude') that sat on an EP alongside covers of two Claude Piron flops, 'Mon cœur bat' and 'Plus grand', the former co-written with Aber. Although older than Piron, and thus less credible as a rock'n'roller, Aber was perfectly at home with the bluesier sound of Ray Charles, and the record was successful enough to warrant a follow-up. This included the easy listening offering, 'Je sais' (Perry Como's 'I Know') and the jazz/gospel standard, 'Down By The Riverside' ('Qu'il fait bon vivre'[326]), with only a big band arrangement of Bobby Darin's 'Dream Lover' ('J'ai rêvé') asserting his commitment to rock'n'roll.

Belgian singer Milou Duchamp was far more interesting. With backings provided by Claude Bolling, he laid down a magnificent EP in 1959 which encompassed the rollicking 'Quand tu m'embrasses' and 'Je t'ai tellement dans la peau', the country-tinged rocker 'Petit poisson', and the creepy 'Tropical' (an uncredited rip-off of Screamin' Jay Hawkins's 'Alligator Wine' that managed to be simultaneously frightening and sensual). With a vocal style verging on the rockabilly yelps common across the Atlantic (dementedly so in the case of 'Tropical'), it was the best rock'n'roll

---

[326] This was buried by a typically forthright and very popular version from Les Compagnons de la Chanson.

**MARIA CANDIDO**

Haute Fidelité
20 909
45 Medium E P
Polydor

11

LA CHANSON D'ORFEU

VENUS

LE PONT DE L'AMOUR

MES FRÈRES

recorded in either France or Belgium to date. Unfortunately, Duchamp looked more like a wine waiter at some posh restaurant than a rock'n'roll singer, and the record flopped. His 1960 LP, *Aïe Aïe Aïe Milou!*, offered further credible slices of rock'n'roll in 'Aïe! Aïe! Aïe!' and 'Hurrah et alléluia' alongside some jazzier material, but once again sales fell short of expectations.

Instead, the next big rock'n'roll hit in France once again came from overseas in the form of Frankie Avalon's 'Venus', a US chart-topper in the summer of 1959. Being watered down to begin with, this was easy meat for the music hall crowd, and covers (adapted into French as 'Vénus') quickly surfaced from Maria Candido, Gloria Lasso, Luis Mariano and (in English) the Allegrettes.[327] All of them, incredibly, were even weaker than the already insipid original, with the Allegrettes failing to maintain their usual high standard, and Candido's and Mariano's polished renditions highlighting the limitations of their show-business representation of rock'n'roll.

Even worse was Francis Linel's attempt, which was sent to market packaged with equally dire versions of Jimmie Rodgers' 'Bimbombey' and Reg Owen's 'Manhattan Spiritual' ('Mes frères').[328] Talented newcomer Babette Bruneau cut worthwhile covers of 'Bimbombey',[329] 'Vénus' and the Platters' 'Smoke Gets In Your Eyes' ('Fumée aux yeux'), but, buried on the tiny GEM label, her emotive performances failed to translate into hits.

### A home-grown rock'n'roll hit

Once the hoopla surrounding Frankie Avalon died down, the next French rock'n'roll hit turned out to be not a cover, but an original tune which surfaced via the 1959 *Coq d'Or de la chanson française* song contest. Performed on the festival's commemorative multi-artist EP by struggling *chansonnier* Hugues Aufray, 'Écoute mon cœur' was a stripped-back finger-snapper that exploded into life on the breaks with punchy horn arrangements and a Scotty Moore-like guitar line that lifted it skyward, marking another step along the road to a decent French rock'n'roll sound. With Aufray a virtual unknown, the song was picked up and watered down by Jean-Louis Tristan and given an instrumental overhaul by Trumpet Boy, while vocal outfit Les Quatre de Paris gave it a French-style doo-wop treatment that was as interesting and enjoyable as it sounds.[330] Besides Aufray's original, the best version was by

---

[327] Among the also-rans were versions by Gil Bernard, Jean-Paul Mauric, Les Compagnons de la Chanson, jazz outfit Richard Bennett et ses Dixie Cats, trumpeter Pierre Sellin and Belgium's Les Chakachas.

[328] 'Mes frères' was also covered in a tedious interpretation by Paul Péri, but both rightly lost out to a version from the ever-effervescent Dalida.

[329] As 'Bim bom bey'.

[330] They gave the same treatment to the not-quite-as-impressive 'Je ne vous le dirai pas'.

Les Chantecler, who surrounded it with covers of Paul Anka's 'Pity, Pity' ('Y'a pas d'question') and Ricky Nelson's 'Lonesome Town' ('Rue des cœurs perdus') on an EP that should have established them as the country's premier rock'n'roll vocal group, but didn't. Or rather, it did, but there wasn't much competition and nobody was really paying attention.

As the summer of 1959 turned into autumn, the growing popularity of rock'n'roll – or, at least, of rock'n'roll-styled songs – brought out a lemmings' rush of singers and musicians trying to grab a piece of the pie. Jazz guitarist André Pyair treated the music as just another dance rhythm, surrounding it with such rubbish as 'When you chachacha' on an EP aimed squarely at dancers. Nevertheless, the instrumental 'Destination lune!' was an excellent slab of guitar-led rock'n'roll and one of the best records of that style yet laid down in a French studio.

Having already issued half a dozen records teaching listeners how to do the latest moves, for his seventh release dance instructor René Vrany turned his attention to rock'n'roll, pompously describing the dance steps on Side One and laying down some music to practise to on the flip, where the very acceptable 'Rock à la carte' could unexpectedly be found lurking. It's debatable how many buyers chose to heed the good professor's instruction.

The ever-impressive Allegrettes took things down soft and low with strong covers of the Crests' 'Sixteen Candles', the Platters' 'Smoke Gets In Your Eyes' and the Teddy Bears' 'To Know Him, Is To Love Him',[331] before picking up the tempo for an enjoyable and worthwhile attempt at the Coasters' 'Charlie Brown', and an even better reading of the Impalas' 'Sorry (I Ran All The Way Home)'.

Letting the side down somewhat, Francis Linel turned in a different adaptation of the Teddy Bears' classic ('Les beaux jours de nos amours'), while veteran Henri Génès turned the clock back several years with a dreadful attempt to poke fun at the music ('Mes chaussures prennent l'eau'). However, Eddie Constantine's low-key shuffle, 'C'est à peine croyable', showed that the collision between music hall and rock'n'roll didn't have to be disastrous. As 1959 wound down, a final slice of comic rock came and went in the shape of André Fandrel's unamusing 'Mademoiselle Rock and Roll', which at least carried a big beat to drive its now-behind-the-game instrumentation.

Making a final stand in favour of big band rock'n'roll, jazz singer Caterine Caps strolled her way through a superb interpretation of Peggy Lee's 'Alright, Okay, You Win' ('D'accord, okay, tu gagnes')[332] before duly returning to

---

[331] For which they procured a female vocalist, lending credence to the suggestion that they were session musicians, rather than a real group.

[332] Her bid for glory was immediately transformed into routine jazz mulch on a version by trumpeter Pierre Sellin.

whence she came. French youth might not have been clear about exactly what it wanted, musically speaking, but it was clear about one thing: it wanted singers who were new, young and fresh.

Perhaps sensing that his time had come, Claude Piron slipped back across the Pyrenees in the autumn to try his hand at further rock'n'roll material. The result was a fourth EP featuring the vibrant 'Rock et guitare', which tapped the gospel-tinged sound brought to prominence by Ray Charles, a reworking of Louis Prima's 'Sing, Sing, Sing', and an impressive adaptation of the Teddy Bears' 'Oh Why' ('Mon amour oublié'). While not as exciting as the best records by the Allegrettes, it was still a step forward from his last release, but once again he failed to reap the reward that was rightly his. 'Mon amour oublié' was nevertheless picked up for a jazz band arrangement by bandleader Billy Nash, as well as by vocal group Les Chantecler in a version closer in spirit to the original, while Rose Mania turned her attention to 'Sing, Sing, Sing' on an EP that did absolutely nothing for her career.

## The first teen idols

Rose Mania also had a flutter at Petula Clark's UK hit, 'Baby Lover' ('Mon cœur danse avec la chance'[333]), but any airplay this might have garnered was forestalled by Clark's decision to cut the tune herself for the French market, blowing Mania's version out of the water. Like Dalida, Clark was one of the few show-business veterans with the ability to mix it in the world of rock'n'roll, even if her recordings always carried more polish and featured clearer enunciation than the average rock'n'roll hit.

While her 1959 UK album, *Petula Clark in Hollywood*, was largely given over to hoary pop standards like 'Too Darn Hot',[334] her French releases offered a more contemporary feel, ranging from the emerging girl group sound of Terri Stevens' 'Adonis' to the doo-wop of 'Ne joue pas' (Linda Leigh's 'What Good Does It Do Me') to the rockaballad 'Dear Daddy' (cut in English and issued on both sides of the Channel). Best of all was 'Prends mon cœur', her swaying take on Elvis

---

[333] As did Jean-Paul Mauric.
[334] First sung in 1948 by Lorenzo Fuller in the stage version of Cole Porter's *Kiss Me, Kate*.

Presley's revival of the old Hank Snow/ Jo Stafford/Tommy Edwards hit, '(Now And Then There's) A Fool Such As I', which, if it lacked the swagger of the King, carried enough easy-rolling charm to outsell Presley[335] and establish Clark alongside Dalida as one of top female performers in French teenage pop.

Despite her fine sense of rhythm, Dalida had as yet made few concessions to rock'n'roll, notwithstanding covers of such hits as 'Passion Flower' ('Tout l'amour') and 'Manhattan Spiritual' ('Mes frères'). Taken as a whole, her 1959 releases exhibited less inventiveness than she had shown during her first two years of glory, as she continued dabbling in exotica even as the wave went out. She did make a decent fist of 'Ne joue pas', but it was only at the end of the year that she took the plunge with an EP containing a further tilt at Clark's market with a version of 'Adonis', as well as a decent cover of Sarah Vaughan's 'Broken-Hearted Melody' ('Mélodie pour un amour'). However, the biggest hit on the EP turned out to be a lightly rocking rendition of Bobby Darin's 'Dream Lover' ('J'ai rêvé') that blew away all competition[336] and soared up the French hit parade, ensuring that she ended the decade as the reigning queen of pop.

As far as French teenagers were concerned, the only choice for king was Sacha Distel. In late 1959, he released his most rock'n'roll-oriented recordings yet, picking up another hit with a cover of Lloyd Price's '(You've Got) Personality' ('Personnalités (Elle a le... Elle a la... Elle a les...)'), despite failing to get anywhere near the relaxed swagger of the original.[337] Indeed, Distel came closer in feel and style to the British version recorded about the same time by Anthony Newley, but in the absence of anything stronger (the luckless Piron and the mysterious Allegrettes aside), he was fêted as the real deal by a teenage audience starved for an idol of their own. While he demonstrated his commitment to the softer end of the rock'n'roll spectrum with a version of Carl Dobkins Jr.'s 'My Heart Is An Open Book' ('Allez! Va!'), the inclusion of a swinging take on Horace Silver's 'The Preacher' ('Drôle de rêve') was a better indication of where his heart lay. But even as Distel's 'Personalités' sallied forth over the airwaves, the storm clouds of change were gathering on the horizon.

Displaying greater commitment to the rock'n'roll cause, the Allegrettes turned in a punchier interpretation of 'Personality' on their next EP, alongside a seemingly effortless version of Freddy Cannon's 'Tallahassee Lassie' that proved once again that they were the best rock'n'roll combo in the land, even

---

[335] A jazz instrumental version by Billy Nash offered little competition.

[336] Including a tougher arrangement by Georges Aber and a weedy cover by the fast-sinking Francis Linel.

[337] Annie Cordy also cut a version which, while inferior, was nevertheless enjoyable and amusing.

if they couldn't quite match the explosive Mr. Cannon. They closed out the year bouncing rhythmically through the Everly Brothers' 'Bird Dog' and getting down and dirty on the Ray Anthony/Duane Eddy hit, 'Peter Gunn'.

With the jazzers having written off rock'n'roll as a failed experiment, Sacha Distel unwilling to commit fully to it, Henri Salvador reluctant to go any further than an easy listening arrangement of the Fleetwoods' 'Come Softly To Me' ('Tout doux, tout doucement'), Danyel Gérard and Gabriel Dalar out of the way and Claude Piron struggling to find the right material, it had initially looked very much like the country's moral guardians had been proved correct and that rock'n'roll had fizzled out in France before it had even taken off. By the autumn of 1959, however, it was clear that the market was ready to move on, with Elvis Presley, Paul Anka, Frankie Avalon and the Platters all enjoying solid sales. It seemed that it would only take one big hit to light the touch-paper and trigger the explosion. As the year drew to a close, that hit duly arrived, courtesy of the one young contender still in the field: Richard Anthony.

### The breakthrough

Still pursuing the breakthrough that had so far eluded him, Anthony also opted to cover 'Personality', but sang it in English to differentiate himself from the more successful Distel. However, he knew that, to reach the hearts of teenage girls, he needed to sing something in French. He seized upon the Everly Brothers' 'Poor Jenny', rewriting it as 'Pauv' Jenny', and also cut a superb bilingual cover of Bobby Darin's 'Dream Lover' ('J'ai rêvé'). To complete the EP, he knocked off a version of the Coasters' 'Three Cool Cats'[338] titled 'Nouvelle vague'.

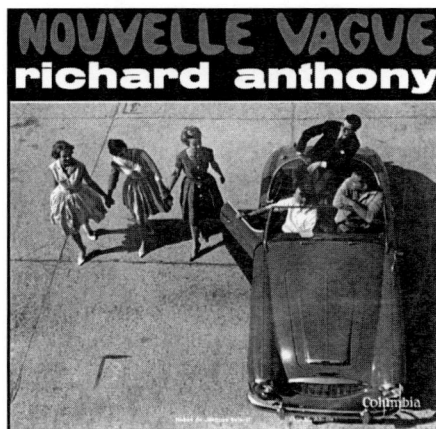

Taking its name from the successful revolution in French film, the song referenced the 'new wave' in teenage fashion, music and culture that was engulfing the world – even in France, where rock'n'roll had still not fully taken off. The lyric's sentiment chimed perfectly with the concerns of its intended teenage audience, and, while the musical backing suffered from the

---

[338] Anthony claimed he'd never heard the Coasters' original (which was on the flip of 'Charlie Brown'), but that he came across the song on a publisher's demo.

189

overtly jazzy sensibilities of the musicians involved, it carried enough of a rock'n'roll kick to make it worth spinning on the jukebox. As the clock ticked down to 1960 and Dalida's version of 'J'ai rêvé' headed up the charts, 'Nouvelle vague' quietly slipped into the listings behind her. Within a few weeks, teenagers across the country were singing it, as the roly-poly Anthony succeeded in becoming what he had set out to be: the country's first truly successful rock'n'roll singer.

A second run of shows by Paul Anka in November 1959 confirmed that the new music was no passing fad and rock'n'roll was now firmly a part of the French musical landscape. With sales of Elvis Presley records on the increase, Richard Anthony vying for Sacha Distel's crown, and the arrival of Gene Vincent in Paris for a sell-out show, as the year drew to a close it became crystal-clear that it was *this*, rather than watered-down music hall rock'n'roll, that teenagers wanted to hear.

# Chapter 12

## UNE BOUM CHEZ JOHN
### The first rock'n'roll stars (1960-61)

*During the late fifties and early sixties, rock'n'roll music took over the music industry of every country in the Western world. It took hold of the teenage audience and rapidly came to be a dominating force in their lives, even if, as Ready, Steady, Go's Cathy McGowan once pointed out, many teenagers were actually more interested in the clothes they wore than the music they listened to – and nowhere would the idea of music as fashion be more assiduously adopted than in France. Yet, even as rock'n'roll was becoming a world force, the quest had already begun to identify its spiritual home: the place from which the music seemed to have begun its journey.*

*In France, as in America, rock'n'roll had many roots, with the jazz clubs of Saint-Germain-des-Prés high up the list of potential starting points. However, neither these, nor the music halls where Claude Piron first whipped up a crowd, nor the EMI studios where Richard Anthony cut the first real French rock'n'roll hit seemed hip enough to be celebrated as the hallowed birthplace of French rock'n'roll. That honour goes to a one-time Parisian tea room on Rue Drouot, situated above the Café d'Angleterre.[339]*

### The Golf Drouot

Converted in the early fifties into a minigolf centre called the Golf Drouot, the place had been a loss-maker from the start, and toward the end of the decade manager Henri Leproux set about converting it into a club for teenagers. Looking to build up an atmosphere, he installed a jukebox, removed most of the jazz and music hall records from the selection and replaced them with rock'n'roll – the genuine article. With a generous selection of tunes by Elvis Presley, Gene Vincent, the Platters, Paul Anka and other American singers whose records had been released in France, he soon found himself with a thriving club and a large clientele who came back repeatedly to listen to their favourite tunes.

Among them was a tight-knit group of local boys who lived and breathed rock'n'roll, including Jean-Philippe Smet, Christian Blondieau and Jacques Dutronc, all of whom would soon become rock'n'roll performers themselves. Occasionally rubbing shoulders with them were a bequiffed bank worker named Claude Moine and the less imposing Daniel Deshayes, who would go on to lead two of the groups that dominated the first wave of French

---

[339] In a depressing sign of the times, the café is now a McDonalds.

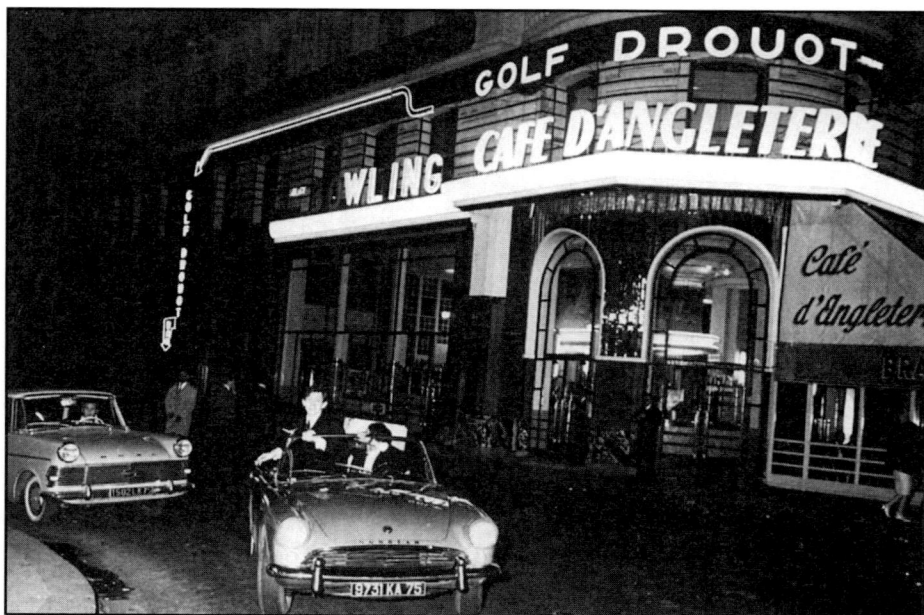

rock'n'roll,[340] as well as countless other budding singers and musicians.

Although rock'n'roll quickly became the club's *raison d'être*, the minigolf course that gave the place its name remained until 1962, when it was finally removed to make way for a stage that would transform it into a live music venue and bring even more teenagers flocking to its doors. By then, the musical landscape of the country had been totally transformed by the activities of the club's regulars, starting with Jean-Philippe Smet.

## Johnny Hallyday

Raised in show business by an aunt after being abandoned by his parents, Smet had spent his childhood travelling around Europe as his two cousins, Menen and Desta Mar, kept the family in food and clothing by dancing on the music hall circuit. Resident for a time in London, the family teamed up with an American dancer, Lee Hallyday, who married Desta and subsequently replaced Menen in the family act. Hallyday greatly impressed young Jean-Philippe, filling his head with tales of cowboys and open plains, instilling in him a lifelong love of all things American. As soon as he was old enough, he learned to play guitar and joined the show, singing the songs of Georges Brassens and others to unappreciative audiences.

When Smet reached his teens, his aunt took the act off the road and settled in Paris to give the boy a chance to get an education, but after a life spent travelling he had no interest in school, preferring to idle away his time in front of the screen at the local cinema. One day in late 1957 or early 1958, he chanced upon Elvis Presley bellowing out 'Party' in *Amour frénétique* (*Loving You*) and instantly fell in love with rock'n'roll.

---

[340] See next chapter.

For the next two years, he and his friends devoured American rock'n'roll wherever they could find it. British efforts were dismissed as a joke until the first records by Cliff Richard crossed the Channel. These demonstrated that, not only was it possible for non-Americans to sing rock'n'roll, but even (in the case of 'Move It' and 'Dynamite') for them to do it as well as the Americans. Richard Anthony's limp cover of 'Move It' ('Chanson magique') showed how far off the mark French artists were at the time, but with the cultural influence of Lee Hallyday behind him and years of experience watching all kinds of entertainers from the side of the stage, Smet was convinced that he could teach the French how to rock. Together with his friends, he began building up a repertoire, singing the hits of Presley and others – in markedly accented English, it has to be said – while accompanying himself on guitar.

When not working on his act, he hung out at the Golf Drouot, swapping ideas with his friends until, in late 1959, a family connection landed him a spot on a radio show, *Paris-Cocktail*. Unremarked by most of the population, the sixteen-year-old (who had recently taken to calling himself 'Johnny Hallyday' in a vain effort to convince listeners that he was American) delivered a ragged version of Presley's 'Party' that proved spirited enough to catch the ear of jobbing songwriters Jil et Jan.[341] The pair alerted the powers-that-be at the Vogue label, who summoned the young singer for an audition in early 1960. Impressing the A&R team with his youth, energy and enthusiasm, Hallyday was duly signed to the label and set about recording his debut EP.

After a furious argument with Christian Blondieau over his decision to record in French rather than English, Hallyday settled on three original songs, 'Laisse les filles', 'J'etais fou' and 'Oh! Oh! Baby',[342] plus a cover of Floyd Robinson's 'Makin' Love' ('T'aimer follement'), which had just entered the hit parade in a not-very-rock'n'roll version by Dalida. Selected as the lead track, the song didn't really rock, even in Hallyday's arrangement, and the backing by session players was decidedly stilted, but his enthusiasm came over well and he delivered the requisite vocal hiccups in a more authentic manner than either Richard Anthony or Sacha Distel. On the other tracks, he made a convincing case for himself as the first truly authentic rock'n'roller in the country, especially on 'Laisse les filles', which popped and crackled with all the fire that could be generated by his largely unsympathetic backing group.

---

[341] Gilbert 'Jil' Guenet and Jean 'Jan' Setti, responsible for such well-known compositions as Maurice Chevalier's 'Le jardinier de Paname', Colette Renard's 'Mon homme est un guignol' and André Claveau's 'Quand les années viendront'.

[342] In the event, Hallyday did sing one of them ('Oh! Oh! Baby') in English, perhaps to placate Blondieau.

The disc was added to the jukebox at the Golf Drouot with much ceremony and everyone sat back and waited for it to take off. Unfortunately for Hallyday, Lucien Morisse, the head of radio station Europe No. 1, showed little interest and declined to play it — a decision that clearly had more to do with supporting his fiancée Dalida than with the relative merits of the two singers' interpretations of the song. Other stations were more receptive, however, and Hallyday's version occasionally joined Dalida's on the airwaves, though sales fell away quickly once his friends in Paris had all bought a copy.

A month later, with his record heading for the deletion racks, Hallyday was offered the chance of a lifetime when he was booked to appear on the 18 April edition of *À l'école des vedettes*, a TV show in which an established star (in this case, Line Renaud) introduced a new performer to the French public. He seized his chance, turning in a fired-up rendition of 'Laisse les filles', complete with stage movements cribbed from Elvis Presley. Across town at the Golf Drouot, Henri Leproux installed a TV set for everyone to watch his performance, while in homes across France,[343] teenagers experienced for the first time the whirlwind that was Johnny Hallyday. Swinging his hips, thrashing hell out of his guitar and falling to his knees as his guitarist ripped into the solo, Hallyday was a revelation to those who had never seen Presley or Gene Vincent in action. While his antics were no more outrageous than those of Gilbert Bécaud seven years earlier, harnessed to the cause of rock'n'roll they were a call to arms across the land.

Despite some negative reviews, the impact was immediate and sales soared in the weeks that followed. Within a few months, Hallyday's EP had shifted over 200,000 copies – a huge number for the time – and he was being touted as the French answer to Elvis Presley. His strategy of singing in French had paid off, and he was well on his way to becoming a phenomenon. In his wake, other members of the Golf Drouot fraternity began fishing around for record deals of their own.

Hallyday's commercial success was also recognised by the French record industry in the now-traditional way: with a plethora of cover versions of 'T'aimer follement'. Ballad singer Jacques Danny and jazzman Guy Lafitte did little to persuade anyone that either of them had a future in rock'n'roll, while vocal quartet Les Riff turned out a bland rendition that likewise did nobody any favours. More enjoyable was the bouncy reading by Bob Azzam, who with consummate ease turned the song into the same silly party music as the rest of his repertoire. None of these held a candle to Hallyday's version[344] and few teenagers were fooled into buying them, marking another clear turning point in French pop. Traditionally it had been the *song* that was important, and music buyers could pick and choose from any number of different recordings; henceforward, the *performer* would matter as much as the song, and fans would rush out to buy their latest release, refusing to accept any substitutes.[345] It would take record companies time to respond to the change, resulting in some major chart battles over the next few years, but gradually the idea caught on and artists began to develop more exclusive repertoires.

### Hallyday's rivals

Johnny Hallyday's rapid rise was a genuine tale of overnight success, neatly bypassing the years of slogging it out on the provincial circuit in front of unsympathetic audiences, as music hall stars had had to do since time immemorial. For him, the rise to the top came before he had set foot on a stage – at least, in his new guise as a rock'n'roller. His show-business family background is often seized upon by Anglo-American critics as proof that Hallyday was not a true rock'n'roller, and that he had merely adjusted his style to suit the times, passing himself off as the real thing when he was in fact a

---

[343] At least, in those few homes which had television sets.

[344] Or Dalida's, for that matter.

[345] Actually, this change probably began with Dalida, whose record sales tended to dwarf those of any rival recordings of her songs, although Hallyday's arrival certainly accentuated it, establishing the way in which the industry would have to function in future.

traditional variety performer. While some credence is lent to this argument by the fact that he went on to record a large number of ballads, one listen to the man at his rocking best is sufficient to dispel all doubt and make the case for Hallyday as the embodiment of French rock'n'roll that record companies had been seeking since the days of Henri Salvador and Mac-Kac. Moreover, the massive sales enjoyed by his debut release demonstrated that French teenagers had no qualms whatsoever about accepting him as their very own rock'n'roll star.

The same could not be said for his main rival, Richard Anthony, who had shot to fame as a rocker and would always profess his love for rock'n'roll, but wanted to be 'more than just a rock'n'roll singer'. He made the mistake of following up 'Nouvelle vague' with the gospel-styled 'Jéricho' (adapted from Louis Armstrong's version of the spiritual, 'Joshua Fit' De Battle'), which achieved nowhere near the success of his breakthrough hit and allowed him to be outflanked by his younger and more dynamic rival. Anthony's love of jazz was genuine, as was evidenced by the inclusion on the EP of an original composition from Claude Nougaro, 'Au fond de mon cœur', and a pleasant adaptation of Sarah Vaughan's 'Broken-Hearted Melody' ('Mélodie pour un amour'). However, such a display of versatility was like a red rag to the rock'n'roll community, who immediately harangued him for selling out. Caught out as much as everyone else by Hallyday's explosive debut, Anthony ignored the criticism and returned to rock'n'roll over the summer of 1960 with a cover of Bobby Darin's 'Clementine' ('Clémentine'), a poppy run through Lance Fortune's 'Be Mine' ('Je suis content... je chante') and an attempt at Marv Johnson's 'You Got What It Takes' in English, but by then he was already playing catch-up in the battle for the affection of teenage girls.

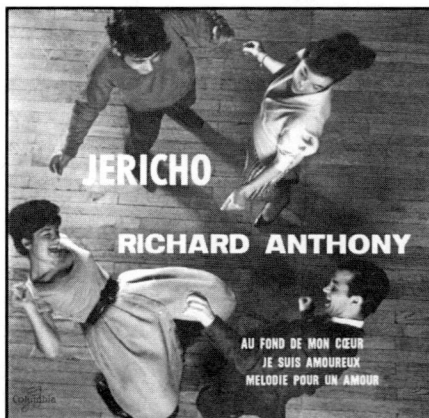

Claude Piron, still brooding on the sidelines, should have been able to take advantage of the Hallyday–Anthony one-two punch to establish himself as the country's third rock'n'roll star, but again squandered the opportunity by watering down his approach for the disappointing 'Carina' and pursuing the exotic sounds of Italian pop two years too late with a cover of Renato Rascel's 'Il mondo cambia' ('Le monde change'), failing to comprehend that the world had changed in the meantime. He tried again later in the year with covers of Neil Sedaka's 'Oh! Carol' and Line Renaud's 'Tilt', easily outclassing the latter in the rock'n'roll stakes, though his performance on Sedaka's hit was woefully poor, even given Sedaka's own limitations as a rocker. Quite simply, the record failed to present Piron at his best and he slunk away to lick his wounds.

Hallyday, meanwhile, was finding his feet as a live performer on a countrywide concert tour, opening for Sacha Distel. Despite losing some of his fans to the newcomer, Distel remained a major force in French pop, racking up rock-lite hits in 1960 'Mon beau chapeau'[346] and a cover of Buzz Clifford's 'Baby Sittin' Boogie' ('Le boogie du bébé'). Distel's and Hallyday's fan bases overlapped considerably at the time and their joint tour was a success, both commercially and artistically, with Distel happily advising the youngster on ways to improve his stage technique.

Gradually though, he realised that Hallyday's arrival made his continued tenure as a teen idol unlikely, and he began to widen his repertoire to include adult fare like 'Les célibataires' (a revival of Frank Sinatra's 'Hey! Jealous Lover'), 'C'est tout, c'est tout' (an adaptation of the standard 'That's All'[347]), and his 1961 hit, 'Bye bye baby' (a revival of Gene Austin's 1926 smash, 'Bye Bye Blackbird') in a successful effort to become an 'all-round entertainer'. This led to an attempt to secure an overseas audience with an English-language LP, *Everybody Loves The Lover*, consisting mostly of standards like 'I Can't Give You Anything But Love' and 'I'm In The Mood For Love'.[348] While the album failed to set the US charts alight, it provided Distel with the material to launch himself onto the international cabaret circuit. After enjoying a hit with a cover of the Don Gibson/Ray Charles country classic 'I Can't Stop Loving You' ('C'était plus fort que tout') in 1962, he was ready to bow out of the teen pop stakes. As the pop hits dried up, he moved sideways into a new career in television, all the while continuing to sell large quantities of records to the mothers and older sisters of the girls who were busy decorating their walls with photographs and posters of Anthony and Hallyday.

Hallyday's ascendancy became even more evident when he returned from tour to cut a follow-up to his breakthrough hit. Issued in June 1960, 'Souvenirs, souvenirs' (adapted from an obscure Barbara Evans recording called 'Souvenirs'[349]) was a massive step forward in terms of sound, style and energy, humming with excitement from the opening bars of the infectious

---

[346] A jazzy original blatantly modelled on Jesse Stone's 'Idaho', most probably cut with the 1959 revival by Dakota Staton in mind.
[347] Recently covered by both Bobby Darin and Ricky Nelson.
[348] Originally hits for Cliff Edwards and Little Jack Little respectively.
[349] Although Hallyday acquired it via a German cover by Bill Ramsey.

guitar riff that ran throughout the song. Superbly played by guitarist Léo Petit (one of the few French musicians to exactly capture the rock'n'roll feel), the distinctive opening notes etched themselves straight into the brain, making cover versions redundant.[350]

The rest of the EP was equally up to the mark, catering to Hallyday's female fans with the teen ballad 'Pourquoi cet amour', seeing him flex his rock'n'roll muscles on the punchy 'Je cherche une fille', and daring to take on the King himself with a cover of 'I Got Stung' ('J'suis mordu') that failed to match the majesty of the original. Unsurprisingly, Hallyday found himself with a second four-sided smash on his hands and 'Souvenirs, souvenirs' dominated the airwaves on *Salut les copains* for the remainder of the year. It was the first of many Johnny Hallyday songs to become a classic of French rock'n'roll.

---

[350] Not that this prevented the Kessler Sisters from attempting to muscle in on the action in high-kicking Las Vegas style.

## Hallyday versus Anthony

With two rock'n'roll stars on their hands, the French press went to work pitting Hallyday and Anthony against one another, painting the polite, well-groomed Anthony as the 'nice' rock'n'roller and the wilder, raunchier Hallyday as the 'bad boy'. The pair played into their hands in the autumn of 1960, when they made their respective debuts on the Paris stage, with Anthony turning in a restrained performance while Hallyday blew the headliner, comedian Raymond Devos, off stage every night during a three-week run at the Alhambra. The adults in the audience were affronted by the raunchy nature of his act and the ferocious power of his music, but in the balcony the gathering clans of teenage fans responded rapturously to their hero – a fact picked up on by the media, who immediately cast Hallyday as a rowdy *blouson noir* to be avoided at all costs. Naturally enough, their stance only increased his appeal to the kids.

On their next releases, Hallyday and Anthony went head to head, both turning out competent versions of the Everly Brothers' 'Cathy's Clown' ('Le p'tit clown de ton cœur') and Bryan Hyland's risible 'Itsy Bitsy Teenie Weenie Yellow Polka Dot Bikini' (mercifully truncated in French as 'Itsy bitsy petit bikini'). The latter was also cut by Dalida,[351] who was refusing to be elbowed out of the limelight and enjoyed continuing support from teenage fans for her efforts.

Attempting to derail the Hallyday express, Europe No. 1's Lucien Morisse gave his version a single spin on his popular radio show, *Le discobole*, and promptly destroyed the disc live on air, declaring to listeners that it was the last time they would hear Johnny Hallyday on the airwaves. Once again, Morisse was probably more motivated by a desire to promote his girlfriend Dalida's recording, than by a genuine dislike of Hallyday's. In any case, the ban didn't last long. All three versions of 'Bikini' became hits, as did the American original – a disproportionate amount of interest for a song that was little more than an annoying novelty in any language. Sales were split more or less evenly between the three French stars,[352] though it was hardly the best work of any of the parties involved.

Hallyday quickly redeemed himself with the kinetic 'Kili watch', a rocked-up tune that had its origins in the Boy Scouts' campfire favourite, 'Ging Gang Goolie'. His lively interpretation left both the original by Belgian group the Cousins and a horribly corny cover by Bob Azzam for dead, providing him with a massive hit as 1960 drew to a close.

---

[351]  Dalida's version, like Anthony's, bore the amended title 'Itsi bitsi, petit bikini'.

[352]  Other versions by Dario Moreno, the Kessler Sisters (who tackled both this and 'Le p'tit clown de ton cœur' in mundane end-of-the-pier arrangements) and a dire cha-cha reading by accordion supremo André Verchuren all proved less popular. Hallyday later dismissed his own version as 'rubbish' and said it was one of the few songs he regretted recording.

## The new contenders

The continued success of both Hallyday and Anthony convinced rival record companies of the need to produce a rock'n'roll star of their own. First out of the stalls were Pathé with François Lubiana, who had earlier attempted a career as a middle-of-the-road crooner, coming close to a hit in 1960 with the old-fashioned 'Notre petit caniche'. His career was relaunched in the spring of 1961, but, though his renditions of Ray Peterson's 'Corrina, Corrina'[353] and Ray Charles's 'Georgia On My Mind' ('Georgia') were worthwhile attempts, they didn't help him find his way into the charts.

Radio Luxembourg disc jockey Camillo Felgen found rather more success on Polydor when his German-language cover of the Teddy Bears' 'Oh Why' ('Sag warum') bizarrely became a major hit in France in 1961.[354] A largely spoken-word effort over a string-laden easy listening backing, the song was the worst kind of teen pap imaginable and owed its success to blanket coverage on the radio station where the singer worked. The rest of the EP comprised German retoolings of the likes of Henri Salvador's 'Le loup, la biche et le chevalier' ('Das kleine Märchen'), though these did not join 'Sag warum' in the hit parade. Felgen released further records in both French and German, and took third place for Luxembourg in the 1962 *Eurovision Song Contest* with the enjoyable if unremarkable 'Petit bonhomme', but despite more hits in West Germany, Canada and Belgium later in the decade, never again managed to replicate the magic that had sparked his unlikely smash.

The Bel-Air label tried to launch Dalida's brother, Bruno Gigliotti, to stardom under the name 'Orlando'. He made a few waves in 1961 with a vocal version of the Shadows' 'Apache' ('L'amour fait la loi') which sounded more like the exotica his sister had built her career on than anything resembling rock'n'roll,[355] but if his take on Gene Austin's 1928 classic, 'Ramona', owed anything to the recent version by Dutch

---

[353] Peterson's hit was in fact a revival of the 1956 R&B hit by Joe Turner, itself a revival of a 1928 country blues by Bo Chatman.

[354] The inspiration for the recording was most likely Dalida's French-language version (the far superior 'Mon amour oublié'), or possibly Claude Piron's earlier attempt.

[355] Though it was no worse than an atypically disappointing effort from the Allegrettes.

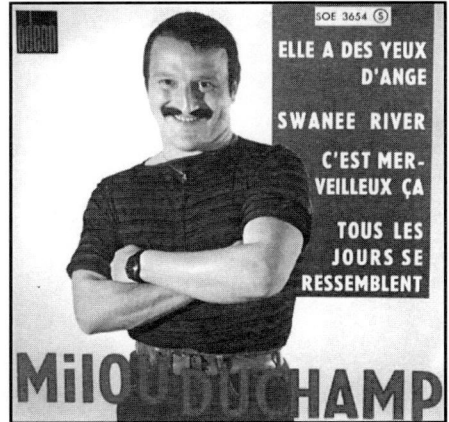

outfit the Blue Diamonds, the evidence was buried in an unsympathetic arrangement that swung rather than rocked. 'Elle a des yeux d'ange' (Johnny Tillotson's 'Poetry In Motion') was marginally better, but Orlando's Italian accent sounded less appealing than his sister's and his lightweight style made Richard Anthony look tough by comparison. His true musical leanings were betrayed by the inclusion of 'C'est si doux', a cover of Bobby Rydell's 'Sway', whose Latin tempo owed more to Dean Martin's 1954 version[356] than to the Philadelphia idol. Although the record was a minor hit, he was given a wide berth by the teenage market, who recognised a bandwagon-rider when they saw one.

Orlando never touched the heights reached by his sister – at least, not in France – despite record sales that were not far below those enjoyed by some of the French teen idols. Oddly enough, he became a big name in Czechoslovakia, with a string of hit records and a fan following to rival that of national pop stars like Karel Gott and Yvonne Přenosilová. As far as France was concerned, though, his cover of Del Shannon's 'Runaway' ('Mon amour disparu') didn't cut the mustard, and he subsequently abandoned his bid for teen stardom to pursue the adult market instead.

'Elle a des yeux d'ange' was given a more impressive treatment by Belgian rock'n'roll pioneer artist Milou Duchamp on an Odéon EP that also boasted a swinging revival of Stephen Foster's 'Swanee River', presumably inspired by Ray Charles's 'Swanee River Rock'. Sadly, this met with no more success than his earlier releases and marked the end of his dalliance with rock'n'roll.

The cute-looking Adamo was signed by Philips in Belgium, but, like many early contenders, he lacked the power and passion to cut it as a rock'n'roller. Inspired more by Charles Aznavour than by Elvis Presley, the Sicilian-born singer wrote his own material, and his early releases were sung in the language of his forefathers. Predictably, both the rock'n'roll-tinged ballad 'Perchè' and the Anka-like 'Cara bambina'[357] failed to sell in a country which has two official languages, neither of which is Italian. After switching

---

[356] Or even to Pablo Beltrán Ruiz's Mexican original, '¿Quién será?'.
[357] Released on Polydor (Philips passed after the first single).

**TU PARLES TROP** 451 099
STANDARD
ODILE
CLIN D'OEIL [DECCA]
FRANKIE JORDAN
OL'MAN RIVER

EDDIE VARTAN
BILLY AYERS

to English for the uptempo but weedy 'Poor fool', he made the sensible decision to move on to French for the big ballad 'Si j'osais' before abandoning rock'n'roll in favour of a more personal style closer to his true musical tastes.

Fifteen-year-old Belgian singer Little Benny was more impressive, although he lacked Adamo's staying power. He enjoyed a domestic hit with 'Petite amie', but an EP release on Festival failed to establish him in the wider French market and he quickly faded from view.

Jacky Delmone was more successful, his 1961 debut single, 'Toi que j'attends', establishing him as a teen idol in Belgium. Although he enjoyed further hits with 'Je n'en veux plus d'autre' and 'Reine d'amour' (an adaptation of Clark Richard's 'Queen Of Love'), the failure of his label, La Voix de son Maître, to promote his records outside the Low Countries drove him to break his contract and seek fresh pastures south of the border.

In France, the most successful of the new wave of rockers was Frankie Jordan, a singing pianist with a neat line in Fats Domino impressions and a love of the New Orleans branch of the rock'n'roll tree. Despite looking even less raunchy than Richard Anthony, he was snapped up by Decca, who launched him with a jolly retread of Joe Jones's 'You Talk Too Much' ('Tu parles trop'). The song was also covered by both Hallyday and Anthony, but Jordan's version was distinctive enough to score in its own right. It set him up for a run of modest hits over the next three years, many of which evinced a good feel for R&B, although the lightweight 'Clin d'œil' hinted at a pop sensibility closer in spirit to Anthony.[358]

**The first rock'n'roll festival**

Jordan joined both Anthony and Hallyday on the bill for the first *Festival de Rock 'n' Roll* staged in Paris at the Palais des Sports in February 1961 This was a cosmopolitan affair which included American singer Bobby Rydell UK hitmakers Emile Ford & The Checkmates and Italy's Little Tony alongside the three French stars, and the show's popularity illustrated how quickly rock'n'roll had taken hold in the wake of Hallyday's success. A rowdy audience largely made up of *blousons noirs* from the suburbs gave the unthreatening Anthony a hard time,[359] but in any event Hallyday stole the show, proving that he was as good as, or better than the more experienced performers from abroad. Aged just seventeen, he had the country's youth at his feet.

His label, Vogue, capitalised on this success by rushing product into the

---

[358] Who also recorded the song.
[359] He had been dropped from the original bill, but attended anyway and was pushed onstage, only to be manhandled off again, allegedly by Hallyday's associates.

stores, including a fake 'live' album, *Johnny Hallyday et ses fans au Festival de Rock n' Roll*, but by now it was apparent to the singer that his records lacked the tough sound of those by his American heroes. While he was able to whip up a storm on stage, his rough-and-tumble version of Little Richard's 'Tutti Frutti' revealed a group unable to replicate the power and drive of the original, and Hallyday started to lobby his record company to put more effort into the recording process. Rebuffed by managers who considered him to be a flash in the pan, he broke his contract and began shopping around for a new deal where his artistic ambitions might be better realised. Already the biggest rock'n'roller in the country, Hallyday was courted by all the leading labels, with the independent Barclay leading the chase, but in the meantime he went back out on the road, honing his act as the most exciting live performer France had ever seen.

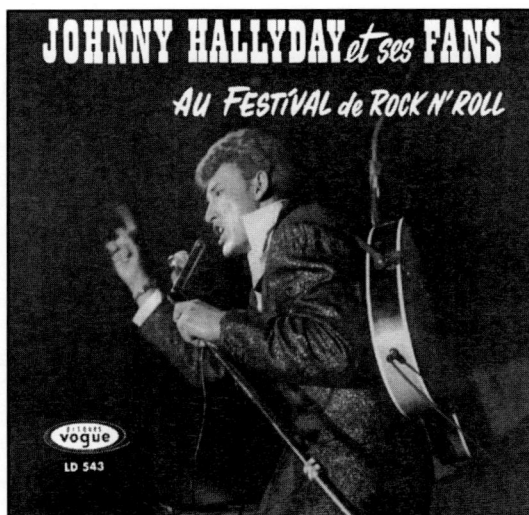

In the months following their joint festival appearance, the divergent paths of Anthony and Hallyday were made clear. While Anthony toured the country as opening act for Dalida, establishing himself as the 'family' rock'n'roller, Hallyday sparked riots across the country, earning himself the nickname *'Prince du tumulte'* – the Prince of Bedlam – for the regularity with which his fans reduced theatres and streets to rubble. On record too, this dichotomy was already being heard, as Anthony charted with covers of Brian Hyland's 'Four Little Heels' ('Cliqueti clac'[360]), Bobby Darin's 'Somebody To Love' ('Dis-lui que je l'aime') and the big band sound of 'Roly-poly', while Hallyday cleaned up with the decidedly raunchier 'Ce s'rait bien' (Brenda Lee's 'Sweet Nothin's') and the ass-kicking original 'Depuis qu'ma môme'.

## Rocky Volcano and Dany Fischer

Hallyday's explosive stage act had as yet only one real rival: a singer from Marseilles by the name of Rocky Volcano. A dynamic live performer, he posed a serious threat to the newly emerged king of French rock'n'roll, and his debut EP on Philips was a breathless effort which spun off a hit with the outstanding 'Comme un volcan'. The record should have been a sensation, with a vibrant saxophone solo topping Volcano's wild rockabilly yelps, but the label seemed uncertain how to promote him. The follow-up picked up good sales too, thanks to a hit adaptation of Del Shannon's

---

[360] Also in the repertoire of the rather older Betty et Suzy, a pair of music-hall-dwelling bandwagonners who were more at home with the likes of Eartha Kitt's 'Uska Dara' ('Uskudara') and were rightly ignored by Anthony's teenage fans.

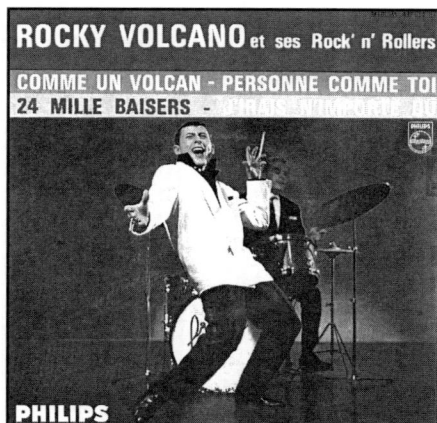

'Runaway' ('Mon amour disparu'), but his cover of Ernie K-Doe's 'Mother-in-Law' ('Belle-maman') was outsold by a rival version by Frankie Jordan, whose friendship with Daniel Filipacchi ensured he received airplay on *Salut les copains* far in excess of that afforded to Volcano.

Sadly, Volcano never managed to translate his live popularity into record sales, despite a run of good releases over a twelve-month period, including rollicking versions of the Flamingos' 'Nobody Loves Me Like You' ('Personne comme toi') and Gene Vincent's 'Brand New Beat', an inspired reworking of the Shadows' 'Saturday Dance' ('Avec les copains') and a blistering take on Cliff Richard's 'Dynamite'. Once Philips had seen off Barclay in the bidding war to sign Hallyday, Volcano's commercial potential swiftly abated and he decamped across the border to seek a new career in Spain.

Volcano was not the only pretender to Hallyday's throne to emerge as other labels found their own young singers to groom for stardom. In the early months of 1961, Polydor came up with Dany Fischer, a former backroom boy who adopted his stage name from the main character in Elvis Presley's *King Creole* movie. He tried hard with four EPs over two years, impressing with an enthusiastic version of Presley's 'Shoppin' Around' ('Je ne veux plus être un dragueur'), a pleasant take on Johnny Burnette's 'You're Sixteen' ('T'as seize ans') and the upbeat original 'Surpat' ', without ever making real headway. A competent vocalist with a good sense of rhythm, Fischer deserved greater success, but his third release saw him sliding backwards toward schmaltz with an uninspiring cover of Sue Thompson's 'Sad Movies' ('Quand le film est triste') in an unsuccessful effort to muscle in on the teen idol market opened up by Richard Anthony.

## Getting down with the kids

While record label bosses were busy searching for the next French Elvis, various hardy individuals from the world of show business continued their attempts to 'get down with the kids' – not least because such an approach had done Dalida no harm whatsoever. Among these opportunist releases were Maria Candido's 'Le pont de l'amour' (a reconstruction of the Teardrops' 'Bridge Of Love') and the thumping 'Taillé dans le rock', a powerful rock'n'roll excursion by music hall entertainer Edmond Taillet which married a wildly enthusiastic vocal to the already dated sound of big band rock. However, the days when such joyous nonsense could inspire rock'n'roll fans were now long in the past.

More creditable was Georges Aber's 'Comme un tigre' (an impressively tight and enjoyable adaptation of Fabian's 'Tiger'), but he almost immediately beat a retreat and opted for a new career as a lyricist, adapting hits of the day into French for the likes of Richard Anthony, who picked up 'Quand tu me diras oui' (his reworking of Johnny Rose's 'Linda Lee') in 1961.

The failure of the show-business elite to replicate Dalida's success was an early indication of the split opening up between the teenage audience and older listeners who had kept the music hall stars in clover for the past decade. French film-makers, ever keen to attract a young clientele, were quick to spot the change, commissioning upbeat, rock-styled theme tunes to draw youngsters in off the street, resulting in such monstrosities as Annie Cordy's 'Rock-a-longa tango', which had plenty of 'tango' but precious little 'rock', other than a breathless vocal. This was featured in *Tête folle* (1960), for which Cordy also delivered a title tune that came a little closer to the required sound, though not close enough for anyone to notice. Far better was André Hossein's 'Rock éclatant' from *Les scélérats* (1960), on which the traditional big band cut loose in the manner of the previous decade's experiments with rock'n'roll.

Michel Legrand worked a similar miracle on the soundtrack to *L'Amérique insolite* (1960), for which he crafted the excellent 'Rock surprise-partie'. This tight, rocking instrumental was topped off with a novelty vocal that might have made it a hit a couple of years earlier, but it was now left redundant by the stripped-down sound favoured by the new young rock'n'rollers. The same could

be said for fellow jazzman Marcel Zanini's 'Dis-moi oui ou non', a near-perfect collision of jazz with rock'n'roll that was issued to general indifference in 1961.

Showing rather less originality, singer François Deguelt attempted to cash in on the new wave with an appalling cover of Elvis Presley's 'His Latest Flame' ('Sa grande passion'), only to be unceremoniously squashed by Richard Anthony's more impressive reading of the song. Meanwhile, Jean-Paul Mauric's attempt at the Allisons' *Eurovision* runner-up, 'Are You Sure' ('Sœur Anne'), was pulled from release in favour of 'Le train d'amitié', which kept him in the running a little longer.

There was also a sense of deperation in Georges Ulmer's final attempts to keep up with the younger generation. His recordings of Bobby Darin's 'Clementine' ('Clémentine') and Bobby Rydell's 'Groovy Tonight' ('Va faire un p'tit tour chez les Grecs') scrabbled for airplay behind Richard Anthony's more joyous renditions. Similarly, while fun on its own terms, Ulmer's big band assault on Dion & The Belmonts' 'A Teenager In Love' ('J'ai toujours peur de l'amour') simply couldn't hold a candle to the original.

Attempting to combine the fast-fading exotica craze with the raunchier sound of rock'n'roll, Belgian showband Les Chakachas produced a passable rendition of the Champs' 'Too Much Tequila' ('Mucho tequila') without exhibiting any sort of real conversion to the cause. Fellow exoticist Dario Moreno made a similarly half-hearted attempt to ride Elvis Presley's slipstream with a version of the Italian classic, 'O sole mio', that was perfectly suited to his operatic tenor but paid scant attention to Presley's inspired reinterpretation, 'It's Now Or Never', and accordingly paid the price. He fared rather better with Ritchie Valens' 'La Bamba', taking it back to its roots in Mexican folk music and picking up a hit for his efforts, although this too had little to do with rock'n'roll.

**Real rock'n'roll**

While these last-ditch efforts by the old guard fell on stony ground, young fans continued to clamour for the latest releases by Johnny Hallyday and Richard Anthony. Some, however, preferred their rock'n'roll to be sung in the original English – something the Allegrettes were well placed to deliver. They entered the new decade exactly where they had left the old, turning out a decent version of the Everly Brothers' '('Til) I Kissed You', a rudimentary stroll through the Fleetwoods' 'Mr. Blue' and a surprising vocal revamp of Johnny & The Hurricanes' 'Red River Rock'.[361] However, their reworking of Floyd

---

[361] Less surprising, perhaps, if one remembers that this began life as the nineteenth-century folk song 'Red River Valley' before becoming an early country music classic in the 1920s thanks to recordings by Carl T. Sprague and Jules Verne Allen as 'Cowboy Love Song'.

Robinson's 'Makin' Love' was buried by Hallyday's and Dalida's hit versions, while an uncharacteristically dry take on the Coasters' 'Poison Ivy' left listeners itching for the real thing. They soldiered on for a couple of years, turning out breezy renditions of the Everly Brothers' 'Cathy's Clown', Bobby Rydell's 'Swingin' School', Buzz Clifford's 'Baby Sittin' Boogie' and Linda Scott's 'I've Told Every Little Star'. Unfortunately for them, most fans opted for the French-language adaptations by Hallyday, Anthony, Distel *et al*, while those who preferred their rock'n'roll in English went for the American originals. By late 1961, the group had run out of steam and disappeared as mysteriously as they had arrived.

Of the newer contenders, Jacky Rider et les Starlettes were a clean-cut outfit who turned out a reasonable cover of Ray Charles's stateside chart-topper, 'Hit The Road Jack' ('Fich' le camp Jack!'). It was a worthy effort, but was ruthlessly outsold by a version by Richard Anthony,[362] as well as by Charles's original, which had recently been released on an ABC-Paramount EP.

Jacky Gordon cut some agreeable jazzy R&B for Véga. He weighed in with a cover of Charles's 'Hallelujah I Love Her So' ('Dieu merci, elle m'aime aussi') and the sparkling 'Laisse entrer le ciel' (Teddy Randazzo's 'Let The Sunshine In'), both issued to little commercial reward, with rival versions from Frankie Jordan and Richard Anthony respectively picking up the lion's share of sales.

Singer/guitarist Chris Sarrel's cover of 'Are You Sure' ('Sœur Anne') did get released, but his routine approach to the Allisons' hit was nothing to write home about. Outclassed by a rival recording by Richard Anthony, he failed

---

[362] Under the amended title, 'Fiche le camp, Jack' (or 'Fich' le camp, Jack' on a later album).

to offer any serious competition.

Worthy though some of these performers were, they all suffered from a lack of support from their record companies, having to make do with jazz musicians who turned up their nose at rock'n'roll and often ruined the records with over-elaborate musicianship or unsympathetic arrangements. This problem plagued Anthony and Hallyday as well, and for all their youthful exuberance, it was evident to most serious fans that the sound and feeling on records like Hallyday's 'Une boum chez John' and 'Je veux me promener' (Fats Domino's 'I Want To Walk You Home'), or Anthony's 'Je suis fou de l'école' (Bobby Rydell's 'Swingin' School') fell far short of those by the leading American artists, and even British acts like Cliff Richard and the Shadows. The solution, self-evidently, was to find musicians who actually *wanted* to play rock'n'roll; musicians like themselves – young, enthusiastic and open to new ideas.

# Chapter 13

## QUAND LES CHATS SONT LÀ
### The groups: The first wave (1960-62)

*Belgian group the Cousins were an offshoot of a traditional showband who began playing rock'n'roll on the side in the late fifties – a decision that allowed them to make a significant impact in the French marketplace. They were highly competent musicians and scored a massive hit in their homeland in 1960 with 'Kili watch', which duly saw release all around the world. In France, their thunder was stolen by a Johnny Hallyday cover, but their version still sold well enough to establish them in the country, and the follow-up, 'Kana kapila', was a best-seller the following year.*

*Their success led to the emergence of a splinter group in the form of the Kili Jacks, whose 1961 debut, 'John Johnson', was likewise a decent rock'n'roll record, even if it lacked the excitement of the Cousins' smash. A moderate hit in Belgium, it was issued in France on an EP together with their second Belgian single, 'Tee-Ya-Ya-Ho!', but they did not succeed in penetrating the French market.*[363]

*Although the Cousins remained popular in Belgium and the Netherlands, enjoying further hits there with 'Marchand de parasols', 'Dang dang' and the extremely silly 'Wadiya',*[364] *their French following rapidly evaporated, and they soon became a mere footnote to the explosion of rock'n'roll groups that followed in 1961.*

### Les Chaussettes Noires

The success of Johnny Hallyday during 1960 had not gone unnoticed at the Golf Drouot, where old friends like Claude Moine cheered his every move. Inspired by Hallyday's example, Moine changed his name to the more American-sounding Eddy Mitchell and got together with four like-minded souls to form Les 5 Rocks, France's first true rock'n'roll group. After rehearsing for several months, they successfully auditioned for Barclay and made their first recordings at the end of 1960. Following a promotional deal between Barclay and clothing manufacturer Stemm to promote a range of socks (yes, really), the record company changed their name without bothering to inform them and issued their debut EP as by Les Chaussettes Noires.

---

[363]  Their third single, the guitar-and-saxophone-heavy 'Polly polly', was not even released there. Some of their records were credited to the Kili Jack's [*sic*].

[364]  For what it was worth, 'Dang dang' and 'Wadiya' were both sung in English. Annie Cordy covered the former for the French market as 'Dingue dingue'.

*Les Chaussettes Noires backstage at Montgeron, 8 April 1961. Eddy Mitchell far right.*

Released in early January 1961, the EP marked a major step forward for French rock'n'roll. It was the first record to be made by a group of rock'n'roll musicians, rather than a singer backed by a team of session players, and the difference was immediately apparent. Tight, ballsy and recorded with liberal use of echo, it leapt out of the airwaves like a bolt of lightning, blowing all competition out of the water.

Among the selections on offer was 'Tu parles trop', a powerful reading of Joe Jones's 'You Talk Too Much' that far surpassed competing versions by Johnny Hallyday, Richard Anthony and Frankie Jordan. With their workmanlike but enjoyable cover of Gene Vincent's 'Be-Bop-A-Lula'[365] joining 'Tu parles trop' on the radio, Les Chaussettes Noires became stars overnight, winning rapturous applause at their first public appearances in February, while a show at the Bobino Theatre in Paris the following month confirmed their potential. Their second EP was also a massive hit, with the rock ballad

---

[365] Oddly, despite Mitchell's near-veneration of Vincent, their version was based on the contemporary arrangement by the Everly Brothers.

'Daniela'[366] becoming the first domestic rock'n'roll record to top the French hit parade,[367] while their third saw them romping through Neil Sedaka's 'Going Home To Mary Lou' ('Ô Mary Lou') like the died-in-the-wool rockers they were.

Although Les Chaussettes Noires were already showing an inclination to diversify into lighter, slower-paced material, there was little doubt that it was their hard-edged rock'n'roll that was bringing the fans out, and their debut LP, *100% Rock*, settled into a long run in the best-seller listings over the spring. Although their take on Chuck Berry's classic 'Johnny B. Goode' ('Eddie sois bon') was uncharacteristically weak, their fast, tight renditions of Elvis Presley's 'Dirty Dirty Feeling' ('Si seulement') and 'I Gotta Know' ('Je t'aime trop') testified to a group in full control of their artistic vision.

Although they could occasionally be sloppy on record, they most definitely *looked* the part, and in Eddy Mitchell they possessed one of the most distinctive rock'n'roll stylists in the country – albeit one with a clear Gene Vincent infatuation.[368] Mitchell lived and breathed rock'n'roll from morning till night, and the enthusiasm of the group meant that they rocked with a furious intensity that pushed their records to sonic heights far beyond anything Johnny Hallyday had so far managed to achieve. By the middle of 1961, they were the hottest act in the country.

## Les Chats Sauvages

Les Chaussettes Noires barely had time to make the climb to the top before they found themselves with a rival in the form of Les Chats Sauvages. Hailing from Nice, they were fronted by fifteen-year-old Hervé Fornieri aka 'Dick Rivers', who could deliver all of Presley's vocal mannerisms in his sleep.[369] Based down on the Mediterranean coast, they frittered away their early opportunities playing shows in Italy before eventually deciding to make the long trek north to Paris in the spring of 1961. After a frenzied audition for Pathé, they were immediately signed and announced their arrival in May with a sizzling debut EP that matched that of Les Chaussettes Noires shot for shot. Both the rip-roaring 'Ma p'tite amie est vache' (a cover of Presley's 'Mean Woman Blues') and the thumping 'Le jour J' (taken from Bobby Doss's little-known 'I've Got You') smashed their way into the charts and Les Chats Sauvages quickly found themselves challenging for the title of the country's best rock'n'roll group.

---

[366] An original song penned by industry insiders André Pascal and Georges Garvarentz.
[367] In *La bourse des chansons*, the chart published by *Le Figaro*.
[368] Best exemplified on their savage assault on 'Everybody's Got A Date' ('Fou d'elle').
[369] Like Dany Fischer, Rivers cribbed his name from a film character played by Elvis Presley, in this instance Deke Rivers from *Loving You* (1957).

Young and dynamic with a powerful live punch, they were a teen sensation, with frontman Rivers quickly becoming a pin-up. Far younger than the already maturing Mitchell, he was no less determined to make a living from the music that had transformed his life. His cute, boyish features looked slightly at odds with the Presley-esque sideburns he insisted on sporting, but his already finely tuned vocal style won him millions of fans across the country and his gentle, tender glances did the rest. Girls flung themselves at the group wherever they played and they milked their success for all it was worth.

Their second EP was another hit, thanks mainly to a popular, if strangely subdued cover of Cliff Richard's 'D In Love' ('Trois en amour'), while their self-titled debut album was a stunning achievement that belied their young age.

The highlight of their first LP was the frantic 'Twist à Saint-Tropez', which dominated the airwaves for months, overshadowing their equally dynamic reworking of Ray Charles's 'What'd I Say' ('Est-ce que tu le sais'), and providing the soundtrack for a thousand parties over the summer. Fuelled by a naggingly insistent guitar riff and driven by Rivers' finest rockabilly yelps, the song was a smash and threw down the gauntlet to their rivals, daring them to come up with something as original[370] and strong. Elsewhere on the album, the group paid further homage to Rivers' hero, Cliff Richard, with a sparkling adaptation of 'Lamp Of Love' ('Yeh! Yeh! Yeh!') that zipped and hummed its way into the memory banks.

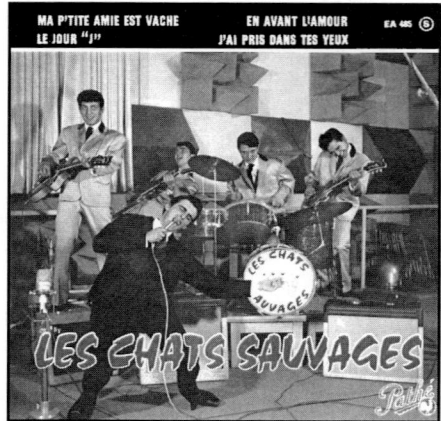

The boys took to the road to promote the release, taking their wild and uninhibited show to every corner of the country, but already internal tensions were threatening to tear them apart. Arrogant and pushy outsiders prone to speaking their mind, they also made few friends and were often at loggerheads with the music business hierarchy in Paris – in complete contrast to the generally well-mannered Chaussettes Noires. Outside the capital, however, they were adored by their legions of fans.

---

[370] Although the song was original, it was not actually written by the band, but by a trio of backroom songsmiths: André Salvet, Guy Lafitte and rising jazz pianist Martial Solal.

## Danny Boy et ses Pénitents

While Les Chats Sauvages at least accorded Les Chaussettes Noires some respect for their musical ability, they were less charitable to the next group to break on the scene, Danny Boy et ses Pénitents, with whom they enjoyed a lengthy and bitter rivalry.

'Danny Boy' was none other than Claude Piron, who had meanwhile resurfaced on the Italian-owned Ricordi label. His group consisted of Madagascan students who had come to France to study, not to play rock'n'roll, and so performed wearing Ku Klux Klan-style hoods to hide their faces from their parents[371] – a trick that also helped to disguise later line-up changes.

Their debut EP was characterised by excellent guitar-work and breathless vocals, as Danny Boy tackled the Elvis Presley songbook. Showing all the prowess that had almost made him a star in his original incarnation, he strolled confidently through 'Un collier de tes bras' ('Wear My Ring Around Your Neck'), 'Un coup au cœur' ('Doncha Think It's Time') and 'Je ne veux plus être un dragueur' ('Shoppin' Around').[372] However, it was the only non-Presley song, 'C'est encore une souris' (adapted from 'Ciao ti diro' by Italian singing star Adriano Celentano) that became a hit.

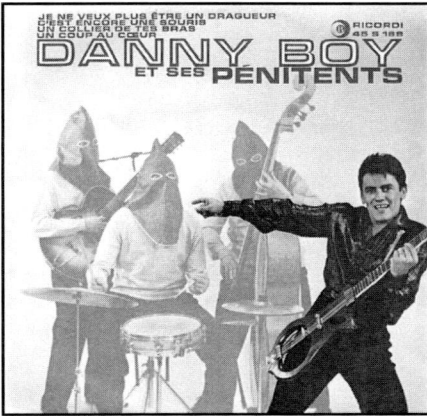

It was followed soon after by 'C'est tout comme' (Presley's 'A Mess Of Blues') from their second EP, that paved the path for a run of other successes over the next two years. The catchy but silly 'Croque la pomme' and 1962's utterly demented 'Ah! Quel massacre'[373] on their fourth, kept the group at the forefront of the rapidly expanding French rock'n'roll scene, but despite Danny Boy's appeal, they never quite managed to reach the same giddy heights as their two more prominent competitors.

The success of these three outfits sparked an explosion in activity to rival the more famous beat group boom then getting underway in Liverpool and other British cities. The difference was that UK record companies' attentions were still firmly focused on solo singers, whereas French record companies, well aware of the limitations of their pool of session musicians, were happy to sign up any ensemble that might be able to deliver the sound that the rapidly growing teenage market wanted to hear.[374]

---

[371] Interestingly, Teddy Raye's band would adopt the same outfits after he decamped to Spain.

[372] Outselling, if not outclassing, rival versions by Teddy Raye and Dany Fischer respectively.

[373] On their second and fourth EPs respectively. 'Croque la pomme' was also recorded, in a more restrained interpretation, by Les Chats Sauvages (as 'Croque, croque la pomme'), but only released on a single in Belgium.

[374] Albeit still in the very traditional manner of 'lead singer plus backing outfit'. The records of Les Chats Sauvages and Les Chaussettes Noires were released under the group name 'featuring' Eddy Mitchell and Dick Rivers respectively.

## Les Pirates

Back at the Golf Drouot, Daniel Deshayes changed his name to Dany Logan and began performing with a group who soon turned professional as Les Pirates. They signed to the Barclay subsidiary Bel-Air and debuted in the summer of 1961 with a passable cover of Del Shannon's 'Hats Off To Larry' ('Oublie Larry') and a rendition of Chubby Checker's 'The Jet' ('Le jet') that trashed the original and showed the group at their rocking best. A talented outfit with a more-than-capable singer, they were soon rubbing shoulders with Les Chaussettes Noires at the upper end of the charts. Although they occasionally overreached themselves – as on their cover of Jerry Lee Lewis's 'Great Balls Of Fire' ('Tu mets le feu') – they had plenty of enthusiasm to spare, and for a while they matched their leading rivals hit for hit.

Their second EP was driven up the charts by their full-scale demolition of Johnny Tillotson's 'Cutie Pie' ('Kioutie paie') and an effective reworking of Jerry Lee Lewis's 'Whole Lot Of Shakin' Going On' ('Mon petit ange') that took the song back to its roots in a manner redolent of the great R&B singer Roy Brown. With the group whipping up a frenzy at live shows across the country, they quickly found themselves with a large following.

## Other early groups

Golf Drouot regular Christian Blondieau missed out on the initial group boom as he was tied up doing military service. As soon as he returned to civilian life in 1962, he too formed a group – Les Daltons – and adopted the name 'Long Chris'. Tall and gangly, he was an unlikely candidate for teen stardom, and despite offering competent versions of Fats Domino's 'My Girl Josephine' ('Hello Joséphine'), Gene Vincent's 'Mr. Loneliness' ('Monsieur «Pas d'Chance»') and Jerry Lee Lewis's 'Big Blon' Baby' ('Beau blond bébé'), his debut EP for the small Pacific label met with little success outside the Golf Drouot faithful. It was only after Johnny Hallyday persuaded the powers-that-be at Philips to offer him a deal that his fortunes began to pick up.

His second EP included a couple of Cliff Richard covers: a tough version of 'I'm Gonna Get You' ('Qui te le dira') that highlighted his excellent rockabilly vocals, and 'Ma verte prairie' ('Evergreen

Tree'). The latter became a minor hit, although it sounded closer to country music than the fuller-bodied rock'n'roll performed by the leading groups of the day. His third EP also produced a small hit, a slowed-down arrangement of Gene Vincent's 'I'm Going Home' ('Je reviendrai'), but the market remained generally unimpressed, and even his friendship with Hallyday seemed unable to open the door to the charts.

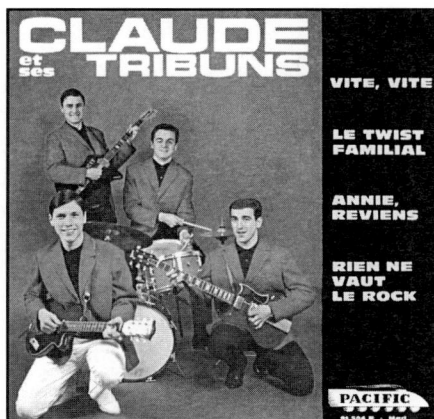

Elsewhere in Paris, groups continued to crawl out of the woodwork. Claude et ses Tribuns started out strongly in 1962 with the gutsy 'Vite, vite' and the celebratory 'Rien ne vaut le rock', but, although they had inadvertently stumbled upon a style very close to true fifties' rockabilly, they proved too rough and unpolished for the needs of the day. More eclectic than many in their choice of material, they turned out an impressive cover of Cliff Richard's 'Got A Funny Feelin' ' ('Avoue c'est formidable') on their second EP, but a bizarre reworking of Patti Page's 'Most People Get Married' ('Quand on sera mariés') took them rather too far from their rocking roots. Subsequent records failed to maintain the quality, although they deserve praise for recording a large number of original songs, rather than relying solely on cover versions. This paid artistic dividends with the wonderful 'Demain c'est dimanche' and the reverential 'Au Golf', but sadly didn't get them into the charts. A formulaic cover of Chubby Checker's 'Twenty Miles' ('Loin de toi') showed their inspiration ebbing away and they never succeeded in making the transformation from live sensations into chart regulars.

Les Vautours were unusual in that they featured a lead singer (Vic Laurens) who also played guitar, rather than standing alone at the front of the stage. They had the potential to become major contenders, but never seemed to take their career seriously, skipping rehearsals to have a laugh and only really coming alive on the concert stage. Their 1961 debut, 'Betty et Jenny' (Bobby Lewis's 'Tossin' And Turnin' '), was a fairly weak effort, but it was a hit anyway. The rest of the EP was far better, especially their impressive run through Gene Vincent's 'Rocky Road Blues' ('Tu me donnes').

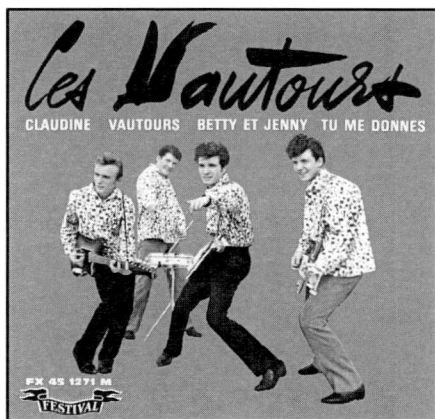

Like many of the first wave of French rock'n'roll groups, Les Vautours roamed far and wide in search of material to record, and, while their opening salvo of hits was drawn from relatively obvious sources, the rest of their catalogue revealed a talent for

215

digging out obscurities.[375] Among their more interesting efforts was a stroll through Elvis Presley's bluesy 'Give Me The Right' ('Permettez-moi'), while perhaps their most impressive piece of crate-digging resulted in 'Ne me dis pas non', a rough and ragged reworking of Woody Harris's 'I Want You With Me'. Never the most powerful group on the circuit, they got their act together sufficiently to turn in a decent cover of the Brook Brothers' 'Warpaint' ('Tu peins ton visage') in 1961, a deserved hit that made clear their stylistic debt to singers like the Everly Brothers.

Belgian outfit Les King Creoles, fronted by singer/guitarist Burt Blanca, also deserve an honourable mention. They produced a decent rock'n'roll sound on a number of domestic singles for the Hebra label, starting with a Flemish version of Neil Sedaka's 'Oh! Carol'. Buoyed by their dynamic live performances, the group enjoyed wide success in their home country, but no attention whatsoever across the border in France.

### Everly Brothers imitators

With much of their material unavailable in France,[376] the Everly Brothers' songbook was ripe for plundering by French singers. The country's leading Everly clones were Les Copains, a duo who based their entire sound and style on that of the brothers from Kentucky. Their 1961 debut EP featured a reasonable stab at 'Problems' ('Problèmes') and a decent original in the style of their American heroes, 'Cet été', but it was only successful in Switzerland, where their version of Ray Peterson's 'Corrina, Corrina' was also a smash.

Over three further EPs,[377] they never strayed from their limited artistic remit, turning out more selections from the Everly Brothers' songbook with 'Mon cœur, mon cœur' ('Muskrat') and an interpretation of Little Richard's 'Lucille' that was clearly modelled on the American duo's arrangement. When they did cut loose with a cover of Dion's 'Runaround Sue' ('Infidèle'), they were outclassed by a rival version from the all-conquering Chaussettes Noires ('Volage'). Despite penning a number of their own songs (notably the excellent 'J'ai besoin d'amour'), Les Copains ultimately owed their existence to their role models' inability to get their records released in France, and once that issue was resolved in 1962, their efforts became largely irrelevant to the wider public.

Franck et Johnny offered a poppier variation on the Everlys' sound, but got nowhere with the four EPs they released in the early sixties. Lacking the joyful intensity of the younger Copains, they struggled through dreary versions

---

[375] It is not clear whether it was the group or their A&R man that was responsible for their inventive choices of repertoire.

[376] Partly due to Warner Bros. not having a distribution agreement at the time.

[377] One of which included another version of 'Tu peins ton visage'.

of the Allisons' 'Are You Sure' ('Sœur Anne') and Johnny Tillotson's 'Poetry In Motion' ('Elle a des yeux d'ange'[378]) without ever striking the right note. By 1963's 'La pluie du printemps' they were aiming squarely at the adult market.

Meanwhile, Les Kimonos, a Vietnamese duo of considerable ability, wasted their talents on the silly 'Mon banjo' and duly disappeared after only one EP, leaving Les Copains as the unchallenged winners in the 'French Everly Brothers' stakes.

## The provincial group scene

Although the French media were focused almost exclusively on Paris, the group scene put down roots everywhere and it was estimated that, by 1962, there were some five thousand of them thrashing away across the country. With the major labels all based in the capital, most provincial outfits had little chance of making the big time and most never bothered to try. For those who wanted to make even a slight impact, the only options were either to finance their own recordings (via regional labels like Soder or JBP in Lyon, who would press and distribute them within their local area), or to sign up with a small independent in the hope of catching the ear of a big-city A&R man.

Among the groups who took the latter route were Les Blousons Noirs from Bordeaux, an amateurish outfit who matched their enthusiasm with a charming level of incompetence on their two 1961 releases. Sounding as if they had bought their instruments in the morning prior to recording in the afternoon, the group took amateurism to a new high (or low, depending on your point of view), years before the likes of the Legendary Stardust Cowboy or the Shaggs were let loose inside an American recording studio. Their slipshod versions of Gene Vincent's 'Be-Bop-A-Lula' and Chuck Berry's 'Johnny B. Goode' ('Eddie sois bon')[379] provided no evidence that they could even play in time with one another, never mind in tune. Similar assaults on the work of Johnny Hallyday ('Depuis qu'ma môme') and Les Chats Sauvages ('Twist à Saint-Tropez') showed that no cow was truly sacred, clearly marking the group out as true precursors of punk fifteen years ahead of time.[380]

Les Diables Rouges from Alsace were hometown heroes who gifted the world the decent 'Comme les diables', but otherwise remain lost in the mists of obscurity. Equally unsuccessful were the ridiculous Les Karting Brothers,

---

[378] Hopelessly outclassed by rival versions by Richard Anthony and Milou Duchamp respectively.
[379] Both modelled on the arrrangements by Les Chaussettes Noires.
[380] Les Blousons Noirs' name had earlier appeared on some more professional, if less interesting, recordings by Bordeaux singer Tony March, although they sound like a different group. March sizzled on versions of Gene Vincent's 'Be-Bop-A-Lula' and Cliff Richard's 'D In Love' ('Trois en amour'), however the songs were already doing good business for Les Chaussettes Noires and Les Chats Sauvages respectively, so he posed no threat to Johnny Hallyday.

old music-business pros from the now-defunct vocal ensemble Les Quatre de Paris, who attempted to join in the fun with a version of Bobby Darin's 'Splish Splash' but made barely a ripple.

Indeed, the only provincial outfit to make any impact in 1961 was Les Chats Sauvages. The only group able to give Les Chaussettes Noires a real run for their money, they were regarded as a major threat by Eddie Barclay, the latter's label boss, and he decided to play on their internal troubles in an attempt to destabilise them. Approaching drummer Willy Lewis (the only Parisian in the line-up), he offered him a deal to found his own group, bringing in guitar wizard Claude Ciari to provide the musical muscle.

Christened Les Champions, the new outfit had great musical chops but chose the unremarkable Jean-Claude Chane as their vocalist, weakening their overall appeal. They launched in 1961 with a hit EP boasting a pair of furious Elvis Presley covers featuring Ciari's sizzling guitar-work, 'Sa grande passion' and 'Le rock du bagne' ('His Latest Flame' and 'Jailhouse Rock' respectively), and a revamp of Cliff Richard's 'Dynamite' that was every bit as good as Rocky Volcano's. Chane's vocals were disappointing, but the group rocked with a passion, and the combination of Ciari's guitar and Lewis's powerhouse drumming made them an instant success. Their second EP carried another Presley cover in the shape of 'Ne me dis pas non' ('I Want You With Me'), complete with more blistering guitar from Ciari, though it was the less frenetic 'Bye bye mon amour' (Ricky Nelson's 'Hello Mary Lou') that became their next hit.[381]

Unfortunately for Barclay, Les Champions' swift ascent had no impact on Lewis's former colleagues. Shrugging off his defection, Les Chats Sauvages signed up a new drummer whose name is lost to history and kept on rocking.[382] Their third EP included a new, utterly superior version of 'Warpaint' ('Tu peins ton visage') alongside the instant classic 'Toi, tu es bath pour moi' and an overcooked but effective bluesy rocker, 'Toi, quel bonheur' (Johnny Restivo's 'Come Closer').

Les Chaussettes Noires matched them hit for hit, selling huge quantities of their autumn 1961 EP thanks to the rollicking but silly 'Dactylo rock', a powerful rampage through Rusty York's 'Sugaree' ('Chérie, oh chérie'), and a rocked-up rendition of Édith Piaf's 'Padam... Padam' ('Madame! Madame!') that blitzed a rival version from Sacha Distel, reaffirming that it was they, rather than Johnny Hallyday, who were delivering the best rock'n'roll in France.

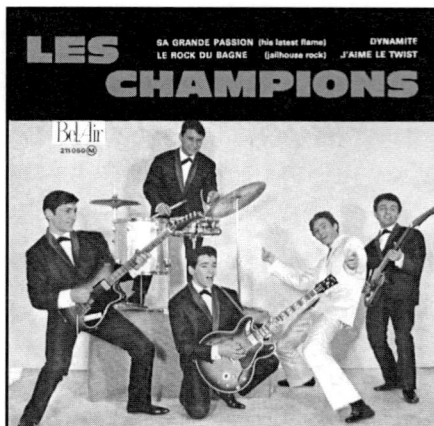

---

[381] Sharing the honours with a poppier reading by Petula Clark.

[382] The band appear to have used session drummers for a while. Their third EP featured a drummer with the surname Rodgers, while the next one featured jazzman Armand Molinetti. The drumstool would not be definitively filled until the arrival in 1962 of André Ceccarelli.

# Chapter 14

# DIEU MERCI, ELLE M'AIME AUSSI
## The early girl singers (1960-62)

*With male groups and singers pounding out rock'n'roll over the airwaves, executives in record companies across Paris were wondering if this new teenage music fad might be broad enough to include girl singers as well. In the absence of any aspiring rockeuses, the mantle of Queen of French rock'n'roll was initially bestowed upon Dalida, the most successful of the old music hall stars when it came to interpreting rock'n'roll songs. Her tentative efforts in the late fifties may not have exactly rocked, but they had been done with far more sincerity than those of Gloria Lasso or Maria Candido, and she enjoyed a loyal following among the youth audience. Possessed of a natural sense of rhythm and a strong, unconventional personality, Dalida was well placed to carry on as the rock'n'roll wave began to wash over France in the early 1960s. It wasn't long, however, before competitors began to gather on the horizon.*

### Dalida and Petula Clark

Dalida opened the the new decade with 'J'ai rêvé' (a capable cover of Bobby Darin's 'Dream Lover') and a version of 'T'aimer follement' that was outclassed by Johnny Hallyday's – though not for want of trying. Over the course of 1960 she covered all bases, scoring a massive hit in the summer with the Paul Anka-like ballad 'Romantica',[383] before returning to rock'n'roll-styled pop in the autumn with a version of 'Itsi bitsi, petit bikini'. The same EP saw her covering Frankie Avalon's 'Why' ('Bras dessus, bras dessous') against stiff competition from Les Compagnons de la Chanson's jaunty singalong rendition.[384] She also scored heavily with 'O sole mio', burying Dario Moreno's over-the-top operatic

70314

T'AIMER
FOLLEMENT

MON AMOUR
OUBLIE

ELLE,
LUI ET L'AUTRE

VA PETITE
ÉTOILE

**DALIDA**

accompagnée par
RAYMOND LEFÈVRE
et son orchestre

*Barclay*

---

[383] Shutting down a rival version by newcomer Maya Casabianca. Jane Morgan subsequently laid down an English-language cover which sneaked into the UK charts.
[384] And less so from a sweet interpretation by the Kessler Sisters.

**La joie d'aimer**
PETULA CLARK
Garde ta dernière danse pour moi  **vogue**
LE TU SAIS OUOI • SUR UN TAPIS VOLANT
PNV 24 077

assault and selling strongly in the face of Elvis Presley's reworking of the theme, 'It's Now Or Never'.

Dalida was not the only old-school performer to record rock'n'roll in 1960, but the efforts of her rivals only served to illustrate how far ahead of the game she was. Maria Candido played it safe with an adaptation of Annette's 'O Dio Mio', while Gloria Lasso focused on the exotic aspects of the music with 'Dans les rues de Bahia' (the Champs' 'Too Much Tequila') and a cover of Connie Francis's 'Valentino'. None of them registered with their intended market, although 'Valentino' was a big hit in its own right anyway. Line Renaud meanwhile released a half-hearted attempt at 'Itsi bitsi, petit bikini', but Dalida was way out in front, taking on Johnny Hallyday and Richard Anthony again in 1961 with 'Tu peux le prendre' (Roy Hamilton's 'You Can Have Her') and 'Avec une poignée de terre' (Gene McDaniels' 'A Hundred Pounds Of Clay').

Dalida's only serious rival in the rock'n'roll stakes was Petula Clark, who affirmed her all-round appeal with 'Moi, j'préfère l'amour à tout ça' (Adam Faith's 'What Do You Want'), the swinging 'Je compte sur toi' (Bobby Rydell's 'We Got Love') and 'Que voulez-vous de plus' (Frankie Vaughan's 'What More Do You Want'), even as her standing in the UK continued to diminish.

In 1961, the market belonged to Clark and Dalida, who went head to head at the start of the year with rival covers of the Drifters' 'Save The Last Dance For Me' (titled 'Garde ta dernière danse pour moi' and 'Garde-moi la dernière danse' respectively[385]). Dalida followed up with 'Vingt-quatre mille baisers' (a remake of Adriano Celentano's '24 mila baci'[386]) that did battle on the airwaves with versions by Johnny Hallyday, Rocky Volcano[387] and

---

[385] However, when it was reissued on the LP *Tête à tête avec Petula Clark*, Clark's recording was retitled to match Dalida's.

[386] Also recorded by Italian star Little Tony, who introduced it to UK audiences in the same year as 'Four And Twenty Thousand Kisses'.

[387] Volcano's version was released as '24 mille baisers'.

Frankie Jordan, and then covered Ben E. King's 'Spanish Harlem' ('Nuits d'Espagne') for a summer hit. Clark meanwhile did good business with Lolita's German smash, 'Seemann', returning to the UK charts for the first time in three years with an English translation ('Sailor') before taking a French-language version ('Marin') high into the national charts. Thereafter, she resumed the rock'n'roll trail with a cover of Neil Sedaka's 'Calendar Girl' ('Tout au long du calendrier') and matched Dalida hit for hit all through the summer.

### Gillian Hills

Clark's English accent was always a large part of her appeal to French audiences and her success led Eddie Barclay to look for another British girl singer to market to the French in much the same way.[388] Gillian Hills was in the right place at the right time. A young starlet who had played a significant role in Adam Faith's 1960 film debut, *Beat Girl*, and was hotly touted at the time as the new Brigitte Bardot, Hills gladly turned her hand to a singing career, but early duet recordings with Eddie Constantine such as 'Spécialisation' (Marilyn Monroe & Frankie Vaughan's 'Specialization') were too mired in the jazz-tinged pop of the previous decade to interest the teen audience. Her cover of Jo Ann Campbell's 'A Kookie Little Paradise' ('Le paradis pour toi'[389]) showed the way forward, and the more rhythmic 'Si tu veux que je te dise' presented her with a minor hit in late 1960.

The Charles Aznavour-penned 'Jean-Lou' repeated the feat early in 1961, but again the jazzy nature of the recording seemed ill-suited to Hills' young, brash style and sales were disappointing. Looking for a commercial breakthrough, she edged toward more of a rock'n'roll sound in 1961 with the creditable 'Allons dans le bois' (Bobby Rydell's 'Good Time Baby'), which brought her much airplay, moderate sales and a large amount of work as a fashion model.[390] A novelty cover of Peter Sellers & Sophia Loren's 'Zoo Be Zoo Be Zoo' ('Zou bisou bisou') kept up the momentum as she searched for that elusive breakthrough, which finally came in 1962 via a hook-up with Les Chaussettes Noires on the dance-floor-friendly 'C'est bien mieux comme ça' from the film *Les Parisiennes*.

### Hédika and Gélou

Although 1960 and the early months of 1961 saw a number of rock'n'roll-styled records released in France by female singers, none of them so far had

---

[388] Clark recorded for Vogue. Barclay wanted to grab a piece of the action for his own label.
[389] Also on the market in an inferior version by Betty et Suzy.
[390] Something that most of the French teen stars of the decade, male and female, would frequently undertake to supplement their often quite meagre earnings.

really come up with anything to compare with the tougher sounds of Johnny Hallyday or Les Chaussettes Noires. This state of affairs was rectified in April 1961 with the debut release by Hédika, the country's first true female rocker.

Other female singers had merely dabbled in rock'n'roll, but Hédika was the real thing. The Hungarian-born wild child transcended the jazzy backings on her records to rip it up with Chubby Checker's 'Pony Time' ('Hey pony'), issued on her 1961 debut EP along with the more sedate 'Journal intime' (Neil Sedaka's 'The Diary'). Later in the year, she cut a rollicking, squealing rendition of Danny Boy's 'Croque la pomme'[391] and the storming, yelping 'L'amour, c'est tout ou rien'. Her live shows were something else too, as she danced up a storm to match the wild, hiccupping way in which she sang, startling audiences who had never imagined a girl singer to be capable of such an uninhibited performance.

Equally wild was Gélou, who sported close-cropped blonde hair and dared to wear trousers on stage. After releasing a handful of bland ballads in the fifties, she put together her own group, Le Machiavel-Rock, and released an uptempo revival of Henri Salvador's mock-gospel effort 'Donne, donne, donne' just two months after Hédika's debut. A dynamic live performer, she was rarely at her best on studio recordings, which tended to be closer to jazz than rock'n'roll, or else hybrids like the rock-tango 'Arrête-toi où l'on danse' or novelty revivals like Robert Stolz's 'Salomé'.[392] However, the fake-live 'Ils croient à leur danse' and 'Dieu m'a faite pour toi' were both a considerable

improvement, featuring jumping rhythms and tight, gutsy guitar lines. Her minor 1962 hit, 'Délivre-moi' (Ray Charles's 'Unchain My Heart'), while a tad too jazzy, still tore Richard Anthony's more commercially successful rendition to shreds.

Unfortunately for both Hédika and Gélou, the French (and, indeed, world) market was just not ready for such uninhibited performers in 1961 – at least, not female ones – and, despite cutting some excellent records, neither singer was able to translate their success into a long-term career.

---

[391] Hédika's version carried the amended title 'Croque, croque la pomme'.

[392] This was also reworked by Petula Clark, in far superior fashion, for a major hit in both English and French versions (as 'Romeo' and 'Roméo' respectively).

## Other early female rockers

Former circus performer turned music hall singer Audrey Arno had fronted Swiss bandleader Hazy Osterwald's sextet at the start of the sixties, even enjoying a minor US hit in 1961 with 'La Pachanga'. After three solo EPs went nowhere at a rate of knots, she made a bid for the teenage market with a cover of a Chaussettes Noires hit, 'Le chemin de la joie',[393] and a decent take on Gene McDaniels'/ Frankie Vaughan's 'Tower Of Strength' ('Toute ma vie') established her as a minor teen star in 1962. She followed up with Little Eva's 'The Loco-motion' ('Loco-motion'), but never succeeded in attaining major star status.

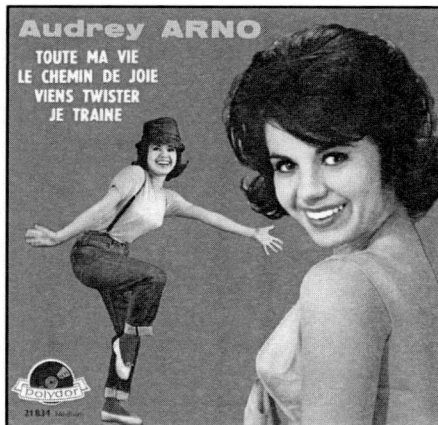

By way of contrast, Jacqueline Néro never really left the sounds of the music hall circuit behind, despite turning in a reasonable cover of LaVern Baker's 'You're The Boss' ('Oui patron') in 1961. Her singing career having hit the buffers, she changed tack and became a force in A&R for the Bel-Air label.

Cris Caroll was no more successful, releasing a 1961 version of Ray Charles's 'Hit the Road Jack' ('Fiche le camp, Jack') that was beaten in the marketplace both by the original and a cover by Richard Anthony. After a second bid for glory with the Hallyday tribute 'Le grand Johnny',[394] she dropped the second 'L' from her surname in 1962 and veered away from rock'n'roll toward a gentler form of pop aimed at teenage girls. This resulted in a cover of Shelley Fabares' 'Johnny Angel' ('Mon ange bleu') and the similarly paced 'Tu as pu me quitter', but neither these, nor the self-penned 'Si tu ne sais pas' brought her much commercial reward.

## Jazz *chanteuses* sing rock'n'roll

The other early contenders mainly came from the jazzy side of the tracks, with Ray Charles again providing the stepping stone from jazz to rock'n'roll. Nicole Croisille was a fine vocal stylist with a feel for soul, and her summer 1961 recording of 'Dieu merci, il m'aime aussi' ('Hallelujah I Love Her So')[395] was one of the better Charles covers on the market. Tapping into the singer's jazz roots, the song was given a full band arrangement lacking from most contemporary covers, but neither this worthy effort, nor Croisille's subsequent jazz-pop recordings found favour with the teen market. Workouts on Frank Sinatra's 'Almost Like Being In Love' ('C'est peut-être l'amour') and Johnny Dankworth's 'African Waltz' ('Ça tourne rond'[396]) were hardly what teenagers

---

[393] Oddly retitled 'Le chemin de joie'.

[394] The first of several attempts over the years by struggling female singers to cash in on Hallyday's star status.

[395] Cut as an 'answer' to the better-known 'Dieu merci, elle m'aime aussi' by Frankie Jordan.

[396] Comprehensively outsold by a near-simultaneous cover by Richard Anthony.

wanted, and the records passed swiftly out of circulation. Croisille continued to record sporadically throughout the first half of the decade, impressing with the swinging 'Un peu plus de chansons' and the keyboard-driven 'Allons-y gaiement' (adapted from Peggy Lee's 'I'm Gonna Go Fishin' '),[397] but she fell between two stools and eventually switched to acting in search of her fortune.

Jennifer was less well known than Croisille and generally stayed true to her jazz and gospel roots with a run of EPs over three years. She finally had a fling at pop in 1963 with a cover of Skeeter Davis's weepie, 'The End Of The World' ('Fait pour durer'), which, contrary to its title, wasn't built to last and marked the end of her career.

Paris-based jazz singer Nancy Holloway helpfully possessed an American accent, and her African-American background enabled her to get with the rhythms that were increasingly being demanded by French teenagers. In her case, this led in 1961 to work as a session singer for budget labels, turning out covers of the hits of the day. Despite the limited remit, the records themselves were rather good, particularly 'Les barbouzes' (a vocal version of the Shadows' 'F.B.I.'), although whether the world really needed her (admittedly powerful) version of Gene Vincent's 'Be-Bop-A-Lula' to add to those already on the market is open to debate. She wiped the floor with her rival version of Les Chats Sauvages 'En avant l'amour' (Cliff Richard's 'I Cannot Find A True Love') and turned out a creditable cover of Brenda Lee's 'Dum Dum', though it was her big-beat assault on Lee's 'Rock The Bop' and a vibrant English-language reading of James Brown's/ Chubby Checker's 'Good Good Lovin' ' that revealed just how good a singer she really was. After her 1962 cover of Ray Charles's 'Hit The Road Jack' ('Fich' le camp, Jack') picked up a modicum of interest, she found the confidence to look beyond session work and sought a deal of her own.

---

[397] From the film *Anatomy Of A Murder* (1959).

le Rythme du Rock c'est...
JACKiE SEVEN

**LE RYTHME DU ROCK**
(movimento di rock)

**SA GRANDE PASSION**
(his latest flame)

**VIENS DANSER LE TWIST**
(let's twist again)

**BLUE-JEAN'S ROCK**

**45 tours L. D. ELP 7892**

**45 tours simples :**
**V 45.875 et V 45.876**

les disques vogue
créent des vedettes

## Jackie Seven and Nicole Paquin

While the links between jazz and rock'n'roll were obvious, none of the jazz-oriented singers (with the possible exception of Nancy Holloway) truly captured the spirit of rock'n'roll. In retrospect, the power and passion of early rock were probably best captured by a pair of short-lived *rockeuses* whose stars shone briefly as 1961 drew to a close.

Belgium's Jackie Seven took the role of female rock'n'roll singer to new extremes, modelling her style on that of Johnny Hallyday. There was nothing remotely feminine about her approach to the music, for she reasoned that there wasn't anything Hallyday could do on stage that she couldn't match.

Dressed in defiantly tomboy fashion and with her guitar slung over her shoulder, she looked every inch a rockabilly hero.

Seven tore through her 1961 debut, 'Le rythme du rock', with complete abandon. Adapted from Adriano Celentano's 'Movimento di rock', the song was a call to arms that saw her squealing and yodelling through the lyric in the manner of a backwoods Tennessee cowboy. Sitting alongside it on the EP was another excellent Celentano cover, 'Blue-jean's rock', and a comparatively stilted version of Elvis Presley's 'His Latest Flame' ('Sa grande passion'). Backed up by some stunning live performances, the record became a moderate hit, but yet again the market couldn't deal with the affront to normal behaviour posed by the singer. Released in 1962, her second EP saw her blasting through Fats Domino's 'Shu-Rah' ('Ça va'), but her career was swiftly stifled once someone more palatable came along.

The same fate befell Nicole Paquin, another rip-roaring performer with an unwillingness to conform, who stormed through a version of Presley's 'Stuck On You' ('Comme un clou') for a minor hit in 1961. She followed up with one of the great French rock'n'roll records of the era: the dazzling 'Mon mari c'est Frankenstein' (based on the obscure Phil Spector production 'You Can Get Him – Frankenstein' by the Castle Kings). Sadly, her brash, rocking style was too raw for mass consumption and she too was left stranded due to the hostility of the media and much of the general public. Ahead of their time, Paquin, Seven, Hédika and Gélou nonetheless blazed a trail that would be followed by countless performers over the next forty years.

## Sylvie Vartan

Dalida and Clark continued to reign supreme, but at the end of 1961 the first true female star of the new era emerged from the shadows to challenge the existing order. Bulgarian-born Sylvie Vartan had actually made her recording debut in the summer of that year with a couple of duets with Frankie Jordan. She got the gig through the record's producer, her brother Eddie Vartan, after Gillian Hills cancelled at the last minute. A cover of Andy Williams' 'I Like Your Kind Of Love' ('J'aime ta façon de faire ça') did little to further Jordan's career, but the other track, 'Panne d'essence' (Floyd Robinson's 'Out Of Gas') was a major hit, proving far more popular than anything he had yet recorded. With solid rock'n'roll backing and Jordan's assured performance, the record leapt out of the airwaves, and, as the record powered up the charts, the public clamoured to know more about the girl whose thin, reedy voice had given it much of its charm.

The young Vartan had hitherto shown no interest in becoming a singer, but she had long been attracted to the jazz and rock'n'roll sounds she had been introduced to by her older brother. The success of her recording gave her the chance to consider more exciting career options than working in a record shop. More than a gawky schoolgirl, but not quite a sophisticated girl about town, Vartan's personality endeared itself to the pop audience. As summer gave way to autumn, her brother and his friends began to see the possibilities in marketing the pretty teenager to the youth audience as one of their own.

Signed to RCA, Vartan proved she had a much better voice than was apparent on her duets. Her first solo release, 'Quand le film est triste' (a highly improved version of Sue Thompson's 'Sad Movies'), was hardly rock'n'roll, but it was a quality ballad and it picked up airplay on *Salut les copains*. The rest of the EP showed off the raunchier side of her personality with a cover of the Coasters' 'Whipper Snapper' ('Le petit lascar') that outpointed a rival version by Frankie Jordan. It certainly helped that *Salut les copains* programme director Daniel Filipacchi was a close friend of her brother's. Filipacchi put his energies into making the record a hit, and over the winter Vartan was rarely off the airwaves, her version of 'Tout au long du calendrier' ('Calendar Girl') comparing well to the hit version by Petula Clark.

Several well-received live shows in early 1962 showed Vartan to be as tough as Jackie Seven without being quite as uninhibited, and despite the predictable catcalls from the *blousons noirs* in the audience,[398] she showed the makings of a decent live performer. With enough of an edge to attract at least some of the rock'n'roll crowd, but conventional enough not to offend the mainstream French audience, Sylvie Vartan was exactly what the market needed.

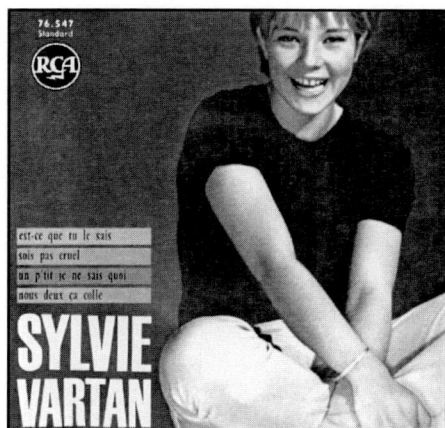

Her next EP featured hit covers of Ray Charles's 'What'd I Say' ('Est-ce que tu le sais') and Bobby Lewis's 'One Track Mind' ('Un p'tit je ne sais quoi'[399]), while a punchy adaptation of Presley's 'Don't Be Cruel' ('Sois pas cruel') proved beyond all doubt that she was an authentic rocker, unlike Dalida or Clark. By the spring of 1962, she was well on her way to becoming the country's leading female star, at least in the youth market.

---

[398] Female singers tended to get short shrift from rock'n'roll audiences, often being greeted with whistles and shouts of *'À poil!'* [Get 'em off!].

[399] Although both were overshadowed commercially by rival versions by Les Chats Sauvages.

## The next wave

Once Vartan had signposted the way forward, other new female singers appeared. Among them was Micky Amline, who had been singing rock'n'roll on stage since 1959, but only made her first record in 1962. Failing to capture the sparkle of her live performances, she nevertheless succeeded in bringing some personality to pseudo-rock'n'roll efforts like 'John, c'est l'amour' (John Leyton's 'Son This Is She'), while tracks such as 'Wy wy' and a cover of Dion's 'Kissin' Game' ('Le soleil de nos vacances') exuded a charm of their own. The following year's 'Donne-moi ma chance' (Babs Tino's 'Too Late To Worry') was also cute in its own way, and the Shadows-like guitars on 'Un garçon manqué' (adapted from the Routers' 'Mashy') added a tasty rock'n'roll edge. Sadly, none of her three EPs truly did her justice and her career soon ground to a halt.

Equally luckless was Maguy Marshall, who cut an impressive cover of Elvis Presley's 'Good Luck Charm' ('Le coup du charme') which lost out to a version by Les Vautours, but was impressive enough to draw a congratulatory telegram from the King himself.[400] Sadly, neither this, nor two further EPs of equally vibrant performances clicked commercially and Marshall soon joined Amline on the back pages of pop history.

By early 1962, Sylvie Vartan had won the race to be France's leading female rocker, following up her early success with an uptempo reworking of Ray Charles's 'Swanee River Rock' ('Fais ce que tu veux') and a stylish version of the Shirelles' 'Baby It's You' ('Baby c'est vous') that swept up the charts in the summer. While Dalida and Petula Clark kept up the competition, Vartan was the most popular among teenagers, her version of the Everly Brothers' 'Bye Bye Love' selling strongly against the contemporary reworking by Ray Charles.[401] She confirmed her as yet uncrowned position as the queen of French pop when she met the uncrowned king, Johnny Hallyday, backstage at the Olympia Theatre in Paris, initiating a long romance that would dominate the French media years to come.

---

[400] Or more likely from his manager, Colonel Tom Parker.
[401] Vartan's version owes more to Charles's arrangement – which was a major hit in France – than to the Everly Brothers' original.

# Chapter 15

## NOUS LES GARS, NOUS LES FILLES
### The growth of French rock'n'roll (1961-62)

*Firmly positioned at the apex of the new rock'n'roll hierarchy, Johnny Hallyday and Sylvie Vartan shared both a manager and a band, and surrounded themselves with kindred spirits like Long Chris and Eddie Vartan, all dedicated to the teen pop revolution. The Hallyday–Vartan clan would be a formidable force in French pop – not least as a result of their links to the most influential man in the pop industry, record producer and presenter of* Salut les copains, *Daniel Filipacchi. With his help, they would become the biggest names in rock'n'roll, throwing down a challenge to the old guard who had dominated French pop since the war.*

*The friendship between the Vartan family and Daniel Filipacchi stemmed from a business relationship between Filipacchi and Sylvie Vartan's brother Eddie, both of whom worked for the Decca label. Although both were passionate jazz fans, they were more than happy to champion the cause of rock'n'roll in pursuit of sales for the label, and, in Filipacchi's case, ratings for his radio show, which was by now aimed more at pop than jazz.*[402]

### *Salut les copains* radio show

By 1961 *Salut les copains* had shaken off its roots in *variétés*, although it never completely abandoned the likes of Charles Aznavour (whose 'Alléluia' was a smash in 1962) or Georges Brassens (whose 'Dans l'eau de la claire fontaine' was also strongly promoted on the show). However, an ever-increasing amount of airtime was now being given over to rock'n'roll – American, British and domestically produced. The show's original theme, Gilbert Bécaud's 1957 recording, 'Salut les copains', had long since given way to Lou Bennett's jazzy 'Brother Daniel', and in 1961 it was changed again, to the Mar-Keys' 'Last Night'.

Such was the programme's popularity that both Bennett and the Mar-Keys enjoyed chart successes with their respective themes. A number of home-grown outfits sought to grab a piece of the pie by cutting covers of the latter, with the faceless Les Barons actually managing to squeeze a hit out of

---

[402] Filipacchi and his business partner Frank Ténot instead indulged their love of jazz on the evening show *Pour ceux qui aiment le jazz*.

their version.[403] Up in Belgium, a rather cheeky group of individuals adopted the name 'The Daniels' in obvious tribute to Filipacchi and unleashed a further version of 'Last Night', picking up a few sales north of the border.

### Âge tendre et tête de bois

Radio was good for generating hits, but with the visuals increasingly mattering almost as much as the music, television was the best medium for creating new stars. In May 1961, Albert Raisner got the go-ahead to produce a pilot for a new youth-oriented TV show called *Âge tendre et tête de bois.*[404] Although a died-in-the-wool jazzman, Raisner was as attuned as Filipacchi to the changing wind and was the first to recognise that the latter's success on radio could be emulated in the newer world of television.

The pilot was filmed live at the Golf Drouot with Les Chaussettes Noires among the featured artists. It was an instant hit with teenagers, who had long felt the need for a show of their own. A kind of audio-visual version of *Salut les copains*, it went into regular production in September,[405] and quickly became essential viewing for every rock and pop fan across the country. Hitherto, the only way rock'n'roll fans had been able to see their favourite performers in action was during the occasional live show that came their way, in one of the risible B-movies that were the French equivalent of American nonsense like *Don't Knock The Rock*, or in cafés that boasted a Scopitone video jukebox.[406]

With image proving as important as substance in French pop, these forerunners of the promotional videos of today were of vital importance in breaking new stars. Practically every major star in French teenage pop made at least one Scopitone film during their career, and those that have survived are sometimes the only remaining record of what these performers were like in a live environment.[407] Johnny Hallyday's 'Laisse les filles', Richard Anthony's 'Itsi bitsi, petit bikini' and Les Chaussettes Noires' 'Je t'aime trop' were among the many records promoted in this way. However, as is evident from surviving clips of Juliette Gréco's 'Jolie môme' and Jacques Brel's 'Madeleine', it was not only teen stars who were showcased in this way.

*Âge tendre et tête de bois* was not initially devoted solely to rock'n'roll any more than *Salut les copains* had been, but gradually the show's content became slanted more and more in that direction. By the time it was rebaptised *Tête de bois et tendres années* in the mid-sixties, it would feature rock singers and groups almost exclusively. Both *Âge tendre* and *Salut les copains* became necessary adjuncts to the daily life of French teenagers, and as such they were ideal places to break new talent. Raisner ran a fairly open booking policy and was not afraid to take a punt on an act who had not yet managed a

---

[403] Even Eddie Vartan had a go, but his rather mundane interpretation fell by the wayside.

[404] Like *Salut les copains*, the show's title was derived from a Gilbert Bécaud song, in this case his 1960 hit, 'Tête de bois'.

[405] In common with many French TV shows, it was broadcast once a month, rather than weekly.

[406] These machines played specially-made film clips. Scopitones were not unique to France, but they do seem to have been more prevalent there than elsewhere.

[407] Most of the clips were mimed, but, as with old footage of the UK's *Ready, Steady, Go*, the Scopitones do a marvellous job of conveying a flavour of the French pop scene of the early sixties.

hit record. For most of the sixties, *Âge tendre* constituted an essential showcase for the country's leading teen-pop singers and groups, and was the most important TV show of its day.[408]

The increasing presence of rock'n'roll singers and groups on television and in the press was matched by their growing prominence on the radio. *Âge tendre* inspired the name of a regular show broadcast by Radio Monte-Carlo, while listeners in the South-West could tune in to *Spécial blue-jeans*, which emanated from Radio Andorra just over the border. Radio Luxembourg weighed in with *Balzac 10-10*, a popular show with a broad audience reach that offered singers an alternative means of exposure to the closed-shop world of *Salut les copains*. Still, it was Filipacchi's pioneering programme that continued to rule the roost, pumping out a ceaseless rotation of hits of the day for an ever-expanding audience.

### Disco revue

The launch in September 1961 of *Disco revue*, the first magazine devoted entirely to pop music, was another indication of the growing importance of rock'n'roll to the French record industry.[409] Its editor, Jean-Claude Berthon, was a young rock'n'roll fan from Nancy who ran the periodical on a shoestring.[410] His preferences were always for the tougher end of rock'n'roll, rather than the polished pop of Richard Anthony, and the early issues of *Disco revue* did much to promote the work of not only Johnny Hallyday, but also Les Chaussettes Noires and Les Chats Sauvages, who remained locked in a fierce competition to be the top group in the country. The magazine's erratic publication schedule prevented it from finding a mass-market circulation, especially outside Paris, but each issue was greeted with fervour by its readers, and record companies were keen to ensure that their latest releases were advertised within its pages. Among the many who noted the possibilities in Berthon's creation was Daniel Filipacchi, who began to draw up plans for a magazine of his own.

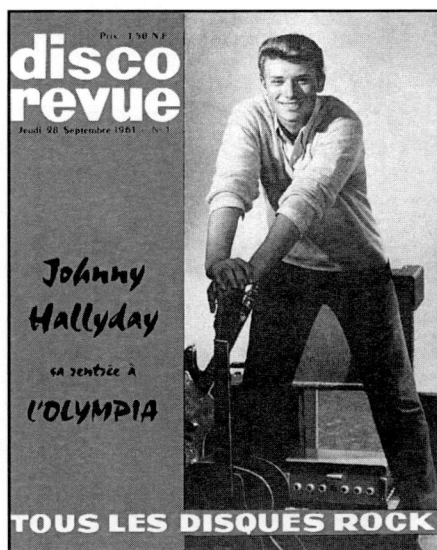

---

[408] Raisner would later tune into the incredible new sounds being made across the Channel in the UK, bringing the leading lights of the beat group scene across to appear on his show. This helped to break down the doors of the French market for a large number of British bands and singers, although in the long run it also helped to sow the seeds of destruction for the French cover version industry.

[409] Strictly speaking, this was a relaunch, as an earlier incarnation had graced the racks for a few months in late 1960 before disappearing from view.

[410] Berthon went on to cut some half-hearted records himself during the mid-sixties, but his main impact was as magazine proprietor and later as chief organiser for rock'n'roll nights staged at the Golf Drouot.

## The Filipacchi – Vartan – Hallyday connection

Filipacchi meanwhile used his radio show to promote the work of those close to him, and producer Eddie Vartan's links to Filipacchi were adroitly exploited by his friend, Frankie Jordan. Jordan's records (often featuring lyrics penned pseudonymously by Filipacchi or his business partner, Frank Ténot, with musical backings supplied by Vartan) were always given generous airplay on *Salut les copains*, and became hits where those by other artists might have struggled. After enjoying massive sales with 'Panne d'essence', a duet with Sylvie Vartan,

Jordan followed up with the atmospheric 'Elle est passée' (an adaptation of Jimmy Jones's 'A Wondrous Place' that owed more than a little to the British version by Billy Fury) and the original 'Le transistor', although a version of Gene McDaniels'/Frankie Vaughan's 'Tower Of Strength' ('Toute ma vie') stretched his vocal capabilities to the limit.

Jordan's success, like that of Vartan, demonstrated that direct access to Filipacchi and Ténot gave singers a fast track to the airwaves, and consequently to the charts. Eddie Vartan exploited this wherever he could, for example ensuring that his protégée Annick Bouquet's version of Elvis Presley's 'Good Luck Charm' ('Le coup du charme') got more airplay than that by Les Vautours. Bouquet duly picked up a hit for her efforts, although in fairness this was due, at least in part, to the fact that her EP also contained superb slices of rock'n'roll like 'Toi c'est pas pareil' (Curtis Lee's 'Under The Moon Of Love') and 'J'ai choisi' (Ben E. King's 'Ecstasy'). She subsequently abandoned this exciting approach in favour of smoother sounds,[411] before

returning to the theatre world from whence she had originally sprung, leaving Vartan to use the same connections to give the best possible career start to his next signing.

Les Pingouins, a rock'n'roll group fronted by singer Lou Vincent, rose rapidly in the spring of 1962. With production by Eddie Vartan, they debuted strongly with an EP on which they opted for a sound drawn from the doo-wop end of the rock'n'roll spectrum. Their rendition of the old Guy Lombardo/ Ted Weems hit, 'Heartaches' ('Pour toi') owed rather too much to the novelty

---

[411] Though she kept the faith with Ben E. King for a polished if unremarkable rendition of his 'First Taste Of Love' ('Le goût d'amour').

version by the Marcels, but the sparkling 'Regarde le ciel' and a tight version of Frankie Jordan's 'Le transistor' testified to their very real abilities. Their rollicking cover of the Marty Robbins/ Rusty York rocker, 'Sugaree' ('Oh, les filles!'[412]), buoyed by regular play on *Salut les copains*, was a deserved hit. Their second EP spun off another in the form of the Coasters' 'Searchin' ' ('Cherche!'), which anticipated the version the UK's Hollies would cut a year later, but their hopes of overtaking Les Chaussettes Noires or Les Chats Sauvages were dashed when Vincent was called up for military service in the summer.

Richard Anthony had been a firm favourite on *Salut les copains* since his first hit, and during 1961 he churned out a several more – all lightly rocking covers of American best-sellers like Ray Peterson's 'Tell Laura I Love Her' ('Dis à Laura') and Bobby Darin's 'Somebody To Love' ('Dis-lui que je l'aime'). Although he lacked the power and the panache of the leading French groups, Anthony was nevertheless a master of the more polished rock'n'roll now coming out of the US and UK, and records like 'Allons dans le bois' (Bobby Rydell's 'Good Time Baby') and 'Trois en amour' (Cliff Richard's 'D In Love') were perfect examples of the family-friendly fodder that he was already coming to define. Despite being bottled offstage at the second *Festival de Rock 'n' Roll* in June 1961, he remained one of the leading rockers in the country, even if serious adherents of the music considered him to be a complete lightweight.

The hardcore rock'n'roller of choice was Johnny Hallyday, who was also rarely off *Salut les copains*, both with fiery outings like 'Sentimental' (Elvis Presley's 'Baby I Don't Care') and rock-tinged ballads like 'Mon septième ciel' (Sal Mineo's 'Seven Steps To Love'). He also came over well in interviews, despite his somewhat rough public image, and did much to ingratiate himself with the hierarchy of French show business – largely thanks to having his manager, Johnny Stark, and long-time role model Lee Hallyday on hand to steer him through the pitfalls of the business. Not everyone was receptive, however: some respected him for his ability as a showman, but others found his rather uncouth, raw approach an affront to everything that the entertainment business stood for.

. Such attitudes were pandered to by actor/comic Jean Yanne, who created the amusing alter ego Johnny 'Rock' Feller as a parody of Hallyday and released the amusing 'J'aime pas le rock', leaving it to the listener to decide who was the victim of his wit – Hallyday or his critics.

Hallyday faced down all such insults and maintained his position at the top through relentless touring and a constant stream of record releases including

---

[412] Already cut a few months earlier by Les Chaussettes Noires as 'Chérie, oh chérie'.

**JOHNNY HALLYDAY**
*nous les gars, nous les Filles*
MON SEPTIÈME CIEL   **vogue**
TU M'PLAIS • CE N'EST PAS MÉCHANT   EPL. 7 825

'Nous les gars, nous les filles' (a catchy reworking of Floyd Robinson's 'Boys And Girls'), the spirited '24.000 baisers' (Adriano Celentano's '24 mila baci') and a cover of Little Richard's 'Tutti Frutti' off his fake-live *Johnny Hallyday et ses fans au Festival de Rock n' Roll* album. With his eye now fixed on bigger and better things, Hallyday jumped ship in the summer of 1961, switching from Vogue to the major-league Philips label. His old record company managed to squeeze one more hit from his final EP, 'À New Orleans' (Gary 'US' Bonds' 'New Orleans'), then settled down to sixty years of recycling the forty or so recordings they had in the can.

Hallyday meanwhile elected to record in London, using a mix of French and British session musicians, resulting in a vastly improved sound. The first results were released in September 1961, his version of Roy Hamilton's 'You Can Have Her' ('Tu peux la prendre') marking a huge leap forward from the tinny sound of his Vogue recordings. The same sessions also produced the classy teen ballad 'Douce violence',[413] which was aimed straight at the hearts of teenage girls across the country and duly became another massive hit, validating the singer's decision to cross the Channel.

But with both Richard Anthony and the leading groups breathing down his neck, and newcomers emerging almost weekly in an attempt to steal his crown, Hallyday was unable to rest on his laurels for long. Most dangerous – in more ways than one – was a performer who first came to prominence thanks to the staging of a *Festival de rock anglais* at the Olympia Theatre in July 1961. The show was a financial disaster, with only a handful of inquisitive youngsters turning out to see a selection of largely unknown British acts, but those who did attend were blown away by a show-stopping performance from a last-minute addition to the bill: the man whom many in France claim was the most exciting rock'n'roll performer ever to walk onstage, Vince Taylor.[414]

## Vince Taylor

Born in England but raised in the US, Taylor had returned to the UK in the late fifties, passing himself off as a genuine American rock'n'roller. Despite cutting a quartet of classic singles including the outstanding 'Brand New Cadillac',[415] and breaking into the UK Top 20 in 1960 with the stunning rocker, 'Jet Black Machine',[416] he had failed to find the stardom he believed he deserved. A nervy, slightly edgy individual, he was in many ways his own worst enemy, and his mood swings did little to impart confidence in those

---

[413] Subsequently the theme of the Elke Sommer film of the same name.

[414] Top of the bill was Wee Willie Harris. Taylor came on as a substitute for an AWOL Duffy Power.

[415] Later a garage band staple across Europe before being revived by the Clash on their *London Calling* album in 1979.

[416] It made No. 15 in the *Record Mirror* chart.

around him – but when he was hot, he was blazing, and, though only a limited singer, he was one of the most dynamic showmen around.

Dressed in black leather in the manner of Gene Vincent, Taylor won rapturous applause from the few hundred spectators at the Olympia, thanks to an animalistic performance during which he clambered all over the equipment, humped the amplifiers and speaker cabinets, writhed on the floor as if in pain and thrashed the stage with a gold chain, leaving the audience – which included Les Chats Sauvages frontman Dick Rivers – in a state of shock. Within hours of leaving the stage, he was signed to an exclusive five-year deal by Barclay, who set about launching his career in France.

Acclaimed by rock fans as the genuine article, Taylor stormed across stages all over the country, driving audiences into a frenzy with a demented act that made Johnny Hallyday look tame by comparison. With concert successes under their belt, Taylor and his group, the Playboys,[417] went into the studio to stamp their own mark on a string of rock'n'roll classics.

With their promotional apparatus running on overdrive, Barclay cranked out an EP every month for six months, beginning in September 1961 with a kickass version of Chuck Berry's 'Sweet Little Sixteen', and flooding the market with product to coincide with Taylor's next scheduled Paris show in November. A hard-driving reworking of Arthur Crudup's 'So Glad You're Mine' (modelled on the more famous rendition by Elvis Presley) gave him a second hit, while a cover of the Jody Reynolds/ Marty Wilde hit, 'Endless Sleep', gave the lie to disdainful claims that he couldn't sing. The latter EP also boasted a stunning treatment of Johnny Kidd & The Pirates' 'Shakin' All Over',[418] and, with the press buzzing, Taylor's releases punched their way onto the airwaves. Despite singing in English rather than French, he looked set to become the biggest rock'n'roll star France had ever seen.

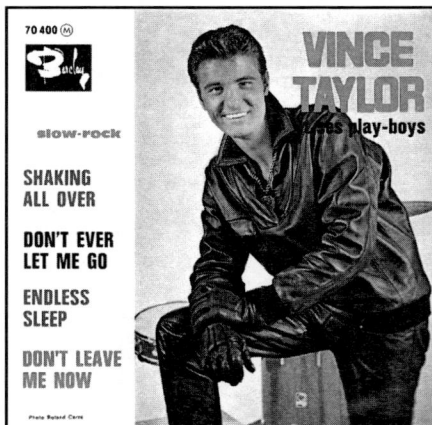

## Other British and American rockers

Taylor was not the only overseas rocker making waves in France, although he was undoubtedly the most successful. Another British outfit to

---

[417] Billed as 'Les Play Boys' in France.
[418] Taylor's version was released as 'Shaking all over'.

235

take the plunge across the Channel were Johnny Taylor et les Strangers, who rocked audiences with a gutsy repertoire and a vibrant stage act. However, they failed to capture the energy of their live performances on any of their four EPs, proving no match for Gene Vincent on a cover of Frankie Laine's 'Jezebel', and disgracing themselves with one of the worst-ever versions of the 4 Seasons' 'Sherry'. Only a triumphant romp through Jerry Lee Lewis's 'It'll Be Me'[419] showed off their talents to good effect. The records flopped and the group missed their big chance, although Taylor stayed on in France, playing guitar in various backing groups over the following months.

Scottish duo Les Travellers were equally unsuccessful in their cross-Channel excursion, meandering musically from the C&W ambience of the Weavers' 'Lonesome Traveler' to a powerful take on Eddie Cochran's 'Twenty Flight Rock'. Their best effort was 'Sœur Anne', a version of the Allisons' 'Are You Sure' that sat uneasily between rock'n'roll, folk and pop, pleasing nobody – apart from, presumably, the duo themselves.

American unit Doug Fowlkes & The Airedales initially found work playing at the American military bases that were still dotted around France[420] before heading for steady employment on the club circuit. A top-notch rock'n'roll outfit boasting a fine African-American singer called Rocky Roberts, they cut a string of EPs which included a tight, ballsy cover of Bobby Lewis's 'Tossin' And Turnin' ', relatively subdued renditions of Ray Charles's 'Hit The Road Jack' and James Brown's/Chubby Checker's 'Good, Good Lovin' ', and a cool and slinky version of the Marathons' 'Peanut Butter'. Sadly, despite consistently excellent musician-ship, they failed to translate their talent into record sales – possibly because they chose to record in English rather than French.

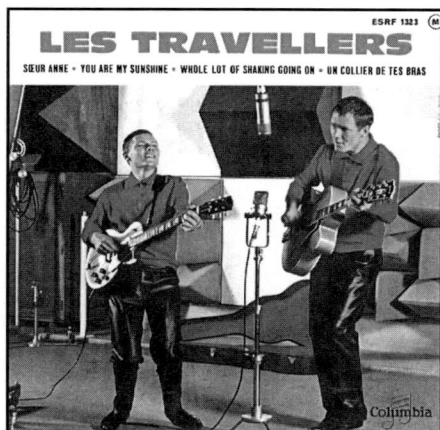

### The French contenders

The softer approach to rock'n'roll brought greater reward to the home-grown Lucky Blondo, a cute, fresh-faced singer with an appealing style, who was the best among the latest bunch of contenders. Released in early

---

[419]  Doubtless inspired by the recent hit version by Cliff Richard.
[420]  Until 1966, when General de Gaulle withdrew from NATO and broke off the American alliance.

*Lucky Blondo.*

1962, his version of Bobby Lewis's 'Tossin' And Turnin'' ('Betty et Jenny') outclassed that by Les Vautours artistically if not commercially, appearing alongside a fine cover of Elvis Presley's 'I Slipped, I Stumbled, I Fell' ('Je bois, je dors et je l'oublie') on an EP that also allowed him to show off his skills as a romantic balladeer on 'C'est merveilleux' (Cliff Richard's 'Travellin' Light'). His second EP was highlighted by an even more effective Cliff Richard cover, 'Dis-moi oui' ('We Say Yeah')[421] and a genuinely exciting reworking of Bobby Darin's 'Multiplication', and set him on the road to stardom.

One of the more impressive newcomers, sartorially at least, was Teddy Raye, who appeared in a lamé suit[422] on the sleeve of a 1962 EP featuring a strong cover of Elvis Presley's 'All Shook Up' ('Crever d'amour'). A second EP offered a decent version of Jimmy Clanton's 'Go, Jimmy, Go' ('Go Teddy go'), but sadly neither went anywhere near the charts. Like Rocky Volcano, Raye ended up having go across the Pyrenees to Spain before he found any significant success.

Belgian outfit Big Brown & The Gamblers were unlikely rock'n'rollers, their leader hiding behind his unlikely *nom de disque* to obscure the fact that he was, by day, a chemist. Backed by a crew of top Belgian jazzmen, he unleashed the frantic 'My Testament', one of the wildest slices of rock'n'roll madness ever conceived outside of the Southern US. Too wild to appeal to the mass market, the record was not a hit, and after two further releases in a jazzier style,[423] he returned to his chosen profession, leaving the rock'n'roll market to younger talents.

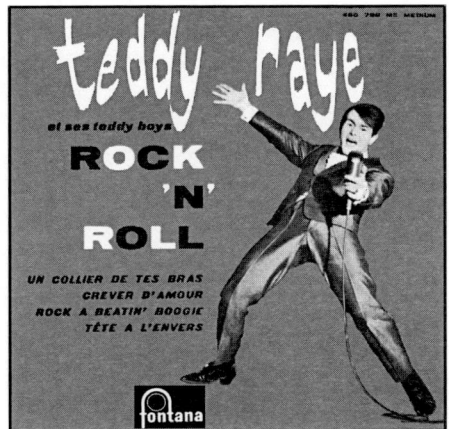

---

[421] Subsequently given a more aggressive treatment by Johnny Hallyday.

[422] Modelled on the one Presley wore on the cover of the *50,000,000 Elvis Fans Can't Be Wrong* album.

[423] Including a credible restrained take on Lionel Hampton's classic, 'Hey! Ba-Ba-Re-Bop', issued as 'Hey ba ba re bop'.

Martinique-born Michel Sydney switched from jazz to doo-wop in 1961 with an engaging stroll through Johnny Maestro's 'Mr. Happiness' ('C'est le bonheur') and an on-the-button cover of Johnny Angel's 'Falling Teardops' ('Au secours'). On the other side of his EP, he upped the tempo for a remake of Belgian singer Adamo's 'Poor fool' ('C'est pas vrai') that outrocked the original but fared no better on the airwaves. Although it was a creditable debut showing Sydney to be a fine stylist with a rich voice perfect for the vocal group sounds then increasing in popularity across the Atlantic, it was not a hit. The more commercial 'Toute ma vie' (Gene McDaniels' 'Tower Of Strength') was an inspired follow-up, but he was beaten to the punch by Frankie Jordan, and, despite his positive approach to the music, he also failed in his bid to become the genre's first star from the French Caribbean.

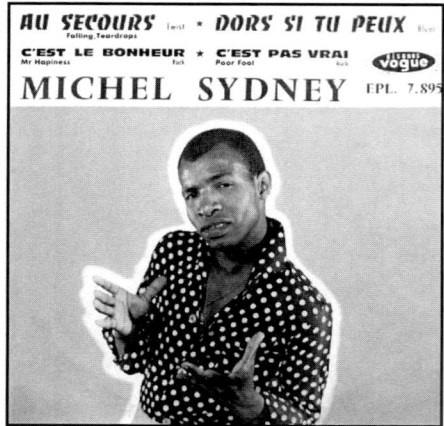

That honour went instead to the French Guianan Henri Salvador — perhaps deservedly so, after all his pioneering efforts. Although he had more or less abandoned rock'n'roll following the death of Boris Vian at the end of 1959,[424] by 1961 he was again knocking on the door with the EP *Classic-Rocks*. Clearly inspired by the latest Hollywood blockbuster, *El Cid*,[425] the stupid 'Le Cid-rock' was less overtly rock'n'roll than his work with Vian and owed more to his sense of the absurd, though 'Athalie-rock' was far better and the silly Ancient Rome narrative 'Horace-rock' showed he had been paying attention to Ray Charles hits like 'Lonely Avenue'.

This was his first release since quitting Barclay in 1961 to set up his own Disques Salvador label,[426] distributed by Philips. The record wasn't a hit, but after rethinking his approach he struck gold the following year with 'Le lion est mort ce soir', a humorous but musically tight adaptation of the Tokens' 'The Lion Sleeps Tonight' that ran a dire instrumental version by Hubert Rostaing and a rival vocal

---

[424] The pair's final effort was a self-proclaimed 'franco-spiritual', 'Donne, donne, donne' which Salvador premièred in concert in 1960. It was caught on tape for the live album *Henri Salvador à l'Alhambra,* also known as *Alhambra Maurice Chevalier,* as this is what is printed on the front cover. The above title is on the reverse.

[425] Released as *Le Cid* in France.

[426] Renamed Rigolo in 1964 when Salvador switched distributor.

reading by Gloria Lasso ('Réveille-toi') off the airwaves. It was the first of a run of successful rock'n'roll covers for him, which included retoolings of Elvis Presley's 'Return To Sender' ('Retour au porteur'), Johnny Cymbal's 'Mr. Bass Man' ('Mr. Boum-Boum') and the 4 Seasons' 'Sherry' and 'Big Girls Don't Cry' ('Grosse fille pleure pas')[427]. He also promoted his records on television, dressing in a succession of ridiculous costumes that reflected the subject matter of each song. Thus he became Zorro for 1964's 'Zorro est arrivé' (the Coasters' 'Along Came Jones'), a hit right across the age spectrum, making him one of the few performers of the era to achieve such broad appeal.

Another veteran of the early days of rock'n'roll to finally achieve a commercial breakthrough was Danyel Gérard. He had returned from army service in 1961 to find he had been overtaken by Johnny Hallyday, Richard Anthony and others. Not wasting any time, he signed a new deal with Polydor and got back to business with 'Laisse crier ton cœur' (a superior adaptation of Bobby Rydell's 'Kissin' Time') and the piano-pumping 'Oh Marie-Line', which confirmed all of his early promise. A talented singer, guitarist and songwriter, and a confident performer on stage, he followed up with a second EP in 1962 which included decent covers of Timi Yuro's 'Hurt' ('Blessé') and the Drifters' 'Please Stay' ('Cœur gros'). But it was 'Marjorie, Marjorie', a powerful rocker in the style of Italian star Adriano Celentano, that stormed the charts and sent him on his way.

Jean-Jacques Debout had started his career just before the rock'n'roll storm broke, and his 1959 hit 'Les boutons dorés'[428] and the following year's 'La corde' had little in common with the sounds now gripping French youth. His first rock'n'roll-flavoured efforts, like his 1961 cover of Conny Froboess's West German smash, 'Midi-Midinette',[429] met with a miserable response, as did the Henri Salvador-inked 'La première fois qu'on aime'. He followed it up in 1962 with an ill-advised adaptation of Hal Kemp's pre-war classic, 'Gloomy Sunday' ('Sombre

---

[427] The French version of 'Sherry' retained the English title.
[428] Also recorded (as 'Boutons dorés') by the *chansonnière* Barbara, which gives some indication of how far removed from rock'n'roll it was.
[429] The French title lost the hyphen to become 'Midi midinette'.

dimanche'), which likewise made little commercial impact.

Debout was also a talented songwriter, penning 'Cette nuit-là' for German diva Marlene Dietrich, whom he supported in concert on her 1962 French shows. Although his first self-penned EP flopped in 1963 (perhaps because the enjoyable 'Les plages de septembre' appeared at the height of winter), his growing friendship with Johnny Hallyday led to several joint concerts that helped establish him in the teenage market. He was thus able to find a niche for his tuneful pop songs, which were closer in style to the Philadelphia sound of Bobby Rydell and Frankie Avalon than to the rough and ready rock preferred by Hallyday, though it was his compositions for Lucky Blondo ('Dans l'eau bleue', adapted from Bobby Vinton's revival of the Clovers' 'Blue Velvet') and Sylvie Vartan ('Tous mes copains') that earned him a place in the world of rock'n'roll.

## Rock'n'roll festivals

Debout and Gérard may have been popular, but neither enjoyed the same level of fan fervour as the country's leading rock'n'roll groups. Les Chaussettes Noires probably had the edge over the competition in terms of musicianship (although rumour has it they were sometimes replaced in the studio by sessionmen) and were the star attraction at the second *Festival de Rock 'n' Roll*[430] in June 1961. For their part, their rivals, Les Chats Sauvages, triumphed in front of their home crowd at *La coupe du monde de rock 'n' roll*, a tournament staged in Juan-les-Pins that August,[431] and turned in such an incendiary performance at the third *Festival de Rock 'n' Roll* in November 1961 that their fans rioted before headliner Vince Taylor was even able to take the stage.

Taylor foolishly allowed himself to be photographed standing amidst the rubble, and, despite taking no part in the incident, somehow managed to attract the blame for what had happened. The press immediately turned against him and began to castigate him as a dark force within rock'n'roll. This turn of events greatly benefitted Johnny Hallyday, who no longer seemed to be such a malevolent figure by comparison.[432] Whatever riots he might go on to provoke in the future, he would always be forgiven by an indulgent press thankful that he wasn't Vince Taylor.

Taylor's star immediately began to fall as bookings dried up, but he soldiered on against the odds, turning out a storming rendition of Gene Vincent's 'Blue Jean Bop' for his fourth EP and performing wherever he could,[433] cementing his loyal following among the rock'n'roll fanatics of Paris. A punchy version of Elvis Presley's 'Mean Woman Blues' maintained the quality of his recorded output, and his debut album, *Le rock c'est ça* (which simply rounded up highlights from his EPs) sold well to his existing fans, but

---

[430]  With the rapid growth in home-grown rock'n'roll, the 'international' element of the first festival was dropped for this and subsequent festivals.

[431]  Actually, any number of bands – including Danny Boy et ses Pénitents and Vince Taylor et ses Play Boys – claimed victory. Irrespective of who was the actual winner, the event boosted all the bands' profiles.

[432]  This despite the fact that Hallyday could be just as wild and unhinged as Taylor, both on stage and on record, as evidenced by his recently released revival of Jerry Lee Lewis's 'High School Confidential' ('Nous, quand on s'embrasse').

[433]  Including the show at the Olympia where Johnny Hallyday first met Sylvie Vartan.

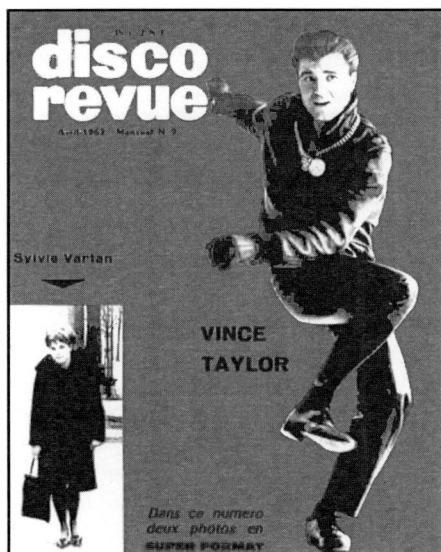

the negative publicity began to take its toll, precipitating a slump in his record sales in the new year.

Attempting to broaden his appeal, he opened a season at the upmarket Folies-Pigalle cabaret in April 1962, headlining a modern revue entitled *Twist appeal – L'érotisme au XXième siècle*. The juxtaposition of Taylor's rock'n'roll antics with motorbikes and strippers caused an enormous fuss among the great and good of Paris, but the late-evening shows were off limits to teenagers and did little to boost his flagging popularity. Those who attended were treated to an experience they were unlikely ever to forget, but the revue did nothing to arrest his commercial fall from grace – despite the fact that he enjoyed continued support in the pages of *Disco revue*.

## The leading groups

Les Chaussettes Noires closed out 1961 with 'Vivre sa vie' (Cliff Richard's 'Gee Whizz, It's You'), 'Petite Sheila' (their hero Gene Vincent's 'She She Little Sheila') and the festive 'Noël de l'an dernier', a rather disappointing effort based on the Scottish favourite 'Auld Lang Syne'. In contrast, Les Chats Sauvages were by now taking their lead firmly from Cliff Richard and the Shadows. Their eponymous debut album included a cover of the British singer's 'I'm In Love With You' ('Oh baby, tu me rends fou'), while their first EP of 1962 contained two: the super-charged 'Laisse-moi rire' ('Lessons In Love') and an attractive treatment of the ballad 'When The Girl In Your Arms Is The Girl In Your Heart' ('Sous le ciel écossais'), which rightly became a hit.

Of course, both groups benefitted from the exposure they received in *Disco revue*, but the mag also did sterling work to promote the other leading French groups of the day, with Danny Boy et ses Pénitents featuring heavily in the third issue, and both Les Pirates and Les Vautours picking up valuable coverage in the fourth.

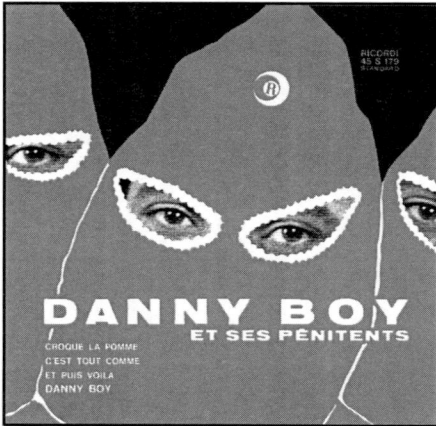

Glossy large-scale photographs and laudatory press coverage never hurt anybody's career, and all three groups saw their popularity boosted as circulation of the magazine rose, with Danny Boy's 'C'est tout comme' enjoying strong airplay, Les Pirates enjoying strong sales for the bluesy 'Dany', and Les Vautours picking up another hit with 'Pas sincère' (Dion's 'Runaround Sue') in early 1962. However, the latter's attempt to go head to head with the all-conquering Chaussettes Noires with a creditable cover of their 'Le chemin de la joie' was unsuccessful.

## New groups

In the wake of these front runners, new groups continued to emerge from the shadows. From the Golf Drouot came the unimpressive El Toro et les Cyclones, who managed a pair of moderately interesting EPs. The first of these saw them employing a prototype beat group sound on a passable version of Little Richard's 'Long Tall Sally' ('Oncle John'), but the rest of the record was given over to somewhat weedy rock'n'roll. Their take on Fabian's 'Tiger' ('Comme un tigre') fell some way below the standard previously set by Georges Aber, while the upbeat 'Je l'aime telle qu'elle est' (Bobby Angelo & The Tuxedos' 'Skinny Lizzie') was outclassed by a far better version from Belgium's Jacky Delmone, neither their guitar assault, nor their vocals truly cutting the mustard.

Their second EP was little better than the first, the lack of drive on a well-played version of Eddie Cochran's 'Twenty Flight Rock' ('Vingtième étage') exposing the group's limitations. Although they succeeded in landing a minor hit with 'Le vagabond' (a cover of Dion's 'The Wanderer'), this too was nowhere near raunchy enough and was deservedly eclipsed by a superior version by Richard Anthony. Even so, they made a decent splash on the Parisian live circuit before falling apart when their lead singer, Daniel Dray (El Toro), and then their excellent lead guitarist, Jacques Dutronc, were called up for army service.

With new groups popping up all over the country, there was little need to import any more, but Italian immigrants Les Brutos made their mark with a strange blend of balladry, rock'n'roll and a wicked sense of the

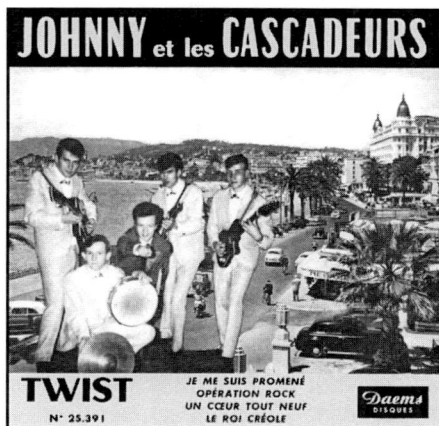

ridiculous. Aiming for a role as the clown princes of the group scene, they cut a passable update of the Gladiolas'/ Diamonds' 1957 hit, 'Little Darlin' ',[434] and found work touring as a support act for Sacha Distel. However, despite becoming a popular live act, they never managed a hit record.

Hailing from Toulon on the Mediterranean coast, Johnny et les Cascadeurs (fronted by child actor/ singer Johnny Monteilhet) recorded a solitary EP for the Paris-based independent Daems. They did a reasonable job on Elvis Presley's 'King Creole' ('Le Roi Créole') and a rather better one on the original 'Opération rock', but sadly remained a purely local phenomenon, victims of music industry inertia. Instead of pursuing the real talent that existed in the provinces, record companies remained content to churn out budget-label identikit covers of hits like Johnny Hallyday's 'Itsy bitsy, petit bikini' and Gilbert Bécaud's 'Tête de bois' by faceless outfits like Les Stéréos.[435] As in Britain, where groups from up and down the country had to go to London to stand any chance of making the big time, so French groups found it necessary to make the trek to Paris and hang out at the Golf Drouot, now the favoured haunt of talent scouts.

### Talent shows at the Golf Drouot

The need to visit the Golf Drouot became even more essential after manager Henri Leproux installed a stage there in early 1962 and established a genuine springboard to success, the aptly named Tremplin. An open booking policy meant that any group with half an ounce of talent could come up to the Golf and ask for a chance to ply their wares before the teenage throng. Leproux made his club the leading teenage venue in town by offering a mixture of amateur nights and regular shows by the leading groups and singers of the day, and it was entirely fitting that *Disco revue* proprietor Jean-Claude Berthon chose to base his operation there.

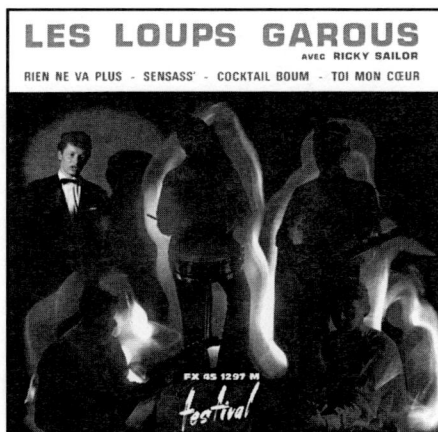

The first group to play on the famous Tremplin stage were Les Loups Garous from Nice, a talented but unpolished unit led by vocalist Ricky Sailor who were trying to follow in the

---

[434] Listed on the sleeve as 'Little darling'.
[435] Much like the Embassy releases sold in Woolworth's stores in the UK.

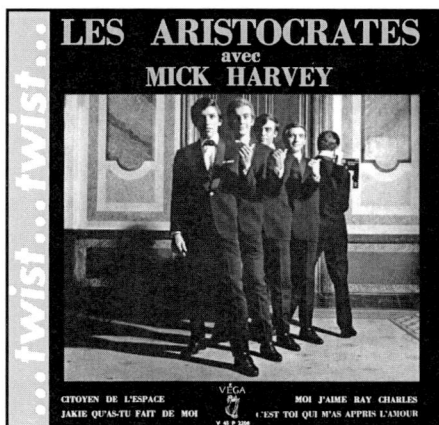

LES ARISTOCRATES
avec
MICK HARVEY

CITOYEN DE L'ESPACE    MOI J'AIME RAY CHARLES
JAKIE QU'AS-TU FAIT DE MOI    C'EST TOI QUI M'AS APPRIS L'AMOUR
VÉGA

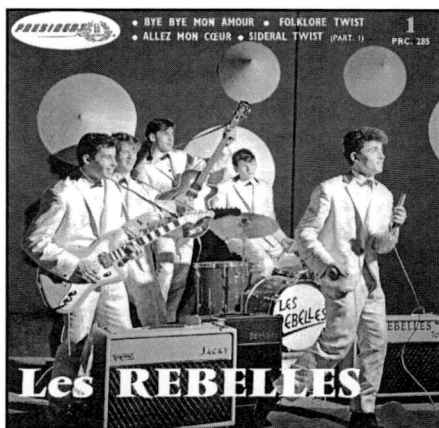

● BYE BYE MON AMOUR ● FOLKLORE TWIST
● ALLEZ MON CŒUR ● SIDERAL TWIST (PART. II)    1    PRC. 285

Les REBELLES

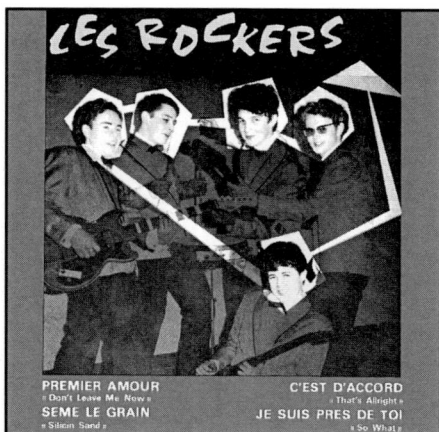

LES ROCKERS

PREMIER AMOUR    C'EST D'ACCORD
« Don't Leave Me Now »    « That's Allright »
SEME LE GRAIN    JE SUIS PRES DE TOI
« Silicon Sand »    « So What »

footsteps of their hometown heroes, Les Chats Sauvages. Despite local followings in both Nice and Paris, and a gutsy debut release on Festival that featured a fast but ragged cover of Elvis Presley's 'Too Much' ('Sensass' ') and the superb 'Cocktail boum' (written for the group by Leproux himself), they never got the major-label support they deserved. Their second EP offered a great Cliff Richard-styled rocker, 'Elle est vraiment jolie',[436] but was similarly unsuccessful despite their tremendous live popularity, and they disintegrated soon after.

Les Aristocrates, a Paris-based outfit led by the excellent Mick Harvey, enjoyed a similarly rapid rise and fall. They wowed the crowds at the Golf Drouot with an energetic style modelled on the country-influenced recordings of Ray Charles, and the superb country-rock shuffle 'Citoyen de l'espace' (Derry Weaver's 'Tonkin' ') captured them at their best. It was, however, the excellent 'Moi, j'aime Ray Charles' and a version of the Hank Snow/Ray Charles hit, 'I'm Movin' On' ('C'est pas méchant'), that laid bare their debt to the great soul master. The group enjoyed a loyal local following, but their minor-label status (they were signed to Véga) and a lack of solid radio support meant that they failed to translate this into sales for either of their two EPs.

'C'est pas méchant' also found its way into the repertoire of Belgian singer Kris Doogan, who teamed up with top-flight Dutch group the Eastern Aces to record a version for the Belgian and Dutch markets in 1962, coupled with the rocking 'Tu l'as trouvé'. The single made a few waves in Belgium, but failed to register across the border in France, and the Eastern

---

[436] Also cut by Les Chats Sauvages in a more polished rendition, which, for some reason, only appeared as a jukebox pressing.

Aces subsequently went their own way, releasing a handful of records in the Netherlands, but never troubling francophone listeners again.

Back in Paris, the newest kids on the block, Les Rebelles, turned out a passable cover of Ricky Nelson's 'Hello Mary Lou' ('Bye bye mon amour') that was blasted off the airwaves by rival versions from Petula Clark and Les Champions in early 1962. They fared just as badly with their second, far better EP,[437] memorable for the rapid-fire 'Je ne peux pas me passer de toi', and never made any real impact beyond the city limits, dogged by line-up changes that kept them firmly locked into the club circuit for several years.

Also making ripples at the Golf Drouot were Les Rockers, who cut some enjoyable covers from the Presley songbook, most notably a tough rendition of 'Slicin' Sand' ('Sème le grain') that outrocked the light-hearted original. The group had an excellent vocalist in Dan Lee Stive, and the highlight of their short recording career was a well-executed cover of Johnny Kidd & The Pirates' 'So What' ('Je suis près de toi'), driven by an excellent descending guitar line. Too rough and ready for mass consumption, they fell victim to poor distribution and remained largely unheard in the wider world.

### *Salut les copains* magazine

While the Tremplin established itself as *the* fast track to rock'n'roll fame in the spring of 1962, across town Daniel Filipacchi readied his plans for a monthly magazine to deliver on the promise of *Disco revue*. Carrying the same title as his radio show, the first issue of *Salut les copains* hit newsstands across the country in June. Sporting a picture of Johnny Hallyday on the front cover and packed full of glossy colour photos, interviews, advertisements, record reviews and a hit parade based on requests to the radio show, it was an instant success. By the end of the year, circulation was in excess of a million copies a month. *Salut les copains* became the magazine of the moment for all fans of rock and pop music, and the chart listing inside became the definitive guide to what was popular in France – at least, among the magazine's readership.[438] Very soon, coverage in the *Salut les copains* magazine became as important as airplay on the radio show.

Filipacchi's decision to diversify his activities would later see him buying up the rival *Âge tendre*[439] and relaunching it as *Mademoiselle âge tendre*, a sister publication for *Salut les copains* aimed exclusively at female readers,

---

[437] Credited to Jean-Pierre et les Rebelles, although the singer was the same on both discs.

[438] See pages 25-28 for a discussion of the problems posed by this and other charts during the period covered by this book.

[439] Initially launched in late 1962, without any connection to Raisner's television show, and without Raisner's permission.

further enhancing his clout within the industry. The move into publishing came at just the right time, as, one month after the first edition went on sale, rival station Radio Luxembourg began broadcasting a daily show featuring songs selected by Golf Drouot proprietor Henri Leproux, posing a direct challenge to the dominance of the airwaves enjoyed up until now by *Salut les copains*.

# Chapter 16

## C'EST BEAU LA VIE
### Holding hard to old traditions (1958-62)

*The first two years of the sixties witnessed the slow but steady rise of rock'n'roll, yet the French charts for this period reveal that a sizeable proportion of the public continued to favour the sounds of the previous generation. For instance, the final* Disco revue *chart for 1961 had Johnny Hallyday at No. 1 with 'Avec une poignée de terre' (Gene McDaniels' 'A Hundred Pounds Of Clay'),[440] but their Top 10 also included Charles Aznavour ('Il faut savoir'), Les Compagnons de la Chanson ('Marin') and 'Poderoso señor (Protégez-moi seigneur)', André Hossein's theme from the film* Le goût de la violence. *Jacques Brel and Marcel Amont could be found further down the Top 20, while on the album chart Léo Ferré joined Brel in the Top 10. The bulk of the hit parade may have been given over to rock'n'roll, but the* chanson *was alive and well, even as the barbarians gathered at the gates.*

*This demonstrated that there was still a substantial audience for a more traditional style of song, one that had its roots in the* chanson *tradition as it had developed over the past sixty years. For them, rock'n'roll was at best an irrelevance and at worst an aberration, a mindless diversion away from 'real music'. Rock'n'roll may have begun moving out of the margins and into the mainstream commercially speaking, but this was more representative of the changing demographic in French society than of a change in taste among the wider listening public, many of whom still craved the emotive quality and depth of the* chanson.

### Stars of *chanson*

The most popular star at the time was Charles Aznavour, whose string of commercial winners was covered by the great and the good of *la chanson française*, although nobody could sing Aznavour's lyrics as well as he did himself. Courting controversy with such carnal offerings as 1958's 'Je te donnerai' and a 1960 reworking of 'Il y avait trois jeunes garçons', his direct approach paid dividends with a run of hits that were rarely off the radio. He joined the expanding Barclay stable in 1960, bidding farewell to his old company Ducretet-Thomson with the excellent *C'est ça* album, which included two further gems in the critical 'Liberté' and a frank commentary on the attraction of young women for older men, 'Tu étais trop jolie'.

He opened the new decade at a creative peak with 'Tu t'laisses aller', a

---

[440]  Also covered by Dalida and Richard Anthony.

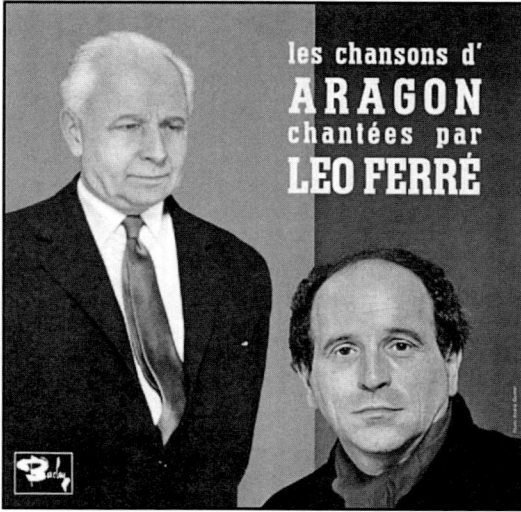

poignant look at the death of a romance which touched the hearts of millions. This set him up for a series of classics that spanned the generations in their appeal, notably 1961's 'La marche des anges' (a reworking of an old Christmas song, 'Les anges dans nos campagnes') and 'Il faut savoir', a discourse on the difficulties of learning from experience set to an effortlessly catchy tune that deservedly topped the charts.[441]

The Barclay label was by now also home to Léo Ferré, who had traded major-label security for greater artistic freedom, though it didn't always turn out that way. *Paname*, his first long-player for the company, generated hits with the title track and the upbeat 'Jolie môme', and boasted several other memorable compositions including 'Les poètes' and the incisive 'Merde à Vauban', whose lyrics were sharply at odds with its mellow arrangement. However, the jazzy 'La maffia'[442] moved the singer closer toward the music hall mainstream than he might have intended.

While Barclay attempted to steer him toward more commercial waters, Ferré sought to emphasise the *chanson*'s traditional links with poetry by setting the works of Louis Aragon to music. The self-explanatory *Les chansons d'Aragon* album included many high spots including the excellent 'L'affiche rouge' and 'Est-ce ainsi que les hommes vivent'.

He continued to show his disdain for convention on the EP *Les chansons interdites*, a selection of songs his label had originally deemed unsuitable for release – among them the anti-militarist 'Miss Gueguerre' and the declamatory 'Thank you Satan', which neatly inverted the sense of most gospel songs.

By turns romantic ('Vingt ans', 'L'amour', 'Les chéris') and viciously sarcastic ('Les Parisiens'), many of Ferré's early sixties' EP tracks went uncollected on album. His support for the anarchists, expressed in songs such as 'Les temps difficiles' and 'Les 400 coups', made it difficult for him to secure airplay or television appearances. And, just as the forthright lyrics of Jacques Brel and Georges Brassens had led to accusations of misogyny, so his work generated criticism for the likes of the ironic 'Les femmes'.

Although Ferré's popularity was on the rise, he remained overshadowed by Brassens, still the genre's greatest exponent. Brassens had gone from from strength to strength in the late fifties, with the nature-loving 'Auprès ce

---

[441] Adapted into English, it was an airplay favourite in the UK in the mid-sixties as 'You've Got To Learn' by Diane Ferraz & Nicky Scott. The same adaptation later became a major hit in Australia for Kamahl.

[442] Recorded first by Catherine Sauvage back in the fifties.

mon arbre' (1956), the emphatic 'La marche nuptiale' (1958) and his light-hearted look at death, 'Les funérailles d'antan' (1960) all establishing themselves as radio favourites within days of their release.

He was also well-represented on LP, as his superstar status warranted. *Georges Brassens No. 4* saw him setting the words of Paul Verlaine ('Colombine') and Victor Hugo ('La légende de la nonne') to music, though it was the gentle 'Je me suis fait tout petit' which stood out from the crowd. *Georges Brassens 5* delivered the superbly observed 'Oncle Archibald', the witty 'Au bois de mon cœur' and the weary 'Le vin'. *Georges Brassens Volume 6* offered a window into the world of the voyeur, 'Le pornographe', and a remarkable treatise on self-sacrifice, 'La femme d'Hector', while the imagery of 'Bonhomme' furthered his reputation as a poet. And, if 'Le vieux Léon' offered nothing new in terms of music, few could deny that his way with a lyric was hard to match.

Brassens eased off the pedal in the sixties, recording far more sparingly but always coming up with the goods. Released in 1960, *Georges Brassens No. 7* contained further classics in 'Pénélope' and 'Le mécréant', while 1961's *Georges Brassens 8* featured the moving 'La ballade des cimitières' and 'Le temps passé', and the remarkable role reversal of 'La traîtresse', in which the singer catches his mistress with her husband. He even managed to hang on to his younger fans, swinging by the *Salut les copains* studio on occasion, and his biggest hits were popular across the whole age spectrum.

The continuing success of the *chanson* mirrored that of the folk revival in the US, representing an alternative to the disposable sounds of the pop marketplace, although musical comparison between the two movements was limited to Brassens' 'L'orage', which inexplicably tapped the sound of Johnny Cash's Sun recordings. Rooted in tradition, the music of the *chansonniers* paid little heed to rock'n'roll, and Brassens in particular remained aloof from the pop world. While younger music buyers fell over themselves in the rush to buy the latest Johnny Hallyday EP, the steady sales enjoyed by Brassens provided a counterbalance to the air of frivolity in the wider marketplace.

### Humour, satire and politics

While Brassens and Ferré took the genre onward and upward, a new generation of performers were taking their first steps in the world of the *chanson*. Ricet Barrier[443] broke through in 1958 with 'La servante du château',

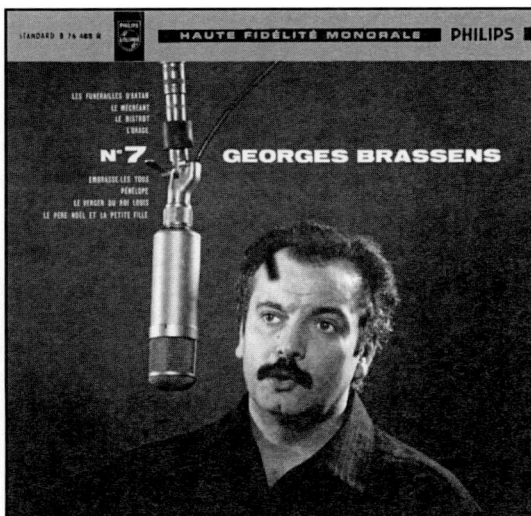

---

[443]  On some releases his name was styled 'Ricet-Barrier'.

which recalled the poetry of François Rabelais in its depiction of character, and, set to a decent tune, gave the singer a well-deserved hit. His self-titled LP offered a handful of similar ditties, all giving full reign to his rib-tickling lyrics, among them 'La java des Gaulois' and 'La demoiselle de Montauban'. Meanwhile, his twenties'-jazz pastiche, 'Dolly 25', was picked up by the still-popular Les Frères Jacques, a group of singing acrobats who included it on an EP along with three of his other tunes. Although Barrier often appeared on stage clutching a guitar, the LP brimmed with contemporary orchestration, none better than the exquisite arrangement on the rhythmic 'Drôle de vie'. And, while the traditional New Orleans jazz backing on 'J'aime les fleurs' may have been decidedly old hat,[444] the more contemporary sound of 'Les pasteurs' anchored the album in the late fifties, and delivered a second winner with the amusing portrayal of 'Le crieur de journaux'.

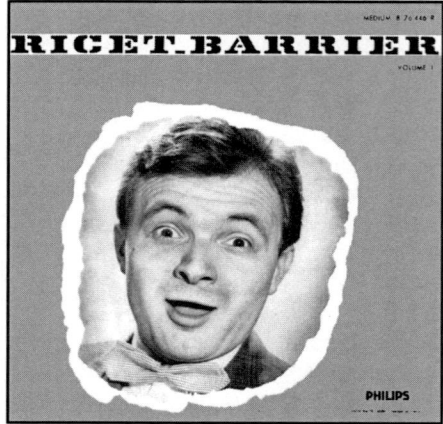

When not covering the works of Barrier, Les Frères Jacques continued to work their distinctive magic on a variety of material, slinking into risqué territory on 'Elle faisait du strip-tease',[445] charging through 'Vas-y Papa' and the brassy 'La demoiselle de bas-étage', and ridiculing the cha-cha fad on 'Shah, shah persan'. Too intellectual for much of the music hall audience, they nevertheless retained a loyal following both for their 1960 LP, *10 chansons de... Jacques Prévert*, and for the atypically restrained 'La violoncelliste'.

A comic approach also paid off for Les Quatre Barbus, when the erotic imagery of 'Les filles de La Rochelle' and 'O, mon berger fidèle' won them a new audience for their *chansons paillardes*.[446] They peaked in 1961 with the infectious 'Le parti d'en rire' (adapted from Ravel's 'Boléro') and the LP *Chansons égrillardes* before regressing into children's songs and sea shanties as their career slowly wound down.

---

[444] Notwithstanding the trad jazz boom across the Channel.

[445] Also given an amusing treatment by Bourvil.

[446] A type of singalong music, often erotic or scatalogical, occasionally political, and usually derived from old folk tunes.

## Singing troubadours

Although at times it seemed that humour, sarcasm, political ideals and derision were the hallmarks of *la chanson française*, there was room for singers who took a diametrically opposed approach. Franciscan monk Le Père Duval made enough impact with his acoustic guitar and gentle songs like 1957's 'La p'tite tête' and 'J'ai joué de la flûte' to become popularly known as *'Le guitariste du bon Dieu'* [God's Guitarist], though outings like 'La paix si douce' or 'Dans le ciel' were unlikely to reach an audience beyond his religious fellow-travellers.[447] Though he did not achieve anything like major success, he was well known enough for Georges Brassens to take a poke at him on his 1962 hit, 'Les trompettes de la renommée'.

*Le Père Duval.*

Félix Leclerc preferred a more traditional approach, and despite spending most of his time in his native Quebec, he remained a respected figure, if not quite in the same league as Brassens. His end-of-decade album, *Les nouvelles chansons de Félix Leclerc*, continued his high standards, with the uptempo 'L'héritage' and the excellent 'Les cinq millionaires' joining his earlier classics as triumphs of fifties' *chanson*.

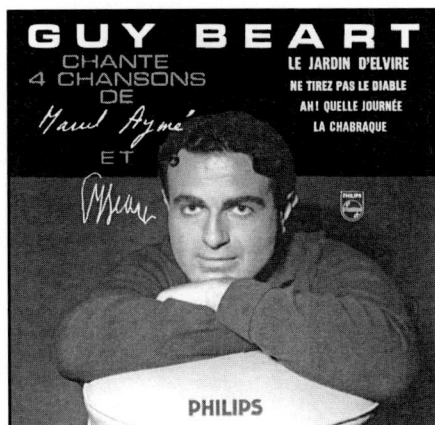

Guy Béart anchored his songs firmly on the Left Bank of the Seine, paying tribute to the area in 'Il n'y a plus d'après', a 1960 hit which he shared with a version by Juliette Gréco.[448] Thereafter, his popularity began to wane, although he continued to enjoy airplay with the cautionary 'Ne tirez pas le diable', the film theme 'Pierrot la tendresse', and the banjo-accented 'Le matin je m'éveille en chantant'.

Robert Ripa had a similarly faltering run, having initially risen to prominence in 1955 with a lovely version of 'Mon pot' le Gitan', a tribute to the recently

---

[447] Religious imagery was also a hallmark of the early songs of Jacques Brel, prompting Georges Brassens to greet him on occasion as 'Abbé Brel' [Father Brel], although by the late fifties Brel had moved on to less mystical discourses.

[448] This song is often subtitled 'À Saint-Germain-des-Prés', though this did not appear on either Béart's or Gréco's original EPs.

departed Django Reinhardt.[449] In 1957, he followed up with readings of Tennessee Ernie Ford's 'Sixteen Tons' ('Seize tonnes') and Léo Ferré's 'Mon p'tit voyou' – the spur for a short run of hits that included the less impressive 'La bague à Jules' and ended in 1961 with the march-tempo 'Magali', a composition from the pen of another emerging writer, Robert Nyel.

Nyel's own, somewhat weaker version of 'Magali' was a hit in its own right, but his recordings generally failed to shift many copies. His greatest success came via covers by Bourvil (who enjoyed a 1961 smash with the pleasant 'Mon frère d'Angleterre') and Juliette Gréco (who recorded 'C'était bien (Le petit bal perdu)' in the same year[450]).

Jean Ferrat was likewise a gifted composer, responsible for the 1955 hit 'Les yeux d'Elsa'[451] by André Claveau. He made a low-key recording debut in 1958 with the anti-militarist 'Les mercenaires', a pseudo-folk song housing a contemporary message. It flopped, although the accompanying 'Frédo la nature' carried an acerbic lyric worthy of Aristide Bruant, suggesting the new singer might be worth watching. A vocal supporter of the Communist Party, Ferrat returned in 1960 with the flamenco-styled 'Federico Garcia Lorca', an anti-Franco treatise paying tribute to the martyr of the Spanish Civil War. A critic of hypocrisy wherever he found it, Ferrat also turned his fire on modern Paris with 'Regarde-toi Paname', couching his assault in a sweet arrangement that failed to win the hearts of modern Parisians. The accordion backing on the romantic 'Ma môme' proved more palatable, achieving widespread radio play without quite translating into a hit.

Another Communist who wore his heart on his sleeve was Francis Lemarque. With infectious melodies and sparkling arrangements, he rode out the decade with 'Une rose rouge', 'Rendez-vous de Paname', and the children's favourite 'La poupée magique'. He sported his political colours on the May Day-referencing 'Le temps du muguet', wrapping his lyric around Vasily Solovyov-Sedoi's Russian favourite, 'Podmoskovniye vyechera',[452] but he also sought out the wider public with romantic offerings like 'Tu s'ras ma mie' and a collaboration with Michel Legrand, 'Les amoureux d'ici'.

Yves Montand was the best-known of the singers who combined their art

---

[449] Written and originally recorded the previous year by Jacques Verrières, the song was also covered by Mouloudji and Yves Montand. Verrières never found the magic touch again.

[450] As did Bourvil, whose version was simply titled 'C'était bien' when it appeared on EP, although subsequent LP releases reinstated the missing subtitle. The subtitle of Gréco's version became 'Le p'tit bal perdu' when it was issued on LP.

[451] The lyrics came from a poem by Louis Aragon, to which Ferrat added the music. Ferrat actually wrote few of his own lyrics, though his rich voice and attractive singing style more than made up for it.

[452] Two years later, British jazzman Kenny Ball reworked the tune into a global smash as 'Midnight In Moscow'.

with support for the Communist Party. A fixture on the silver screen, he maintained a presence on the airwaves as well, assuming the political stance that would in part define him on the anti-militarist 'Le dormeur du val', and triumphing with interpretations of Lemarque's 'Rendez-vous de Paname' and Édith Piaf's 'Mon manège à moi' on the 1958 album, *10 chansons pour l'été.* Time spent in Hollywood filming with Marilyn Monroe in 1960's *Let's Make Love* meant time away from home, but he returned in 1961 with another radio favourite, 'La chansonnette', and the LP

*Dansez avec Yves Montand*, which yielded the classic 'La fête à Loulou'.

## Music hall and *chanson*

Marcel Amont continued to amuse with 'Cha cha boum' (1957) and the impressive 'Le balayeur du Roy' (1958). The latter was gifted to him by Claude Nougaro, who also penned the lyrics for 'Le barbier de Séville', adapted from a melody in Rossini's opera of the same name. Amont was one of many performers to take on Guy Béart's 'L'eau vive', Charles Aznavour's 'Si je devais mourir mon amour', and the much-covered 'Aïe mon cœur'. Even so, his record sales trailed some way behind those of his contemporaries until he turned things around in 1961, topping the charts with 'Dans le cœur de ma blonde', a vocal version of the String-A-Longs' US smash, 'Wheels'.[453]

Following Amont's success in 1958, Nougaro was offered a recording contract by the small Président label, his debut EP including two songs co-written with Michel Legrand, 'Vachement décontracté' and 'Tiens-toi bien à mon cœur'. Neither the EP, nor his debut album, *Nougaro*, which contained an eloquent lament for the destruction of Hiroshima and Nagasaki titled 'Il y avait une ville', enjoyed many sales, but Nougaro benefitted from an increasing number of recordings of his songs by the likes of Jacqueline François ('Le piano de mauvaise vie', adapted from Gerry Mulligan's 'Jeru'), Lucienne Delyle ('Seulement') and Philippe Clay ('Vise la poupée' and 'À perpète', an adaptation of Guy Mitchell's 'Ninety-Nine Years (Dead Or Alive)').

Clay continued to mix serious material like 1957's 'Festival d'Aubervilliers' with pop fluff like the following year's

---

[453] Amont shared the honours with a version by Georges Guétary.

'Les clochards', while championing new writers like Jean-Roger Caussimon,[454] who composed the swirling 'Bleu, blanc, rouge'. The hits ran on to the end of the decade with 'La gamberge', a cover of the Kingston Trio's 'Tom Dooley' ('Fais ta prière') and 'Dans la légion', but after 1961's 'La sentinelle' slipped off the airwaves, he found richer pickings in the cinema.

Mouloudji likewise found it hard to maintain a presence on radio. In 1959, he recorded an impressive version of 'La complainte de Mackie' (a French version of the Kurt Weill song then topping the US charts for Bobby Darin as 'Mack The Knife') and managed a moderate hit in 1961 with 'Patricia'. However, as the new decade drew on, he found himself increasingly out of favour, though the self-penned 'Madame Garbo' proved popular in 1962 after he performed it on television.

Gilbert Bécaud rode out the fifties in style, scoring hits in 1959 with 'Le rideau rouge', 'Pilou...pilou...hé' and the amusing 'L'enterrement de Cornelius', and displaying his romantic side with the lovely 'Quand tu n'es pas là' and 'La princesse de juillet'. His soundtrack work for the film *Babette s'en va-t-en guerre* (1959) starring Brigitte Bardot meanwhile resulted in the excellent 'La chanson pour Roseline', and he confirmed his status as a superb live act with a further season headlining at the Olympia Theatre.

By then, Bécaud was wanting to play down the youthful excesses that had earned him the nickname *'Monsieur 100.000 volt'* and was yearning to do something more creative. In 1960, he set to work on a Christmas cantata, *L'enfant à l'étoile*, designed to establish him as a serious composer. It was a commendable achievement, but once this was out of his system he reboarded the commercial gravy train. In the interim, the hits continued regardless, varying in style from a forties' guitar sound on 'Je te promets' to the more contemporary 'Je me balance'. After dominating the airwaves with 'L'absent', Bécaud closed out the year with 'C'était moi'. In 1961, he rose to the challenge of the youth revolution, hitting the heights with the bluesy 'Quand l'amour est mort' and the electric-guitar-laden 'Abrina birchoué (Le fond des rivières)', while amusing listeners with the seductive 'Ma châtelaine'.

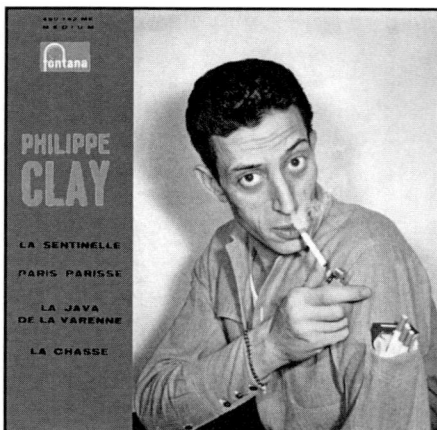

---

[454] A frequent songwriting partner for Léo Ferré.

## Female *chanson*

Édith Piaf continued to use her success to help further the careers of her favourites. A short-lived liaison with Félix Marten saw him falling rapidly into the debris when their romance came crashing to a halt, taking half-decent songs like 'Splendide' down with him. Piaf fared little better with bohemian songwriter Jo Moustaki, although their relationship resulted in some great recordings, among them 'Eden blues' and the dramatic 'Les orgues de barbarie'. However, these paled into nothing compared with her 1959 hit, 'Milord', a strident *chanson* that proved equally accessible in any language and gave Piaf her biggest ever international hit. It marked the end of her relationship with Moustaki, who picked up his royalty cheque, changed his first name to Georges, and went off in search of wine, women, and a career of his own.

Piaf entered the sixties with a new album fit to rank with her best, *Édith Piaf*. The gentle opener, 'C'est l'amour', suggested that she was mellowing her approach, but despite the occasionally intrusive presence of a big band, 'Ouragan' and 'Opinion publique' proved that she had lost none of her fire. Best of all was the mordant 'Le vieux piano', which stripped things back to the classic voice-and-piano combination of her earlier successes, bringing in other instruments to support the song, rather than decorate it. Elsewhere, she bared her soul for all the world to see on the self-explanatory 'Cri du cœur'.

Moustaki's place at Piaf's side was taken by Charles Dumont, with whom she cut the best-selling duet, 'Les amants', in 1960. Although she recorded several more of his compositions including the magnificent 'C'est peut-être ça', Dumont proved unable to match this success in his own right. Both 'Inconnu excepté de Dieu' and 'Les rues de mon quartier' were worthy attempts, but his recordings lacked charisma and he quickly fell back on crafting high-class songs for Piaf to supplement his income.

In 1961, this collaboration resulted in her biggest ever hit, the defiant 'Non, je ne regrette rien', which was to serve as her theme song for the rest of her life. A statement of self-confidence that makes Frank Sinatra's 'My Way'[455] sound like an apology, it travelled

---

[455] This song is also French in origin. The story of its creation and diffusion around the globe will be covered in Volume 2.

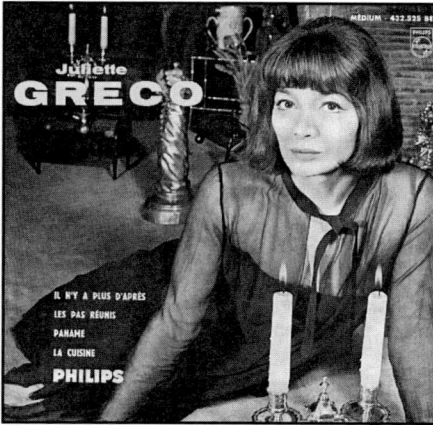

across linguistic boundaries to become a catchphrase around the world[456] (Piaf also recorded it in English as 'No Regrets', although the new lyric failed to do it justice). With its rolled r's and a vibrato that still sends shivers down the spine, it is the quintessential Piaf recording, and none of her subsequent releases could match the power of this supreme example of the *chanteuse réaliste*'s art.

Barbara preferred to hide behind her piano rather than take the front of the stage, holding down a residency at the Écluse club in Paris but struggling to make herself heard in the wider world. She showcased the works of the country's leading songsmiths on the LPs *Barbara chante Brassens* (1961) and *Barbara chante Jacques Brel* (1962), although her totally ignored 1959 debut album, *Barbara à l'Écluse*, had contained a greater variety of material. Her revival of Harry Fragson's 'Les amis de monsieur' made little headway, even as striking versions of Brassens' 'La marche nuptiale' and 'Il n'y a pas d'amour heureux' made the case for her as an interpretive singer. Her 1961 EP was also worthy of attention, featuring a superb reading of Moustaki's 'De Shangaï à Bangkok', but it was the self-penned 'Chapeau bas' that laid down a template for the future, helping her build an audience to match her talent.

Juliette Gréco resumed the concert trail in 1958 after a frustrating time acting in Hollywood movies, although links to the cinema peppered her new recordings. Her melancholy theme to Otto Preminger's *Bonjour tristesse* was released as a single, but the orchestrated flip, 'Demain il fera jour', was more typical of the Gréco that audiences had come to know. A year later, she cut 'Comment voulez-vous' (the theme to François Truffaut's *Les quatre cents coups*) and the warning 'Méfiez-vous de Paris'. Neither sold well, but she returned to favour in 1960 with a reading of Léo Ferré's 'Paname', and enjoyed a big hit in 1961 with a bright, upbeat version of his 'Jolie môme'. However, her days as one of the country's biggest recording stars were behind her.

## Jacques Brel

Gréco was impressed with Ferré's recent songs and she was equally enamoured of Jacques Brel, frequently recording the ever-improving works of the Belgian *chansonnier*, most notably a version of the downbeat 'On n'oublie rien'.[457] Michèle Arnaud was also a fan, enjoying success in 1959 with a subdued version of Brel's 'Les Flamandes' that helped the song reach an audience who might have been put off by the composer's own declamatory approach. With his name increasing in prominence thanks to Arnaud and Gréco, Brel hit a rich run of form and saw his star rise dramatically as the

---

[456] It was famously quoted by UK Chancellor of the Exchequer Norman Lamont to justify his disastrous handling of the 1993 exchange rate crisis.
[457] A recording that did rather more justice to the song than Brel's own churning rendition.

decade drew to a close.
Released in 1959 and benefitting from a more sympathetic production than before, the LP *Jacques Brel No. 4* was his first masterpiece. A flawless set of songs that confirmed his outsider status with vigorous attacks on the hypocrisies of social norms, it spun off hits with 'La valse à mille temps', 'La mort' and 'Les Flamandes'. Most popular of all was 'Ne me quitte pas', as bleak a love song as has ever been written and an instant standard[458] which survived a mid-sixties adaptation into English by Rod McKuen as 'If You Go Away' to become a favourite among both the supper club circuit and the 'bedsit' generation of the seventies.[459]

His next album, 1961's *Jacques Brel No. 5*, was equally hard-hitting and yielded a hit with the wry death-bed humour of 'Le moribond', a classic that deserved a far better fate than its subsequent reworking by McKuen into the kitschy 'Seasons In The Sun'.[460] Other highlights included the sad 'Marieke' and his dismissal of bourgeois society, 'Les singes', while the slurred 'L'ivrogne' perfectly complemented the lyric's examination of a drunkard's lot. Critically lauded, the album sold steadily, but Brel remained dissatisfied and jumped ship from Philips to the more adventurous Barclay label.

### Serge Gainsbourg and Boby Lapointe

Serge Gainsbourg struggled to come anywhere near the level of success enjoyed by Brel, and by 1961 two more long-players had joined his debut album on a pile of flops. Tracks like the finger-snapping 'Le claqueur des doigts' and the exotic parody 'Mambo miam miam' (both on 1959's *Serge Gainsbourg No. 2*) were catchy enough, and 'La chanson de Prévert', his tribute to the French poet and his lyric for Yves Montand's 'Les feuilles mortes' (on 1961's *L'étonnant Serge Gainsbourg*) immediately engaging. However, material like 'En relisant ta lettre' (also on the *L'étonnant* LP), in which he read through a lover's suicide note while criticising her spelling and grammatical mistakes, was hardly likely to propel him into the charts.

A fourth album, imaginatively titled *Serge Gainsbourg No. 4*, contained

---

[458] Among those turning in quality interpretations were Jacqueline Danno, on her debut release, and Barbara, on the excellent *Barbara chante Jacques Brel* LP. It was also famously covered by Nina Simone.

[459] It was a minor US hit in 1966 for Damita Jo. Frank Sinatra, Neil Diamond, Scott Walker and Dusty Springfield also recorded notable versions.

[460] A minor hit in the US for the Kingston Trio in 1964, the song was then a 1969 European hit for UK group the Fortunes and a global smash in 1974 for Canadian singer Terry Jacks. Jacks recorded 'If You Go Away' as the follow-up.

some of his most accessible work to date, but the jazzy, late-night sounds of 'Intoxicated man' and 'Black trombone' did little to raise his standing in the marketplace. With song-writing currently his main source of income, Gainsbourg also turned to composing for the cinema – a move which generated his first hit in 1960 with the lascivious 'L'eau à la bouche', though it was covers such as Michèle Arnaud's 'La chanson de Prévert' that accorded him what little fame he enjoyed.

Boby Lapointe was a wildman of a performer who brought with him a surreal sense of humour, and a love of literary invention and word games to match Gainsbourg's own. Following an appearance in François Truffaut's 1960 film, *Tirez sur le pianiste*,[461] he became the darling of the intellectual fringe. The anarchic jazz opus 'Framboise' and the music hall knockabout 'Aragon et Castille' garnered Lapointe a cult reputation, but, despite his unique talent, he failed to carve out a niche in the wider marketplace.

## The continuing popularity of *musette*

Lapointe and Gainsbourg may have appealed to the intelligensia, but not everyone wanted cerebral stimulation in their musical distractions, and the purveyors of *musette* and other folk traditions remained hugely popular. This grass-roots movement even produced a major star in accordionist André Verchuren, who was savvy enough to mix traditional material with pop covers in pursuit of record sales. A version of the much-covered 'Java', sold well in 1956,[462] but his biggest success came at the dawn of the sixties when the old-fashioned 'Les fiancés d'Auvergne' and 'Si tu m'écrivais' both became massive hits in the eye of the rock'n'roll hurricane.

---

[461] The film starred Charles Aznavour in one of his best roles.
[462] He even had a stab at rock'n'roll in 1957 with the frightful 'Rock'n polka'.

Yvette Horner opened the new decade with 'Rapid' BB', 'Bergère des Pyrénées' and 'Mon tour de France', as well as turning Édith Piaf's 'Milord' and Hugo Alfvén's 'Swedish Rhapsody'[463] ('Rapsodie suédoise') into accordion-swamped dance music. Whether celebrating her country's heritage with 'À la pétanque', reinterpreting the *Exodus* movie theme, or trying to rock on a cover of Charles Aznavour's 'Il faut savoir', Horner was a fixture on both the airwaves and the small screen, if not in the charts.

Aimable also kept the accordion at the forefront of French pop, paying tribute to the denizens of funfairs on 1959's 'Le chemin des forains', and covering Dalida's 'L'arlequin de Tolède' and Gilbert Bécaud's 'Tête de bois' in 1960. He also tried to rock on a dreadful cover of Brian Hyland's 'Itsy Bitsy Teenie Weenie Yellow Polka Dot Bikini' ('Itsy bitsy, petit bikini'), but it was 1961's *Aimable en Auvergne* EP that showed off what he did best.

Jacky Noguez struggled to match his compatriots, but he managed a feat that eluded all but a few French entertainers when he broke into the US charts, landing three hits in the *Billboard* 'Hot 100' in 1959-60.[464] The biggest of these was a reinvention of the widely-recorded 'Ciao, ciao bambina',[465] which made the Top 30, though he turned his hand to everything from Henri Salvador's 'Les Papous' to Ben E. King's 'Spanish Harlem' ('Nuits d'Espagne').

### Easy listening orchestras and chorales

Bandleader Franck Pourcel[466] favoured violins over accordions, establishing himself as the French equivalent of Joe Loss, Lawrence Welk or Bert Kaempfert. An arranger and producer on numerous pop records, Pourcel had been inspired by Stéphane Grappelli to form a violin ensemble in the late 1940s. By the fifties, his lounge-style reworkings of contemporary hits were

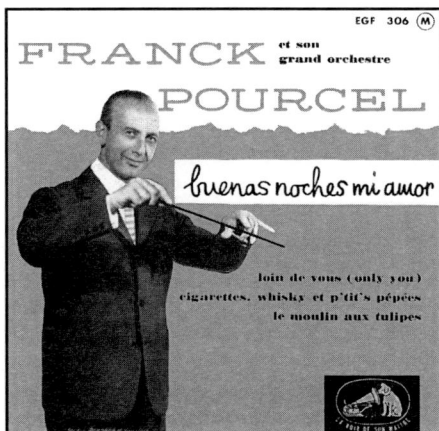

being issued around the world under the name Franck Pourcel's French Fiddles – notably 'Tango bleu' (Leroy Anderson's 'Blue Tango'), which provided him with a hit in 1952, and his reworking of the Platters' 'Only You (And You Alone)', which made the US Top 10 in 1959. His instrumental take on Édith Piaf's 'Milord' was coupled with the original for a US single release, both sides tiptoeing around the lower end of the *Billboard* charts in 1961.[467]

Raymond Lefèvre was almost as successful, peaking at No. 30 in the

---

[463] A hit in the fifties for both Percy Faith and Mantovani.

[464] 'Ciao, Ciao Bambina', 'Marina' and 'Amapola', all on the Jamie label.

[465] This was originally an Italian hit by Domenico Modugno titled 'Piove'. Noguez's title came from Dalida's successful cover of the song for the French market.

[466] Well known today for his 'cheesy listening' albums of the sixties.

[467] Piaf peaked at No. 88 in the *Billboard* 'Hot 100', while Pourcel had to be content at No. 112 in the 'Bubbling Under' chart. Pourcel's Platters cover lost the subtitle and was issued simply as 'Only You'.

*Billboard* 'Hot 100' in 1958 with 'The Day The Rains Came', an instrumental arrangement of Gilbert Bécaud's 'Le jour où la pluie viendra'. Repeating the trick proved to be a more difficult proposition, but Lefèvre continued to record instrumental pops as well as lending his powerful sound to covers of film themes such as *Exodus* and *Les mercenaires* (*The Magnificent Seven*).

Listeners desiring soothing lyrics rather than instrumentals could rely on Danielle Darrieux, whose gentle 1958 reading of Charles Aznavour's 'Mais moi, je m'ennuie' was typical of her performances. Darrieux was comfortable remaking sentimental old hits like 'Les fleurs sont des mots d'amour', and, while her sales never matched her popularity on the silver screen, she continued to serve up more of the same for her fans for many years to come.

Those looking for ultra-smooth wallpaper music needed to look no further than Les Djinns, a massed group of female singers who turned everything into a mushy stew of sleep-inducing harmonies, but were highly palatable to those for whom music remained just an accompaniment to other activities. Their versions of Francis Lemarque's 'Une rose rouge' and Gilbert Bécaud's 'Marie, Marie' sold steadily, and they peaked commercially with the banal 'Les criquets' in 1961.

**Jazz at the turn of the decade**

Michel Legrand made a living on the borderland where easy listening met jazz, but found his richest rewards in the world of cinema. His 1957 EP of music from the film *Paradis des hommes* proved popular, and he enjoyed a decent-sized hit with 'Chanson de Lima' from *L'empire du soleil*. In 1959, he went back to his roots for the album *Paris jazz piano*, which featured ten songs about Paris (including most of the usual suspects), plus a handful of tunes by American songwriters – notably Freddy Martin's 1933 hit, 'April In Paris' and Cole Porter's classic, 'I Love Paris'.[468]

Claude Bolling enjoyed success with covers of hits like Frank Sinatra's 'The Lady Is A Tramp' ('La vie mondaine'), but he also dabbled in film music, scoring the 1960 opus *Les mains d'Orlac*. One of the country's leading jazzmen, he was popular enough to warrant a TV special in 1961, the *Claude Bolling Special Show*, which featured the imaginative 'Bach to swing', a successful attempt to combine classical music and jazz rhythms. He probably picked up on the idea from pianist Jacques Loussier, who had reconstructed

---

[468] Legrand had already recorded this earlier in the decade for his album of the same name, albeit in a very different arrangement.

Bach's melodies as jazz for a major hit in 1959 with the *Play Bach* album. Featuring well-known compositions rearranged for a jazz trio,[469] the results were astounding and led to a whole new career for a man previously best known as an accompanist for Charles Aznavour.[470]

Richard Bennett et ses Dixie Cats[471] took a less adventurous approach on a 1960 EP including covers of Sacha Distel's 'Mon beau chapeau' and Fats Domino's revival of the Glenn Miller classic, 'Blueberry Hill'.[472] However, without a fresh young face to attract teenage girls, the band were dead in the water and their career came slithering to a halt as rock'n'roll began to outstrip jazz in popularity.

Meanwhile, Lamar Ward Swingle and Christiane Legrand emerged from the ranks of Les Blue Stars to join another jazz-vocal ensemble, Les Double Six. Ignoring the pop covers that had blighted their previous group's repertoire, their self-titled LP enjoyed big sales thanks to inventive renditions of songs like Ray Charles's 'Moanin' ' and Cliff Edwards' 'Fascinating Rhythm'.

### Blues in France

Backed by Claude Luter and Benny Vasseur,[473] Phily Form (one-time sports star René Clausier under a pseudonym) recorded an EP of late-night blues for the Lyon-based Teppaz label. The results came out closer to jazz than electric blues, although 'Blues pour ma p'tite amie' and 'Sur le boulevard des allongés' were decent attempts to carve out a style that was all his own, with scat singing and jazz blowing over a tight rhythm section. Issued in 1958, several years before anyone would be interested in the blues, it died a commercial death, sending all concerned back to the drawing board.

The early sixties saw the arrival of American pianist Memphis Slim, who provided countless musicians with first-hand experience of a blues master at work. Having enjoyed a number of R&B hits in the States in the late forties and early fifties, Slim arrived in Paris in 1961 and went on to cut a series of blues albums for the French market. Although efforts like 1963's *Aux Trois Mailletz*

---

[469] With rock'n'roll pioneer Christian Garros on drums.

[470] Loussier issued four more volumes in the *Play Bach* series during the early 1960s, as well as a set dedicated to Kurt Weill, *Jacques Loussier joue Kurt Weill*. The trio toured the globe, captivating audiences with their blend of classical virtuosity and improvisational skills, and selling millions of records along the way to become one of the most commercially successful jazz outfits of the decade.

[471] Bennett made a good living on the club circuit and had earlier cut a version of the standard, 'When The Saints Go Marching In', for a 1959 EP. For all that, his band would probably be forgotten today were it not for his bass player, Nino Ferrer, who would go on to back Nancy Holloway before establishing a successful career as a pop/R&B star in the mid-sixties (see Volume 2 for details.)

[472] The latter retitled 'Blue Berry Hill', presumably in error.

[473] Aka the French 'Benny Rock'.

failed to make the charts, they proved to be a huge influence on a generation of musicians who would come to prominence later in the decade.[474]

More immediately significant was the role of Mickey 'Guitar' Baker, formerly one half of the duo Mickey & Sylvia, whose 'Love Is Strange' remains a classic of fifties' pop. Baker settled in France at the start of the decade and found regular work as a session guitarist and producer for a number of the early rock'n'roll singers, including Sylvie Vartan and Frankie Jordan, as well as cutting a string of fine blues albums on the side.

Henri Salvador had dabbled in blues back in the mid-fifties with the scatted hybrid 'Salvador plays the blues', while also laying down his mark with jazz, pop, easy listening and rock'n'roll. Too eclectic to stick with any one style for long, he opened the sixties with a revival of Maurice Chevalier's 'Ma Louise' and 'C'est un gigolo' (a reworking of Fritz Imhoff's Austrian classic, 'Schöner Gigolo'[475]), which allowed him to indulge his sense of humour. Salvador's love of the ridiculous was also evident on 'Ça, c'est d'la musique' and 'Je ne peux pas rentrer chez moi', both featured on an EP of mock-Chinese vocalising that is scarcely believable in these more enlightened times.

Continuing to mix styles at will, he raised further laughs with the comic jazz offering 'Pas mon papa' and reunited with Quincy Jones for 'Soleil de minuit',[476] which was as smooth a slice of big band jazz as he would ever create. These pleasant sounds continued with the 1960 summer hit, 'Le soleil, ton visage et la mer', and the relatively contrived 'L'amour est là', but Salvador could never stay in one place for very long and would soon be back knocking at rock'n'roll's door.

### The tail-end of the exotica boom

Laura Villa, on the other hand, ignored rock'n'roll and mined the still-viable exotica seam instead, with 'Le soukou-soukou' (a French version of the South American hit, 'Sucu Sucu').[477] Villa's performance was competent enough, but Swiss star Lys Assia and veteran bandleader Jacques Hélian (who retained the original title) got the lion's share of the sales.

Dario Moreno also kept the exotica flag flying, opening the decade strongly with a rendition of Jan & Kjeld's 'Banjo Boy'. In 1961, 'La marmite' (a revival of Marlene's 1953 Brazilian hit, 'Zé marmita') provided him with a colossal hit, the song's party atmosphere and his jocular image proving a

---

[474] See Volume 2 for a discussion of the sixties R&B boom in France.

[475] Introduced to English-speaking audiences in 1931 by Bing Crosby as 'Just A Gigolo'.

[476] Jones would also go on to record it as 'The Midnight Sun Will Never Set'.

[477] Well-known to UK audiences through five different versions in 1961. The biggest of these was Laurie Johnson's, which was used as the theme to the television series *Top Secret*.

perfect match. He stayed with the Brazilian sound for a follow-up hit with a cover of Jorge Veiga's tribute-in-samba, 'Brigitte Bardot'.

Based in Belgium, Italian-born Rocco Granata came to prominence in 1959 with the ultra-catchy 'Marina', which fought its way into a US Top 40 packed with rock'n'roll and sold millions around the world. Nothing else Granata did matched this success, but he enjoyed further hits across Europe well into the sixties (and was still charting in Belgium a decade later), scoring in 1960 with 'Rocco cha cha' and the rhythmic 'La bella', awash with accordion backing. The flip side of the latter, the Italian classic 'Torna a Surriento', was best known to English-speaking audiences at the time as Dean Martin's 'Come Back To Sorrento', but earned its place in rock's history books a year later when it was reworked into a transatlantic chart-topper by Elvis Presley as 'Surrender'.

Newcomer Colette Deréal plundered the Italian market for her 1959 hit, 'Moi' (Domenico Modugno's 'Io'[478]) before joining the premier league with the poppy 'Ne joue pas' (Linda Leigh's 'What Good Does It Do Me'), successfully fighting off rival versions from the likes of Dalida and Tino Rossi. She subsequently strutted her way through such variety-show offerings as 'Amour, soleil et cha cha cha', 'Emmène-moi au bout du monde', and the Latin-tinged 'Pourquoi?'. Though her rather anodyne 1960 reading of 'Jéricho' lost out to Richard Anthony's version, 'Rendez-vous à Brasilia' kept her name alive and she returned later that year with 'Notre concerto'. A superb cover of Umberto Bindi's Italian smash, 'Il nostro concerto', it faced down all challengers,[479] setting her up for a tilt at *Eurovision* in 1961, representing Monaco with 'Allons, allons les enfants'.[480]

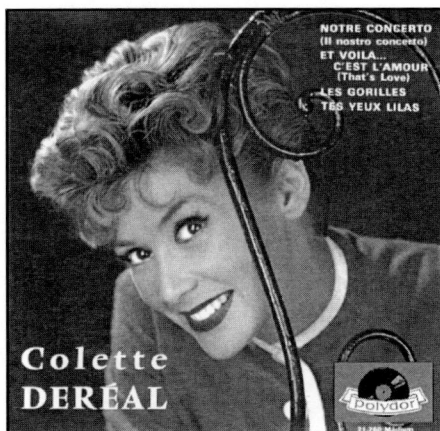

The ultimate expression of the fad for exotic sounds was the success of Los Machucambos, a Paris-based trio featuring singing male guitarists from Spain and Peru backing a Costa Rican chanteuse. They first came to fame in late 1959 with a bright rendition of the Mexican folk song 'La Bamba' that had nothing to do with the recent US recording by Ritchie Valens. It was the first of a string of hits for the trio, whose colourful costumes and joyful

---

[478] Transformed five years later into 'Ask Me' by Elvis Presley.
[479] Including Les Compagnons de la Chanson, André Dassary and Tino Rossi.
[480] She was placed joint 10th.

rhythms made them ever-welcome on TV variety shows and concert stages. The catchy 'Dos horas de balazos' and 'Canção dos jangadeiros' (from the 1961 Brazilian film, *Os Bandeirantes*) brought them further glory before they hit paydirt again with the vibrant 'Pepito'. They later came up trumps again with the revolutionary tune 'La cucuracha', 'Otorrino laringologo' and the eminently danceable 'La boa', their fame spreading across Europe to South America.

Bernard Stéphane began by ignoring exotica in favour of 'Garde-moi la dernière danse' (a cover of the Drifters' 'Save The Last Dance For Me'), before grabbing a hit with 'Le petit tramway'.[481] He shamelessly catered to the summer holiday audience with 1961's 'En vacances en Italie' and the following year's 'L'enfant du port' (adapted from Mary Lo's Greek hit, 'O Vassilikos').[482] He repeated the trick again in 1963 with 'Sous la lune bleue', but his later attempts to sustain the exotica boom wound up lost in the shuffle.

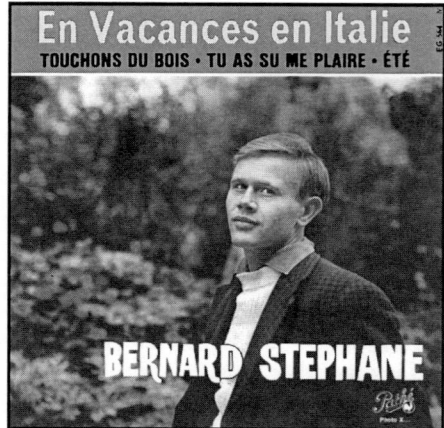

## Greek and Middle Eastern influences

One of the biggest international hits of 1960 was Greek actress/singer Melina Mercouri's recording of the theme to *Never On Sunday*, 'Ta pedia tou Piréa'.[483] It was covered for the French market as 'Les enfants du Pirée' by Dalida, Gloria Lasso, Patrice et Mario, Dario Moreno, Maria Candido and many others, although it was Dalida who grabbed most of the sales. The song was also recorded, with rather less success, by another Greek-born singer, Nana Mouskouri, who had recently signed with the French division of the Fontana label after winning first prize at the *Festival de la Canción Mediterránea* in Barcelona with 'Xypna, agapi mou'.[484]

Having moved to France to establish an international career, Mouskouri found enormous popularity in West Germany, where 'Weiße Rosen aus Athen' became a million-seller in

---

[481] Also recorded, with less success, by André Claveau.

[482] Although Eddie Calvert's instrumental version, 'The Greek Flower Song', was the likely inspiration.

[483] Mercouri was also nominated for an Oscar and won Best Actress award at the *Cannes Film Festival* for her role.

[484] Her recording of the song also topped the Spanish charts in December 1960.

1961.[485] French record sales were slow to follow, however. Offerings from Charles Aznavour (who adapted Milva's Italian ballad, 'La risposta della novia', into French for her as 'Salvame Dios') and Gilbert Bécaud ('Crois-moi, ça durera'), and reworkings of Bobby Vinton's 'Roses Are Red (My Love)' and Mr. Acker Bilk's 'Stranger On The Shore' ('Je reviendrai my love' and 'Savoir aimer') failed to make even a minor impact. Apart from a small hit with 'Roses blanches de Corfou' (adapted from her 1961 German breakthrough hit), her EPs resolutely refused to sell.

Israeli-born singer Rika Zaraï acknowledged her roots with hit versions of the folk song 'Hava Nagila'[486] and the theme to the 1960 film *Exodus*, though the latter was overshadowed by a powerful reading from Édith Piaf. However, her cover of Manos Hadjidakis' Greek hit, 'Zingara', was less well received, so she switched to rock'n'roll instead, with a cover of Ricky Nelson's 'Hello Mary Lou' ('Bye bye mon amour'). In the event, it was Petula Clark who got the hit, sending Zaraï scuttling back to the middle of the road for a revival of the Andrews Sisters' 'Bei mir bist du schön'.

Bob Azzam's career peaked in 1960 with a pair of Arabic-styled novelties: a reworking of the folk song 'Mustapha'[487] and the irrepressible 'Fais-moi le couscous, chéri', which, together with the Mediterranean pop of 'C'est écrit dans le ciel', briefly made him one of the country's most bankable performers. Riding in his slipsteam were the risible Staïffi et ses Mustafa's, who covered 'Mustapha' as a cha-cha-cha,[488] without bringing any of the joy that pervaded everything that Azzam recorded.

---

[485] This came after its use in a German documentary about Greece. The song was the first of several massive hits for her across the Rhine. She also recorded it in English as 'The White Rose Of Athens', enjoying a minor hit in the US, where she also recorded the excellent jazz album *Nana Mouskouri In New York* with Quincy Jones.

[486] More dynamic than the French adaptation by Dalida, 'Dansons mon amour', Zaraï's version was titled 'Hava naguila'.

[487] The song had already been a hit in Egypt in the fifties for Dalida's brother, Bruno Gigliotti aka 'Orlando', prior to his relocation to France following his sister's huge success.

[488] The group's name had a typically imprecise French placement of the apostrophe. Sensibly retitled 'Mustafa – Cha cha cha oriental', their version briefly tickled the lower reaches of the charts across the Channel in the UK.

## Operetta and music hall

Bourvil usually played things for laughs, but he hit a commercial peak in 1958 with the romantic ballad 'Ballade irlandaise (Un oranger)'. He also proved an able duet partner to Pierrette Bruno on the sweet 1959 hit, 'On a vécu pour ça', and the entertaining 'Ah! C'que t'es bête'. 'C'est du nanan' parodied the exotica boom, while 'Les pruneaux' was a comic masterpiece from the country's leading musical jester. Bourvil saw pop music as escapism and never let anything prevent him giving his audiences an enjoyable time, although he also enjoyed steady sales with the mournful 'Vieux frère'.

Along the way, Bourvil teamed up with Georges Guétary for the amusing 'Duo des célibataires' and the operetta *Pacifico*, which featured the pair dueting on the jazzier-than-usual 'Casimir'. By this time, however, Guétary's appeal was beginning to fade and his 'Chanson de Ben-Hur' (from the 1959 MGM blockbuster) failed to mirror the success of the film from whence it came.

André Dassary also slipped down the ladder after such ill-chosen efforts as 'Le grand Sam' (a reworking of Johnny Horton's 'North To Alaska') and 'La ballade d'Alamo' (Marty Robbins' 'Ballad Of The Alamo') failed to generate interest as the French fascination with America shifted from western movies to more contemporary matters.

Eddie Constantine's American image was also no longer enough to sustain a career, and by the turn of the decade his young fans were likewise beginning to move on. As his sales went into decline, he turned to the Aznavour songbook for the Sinatra-esque 'Quand tu viens chez moi, mon cœur', but the writing was clearly on the wall.

Jacqueline François also found the going difficult, although a vocal version of Sidney Bechet's 'Petite fleur'[489] kept her name up in lights during 1960. The following year, she joined the pack rushing to cover Charles Aznavour's 'La marche des anges', but sadly few people rushed to buy her version.

Time was running out too for Maria Candido, whose jolly 1961 effort, 'D'amour et d'eau fraîche', missed its target. In 1962, she was one of many artists to cover Robert Nyel's 'Magali', but this likewise failed to catch on.

Fortune smiled more favourably upon actress Jacqueline Danno, who crossed over into *chanson* with her 1959 cover of Gilbert Bécaud's 'Marie, Marie'.[490] After reworking Rosemary Clooney's 'Many A Wonderful Moment' ('Pour nous seuls'), she developed a distinctive style with the 1961 hit 'Alors (Les amants orgueilleux)' and

le manteau gris
marie-marie
ne me quitte pas
Billy

---

[489] Also given a swinging arrangement by Annie Cordy.
[490] This was featured on her debut EP. She had, however, appeared on around a dozen Various Artists EPs on the independent Baccara label over the previous two years, rendering hits of the day in a rather bland style.

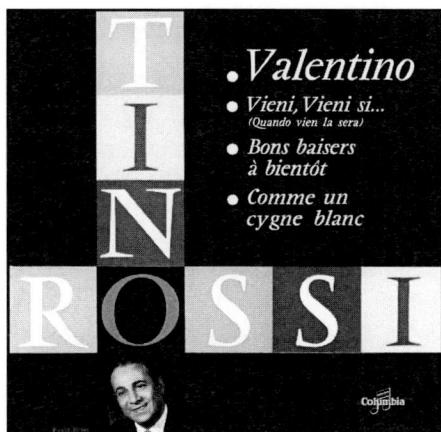

**.Valentino**

- *Vieni, Vieni si...*
  (Quando vien la sera)
- *Bons baisers*
  *à bientôt*
- *Comme un*
  *cygne blanc*

Columbia

the sweet 'Les mouettes de Saint-Malo'. Danno held her own through the early years of the decade, with an atmospheric reading of the film theme 'L'île nue' and the excellent 'Quand j'étais blonde' (adapted from Albert Van Dam's 'Instrumental Continental'), but wisely never abandoned her acting career.

For pure nostalgic pleasure, however, there was nobody to touch Tino Rossi, who, despite his advancing years, remained a major draw, selling strongly in 1960 with the romantic 'Bons baisers, à bientôt'. The hits dried up after 1961's 'Une simple carte postale',[491] but by then his position was secure, and his LPs and EPs continued selling steadily throughout the decade.

The affable Henri Génès also presented a unthreatening form of pop music to an audience looking simply to be entertained. Content to ride the exotica boom for 1957's 'Calypso 6', he was also comfortable sending himself up on the same year's 'Le chanteur sexy'. Increasingly busy with film roles, he enjoyed his last major hit in 1958 with 'Fatigué de naissance' before returning to exotica for 'Le millionnaire' (a reworking of Pérez Prado's 'The Millionaire').

Annie Cordy also played it for laughs on 1958's 'Au zoo de Vincennes' and 'Bottle cha cha', before tangoing across 'Attends, je viens' and switching to the mambo for a take on Prado's US chart-topper, 'Patricia'. In 1959, she bagged one of two hit versions[492] of 'La marche des gosses' (Cyril Stapleton's 'The Children's Marching Song'[493]), dabbled in exotic parodies like 'Le tango ruminant' and 'Tango militaire', and scored strongly in 1960 with a cover of Jan & Kjeld's 'Banjo Boy'.

Good humour was the entire selling point of Nick Kartoon et ses Tueurs à Gages. Effectively a French response to America's Spike Jones & His City Slickers, Kartoon's approach was typified by his 1960 cover of Henri Salvador's 'Faut rigoler'. Although his records were advertised as being *'pour danser'*, only the demented would have attempted such a feat, and his recording of John Dankworth's 'African Waltz' ('Ça tourne rond') was best

LE
**CHANTEUR SEXY**
*(FOX-TROT)*
*CRÉÉ ET ENREGISTRÉ PAR*

PAROLES DE
NOËL ROUX
ET
HENRI GENÈS

MUSIQUE
DE
GABY
WAGENHEIM

**HENRI GENÈS**
DISQUE PACIFIC

ÉDITIONS ET PRODUCTIONS MUSICALES
PATHÉ - MARCONI - S.A
1 RUE LAFFITTE - PARIS - 9e

---

[491] Rossi shared the honours with a bright version by Maria Candido.
[492] The other was by Les Compagnons de la Chanson.
[493] Itself a revival of an old folk song revived in the film *The Inn Of The Sixth Happiness*.

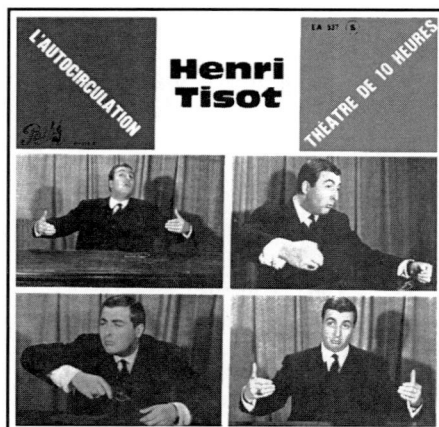

enjoyed sitting down with an inane grin and a belly laugh.

In 1961, jazzman Marcel Zanini's light-hearted approach delivered a turntable hit in the shape of 'Arrête' (the 1931 Guy Lombardo hit 'Heartaches', which had recently been given a doo-wop makeover by the Marcels[494]), thanks to an audience who appreciated humour as much as musical ability. This was also good news for veteran comic and singer Fernandel, who continued to record into the sixties, turning out enjoyable ditties like 1961's 'Ah! Le tango corse'.

Recordings of straight comedy sketches also proved commercially viable in the early sixties, and the actor/comedian Henri Tisot enjoyed a major hit with the hysterical 'L'autocirculation'. Tisot, who was renowned for his impressions of President Charles de Gaulle, enjoyed further success with the equally ridiculous 'Conference de presse sur la dépigeonnisation', and the hits kept coming until the novelty eventually wore off.

John William rode out the changes in taste to remain a popular live draw, and as the sixties progressed he enjoyed steady, if unspectacular record sales. Although he had briefly flirted with easy listening on his 1959 revival of the Four Aces' 'There Goes My Heart' ('Tu prends mon cœur'),[495] it was usually film themes that formed the basis of his repertoire, and he enjoyed hits in 1961 with big-voiced covers like 'Le bleu de l'été' ('The Green Leaves Of Summer' from *The Alamo*) and 'Navarone' (from Joe Reisman's theme for *The Guns of Navarone*).[496]

Fortune also continued to smile upon Les Trois Ménestrels, whose 'Tango de l'assassin' served to keep the wolves from the door in 1960. A year later, they were one of many to have a stab at Guy Béart's 'Il n'y a plus d'après', but it was their bouncy take on modern life, 'Les employés de bureau (Bureaucratique-tango)', that best exemplified their appeal.

Les Compagnons de la Chanson maintained their hit run through the

---

[494] The song had also been revived in 1947 by Jimmy Dorsey, Eddy Howard, Harry James and Ted Weems, although it was most likely the Marcels' reworking that inspired Zanini to have a go at it.

[495] Possibly inspired by Joni James's 1958 revival in the US.

[496] Both were also successfully covered by Les Compagnons de la Chanson. 'The Geeen Leaves of Summer' was also a big international hit – including in France – for the Brothers Four, whose recording inspired the cover by Les Compagnons.

early sixties, plundering the songbook of American folk outfit the Brothers Four for 'Verte campagne'[497] ('Greenfields') in 1960, and likewise picking up good sales with a version of Charles Aznavour's 'La marche des anges'. Staying as close to the middle of the road as they could without getting run over, they picked up further hits with 'Si tous les oiseaux' and a cover of Petula Clark's 'Roméo'.

## Cabaret queens

Zizi Jeanmaire largely ignored the record market, focusing instead on all-singing, all-dancing revues that were highlights of the Parisian cabaret circuit, although a 1959 revival of the twenties' standard, 'Charleston', kept her recording career alive. However, it was on stage that she truly came into her own, with albums such as *Zizi à l'Alhambra* driven by the vibrant sounds of a flamboyant performer at the top of her game. Jeanmaire hit a second commercial peak in 1961 with the infectious 'Mon truc en plumes'. A stereotypical piece of music hall whimsy that gave maximum space to her dynamic personality, it was a major chart success, ensuring that she would remain a star long after the hits had run out. Indeed, it would serve as her theme tune for the rest of her career.[498]

Line Renaud was an equally dynamic performer, and she took on Dalida in 1959 with a cover of 'Ciao, ciao bambina' (Domenico Modugno's 'Piove'), holding her own with the Queen of Exotica while also keeping the genre alive with 'Mon cœur au Portugal' and the summer swayer, 'Un amour d'été'. Her cover of Doris Day's 'Everybody Loves A Lover' ('Dis, oh! Dis...') was another triumph, allowing the vivacious personality that had captivated Las Vegas to shine across her native land.

Patachou closed out the fifties with a version of Guy Béart's 'Vous', although it was her cover of Bourvil's 'Ballade irlandaise' that rang the commercial bell. However, it was albums such as 1960's *Les chansons que j'aurais aimé créer*, with on-the-nail readings of classics like Georges Ulmer's 'Pigalle', Édith Piaf's 'Padam... Padam' and Yves Montand's 'C'est si bon' that better typified her appeal. In 1961, she picked up the Charles Aznavour songbook for 'C'est ça qui m'intéresse', but her moment had passed and the sweet 'Voyage de noces' and the rhythmic 'La chansonnette' were no longer the stuff of hit records. The *chanson*-by-numbers 'Cherbourg avait raison' was a more commercial effort, although it was newcomer Frida Boccara who got the hit – not that it did much to further the commerical standing of either singer.

Dalida meanwhile remained one of the country's biggest stars, turning her

---

[497] Also a moderate hit for both François Deguelt and Henri Salvador.

[498] The EP it appeared on also included a rock'n'roll number written by Johnny Hallyday ('Je te tuerai d'amour'), on which she tried – and failed – to get with the big beat.

hand to anything she fancied. She revisited Italian waters for 1960's 'C'est un jour à Naples' before having a go at the themes from *The Unforgiven* ('La joie d'aimer') and *Le goût de la violence* ('Protégez-moi seigneur') in 1961, though it was her more rock'n'roll-influenced material that kept her high in the hit parade.

Gloria Lasso enjoyed a hit in 1961 with a version of 'Pepito', but by 1962 her sales were slumping dramatically and a dull-as-ditchwater revival of Jim Dale's 'Be My Girl' ('Je ne veux pas que nous restions amis') swiftly sank. The finger-snapping 'Oh! Quelle fête' showed that she could be comfortable with more rhythmic material, but, unlike Dalida, she seemed irrevocably saddled with the baggage of her exotic past.

Much of Dalida's and Lasso's initial appeal had come from their headstrong personalities and ability to make headlines in the glossy press. Glamour, as much as musical talent, was the key to their success and it was perhaps predictable that they would be followed by a singers for whom image was everything, and musical talent merely a secondary consideration.

Rita Cadillac took the exotica concept to its logical conclusion, moving from a career as an 'exotic dancer' to a new one as a singer of risqué material like 1960's 'Ne comptez pas sur moi (pour me montrer toute nue)' and 1962's 'J'ai peur de coucher toute seule'.[499] Meanwhile, Silvana Blasi attempted a similar crossover in 1960 with the charming 'Bons baisers, à bientôt' that struggled for space among a plethora of rival versions headed by Tino Rossi and the Kessler Sisters,[500] but by then the exotica craze was in decline.

### Eurovision

André Claveau was less able to move with the times, although his 1956 effort, 'Mon p'tit paradis', had been popular enough with his fans to keep him in favour for some time. He hit a career peak in 1958, when he won the *Eurovision Song Contest* for France with the ballad, 'Dors, mon amour'. Not the most memorable of songs to win the competition, it nevertheless widened his audience still further, allowing him ride out the decade with a cover of Jacques Brel's 'La valse à mille temps'.

Newcomer Jean Philippe launched himself via the 1959 *Eurovision Song Contest*, coming third with 'Oui, oui, oui, oui'. One of the earliest *Eurovision* entries to consist of little more than a title, it was a catchy, repetitive tune and

---

[499] She also cut a version of Johnny Hallyday's 'Souvenirs, souvenirs' and a relatively straight take on Petula Clark's 'Adonis', which was buried by a rival recording by Gloria Lasso, as well as Clark's own version.

[500] The song was also recorded by black singer Dominique, who had cut a revival of Judy Garland's 'Over the Rainbow' in 1958. Despite possessing a decent voice, she never truly established herself in the pop marketplace.

**GRAND PRIX EUROVISION DE LA CHANSON 1960**
Tom Pillibi          Gouli Gouli Dou
Le village de Sainte Bernadette          Toute jeune          Columbia

became a substantial hit.[501] Sadly, it failed to sustain his career beyond the early sixties, with recordings like the mid-tempo 'Dis-lui que je l'aime' and the pretty 'J'ai mis notre amour au monde' testifying to a talent that was unfairly overlooked.

In 1960, Jacqueline Boyer[502] won *Eurovision* with the inane 'Tom Pillibi', which basked in its own glory to become a smash across much of Europe. She managed a second hit with the dreamy follow-up, 'Comme au premier jour',[503] but this success and exposure failed to translate into a lengthy chart career, though she remained a popular live draw for many years.

Among those vanquished by Boyer's march to *Eurovision* glory was François Deguelt, who represented Monaco that year.[504] Having enjoyed a hit in 1959 with the cod-Mexican 'Je te tendrai les bras',[505] he had subsequently slipped into a routine of pop ballads like 1960's 'Marie Mirage'. His career climbed to an international peak with his 1960 *Eurovision* entry, 'Ce soir-là', which finished third on the night and became a moderate hit.

Jean-Paul Mauric, who combined romantic ballads with silly novelty songs, represented France in the sixth *Eurovision* contest in 1961. The nonsensical 'Printemps, avril carillonne' finished a respectable fourth, though nothing else in his repertoire found much support among the pop audience.

More successful was Luxembourg's entry, Jean-Claude Pascal, who was well established at the time of his 1961 *Eurovision* victory with 'Nous, les amoureux'.[506] Having already laid down 'easy' treatments of the works of Gilbert Bécaud ('C'était moi' and 'L'absent'), Jacques Brel ('On n'oublie rien') and Guy Béart ('Les pas réunis'), he now applied the same touch to the songs of Serge Gainsbourg, whose 'Les oubliettes' was included on the same EP as his *Eurovision* winner. Pascal's unthreatening style kept him in favour for some time, but in the long term his *Eurovision* triumph did him no more good than it had Claveau or Boyer.

---

[501] Although it was outsold by a massively popular and timely cover by Sacha Distel.
[502] Daughter of Lucienne Boyer and Jacques Pills.
[503] The song was also available in rival versions by François Degeult and Rika Zaraï.
[504] And would do so again in 1962.
[505] Also a hit for Dalida.
[506] The third French-language win in four years and the fourth since the contest began in 1956.

## Other song contests

Song contests were a big part of the music publishing world during the early sixties, with any number of them being held across Europe during the decade. After *Eurovision* and the Italian festival at San Remo, the best known was probably the *Festival de la Canción Mediterránea*, staged annually in Barcelona, which had first brought Nana Mouskouri to international attention in 1960. The winner of the contest in 1961 was French entrant Robert Jeantal with 'Dans le creux de ta main', the only significant hit he ever had. Jeantal was an above-average singer with a style midway between teenage pop and traditional music hall sounds, but despite cutting quality versions of international hits like Augusto Algueró's 'La montaña'[507] ('La montagne') and the *West Side Story* favourite, 'Maria', he was unable to repeat his success.

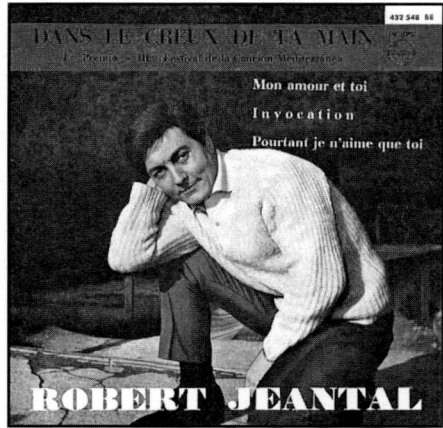

Back in France, another festival, the *Coq d'Or de la chanson française*,[508] was responsible for the emergence of Alain Barrière in 1960 with the hit ballad 'Cathy', which he followed up a year later with the pop hit 'Une fille pleurait'. Ensconced at the easy listening end of the market, he dabbled in pseudo-country pop on the cornball 'Mon vieux Joe', and the uptempo 'Je reviendrai d'Al Cantara' was equally contrived but no less enjoyable. Barrière's participation in the *Coq d'Or* contest carried a lower international profile than that of a *Eurovision* laureate, but it served him well and he went on to carve out a successful career over the decade.

Barrière's success – and the song contests' continuing support for old-fashioned balladry – demonstrated that there remained a substantial audience for music that owed little or nothing to rock'n'roll. The market for 'quality' songs and traditional French pop would in fact never go away, and the coming decade would see the emergence of some of the most popular ballads and *chansons* ever written.

---

[507] Best known to anglophone audiences as Anthony Newley's 'If She Should Come To You'.
[508] Jointly sponsored by radio station Europe No. 1 and the Olympia Theatre.

# Chapter 17

## VIENS DANSER LE TWIST
### Rock'n'roll takes over (1961-63)

*The story of the twist has been endlessly retold over the years, and, along with the rise of the Philadelphia school of* American Bandstand *idols, it has often been cited as evidence of the decline of rock'n'roll in the early sixties. This may well be true, although it obscures the fact that there were some excellent records released during the period of its greatest popularity, among them Sam Cooke's 'Twistin' The Night Away' and the Isley Brothers' 'Twist And Shout'.[509] More importantly however, the dance proved popular with young and old alike, marking the first occasion that any form of rock'n'roll won mainstream acceptance beyond the teenage market.*

*Nowhere was this more true than in France, where the sudden arrival of the twist brought rock'n'roll in from the margins and placed it centre stage. Indeed, it is unlikely that the music would have made such huge commercial leaps forward without it. While the rock'n'roll beloved by the* blousons noirs *was rough, tough and synonymous with violence, the twist was greeted as simply good, clean fun and the French music industry eagerly embraced the new dance, hastening to proclaim it as the Next Big Thing.*

### The twist arrives in France

Chubby Checker's cover of Hank Ballard's 'The Twist' had made a few waves in France in March 1961, when it came out on a Columbia EP. At the time, it was received simply as the latest rock'n'roll import from America, and failed to make any significant impact on the national consciousness, being outsold by a gutsy cover of one of the other tracks, 'Pony Time' ('Hey pony') by Les Chaussettes Noires.[510] Two events then took place more or less simultaneously, setting off a bout of twist fever that would not fully subside for several years.

The first, in the autumn of 1961, was the arrival in Paris of the cast of the Broadway musical *West Side Story*, one of whom brought across a copy of Checker's record (probably unaware that it was available in France). Passing it to the disc jockey at Chez Régine,[511] he set about teaching the great and good of French society how to dance the twist.

---

[509] Originally recorded by the Top Notes, although their version, an early Phil Spector production, was a poor recording totally unlike the Isley Brothers' vibrant reading.

[510] And by a less stellar attempt by Johnny Hallyday.

[511] A chic nightclub run by cabaret singer Régine Zylberberg.

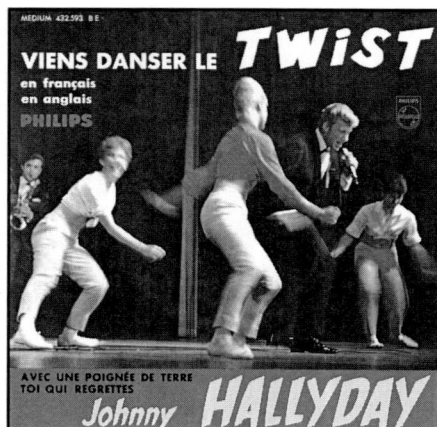

The second was Lee Hallyday's return from a holiday in the US with a copy of Chubby Checker's latest recording, 'Let's Twist Again', in his bag. The record was duly passed to Johnny Hallyday, who decided to cut a cover during his first sessions for Philips.[512] The bilingual 'Viens danser le twist' duly appeared in October 1961 on his second EP for the label. Checker's original and an English-language version by Richard Anthony were also released in the same month, and all three sold briskly.

This was due in no small part to Hallyday's decision to demonstrate the twist on stage in September 1961, during his first headlining season at the Olympia Theatre, after which it exploded, virtually overnight, into the biggest dance craze the country had seen since the tango.

'Viens danser le twist' became a hit across much of Europe. The first of Hallyday's records to sell in significant quantities beyond the borders of France,[513] it gave him his first gold record and the biggest-selling EP of his career. He followed up with further twist-appeal tunes like 'Danse le twist avec moi' and 'Twistin' U.S.A.' (a straight cover of the Danny & The Juniors original) as his popularity soared. Richard Anthony's career also rocketed skywards, with his version of 'Let's Twist Again' chasing Hallyday's across the airwaves. In their wake, the music industry rallied to cash in on this new craze of which it seemed the whole country wanted to be a part.

### French and Belgian twist tunes

Among the first to join the rush were Les Chaussettes Noires, who made a Christmas twist, 'Le twist du Père Noël', before following up in early 1962 with versions of Hank Ballard's/Chubby Checker's 'The Twist' ('Le twist') and Joey Dee & The Starlighters' 'Peppermint Twist',[514] adding a saxophonist to their line-up to give them the requisite new sound.

They were quickly joined by Doug Fowlkes & The Airdales (who cut the original 'Twistin' Time' alongside covers of 'The Twist' and 'Let's Twist Again' for their debut EP), Gillian Hills ('En dansant le twist', a passable reworking of the Shirelles' 'Mama Said'), Gélou (the unimpressive fake-live 'Viens twister!'[515]), Belgian *rockeuse* Jackie Seven (a squealing take on 'Viens danser le twist') and Elvis impersonator Teddy Raye ('Twist stop', adapted from Chubby Checker's 'Ray Charles-ton'), all of whom got their records out in time for the 1961 Christmas market, although only Hills enjoyed any

---

[512] These took place over four days in London with studio musicians including Joe Moretti and the soon-to-be famous Georgie Fame.

[513] Although he had already developed a following in Spain, where 'Souvenirs, souvenirs' had entered the Top 20.

[514] Also covered by the Cousins.

[515] Also recorded (without the exclamation mark) by Audrey Arno.

commercial success.

More cynical were the punningly-named Oliver Twist et ses Twisties, who cut a throwaway version of Les Chats Sauvages' 'Twist à Saint-Tropez' (which, despite the title, was more rock'n'roll than twist) and Les Twistin' Tigers, a faceless studio outfit who cut a pair of instrumental EPs that failed to convince anybody to dance the twist or anything else, despite offering a bright, bouncy sound on the saxophone-fuelled 'La machine à danser'.

Les Philosophes cut the abominable 'Chicken curry twist', while orchestra leader Paul Mauriat's pseudo-rock'n'roll outfit, Les Satellites, titled their latest instrumental EP *Slow-rock and twist*. In truth, only the first word was applicable, and anyone foolish enough to attempt to twist to their abominable cover of Teddy Randazzo's 'Let The Sunshine In' ('Laisse entrer le ciel') soon gave up on the idea. In the same boat were the idiotically named Rocky Twist & His Bips Bips, whose cheesy versions of 'The Twist' ('Le twist') and Fausto Papetti's 'Twist – twist' ought to have been thrown overboard at the first opportunity, although the former at least had a decent saxophone break to offset the dreadful organ that dominated the record.

Nancy Holloway, whose budget-label reworking of 'Viens danser le twist' was followed by an excellent English-language reading of 'The Twist', was more impressive. So too was Maguy Marshall, whose 'Mademoiselle Twist' served as a theme song for the rest of her (short) career.

Chubby Checker's records also sparked a bout of twist fever up in Belgium, where Brussels-based American singer Jack Hammer[516] added fuel to the fire with the nonsensical 'Kissin' twist', which enjoyed major success in both halves of the linguistically-divided country. He followed up with a clutch of other twist singles over the next year, mostly formulaic junk like 'Crazy twist' and 'Boogie woogie twist', none of which achieved anything more than domestic success. An enthusiastic and versatile showman and performer able to drop seamlessly into impersonations of other singers, Hammer never made any great headway in France, where Hallyday quickly became King of the Twist.

---

[516] Hammer (whose real name was Earl Burroughs) was also responsible for writing or co-writing a number of rock'n'roll classics including Jerry Lee Lewis's 'Great Balls Of Fire' and 'Milkshake Mademoiselle', Wanda Jackson's 'Fujiyama Mama', and the Treniers' 'Rock'n'Roll Call'.

The dance was also grist to the mill for Belgian rockers the Kili Jacks, whose 'Rag mop' and 'Bowling twist' were both passable, if unexciting efforts. Meanwhile, their erstwhile colleagues, the Cousins, made a better fist of it with 'Pour twister' and 'Quand les Cousins s'en vont twister', the latter a surprisingly decent reworking of the jazz standard 'When The Saints Go Marching In'.

Cruising along behind them were fellow Belgians Les Croque-Morts with 'Suzy twist' (a more-than-acceptable remodelling of 'De hele stad is gek en dol' by Dutch rock'n'roll outfit Peter en zijn Rockets) and 'Jenny dans le miroir' (a decent, if ragged take on Del Shannon's 'Ginny In The Mirror'), while the Daniels unleashed a pair of EPs replete with cash-ins like 'Easy twist', 'Twist a ree' and 'Scotch twist'. Probably the most interesting of these opportunistic releases was 'Twist – twist' by Les Chakachas, survivors of the exotica boom of the early fifties, whose superior version charted in a number of European countries, including the UK.

## Twistmania

In early 1962, Petula Clark waded into the fray with a retooling of Lee Dorsey's 'Ya Ya'. Delivered in French over a danceable rhythm as 'Ya ya twist', it was a massive hit across Europe – including the UK. Too shrewd to hitch her fortunes entirely to the new dance fad, she avoided any more songs with the word 'twist' in the title (even though recordings like 'Dans le train de nuit' continued to bounce along to the same beat) and soon reverted to more straightforward rock and pop material.

Richard Anthony also elected to keep his distance from the phenomenon he had helped to launch, but not before unleashing the next major twist hit on the French public, 'La leçon de twist'. Originally knocked out as 'Twistin' the twist' by bandleader Jerry Mengo (under the pseudonym Teddy Martin & His Las Vegas Twisters, in attempt to pass the record off as American), it had been retitled when turned into a guitar instrumental by Danyel Gérard's backing group, Les Danger's. Anthony's rendition (with lyrics by Gérard) was a rocking effort far stronger than the average twist tune and became a huge hit. His success engendered a plethora of rival versions, among them a great cover by by Les Chaussettes Noires and a sizzling take by Gérard himself, both of which also charted. [517]

Gérard went on to cut the formulaic 'Chattanooga twist'[518] and 'Le petit Gonzalès' (a version of David Dante's 'Speedy Gonzales') that reached the racks in France even before Pat Boone's effort had charted in the US and

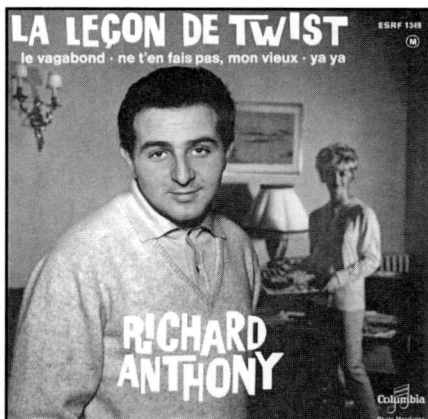

[517] The versions by Gérard and Les Danger's were released simply as 'Leçon de twist', without the definite article.
[518] Covered in Belgium by Jacky Delmone but not issued in France.

became a monster hit. Although the song made no mention of the twist, musically it was in keeping with the style and confirmed that the twist fever that was sweeping the country had brought with it a change in taste among the rock'n'roll audience. Hard-hitting rock'n'roll was now on the way out and more light-hearted, danceable pop on the way in.

Picking up on the change, most of the rock'n'rollers in the country hastened to adapt their style and climb aboard the twist bandwagon. Danny Boy et ses Pénitents rushed out the enjoyable 'Twistez' on their third EP, followed by the unbelievably silly 'Le twist de Schubert' (adapted[519] from said composer's *Piano Quintet in A Major*, better known as 'The Trout Quintet') and a dire cover of Jack Hammer's 'Kissin' twist'.[520] Although commercially successful, the group lost much of their appeal when they abandoned their hard-rocking style. 'Stop!' (a punchy take on the Stereos' 1961 doo-wop hit, 'I Really Love You') kept their heads above water for a while, but by the end of the year their career was sinking fast.

Dany Fischer also had a stab at 'Kissin' twist', while Frankie Jordan recorded the inane 'La marche des twisters' (Kenny Dino's 'Your Ma Said You Cried In Your Sleep Last Night'), both to no avail. Equally unsuccessful were Michel Sydney (with 'Tais-toi et twiste' and another version of 'Le twist de Schubert'), Rosy Armen ('Mon amour twiste') and Nicole Croisille ('Leçon de twist'), while the little-known Billy Watch cut the underwhelming 'Let's twist infernal' for the tiny Star Success label to complete indifference. Of these, only Armen showed sufficient grasp of the new style to stand a chance in the marketplace – albeit not enough to take her effervescent adaptation of the Paris Sisters' 'All Through The Night' ('Toutes les nuits') into the charts.

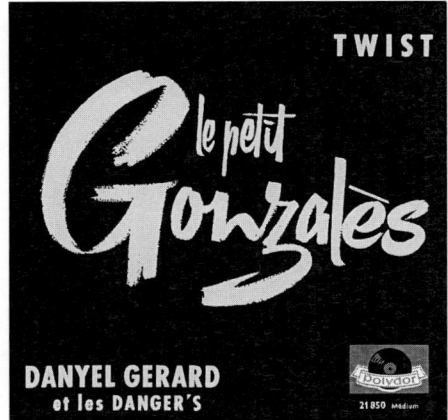

Trying desperately to keep their careers afloat, Jacky Rider and Vince Taylor both took a punt at 'Peppermint Twist'. Rider's record disappeared down the dustpipe, but Taylor's English-language version became a moderate hit. His near-simultaneous release of 'There's a lot of twistin going on' (a bastardised version of 'Whole Lotta

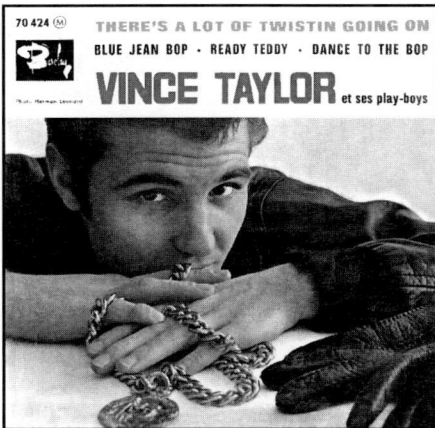

---

[519] Like Les Frères Jacques' 'La truite' before it.
[520] Les Chats Sauvages also recorded the song, in English. It was released as a single in Belgium but went unissued back home in France, perhaps because it was below their usual standard.

Shakin' Goin' On') was not without its merits either, but its moderate commercial impact showed how badly the twist had derailed the career of the country's most exciting rock'n'roll singer. Desperate to keep himself afloat, Taylor resorted to cutting 'Mimi', a substandard French-language pop confection that bore little resemblance to his earlier rock'n'roll classics. Despite including a lascivious rendition of Jerry Lee Lewis's 'Big Blon' Baby' (retitled 'B.B. Baby' in honour of Brigitte Bardot) and a decent stab at Little Walter's 'My Babe', the EP flopped. In the middle of 1962, Eddie Barclay abandoned the attempt to topple Johnny Hallyday from his throne.

## Hallyday in the USA

Intent on broadening his audience, Hallyday mixed his twist records with traditional rock'n'roll like 'Sam'di soir' and even smooth ballads such as 'Retiens la nuit', written especially for him by Charles Aznavour and Georges Garvarentz. Another massive hit, the latter helped him connect with the huge female audience that had hitherto preferred the less-threatening Richard Anthony, ratcheting up their ongoing battle to be the King of French rock'n'roll.

Never one to rest on his laurels, Hallyday set his sights on the market that counted most – the USA – and spent much of early 1962 in Nashville cutting his first English-language LP, *Johnny Hallyday Sings America's Rockin'
Hits*. Opting to cover a set of rock'n'roll classics was not the greatest of ideas, as the album invited comparison with the originals in a way that his French adaptations often avoided. It failed miserably in the international market,[521] although it became a modest hit in France, as did a spin-off EP featuring his take on Ray Charles's 'I Got A Woman'.

Hallyday also reworked some of the material into French, resulting in the hits 'Serre la main d'un fou' (Titus Turner's 'Shake The Hand Of A Fool') and 'Dans un jardin d'amour' ('Garden Of Love').[522] Putting the disappointment of the album behind him, he scored another hit in the summer of 1962 with 'Pas cette chanson' (Ben E. King's 'Don't Play That Song') before returning to the twist with a great cover of Sam Cooke's 'Twistin' The Night Away' ('Laissez-nous twister').

---

[521] However, two spin-off singles ('Shake The Hand Of A Fool' and 'Be-Bop-A-Lula') were regional hits in the US, with the former figuring in the *Cash Box* 'Coming Up' chart and both briefly bubbling under the *Music Vendor* chart.

[522] Hallyday's English-language version of 'Garden Of Love' was not included on the US album, though it was issued on a single in the Netherlands. The song's composer, Gene Pitney, did not release his own interpretation until after Hallyday's version had been and gone.

## Twist groups

While Hallyday was exhausting his energies on his American campaign, back in France the twist bandwagon lumbered on and almost every group in the country felt the need to clamber aboard as it went past. Following in the footsteps of Les Chaussettes Noires, Les Champions slipped the perfunctory 'J'aime le twist' onto their 1961 debut EP. They included 'Ne me plus passer du twist' and a version of 'Ya ya twist' on their second, but Claude Ciari's guitar was buried in a muddy mix that did little to enhance his reputation. They fared rather better with a version of 'Petit Gonzalès',[523] which became a modest hit, but the group's gutsy sound sat poorly within the framework of the twist. They only revealed their true qualities on a cover of Elvis Presley's 'Good Luck Charm' ('Le coup du charme') and a rollicking version of Teddy Martin's 'Pardon Me' ('Pardonne-moi'), which rightly put the emphasis back onto Ciari's guitar-picking.

Their early records had sold reasonably well, but, saddled with a vocalist as unimpressive as Jean-Claude Chane, the group were soon struggling. While their 'J'aime, j'aime, j'aim' ' picked up more airplay than another version by Jean-Pierre et les Rebelles, neither this, nor their cover of Ricky Nelson's 'Travelin' Man' ('Si j'avais un bateau') made even a minor ripple. A year into the twist boom, their 1962 take on Chris Montez's 'Let's Dance' ('Dansons') tickled the eardrums of those who heard it, but did little to dispel the impression that the group was in decline – a fate confirmed when drummer/leader Willy Lewis quit for a solo career. His bid for independence as Willy Twist resulted in a pair of rather tedious EPs based around the likes of 'Hallali twist' and 'Galoping twist', which were as unimaginative as they sound and failed to propel his career into orbit.

Across town, Les Pirates scuppered their career with a series of uninspiring twist records, starting with 'Twist twist baby' (Perry Como's 'Juke Box Baby') in early 1962. Things got worse with the banal 'Twist de Paris' and 'Spring twist', although 'La route du twist', a reworking of the King Cole Trio classic, '(Get Your Kicks On) Route 66',[524] added some sorely needed thump to the proceedings. They confirmed their continued devotion to rock'n'roll with 'Le slow twist' (an impressive cover of Chubby Checker & Dee Dee Sharp's 'Slow Twistin' ') and a sparkling saxophone solo on 'Danse un twist' (Checker's 'Dance-A-Long'), but their desperation was evident on 'Laissez-nous twister' (a substandard assault on Sam Cooke's 'Twistin' The Night Away') and by the end of the year they were beginning to fall apart.

All over the country, groups scrabbled to get a piece of the action as twist

---

[523] Unlike Danyel Gérard's recording, the title of Les Champions' version appeared without the definite article.

[524] Doubtless inspired by the recent version by Chuck Berry.

mania showed no signs of abating. Many hard-rocking outfits felt obliged to record at least one twist number, among them Les Loups Garous ('Twist à La Baule'), Les Pingouins ('Voo-doo-twist', adapted from LaVern Baker's 'Voodoo Voodoo'), Les Rebelles ('Folklore twist', an instrumental built on the traditional 'Frère Jacques'), Les Beaver's ('Loup blanc twist'), Les Gones Rock ('Allez, twistez') and Claude et ses Tribuns ('Le twist familial'). Others simply added the suffix 'twist' to the titles on their records in an effort to entice people to buy their wares.[525]

Nice-based outfit Les Trim's wasted their abilities covering twist hits of the day, though their original 'Amour twist' suggests they might have been better off sticking to their own material. Six-piece vocal ensemble Les Collégiennes applied a girl group sound to the inane 'Twiste collégienne' and 'Good morning twist', while the only original attempted by the endearingly incompetent Les Blousons Noirs, the truly amateurish 'Les fous du twist', can be placed in the same category.

Also trying to grab a piece of the lucrative twist action was songwriter Jacques Verières, who teamed up with Django Reinhardt's guitar-strumming son Babik to form Glenn Jack et ses Glenners. They impressed with 'Zizi la twisteuse' on their 1962 debut EP, but despite their musical pedigree, they lacked the necessary teen appeal to succeed. Although guilty of recording 'rock'n'roll by numbers', it has to be said that their version of Ray Charles's 'Unchain My Heart' ('Délivre-moi') was far from a disgrace. However, sales were minimal and Verières returned to his roots, where he remained a shadowy figure on the fringes of the French music scene.

Not all groups professed to like the twist, but such was its promotional pull that few could afford to disregard it. Les Vautours tried to stand against the tide, cutting the defiant 'Jacky qu'as-tu fait de moi' instead, but when they eventually succumbed, they made a reasonable fist of 'Ya ya twist' and 'Laissez-nous twister' while retaining enough integrity not to sell out completely. Never dedicated sufficiently

---

[525] This, of course, was a time-honoured ploy: early rock'n'roll releases around the world had similarly been designated 'foxtrot'. In France, record companies continued to append the names of dances to song titles on record sleeves well into the sixties.

to their career to reach the heights scaled by Les Chats Sauvages or Les Chaussettes Noires, they remained true to their rock'n'roll roots thanks to an ability to unearth good material like 'Hey Little Angel' by New Zealand's Johnny Devlin (reworked into into French as 'Petite Angèle') and Jay B. Loyd's little-known 'You're Just My Kind' ('Hé! Tu me plais'). Although their twist records sold moderately well, they did the group few favours and by the end of the year, they too were on the ropes.

Les Chats Sauvages actively hated the twist, but even they felt obliged to record a version of 'Laissez-nous twister' (Sam Cooke's 'Twistin' The Night Away') for their second LP, *1ère Anniversaire*,[526] in 1962. They had fewer problems watering down their sound to include ballads and less frantic sounds, and enjoyed substantial sales with a version of Cliff Richard's 'Theme For A Dream' ('C'est pas sérieux') in the spring of that year,[527] but it was a belated issue on EP of the seven-month-old 'Twist à Saint-Tropez' that proved to be the bigger hit. The song had long been a favourite among the group's fans, but the popularity of the twist helped it find a new audience. Musically it had nothing in common with the sound dominating the airwaves, but it gave them their biggest hit to date – not only in France, but also in Scandinavia, where it remains something of a classic.

Having to pander to the needs of twisters was one thing, but the group also had its own internal problems, with members frequently squabbling over rehearsal time and the choice of material. They rocked up a storm with covers of Gene Vincent's 'Dance To The Bop' ('Quand les Chats sont là') and 'I'm Going Home' ('Je reviendrai'),[528] Helen Shapiro's 'Tell Me What He Said' ('Tout ce qu'elle voudra') and an airy rendition of Eddie Cochran's 'Weekend' ('Toute la nuit'), but it was the unimaginative ballad 'Oh! Lady' that generated a sizeable hit. Midway through their next tour, the arguments came to a head and frontman Dick Rivers quit for a solo career.

Their main rivals, Les Chaussettes Noires, were poorly placed to take advantage of this state of affairs, as their own lead singer, Eddy Mitchell, had been called up for miltary service. When he could make it to a recording session, they turned out rockier material like the savage 'Je reviendrai bientôt' (Johnny Otis's 'Willie And The Hand Jive'[529]). A return to their roots, the number appeared on a 1962 EP that also saw them pursuing the prevailing

---

[526] The album was actually untitled, but was popularly referred to as this in the press, as it was released roughly a year after their recording debut.

[527] The song was also covered by Orlando, who likewise enjoyed good airplay, though it was Les Chats Sauvages who garnered most of the sales.

[528] Cut by Dick Rivers with session players following one argument too many in the band. According to Rivers, the only track on the EP to actually feature the Chats was 'Oh! Lady'.

[529] Which bore more than a passing similarity to the 1960 cover by Cliff Richard and the Shadows.

trends with 'Shout, shout' (a decent attempt at Ernie Maresca's 'Shout! Shout! (Knock Yourself Out)') plus a rather perfunctory version of Joey Dee & The Starlighters' 'Hey, Let's Twist'. However, Mitchell's absence from the scene left the twist field free for new singers and groups to make their mark.

### New twist singers

The best of the newcomers were the charismatic Gary 'L'Ange Noir' et ses Démons. L'Ange Noir yelped his way through James Brown's/Chubby Checker's 'Good Good Lovin'' ('De t'aimer, de t'aimer[530]) and also cut excellent versions of 'Ya ya twist' and Checker's 'The Fly' ('Le «fly»') for a pair of 1962 EPs that met with surprisingly little success. Offering a lighter feel than Les Chaussettes Noires, the group hit new artistic heights with a tight and powerful version of Eddie Cochran's 'C'mon Everybody' ('J'ai le cœur qui chavire'), but neither this, nor a kicking organ-led assault on Bobby Darin's 'Multiplication' found the audience they deserved.

Black American singer Gerry Beckles and his group, Les Toppers, offered a much fuller sound complete with horn section, but despite their popularity in the clubs, their 1962 release 'Savez-vous danser le twist?' went nowhere. The group's live appeal was perfectly captured on a passable cover (in English) of Ben E. King's 'Stand By Me', but by then they were falling apart, leaving Beckles to pursue a solo career in 1963 with the smooth 'L'amour est roi' (Frank Ifield's 'Your Time Will Come') and a cool, finger-snapping rendition of the Majors' 'A Little Bit Now' ('Tu connais la suite'), with equal success.

Lyonnaise singer, actress and dancer Arielle was nicknamed '*La Minou Drouet du twist*'[531] and showed how much she deserved the appellation with a bouncy version of Frankie Lymon's revival of Benny Goodman's 'Good Goody' ('Goody goody (Ça va, ça va)') and the inevitable 'Petit Gonzalès', both of which appeared on the same 1962 EP. She subsequently turned to girl group pop for the worthwhile 'Je n'aime que Bobby' (Marcie Blane's 'Bobby's Girl') in 1963, but failed to make any significant impact with any of

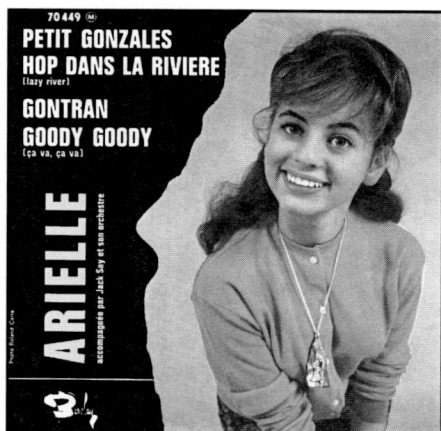

her four EPs, despite a strong voice and a charming style.

Such was the hunger of the French record industry for the twist that Belgian rocker Burt Blanca set to work on a series of records that made little use of the powerful rocking style that had been evident on his domestic recordings with Les King Creoles. Leading a schizophrenic musical existence, he recorded rock'n'roll for the Belgian market and twists for the French one, opening the latter account with a pointless cover of 'Ya ya twist' and a more worthy attempt at Ray

---

[530] Les Vautours did better with the song.

[531] A reference to her young age and multiple talents, which drew comparisons with the Breton child prodigy, Minou Drouet (see pages 143-4).

Anthony's 'Bookend Twist' ('Week end twist'). He followed up with 'Quand tu twistes avec moi' and a take on the Billy Joe & The Checkmates instrumental, 'Percolator (Twist)'. However, neither of these came close to the sound he pounded out in the clubs, and his best French releases featured more rocking material such as 1962's 'Ohé la fille' (Dee Clark's 'Hey Little Girl'), or the more-powerful-than-usual twist effort, 'Twist, twist señora' (adapted from Gary 'US' Bonds' rollicking 'Twist, Twist Señora').

Travelling southwards at the same time as Blanca, British singer Dave Dacosta teamed up with Shadows wannabes the Strollers and slipped across the Channel to try his luck with yet another version of 'Let's Twist Again'. This offered little in the way of originality, but his slow, bluesy remake of Gene Vincent's 'Be-Bop-A-Lula' was far better and indicated where his real interests lay. Unfortunately for Dacosta, it was the twist, rather than rock'n'roll, that was ruling the roost and his EP passed into obscurity. For a follow-up, he turned to the Little Walter standard 'My Babe', but a lifeless version of Sam Cooke's 'Twistin' The Night Away' effectively put an end to his hopes of finding fame and fortune in France.

Dacosta was by no means the worst offender, but in truth very few singers or groups gave any thought as to how they could establish their own identity within the context of the twist. Indeed, very few attempted anything new with the formula, although Moroccan girl singer Malika took the brave (for the time) step of recording 'Ya ya twist' in Arabic for the North African and Middle Eastern market. On a similar tack, 'Le nabout twist' by Kôkô (drummer Claude François under a pseudonym[532]) was a hit in the Middle East, but was roundly ignored back home in the aftermath of the Algerian War (1954-62).

**Grown-up twisters**

Such releases were aimed squarely at the teenage market, but the twist's popularity on the dance floor at the upmarket Chez Régine convinced many of the old guard that they too could grab a piece of the action in a craze that was open to all ages. Unfortunately, like Frank Sinatra's 'Everybody's Twistin' ', most of the records that resulted were far from impressive, with Jean-Paul Mauric's 'Twist avec Maman', Annie Cordy's version of 'Zizi la twisteuse' and Line Renaud's 'Double twist' failing to generate much excitement. Cordy was amusing as ever, but Renaud's attempt was simply disappointing, though she did hit a Ray Charles-like groove on the enjoyable 'Dieu, que c'est bon'.

Marcel Amont's 'Percolateur' (Billy Joe & The Checkmates' 'Percolator (Twist)') was another release that failed to live up to its promise, but he did at least redeem himself with 'Françoise aux bas bleus', which name-dropped

---

[532] Among other things, François had played on Los Machucambos' 1961 smash, 'Pepito'.

Johnny Hallyday and advertised itself as a twist – a boast it did a reasonable job of living up to, even if the orchestration diminished the effect.

Taking a more sensible approach, Maurice Chevalier teamed up with Les Chaussettes Noires to record the amusing and catchy 'Le twist du canotier'. A surprisingly decent twist outing, it was a huge hit into the bargain.

Far less impressive were the efforts of songwriter Jean Renard, who posed as 'Big Twist' for the dreadful 'Rocket-bye-bye' and 'Sacré Big Twist', and comic actor Jean-Claude Massoulier, who debuted in early 1963 with the downright bizarre 'Le twist agricole'. 'Le twist militaire' by famous clown Achille Zavatta was equally poor, but at least had the benefit of being amusing, although not quite as much as Nick Kartoon's hysterical 'Chickadee-twist'. At the other end of the spectrum, Pierre Brun's attempt to relive the glories of Jean Sablon by turning 'Sur le pont d'Avignon' into a twist (titled, yes, 'Twist sur le pont d'Avignon') and Jean Ségurel's accordion-drenched 'Twist auvergnat' were simply laughable – or would have been, if they hadn't been so awful. Bringing up the rear were Les Sœurs Rosio, two middle-aged ladies whose dreadful 'novelty' cover of 'Viens danser le twist' was, amazingly, given space within the pages of *Disco revue* during 1963.

Predictably, the two old-school singers who enjoyed the most success with the twist were those who already enjoyed large followings in the teen pop market, Henri Salvador and Dalida.

Salvador, who had already dabbled in dance crazes with the novelty 'Dracula cha cha cha' eighteen months earlier, picked up a massive hit in early 1962 with 'Twist S.N.C.F.', one of several tongue-in-cheek twists recorded during the year by the master of musical humour. He was a shrewd operator and a consummate showman who fully understood the marketplace, and he made sure of his own continued place in it with recordings like 'J'm'en fous twist' and 'Twist de l'enrhumé', which played it strictly for laughs.

While Salvador kept his tongue firmly in his cheek, Dalida took her material rather more seriously. Still reaching out across all age groups, she cut yet another version of 'La leçon de twist', which incredibly made the charts, and the more all-purpose 'Achète-moi un juke-box', on which

she nailed her teen pop credentials to the mast. After taking on Danyel Gérard with a good cover of 'Le petit Gonzalès' during the summer of 1962, she let her standards drop significantly with the banal 'Petit éléphant twist' (based on Henry Mancini's 'Baby Elephant Walk'), but by then the teen audience was looking for new idols of its own and had lost interest in the efforts of a singer who had been around for too many years. Her EP initially sold poorly, but was saved from complete failure by the inclusion of 'Le jour le plus long' (Paul Anka's theme from the 1962 film, *The Longest Day*). This presented her with a smash hit and an opportunity to move away from the teen-pop market to consolidate her hold on an older audience with a more sophisticated, but no less enjoyable repertoire.

### From jazz to twist

Dance music had never been the preserve of the young, previous generations of adults having gone overboard for the foxtrot, the Charleston and the tango. Indeed, dance music still provided a great deal of work for the country's jazz bands, as was evidenced by the 1960 LP *Dansons avec Claude Bolling*. Always keeping one eye open for opportunities for crossover success, Bolling kept up with the times with 1962's *Claude Bolling joue les succès de Ray Charles*, on which he perfectly reflected the American singer's roots in jazz.

The same attitude pervaded the unashamedly backward-looking records of Jack Ary et son 'High Society' Cha Cha, who unsurprisingly cha-cha-cha'ed their way through such nonsense as 'Théodore le dinosaure' and the clichéd 'Défendu, défendu', attracting the interest of those still lamenting the passing of the exotica boom, but few others.

Jazz bands found that the twist provided easy pickings, even if, from their perspective, it marked a new low in musical oversimplification. For a short while, the market was swamped with substandard jazz-twist offerings like Guy Lafitte's variation on 'Peppermint Twist', Claude Luter's 'Dixie twist', and trumpeter Peter Dean's 'Voulez-vous twister, Grand-Mère?' (a revival of Lina Margy's 'Voulez-vous danser, Grand-Mère?') that had little in common with the sounds that were enticing teenage dancers out onto the floor.

285

Trad jazz enthusiast Maxim Saury in particular sold out to the teenage beat with odd reworkings of 'Let's Twist Again', 'Twistin' the twist' and 'Twistin' The Night Away'.

Claude Vasori, who could usually be found churning out easy listening albums rather than jazz, at least tried something a little different with the Afro-twist sound of 'Tanganika twist', although whether it was worth the effort is open to question. Meanwhile Trumpet Boy's instrumental takes on 'Viens danser le twist' and 'Peppermint twist' sounded exactly as one might have imagined.

This explosion of interest in the twist was mirrored across the globe. Between 1960 and 1963, twenty different twist records made the *Billboard* Top 40 in the US, with eleven doing likewise in the *Record Retailer* chart in the UK. While Chubby Checker was responsible for many of these, there were also chart strikes by artists as diverse as Gary 'US' Bonds ('Dear Lady Twist'), King Curtis ('Soul Twist'), Frankie Vaughan ('Don't Stop – Twist!') and even the Chipmunks ('The Alvin Twist'). On the other side of the globe in Australia, leading rockers like Col Joye ('Sweet Little Sixteen Twist') and Johnny O'Keefe ('Twistin' Australia Way') added twist tunes to their repertoires in an effort to stay hip, while Europe was swamped by twist records in a variety of foreign languages. In West Germany, Charly Cotton charted in 1962 with the ludicrous 'Der Liebestraum als Twist', based on the classical piece by composer Franz Liszt.[533] In Italy, Peppino di Capri topped the charts the same year with the ubiquitous 'Let's Twist Again'. In Spain, the biggest hit of the year was the massively popular EP track[534] 'Bailando twist' by Dúo Dinámico, while up in Denmark Buster Larsen og Lille Marlene scored with 'Baby Twist' in 1963.

Nowhere though, did the twist enjoy such tremendous popularity as in France. Indeed, by the late summer of 1962, it was the dominant force in French pop – so much so, that Eddie Vartan felt obliged to record 'S.L.C. twist' as a new theme for the *Salut les copains* radio show. Already though, many in the business were on the lookout for the next dance craze, and the answer duly arrived in the form of the jazz-tinged Madison.

**The Madison**

Sometimes seen as the jazzers' revenge for the simplicity of the twist, the Madison had a more complex rhythm that crippled many of the amateur groups who tried to play it, but nevertheless proved to be hugely popular in France – far more so than in the US, where it had enjoyed a brief run of popularity back in 1960.

---

[533] Immediately adapted into French for the hilarious 'Papa Liszt twist' by Henri Salvador.
[534] Spain, like France, favoured EPs over singles for much of the sixties.

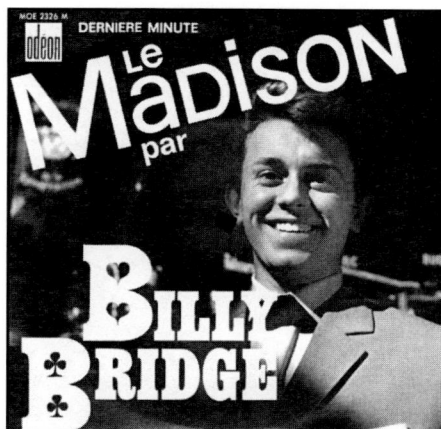

Its leading exponent was Billy Bridge, who debuted in the spring of 1962 with the tough rocker 'Surboum'[535] and a stomping take on Hank Ballard's 'Triple Twist' before shooting to glory in the summer with 'Le grand M'. The song caught the ear of audiences across the country, and within weeks everyone was doing the Madison along with Bridge, whose EP also offered 'Ça, c'est l'Madison'.

Madison fans and twist- and Hallyday-haters rushed to proclaim Bridge *'Le prince du Madison'*, the idol of the hour, and the man who would end Hallyday's reign at the top, but such claims quickly proved to be premature. Although his third EP contained a powerful cover of Elvis Presley's 'Anything That's Part Of You' ('Ce qui me vient de vous'), it was the catchy 'Madison flirt' that became his next hit and the public association of singer and dance proved difficult to break. Despite cutting a series of good records with producer Mickey Baker over the next two years, including another Presley cover, 'Cours, mon cœur' ('Night Rider'),[536] and a quality Charles Aznavour-penned offering in the same style, 'Notre amour renaîtra', he never succeeded in matching the success of his breakthrough hit.

Bridge's success brought forth a spate of Madison records from a variety of sources, among them Les Collégiennes with the straightforward 'C'est le Madison', bandleader Jacques Denjean's dire version of 'Le grand M'[537] that was just as awful as his earlier interpretation of 'The Twist', and a 1962 Barclay EP by an anonymous Belgian group calling themselves the Madison's which contained surprisingly listenable late flowerings of big band rock like 'Madison shake' and 'Mad Madison'.

Cris Carol updated the ideas of Les Chats Sauvages for her 1962 release, 'Madison à Saint-Tropez' (which, despite the similarity in title to 'Twist à Saint-Tropez' was actually a different song), before coming over all jazzy with 'Je souris sous la pluie' (a cover of Mr. Acker Bilk's 'Acker's Lacquer'). Jazz and the Madison also collided on Claude Bolling's *Madison Twist* LP, whose contents require no further elaboration.

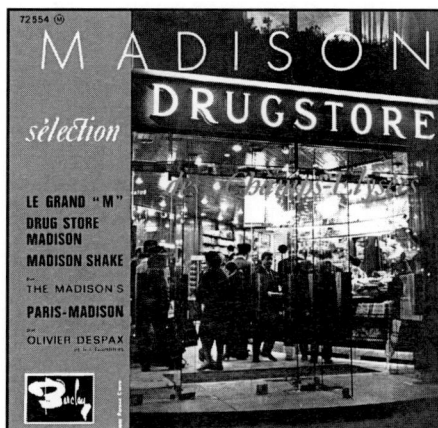

---

[535] Although credited as an original, the song was loosely based on Chuck Berry's 'Reelin' And Rockin' '.

[536] Which compared favourably with a version on Dick Rivers' first solo album at the end of 1962.

[537] Retitled 'The Big «M»', presumably in an attempt to pass it off as an American title.

Although Les Vautours professed disinterest, in 1962 the Madison was duly added to the repertoire of most other French groups including Les Pirates ('L'A.B.C. du Madison'), Glenn Jack et ses Glenners ('Quand Maddy sonne') and Les Loups Garous (a cover of Billy Bridge's hit, 'Le grand M').

Up in Belgium, Les Chakachas came up with the equally interesting 'Big strong Madison' and 'Madison 62'. Their fellow countryman Burt Blanca dipped into the new craze in late 1962 with 'Twistons le Madison', while the Kili Jacks produced the perfunctory 'Madison Knokke'. Although the latter generated some moderate interest, it was the rough-and-ready flip, 'Cassons la baraque', that was chosen for the lead track on their next French EP. Despite this, chart success still eluded them.

Paris-based American singer Harold Nicholas[538] had cut a substandard 'Ya ya twist' in early 1962 before entering the Madison fray with the big band sound of 'Le Madison' (adapted from Chubby Checker's 'The Hucklebuck'[539]) and 'Le Madison des Madisonnistes'. Nicholas was a fine vocalist in the manner of Gene McDaniels, as is evidenced by his swinging 1963 cover of the Lafayettes' 'Nobody But You' ('Personne que toi') and superb take on Solomon Burke's 'Cry To Me' ('Elle en pleure').

Strangely enough, despite the plethora of Madison records, the only singers to offer Billy Bridge any real competition were Sylvie Vartan and Johnny Hallyday, both of whom took the hybrid 'Madison twist' (Johnnie Morisette's 'Meet Me At The Twistin' Place') into the charts late in the summer of 1962.

## Old-time dancing

Rather less expected was the emergence of a backlash against both the twist and the Madison in the form of a tango revival. This short-lived affair was kicked off by a 1962 Guy Béart EP titled *Béart tangos*, which featured the excellent 'Plus jamais' and 'Je ne sais jamais dire non'. Joining in the nostalgia, Charles Trenet landed a hit with 'L'horrible tango', Gina Gardel turned out the decent 'Mi Buenos Aires querido' and Marcel Amont doubled the pleasure with 'Le tango des jumeaux'. Amont also attempted to keep the polka alive with the unsuccessful 'Les filles de Copenhague', as did Georges Guétary with 'La polka des lampions'. Meanwhile, Annie Cordy poked fun at the whole affair with the mock-German nonsense of 'Choucrouten tango'.

While the occasional hit by old-school singers like Gloria Lasso (such as

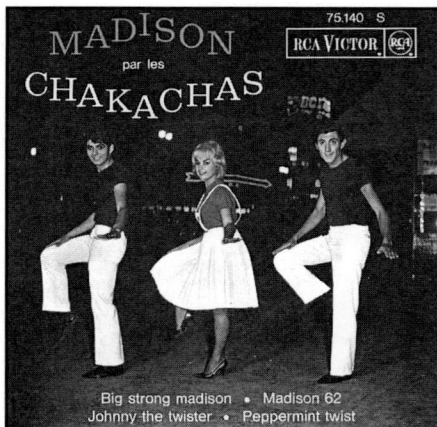

---

[538] Formerly one half of the Nicholas Brothers dance duo, he had initially dabbled in rock'n'roll in Sweden before heading for France.

[539] A huge hit in 1949 for Tommy Dorsey, Lionel Hampton, Roy Milton, Frank Sinatra and Paul Williams.

'Le cha cha cha', her cover of Bobby Rydell's 'The Cha-Cha-Cha') or Jacques Brel, whose 'Tango funèbre' would be a highlight of his 1964 concert season, might have held out faint hope of a return to the 'good old days', the reality was that the polka, the tango and all the other dances of the past had been steamrollered by the younger generation.

Older music fans could, however, still rely on evergreen accordionist André Verchuren, whose 1960 waltz, 'Carillon d'Alsace', had been a major smash shortly before Johnny Hallyday turned the charts upside down. Verchuren's recording was included on an EP alongside a Charleston ('Le vieux pianola') and a paso doble ('L'ardent matador'). He would later also return to the java, on 1962's 'Java des beaux dimanches'.

Despite his remarkable ability to take any style and arrange it for the accordion, his attempts to get down with the kids were less impressive, resulting in dire arrangements of Ben E. King's 'Spanish Harlem' ('Nuits d'Espagne') and Johnny Hallyday's 'Retiens la nuit', although his popularity among older record buyers ensured a healthy flow of royalties to the songs' composers, regardless of what Hallyday's fans might have thought.

## New dance crazes

In 1962, the mashed potato was introduced to French audiences by Johnny Hallyday via 'C'est le mashed potatoes' (Bobby Day's/Thurston Harris's 'Little Bitty Pretty One') and Henri Salvador's adaptation of Nat Kendrick & The Swans' 'Mashed Potatoes' ('Purée de pommes de terre'). Pre-teen Moroccan singer Malika also turned out an impressive cover of 'C'est le mashed potatoes',[540] although it quickly disappeared in the wake of Hallyday's success. Her sparkling rendition of Dee Dee Sharp's 'Mashed Potato Time'[541] was also unsuccessful, despite a vocal performance equal to or better than almost any of the French *rockeuses*.

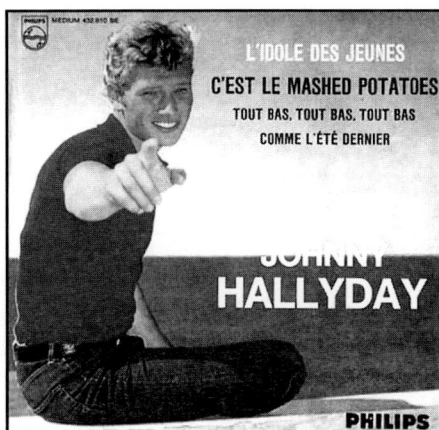

Meanwhile, Sylvie Vartan went to town on 'Le loco-motion', a top-notch adaptation of Little Eva's 'The Loco-motion'

---

[540] As did Lucky Blondo.
[541] Sung in French and issued under the misspelt title 'Mashed potatoe time'.

that left rival versions[542] standing at the station as 1962 dissolved in a flurry of dance crazes, each aimed at reigniting the commercial bonfire of the twist. Danny Boy and Chris Valois tried to convince audiences to do 'Le climb',[543] Jack Hammer exhorted them to do 'The wiggle', while the Kili Jacks promoted the slop via the guitar instrumental 'Slop well'.[544]

The fad for new dances continued into 1963, with both Harold Nicholas and the Lions doing their bit for the hully gully. The best the latter could offer was the unimaginative 'Stompin' the hully gully', but Nicholas found his stride with a superb remake of George Hudson's 'Hully Gully Fire House'.[545] He went on to rework Ma Rainey's blues classic 'See See Rider' as 'Hully baby', which was joined on a 1963 EP by the floor-filling groove of 'Hully gully Sue' (a superb cover of the Righteous Brothers' 'Little Latin Lupe Lu').

As well as recording straightforward pop material, such as his 1963 cover of the Cookies' 'Chains' ('Chance'), Nicholas would jump on every passing

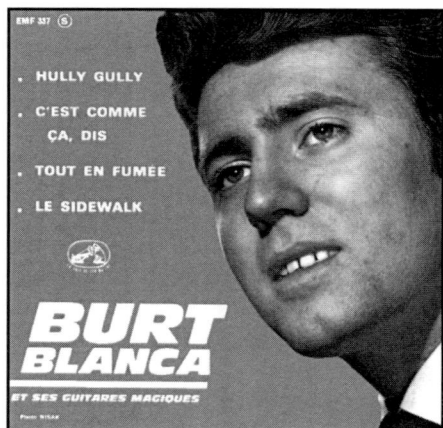

dance craze for the rest of the decade. Though some of his recordings sounded rather contrived, his top-notch revamp of Cornell Muldrow's 'You Can't Sit Down'[546] deserved greater success, as did his romp through the Exciters' 'He's Got The Power' ('Elle a le truc'). Regrettably, none of these prevented him from disappearing off the radar.

Up in Belgium, Burt Blanca also took a punt at the hully gully with covers of 'Hully Gully Fire House' and the Olympics' '(Baby) Hully Gully' ('Hully gully'), while also dabbling in the limbo

---

[542] By Les Pirates, Burt Blanca and Danny Boy, among others.

[543] Danny Boy retained the original title, 'The Climb', as used by the Coasters. Johnny Taylor et les Strangers also had a go at this one (as 'Le climb' '), as did bandleader Jacques Hendrix (yes, really!), with no more success than his other failed attempts to ride 'Le loco-motion' or to date 'Miss Madison'.

[544] This actually preceded their Madison singles, although the slop's rise to European popularity came later.

[545] This tasty slice of dance-floor-friendly pop was also cut in impressive fashion by Johnny Hallyday's backing band, Les Golden Stars, and British import Dave Dacosta, and less well by jazzmen Hazy Osterwald and Claude Bolling.

[546] Best known as an instrumental by the Phil Upchurch Combo, though Nicholas's version was most likely inspired by the Dovells' 1963 vocal hit, which name-checked several different dance crazes.

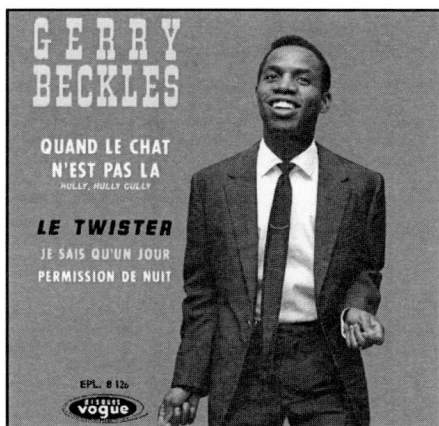

GERRY BECKLES

QUAND LE CHAT
N'EST PAS LA
*HULLY, HULLY GULLY*

*LE TWISTER*
JE SAIS QU'UN JOUR
PERMISSION DE NUIT

EPL. 8 126
vogue

for an engaging version of Chubby Checker's 'Limbo Rock' (retitled 'Limbo bossa' for no apparent reason).

Girl singer Vicki teamed up with instrumental outfit Les Jokers for the excellent 'L'heure du hully gully' (a reworking of Johnny & The Hurricanes' 'Red River Rock'), issued on the flip of an equally impressive girl group effort, 'Si j'étais un garçon'. The Kili Jacks had a fling with 'Hey, hully gully girl', and the Cousins settled for 'Hully gully boy'.

Back in France, Trumpet Boy weighed in with 'Viens danser le hully-gully', while Gerry Beckles made rather better use of the new rhythm, transforming '(Baby) Hully Gully' into the enjoyable 'Quand le chat n'est pas là', a tribute to the departed frontman of Les Chats Sauvages, Dick Rivers. Sadly, despite the media frenzy accompanying the group's split, the record failed to find an audience.

Searching for fresh pastures, Claude et ses Tribuns attempted to persuade audiences to do 'Le stomp' (Bobby Comstock's 'Let's Stomp'). Meanwhile, neither the Kili Jacks' 'Aloha tamouré', nor Annie Cordy's daft 'Anaé atoa (Le vrai tamouré)' succeeded in kick-starting a craze for Tahitian dancing. Danyel Gérard's dubious 'Youpi ya tamouré' was submerged by the same wave, while the more original 'Le Marsupilami' failed to turn the famous comic-book character of the same name into a dance-floor hero.

In 1964, Sylvie Vartan introduced the surf on the Paul Anka-penned 'U.S.A.', but an attempt by singing drummer Conrad Pringel to get audiences to do the snap found few takers, despite the catchy melodies and decent enough rhythms of such Mickey Baker-Albert Raisner compositions as 'Le snap' and the swinging 'Snapez à mes côtés'.

Dick Rivers summed up the dance craze phenomenon on his first solo EP with 'Voulez-vous danser?' (adapted from the Bobby Freeman/Cliff Richard hit, 'Do You Want To Dance'), as did Sylvie Vartan with 'Dansons' (Chris Montez's 'Let's Dance') and Long Chris with 'Comme l'été dernier' (an energetic reworking of Chubby Checker's 'Dancin' Party'[547]). Valéry satirised the trend on the enjoyable (and danceable) pastiche, 'Vous dansez Mademoiselle', while Laura Villa set the seal on the whole affair

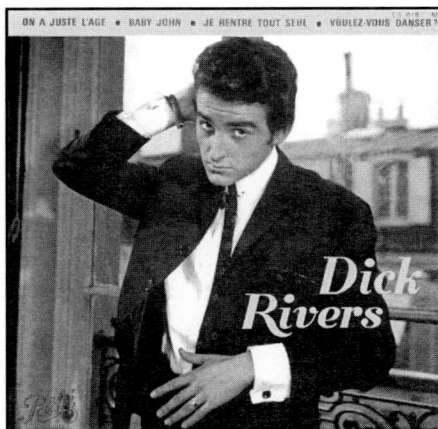

ON A JUSTE L'AGE • BABY JOHN • JE RENTRE TOUT SEUL • VOULEZ-VOUS DANSER ?

*Dick Rivers*

---

[547] Also recorded, with greater commercial success, by Johnny Hallyday.

with the LP *Toute la danse avec Laura Villa*, a catch-all party album aimed at all the family that mixed twists, Madisons, cha-cha-chas and sundry other dances.

The twist explosion had been a watershed in French pop, with less abrasive sounds and more commercially appealing tunes serving to break the rock'n'roll market wide open. As dance craze followed dance craze, the once-threatening sounds of rock'n'roll came to seem more and more like harmless fun. Some more broad-minded souls even began to consider it to be *music*, although it was still held in lesser esteem than *chanson* or jazz. This breakthrough in public acceptance was given added impetus by a younger generation of French musicians who saw rock'n'roll not through the prism of jazz, but as a vital music in its own right, and who found the perfect template to follow when learning to play, courtesy of the UK's leading instrumental group, the Shadows.

# Chapter 18

## COMME UNE OMBRE
### The groups: The second wave (1961-64)

*Pop music historians are prone to date the start of the 'British invasion' to the advent of the Beatles, but even setting aside such hits as the Tornados' 'Telstar' (a stateside chart-topper over a year before the Fab Four landed in New York), this analysis overlooks the enormous success of Cliff Richard, who was the biggest-selling artist worldwide in 1963, ahead of Elvis Presley.[548] His early rock'n'roll recordings 'Move It' and 'Dynamite' were both minor hits in France during 1959, where he began to make real headway as the sixties progressed. However, once he began including too many ballads in his repertoire, his following fell away slightly and he was overtaken in popularity by his backing group, the Shadows.*

*Their 1960 breakthrough hit, 'Apache', was also a major hit in France, establishing their cleanly played instrumental style as one of the most popular sounds in the country. In June 1961, their performance at the now-legendary* Rock Across The Channel *festival in Calais was warmly received by a largely male audience, almost all of whom paid close attention to their sound and stage manner before rushing home to practise the group's licks themselves. Such dedication paid off, and within days Les Guitares du Diable had their first record, 'Lover of Saint-Jean' (a revamp of Lucienne Delyle's 'Mon amant de Saint-Jean') on the market in an attempt to become France's answer to the British quartet.*

### The first French instrumental groups

Les Guitares du Diable were actually a studio group formed by several session players and were never intended to be a performing outfit. Led by guitarist Léo Petit (who had played the superb lead on Johnny Hallyday's recent smash, 'Souvenirs, souvenirs'), they aped the sound of the Shadows with a repertoire drawn from the hits of the day, making an impact commercially at the end of 1961 with a version of Ray Charles's 'Hit The Road Jack' ('Fich' le camp, Jack!'). Although their recordings veered toward the middle of the road too often for them to qualify as a true rock'n'roll outfit, they were redeemed by their impeccable musicianship, and their clean sound swiftly established them as radio favourites. Sadly, they wasted their talents

---

[548] Incredibly, Françoise Hardy (see pages 331-2) came eighth in the same ranking published in *Billboard*, demonstrating the existence of a large international market for French recordings in the early sixties, even in the face of the American rock'n'roll explosion.

on poorly conceived arrangements of Johnny Hallyday's 'Retiens la nuit' and Petula Clark's 'Ya ya twist', although a rocked-up version of Paganini's 'Moto Perpetuo' ('Mouvement perpétuel') and the occasional original such as 1963's spacey 'Galaxie' demonstrated that they were capable of more than they achieved. They did became stars in Japan[549] on the back of an instrumental version of the much-recorded 'Leçon de twist', but the competition in France was much fiercer and they only ever enjoyed minor success back home. After soldiering on up to the middle of the decade, they returned to session work.

Léo Petit also cut a string of solo releases,[550] including a decent, though somewhat pointless cover of 'Apache'. The same EP also saw him revisiting his work with Johnny Hallyday on instrumental covers of three of the star's early hits, including a reworking of 'Souvenirs, souvenirs' that saw him recreating his original solos to perfection. The record was not a big seller, but it did well enough to encourage further forays in the same vein, ranging from Hallyday's 'Viens danser le twist' ('Let's Twist Again') to Danyel Gérard's 'Le petit Gonzalès' ('Speedy Gonzales'). Sadly, although Petit's feel was second to none, his records failed to sell in any great quantity, and in 1964 he decided to put his solo career on ice.

A year after the Shadows' first appearance in front of French audiences, the country produced a more worthy contender in the form of Les Fantômes. The best of all the instrumental units who flooded France in the early sixties, they released their excellent debut EP[551] in 1962, introducing the world to their 'Big Sound' guitars. Although their early recordings included some vocal numbers – their first hit, 'Le diable en personne', was a cover of Johnny Kidd & The Pirates' 'Shakin' All Over'[552] – the emphasis was always on their crisp, clean guitar-picking.

The standout track on their first

---

[549] Where instrumentals would, by 1965, be the preferred form of rock'n'roll. America's top instrumental group the Ventures were – and still are – superstars in Japan.

[550] Indeed, he had already begun to do so before forming the group, albeit in a more easy listening style.

[551] They had actually appeared on record before, backing singing duo Les Copains on their second EP.

[552] Most likely modelled on the recent cover by Vince Taylor.

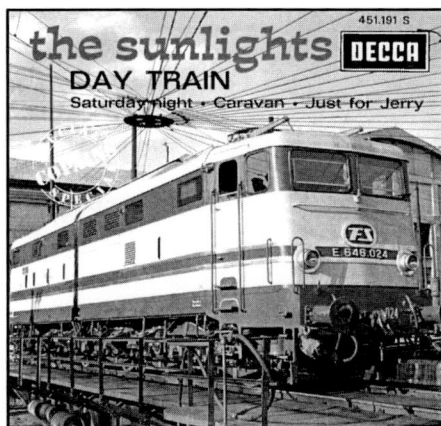

EP was 'Fort Chabrol', an ominous number penned by guitarist Dean Noton (freshly arrived from Scotland) and El Toro et les Cyclones' guitarist Jacques Dutronc, while the bluesy 'Cafard' was a highlight of the second. The latter also generated a hit with a cover of Duane Eddy's 'Shazam!' that aped the recent remake by the Shadows. They followed up with 'Twist 33', powered along by a killer guitar riff from Noton, who was fast establishing himself as a rival to Claude Ciari of Les Champions as the country's leading rock'n'roll guitarist. A more complex arrangement of Bobby Parker's 'Watch Your Step' testified to their musical skills, and by the end of the year they were arguably the most respected outfit in the country.

With Les Fantômes leading the way, instrumental fever struck record companies as hard as twist fever had a few months earlier, and labels scrambled to get a piece of the action. Among the best of the early groups to emerge were the Sunlights and Les Bourgeois de Calais.

The Sunlights were built around Serge, Aldo and Bruno Cogoni, three immigrant brothers from Italy who whipped up a storm in dances across Belgium, where they released a number of singles as I Cogoni before setting their sights on the French market. Their first EP as the Sunlights appeared in 1963 and featured the rollicking 'Day train' alongside their take on Duke Ellington's 'Caravan', which drew on the recent US remake by Santo & Johnny. On their second, they turned out a revival of Vaughn Monroe's 'Riders In The Sky'[553] ('Les cavaliers du ciel') and a worthwhile rendition of José Padilla's 'Valencia' in the manner of the Shadows.[554] Casting their net wider for their third EP, they dabbled in country music on 'Black rider'[555] and picked up airplay for 'Les malheurs de Sylvie', the theme to a radio show dedicated to Mademoiselle Vartan.

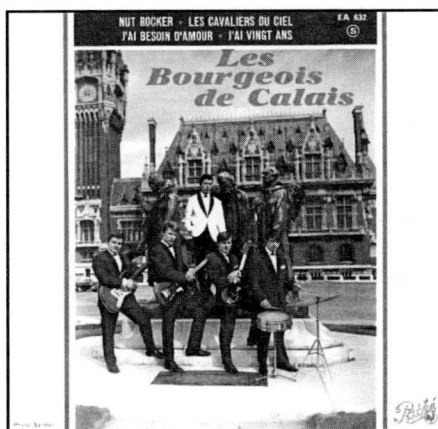

Les Bourgeois de Calais added an organ to the mix and recruited a Cliff Richard clone in the shape of British rocker Jeff Parker before proceeding

---

[553] Doubtless recorded in imitation of the recent US hit by the Ramrods, '(Ghost) Riders In The Sky'.

[554] Who in turn cut it for their 1963 *Los Shadows* EP.

[555] Victim of another misspelling: although the back cover was correct, the front cover had it as 'Black Reader'.

to cut 'Riders In The Sky' ('Les cavaliers du ciel') and a guitar-led version of B. Bumble & The Stingers' 'Nut Rocker'[556] in 1962. Their debut EP contained a mix of vocal and instrumental tunes, of which the mellow 'J'ai vingt ans' proved particularly popular. Their second contained more vocals, offering highlights like the rocking 'Je vous l'avoue' and a jazzy take on Larry Clinton's 'In A Persian Market' ('Sur un marché persan'). A cover of the Shadows' 'Round And Round' on the same EP demonstrated that they were more than competent, but it did little to win them an audience, and by the end of 1963 their moment had gone.

Further north, countless outfits formed in emulation of the Shadows, as a wave of guitar instrumentals broke over Belgium. From the coastal town of De Panne, the Ghosts shone on a cover of Jet Harris & Tony Meehan's 'Scarlett O'Hara', while Brussels-based outfit the Rowdies turned out the rhythmic 'Kafka', but failed to secure a French release. Making a rather bigger splash, Les Waikiki's staked their claim as Belgium's biggest instrumental act with the jolly steel-guitar sounds of 'Hawaii tattoo', a smash hit in 1961 not only in their home country, but also in the Netherlands and in West Germany. German fans also went for the follow-up, 'Hilo kiss', though French listeners were less impressed. However, this didn't stop the group from riding the Hawaiian wave for a few more years, which eventually saw their records chart in Britain and in the United States.[557]

## Switching from vocals to instrumentals

There were compelling reasons why the instrumental style took off so strongly in non-English-speaking countries like France. Hitherto, a home-grown rock'n'roll group wishing to make it big was faced with the choice of singing in (usually thickly accented) English, or adapting the international hits of the day into their own language – something that the likes of Les Chaussettes Noires had proved adept at doing. Instrumentals made the process simpler: all that was needed was a rudimentary musical ability, and the road to gigs, records and fame (if not fortune) was wide open. In this respect, they served the same function for the French as skiffle had done for the British a few years earlier.

Rock'n'roll instrumentals had, of course, been around since the fifties and some of the established French and Belgian groups had been dabbling in the form since their inception – notably Les Vautours, who opened their first EP with a Link Wray-styled powerhouse titled simply 'Vautours'. The Cousins had likewise long been laying down instrumentals alongside their vocal recordings, picking up a hit in Belgium with the silly oriental sounds of 'Bouddha' back in 1961. Leaping onto the bandwagon, they cut the space-age 'The robot'[558] and the easy listening 'Dansevise' (lifted from Grethe & Jørgen Ingmann's 1963 Eurovision-winning smash), scoring hits with both in their homeland. Skittering around behind them, the Kili Jacks laid down 'Lost

---

[556] Itself adapted from Tchaikovsky's *Nutcracker Suite*.

[557] 'Hawaii Tattoo' briefly made the UK Top 50 in 1965. Both this and the trite 'Hawaiian Honeymoon' made the *Billboard* 'Hot 100' in 1964 and 1965 respectively.

[558] Released in France as 'Le robot', this was not a cover of the Tornadoes' 1963 UK hit, 'Robot', but an original that grooved along in the manner of Booker T. & The MG's.

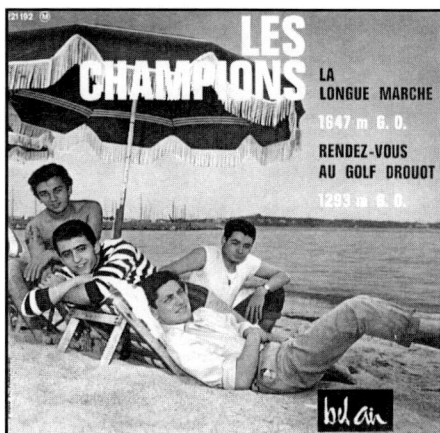

island' in a style derived from the Shadows before cutting loose with the organ-and-sax-led 'Square dance' and the powerful 'Jingles', albeit never quite escaping the influence of their British role models.

One benefit of the fad for instrumentals was that groups whose lead singer had left were able to reinvent themselves as instrumental units. Les Champions, having lost Jean-Claude Chane to ill health, were actually a better group as a result, with the spotlight now firmly on Claude Ciari's guitar wizardry. American rock'n'roll legend Gene Vincent was a fan, choosing them to back him on his Paris shows in October 1962. A photo of Vincent surrounded by the group appeared on the back cover of their LP *Pan dans le 1000!*, which generated another hit in early 1963 with the clean-cut 'Poupée brisée'.[559] Other high spots on the album were the rumbling 'L'infini au soleil' and a tasty reworking of Al Caiola's theme tune from *The Magnificent Seven*, 'Les mercenaires'.

Les Champions were also in high demand for sessions and stage performances, even backing such avowedly non-rock'n'roll singers as Guy Béart and Mouloudji, who also briefly hired Les Fantômes as his backing group. In purely musical terms, Les Champions were the most respected outfit in the country. While Les Fantômes had the Shadows sound down to a fine art, the versatility offered by Claude Ciari made Les Champions unbeatable in any hypothetical battle of the bands.

Unfortunately, their choice of material was not always inspired, and their next EP featured a poor cover of Little Eva's 'Let's Turkey Trot' ('Le pas du dindon'[560]) that lacked the appeal of their earlier work, though it did spin off minor hits with the uptempo 'T'shirt' and a rendition of the much-covered 'Galaxie'. However, the damage was done and their career never recovered. The subdued 'La longue marche' and the rockier '1647 mètres G.O.'[561] on their next EP raised standards considerably, and they picked up a hit with a cover of the Ran-Dells' 'Martian Hop',[562] but after their impressive, string-laden cover of the Dakotas' 'The Cruel Sea'[563] briefly scraped into the *Salut les copains* charts at the end of 1963, they slid off the hit parade altogether, never to return.[564]

Dean Noton of Les Fantômes and Belgian star Burt Blanca were Claude Ciari's closest rivals for the crown of guitar king. Blanca's EPs had for a long time mixed vocal efforts with instrumentals designed to show off his abilities.

---

[559] A vocal version was a simultaneous hit for Johnny Hallyday.
[560] This appears to be the French title and is listed thus on the back of the EP sleeve. On the front, it is shown as 'Le turkey' trot'.
[561] The broadcast frequency of radio station Europe No. 1.
[562] A vocal version by Henri Salvador, 'Le martien', was just as silly and even better.
[563] Les Champions' version was simply titled 'Cruel Sea', without the definite article.
[564] At least, not in their own right. They did go on to have hit records as the backing band for Danyel Gérard.

As early as 1961, he had made a name for himself with 'Texas rider' and the gutsy 'Shamash', but it was his 1962 reworking of the Virtues' 'Guitar Boogie Shuffle' (retitled 'Guitar boogie twist') that cemented his reputation, even if the same year's 'Joanna' leaned too close toward easy listening. Blanca continued the good work in 1963, with the swirling 'Rocking the twelve eight' and the clip-clop rhythms of 'Je partirai' confirming his standing among the cognoscenti, though he never broke through to the wide audience who followed Les Champions.

Les Cyclones and Les Pingouins, both of whom had lost their lead vocalists to military service, were less successful. Les Cyclones crumbled following the departures of both singer El Toro and guitarist Jacques Dutronc to the colours, leaving bassist Hadi Kalafate to rebuild the group from scratch. The new line-up's first EP included 'Lucky Luke', one of the better instrumental tunes to hit the market, although commercial success did not follow. Their cover of the Routers' 'Let's Go' lacked sufficient power to succeed, but they shone brilliantly on the harmonica-led 'Firewater', a sprightly effort that stood out from the massed ranks of Shadows wannabes. Their second was even better, featuring a percussive take on Adriano Celentano's 'Teddy girl' and a remake of the Newport Nomads' 'Blue Mallard' ('À tombeau ouvert'), which rocked with a passion completely missing from their earlier records, yet still failed to set the airwaves alight.

Released in July 1962, Les Pingouins' first instrumental EP was also a flop, despite offering some well-made and entertaining recordings like the chugging 'Alaska' and the Ventures-styled 'Groenland', as well as a tip of the hat to the country's leading *yé-yé* chanteuse in the form of 'Sylvie'. Their second was a disappointing affair headlined by the corny 'Bach' that was only partially redeemed by the tasty 'Yéti'.

Ably led by singer/guitarist Olivier Despax, Les Gamblers drew on a repertoire mixing jazz, R&B and rock'n'roll, and in 1962 tapped the sounds of the twist and the Madison for the album *Au Madison.*[565]

---

[565] This featured the first recorded appearance by future *yé-yé* superstar Claude François, then still known as Kôkô, who played percussion on 'El nabout' – the original, markedly different and largely instrumental version of the song that would subsequently resurface on his 1962 Kôkô EP as 'Le nabout twist' (see page 283).

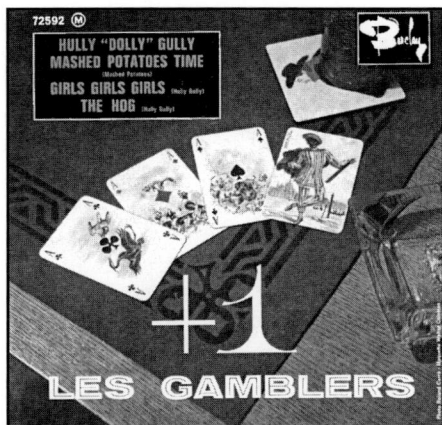

Ostensibly a live set, it was a classy showcase for the group, with a cover of Nat Kendrick & The Swans' 'Mashed Potatoes' and the self-explanatory 'Paris Madison (City gate)' placing the emphasis on their musical prowess, although Despax's lead guitar contributions more than justified his top billing. A cover of the Phil Upchurch Combo's 'You Can't Sit Down' further testified to the group's credentials, but the album did little for Despax's personal ambitions and he soon set sail for a solo career.

Left to their own devices, the group turned heads with 1963's 'Hully "Dolly" gully', but their jazzier variety of instrumental rock found few takers. The same EP offered more substance on an organ-dominated cover of the Coasters' 'Girls, Girls, Girls',[566] but it was their treatment of the Phil Upchurch Combo's 'The Hog' that best showed off their talents. For their next, they cut routine run-throughs of recent hits like Dion's revival of the Drifters' 'Ruby Baby' and Gene Vincent's 'Say Mama', but their approach was too far removed from the clean guitar sound of the leading instrumental groups and the record flopped.

Les Chaussettes Noires were also without a singer, although Eddy Mitchell had every intention of returning to the line-up as soon as the army finished with him. Shortly before his departure in 1962, the group had knocked out some songs for the soundtrack to the film *Comment réussir en amour*. One of them, a ballad called 'Parce que tu sais', was selected as the lead track for their next EP, where it joined two tributes to Gene Vincent, 'C'est la nuit' (a cover of 'The Night Is So Lonely') and 'Le temps est lent' ('Right Now'). The film soundtrack also featured another classic rocker in

'Oublie-moi', and the group were given the chance to show off their instrumental prowess on the upbeat 'Golf Drouot' and an instrumental version of 'Parce que tu sais', which subsequently appeared on their final EP release of 1962.

Despite suffering from multiple cases of military call-up and precious few opportunities to get everyone together to record, the band's popularity remained high. Eddy Mitchell's absence forced those members still in civilian life to focus on instrumentals for a while, pushing the saxophone to the

---

[566] As recently revived by both Elvis Presley and Danny Boy (now minus Les Pénitents).

fore on the self-penned groover 'Boom-rang' and the simple yet effective 'Oui chef, bien chef'. Meanwhile, the more traditional guitar-picking on the fast and frantic 'Pow-wow' generated a moderate hit for them in the spring of 1963 as they awaited Mitchell's return and a chance to reassemble the whole group.

## Backing bands seize the spotlight

Other groups didn't even wait for their singer to become unavailable, but simply took the opportunity to enjoy their own moment in the sun. Johnny Hallyday's backing band, Les Golden Strings, ducked out from under his shadow to cut an unremarkable cover of Duane Eddy's 'Rebel Rouser' and a handful of originals, of which the upbeat 'Golden twist' was the pick of a fairly poor bunch. Their career ended when Hallyday quit Vogue for Philips in late 1961 and put together the similarly named Les Golden Stars to replace them. The new outfit cut another version of 'Rebel Rouser' with Hallyday helping out on guitar, and a thumping arrangement of the Mar-Keys' 'Last Night' that was better still. Their second EP saw them acknowledging the Madison craze with the swinging 'Madison chez Johnny' and 'Marc's Madison', but despite their talent they failed to establish a name for themselves away from their frontman.

On their 1961 debut EP, Danyel Gérard's group, Les Dangers, nodded politely in their leader's direction with instrumental covers of three of his hits, including a sparkling reading of 'Oh! Marie Line'. Their second, 1962's *Madison*, featured the dire 'Play Madison', but a jazzy take on Bill Doggett's 'Ram-Bunk-Shush' ('Toute ma chance') showed them looking further than usual for inspiration.

Maguy Marshall's backing crew, Les Drivers, acknowledged their leader on the formulaic 'Mademoiselle Twist', an instrumental version of Marshall's contribution to the twist fad and the lead track on the first of three fairly poor instrumental EPs. The second of these included a dismal guitar-led attempt at Johnny & The Hurricanes' 'Red River Rock', but was saved from total anonymity by an impressive remake of Bruce Channel's 'Hey! Baby'.

Les Mustangs were Billy Bridge's backing group, but they likewise took advantage of the fad for instrumentals to cut two EPs under the watchful eye of Mickey Baker. Musically they were a mixed bag, their material ranging from polished Baker originals like 'Sur la plage' and the gutsy 'La main du diable', to competent covers of Dave 'Baby' Cortez's 'Rinky Dink' and the Cougars' adaptation from Tchaikovsky's *Swan Lake*, 'Saturday Night At The Duck Pond' ('Thème du Lac des cygnes').

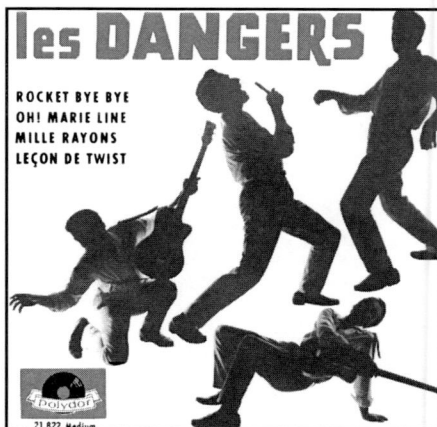

**les DANGERS**

ROCKET BYE BYE
OH! MARIE LINE
MILLE RAYONS
LEÇON DE TWIST

polydor

21.822 Medium

## American and British groups

The same style appealed to Doug Fowlkes & The Airdales, who laid down a dance-floor-friendly version of the Phil Upchurch Combo's 'You Can't Sit Down' and a remake of Duane Eddy's 'Peter Gunn' before Fowlkes quit to become the group's manager late in 1962, with lead singer Rocky Roberts now rightly taking star billing.

Les Play Boys recorded their first instrumental EP in 1961, shortly after their leader, Vince Taylor, had made his explosive French debut.[567] This included versions of Larry Clinton's 'In A Persian Market'[568] ('Sur un marché persan') and Duane Eddy's 'Moovin' And Groovin' ', the latter slightly marred by some over-intrusive organ-work. For the follow-up, they knocked out covers of three Hallyday songs from the 1962 film *Les Parisiennes*,[569] but their polished arrangements of the likes of 'Sam'di soir' lacked the raunch of the originals. Their third EP, released in March 1963 after Taylor's career had stalled, contained four twist numbers including the Bill Justis/Ernie Freeman hit, 'Raunchy' ('Raunchy twist') and a fine interpretation of Stan Kenton's jazz classic, 'Artistry In Rhythm' ('Artistry in twist'). A couple of months later, they recorded four vocal tracks including versions of Chuck Berry's 'Bye Bye Johnny' and Buddy Holly's 'Peggy Sue' for a competent, but unsuccessful fourth EP.

Nero & The Gladiators, who had likewise appeared at the 1961 *Festival de rock anglais*, were a British instrumental outfit who performed on stage dressed in Roman costume. Having been unable to sustain the success of their two 1961 UK hits, 'Entry Of The Gladiators' and 'In The Hall Of The Mountain King', the original members were gradually replaced by a new line-up who rebranded themselves 'The Gladiators' and decided to follow in Vince Taylor's footsteps, crossing the Channel in 1963 to pick up work on the live circuit in France. They found the going harder than expected, and after cutting an EP containing several Hank Marvin-influenced tracks including the incisive 'Wigwam', 'Tram', and a version of Kai Winding's 'More', they fell into work backing various singers

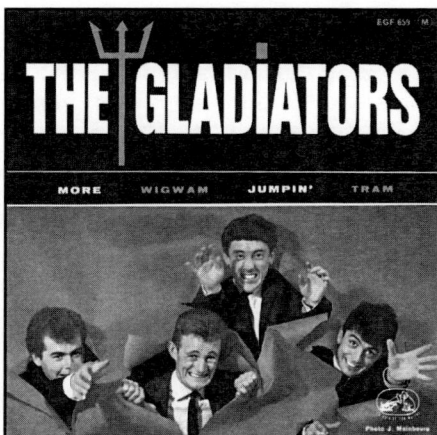

---

[567] See pages 234-6
[568] Probably inspired by the version released in the UK by the Charles Blackwell Orchestra.
[569] The lead track on the *Musique du film 'Les Parisiennes'* EP was 'C'est bien mieux comme ça' by Gillian Hills and Les Chaussettes Noires.

on the concert trail. After a while, the
group splintered, but mainstays Micky
Jones[570] (guitar) and Tommy Brown
(drums) stayed on in France as
musicians for hire, eventually ending
up providing live support for Sylvie
Vartan.

More impressive were the Krew
Kats,[571] who had enjoyed small-time
fame in the UK with their 1961 hit,
'Trambone', before losing drummer
Brian Bennett and bassman Licorice
Locking to the Shadows and setting off
for the Continent. After first travelling
to Hamburg to back Tony Sheridan at
the Star-Club when the Beatles returned to Liverpool, they then gravitated to
Paris to put in time behind Dick Rivers.[572] While there, they also cut a couple
of EPs for La Voix de son Maître. Highlights included a version of the West
Side Story hit 'Tonight' and the contagious 'Tuxedo twist', both complete with
chiming guitars and rolling drums, and the Shadows-like 'Polaris', however
neither their live work, nor their recordings brought them much commercial
success.

Fellow Brits abroad Dave Dacosta & His Strollers squeezed no fewer than
six instrumentals onto their Twist LP, impressing with the classy '3:30 Blues',
a slow ramble that deserved to become a hit, and 'Drinkin' ' (a cover of Boots
Brown's Latin-tinged 'Cerveza'). Sadly, the long-player fared no better than his
two earlier EPs, and Dacosta subsequently quit France to forge a new career
in West Germany.

**Studio groups**

None of these records made even a dent in the market, but at least they
gave the musicians a chance to express their own artistic desires. The
majority drew their inspiration from the Shadows, but others were impressed
by the success of Les Guitares du Diable, who served as a beacon to a host
of session musicians. The result was a number of faceless releases by the
likes of the totally uninspired Les Ambassadors, whose version of 'Madison
twist' plumbed new depths of awfulness, or Les Kili-Cats, whose records,
including dire covers of the Cousins' 'Kana kapila' and LaVern Baker's 'You're
The Boss' ('Oui, patron'), were only worth buying for the cover art, which
foreshadowed the late sixties' fashion for putting scantily clad ladies on the
sleeves of equally dull and faceless records. Meanwhile, Les Mutants, whose
'Original climb U.S.A.' was anything but original, hid behind a comic strip on
the sleeve to protect the identities of the guilty parties.

As had been the case in the fifties, jazz musicians also sought to get in on

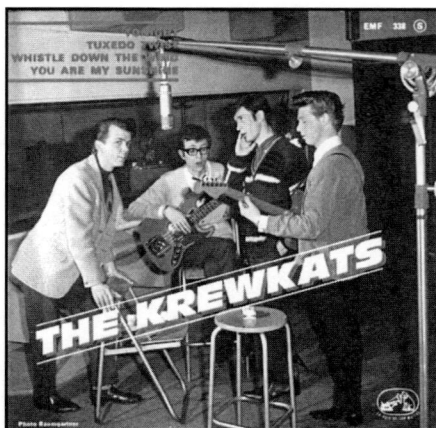

---

[570] Jones was to play a major role in the development of French pop during the sixties. He later
went on to play with Wonderwheel, Spooky Tooth and Foreigner.
[571] Formerly Marty Wilde's Wildcats. Their name was styled 'Krewkats' in France.
[572] Rivers also used the Gladiators for a time.

the act – usually with disastrous consequences. The Roger Blanchard Quintet were one such example, offering stilted fare like 'Week-end hully gully' for an undemanding audience. Even worse were the latest releases by Trumpet Boy, who had at least entered the new decade with a decent cover of Johnny & The Hurricanes' 'Reveille Rock' ('Réveil rock'). Ignoring the exciting guitar sound now in vogue, he targeted an older audience who found his trumpet-fuelled arrangements[573] of contemporary sounds like Bert Kaempfert's 'Afrikaan Beat' and Bobby Darin's 'Dream Lover' ('J'ai rêvé') more palatable than his occasional attempts at rockier material, such as a dreary take on Dion's 'The Wanderer' ('Le vagabond').

Of the jazzers, only Raymond Le Sénéchal and Swiss guitar maestro Pierre Cavalli managed to turn out anything listenable. Cavalli mimicked Duane Eddy in an acceptable fashion on his 1962 cover of 'The Avenger', while Le Sénéchal covered the same ground with an arrangement of Buzz Clifford's 'Baby Sittin' Boogie'[574] before gravitating to soundtrack work for 1963's *La bonne soupe*.

Les Fingers, who turned out note-perfect versions of the hits of the day, provided a better example of studio craftsmanship. Sadly, their unimaginative choice of material (like their 1962 version of Billy Bridge's 'Le grand M') let them down. Their keyboard-free take on 'Telstar' paled in comparison to the Tornados' vibrant original,[575] however a decent cover of Jet Harris & Tony Meehan's 'Diamonds' ('Diamant') confirmed that they were better advised to stick with the sound of the Shadows. Like Les Guitares du Diable, they also recorded occasional originals such as 'Les cavaliers du feu' and 'Finger print', the latter a polished Shadows-style rocker which towered over the rest of their output. Despite their shortcomings, Les Fingers enjoyed tremendous popularity, their recording of 'Spécial blue-jeans' serving as the theme for the show on Radio Andorra in 1963. However, a decision to cover Ronnie Carroll's schlocky UK *Eurovision* entry, 'Say Wonderful Things', exposed their lack of vision, and their mainstream allegiances were further confirmed when they backed Line Renaud on yet another version of 'Hully gully'.

The Four Dreamers, another session crew, pretended to be British and even went out on the road like a proper group. They launched their career with the album *Claudia Cardinale présente the Four Dreamers*, cashing in on Cardinale's prominence as a film actress to deliver a set full of easy-rolling arrangements of Caterina Valente's 'Twist à Napoli', Mr. Acker Bilk's 'Stranger On The Shore' and the like, before taking the Madison route with yet another a retread of Billy Bridge's 'Le grand M'. None of these releases came anywhere near the sound currently in favour with the teenage audience, but they made amends on their third EP with the space-age 'Nautilus'. Their fourth featured their first original tune, 'Attila', which far outshone the rest of their efforts, but they soon descended into blandness again with dull versions of Charles Aznavour's 'La mamma' and Bert Weedon's 'Ginchy'. Ultimately,

---

[573] Almost a French parallel for the success of Al Hirt or Herb Alpert in the US.

[574] Titled 'Le boogie du bébé' after Sacha Distel's adaptation – perhaps because Le Sénéchal earned his living playing in Distel's band.

[575] Though it stomped all over a dire interpretation by jazzman Noël Chiboust, and a strange, also organless version by Johnny Taylor et les Strangers.

the Four Dreamers' slick approach prevented them from finding a niche in an overcrowded market, but they remained a popular live draw with a comforting style that appealed across the generations. Their records sold slowly but steadily, and they were able to sustain their career into the mid-sixties before settling back into session work.

## Surf music

One of the Four Dreamers' better releases was a 1964 take on 'Bombora', the classic surf tune created a year earlier by Australian group the Atlantics. Surf music had exploded out of California in 1962, propelled across the world by Dick Dale's 'Let's Go Trippin' ' and 'Surf Beat',[576] joined in 1963 by the Surfaris' 'Wipe Out' and the Chantays' 'Pipeline'. The piledriving guitar sound gave the instrumental movement a shot in the arm at a time when many groups were verging on easy listening. The result was another clutch of guitarists attempting to ride another new wave.[577]

The first surf-style instrumental record made in France was probably the top-drawer 'No man's land', released in the autumn of 1962 by Les Fantômes, who remained the group to emulate. The same EP featured a well-executed cover of the Shadows' 'Mustang' which delivered them their fourth hit in a row. As usual, the emphasis was squarely on the powerful yet melodic playing of guitarist Dean Noton, but the group were more than just support for his guitar workouts, as demonstrated by the remarkable 1963 release 'Bastic', a bass-guitar-driven tango that tipped the hat to Jet Harris, and the same year's rollicking 'Tolhrac', which put the spotlight on drummer Charles Bennaroch. However, it was a mundane cover of Johnny Thunder's 'Loop De Loop' that gave them the biggest hit of their career.

With surf music overtaking the Shadows' style as the sound to emulate, Les Fingers hastened to rejig their approach. The impressive 'Teenage trouble' tapped exactly the right blend of rocking rhythm and rumbling bass, proving that they were better than much of their output suggested, but their bland instrumental remake of the Beach Boys' 'Surfin' Safari' was hardly what the market needed. The sprightly 'Banjo song' raised standards again in early 1964, but, although they continued to release EPs until 1965, they never came close to challenging Les Fantômes in the teenage marketplace.

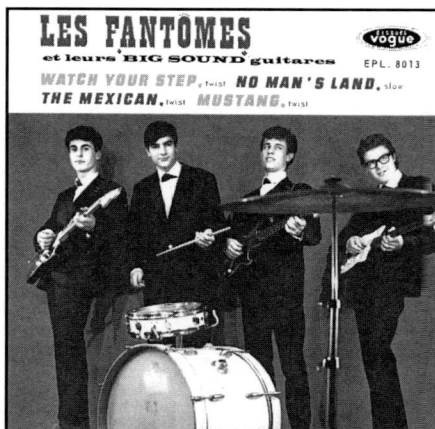

Surf music provided a timely boost to the popularity of guitar-based groups, many of whom adopted the thunderous

---

[576] The latter was covered in fine style in early 1964 by the Sunlights.

[577] Among them Les Pénitents (recently abandoned by Danny Boy, who was touring with Les Pingouins instead), whose appalling rendition of 'Wipe Out' demonstrated a total lack of feel for the genre. They also cut a dire version of Jimmy Gilmer & The Fireballs' 'Sugar Shack' ('Shugar shack').

approach of the American surf bands. Foremost among the latecomers were Les Flash, whose rendition of Bert Weedon's 'Ginchy' was as impressive a record as anything on the market, but the surf-style 'Prends la Caravelle' failed to take off and they soon vanished from sight.

Les Gardians tried to position themselves as the Mediterranean Coast's answer to the Tornados with the worthwhile 'Gardian's time', but the bulk of their repertoire was too cheesy to gain them much attention in the rest of the country.

Lyon group Les Korrigans, who had cut an EP of formulaic instrumentals for the local JBP label before discovering surf music in 1963, made a better fist of it on their second with the genuinely exciting 'Atlanta' – not that anyone could go surfing in Lyon. The record was the equal of anything recorded in Paris, though provincial outfits stood little chance of hitting the big time.

Also from Lyon, Les Gadgets featured three guitarists rather than the usual two, but the extra strings did not translate into extra sales for the uninspired 'Insa twist', released on Teppaz in 1962. Switching to the Soder label, they redeemed themselves in 1963 with the crackling 'Sunset' and the equally vibrant 'Neptune', but by then the world was looking for more than well-executed guitar instrumentals.

Les Players from Paris were a fine outfit, who drew as much inspiration from Duane Eddy as they did from the Shadows or from surf music. They were also one of the few groups to carve out a distinctive style and generate anything resembling a serious career. Debuting in 1962 with the striking 'Out of this world' and a rumbling cover of the Sunsets' 'Manhunt', they cut a number of moderately successful EPs[578]. With a line-up blending keyboards

and guitars, their sound offered more variety than most, and the musical flexibility this afforded was exemplified by the drum-heavy, oriental-sounding 'Sheiba' – one of the more interesting instrumentals to grace the record racks in 1963 – while the chunky rockers 'Nashville', 'Your other love' and 'Watusi stomp' testified to their rock'n'roll prowess. Although less commercially successful than Les Fantômes, they were arguably a more inventive unit, and they remained widely respected by their peers.

---

[578] While also providing musical backing for Nancy Holloway.

## Provincial instrumental groups

Although few made the jump to Paris and the big time, provincial groups made a reasonable living from live appearances and every sizeable settlement boasted at least one outfit working its way through the Shadows' songbook. Most never even made a record, but among those who scraped together enough money for a private pressing were the Arvern's from the Auvergne region.[579] They weren't bad, though a copycat rendition of the Spotnicks' 'Spotnicks' Theme' and a jazzy stroll through Lesley Gore's 'It's My Party' ('C'est ma fête') revealed why they deserved to stay on the provincial circuit.

Les Gones Rock from Lyon mutated into Les Gun's Rock in 1964 for their second EP on the independent JBP label. Their best effort was 'Pal d'Hiv' ', which paid tribute to the city's leading venue, the Palais d'Hiver, but nothing they recorded found an audience anywhere beyond the city limits. Across town, Les Sphinx aped the Shadows on two enjoyably amateurish EPs which included a take on the latter's '36-24-36', while Les Vampires from nearby Grenoble mixed originals like 'Les copains' with covers of the Spotnicks' 'Last Space Train'[580] and Brenda Lee's 'My Whole World Is Falling Down' ('Si je chante').

Up in the north-east, Strasbourg offered up Les Blue Rockets, whose 'Shadooguitar' paid open tribute to their heroes, while on the Mediterranean coast Nice's Les Milords bestowed upon the world the impressive reverb-heavy original, 'Chevauchée du diable'. They were also sufficiently inspired by B. Bumble & The Stingers' 'Bumble Boogie' to lay down a sparkling reworking of Rimsky-Korsakov's 'Flight Of The Bumblebee' ('Le vol du bourdon'), but to no avail.

Also on the Côte d'Azur, Les Schtroumpfs made their mark with a series of cheeseball tracks such as 'T.V. d'Antibes' and the summer swayer 'Along

the Croisette',[581] enjoying sufficient local popularity to justify the release of two albums' worth of novelty pop,[582] all driven by the electric organ of band-leader Patrick Logelin. They recorded as many vocal numbers as they did instrumentals (most notably the fast-paced 'Le temps des juke-boxes'[583] and the punchy 'Boom-twist'), but the heart of their appeal lay in infectious reworkings of classical themes. These were cunningly disguised as original compositions, for instance 'Antique Schtroumpfs' (which was adapted from Grieg's 'In The Hall Of The Mountain

---

[579]  Actually members of a popular ballroom band led by André Thivet.

[580]  Itself composed by veteran French jazzman-turned-TV presenter Albert Raisner as 'Le dernier train de l'espace'.

[581]  The famous seafront road in Cannes.

[582]  *Ça va schtroumpfer* and *Ça schtroumpf encore*, both issued in 1963.

[583]  When pulled for EP release, the song became the more grammatically correct 'Le temps des juke-box'.

King[584]), although they also impressed with the circus-like original, 'Val de Cuberte'. With high-pitched keyboards and uptempo arrangements, their records were either enjoyably cheesy or hideously annoying, depending on the taste of the listener, but they presumably sold well down in Antibes.

Les Dean's from Maubeuge, near the Belgian border, released a privately pressed EP containing a decent version of Santo & Johnny's 'Sleepwalk', but the record industry preferred to sleep rather than walk and they were never heard from again.

Hailing from Saint-Étienne, the Gentlemen had a visual gimmick, sporting top hats and evening dress for stage performances. Original tunes like 'American twist' and 'Gentlemen indicatif' hinted at above-average talent, but they remained buried on the local club circuit.

Normandy's Les Shazams delivered covers of Shadows hits like 'Foot Tapper', but given the huge sales enjoyed by the originals, one wonders why they bothered.

Les Spirits from Douai in northernmost France opted to tackle Les Paul favourites like 'How High The Moon', but seemed uncertain whom their records were aimed at and failed to hit any target at all, despite some sporadically impressive guitar-work.

Les Messagers du Diable made the trip from Saint-Nazaire to Paris to play at the Golf Drouot and cut covers of Les Fantômes' 'Twist 33' and the Shadows' 'The Stranger' ('Toi, l'étranger'), but failed to generate any interest and returned to whence they had come.

Les Panthères from Besançon made the same mistakes as many of their contemporaries – with the same results – although the western-tinged 'N'oublie jamais' showed they were capable of better things.

From further afield in Morocco, Les Jaguars released a stunning EP, but few copies found their way across the Mediterranean and their inspired reading of the Shadows' 'The Savage' remained a local success story. They made a second bid for glory with a vocal EP with a superb cover of Les Chaussettes Noires' 'Toi, quand tu me quittes', but once again the difficulties of breaking out of their home market proved impossible to overcome.

## Swiss and Belgian groups

Given the glut of groups across the country, there seemed little point in importing more, but Switzerland's Les Aiglons proved individual enough to find their way over the Alps to become one of the first signings to the Golf Drouot label, an offshoot of the mighty Barclay empire for whom club manager Henri Leproux acted as talent scout.

---

[584] By way of the superb version laid down across the Channel by Nero & The Gladiators.

Easily one of the best groups around at the time, Les Aiglons debuted in 1963 with 'Stalactite', a swirling Tornados-like track that rode the surf wave to perfection. With an organ-driven sound that set them apart from the hordes of second-string Shadows clones, the record deservedly became a major hit.[585] Aside from the bubbly 'Marie-Line', the rest of their debut EP didn't quite measure up, but 'Panorama' on their second was another irrepressible tune with a harsh, metallic edge, again highlighting their trademark sound. Although not as big a hit, it served to confirm their place in the French market. Also deserving of mention is the track 'De l'amour', whose slow-building interplay between organ and guitar presented a sound unique in French pop. Highly sought after as a backing group in the studio, they provided accompaniment for many of the Golf Drouot label's singers while releasing further recordings of their own, most notably 1964's country-styled 'Tennessee'. However, when their relationship with their producer, fellow Swiss exile Ken Lean, fell into disorder following a disastrous tour, their career ebbed away.

There were two other Swiss instrumental outfits who worked with Lean and made a small mark on French pop during the sixties. Les Sorciers released two EPs featuring such delights as 'Cyclone', 'Caravelle', 'Indicatif' and a scintillating cover of the Astronauts' 'Baja' ('Baya') before the tide turned. The Four Shakers delivered a tasty debut EP in 1963, featuring the upbeat stroller 'Natacha' and the gentle guitar ballad 'Spleen'. The follow-up included the cool, rumbling 'Convoi' and the western-styled 'O'Casey ranch', which sounded a little like the UK's Outlaws, but by then the sun was already beginning to set.

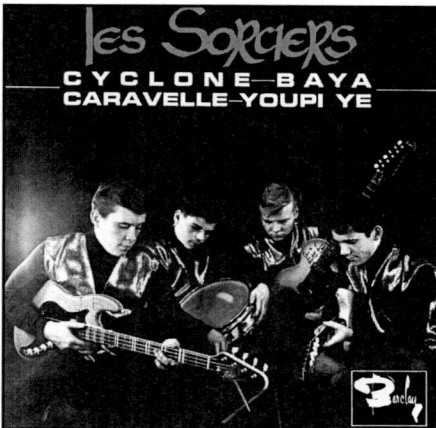

Fast establishing himself as the French counterpart of British independent producer Joe Meek, Lean was also at the controls in 1964 for the recording debut of a guitar/organ/drums trio called Les Français. The punchy 'Palpitations' and the soulful 'Suspenses' should have set the cash registers ringing, but sadly came too late in the day to propel the group into the major league, leaving them, like many of their rivals, eking out a living backing the country's pop stars on the concert trail.

Equally competent and enthusiastic

---

[585] It was even released in the US on the Smash label, credited to 'The Eagles'.

were Belgium's Black Angels, whose muscular 'Feu des anges' was a great surf record in a country where surfboards were as common as icicles in a desert. Meanwhile, fellow Belgians Les Bourreaux beat a path back to the beach for the lively 'Surfin' rope' without getting their feet wet in the turbulent waters of the hit parade.

## Vocal recordings

Not all groups opted to go down the instrumental route. One outfit who might have been expected to do so were Les Chats Sauvages, who had lost Dick Rivers to a solo career, but aside from one desultory attempt, 1963's 'Horizon', they decided against this option. Instead, they drafted in a new singer, Mike Shannon, and in late 1962 scored the biggest hit of their career with 'Derniers baisers' (Bryan Hyland's 'Sealed With A Kiss'). The same EP also saw them tackling American harmony pop with a somewhat weak-kneed take on the 4 Seasons' 'Sherry', while trailing kisses at the fading twist phenomenon with 'Tout le monde twiste' (Billy Fury's 'The Twist Kid').

Thereafter, they resumed ransacking the UK chart for hits to cover – among them Cliff Richard's 'Please Don't Tease' (rendered in French as 'Au moins huit jours') and 'Dancing Shoes' ('Allons, reviens danser'), and John Leyton's 'Johnny Remember Me' ('Johnny, rappelle-toi'), but something of the group's spirit seemed to have left with Rivers. Their (and Pathé's) determination to cope without him was emphasised when his vocal was wiped from the Cliff-like movie theme 'Venez, les filles'[586], and replaced with a new, admittedly excellent, performance from Shannon. Even so, their later material seemed to lack the sense of urgency that had made their early records so exciting. It wasn't that Shannon was a weaker vocalist – replacing Rivers wouldn't have been easy for anyone – more that their enthusiasm was being sapped by the continuing personality clashes within the group.

Another group to keep vocals to the fore were Les Ranger's Star, whose ramshackle versions of Gene Vincent's 'Say Mama' ('Il revient') and Elvis Presley's 'Gonna Get Back Home Somehow' ('Ne délaisse pas') were nothing

more than poor-quality facsimiles of the far superior interpretations laid down a little earlier by Les Chaussettes Noires.

Belgian guitar-pickers Les Saphirs stuck with vocals for the wild and rocking 'Jivaros', an absolute gem that somehow failed to become the smash it should have been. The tune was also cut by Les Castors, a group from the Dunkerque area who deserved far more success than they enjoyed.

Offering both instrumentals and vocals, Les Klébers from Mulhouse in eastern France won the major talent

---

[586] From *Le roi du village* (1963).

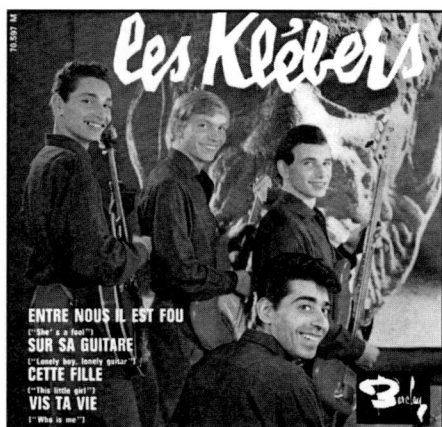

contest *La Guitare d'Or* at the Olympia Theatre in June 1963, earning themselves a contract with Barclay. Unfortunately, neither of their superb remakes of Duane Eddy's 'Lonely Boy, Lonely Guitar' ('Sur sa guitare') and Dion's 'This Little Girl' ('Cette fille') resulted in a hit. Cruelly, their night of glory remained the high-point of their brief career, with military call-up demolishing the ensemble shortly after.

By the end of 1963, the fad for instrumentals appeared to be fading as vocalists once more began to claim the spotlight. Seeing the writing on the wall, Claude Ciari quit Les Champions in early 1964, abandoning rock'n'roll for a career as the king of easy listening guitar, with a run of immaculately recorded albums that did little justice to his guitar hero status. He debuted his new style with a reading of Peter, Paul & Mary's 'Hush-A-Bye', but it was the follow-up that established him as a household name. Cribbed from the songbook of Belgium's Les Waikiki's,[587] the gentle 'La playa' went on to become a major hit across France and around South America. After enjoying further minor hits at home, Ciari eventually moved to Japan, where his subdued brand of guitar-picking enjoyed a huge following.

In the final analysis, where most of the French instrumental groups went wrong was in their insistence on slavishly copying tunes and arrangements from their overseas role models, leaving fans with little incentive to choose the home-grown version over the original. Others opted for instrumental versions of the hits of the day instead, but were often guilty of a severe lack of imagination, expecting the song to sell the record without putting much thought into how an instrumental arrangement with hit potential should sound. The outfits which thrived were those who chose a different approach and either wrote their own material, or grafted distinctive arrangements onto old songs in order to recreate them as something new, or both. However, the success – or lack of it – enjoyed by most of the instrumental groups turned out to be of secondary concern.

The real legacy of the instrumental boom was that, by encouraging young men to pick up guitars, it helped to create a pool of musicians who would provide both the musical backbone for the groups of the late sixties, as well as the core of the session musicians who would prove so crucial to the development of French pop. Even though new hopefuls continued to surface, the boom was over pretty quickly, with groups crippled by line-up changes forced by military service, the singer fixation of the entertainment industry, and the huge power wielded by *Salut les copains*, a magazine far more suited to solo singers.

---

[587] By way of fellow Belgians Los Mayas, who first cut it at the start of the year.

# Chapter 19

## TOUS LES GARÇONS
## ET LES FILLES
### The *yé-yé* explosion (1962-64)

*The success of the twist was one of the most important factors in leading the French market away from rock'n'roll to less abrasive forms of teenage pop, but it was not the only thing that drove the change. Hard rock'n'roll had not gone away and many performers – such as Les Chaussettes Noires – defiantly continued to record it, albeit with less commercial success than they had once enjoyed. Gradually, however, rock'n'roll was smoothed out for mass consumption, developing into a less raucous style that over time came to be known as yé-yé.*

*The term had its origins in the English expression 'yeah', which cropped up in so many American pop songs of the time[588] and was eagerly seized upon by many French singers. Coined by journalist Edgar Morin and used by him for the first time in early July 1963 in an article for* Le Monde, *yé-yé was originally a term of derision.[589] Over the years, however, it has become a catch-all label for the whole of French teen pop from the early to the mid-sixties, and has to a large extent been divested of its initial negative connotations.*

*Much has been written about it over the years, but strictly speaking the term does not define a style of music, French or otherwise. Yé-yé was not, as has been suggested by some commentators, a fusion of rock'n'roll with traditional French* chanson. *If it was anything in particular, it was contemporary American and British pop (as opposed to rock'n'roll) filtered (occasionally) through French accents and (usually) the French language. The yé-yé 'revolution' was the French equivalent of the* Bandstand-isation *of American rock'n'roll, in which the 'jungle music' of the original rock'n'rollers was replaced with a tamer sound delivered by interchangeable teen idols. The leading yé-yé stars were, by the same analogy, the home-grown equivalent of the 'Bobbies' (Messrs Vee, Rydell, Darin, Vinton, etc.) who watered down American rock'n'roll in the years between the death of Buddy Holly and the arrival of the Beatles, although the enthusiasm and energy of the French performers generally ensured that their records far outclassed those of the Philadelphia scream team.*

---

[588]  It predates the Beatles' 'She Loves You', which took use of the expression to extremes.
[589]  Although Morin's article was actually more supportive than is often remembered.

## From rock'n'roll to yé-yé

The transition from rock'n'roll to yé-yé was perhaps most obvious in the records of Richard Anthony. He opened 1962 with a clutch of twist tunes and covers of Ray Charles's 'I Can't Stop Loving You' ('C'était plus fort que tout') and Roy Orbison's 'Dream Baby' ('Cri de ma vie'), but in the summer he changed tack and released 'J'entends siffler le train', a plaintive adaptation of the old country folk song 'Five Hundred Miles'. Against his record company's expectations, it went on to become his biggest ever domestic hit,[590] a multi-million-seller that moved him — temporarily, at least — way out in front of Johnny Hallyday. He followed up with a vocal version of Dave Brubeck's jazz hit, 'Take Five' ('Ne boude pas'), beginning a gradual move toward a more polished, yet still uptempo style.

Johnny Hallyday also joined the trend toward a softer form of rock'n'roll in 1962, albeit rather more reluctantly. After Anthony had kept him off the top of the *Salut les copains* chart all summer, he returned with a vengeance, scoring back-to-back chart-toppers with ballads adapted from Rick Nelson's 'Teen Age Idol' ('L'idole des jeunes') and George Jones's 'Tender Years' ('Tes tendres années'). While the girls swooned over Hallyday's new, gentler image, he kept his male fans happy with liberal doses of rock'n'roll on the side, including a raucous cover of Eddie Cochran's 'Somethin' Else' ('Elle est terrible') and a wild in-concert version of Elvis Presley's 'Trouble' ('La bagarre').

The growing acceptability of a less frantic style of pop opened the door to a number of performers who might otherwise have found it slammed in their faces. Singer/pianist José Salcy from Nice took his lead from Ray Charles, but sensibly set out his stall with a batch of self-penned songs including the bluesy 'Barbara' and the uptempo tribute 'Ray Charles', rather than trying to beat the Genius at his

---

[590] Anthony discovered the song on an album by the Journeymen. The commercial success of his French cover version, which appeared some time before before the highly regarded American versions by Bobby Bare and Peter, Paul & Mary, did much to bring the original to international popularity.

own game. It took a cover of Dion's '(I Was) Born To Cry' ('Je suis né pour pleurer') to get him underway, but it was the crunching 'Oublie et recommence' that showed his true colours. However, it was now girl fans, rather than the *blousons noirs*, who were calling the shots, and in early 1963 Salcy obliged with the maudlin 'Moi, je tutoie les anges', relegating the harder-hitting, guitar-driven 'Écoute-moi' and the R&B throwback 'C'était mon quartier' to the status of fillers on his EPs. Later in the year, he launched an anonymous dance craze with 'C'est la danse sans nom', and subsequent releases – almost all of them containing original songs with a nice, soulful touch – kept him in the picture until the mid-sixties.

Lucky Blondo, never altogether convincing as a rocker, took to the new style like a duck to water, hitting the jackpot at the end of 1962 with a bouncy take on Tommy Roe's 'Sheila' that elbowed aside a cover by Les Pirates to become the biggest-selling of the many versions available on the French market.[591] The EP also allowed Blondo to continue his fascination with Bobby Darin with 'Isabelle', utilising an arrangement lifted from Darin's recent revival of 'You Must Have Been A Beautiful Baby'.[592] Taking an eclectic route toward a succession of hits, Blondo subsequently cut versions of Darin's 'Things' ('Filles') and the Beach Boys' 'Ten Little Indians' ('Dix petits Indiens'), but it was

the countryish 'Au cœur du silence' that best reflected his new image. A crooner for the young generation, he continued to record passable teen pop like 1963's 'Tout haut, tout bas', but increasingly drifted off toward a diet of ballads that saw him left behind when the next wave of idols appeared.

At least Blondo enjoyed a spell at the top, which was more than the Yugoslav-born singer Karlo Metikoš aka Matt Collins ever managed, despite briefly being considered as a replacement in Les Chaussettes Noires for the absent Eddy Mitchell. However, Collins found it difficult to secure decent material and his debut, 'En écoutant la pluie' (the Cascades' 'Rhythm Of The Rain') was buried by

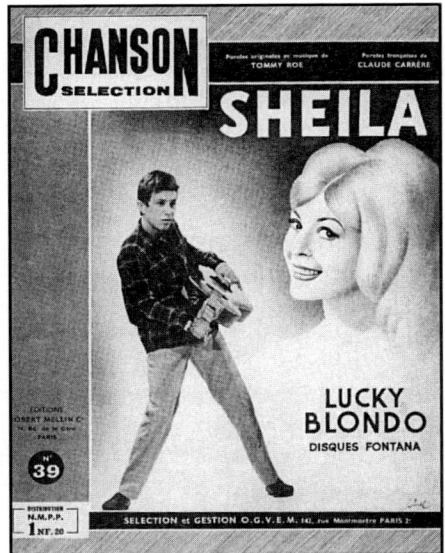

---

591 Among the vanquished were recordings by Johnny Taylor et les Strangers and Chris Valois, and an instrumental interpretation by Les Guitares du Diable.

592 Originally a hit for both Dick Powell and Bing Crosby.

MATT COLLINS

J'AI CHANGÉ D'AVIS
POURQUOI
PETITE FILLE SAUVAGE
VIS TA VIE

MEDIUM 434 856 BE

PHILIPS

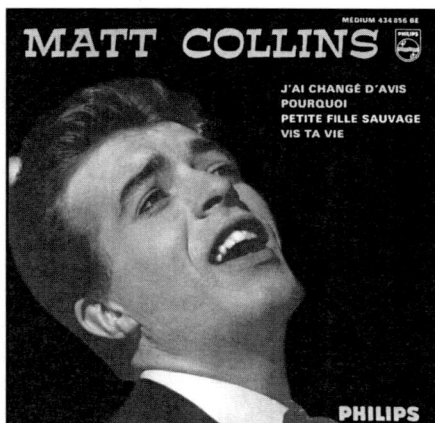

rival – and superior – versions by Sylvie Vartan and Richard Anthony. He did however score a minor hit with the pleasant 'Il faut choisir' (Rick Nelson's 'It's Up to You').[593] A second EP released in late 1963 contained excellent readings of Frankie Vaughan's 'You're The One For Me'[594] ('J'ai changé d'avis') and Helen Shapiro's 'Woe Is Me' ('Vis ta vie'), but failed to maintain his momentum. He remained a visible presence for several years but he never cracked the charts, eventually decamping back behind the Iron Curtain for further releases and concert tours that took him from the Middle East to Moscow.

Alongside his string of twist recordings, the latest of which, 'Ça n'finira jamais' (aka Gary 'US' Bonds' 'Dear Lady Twist') had fared less well than hoped, Danyel Gérard also drew on American R&B for inspiration, cutting the Marathons' 'Peanut Butter' and a wild reworking of the Ikettes' 'I'm Blue (The Gong Gong Song)' issued as 'Gong gong'. Increasingly though, it was his self-penned material that proved more impressive, from the sweetened rock'n'roll of 'Mon cœur sera roi' to the organ-fuelled 'L'incendie',[595] although it was the ballad 'Reviendra-t-il le temps' that was most in keeping with the times.

Georgie Dann, on the other hand, started out trying to cash in on the twist and Madison crazes with two undistingushed EPs. After a run of self-penned material including the teen-pop 'Une fille de mon âge', he rebranded himself as a cowboy in 1963, covering Frank Ifield's remake of Hank Williams' 'Lovesick Blues' ('Je ne pense qu'à l'amour'). The smooth 'Arizona' made the case for him as a crooner, but he failed to find many takers and eventually went across the border to Spain to forge a new career.

### Country music

Long Chris was likewise attracted to the less commercial sounds of country music, and after his third EP with Les Daltons had failed to register anything more than a minor hit, he abandoned rock'n'roll completely in favour of such C&W-tinged efforts as 'Ma guitare et mes bottes' and 'The ballad of Jesse James' and watched his sales slide ever downward.

The country sound also drew in Les Mercenaires, a competent six-piece outfit who had introduced themselves to the world in 1962 with a twist EP, although the sprightly 'Donne' had a rockier edge than was usual, while the upbeat 'Les conseils de Papa' would have been perfect for Cliff Richard and the Shadows. However, it was their second disc that best showcased their

---

[593] The record fared better in Collins' native land, prompting the release of a Yugoslav-only follow-up given over to covers of such hits as Ray Charles's 'What'd I Say' and the Ronettes' 'Be My Baby'.
[594] A sizeable Scandinavian hit for Vaughan, although it missed in the UK.
[595] Which was quickly covered by Richard Anthony.

country leanings. With ensemble vocals to the fore, this was an excellent release, headlined by the harmonica-led stroll 'Les mercenaires de l'amour' (a truly inspired reworking of Dickie McBride & The Village Boys' western swing classic, 'Tulsa Twist'). Sadly, neither this nor the statutory twist tune, 'Allez mon cœur' (Sam Butera's 'Come On And Do The Twist'), made any impact on the wider teenage audience. On their third EP, Les Mercenaires took a confident stab at the Serge Gainsbourg-penned 'Quand tu t'y mets',[596] but after the lead track, 'Moi, je pense encore à toi' (a weedy adaptation of Neil Sedaka's 'Breaking Up Is Hard To Do') went nowhere, they hung up their guns.

This was far better than the fate enjoyed by Marc Anderson, who led Les Discoverers 'V' to oblivion following the failure of one half-decent EP offering a revival of Ritchie Valens' 'Donna' and a Danyel Gérard-penned original, 'Leena'.

## Frontmen to solo singers

Les Pirates took to the road laid down by Cliff Richard with a moderately impressive cover of 'The Young Ones' ('De tout mon cœur'), but the simultaneously issued cover of his 'Thinkin' Of Our Love' ('Sur ma plage') was too far removed from their roots to be convincing. Frontman Dany Logan gave his all in a decent impersonation of Britain's leading rocker, but the limp instrumental backing only served to illustrate how far their standards had slipped. Increasingly outshone by newer, more clean-cut rivals, the group were at a low ebb, and their morale was hardly helped when their creditable take on Chubby Checker's 'Dancin' Party' ('Comme l'été dernier') was buried by rival versions from Johnny Hallyday and Sylvie Vartan. Falling sales sapped their inner harmony and Logan quit for a solo career. The group attempted to keep things going with new vocalist Tony Morgan, but they were already history, and after a final EP offering a cover of Del Shannon's 'Cry Myself To Sleep' ('Je pleure aussi'), they called it a day.

Les Vautours too had bitten the dust after a final EP highlighted by a vocal version of Gene Vincent's 'Be Bop Boogie Boy' brought to an end two years of diminishing returns. Their frontman, Vic Laurens, sat in on guitar with Les Chaussettes Noires for a while before he too embarked on a solo career.

Having abandoned Les Chats Sauvages to whatever fate awaited them, Dick Rivers initially seemed unsure how to proceed as a solo singer. His debut EP included 'Baby John', a clumsy Hollywood-styled country opus that sold well, but hardly set the world on fire. After alternating Cliff Richard-style

---

[596] Written for, but not recorded by, Long Chris.

rockers like 'Pour une fille' (Shane Fenton's 'Why Little Girl') with bizarre orchestral experiments like the minor hit 'À Seville', which had nothing whatsoever to do with rock'n'roll, he got back on track in 1963 with another countryish effort, 'La fille qu'on a tant aimée', and covers of Joe Brown's 'A Picture Of You' ('Au cœur de la nuit') and 'That's What Love Will Do' ('Ça ne s'oublie pas'). It was a far cry from the excitement of Les Chats Sauvages, but Rivers' new recordings were perfect for the post-twist era, setting him on the road to solo stardom.

## Claude François

The crystallisation of the as yet unnamed *yé-yé* movement came in late 1962 with the overnight success of Claude François. Having made an inauspicious start that summer with an unuccessful EP released under the name 'Kôkô', François hit on a winning formula with his second, on which he turned the Eddie Hodges hit, '(Girls, Girls, Girls) Made To Love'[597] into a bouncy piece of pop and landed a huge hit with 'Belles! Belles! Belles!'.

With his jolly, upbeat, infectious tunes, the squeaky-clean singer was the complete antithesis of Vince Taylor and Johnny Hallyday – and perfect pin-up fodder for the *Salut les copains* magazine. A Philadelphia-style teen idol, albeit with rather more talent than most, François' cheery, boyish demeanour, dynamic dancing and persistent smile made him a huge star among teenage girls, even if he was often loathed by their boyfriends. His breakthrough success was soon joined on the airwaves by the winsome 'Vénus en blue-jeans' (a slick adaptation of the Jimmy Clanton/Mark Wynter hit, 'Venus In Blue Jeans'), which deservedly shunted aside an inferior rendition by Les Champions and provided him with a second hit before the year was out.

Throughout 1963, François unleashed a string of winners, all bouncy covers of the most obvious overseas smashes he could get his hands on. Spending hours poring over the American charts looking for material, he coated all his releases in a shiny production gloss, resulting in a candy-pop sound that was a precursor to bubblegum. Nonetheless, he was a capable singer and his records were never less than professional, their catchy arrangements conveying a genuine sense of excitement. The year's releases saw him taking in the the girl group sound of the Exciters' 'Tell Him' ('Dis-lui'), the balladry of 'Pauvre petite fille riche' and the calypso-soul of Jimmy Soul's 'If You Wanna Be Happy' ('Si tu veux être heureux...') with equal ease. With regular airplay on *Salut les copains*, he quickly eclipsed most of the stars of the day and by the end of the year he was challenging Johnny Hallyday and Richard Anthony for the position of most popular singer in the country.

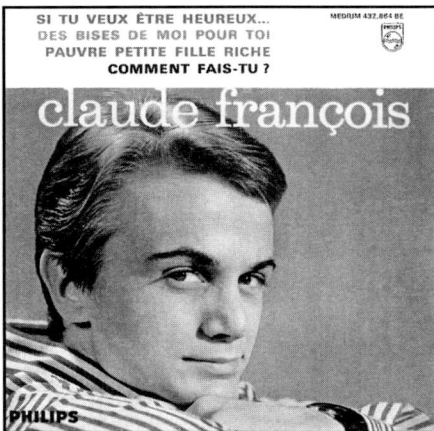

---

[597] This song had started life as an album track by the Everly Brothers, who also wrote it.

The lengths François would go to in order to secure a hit made him many enemies within the industry, as he contacted overseas publishers directly to secure exclusive rights to international hits, thereby blocking potential rival versions. The practice soon became widespread, putting an end to the chart battles that had characterised the early rock'n'roll years in France. The energy which typified both his stage act and his commitment to his career was best exemplified by his late 1963 smash, 'Si j'avais un marteau' (a cover of Trini Lopez's arrangement of Pete Seeger's 'If I Had A Hammer'[598]) which was in the shops barely a week after François first heard it on Radio Luxembourg.

### Enter the *yé-yés*

François had got his start in the music business playing drums with Les Gamblers, backing singer/guitarist Olivier Despax as he worked his way around the casinos and nightclubs of the Mediterranean coast. A ladies' man in the manner of Sacha Distel, Despax was too sophisticated for the fans who followed his former drummer. Although he initially found hit records hard to come by, he did manage a minor chart strike in 1963 with a version of Duane Eddy's '(Dance With The) Guitar Man' ('L'homme à la guitare'). Fortunately, his matinée idol looks secured him regular work on television and in adult nightspots around the country while he bided his time until the wind changed in his favour.

François' rocket ride to the top had left Despax stranded in his wake, and it also helped put an end to the flickering career of Frankie Jordan. Having watched successive releases struggle to recreate the glory of 'Panne d'essence', Jordan agreed to guest on an EP by Sylvie Vartan in 1962, sub-consciously acknowledging how far her career had now outstripped his own. The pair's cover of Dinah Washington & Brook Benton's 'A Rockin' Good Way' ('C'est une drôle de façon') was a good recording, but it was not a hit, being overshadowed by one of Vartan's solo efforts on the EP, 'Qui aurait dit ça' (Ray Charles's 'Talkin' 'bout You').

Returning to his own devices, Jordan paid tribute to the Fat Man with the *Frankie Jordan rencontre Fats Domino* EP. This included an excellent

---

[598] Peter, Paul & Mary had enjoyed a US Top 10 hit with the song in 1962, but it was Lopez's upbeat arrangement that provided the basis for François' cover.

reworking of 'Walking To New Orleans' ('M'en revenant de guerre') which boasted one of the first anti-war lyrics to show up on a French teen-pop record, but sales were pitiful. The follow-up, a breezy take on the Rooftop Singers' folk-pop hit, 'Walk Right In'[599] ('Marche tout droit'), was made redundant when Claude François covered it in his usual bouncy fashion, grabbing most of the airplay and the lion's share of the sales. Jordan subsequently threw in the towel, ultimately settling into a new life as a dentist and making way for a posse of new performers who adopted a stridently commercial approach to their material, with varying degrees of success.

Alain Dumas cut a pair of entertaining EPs, earned a modicum of interest for his 'teen idol' renditions of Johnny Nash's 'What Kind Of Love Is This' ('Ça fait un drôle d'effet') and Arthur Alexander's 'You Better Move On' ('Tu peux t'en aller'), but failed to build this limited success into a long career.

Having gone as far as he could back home, Belgian singer Jacky Delmone headed south in 1963 to launch a career in France with 'Pour les filles' (Heinz's 'Just Like Eddie'), which suited his singing style perfectly. Sadly, it didn't suit anybody else, and although his 1964 cover of Terry Stafford's 'Suspicion' ('Obsession')[600] became a sizeable hit in Belgium, he never achieved major success in France.

Another Belgian singer, Adamo, found a route to the airwaves with a series of engaging light rockers commencing with 'Sans toi, mamie', which topped the Belgian chart in 1963. He picked up a second chart-topper later in the year with the dreamily romantic 'N'est-ce pas merveilleux', complete with cheesy organ arrangement. The bluesier 'En blue jeans et blouson d'cuir' also received a modicum of attention south of the border, but he meant little in France until he recorded the fifties-styled ballad 'Tombe la neige' at the end of the year.[601] A huge hit in Belgium and the Netherlands, it generated enough

---

[599] Originally recorded in 1929 by Cannon's Jug Stompers.

[600] Originally recorded in 1962 by Elvis Presley for the LP *Pot Luck*, the song became a massive hit when covered by Stafford in 1964.

[601] Issued in Japan a few years later, it became one of the biggest hits of the decade there and remains a big karaoke favourite today.

319

interest in France to prompt him to head for Paris, though the follow-up, also a ballad, called 'Quand les roses' failed to deliver the breakthrough he'd hoped for.

At least Adamo wrote his own material, rather than stalking the American charts like most of his rivals. Michel Paje displayed a similar degree of originality, combining dreamy ballads with light rockers to win the hearts of teenage girls across France. Hits like 'Tu peux pleurer' and 'Nous, on est dans le vent' may have lacked excitement, but they were still impressive efforts that made the more cynical approach of Claude François seem lazy by comparison. Equally adept at ballads like 'Notre amour sur le sable' or mid-tempo offerings such as 'Tous les jeunes', Paje wrote the bulk of his material himself – including all the tracks on his first three EPs. In this, he displayed a creativity that put many of his leading rivals to shame, although the slushy stentiments of 'Ton chouchou' were little different from those found in Adamo's romantic balladry.

Original or not, sales of Paje's records came nowhere near those of the big names in French pop, which perhaps demonstrated that François, Hallyday and the others had a better idea of what their public wanted than he did. Paje eventually resorted to cover versions, having a flutter at Dean & Jean's 'Tra La La La Suzy' (oddly retitled 'Tra-la-la Suzie') and the Beach Boys' 'I Get Around' ('Elle aime tout sauf moi'), but while the former was a decent enough attempt, the latter was an artistic faux pas from which his career struggled to recover.

The Beach Boys' banner was also taken up by balladeer Jean-Pierre Fall, who cut a cover of 'Don't Worry Baby' ('J'ai peur de l'été') to negligible impact. Having initially set out his stall with some middle-of-the-road efforts, the most impressive of which was 'Dis-moi pourquoi?' (a cover of Udo Jürgens' 1964 *Eurovision* entry, 'Warum nur, warum'),[602] he did rather better with 'Du chagrin pour toujours', a beat-ballad rendition of Maxine Brown's 'Yesterday's Kisses'. However, none of his records succeeded in rattling Claude François' cage.

Of all the singers to debut in the months following François' rapid rise

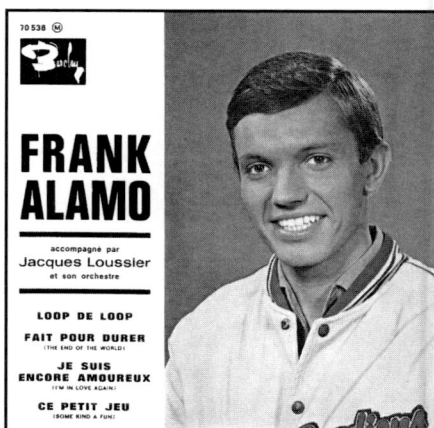

---

[602] Though he failed to replicate the success that Matt Monro's version of the same song ('Walk Away') had enjoyed in the UK.

to stardom, the only one to offer any real threat was the similarly squeaky-clean grinmeister Frank Alamo. Sometimes unfairly dismissed as a poor man's Claude François, Alamo had a decent voice and an engaging manner, but his early recordings suffered from weak arrangements which lacked the sonic punch that made François irresistible to the airwaves.

His first release, a cover of Johnny Thunder's 'Loop De Loop' was pop at its most vapid, while his second offered a limp attempt at the Crystals' 'Da Doo Ron Ron' ('Da Dou Ron Ron'), but the hits eventually began to flow with the infectious 'File, file, file' (the Crickets' 'My Little Girl') and he soon had the girls swooning every time he appeared on television. Ransacking the songbooks of the leading American vocal groups, he scored with reworkings of Randy & The Rainbows' 'Denise' ('Sylvie') and the Ronettes' 'Be My Baby' ('Reviens vite et oublie'), though his popularity had more to do with his teen-appeal than the quality of his recordings, none of which came close to the highly superior originals.

Like François, Alamo was perfect for TV variety shows: a safe, wholesome presence whom even the squarest parent could tolerate – quite unlike that 'nasty' Hallyday character. Both singers were also perfect for the glossy magazines springing up to catch the youth market, and saturation coverage in the teenage press encouraged fans to demand more airplay for their heroes on *Salut les copains*. Sales of the magazines thus began to affect radio playlists and the composition of the charts. This further reinforced the position of *yé-yé* at the expense of the old guard of rock'n'roll singers – which was good news for François and Alamo.

## Sylvie Vartan and Petula Clark

*Yé-yé* was also good news for female singers, who had long been struggling to find a way to break into the new and exciting world of teen pop. Even Sylvie Vartan, who *had* managed to translate her appeal into record sucess, needed to change direction to survive.

By 1963, she had already embarked on a long journey from the exciting rock'n'roll of her first recordings toward a more accessible, less frenetic style that still possessed enough of a commitment to the big beat to affirm her position as the queen of teen pop. Moving away from her decidedly tomboyish stage demeanour, she had worked hard at her craft, extended her vocal range, learned to dance, and was gradually moving down the road to highly choreographed stage shows and an audience that spread far beyond the young fans who made up her original following. Musically too, she was slipping into a more polished form of pop that chimed perfectly with the emerging *yé-yé* movement.

Her first hit of 1963, the Jean-Jacques Debout composition 'Tous mes copains', was a gentler affair than usual. The highlight of her debut album, *Sylvie*, it was her biggest chart success to date. One of the few hits of the era to directly address the issue of the military service that would blight so many young lives for the remainder of the century, 'Tous mes copains' demonstrated that Vartan could *really* sing and ushered in a sporadic partnership with Debout that brought much-needed royalties to them both.[603]

---

[603] Its lilting refrain also lent itself to easy listening instrumental arrangements, such as the cover recorded by session guitarist Léo Petit.

**76.602 S**

**RCA VICTOR**

**Sylvie Vartan**

Moi je pense encore à toi

Dansons

M'amuser

Tous mes copains

Subsequent hits such as 'Chance' (the Cookies' 'Chains') offered a glossy vision of rock'n'roll, though she kept the faith with a reading of Gene Vincent's 'Say Mama' ('Il revient') and the ominous 'Réponds-moi'.

By the summer of 1963, Vartan was beginning to rival the leading male stars in popularity, topping the *Salut les copains* chart with the English-language rocker 'I'm Watching' – a gift from admirer Paul Anka, whose own version would be completely eclipsed when it appeared on EP in France later that year.[604] The first time that a French singer had taken an English-language recording to the top of the charts, it was subsequently reworked into French as 'Je ne vois que toi' for her next EP release.

Petula Clark meanwhile confirmed her position as one of the country's biggest stars, boosting her standing with original hits like 'Je chante doucement'.[605] She hit the jackpot with 'Chariot', a classy piece of girl-group pop that became a massive hit in France in the summer of 1962[606] and even scraped into the UK Top 40 in 1963 – a rare achievement for a French-language recording. It also became the first rock'n'roll hit from France to top the US charts, albeit by proxy, in the form of Little Peggy March's English-language cover, 'I Will Follow Him'.[607]

Clark maintained the pace into 1963 with vocal covers of the Shadows' instrumental hits 'Dance On' ('Je me sens bien (auprès de toi)') and 'Foot Tapper' ('Mon bonheur danse').[608] Although older than most of the competition, she entrenched herself as a regular on *Salut les copains* with enjoyable teenage fluff like 'Elle est finie (La belle histoire)' and a strong cover of Barbara Lynn's 'Second Fiddle Girl' ('Que ton cœur me soit fidèle').

Ever versatile, Clark dabbled in country-tinged pop for 'J'ai tout oublié' and even managed to sing 'Plaza de toros' (Herb Alpert's 'The Lonely Bull'[609]) with a straight face. Despite extending her reach to West Germany on the back of the chart-topping 'Monsieur' (sung in German, despite the title), she found it difficult to get back into the charts in her native UK, where her last English-language hit had come and gone in February 1962.

---

[604] The song was also minor US hit for Little Peggy March the following year, albeit as a vastly inferior rendition titled '(I'm Watching) Every Little Move You Make'.

[605] Although not in the UK, where her English-language version ('The Road') flopped.

[606] The song began life in 1961 as an instrumental by Franck Pourcel. After Clark made it a hit, it was quickly covered by a raft of instrumental groups, among them Les Guitares du Diable and the Four Dreamers.

[607] Clark had earlier recorded 'I Will Follow Him' for the UK market, without success.

[608] Issued on consecutive EPs. The first of these probably inspired UK singer Kathy Kirby to cut the tune in English (as 'Dance On') in the summer.

[609] Originally recorded by Sol Lake as 'El solo toro' before Alpert took it around the world.

*Petula Clark on stage in Juvisy-sur-Orge, 1964.*

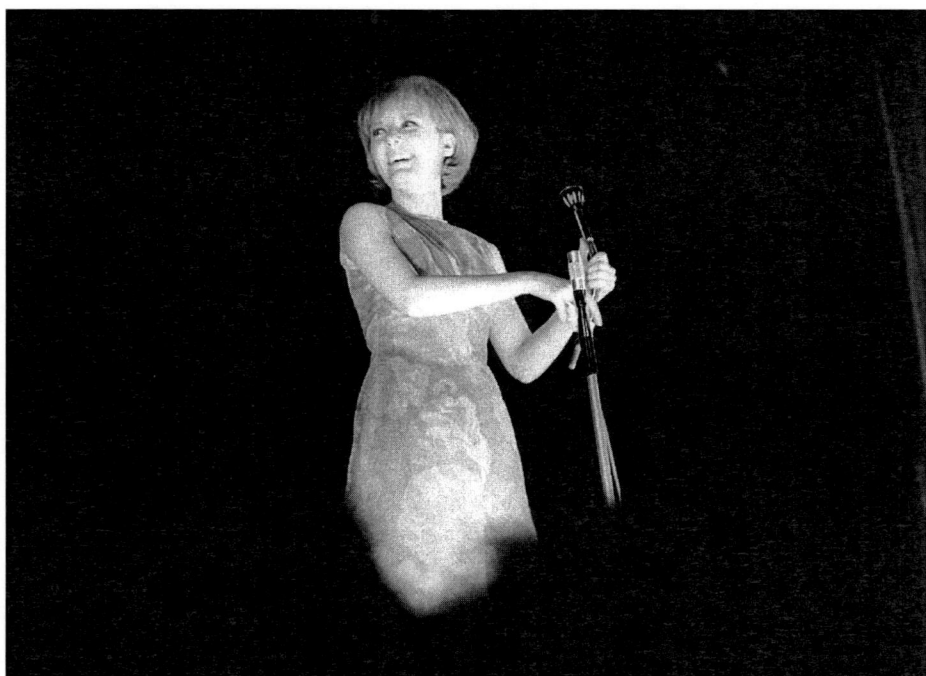

## Sheila

As twist fever subsided, French pop unveiled its next major female star: a gawky schoolgirl with a nauseatingly winsome smile. Discovered and managed with Svengali-like control by songwriter/producer Claude Carrère,[610] the pigtail-wearing Sheila was unveiled to the public in late 1962 with a mundane version of the Tommy Roe hit that provided her stage name, but it was her second EP, released in early 1963, that made her a star. 'L'école est finie' was an original song[611] packed with teen appeal and established a pattern that would last for most of her career.

Sheila's hits were often the most inane kind of pap: twee, bright, cheesy pop, often from foreign sources, sung with an audible smile and tailored to a readily definable image. Even decent American or British songs were adapted into disposable school-age pop that appealed to both pre-teens and grandparents, although those in between sometimes found themselves cringing at the wholesome *niceness* of it all.

The easy listening 'Le ranch de mes rêves' (Brook Benton's 'Hotel Happiness') and the upbeat 'Ne raccroche pas' (the Orlons' 'Don't Hang Up') followed her breakthrough onto the airwaves, and, with the teen press adopting her as an ideal role model for teenage girls, Sheila was catapulted to the front rank of the *yé-yé* pantheon. As the spring of 1963 gave way to summer, she returned to the charts with a revival of the Everly Brothers' 'All I Have To Do Is Dream'. In a logical progression from the previous release, it was titled 'Pendant les vacances',[612] celebrating the school holidays in a sweet, inoffensive vocal performance. Unsurprisingly, it presented her with a second consecutive smash. Elsewhere on this, her third EP, she turned her hand to the latest dance craze on 'Viens danser le hully-gully', while the more exciting 'Première surprise-partie', an upbeat, rocking number with nice guitar accompaniment, chased 'Pendant les vacances' up the chart to give her another major hit.

---

[610] A former singer, Carrère's closest brush with fame had come in 1957 when he was one of many to record the hit 'Cigarettes, whisky et p'tites pépées'.

[611] It was quickly covered in English as 'School Is Over' by Billie Davis. Although the single flopped in the UK, it became a sizeable hit in parts of Scandinavia.

[612] It had already been covered a year earlier by Les Chausssettes Noires as 'Line'.

Sheila's success was a triumph for Carrère's marketing strategy, which was designed to establish her as a *yé-yé* star for all the family. With her distinctive schoolgirl appearance, she was designed to be as unthreatening as possible, and the sleeve of each release contained a brief, handwritten message from the singer to her fans – a cute marketing ploy that served to endear her to young teens, pre-teens and their parents. Her records sold by the bucketload, establishing her as a surrogate older sister for her young fans, and in less than a year she was challenging Sylvie Vartan for the title of the country's most popular *chanteuse*, coming second in the 1963 popularity poll in *Salut les copains*. However, following a disastrous concert tour which ended with her suffering a nervous breakdown, Sheila refused to go on the road again,[613] reaching out to her fans via the medium of television instead.[614]

### Yé-yé girls

Sheila's colossal success spawned a mass of imitators, all of whom had the same 'little girl' charm, and many of whom were far younger than the original. However, none of them had a manager with such a single-minded vision as Carrère and few had anything more than a limited impact.

Chantal turned out a pair of reasonable EPs in 1963 to near-universal indifference, despite such enjoyable outings as 'Uh huh' and 'J'ai flirté quatre fois', but at least she proved to be worthy of the effort.

Peggy likewise used her cute-as-a-fluffy-bunny voice to good effect on the catchy 'Ne me laisse pas l'aimer', as well as a big-beat rendition of Betty Everett's 'You're No Good' ('Recherché pour...'), but to little avail.

Diana sang her heart out on three EPs, shaking up dance floors with 'Hully gully', but otherwise passing completely unnoticed.

Konnie, on the other hand, was nothing to write home about, struggling to establish an identity with the disappointing 'Le juke-box des copains' and deservedly vanishing after her one and only EP sank without trace.

Similarly, British import Lynn had a bubbly personality but little else to offer, and her 'Dis-moi Maman' (Christine Quaite's 'Tell Me Mama') inevitably went nowhere.

Rather more successful was Claudine Coppin, who cut the joyful 'Le twist du bac' in 1963, as well as a creditable cover of the Sherrys' 'Pop Pop Pop-Pie' which gave her a minor chart strike. She followed this with the girl group-styled 'Rêver d'un garçon', but despite more stylish releases over

---

[613] Cast adrift, her support band, Les Guitares, attempted to make ends meet with a pair of instrumental EPs. The first featured an arrangement of Les Guitares du Diable's 'Galaxie' that was closer in style to the Tornados than the Shadows, while the second generated a minor hit with the space-flavoured 'Chris-craft'.

[614] Making her one of the forerunners of the video age.

Claudine COPPIN
AVEC GUY MOTTA ET SON ORCHESTRE
LE TWIST DU BAC
NE T'EN VA      SAINT-TROP' EXPRESS
PAS SANS MOI    POP...POP...POP...PIE
(DON'T GO AWAY)

the next year, success continued to elude her until she crossed the Pyrenees into Spain.

The explosion of interest in girl singers was not confined to France and it had its parallels in the girl group sound that was dominating American pop at the time. While the French pop industry was slow in producing female singing groups of its own, it was certainly amenable to the sounds of such giants of the genre as the Chiffons or the Ronettes, with both male and female singers rushing to cover the latest sounds to come out of the Brill Building or off Phil Spector's Gold Star production line in Los Angeles.

The same trend was also apparent in the UK, where beat groups may have been attracting all the attention, but record companies remained wedded to the idea of female solo singers for many years. Even before Cilla Black, Dusty Springfield and Sandie Shaw relegitimised girl singers in the eyes of British teenagers, the likes of Julie Grant, Helen Shapiro and Susan Maughan set the agenda.

Among those enjoying success in the UK was Louise Cordet,[615] daughter of French actress Hélène Cordet and Second World War hero Marcel Boisot. After an EP rounding up the tracks from two UK singles made a little noise in France, she decided to follow in Petula Clark's footsteps. Singing in English, she released 'She's Got You' on both sides of the Channel, but in 1963 switched to French for the jolly rocker 'Que m'a-t-il fait' and the lightweight girly pop of 'L'amour tourne en rond', which was the closest she ever came to troubling the French charts. Cordet's main claims to fame were a family tie to the Duke of Edinburgh (publicity material noted that he was her godfather) and a demeanour that would have been better suited to an adult audience.

The same sophistication under-pinned the appeal of actress Dany Saval,[616] who appeared on a couple of recordings taken from her films before attempting to strike out as a singer in 1963 with the surprisingly good 'Ne dis pas du mal de mon amour' (the Cookies' 'Don't Say Nothin' Bad (About My Baby)'). Despite favourable reviews, it was not a major seller and Saval sensibly opted not to quit her day job.

454.089 S
DECCA
Sweet enough
Someone else's fool
I'm just a baby
In a matter of moments

Louise
Cordet

Orchestre Tony Meehan

---

[615]  Cordet hit the UK Top 20 in 1962 with 'I'm Just A Baby', later adapted into French for a rare single release as 'Je ne suis qu'un baby'.

[616]  Saval had had a bit part in the 1958 cinematic classic *Les tricheurs*.

Fellow actress Marie Laforêt was widely known on account of her appearances in films. She debuted in *Plein soleil* (1960),[617] co-starring with Alain Delon, and *Saint-Tropez blues* (1960), for which she also recorded the theme song. A surprise hit in Japan, it prompted her to embark upon a parallel career as a singer. Her first hit in France was 1963's 'Les vendanges de l'amour', a jaunty piece of pop fluff written for her by Danyel Gérard with journeyman songwriter Michel Jourdan, and she continued to release records at regular intervals, interspersing pretty pop ditties with more world-weary material drawn from folk music and gospel. The unusual medieval-styled 'Le roi a fait battre tambour' was a cut above the average pop recording, and the folk-pop confection 'Au cœur de l'automne' was equally enticing, but it was her pretty take on the Victorians' 'What Makes Little Girls Cry'[618] ('Qu'est-ce qui fait pleurer les filles') that propelled her back into the charts.

Sophie had a real feeling for rock'n'roll, and, had she emerged a year earlier, might have given Sylvie Vartan a run for her money. She enjoyed a substantial hit in 1963 with 'Quand un air vous possède' (the Drifters' 'When My Little Girl Is Smiling'[619]), and she impressed with a bluesy take on Ann-Margret's 'I Just Don't Understand' ('Je ne comprends rien'). She followed up with two more hits later that year, although neither the catchy 'T'es pas seul au monde' (Paul Anka's 'Remember Diana'), nor 'Reviens vite et oublie' (a stripped-down version of the Ronettes' 'Be My Baby') enjoyed quite the same success. In truth, her gutsy style was at odds with the prevailing sound, and, although she turned out further worthy recordings until the middle of the decade, only the shuffling ballad 'Ton au revoir est un adieu' (the Shirelles' 'Don't Say Goodnight And Mean Goodbye') set the cash registers ringing. Not everything she cut was tough rock'n'roll, but she did achieve a remarkable consistency in her recordings and stayed in the game long enough to cut a cover of the

---

[617] Remade in the 1990s by Hollywood as *The Talented Mr. Ripley*, after the book on which the French film had originally been based.

[618] The original version bubbled under the *Billboard* 'Hot 100' in 1963.

[619] Most likely lifted from Jimmy Justice's UK cover. A rival version by Johnny Hallyday stole most of the sales.

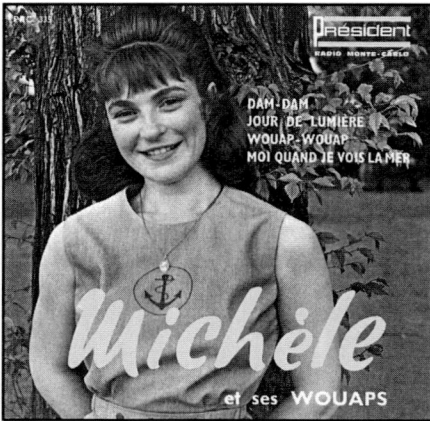

Merseybeats' take on Dionne Warwick's 'Wishin' And Hopin'' ('Tente ta chance') that totally outclassed the British waxing, if not Warwick's original. A cut above the average *yé-yé* chanteuse, Sophie deserved far more success than she ever achieved.

The coy-but-cool Nathalie Degand also cut her share of quality girlie pop over five EPs between 1963 and 1965, kicking off with rhythmic versions of Jan Bradley's 'Mama Didn't Lie' ('Maman m'a dit') and Paul Anka's 'Love' ('Je n'y comprends plus rien') that won her support among the readers of *Bonjour les amis*, a self-evidently imitative magazine trying to establish itself as a credible rival to *Salut les copains*. Subsequent releases such as 'Je suis perdue' saw her edging into Sylvie Vartan territory, while 1964's beat group-styled 'Pour être belle' was the closest she came to a *bona fide* hit. Even when her image matured into that of a stylish girl about town for the indignant 'Je n'ai pas vingt ans' and a high-class composition by Jean-Jacques Debout and Charles Dumont titled 'Mon ami Dominique', she proved unable to find an audience for her undeniable charms.

Down on the Mediterranean coast, Radio Monte-Carlo discovered Michèle et ses Wouaps, a group with country roots and an appealing female singer who set them apart from the host of Chats Sauvages clones playing the provincial circuit. Unthreatening, yet anchored in rock'n'roll, Michèle and the boys impressed with the jaunty 'Moi, quand je vois la mer', the harmonica that underpinned both this and the countryish stroll 'Dam-dam' anticipating the sound of the Beatles. Sadly, their one excellent EP remained a treasure little known beyond the South of France.

Taking a different tack, the independent Orly label signed up Angélica, a powerful singer who attempted to succeed where Adamo had failed, cutting his 'Sans toi, mamie' and 'N'est-ce pas merveilleux' on successive EPs that met with even less success than the Belgian singer's own work.

### Foreign *yé-yé* girls

Equally deserving was Ria Bartok, a German-born singer who released a string of impressive EPs in France during the mid-sixties. She launched her career in 1963 with a cover of Dickey Lee's 'I Saw Linda Yesterday' ('Parc'que j'ai revu François') that was obliterated by Johnny Hallyday's version ('Parc'que

j'ai revu Linda'). Undaunted, she followed up with a bouncy cover of the old Hank Williams hit 'Hey, Good Lookin' '[620] ('Tu sais me plaire') that compared favourably to a contemporary version by Belgian star Burt Blanca, but again was unsuccessful. Her third EP offered an unfairly overlooked take on Ruth Brown's 'Lucky Lips' ('Sans amour'), inspired by Cliff Richard's UK Top 5 entry.[621] It sat alongside the dramatic ballad, 'Cœur' (adapted from Kenny Chandler's recent US hit, 'Heart'), which had all the necessary ingredients for a smash and duly became one... for Italian singer Rita Pavone, whose version was released in France at the same time and left Bartok's in the starting blocks.

It is possible that Ria Bartok's German-accented vocals were an impediment to chart success, but no such problems afflicted Gillian Hills, whose cool British charm had long made her a favourite among French teenagers. Having lost her way in the summer of 1962, when her cute remakes of Helen Shapiro's 'Walking Back To Happiness' ('Je reviens vers le bonheur') and 'Don't Treat Me Like A Child' ('Mon cœur est prêt') were outsold by the originals, she abandoned cover versions to write her own material. She came back strongly in 1963 with the horn-led floor-filler 'Tu mens' and the jazzily atmospheric 'Ne t'en fais pas', displaying a sophistication far beyond that of most of her rivals. The blues-tinged 'Maintenant il téléphone' offered further proof of Hill's developing talents, but despite her artistic leaps forward, she languished some way behind Sheila in the marketplace. The slinky sounds of 'C'est le garçon' maintained the same high quality into 1964, though she had to regress toward more formulaic teen pop to get a hit with the cutesy 'Qui a su' as she struggled to reassert her presence in what was now an overcrowded market.

Across the border in Belgium, the youthful Rita Dee turned out a pair of lightly rocking efforts, 'Il viendra... le garçon que j'attends' and 'Ne crois pas

---

[620] Doubtless inspired by Connie Stevens' 1962 revival.
[621] It was also a chart-topper for Richard in West Germany as 'Rote Lippen soll man küssen'.

qu'avec moi', but despite some attractive guitar flurries,[622] the record lacked sufficient spark to set her career alight.

Fellow Belgian Catherine Alfa cut the twee 'Tu es pris au piège' (based on Eydie Gormé's 'Don't Try To Fight It Baby') in 1963, but neither this, nor the following year's 'Tu m'as trahie', succeeded in ensnaring the French audience.

Swiss-born Betty Clair crossed over from the world of modelling[623] to try her luck as a singer. She made barely a ripple with 'Quand tu joues avec moi', a pleasant if unremarkable first effort. For the follow-up, she borrowed a leaf from Sheila's book and raided the Tommy Roe catalogue for 'Tout le monde sait tout' ('Everybody'), a convincing attempt at the girl group sound that likewise failed to fly off the racks.

From further afield, Bach Yen and Tiny Yong were a couple of female singers from French Indo-China attempting to carve out a career in Paris during the early sixties. Saigon-born Yen had an enticing style that made her work highly enjoyable, especially the polished 'À bas la rentrée'. Despite heavy television exposure, she failed to score any hits over three EPs and settled instead for a more lucrative career as an international cabaret star.[624]

Yong, from Phnom Penh in Cambodia, enjoyed rather more success thanks to her association with Henri Salvador, to whose label and production house she was signed. After some early misses in a cabaret style recorded under her real name, Thiên Huong, Yong went pop in 1963 with a Salvador-penned adaptation of Roy Orbison's 'In Dreams' ('En rêve') and a hit cover of the Shirelles' 'Foolish Little Girl' ('Tais-toi petite folle'), the first of a short run of hits for her in the first half the decade.

Yong never quite abandoned her cabaret roots, but she proved a dab hand at marrying the old exotica sound with the feel of yé-yé, picking up a hit with 'Un seul garçon sur la terre' (Shirley Jackson's 'The Boy Of The Year'). However, her records were remarkably hit and miss, as if she seemed uncertain where her audience lay. Occasional forays into girl group territory, such as her take on Skeeter Davis's 'I Can't Stay Mad At You' ('Je ne veux plus t'aimer') and her 1964 hit 'Les garçons m'aiment' (the Chiffons' 'When The Boy's Happy') provided the answer and confirmed that this was the direction she needed to take if she was to keep her career afloat.

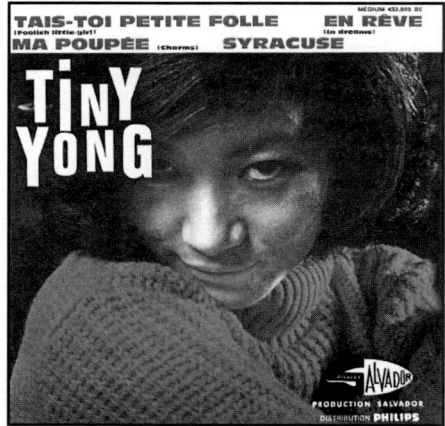

---

[622] These recordings marked the return to rock'n'roll action of jazz guitarist Harry Frékin (aka Rockin' Harry).

[623] Her face appeared on advertisements for Clearasil anti-acne cream – an important part of teenage life then as now.

[624] She went on to work with Bob Hope for several years and also appeared in the 1968 John Wayne film, The Green Berets.

## Françoise Hardy

The biggest new star of *yé-yé*, however, was one who was born and bred in France. Françoise Hardy wrote much of her own material, and she went on to become one of the few French artists of the decade to make a sustained impact on the English-speaking world. Cool, stylish, intelligent and beautiful, she burst into view in late 1962 and quickly came to represent the intellectual end of the *yé-yé* spectrum as one of the few pop singers it was deemed acceptable to like in polite society.

Signed by Vogue, she was launched with a catchy if inane cover of Bobby Lee Trammell's 'Uh Oh' ('Oh oh chéri'). It was a poor recording and failed to sell, but fortuitously she had recorded some of her own songs too, and it was one of these that brought her success. Her debut hit, 'Tous les garçons et les filles', was a sad lament on behalf of teenage wallflowers everywhere. A plaintive, almost folksy number, it was picked up by radio, saving her EP from the bargain bins and selling over a million copies as it charted across much of Europe, laying the ground for a string of smash hits.

Hardy's early recordings were characterised by a restrained sound, with prominent use of acoustic guitar and light string accompaniments on gentle tunes that had many rock'n'roll fans wondering why she got airplay on *Salut les copains* at all. Irrespective of the musical backings, though, there was no doubt that her wistful ballads spoke directly to the heart of the teenage audience, and her follow-up EPs were all huge sellers, with 'C'est à l'amour auquel je pense', 'Ton meilleur ami', 'Le temps de l'amour'[625] and 'L'amour s'en va' (her 1963 *Eurovision* entry, representing Monaco) swamping the airwaves.

With a Chet Atkins-style electric guitar dominating the arrangements, her debut LP, *Françoise Hardy* (simply the contents of the first three EPs cobbled together), was more restrained than most pop albums of the time, relying on her distinctive voice to carry the songs. Indeed, these early recordings could have marked her out as a budding *chansonnière*, but she revealed her true artistic ambitions when she began adding more rock instrumentation

---

[625] A vocal version of Les Fantômes' 'Fort Chabrol', previously recorded under its new title by labelmate José Salcy.

331

to her songs, starting with 'Je pense à lui' (a rare cover, based on the Majors' 'Wonderful Dream') and the lilting ballad 'J'aurais voulu'. These were followed at the end of the year by the Shadow-esque 'Va pas prendre un tambour' and 'Le premier bonheur du jour', a beautifully atmospheric ballad kitted out with a string arrangement that was easy listening gold. It remains one of her loveliest recordings and became one of her biggest international hits. Released in 1963, her second LP[626] attested to her artistic progress, the organ-led 'L'amour ne dure pas toujours' tapping the same sound that would soon deliver international hits to the UK's Georgie Fame.

## Songwriting *chanteuses*

With her ethereal style and ability to look great in almost any fashion, Hardy had few rivals as the classy pin-up of French pop. Musically, too, she was largely in a league of her own, although other record companies quickly set about trying to find her some competition.

Pathé had originally turned Hardy down, thinking she was just reworking the ideas of the now-faded Marie-Josée Neuville, whose mid-fifties hits had been such a breath of fresh air. Neuville had attempted to reboot her career in 1961 with 'Tout recommence', but, despite strong media support, the record had flopped. She tried again at the end of 1962 in the slipstream of Hardy's success, picking up interest for the excellent 'La maison'. Sadly, it wasn't enough to refloat her career, and within a year she was shopping around for a new deal, left stranded as her youthful rival stole centre stage.

Fifties' child prodigy Minou Drouet also failed to make the most of the opportnuities on offer, despite a new deal with the powerful Barclay organisation. Released in 1963, her pretty 'J'ai rendez-vous ce soir avec le clair de lune' was too old-fashioned in its approach to achieve the wistful beauty of Françoise Hardy's recordings. There was no doubting her talent (she had meanwhile published three books of poetry and toured most of Europe), but even at the age of sixteen there was something about her scholarly image

---

[626] Hardy's early albums were all untitled, but her second was (and still is) commonly referred to as *Deuxième album*.

that set her apart from the mainstream teenage market. Even her blatant tip of the hat to passing fads, 'Le twist du bon Dieu', missed its target and, while she remained a well-respected popular figure, she never landed the hit her talent deserved.

Alice Dona's early releases were fine pieces of rock'n'roll-flavoured pop, and the strikingly original and atmospheric 'Mon train de banlieue', the slightly cheesy 'Les garçons', and the jazz-tinged 'C'est pas prudent' were all hits during 1963. However, 1964's 'Je n'sais pas' only managed to struggle into the bottom end of the chart, and a series of miscalculations thereafter sent her spinning into the void. Uncertain which way to jump, Dona first alienated the teen audience with the frightful 'Plus je t'embrasse' (a singalong rendition of the Don Cornell/Alan Dale/Johnny Desmond hit, 'Heart Of My Heart'[627]), then confused the adult market with the teen-pop sound of 'On t'a vu danser', leaving her without any market at all.

Dominique Grange had the right look of seriousness about her, and her 1963 debut EP delivered the thoughtful 'Je ne suis plus ton copain (La lettre)'. Caught midway between *yé-yé* and the *chansons* of the Left Bank that were her preference, she began writing her own material, although her over-earnest attempt at poetry, 'Cinq-en-tin (Le chien)', failed to hit the mark. A third EP, featuring the much better 'Si le soleil s'en va', might have done the trick, but didn't, and by the middle of the decade Grange had abandoned pop altogether in favour of a more cerebral form of *chanson*.

Italian-born Patricia Carli wrote gentle ballads that appealed equally to teens and adults, and sang them with an accent that would have made her a

star during the exotica boom of the late fifties. The upbeat 'L'amour en cage' was an obvious tilt at the youth market, and her breakthrough hit, 'Demain tu te maries (Arrête, arrête, ne me touche pas)', was worthy of Françoise Hardy. It was one of the biggest chart successes of 1963, although most of its sales came from an audience older than the one listening to *Salut les copains*. Her second EP fared less well, despite offering the lush 'Nous on s'aime' and the quality ballad 'Je ne voudrais pas pleurer'. A big-production cover of Gigliola Cinquetti's

---

[627]  Presumably inspired by Trini Lopez's recent version.

1964 *Eurovision*-winner, 'Non ho l'età' ('Je suis à toi'), kept her in the public eye for another few months, but the gentle 'Nous sommes là' and the strident 'Hier, j'ai rencontré ma mère' both failed to click and her sales went into a rapid decline. The richly orchestrated 'L'amour va toujours' similarly fell into the gap that was opening up between the adult and the teen audiences and disappeared without trace.[628]

Stella was another singer who deserved her reputation as an intelligent performer. She set aside the usual teen vapidities to devote herself to the art of satire; although only thirteen years of age, she had a wicked sense of humour. In conjunction with her uncle and collaborator, Maurice Chorenslup, she set about poking fun at the very songs that her peers were buying. Her debut, 'Les parents twist', ridiculed parents trying to be hip in much the same way as Kay Starr's 'The Rock And Roll Waltz' had back in 1955, albeit to a rhythm that was perfect for twisting. A favourite target for her musical barbs was Sheila, who copped it head-on with the *yé-yé* parody 'La surprise est partie'.[629] Too clever by half, Stella never enjoyed even a fraction of the sales accruing to the victims of her humour, but nevertheless gradually built up an audience for her insight and sense of fun, neatly filling a niche that nobody else seemed to want to occupy.

Bessie Smith-style blues singer Colette Magny was an unlikely candidate for pop stardom, but she somehow landed a fluke hit on *Salut les copains* in 1963 with 'Mélocoton', carried along on a catchy keyboard riff that sat somewhere in an undefined middle ground between jazz, blues and pop. Magny cut a handful of similar-sounding commercial efforts, notably the *chanson*-like 'Les Tuileries', but an eclectic style that veered from the percussive 'Monangamba' to a cover of the Louis Armstrong hit, 'St. James Infirmary' (in English), to the jazzy blues of 'Rock me more and more' ensured that her chart presence was only temporary. An assertive performer who had nothing in common with the teenagers who bought her record, she was also fiercely political and ill-suited to pop stardom. She failed to achieve follow-up success, but soldiered on with the music she loved for many years, completely oblivious to the pop market of which she had briefly been a part.

---

[628] Carli nevertheless went on to enjoy a long career as a recording artist and later became a songwriter of some renown.

[629] Even the title recalling Sheila's 'Première surprise-partie' was part of the joke.

# Chapter 20

## L'IDOLE DES JEUNES
### The triumph of *yé-ye* (1963-64)

*One date marks the point at which the youth revolution in French pop was won: 22 June 1963. On that night, Daniel Filipacchi elected to celebrate the first anniversary of the launch of the* Salut les copains *magazine by staging a free concert at the Place de la Nation in Paris with a line-up drawn from the upper echelons of French teen pop. Although the bill for* La Fête de la Nation *included the fast-fading Les Chats Sauvages and instrumental outfit Les Champions, keen to promote the release of new EPs featuring the syrupy 'Dis-lui que je l'aime' and the crackling 'Rendez-vous au Golf Drouot' respectively, the bulk of the show featured singers rather than groups, reflecting the magazine's preference for recognisable faces who could be presented to the readership as 'copains' (pals).*

*Filipacci optimistically expected to draw a few thousand teenagers to the event. To his amazement, 150,000 fans converged on the site from all over Paris, its suburbs and the country at large. Walking, cycling, cruising in on mopeds and motorbikes and in cars, swamping bus, train and Métro services, teenage boys and girls (and a few older fans as well) came together to enjoy the first large-scale free rock concert in history. All order was lost as hundreds of screaming girls scaled the barriers to get at the stars and the scheduled order of appearance was torn to ribbons by the billowing mass of fans, forcing singers to get to the stage as best they could. Despite it all, the event itself passed off comparatively peacefully, though many reporters criticised the music on offer[630] and were appalled both by the size of the crowd and the small-scale violence and vandalism that occurred around the fringes. Nonetheless, it did for* yé-yé *what the* Monterey Pop Festival *would later do for American rock, confirming that there was a huge market for rock and pop music, and that the teenage franc was there for the taking.*

### La Fête de la Nation
Top of the bill was Johnny Hallyday, currently storming the airwaves with the western-styled 'Les bras en croix' and a cover of the Crystals' 'Da Doo Ron Ron' ('Da dou ron ron'), which, although no match for the original, brimmed with his usual energy. Unchallenged as the country's leading male star and often referred to simply as *'L'idole'*,[631] he chalked up further hits with

---

[630] It was this concert that prompted Edgar Morin to coin the expression '*yé-yé*' in his famous article for *Le Monde*.

[631] After his hit from a few months earlier, 'L'idole des jeunes'.

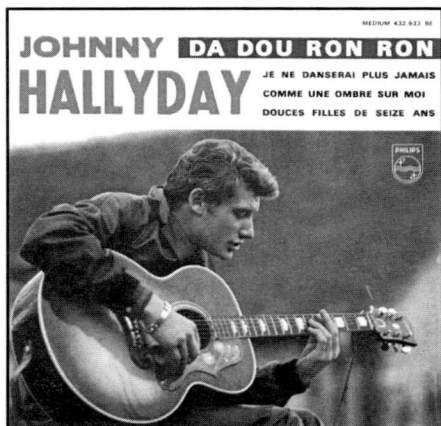

the blues-edged rock'n'roll of Chuck Berry's 'Sweet Little Sixteen' ('Douces filles de seize ans'[632]) and a cover of Bobby Rydell's 'I'll Never Dance Again' ('Je ne danserai plus jamais'). Better still, his film *D'où viens-tu, Johnny?* became a box office smash upon its release in late October and spun off a million-selling EP, with the ballsy 'Ma guitare' and the country-tinged 'Pour moi la vie va commencer'[633] charting across much of Europe.

At Hallyday's side – both on the bill and in real life – was Sylvie Vartan. The show coincided with the release of her second album, *Twiste et chante*, which generated hits with the title track (a cover of the Isley Brothers' 'Twist And Shout') and with 'Ne t'en vas pas' a swinging take on Herbie Mann's 'Comin' Home Baby'.[634] It was a first nod in the direction of the jazz-tinged R&B that was starting to catch on in the late-night clubs of London and Paris. She hit the jackpot at the end of the year with the chart-topping 'Si je chante'[635] (Brenda Lee's 'My Whole World Is Falling Down'). Meanwhile, 'Te voici' (a reworking of Elvis Presley's 'Mean Woman Blues')[636] emphasised her position as the queen of French rock'n'roll. Vartan had recorded the songs in Nashville after deciding that the French studios were unable to deliver the sound she wanted.

Richard Anthony likewise received a rapturous reception at *La Fête de la Nation*. He too was now recording abroad, at EMI's Abbey Road studios in London, where he laid down a cover of the Crystals' 'Then He Kissed Me' ('Et je m'en vais') that outclassed Hallyday's assault on the Phil Spector songbook. This appeared alongside the swinging 'Tchin tchin'[637] and a highly danceable arrangement of the Jaynetts' 'Sally, Go 'round The Roses' ('Rose (parmi les roses)'), topping off a

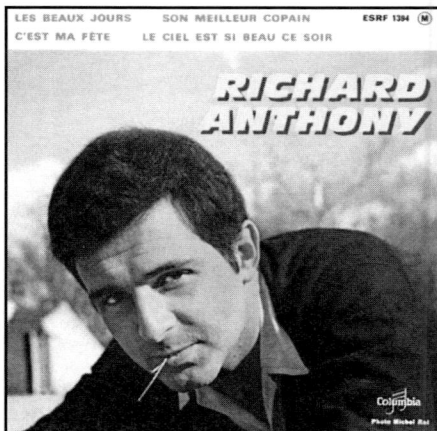

---

[632] Although the lyric was clearly inspired by Berry's original, the arrangement owed more to its recent reworking by the Beach Boys as 'Surfin' U.S.A.'.

[633] Also recorded less impressively by the song's composer, Jean-Jacques Debout.

[634] Clearly inspired by Mel Tormé's vocal version.

[635] It was a No. 1 hit in the *Salut les copains* chart during Vartan's early 1964 season of shows at the Olympia Theatre.

[636] Influenced by a recent cover by Roy Orbison, it was included on the LP *Sylvie à Nashville*, released in early 1964.

[637] An international hit for Anthony, it charted in Italy, Spain and West Germany (in the respective local languages), as well as across much of South America.

year that had already delivered hit renditions of Babs Tino's 'Too Late To Worry' ('Donne-moi ma chance')[638] and Lesley Gore's 'It's My Party' ('C'est ma fête').

**GÉRARD DANYEL**
JE
SORTEZ SANS MOI
TOUJOURS
CETTE GUITARE
ELLE EST TROP LOIN
941 MEDIUM
disc AZ

Further down the bill was Danyel Gérard, the first artist to sign with the new Disc AZ label, owned and run by the boss of radio station Europe No. 1, Sylvain Floirat. Needless to say, Gérard became a favourite on the station – including on *Salut les copains* – and his subsequent releases were all sizeable hits. After scoring with the rocker 'Je', he teamed up with Les Champions[639] for hit covers of Jimmy Gilmer & The Fireballs' 'Sugar Shack' ('Sugar shake') and Trini Lopez's arrangement of 'America' from *West Side Story* to claim his place as one of the country's leading pop vocalists. Gérard also took time out to pen 'Que la vie était jolie' for Dalida before cutting the sweet 'Elle est trop loin' and 'Les roses sont fânées' to win the hearts of female fans across the country.

*La Fête de la Nation* was Frank Alamo's major concert debut, and he followed up his first hits with a run of EPs drawn mainly from the work of the vocal groups then dominating the US hit parade. He scaled the charts with 'À Broadway' (the Drifters' 'On Broadway'), 'Pas de larmes' (the Cascades' 'Shy Girl') and 'Ma mère' (Del Shannon's 'Hey Little Girl'), but overall the sound of his records left a lot to be desired. It was only with 1964's 'Âllo... MAI 38-37?' (Lorraine Gray's 'Are You Getting Tired Of Your Little Toy') that his releases acquired sufficient punch to match those of his main rivals.

**Girl groups**
Also making their debut on the show were Les Gam's, four protégées of Lee Hallyday who had escaped the easy listening hell of Les Djinns to form a girl group in the manner of New York's finest. After their first EP strayed too far into easy listening territory – only 'Adieu bye bye' (a reworking of Leroy Van Dyke's 'Walk On By') hinted at their ability – they finally broke through in 1963 with the vibrant 'Il a le truc' (the Exciters' 'He's Got The Power'). Lead vocalist Annie Markan proved to be one of the more powerful girl singers around and the group's early releases brimmed with teenage *joie de vivre*, despite the fact that the 'girls' themselves were far older than their American role models.

Les Gam's were a revelation to French audiences, capable of turning their hand with equal aplomb to the cavernous thump of Bob B. Soxx & The Blue Jeans' 'Why Do Lovers Break Each Other's Heart?' ('Oui les filles') or the rougher sounds of the Cookies' 'Don't Say Nothin' Bad (About My Baby)' ('Ne dis pas du mal de mon amour'), and throwing down the gauntlet to

---
[638] Which stole the thunder from a hapless version by Gloria Lasso.
[639] Who also backed him at *La Fête de la Nation*.

337

Claude François and Frank Alamo, whose renditions of girl group hits couldn't hold a candle to the power they were able to unleash. They consolidated their position with an excellent cover of the Beach Boys' 'Shut Down' ('Attention! Accident') and an on-the-nail reworking of Lesley Gore's 'Judy's Turn To Cry' ('C'est bien fait pour toi').

Just how good Les Gam's were was thrown into stark relief by the weakness of the competition. The country's first girl group, Les Quatre de Cœur, had begun recording in 1962, but wasted their talent on such unhip material as 'T'aimerai toujours' (a dull adaptation of Elvis Presley's 'Wooden Heart'[640]) and were bypassed by an audience looking for a bit more 'oomph' in their music.

Meanwhile the vocal trio Les B3 offered a slimmed-down version of the girl group sound on passable renditions of Paul & Paula's 'Something Old, Something New' ('Tout ce bleu') and Little Cheryl's 'Mama, Let The Phone Bell Ring' ('Maman ne répond pas') before heading off into the sunset.

Les Jumelles, identical blonde twins who came across as a younger, hipper version of the Kessler Sisters, offered a better alternative. They were among the signings to the Golf Drouot label, but despite waxing a vibrant take on the Orlons' 'South Street' ('Rendez-vous jeudi') and the traffic-stopping 'L'embouteillage', they never expanded their audience into the wider record market.

A similarly hip image should have helped the femme duo Les Ruby Baby to a hit in 1963 with the creditable 'Que faut-il que je fasse', but radio programmers and listeners felt otherwise. Going solo, Nicole Legendre released the creditable 'Ne perds pas la tête' in 1963 and 'J'attendrai demain' (a cover of Dee Dee Sharp's 'Where Did I Go Wrong') in 1964, but soon ran out of steam.

Indeed, Les Gam's' only serious competition came from Les Surfs, a group of six siblings (four male, two female) from Madagascar who were equally at ease with rock, pop or jazz. They kicked things off in 1963 with a fine reading of the Ronettes' 'Be My Baby' ('Reviens vite et oublie') which outshone contemporaneous versions by Sophie and Frank Alamo, and an

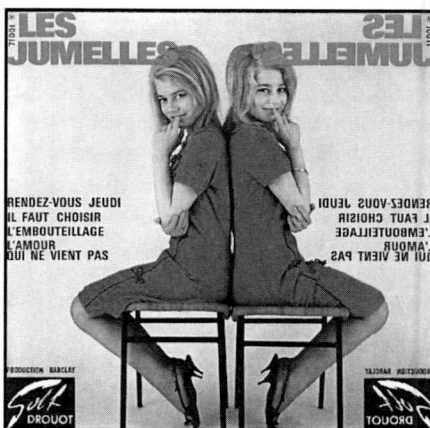

---

[640] Itself adapted from a German folk song called 'Muß i denn' that Presley had picked up whilst on military duty in that country.

even better take on the Essex's 'Easier Said Than Done' ('Pas si simple que ça'). After their cover of 'Si j'avais un marteau' (Trini Lopez's 'If I Had A Hammer') lost out to Claude François, they bounced back in 1964 with a thumping rendition of 'À présent tu peux t'en aller' (Dusty Springfield's 'I Only Want To Be With You') that took the song back to its roots in black American R&B.

Les Surfs benefited from being on the Radio Luxembourg-affiliated Festival label,[641] which enabled them to scoop up airplay that might otherwise have favoured a recording of the latter by Richard Anthony (though he did grab the bulk of it on *Salut les copains*). They also revealed a fondness for rifling through the Phil Spector songbook, most notably the Ronettes' 'Baby I Love You' ('Je te pardonne'), but it was their laid-back interpretation of Betty Everett's 'The Shoop Shoop Song' ('Shoop shoop... va l'embrasser') and the superb 'Chaque nuit' (Barbara Chandler's 'I'm Going Out With The Girls') that were winners at home and abroad, entrenching the group as a popular live draw on the European circuit. Disappointingly, TV appearances in the UK and the US failed to break them into the English-speaking market, but they did become major stars in Italy, where they were regulars at the *San Remo Song Festival* and a constant presence on the airwaves.

### The *yé-yé* singers

Of course, not everybody could appear at *La Fête de la Nation*. Claude François was a notable absentee, although he remained a dominant force on the airwaves with covers of the Angels' 'My Boyfriend's Back' ('Ma petite amie est de retour') and Steve Lawrence & Eydie Gormé's 'I Want To Stay Here' ('Je veux rester seul avec toi'). By the end of the year, François was one of the biggest stars on the block, even if diehard rock fans detested him.

He opened 1964 with a huge hit, 'Chaque jour c'est la même chose' (Steve Alaimo's 'Every Day I Have to Cry'), and continued working fans into a frenzy with his all-singing, all-dancing shows. The thumping 'Petite mèche de cheveux' gave him a smash in the spring, while the more measured 'Maman chérie' (Gene Pitney's 'Twenty-Four Hours From Tulsa') proved the perfect choice to keep older listeners

---

[641] Just as Danyel Gérard benefitted from being on a label owned by Europe No. 1.

happy as well.

Billy Bridge was less successful but he was still in the race, laying down a cover of Neil Sedaka's 'Happy Birthday, Sweet Sixteen' ('On est heureux à 16 ans') in 1963 that transformed the Brill Building pop song into a gutsy rocker. He kept up the campaign with 'Fâchée' and the rampaging 'Ne la fais pas souffrir', a Chuck Berry-esque rocker propelled by a dynamic piano line. However, Bridge remained eternally linked in the public mind to the fading Madison craze and the *blousons noirs* were unimpressed.

Jean-Jacques Debout took time out from penning hits for Johnny Hallyday and Sylvie Vartan to finally register some of his own. 1963's 'Les feux rouges' was an ill-advised and somewhat clumsy attempt to merge rock'n'roll with music of the music hall era, but the guitar ballad 'Nos doigts se sont croisés' proved to be more satisfying for both singer and audience. However, it was the easy listening end of *yé-yé* that proved to be his natural *métier*, and Debout's ability to pen catchy ditties like the understated 'Je ne sais pas, ne sais pas' and the string-swept 'Les filles de ton âge' gave him a ready source of material. The pleasant 'Préviens les amis, préviens les copains' established him in the marketplace, and 'La lanterne rouge', 'Si tu vois Christine' and the mix of *chanson* and pop on 'Aux accords des guitares' all made for most enjoyable listening. However, the silly 'J'embrasse les filles' was far less impressive, though it was a bigger hit. Such musical junk hardly endeared him to serious music fans, and as a result Debout remained a second-tier *idole*, the bulk of his income coming from outside commissions.

At least Debout got into the charts – which was more than many others managed. Jamy Olivier[642] cooked up an appealing version of the Poni-Tails' classic, 'Born Too Late' ('Interdit aux moins de 16 ans') in 1963, and turned the Islanders' 'The Enchanted Sea' into the equally unsuccessful teen ballad 'Un bateau s'en va'.[643]

Surfing the same wave was Jessy, whose two EPs were notable only for the moderately interesting 'Que demandent les jeunes?' and met precisely the same response as a trio of releases by Alain Kan – almost none. Kan was, in fact, a better-than-average vocalist, but formulaic *yé-yé* fluff like 'Tu le sais' (Buddy Holly's 'Everyday') did him few favours and he swiftly disappeared from view.[644]

The same fate befell François Lubiana, whose self-penned 1963 opus 'Ma mie' was undeservedly overlooked. By 1964, he recognised that the pop star game was up, crooning 'Il faut que tu reviennes' ('Over The Rainbow') as

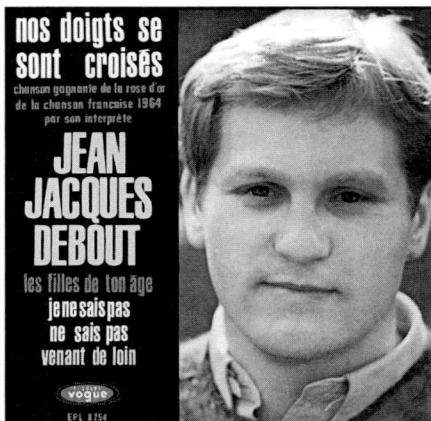

---

[642] Son of fifties' star Anny Gould.

[643] Also recorded, with more commercial success, by Sheila.

[644] Both Jessy and Kan would resurface later in the sixties and seventies, the former as 'Jean-Claude Decamp'.

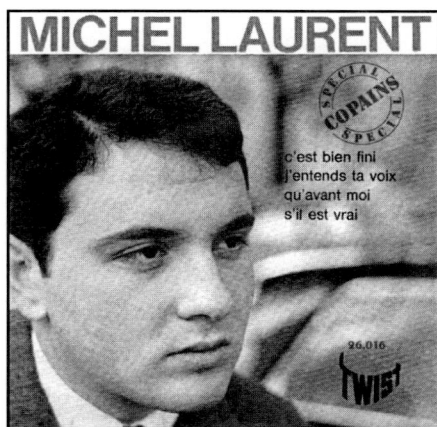

his career disappeared over the horizon.

Also left behind was Alain Gaunay, formerly one half of Swiss duo Les Copains and now intent on a solo career. Despite his talent as a song-writer, his debut solo release, 'Mes belles saisons', lacked the necessary sparkle, offering a weedy organ and a meandering melody in the style of the worst teen drivel. The record flopped, sending him scurrying back over the Alps.

Swedish-born yachtsman-turned-singer Bob Asklöf wooed the ladies with a vocal style that is epitomised by his rendition of Matt Monro's 'From Russia With Love' ('Bons baisers de Russie'). He probably should have stuck to supper-club material, as his interpretations of Frank Sinatra's 'Witchcraft' ('Mon cœur est brisé') and Fred Astaire's 'Night And Day' (in English) were perfect for an older audience. Although he did enjoy a hit in his Swedish homeland with 'Dis-moi pourquoi' (Udo Jürgens' 'Warum nur, warum'), his cover of Terry Stafford's 'Suspicion'[645] ('Obsession') laid bare his limitations as a *yé-yé* singer. Despite covering obvious winners like Bobby Vee's 'The Night Has A Thousand Eyes' ('La nuit ne veut pas finir'), his only French hit was a version of Rick Nelson's 'It's Up To You' ('Il faut choisir'), although even this was outperformed by a better version from Sylvie Vartan.

Only the moody-looking Michel Laurent seemed to have the musical talent to back up his physical attributes. Aided by producer/guitarist Mickey Baker, he debuted in 1963 with a beat-heavy revival of Fats Domino's 'Ain't It A Shame' ('C'est bien fini') cribbed from the recent reworking by the 4 Seasons[646] – although he thankfully didn't attempt to replicate Frankie Valli's falsetto. The record flopped, but Laurent hit the charts later in the year with the circus-themed 'Le pantin', a light rocker that was a favourite on *Salut les copains*. The same EP included two further hits, the fifties throwback, 'Laisse-moi rêver', and the bluesier 'Perdu'. Although his subsequent releases were less successful, the quality seldom dipped and 'Avant de sortir' presented him another hit at the end of the year.

## Vocal group sounds

With the teenage music industry geared toward good-looking solo singers, it was no surprise that vocal groups tended to get short shrift from the pop audience. Although Les Compagnons de la Chanson continued to pack them in at live shows (this despite coming no closer to the pop sounds of the

---

[645] Like Jacky Delmone (see *Chapter 19*), Asklöf was inspired by Stafford's hugely successful 1964 cover version, rather than the Elvis Presley original. The song was also recorded by Les Chats Sauvages.

[646] Like most covers of the song, the 4 Seasons' version was retitled 'Ain't That A Shame', which is what Domino actually sings.

341

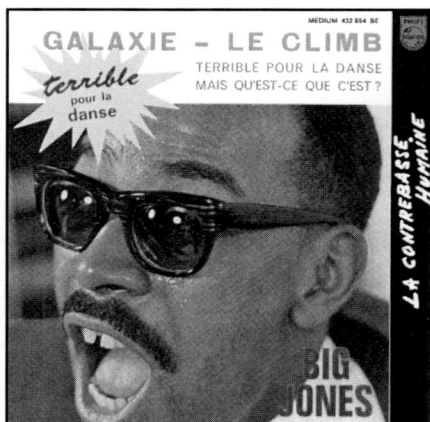

day than a vocal version of the Tornados' 'Telstar'), apart from Les Surfs and Les Gam's none of the newer French singing groups enjoyed much in the way of commercial success.

Les Solistes' claim to fame was that they provided vocal backing on record and stage for Johnny Hallyday. *L'Idole* lent his support to their reworking of Chubby Checker's 'Black Cloud' ('Comme une ombre'), but only to the extent of appearing with them on the EP's cover photo,[647] and none of their other recordings attracted the slightest amount of interest.

Les Célibataires were more interesting, straddling jazz and pop on the dance tune 'Le five', and tackling rougher material like the Rivingtons' 'Papa-Oom-Mow-Mow'. They also tried their hand at the Beach Boys' songbook, picking up a minor hit with a cover of 'Surfin' ', although their take on 'Surfer Girl' ('Ne pleure pas') compared poorly with the original. After their next EP bit the dust, they drifted into easy listening with a revival of Édith Piaf/Les Compagnons de la Chanson's 'Les trois cloches'.

Big Jones, a black American doo-wop specialist, used his deep voice to replace the bass guitar on a version of the instrumental favourite, 'Galaxie'. It was an impressive gimmick, and the nonsense doo-wop 'Mais qu'est-ce que c'est' could have set him up as a rival to Henri Salvador as the country's leading singing clown, but he soon gravitated toward a more adult sound.

Jean-Pierre et Nathalie came on like the French answer to old-fashioned UK duo Miki & Griff, though they also made a pass at a younger audience with the uptempo 'Oh! Ne dis pas' on their 1963 debut EP. Later that year, they went for broke with covers of Paul & Paula's 'Hey Paula' and 'First Quarrel' ('Leur première dispute'),[648] but the teenage audience showed little interest.

### Staying true to rock'n'roll

All of these performers followed the trend toward a more pop-oriented style, but hovering on the fringes were some who refused to accept the idea that rock'n'roll should be watered down.

---

[647] Hallyday also recorded the song himself (as 'Comme une ombre sur moi'), which didn't help their commercial chances.

[648] On which they were backed by Les Fingers.

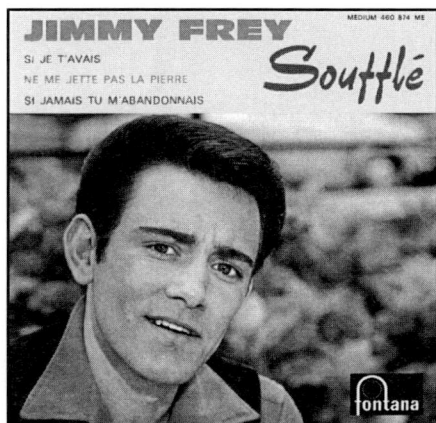

Belgian singer Jimmy Frey was too old to succeed as a teen idol, but he cut an impressive figure on the swinging 'Si jamais tu m'abandonnais' and the fiery 'Soufflé' (a revival of Jerry Lee Lewis's 'Breathless' with lyrics by Eddie Mitchell), one of the harder-hitting records of 1963. Indeed, Frey turned in a breathless performance, but in a world dominated by the young, he didn't fit and the record fell stillborn from the presses.

Frey's fellow countryman William Tay fared no better with the powerful 'Tant pis pour moi', despite a rocking backing by Les Rockets. His cover of the Lafayettes' 'Life's Too Short' ('Bien trop court') made a little noise in Belgium, but with Dick Rivers doing good business with the song in France, it stood no chance south of the border.

Swiss singer Larry Gréco led his group, Les Mousquetaires, through a run of torrid rock'n'roll releases. This approach generated hits with the piledriving Little Richard rip-off 'Mary-Lisa' and the ballsy 'Adieu, il faut partir', on which he fought his way past the strings and horns to transform a slice of routine pop into something special. On the whole, Gréco managed to straddle the line between rock'n'roll and *yé-yé* successfully, and his EPs contained a number of treats, most notably the tight rocker 'J'ai fini de tricher' and the beat ballad, 'Yolène'. A ballsy cover of Elvis Presley's 'Bossa Nova Baby' ('Oui, c'est pour toi'[649]) presented him with a third hit in early 1964, after which he stormed his way through the nihilistic 'Bientôt'. The punky 'Comme chaque fois' anticipated the sounds of American garage bands like the Shadows of Knight, but Gréco was out of synch with the wider pop market and the record ran aground on the *yé-yé* beach.

Rocking duo Les Faux Frères[650] also hailed from Switzerland, where their Everly Brothers-styled harmonies generated winners with the folksy 'Oh! Oui' and a cover of the Americans' retread of Gene Vincent's 'Be-Bop-A-Lula' that picked up from where the now-defunct Les Copains had left off. With a backing group behind them, the boys turned in a perfect imitation of Don and Phil on the rolling 'Quinze ans', and kept the rock'n'roll faith with 'Les cent pas'. Despite the quality of their recordings, they failed to crack the French market,

---

[649] Presley's version was itself a cover of the original by Tippie & The Clovers.
[650] Billed as 'Les (Faux) Frères' on their first EP.

where their beautiful interpretation of the Everlys' 'Some Sweet Day' ('Jours heureux') remained a secret known only to those fortunate enough to catch them drifting over the airwaves from the other side of the Alps.

Back in Paris, the Golf Drouot became the stamping ground of the most lunatic performers yet thrown up by the French rock'n'roll industry. With hair way over his shoulders, a fondness for evening suits, and a chauffeur to ferry him to gigs, Hector was the joker in the pack: Screaming Lord Sutch, French-style. Nicknamed *'Le Chopin du twist'*, he belied his title with a vintage rock'n'roll show that was sadly under-represented on record. After cutting a storming version of Eddie Cochran's 'Somethin' Else'[651] in 1963, he teamed up with comic Jean Yanne to create some wonderfully funny rock'n'roll pastiches, among them 'T'es pas du quartier' and the hysterical diatribe 'Je vous déteste', but he was just too weird for the *Salut les copains* star-making machine. A true rebel without a cause, he won headlines for frying an egg on the eternal flame at the Tomb of the Unknown Soldier, but no amount of publicity could get his records into the charts.

Equally popular at the Golf were Ron et Mel, two brothers from the UK whose most notable recording was a cover of Jan & Dean's 'Surf City' ('Deux filles pour un garçon') which failed to eat into the sales of the original. The EP also saw them in rock'n'roll territory, cutting a swathe through Wilbert Harrison's 'Kansas City', while the follow-up featured the rocking 'Oui, c'est fou'. Regrettably, their acrobatic stage show distracted from their music, and

neither record made even a ripple before the pair returned to the UK.

Tony Victor had already made some unsuccessful recordings for Joe Meek in his native UK[652] before crossing the Channel in 1963 to try his luck in France. His debut EP offered up the passable 'Merci Mr. Armstrong', but by the time of its release French audiences were falling under the spell of a new generation of British performers and his attractive, husky beat ballad 'Oh! Prends ma main' was quickly consigned to the scrap heap.

Altogether more successful was

---

[651] The EP also allowed his band, Les Médiators, to show off their chops on the tasty guitar instrumental 'Tchang'.

[652] Notably a punchy, hard-rocking cover of Larry Finegan's 'Dear One'.

Jacky Moulière, a protégé of Henri Salvador who proved to be the complete package. A frenetic live performer, competent songwriter and more-than-capable singer, the multi-talented Moulière found instant success with covers of Neil Sedaka's 'Next Door To An Angel' ('À deux pas d'un ange') and 'Alice In Wonderland' ('Alice au pays bleu'), while showing off his guitar prowess on 'Jacky la guitare' (Duane Eddy's '(Dance With The) Guitar Man'). Often given sub-standard material like the sickly 'Mon père' (Paul Peterson's 'My Dad'), and occasionally let down by his producer (as on the limp 'C'est la seule fille que j'aime' aka the Crystals' 'He's Sure The Boy I Love'), when he was on form he was superb, as 'Un beau jour' (the Chiffons' 'One Fine Day') attests. Later on in 1963, he cut 'Lam'di lam' ', a storming cover of the Miracles' 'Mickey's Monkey' that led Brian Holland to invite him to come to Detroit and sign with Motown. Declining the offer, Moulière scored another hit in early 1964 with the rumbling rocker 'Tout ou rien', which displayed all of his talents to good effect.

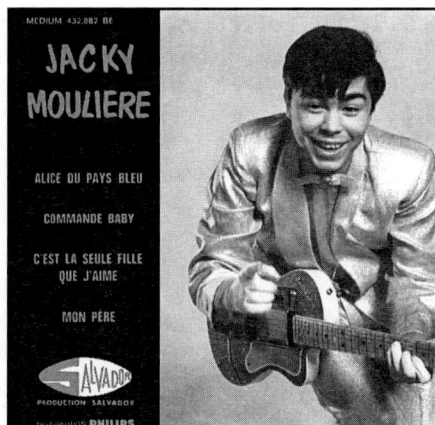

## Breaking up the group

The boom in solo singers vindicated Dick Rivers' decision to go it alone back in 1962. Having got his career on track by the summer of 1963, Rivers went from strength to strength with covers of the Crickets' 'Maybe Baby' ('Mais oui baby') and Roy Orbison's 'Blue Bayou' ('Tu n'es plus là'), keeping him high up the charts as the year drew to a close. While girls screamed over his remake of Cliff Richard's 'Let's Make A Memory' ('Laisse parler ton cœur'), he kept their boyfriends happy with a mid-tempo stroll through Chuck Berry's 'Sweet Little Sixteen' ('T'as seize ans demain'), although the powerful sound he had favoured with Les Chats Sauvages was rarely in evidence. Ever conscious of trends on both sides of the Atlantic, Rivers transformed Fats Domino's 'There Goes My Heart Again' into 'Mon cœur, tu remets ça', but it was his bubbly reworking of Gerry & The Pacemakers' 'How Do You Do It?' ('L'effet que tu me fais') that best sign-posted the future.

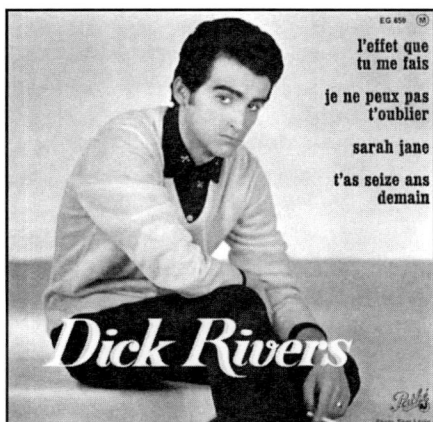

Fortune smiled less kindly upon former Pirate Dany Logan, who launched his solo career with the impressive 'Donne tes seize ans', a Charles Aznavour-penned effort that was inexplicably overlooked by the radio stations.[653] They did pick up on his enjoyable cover of Neil Sedaka's 'Keep A-Walkin' ' ('Vous... les filles'), but his quality interpretation of the Exciters' 'Tell Him' ('Dis-lui') was unfairly buried by a rival reading from Claude François.

Logan should have made the jump to solo stardom, but his rocking updates of Eddie Cochran's 'Summertime Blues' ('Le soleil d'été') and Les Fingers' 'Spécial blue-jeans' both failed to click, while a diversion into Cliff Richard-styled balladry on 'Mon cœur à Juan-les-Pins' was a disastrous error of judgment that saw him moving too far away from rock'n'roll in pursuit of the new *yé-yé* market. Despite a strong track record fronting one of the biggest groups in the country, he suddenly appeared to be a man out of time as his career was ruthlessly steamrollered by the incoming horde of new *idoles*.

Logan was not the only pioneer to find the going tough in the *yé-yé* era. By 1963, Danny Boy, having abandoned his Pénitents to go solo with covers of the Everly Brothers' 'Bye Bye Love' and Little Eva's 'The Loco-Motion' ('Locomotion') – both flops – found himself dropped by his record label, a rapid fall from grace for one of the country's leading rockers. Picking himself up and dusting himself off, he joined the fast-growing Barclay stable and attempted a comeback with the ballad, 'Fin de vacances' (the Crickets' 'Teardrops Fall Like Rain'), for which his former group provided the backing. However, the style didn't suit him and this record also flopped. He persevered with teenage fluff like 'Pourquoi l'été' (adapted from the Fleetwoods' 'They Tell Me It's Summer') and the rather better 'Ma solitude',[654] but these likewise failed to generate much in the way of sales. By the end of the year he too was sagging on the ropes.

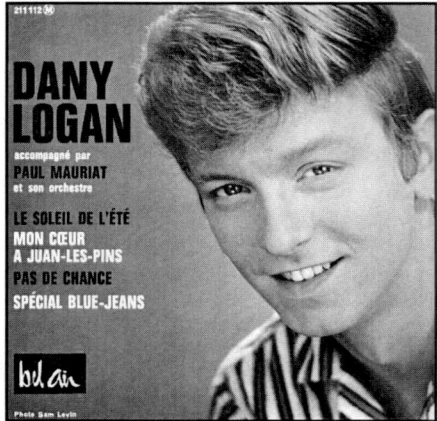

The same fate awaited ex-Vautour Vic Laurens, although he at least managed a few solo hits before the dream went sour. The rocking 'Quand je te suis des yeux' (Rick Nelson's 'I've Got My Eyes On You') got him off to a flying start in 1963, but 'Je ne peux pas t'oublier' (Andy Williams' 'Can't Get Used

---

[653] The risqué lyric hardly helped, and neither did the release of Aznavour's own version of the song.

[654] This was also written by Charles Aznavour, who had established a lucrative sideline penning material for the *yé-yé* market.

To Losing You') was blown off the airwaves by a superior version by Dick Rivers.[655] Laurens' solo recordings lacked the polish that turned less classy performances into gold for the country's *yé-yé* stars, and things got tougher as the competition grew ever more intense. While an impressive version of Elvis Presley's 'Mean Woman Blues' ('Te voici') gave him his biggest solo hit later in the year, ballads like 'Mon cœur sans ton amour' (Frankie Avalon's 'Boy Without A Girl') and 'Seul parmi les autres' (the Elektras' 'All I Want to Do Is Run') did little to satisfy his long-term fans. Although he was still in the race at the end of the year, his time in the spotlight was pretty much over.

### Eddy Mitchell

Laurens' decision to go solo had put an end to Les Vautours, but the ripples this made to the group scene in France were as nothing compared to Eddy Mitchell's seismic decision to go solo as well, effectively killing off Les Chaussettes Noires as a viable proposition. With military service claiming one member after another, there was in any case hardly any group left.

In late 1962, Mitchell made a series of experimental recordings with an orchestra which yielded the commercially successful, if artistically unimpressive 'Mais reviens-moi' (Bryan Hyland's 'The Night I Cried') and the somewhat better 'C'est à nous' (Elvis Presley's 'Something Blue'), but it was a long way from his roots in rock'n'roll. A second EP followed in early 1963, including the hit ballad 'Oui je t'aime' and a jazzy remake of Gene Vincent's (and Les Chaussettes Noires' own) breakthrough hit, now retitled 'Be bop a lula 63',[656] while 'Je ne pense qu'à l'amour' (adapted from Frank Ifield's revamp of Hank Williams' 'Lovesick Blues') reached out across the generational divide to their parents.

After these disappointing releases, Mitchell rejoined the Chaussettes for a final EP which generated two hits in 'Il revient' (Gene Vincent's 'Say Mama') and 'Ne délaisse pas' (Elvis Presley's 'Gonna Get Back Home Somehow') before quitting on a high note in pursuit of wider artistic visions.

On his 1963 LP, *Voici Eddy ...C'était le soldat Mitchell*, he again combined rock'n'roll with large orchestral backings. There was sufficient commitment to the Big Beat on Del Shannon's 'Little Town Flirt' ('Si tu penses') and Sam Cooke's 'Chain Gang' to generate minor hits, although it was a rendition of Cozy Cole's revival of Bob Crosby's 'Big Noise From Winnetka' ('Quand une fille me plaît') that won out on *Salut les copains*. The album also included a credible attempt at Gene Vincent's 'I'm Going Home' ('Je reviendrai'),

---

[655] There were also some interesting covers by Dunkerque's Les Castors and Besançon-based Shadows wannabes Les Panthères.

[656] Presumably inspired by Vincent's own remake, 'Be-Bop-A-Lula '62'.

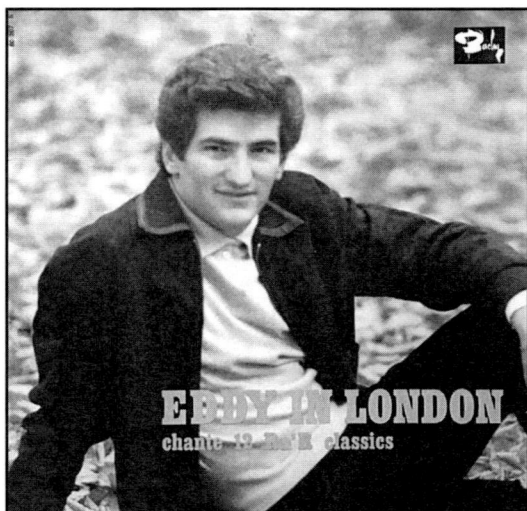

which became a minor hit in late 1963.[657] The remainder, however, was disappointing, and he realised that his new musical direction was taking him towards an artistic dead end.

Following his discharge from the army in September 1963, Mitchell went back to his roots, travelling to London to commence his solo career proper with the album *Eddy in London*. Recording with a team of crack British sessionmen including the legendary Big Jim Sullivan, Reg Guest and Bobby Graham, he ripped through a string of rock'n'roll classics including Gene Vincent's 'Blue Jean Bop', Elvis Presley's 'Baby I Don't Care' and 'Mean Woman Blues' (reworked as 'Sentimentale'[658] and 'Te voici' respectively), a beefy version of Buddy Holly's 'Peggy Sue', and a piano-bashing assault on Eddie Cochran's 'C'mon Everybody' ('Comment vas-tu mentir?'). Moreover, his rearrangement of the latter into a thumping beat stomper in the manner of the newer groups starting to make waves in the UK demonstrated that he was intent on more than simply recreating the sound of his heroes.

He followed up with an EP containing three remnants from the London session including the Doc Pomus & Mort Shuman-penned 'Ma maîtresse d'école',[659] which kicked along to a sliding groove akin to the current work of Johnny 'Guitar' Watson, and a cover of Elvis Presley's '(You're The) Devil In Disguise' ('Tu n'as rien de tout ça') which outclassed a rival version by Johnny Hallyday.

Mitchell was something of an anomaly in this new world of *yé-yé* singers, staying loyal to the harder-edged sounds of good old rock'n'roll. Fiercely championed by Jean-Claude Berthon in *Disco revue*, he retained a loyal following among the country's growing community of '*rockers*'.[660] Hallyday, on the other hand, began to attract criticism for imitating Elvis Presley in courting the teenage girl market. Although Mitchell was not above cutting the occasional slower-paced number himself, such as his late 1962 take on the Presley's 'Angel', *Eddy in London* made no concessions to the *yé-yé* market and sold in the thousands to those who resented the hijacking of rock'n'roll by the likes of Claude François and Frank Alamo.

---

[657] The song had previously been taken to market by Long Chris.

[658] Previously (and less impressively) recorded by Johnny Hallyday as 'Sentimental'.

[659] The original English-language title was 'Don't School A Fool', although it does not appear to have ever been released in that form. Mitchell wrote the French lyrics.

[660] The term used in France to describe fans of real rock'n'roll as opposed to *yé-yé*. 'Rockers' in the British sense of the word (i.e. leather clad bikers and the antithesis of the mods) were '*les blousons noirs*' ['the black jackets'].

## Between *yé-yé* and *chanson*

While Mitchell remained true to rock'n'roll, some young contenders opted for a mature approach, eschewing both rock'n'roll and *yé-yé* for a style that owed more to French *chanson*. One of the better proponents of this new trend was Jean-Claude Annoux, whose 1963 debut EP featured such offerings as 'La messe de Pâques' and 'La fête à la java'. When these failed to set the airwaves alight, he laid down a cover of Gene Vincent's 'There I Go Again' ('Sans que tu t'en doutes') which failed to make the case for him as a rocker. Seemingly unable to decide which direction to take, he set sail for Spanish waters on 1964's 'Le signe du taureau', but neither this, nor the laboured big ballad 'Plus jamais' found enough favour to set him on course for stardom.

Jacques Revaux was best known as a lyricist adapting American hit tunes for others, although he had attempted to foster a parallel singing career since 1959. In 1963, he made an unsuccessful bid for glory with a cover of Cliff Richard's 'Summer Holiday' ('Quand revient l'été'),[661] and tried again later in the year with an acceptable take on Billy Adams' 'Go (Go On, Get Out Of Here)' ('Va, va-t'en'), plus covers of two girl group classics, the Crystals' 'He's A Rebel' ('J'attendais') and the Four Pennies'[662] 'My Block' ('Oh! Peggy'), but these added nothing to the originals and the EP did little to bolster his hopes of making it as a singer.

Claude Nougaro was another who refused to conform to the rules of teen popdom. Essentially a jazzman, he succeeded in being accepted as a sort of French answer to Ray Charles, delivering jazzy *chansons* in a warm, soulful

voice that found a wide following among teenagers and adults alike. Championed as an 'acceptable' star by the less excitable teen press (such as the Communist Party-run *Nous les garçons et les filles*) and with a new record contract from Philips in his pocket, he dusted off four years of disappointment and picked up regular airplay on *Salut les copains* with his smooth-rolling 1962 release, 'Une petite fille'. So strong was the EP that all four tracks were hits in their own right, the late-night shuffle 'Le cinéma' and the bluesy 'Les Don Juan' finding favour

---

[661] The fact that Dalida also recorded the song probably didn't help.
[662] A pseudonym used for this release by the Chiffons.

with the 'cool' crowd, and the airy, upbeat 'Le jazz et la java' winning him a somewhat older audience.

Tours alongside the likes of Johnny Hallyday helped to consolidate his position, making Nougaro one of the few older performers along with Charles Aznavour and Gilbert Bécaud still greeted warmly by the teenage audience. His next EP sold less well, but 1963 saw him back on top, promoting the lyrical 'Les mines de charbon' on television, although it was the pretty 'Cécile, ma fille' that provided him his biggest hit. He retained a large following across the generations until he was sidelined later in the year by a road accident that put him out of action for some considerable time.

### Singers getting ever younger

Fifteen-year-old Michel Berger wrote his own candyfloss-pop confections and lit up the hearts of pre-pubescent schoolgirls everywhere. A decent melodist with a flair for irresistible musical hooks, he wasn't at all bad and his debut release, 'Tu n'y crois pas', became a hit on the back of copious airplay on *Salut les copains*. His early releases were pure pop, typified by the subject matter of 'Amour et soda', and his face featured regularly in the teen press, even though sales of his records actually offered little to celebrate.

Even younger was Le Petit Prince,[663] an eleven-year-old from Switzerland who was launched to stardom in 1963 as the opening act on Claude François' end-of-year live shows. A cute novelty act foreshadowing the seventies' triumphs of Little Jimmy Osmond, he enjoyed significant, if short-lived success beginning with the nauseating late 1963 smash, 'C'est bien joli d'être copains'. Jean-Jacques Debout joined François in supporting the youngster's aspirations, penning 'C'est pas drôle' for him to deliver in his twee, irritating manner. Both this and the awful 'La copine que j'ai choisie'[664] (Jan Burnette's 'The Boy That I Used To Know') featured backing by Les Aiglons, but even such stellar support failed to prevent his career from sliding inexorably downwards as the novelty wore off. Undaunted, the Prince bounced his way through 'Evy aime Jerry' (Donna Lynn's 'Donna Loves Jerry'), threatened but failed to turn into a rocker on the self-penned 'Ma sœur et moi', and reworked the 4 Seasons' 'Rag Doll' into a dire Christmas song, 'Triste Noël'. He managed a few more hits in 1964, most notably the pleasantly crooned 'Tout sauf une rose', before his voice broke and he retired from the fray to a chorus of relief.

Such was the obsession with youth that France also produced a female

C'EST BIEN JOLI D'ETRE COPAINS
MAMAN NE M'A JAMAIS DIT
J'AIME BIEN LES FILLES
C'EST PAS DROLE

---

[663] Born Pascal Krug, he took – or was given – his stage name from the classic children's story by Antoine de Saint-Exupéry.

[664] It wasn't a bad song, so much as an awful recording – as was proven when Les Bourgeois de Calais turned out a fine version a few months later.

*Malika with producer Lee Hallyday.*

equivalent to Le Petit Prince in the person of Patricia Patoune, an equally winsome figure with a toothy grin. She wisely devoted most of her attention to recording children's ditties, but dipped a toe into the pop market with 'Quand j'aurai l'âge', without success.

Rather more impressive than Patoune was the rapidly maturing Malika, who moved on from Arabic twist novelties to a swinging adaptation of Brenda Lee's 'Anybody But Me' ('L'amour est fini') without anybody noticing. Attempting a career relaunch, she changed her name to Maguy Banon[665] for 'Je m'éveille à l'amour', a rhythmic effort that sat alongside the catchy 'Je suis trop jeune pour aimer' and a cover of Christine Quaite's 'Tell Me Mama' ('Dis-moi Maman') on an EP that went down the dustpipe shortly after its release in 1964.

Fulfilling the demand for a 'French Brenda Lee' more successfully was thirteen-year-old Jocelyne, who debuted in 1964 with the doo-wop-styled 'La vie c'est bon' and a full-tilt assault on Darlene Love's 'A Fine Fine Boy' ('Il a tout pour lui'), complete with a big Spectorian production as yet unmatched in France. Next up were the excellent 'J'ai changé de pays' (Jackie DeShannon's 'Heart In Hand') and the catchy 'Le dimanche et le jeudi'

(Brenda Lee's 'Lonely Lonely Lonely Me'), both of which became hits as spring merged into summer. Far younger than most of her rivals, Jocelyne quickly established herself as one of the most accomplished girl singers in the country, reinforcing her pop credentials with the magnificent girl group sounds of 'Les garçons' (Lesley Gore's 'Boys'), and restating her fondness for Brenda Lee with a thumping cover of her 'Is It True' ('Oui j'ai peur') that made mincemeat of a rival version by Frank Alamo.

With a powerful voice that belied

---

[665] Her real name was Allegria Banon. She would later also record as 'Tina'.

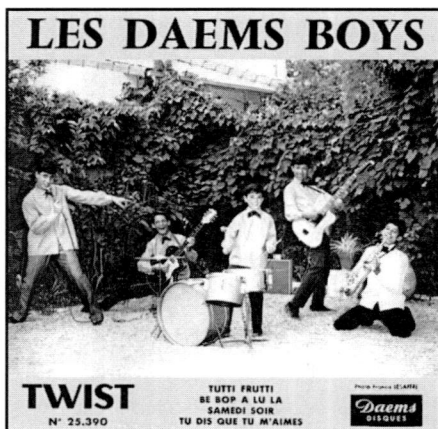

her young age, Jocelyne stunned audiences with her show-stopping rendition of Édith Piaf's 'Exodus' (a highlight of her 1965 LP, *Jocelyne*) and should have gone on to be a major star. Unfortunately, she lacked a clear-headed manager who could steer her through the pitfalls of early fame, and she never came close to challenging the hegemony of Sylvie Vartan and Sheila.

The fad for youth reached its zenith with Les Daems Boys, a group from Grenoble featuring eleven-year-old drummer Michel Torelli. They made some amateurish and utterly dreadful recordings of staples like Little Richard's 'Tutti Frutti' and Johnny Hallyday's 'Sam'di soir'[666] for a 1964 EP on the Daems label which allowed them a few minutes in the spotlight before somebody thankfully realised that they ought to be in school and put the brakes on their career.

Equally unpolished but rather more competent, Toulouse-based Germinal Tenas et les Caïds shone on a dance-floor-friendly rendition of Chris Montez's 'Rockin' Blues' ('Tu es trop belle'), but neither this, nor the decent rocker 'Sitôt qu'elle est là' (Cally Dodd's 'You've Discovered Love') managed to pull the group out of obscurity. However, regular airplay on Radio Andorra ensured them some sales in the South-West.

### The *yé-yé* girls

Sheila hit a rough patch at the start of 1964, when a below-par cover of the Fourmost's 'Hello Little Girl' ('Hello petite fille') on her fifth EP failed to match the success of her late 1963 hit, 'Le sifflet des copains'. The rest of the record was similarly upbeat, but neither 'L'ami de mon enfance', nor the party rhythms of 'Oui, c'est pour lui' did more than scrape the bottom of the charts. Any sense of panic this might have aroused was short-lived, for she soon resumed the onward march to superstardom with 'Chaque instant de chaque jour' (a cover of Dionne Warwick's 'Any Old Time Of Day') which outsold a competing version by Dalida.

Françoise Hardy continued to triumph, scoring heavily with 1963's 'Qui aime-t-il vraiment' and the following

---

[666] Listed as 'Samedi soir' on the sleeve of the Daems Boys' EP.

year's 'Pourtant tu m'aimes' in a run of hits across most of Europe. Thereafter, she set her sights on recording in the UK, releasing a beat-heavy English-language arrangement of Perry Como's 'Catch A Falling Star' in 1964 to establish herself on the UK pop scene. Her second British single, a belated issue of her 1962 French smash, 'Tous les garçons et les filles', made the UK Top 40. Recording material in both English and French, Hardy experimented with different producers before finding a kindred spirit in UK girl group specialist Charles Blackwell. Under Blackwell's auspices, she cut the fuzz-guitar-decked 'Je n'attends plus personne' (adapted from Little Tony's 'Non aspetto nessuno'[667]) and the cantering 'Je veux qu'il revienne' (also cut in English as 'Only You Can Do It') – records which confirmed her status as one of the major pop vocalists in the world. She followed up with the Spectoresque 'Et même', which gave her a second Top 40 UK hit at the start of 1965.[668]

Petula Clark was unable to replicate Hardy's success in the UK, where none of her English-language singles had made the charts since 'I'm Counting On You' stalled at No. 41 and dropped from view in February 1962, with later singles like 'Baby It's Me' and 'Thank You' being roundly ignored. Clark nevertheless continued to score hits in France and elsewhere in Europe with the likes of Lesley Gore's 'She's A Fool' ('Entre nous il est fou') and the Shadows-influenced 'Prends garde à toi'. In terms of quality, there was little to separate the records being released on either side of the Channel, so Clark's inability to maintain her profile in her homeland was undeserved.[669]

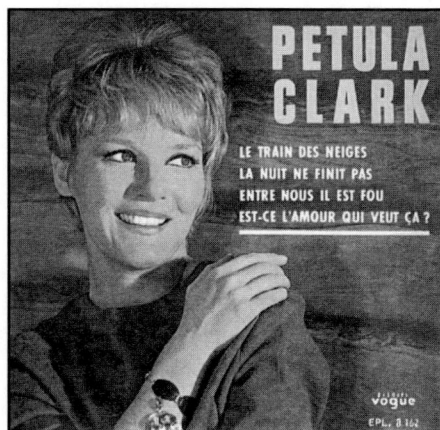

In France, she finished off the year with the engaging 'Est-ce l'amour qui veut ça?' and 'Le train des neiges', opening 1964 with a superb cover of Dionne Warwick's 'Anyone Who Had A

---

[667] Later recorded in English by Lesley Gore as 'I Cannot Hope For Anyone'.

[668] Hardy also recorded 'Et même' and 'Tous les garçons et les filles' in English (as 'However Much' and 'Find Me A Boy' respectively), but it was the French-language originals that made the UK charts.

[669] Especially considering that 'Baby It's Me' had much in common with the sound that was turning to gold for her producer Tony Hatch's latest signings, the Searchers. Clark later blamed her commercial decline on her fans viewing her relocation to France as a desertion, although it probably had as much to do with the UK experiencing a sea change in listening tastes at the time as the beat group boom got underway.

Heart' ('Ceux qui ont un cœur'). This should have given her a chance in the UK market, but she never recorded it in English, stymied by a contemporaneous cover by new Brit girl-about-town Cilla Black.

Petula Clark and Sheila were not alone in plundering the repertoire created for Dionne Warwick by the Burt Bacharach & Hal David songwriting team. Les Surfs had a go at 'You'll Never Get To Heaven' ('Tu n'iras pas au ciel'), but Warwick's best French interpreter was Nancy Holloway, who had recently quit budget label work to launch her career with a smoky version of the Cliff Richard/Peggy Lee hit, 'I'm Looking Out The Window' ('Déjà le jour se lève'). Her jazzy intonation was perfect for the three hits she enjoyed during 1963: Warwick's 'Don't Make Me Over' ('T'en vas pas comme ça'),[670] the Bob Crosby standard, 'Big Noise From Winnetka'[671] and a well-executed reworking of Jackie Wilson's 'Sing, Sing, Sing' ('Chante').[672] Despite a continuing run of classy EPs, only 1964's 'Désappointée' (Dionne Warwick's 'Disappointed') built on this commercial promise, although the bluesy 'Tu n'es pas venu' (Wanda Jackson's 'Whirlpool') and the soulful 'Prends tes clés', which gave Holloway the chance to stretch out and really sing, were a better reflection of her talents.

Rosy Armen moved on from the twist to mix 'exotic' pop songs like Los Hermanos Rigual's 'Cuando calienta el sol' ('Quand le soleil était là') with occasional R&B covers like her 1962 punt at Ben E. King's 'Stand By Me' ('Tu croiras').[673] Unconvincing on such contemporary material, she quickly abandoned the attempts at teen appeal in favour of a career as an adult-orientated pop singer, going on to enjoy moderate success with a more original repertoire.

Marion's melancholy 'Ils ont voulu nous séparer' saw her aiming at the Françoise Hardy end of the market, but, as this particular niche was firmly filled, she found no more commercial reward than British-born Vency, who had the requisite toothy grin but little else to offer. Having set up home in Versailles, Vency laid down two EPs of pedestrian pop-by-numbers featuring disposable ditties like 'N'hésite pas' (Grazina Frame's 'Don't Be Shy') and 'Quand tu m'as demandé' which were rightly avoided by discerning record buyers.

Fellow Brit Patti Lynn was a singer with real potential. She had charted in the UK back in 1962 with a cover of Shelley Fabares' 'Johnny Angel', but when she tried to find fame in France in 1964 with the girl group-styled 'Stop c'est merveilleux' (adapted from the 1939 Orrin Tucker hit, 'Stop! It's Wonderful'), she found herself eclipsed by Sheila's ever-lengthening shadow.

Anne Kern from Lyon sounded convincing on her 1964 effort, 'Mon copain, mon amour', but not enough to persuade people to actually buy the record. Two more EPs appeared in quick succession, mostly containing original songs like 'Mon bonheur c'est toi' rather than covers, but they were

---

[670] Also cut by Les Surfs.
[671] As recently revived by Cozy Cole and Eddy Mitchell. She used the same lyrics as Mitchell, with appropriate gender changes, for her version, 'Quand un garçon me plaît'.
[672] This effortlessly outclassed a contemporary cover by Sheila ('Chante chante chante').
[673] Also covered by Dalida the following year under the same title, and by François Lubiana as 'Vienne la nuit'.

*France Gall, unknown venue, 1964.*

not strong enough to find a home on the airwaves and she disappeared from view as quickly as she had arrived.

The only singer to mount an effective challenge to Sheila as queen of school-girl pop was France Gall, a bubbly teenager with a pleasantly squeaky voice who announced her arrival in 1963 with the chirpy 'Ne sois pas si bête' (the Laurie Sisters' 'Stand A Little Closer'). Daughter of songwriter Robert Gall, the doll-like singer was in many ways the ultimate *yé-yé* girl: cute without being cloying, innocent without being overly childish, and enthusiastic above and beyond the call of duty. Although she was hardly the world's greatest vocal stylist, her naive little-girl charm enabled her to transcend sometimes mundane material and turn rough diamonds like the inane but catchy 'Ça va je t'aime'[674] into pop gems.

Gall was in many ways a textbook example of a *yé-yé* starlet, with well-placed show-business connections opening the doors to the record industry before she had ever walked onto a stage. If Sheila was the prototype, then Gall was the finished article, and though she rarely touched the commercial heights reached by her rival, artistically she quickly moved way out in front. Conveying an impression that she was younger than her sixteen years, she found an audience among pre-teens and parents alike, the latter drawn to her penchant for jazzy arrangements like the Dave Brubeck-styled 'Pense à moi'.

Gall's real talent, though, was delivering high-class, bouncy pop and her debut EP set her off on a run of similarly infectious hits. Her second offered further variations on the teen-pop formula like 'Si j'étais garçon' and the pretty ballad, 'Les rubans et la fleur', but she really hit her stride when she joined forces with songwriter Serge Gainsbourg for the infectious 'N'écoute pas les idoles'.

Gainsbourg, who had long been a favourite among music hall *chanteuses*, had earlier assisted actress Brigitte Bardot with her debut album

---

[674] A track on her debut EP, this later became a substantial hit for her in Quebec.

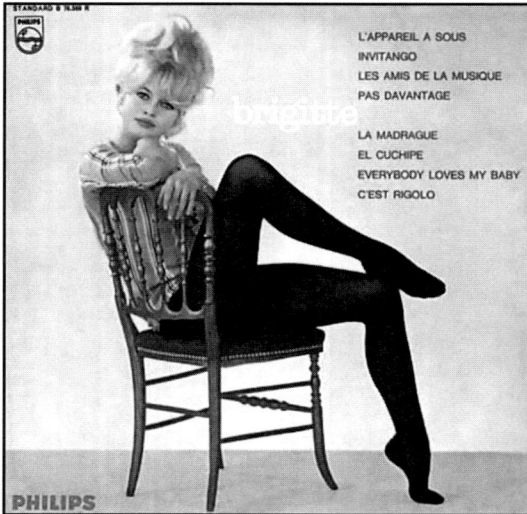

after she landed a surprise hit with the acoustic ballad 'Sidonie'[675] in 1962. Released in early 1963, the LP *Brigitte*[676] was a worthwhile effort which generated hits with the nostalgic 'La Madrague'[677] and Gainsbourg's witty, *yé-yé*-styled 'L'appareil à sous'. Playing on Bardot's image as a sex symbol, the more mature 'Je me donne à qui me plaît' was another excellent offering from Gainsbourg's pen, but it was the mock-Latin 'Invitango' that provided yet another hit from the set. Veering from the jazz of 'C'est rigolo' to the easy listening of 'Rose d'eau', the album was too diverse to take the teenage franc, though the combination of Bardot's charming vocals and Gainsbourg's typically twisted lyrics on the two songs in which he had a hand revealed to him that a shift from *chanson* to *yé-yé* might be worth pursuing.

With every month throwing up a new *idole* for the youth market to devour, keeping track of who was hip and who wasn't became an increasingly demanding task. Reading and listening to *Salut les copains* became an ever more essential part of life for French youth as both the magazine and the radio show took a stranglehold on the *yé-yé* market. Proof of the show's omnipotence, if any were needed, came when Daniel Filipacchi decided that the cartoon character Chouchou, who served as the magazine's mascot, should become a pop star. Subjecting Jean-Jacques Debout's voice to a Chipmunks-style treatment, he wound up with a pair of best-selling EPs for his pains, the first of which included the hit 'Johnny, Françoise et Sylvie', an all-too-obvious tribute to the three leading *idoles* which climbed the charts in the summer of 1964. History does not record whether Debout was miffed to see Chouchou's records selling better than his own, but the royalties would have provided welcome compensation.

By the end of 1963, it seemed that the music industry and France as a whole was obsessed with the activities of the *yé-yé* stars. Indeed, a casual observer might have been forgiven for assuming that the traditional forms of French pop had been all but wiped out. However, nothing could have been further from the truth. Away from the glare of the front pages of the music press, traditional *variétés* was not only enjoying the same level of success, but was even undergoing a creative renaissance.

---

[675] The theme from Louis Malle's 1962 film, *Vie privée*, in which she also starred.
[676] It was available in both 10" (eight-track) and 12" (twelve-track) formats.
[677] A tribute to her luxury mansion of the same name in Saint-Tropez.

# Chapter 21

## NON, JE NE REGRETTE RIEN
### Evolution and counter-revolution (1961-64)

*The triumph of yé-yé in France was greeted with a groan of disapproval by the self-appointed guardians of the country's morals and culture, its critics sniping at the supposed lack of melody and the preponderance of inane lyrics. While this seems in retrospect to have been a collective case of tin ears that completely missed the music's appeal, for those who felt lost in a sea of alien sounds, comfort was close at hand. Away from all the noise, the old-timers of music hall and* chanson *(many of whom, ironically, had aided and abetted the rise of rock'n'roll in the first place) were going about their business as before, turning out records as good as, or better than, those they had released in the days before rock music shattered the silence.*

### The stars of *chanson*

The growth in popularity of teen pop was counterbalanced by a similar upsurge in demand for a more poetic form of popular music, perhaps as a reaction to the juvenile inanities favoured by the young. Certainly, sales of Jacques Brel's records saw a sudden uplift at the start of the sixties and remained consistently high throughout a decade in which he stamped his mark ever more firmly on the evolution of the *chanson*.[678]

Released in 1962, Brel's first LP for Barclay[679] was a massive success,[680] spinning off a hit with 'Les bourgeois', on which his wickedly funny lyric pointed the finger at both the petty bourgeoisie and their young critics, fated to become those whom they deride, while the bittersweet 'Rosa' likewise shone a spotlight on the frauds he was eager to expose. Brel's new songs adopted a more conversational flow, and, stripped of the orchestration that had overpowered his earlier work, the album allowed the words to breathe, bringing to life the German soldier in 'Casse-Pompon' and the over-eager youth stood up by the flirtatious 'Madeleine', while looking homeward with rare affection on 'Bruxelles'[681] and the moving 'Le plat pays'.

---

[678] It would, however, be a mistake to assume that Brel's audience was necessarily older. A considerable portion of the youth market also flocked to his concerts, even if he was never heard on the airwaves during *Salut les copains*.

[679] The abum was untitled, but is informally known as *Les bourgeois*. It was available in both 10" (eight-track) and 12" (twelve-track) formats.

[680] This despite the release by Philips of a 'spoiler' LP featuring several of the new songs recorded in concert at the Olympia Theatre before he left the label.

[681] Covered in fine style two years later by Frida Boccara.

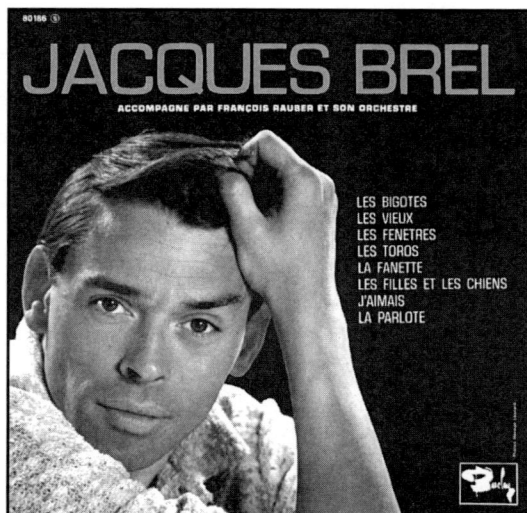

LES BIGOTES
LES VIEUX
LES FENETRES
LES TOROS
LA FANETTE
LES FILLES ET LES CHIENS
J'AIMAIS
LA PARLOTE

As Brel's assaults became ever more direct, ruthlessly slamming the hypocrisies he saw in polite society, so his sales continued to rise. Issued in 1963, his second Barclay LP[682] generated hits with 'Les bigotes', a rant in search of a tune; 'Les vieux', a spooky ballad about the desperation of being old; and 'Les toros', a condemnation of the bullring that served as a wider metaphor for inhumanity. And, while the cutting but misogynistic 'Les filles et les chiens' attracted some criticism, Brel was equally capable of being tenderly nostalgic, as on the lovely 'La Fannette'.

Georges Brassens was also willing to experiment with gentle orchestrations, though the guitar remained his principal form of musical expression. His ninth LP, 1962's *Georges Brassens No. 9*, used a light orchestral backing to add colour to the tracks, particularly on the ballad 'Les amours d'antan'. Highlights included a bouncy tune about the First World War, 'La guerre de 14-18', which upset the country's veterans (no doubt the provocative Brassens' intention) and the self-mocking 'Les trompettes de la renommée'. He experimented with a medieval ballad feel on 'Je rejoindrai ma belle', while 'Jeanne' saw him adopting an almost free-verse approach to the

léo ferré

la langue française
mister giorgina
les bonnes manières
l'on chouette
ça s'va
la vie est louche
ça s'lève à l'est
la vieille pèlerine
les tziganes
ep love
plus jamais
t'es rock, coco!

art of lyric writing. Brassens followed up the album in 1964 with the film theme 'Les copains d'abord', a smash hit on which he varied his style to include a hint of boogie-woogie in its Django Reinhardt-styled arrangement.

Léo Ferré likewise found himself with a steadily growing audience, albeit not quite as large as that enjoyed by Brel or Brassens. His style continued to evolve through 'T'es rock, coco!', which, along with the dramatic 'Mister Giorgina' and the easy listening 'La vie est louche', was a highlight of his

---

[682] All of Brel's early Barclay albums were untitled. This one is informally known as *Les bigotes*, and, like the following three, was only available as a 10" release.

1962 LP *La langue française*, the title track of which vigorously defended the French language against increasing anglicisms. Ferré found his most loyal fans on the Parisian concert circuit, and some of his shows were captured for posterity on the live albums *Récital Léo Ferré à l'Alhambra* (which included the stunning 'Thank you Satan') and *Flash! Alhambra – A.B.C.* (featuring the show-stopping anti-de Gaulle diatribe, 'Mon général'), heightening his reputation among those who regarded him, rather than Brel, as the future of the *chanson*.

Catherine Sauvage fared less well, her 1961 reading of Ferré's 'Jolie môme' losing out to an interpretation by Juliette Gréco. Undeterred, she kept her finger on the pulse with a 1962 EP featuring four songs by Serge Gainsbourg, including the late-night jazz of 'Black trombone' and 'Baudelaire',[683] and the otherwise unavailable 'L'assassinat de Franz Lehar'. More successful were a brace of EPs given over to the Kurt Weill songbook, where Sauvage shone with her interpretations of 'La chanson de Barbara' and 'La fiancée du pirate'. Themed LPs dedicated to individual writers, such as *Catherine Sauvage chante Louis Aragon*, *Chansons de Louis Aragon* and two volumes of *Catherine Sauvage chante Léo Ferré* kept her in the public eye, alhough she would never regain the popularity she had enjoyed during the fifties.

Juliette Gréco, on the other hand, was able to retain a dedicated following, enjoying considerable airplay in 1962 with the Gainsbourg composition 'Accordéon'. She raised eyebrows with 'Les mariés', a frank discussion of marital unhappiness, before delivering a top-notch rendition of Gainsbourg's 'La javanaise' a year later. Although not as smooth as the composer's own version, Gréco's proved the more popular of the two and her support did much to boost Gainsbourg's public profile. For Gréco, though, record sales always took second place to live

---

[683] A rare example of Gainsbourg setting music to somebody else's words – in this instance, the poet Charles Baudelaire.

performances, her only albums of the period being drawn from concert seasons in Paris in 1962 (*Juliette Gréco à l'A.B.C.*) and 1964 (*Juliette Gréco à Bobino*).

Gainsbourg meanwhile remained in the background, enjoying success by proxy with the much-covered 'La chanson de Prévert', which by now was well on its way to becoming his first 'standard',[684] and a 1963 cover of 'Vilaine fille, mauvais garçon' by Petula Clark. The occasional inclusion of rock'n'roll rhythms in his work (such as 1961's 'Le rock de Nerval') did little to find him an audience, while his 1962 release, 'Requiem pour un twisteur', was set to one of the least twistable rhythms ever – which may have been the point, but would hardly have helped the song find a home on *Salut les copains*, or anywhere else for that matter.

In 1963, Gainsbourg released the *Confidentiel* album, which included his first real play for the youth market, 'Chez les yé-yé', although nobody paid it much attention at the time. This was a shame, as it was his strongest set to date, with the wordplay of 'Elaeudanla Téïtéïa' and 'Le temps des yoyos' wrapped around catchy melodies that were the equal of anything on offer from the rest of the country's *chansonniers*. A year later, he dabbled in Latin and African rhythms on *Gainsbourg percussions*, another excellent set including the tribal chant 'New York – U.S.A.' and the Latin swinger 'Couleur café'.[685] When these sophisticated word games and up-to-date sounds failed to sell, Gainsbourg reflected on the sales he had enjoyed when writing for *yé-yé* chanteuse France Gall and decided to turn his back on *chanson* to enter the *yé-yé* market as a songwriter for hire.

### Left Bank *chanson*

Suzanne Gabriello had built up a modest following during the late fifties[686] with her parodies of other singers, and she continued to perform in the cafés and theatres of the Left Bank during the new decade. In 1963, she teamed up with Les Players for 'Rata twist', which worked both as a parody and a genuine twist record, and satirised the *yé-yé* craze with the rocked-up nursery rhyme 'Le kilomètre à pyé yé yé', but the subtleties of her work were lost on most of the record-buying public. Two years later, she turned her attention

---

[684] It was covered by Gloria Lasso and a host of others.
[685] The same swinging vibe also coloured the work of Robert Cartier, who debuted in 1964 with the 'Deux allers pour l'amour' (Brook Benton's 'Two Tickets To Paradise'), a surprisingly cool effort that deserved a wider hearing.
[686] She was also Jacques Brel's paramour at the time, and the inspiration for his 'Ne me quitte pas'.

away from *yé-yé* to take a pop at the *chanson*, reworking Brassens' 'Les copains d'abord' as 'Les potins d'abord'.

Boby Lapointe offered a richly varied repertoire, indulging in deft verbal acrobatics on 'Ta Katie t'a quitté' and the Hawaiian-flavoured 'La peinture à l'huile', lampooning the Central European kletzmer sound on 'Bobo Léon' and gently ribbing the world of *Salut les copains* with the pastiche 'Eh! V'nez les potes'. However, despite the quality of his output, he proved to be too cerebral for the wider audience and, like Gainsbourg, languished in undeserved obscurity.

Ricet Barrier had bowed out of the fifties with a strong EP featuring the inventive 'Neurasthénie' and the neoclassical 'L'espionne'. His second LP, 1962's *Ricet Barrier 2*, was equally worthwhile, containing standouts like the witty 'Rendez-vous (Stanislas)', 'Quatorze juillet bizarre' and 'Sur les bords de la Loire', an amusing account of riverbank life set to an old-school jazz backing. Sadly, he was left behind as the pop explosion rocked the world. Despite releasing several EPs over the next few years, the highlight of which was 1963's so-silly-it-was-good 'La java des hommes-grenouilles', the general public remained unimpressed.

Once again, Les Frères Jacques came calling, laying down a superb version of 'Rendez-vous (Stanislas)' – one of nearly two dozen songs they ended up cribbing from Barrier. LPs were now the quartet's natural setting, and occasional EP releases, such as 1961's *Don Léon* were overshadowed by albums like the live *Récital à la Comédie des Champs-Elysées*.

Riding a different wave, Les Quatre Barbus recorded an album of sea shanties, *Chansons de la marine à voiles*, in 1964. These were performed straight, rather than as comic songs, although, as with many sea shanties, the results were not without humour. Four of the best performances, among them the reflective 'Sur l'pont d'Morlaix', also surfaced on an EP, while their next included the memorable 'L'alcool', a thoughtful discourse on the demon drink. However, their hit-making days were now long in the past.

Philippe Clay was another *chansonnier* who found the sixties hard going, despite the quality of offerings like 1962's 'Les touristes'. The same year brought a sniff of a hit with 'Les baleines', but by 1963 his sales were falling fast and the Gainsbourg-penned 'Chanson pour tézigue' was all but ignored. His 1964 cover of Louis Armstrong's recent US chart-topper, 'Hello, Dolly!', likewise met with widespread indifference[687] and by the end of the year his singing career was virtually at a standstill.

Guy Béart also struggled in the early sixties, and after his excellent 1963 effort, 'Suez', failed to catch fire, he parted company with Philips. It took his own TV series, *Bienvenue*, and a 1964 duet with Marie Laforêt, 'Frantz', to return him to the public eye. Adapted from an Austrian folk song,[688] 'Frantz' was the first release on Béart's own Temporel label, through which he set about establishing complete control over his career.

Mouloudji took a similar step once the hits dried up. After 1963's romantic 'L'amour, l'amour, l'amour' did little to rebuild his fortunes, he quit Vogue and launched the Mouloudji label in 1964 with revivals of Yves Montand's hit, 'Les feuilles mortes', and his own/Boris Vian's 'Le déserteur', a song that had lost none of its power in the intervening decade.[689]

Georges Moustaki had earlier penned the lyrics to Édith Piaf's 'Milord' and Maria Candido's 'Donne du rhum à ton homme', so he had a ready audience for his next efforts. His 1962 hit, 'Mon Île de France', augured well for his career, but neither 'Un jupon d'Italie' nor 'Jeux dangereux' caught the ear of the record-buying public sufficiently to generate a second hit EP. An easy-going writer without the intensity of Brel or Ferré, he found himself struggling by the middle of the decade to retain any kind of following.

Joël Holmès had first surfaced in 1958, but failed to attract attention until he teamed up with Moustaki to

---

[687] Petula Clark got the hit instead.

[688] Previously rendered in English by Harry Belafonte & Miriam Makeba as 'One More Dance', the song was later restored to its original language as 'Noch einen Tanz' and was a hit in 1966 in West Germany for Israeli duo Esther & Abi Ofarim. They then closed the circle by recording it in English for a UK hit in 1968.

[689] Peter, Paul & Mary had covered it on their best-selling *In Concert* double album, which at that time was on the US album charts.

write 'La mer m'a donné' in 1960. Exhibiting a love-lorn streak, he tickled the airwaves in 1963 with 'La romance' and 1965's 'L'amour', but was unable to find commercial success.

Barbara found the going just as tough, with a repertoire that seemed far too personal, even in the world of the *chanson*. Backed by a bigger-than-usual orchestra, she set out her stall in 1962 with an EP of original songs, among them the classy 'Dis, quand reviendras-tu' and 'Le temps des lilas'. Although not a hit, the record was proof that she was developing a style of her own. It reached fruition in 1963 with the piano-led 'Attendez que ma joie revienne', a moving dissection of an unsatisfactory love affair. Her first truly great recording, it was, however, another commercial failure.

The amusing Pierre Perret had also hovered around the margins since the late fifties, when his two Barclay LPs disappeared quicker than an iceberg in Arabia. After moving to Vogue, he scored a fluke hit in 1963 with the accordion-decked 'Le Tord-Boyaux', a humorous yet incisive description of a terrible, if not downright unhygienic restaurant. Coupled with 'L'idole des femmes', an amusing response to the Johnny Hallyday phenomenon and an obvious rejoinder to the latter's 'L'idole des jeunes', it kicked off a run of similarly rib-tickling hits. Perret had no qualms about varying his musical palette, referencing James Bond soundtracks on 'La petite' and stripping things down to bare bones for 'Pépé la jactance'. He established himself as an endearing figure, building a reputation that songs such as 'Trop contente', 'Les filles ça me tuera' and the major hit 'La corrida' could only enhance.

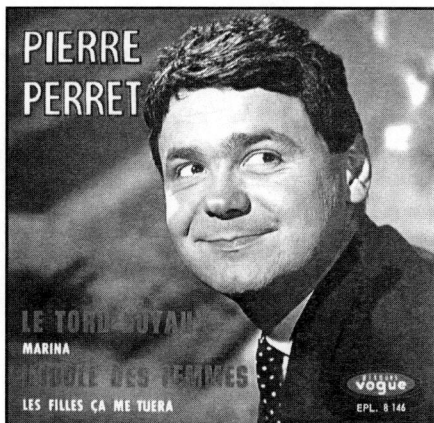

Anne Sylvestre was far more serious. A Joan Baez-like presence who spoke for the rural heartland of France, she delivered pretty songs to simple guitar accompaniment. Combining the Left Bank style of *chanson* with the rural feel of Brassens, she broke through in 1961 with the churchy 'Les cathédrales', while her 1963 hit, 'Vous aviez ma belle', brought a feminine – even feminist – perspective to the *chanson*.

anne **sylvestre**

Mischievously described as being simply 'Brassens in a skirt', Sylvestre bridged the gap between the French *chansonniers* and the folk songs of their American equivalents. Never a major star, she charted her own course with 'Eléonore', a ballad about a prostitute, and 'La femme du vent', an assault on petty morality set to an accompaniment not far removed from the sound that was earning a fortune for Baez across the Atlantic.

## Political activists

Jean Ferrat passed the early years of the decade writing songs for the likes of Zizi Jeanmaire, who recorded his 'Eh l'amour!'[690] and 'Mon bonhomme' for a 1961 EP. A left-wing activist unafraid to put his money where his mouth was, Ferrat was much disliked by the Right. Released in 1961, his third EP went the same way as the first two, his latest resetting of a Louis Aragon poem, 'J'entends, j'entends', faring less well than 'Les yeux d'Elsa' had for André Claveau back in the fifties, and the Victor Hugo sentiments of 'Paris gavroche' sitting poorly with a too-jolly orchestration.

Decca quickly recycled Ferrat's last two EPs on a 10-inch LP rounded out with two new songs, including the great opening track, 'Deux enfants au soleil'.[691] A summer ballad akin to Charles Trenet's 'La mer' and borne aloft by a warm vocal delivery, it swept the airwaves to give Ferrat his breakthrough hit, selling by the thousand, although the sentiments were at odds with much of his other material.

---

[690] The sleeve of Jeanmaire's version relocated the exclamation mark ('Eh! L'amour'), which actually makes more sense.

[691] The album was untitled, but is generally known as either *Jean Ferrat* or *Deux enfants au soleil.*

The LP was reissued as a 12-incher[692] at the end of 1962 with six of the original songs and six new ones. 'La fête aux copains' rang all the right bells, although the song celebrated traditional working-class friendships rather than the modern *copains* catered for by Daniel Filipacchi's radio programme. Ferrat tackled a similar theme on 'Les petits bistrots', while on 'Les noctambules' he took the mickey out of nightclub habitués – the latter set to a twist-friendly rhythm that might, had he been younger, have found a home alongside Filipacchi's *idoles*. Elsewhere, he paid tribute to the Dutch painter Vincent van Gogh on 'L'homme à l'oreille coupée', and to the gypsy lifestyle on the poignant 'Les nomades', but only the bolero rhythms of 'Mes amours' reflected the sentiments of his breakthrough hit.

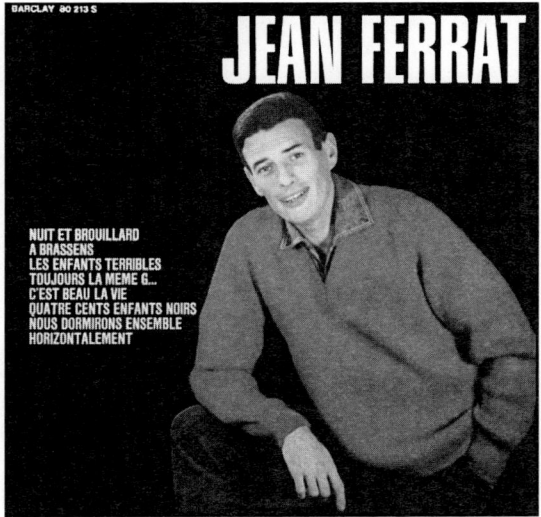

In 1963, Ferrat scored a major hit with 'Nuit et brouillard', a haunting treatment of the Holocaust that paid homage to the deportees of the recent war[693] – despite, or perhaps because of, a ban by state radio stations nervous of disturbing the blossoming post-war Franco-German relationship.[694] The song's success allowed Ferrat to shake off his crooner's image and restate his political credentials. It rightly served as the opening track on his untitled third album, on which he also took time out to acknowledge one of his major influences with the excellent 'À Brassens'. However, it was stronger material like the anti-racist 'Quatre cents enfants noirs' and the celebratory 'C'est beau la vie', which made him a household name. And, while the gentle 'Horizontalement' marked another fruitless stab at a younger sound, the closing track, a beautiful love song titled 'Nous dormirons ensemble', presented him with another smash in 1964.

Although Ferrat was much covered by the likes of Juliette Gréco (who recorded 'La fête aux copains' in 1963), his main interpreter was Isabelle Aubret, who also shared his political concerns. Her glossy repertoire mixed *chansons* by Ferrat ('Deux enfants au soleil') and Serge Gainsbourg ('La chanson de Prévert') with pop ditties such as 'Le premier rendez-vous' and 'Tintin et la toison d'or', the theme from the 1961 children's film *Tintin et le mystère de la toison d'or*. This odd mixture of material did her no harm at all, and in 1962 she won the *Eurovision* song contest with the ballad 'Un premier

---

[692] The 12" album *did* carry *Deux enfants au soleil* as the title.
[693] Something that had directly impacted Ferrat's family, several of whom perished in the Nazi death camps.
[694] At the time of the record's release, West German chancellor Konrad Adenauer was paying a formal visit to Charles de Gaulle.

amour' – almost certainly the only time a left-wing activist has carried off the prize. In 1963, she enjoyed further success with Jacques Brel's 'La Fannette' and a rare songwriting collaboration between Serge Gainsbourg and Henri Salvador, the lovely 'Il n'y a plus d'abonné au numéro que vous avez demandé'. Aubret's career was subsequently interrupted by a bad car accident, but she returned in 1964 with a cover of Ferrat's 'C'est beau la vie' that lacked the warmth of the composer's own rendition, but was closer in spirit to the music hall of the past.

MEDIUM B 372.577 F

Avec **"UN PREMIER AMOUR"**
Isabelle AUBRET représente la France au grand prix de l'EUROVISION le 18 mars 1962

au verso de ce disque " POLY-POLISSON " bande originale de l'émission télévisée de la RTF

Francis Lemarque tapped the same political sentiment that fired Ferrat, and his words invariably came wrapped in attractive musical packages. The lush 'Écoutez la ballade' was as deceptive as Ferrat's romantic moments and the criminal's lament 'Miséricorde' also carried a powerful punch, but Lemarque struggled with opposition from the censors and was rarely seen on television, paying a heavy commercial price for his beliefs.

Quebec's Félix Leclerc stuck to what he did best, although he was by now beginning to sweeten his sound with wind instruments, the pretty 'Le bal' on his 1962 LP *Le roi hereux* being a case in point. In 1964, he released a self-titled album offering the light-hearted 'La fête', and the reflective 'Le jour qui s'appelle aujourd'hui' and 'Premier amour'. However, his prolonged absence from the French music scene meant sales were disappointing.

Canada's new breed of *chansonnier* was perhaps best represented by Jean-Pierre Ferland, who was introduced to European audiences in 1962 when he won the *Chansons sur mesure* song contest in Brussels with 'Feuilles de gui'. A handful of releases followed, including the 1963 live album *Jean-Pierre Ferland à Bobino*, but, although well-received in concert, none of his well-crafted *chansons* found a wide audience. However, compositions such as 1962's 'Les immortelles' and the following year's 'Les fleurs de macadam' were hits for him back home in Quebec, where, like Leclerc, he became a major star.

JEAN-PIERRE FERLAND
à BOBINO

## Interpreters of *chanson*

Pia Colombo had hovered on the fringes of the *chanson* world since the late fifties, drawing her repertoire from other, more prominent singers and finding an audience in 1960 with covers of Jacques Brel's 'La valse à mille temps' and 'La colombe'. Equally interesting was 1962's 'Le rouge et le noir', a title borrowed from the literary classic by Stendhal for a musical collaboration between Claude Nougaro and Michel Legrand, but even these stellar talents couldn't make this most cerebral of singers into a household name. It was only on stage that she truly came to life, wowing audiences with a dramatic reading of 'L'écharpe'. Released in 1964, it was as close as she ever came to making the charts.[695] Of the other tracks, the sprightly 'À la Jésus' deserved more airplay than it got, while 'Il y a si peu de temps' offered a pause for reflection in a decade that was fast gathering pace.

Yves Montand scored a hit in 1962 with a cover of Claude Nougaro's 'Le jazz et la java', while his album *Yves Montand chante Jacques Prévert* included a reworking of his classic 'Les feuilles mortes' alongside other Prévert offerings like 'Le jardin', 'Page d'écriture' and 'Quelqu'un'. Still capable of drawing huge crowds, his dynamic performances were captured on the superb *Récital 63* and *Yves Montand à l'Étoile* live albums as he took time out from his still-buoyant cinematic career.

Patachou found it easier to sell albums to the adult market than to carry on the business of getting pop hits. She enjoyed steady sales with in-concert recordings like *Patachou à l'A.B.C.* (1962) and themed sets like *Patachou chante Bruant* (also 1962), while a 1963 trip to New York resulted in the US-only *Patachou At Carnegie Hall* set, which, as one might imagine, saw her performing a selection of

---

[695] Written by Colombo's husband, Maurice Fanon, upon their separation in 1963, the song had originally appeared on his debut album, *Avec Fanon*. (Fanon had first become known after Colombo recorded his 'Jean-Marie de Pantin' in 1960.) His co-writer, Joël Holmès, also recorded it in less dramatic style, enjoying moderate commercial success.

recent and classic *chansons* on the stage of the prestigious New York venue. However, as *yé-yé* continued to overtake *chanson* in the marketplace, her sales began to fall and she parted company with her record label, Philips, following her 1964 release, 'Je quitterai Paris'.

Michèle Arnaud stuck to the safe option of covering contemporary *chansons*, picking up early on Jean Ferrat's 'Deux enfants au soleil' and bringing Léo Ferré's 'Pauvre Rutebeuf' to the airwaves in 1964. Along the way, she adapted the old folk song 'The Ballad Of Lady Jane' into French ('La ballade de Lady Jane')[696] before embarking on a parallel career as a television producer – a move that would eventually see her moving toward a more contemporary repertoire, if still some way from rock'n'roll.

## Popular *chanson*

Not all *chansonniers* shared the perception that rock'n'roll was a bad thing; indeed, some welcomed its sense of fun and liberation. Pierre Barouh appeared in the film *D'où viens-tu, Johnny?* with Johnny Hallyday and wrote lyrics for artists like Danyel Gérard ('D'accord, d'accord'), Dalida ('Eux') and Bob Asklöf ('Moi qui n'ai plus rien').[697] A man of many talents, he failed to achieve the same level of success with his own records, and even pleasant teen fodder such as 'Tes dix-huit ans' went absolutely nowhere.

Charles Aznavour was also happy to dip his toe into rock'n'roll waters, writing for both Hallyday ('Retiens la nuit') and Sylvie Vartan ('La plus belle pour aller danser'), while simultaneously recording some of the best music of his career. Ever eclectic, he stuck to traditional arrangements for 'Esperanza'

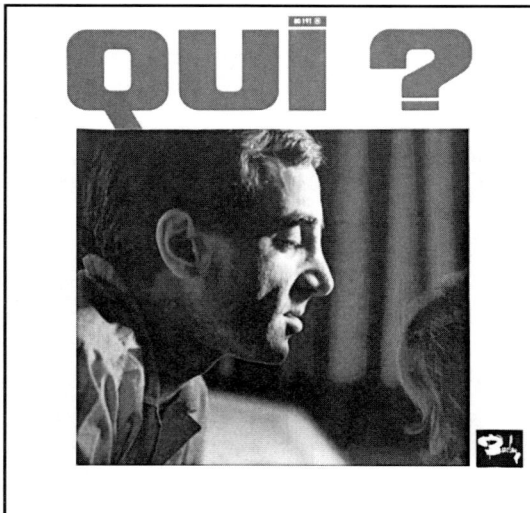

(a rare adaptation, based on Ramón Cabrera's Cuban classic of the same name) and 'J'ai tort', dabbled in gospel for 'Alléluia', and headed deep into *American Bandstand* territory for the rhythmic 'Les comédiens'[698] in 1962.

By the time his 1963 LP *Qui?* came out, Aznavour was firing on all cylinders. Among the highlights were 'Bon anniversaire', a witty account of a disastrous birthday celebration, and the Sinatra-esque swinger 'For me... formidable'. Indeed, the album made the case for Aznavour as a Gallic rival to

---

[696] After the American singer formerly based in Paris, Jane Morgan, had included it on her 1960 LP, *The Ballads of Lady Jane*.

[697] A cover of Joe Sentieri's 'Uno dei tanti', best known internationally as Ben E. King's 'I (Who Have Nothing)'.

[698] The song was quickly covered by both Les Compagnons de la Chanson and the fading Jacqueline François.

the Chairman of the Board as he swung his way through such jewels as 'Dors' and 'Jolies mômes de mon quartier', and emoted with style over the piano-heavy 'Trop tard'. He was ready to take on the world, and later that year would cross the Atlantic to wow audiences at Carnegie Hall in New York.[699]

Gilbert Bécaud opened 1962 with the dynamic 'Et maintenant', a massive hit that was subsequently covered by Gloria Lasso, Isabelle Aubret, Jacqueline Danno and many others.[700] The recording took the dramatic tension inherent in the best *chansons*, married it to a bolero-style arrangement and gave it a contemporary makeover. The song's runaway success completely overshadowed the rest of a strong EP, which featured the stinging protest song 'Le condamné', which put the singer in the role of a man sentenced to the guillotine and deserved to be a hit in its own right.

1962 also witnessed the release of a self-titled LP that found Bécaud dabbling in percussive jazz on 'Contre vous' and easy listening on 'Fanfan', though it was the more typical 'Le bateau blanc' that became a hit. It contained more challenging material too, like 'Le jugement dernier' and the anti-war 'Nicolas', which was banned from the airwaves.

Bécaud meanwhile took time out to pursue grander ambitions, following up his 1960 cantata with a full-length operatic work, *L'opéra d'Aran*, also released on album in 1962. With this out of his system, he returned to the task of crafting hits, scoring with the lush 'Crois-moi',[701] 'Je t'attends', 'Dimanche à Orly' and the superb 'Quand Jules est au violon'. The sweet 'Trop beau' was another fan favourite, though not a hit. Although toned down from the youthful excesses of a decade earlier, Bécaud's live performances remained a major event of the concert season, and his 1963 live album, *Gilbert Bécaud à l'Olympia*, with standout performances of the comic 'La grosse noce' and the swinging 'Les tantes Jeanne', perfectly demonstrated his way of inhabiting a song.

Although Bécaud and Aznavour had successfully managed to straddle the *yé-yé* and adult markets, the balance of their work began to lean toward their older fans as the decade wore on. Only Petula Clark walked that

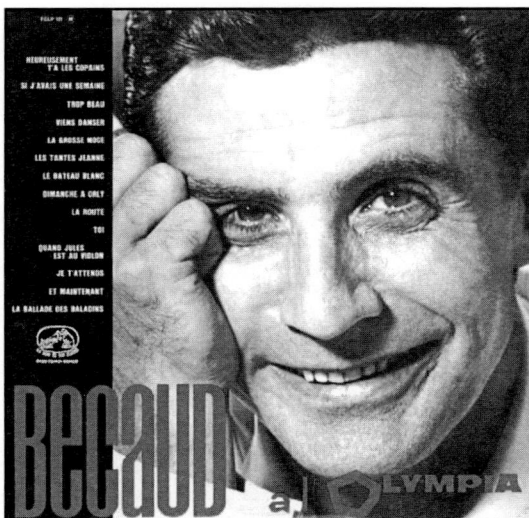

---

[699] Bob Dylan, who was there, later recalled being blown away by the diminutive singer.
[700] Reworked into English for Shirley Bassey as 'What Now My Love', it became an international standard, with versions by Elvis Presley, Frank Sinatra and Connie Francis joining countless others on the shelves over the next two decades.
[701] Some French covers of this song were titled 'Crois-moi ça durera'. It was also recorded in English and French by Nat 'King' Cole as 'You'll See'.

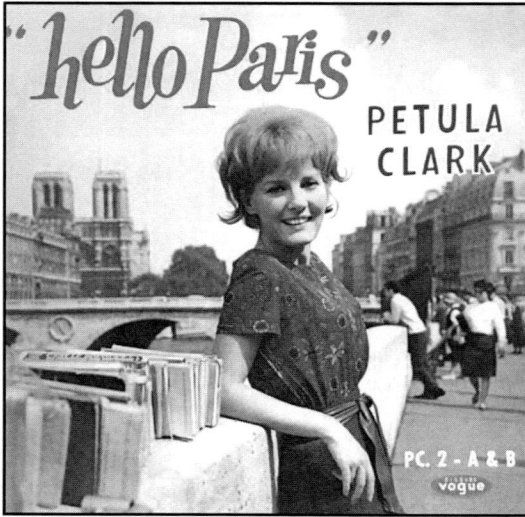

tightrope to perfection, mixing easy listening efforts like 'Toi, tu joues à l'amour'[702] and 'Il n'a chanté qu'un soir' with well-made teen pop like 'J'ai pas le temps' (a cover of the Beach Boys' 'No-Go Showboat'), finding success on both sides of the generational divide.

Although Clark's recordings were primarily aimed at the teenage audience, it was their parents who had first embraced her when she moved to France. She thanked them in 1964 with the double album *Hello Paris*, rounding up two dozen classics of French music hall, jazz and *chanson*. Her readings of such jewels as Charles Trenet's 'Vous qui passez sans me voir' and 'La mer', Mistinguett's 'Mon homme', André Claveau's 'Cerisier rose et pommier blanc' and Édith Piaf's 'La vie en rose' reminded listeners of her roots, even as her latest pop EP was in heavy rotation on *Salut les copains*.

Dalida, on the other hand, had completely embraced teen stardom and her career was rocked when the market rejected her 1963 cover of Johnny Thunder's 'Loop De Loop' in favour of a version by Frank Alamo. On her next EP, the former queen of exotica retreated to safer ground with 'Sois heureux' (Domenico Modugno's 'Lettera di un soldato'), and for the following two years she veered from pillar to post in an effort to find her way back to the top, turning to Italian pop with 'La partie de football' (Rita Pavone's smash, 'La partita di pallone'), *yé-yé* ballads like 'Quand revient l'été' (Cliff Richard's 'Summer Holiday') and easy listening efforts like 'Je t'aime' (Roy Orbison's 'It's Over') with varying degrees of success.

### The world of light entertainment

Although some way down from her late-fifties' peak, Dalida's continuing popularity proved that traditional *chanson* was not the only alternative for older listeners alienated by rock'n'roll and *yé-yé*. The escapist world of music hall was also alive and well, and the country's venues were packed to the rafters with audiences happy to sit through shows that combined comedy, *chanson*, jazz, *musette*, romantic balladry, magic acts and even a little rock'n'roll on occasion. Although teenagers were beginning to demand all *yé-yé* bills, and some performers were putting on lengthier recitals and 'one-man' concerts, the traditional variety show, with its 'something for everyone' approach, remained the preferred mode of an evening's entertainment. For

---

[702] This was an American song written by Buddy Kaye & Paul Springer, 'I'm Looking At The World Through Teardrops', however it does not appear to have ever been recorded under that title.

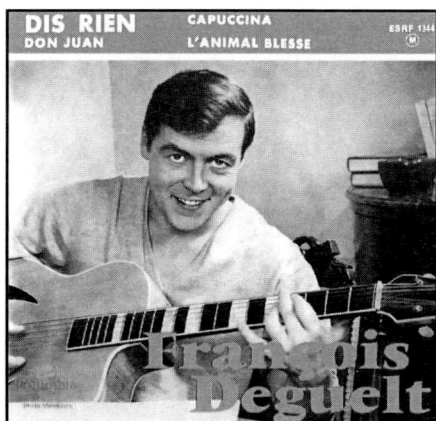

artists struggling to get hit records, they also provided a means to connect with a far larger audience than they might otherwise have attracted on their own.

One such artist was François Deguelt. His early attempts at rock'n'roll long behind him, he was now scratching a living purveying easy listening material like 'Les voiliers'. In 1962, he got the chance to perform at *Eurovision* for the second time, representing Monaco with a better-than-average ballad from the pen of Henri Salvador titled 'Dis rien', finishing second. Deguelt persevered with Salvador's 'C'était un jour comme celui-là' and covers of Claude Nougaro's 'Une petite fille' and Cliff Richard's 'Evergreen Tree' ('Ma verte prairie'),[703] all of which proved commercially disappointing. By the middle of the decade, his career was fast shipping water.

Jean-Claude Pascal's career had hit a peak with his *Eurovision* triumph in 1961, but, although he covered quality *chansons* like Serge Gainsbourg's 'En relisant ta lettre', his style seemed irredeemably bland as the decade wore on. A 1963 cover of Brigitte Bardot's 'L'appareil à sous' hit did him few favours, and his take on Françoise Hardy's 'Le temps de l'amour' was little short of embarrassing. Even so, he remained a draw on the European cabaret circuit, picking up hits in West Germany and Austria, and championing the work of songwriters like Guy Béart ('Un enfant écrit') and Charles Dumont ('Le rendez-vous des routiers').

Italian-born singer Franca di Rienzo represented Switzerland at the 1961 *Eurovision Song Contest* with 'Nous aurons demain', taking third place on the night. The exposure she received as a result of the show led her to set up home in France, where she released half a dozen EPs over the next three years. These included covers of hits like Adam Wade's 'Take Good Care Of Her' (Je ne t'aime plus') and Lonnie Donegan's 'The Party's Over' ('Mon rêve est cassé')[704] alongside some excellent home-grown material, most notably 1963's 'Tu as beau sourire'.

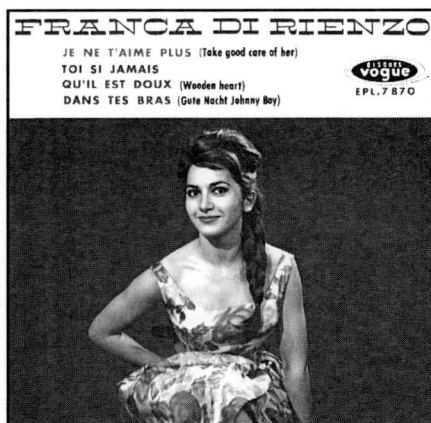

---

[703] Hopelessly outclassed by a contemporary cover by Long Chris.
[704] This song began life in the 1956 musical *Bells Are Ringing* and had already been recorded by Nat 'King' Cole and Shirley Bassey, among others, although it was likely to have been Donegan's recent UK hit, or possibly Lesley Gore's version on her 1963 LP *I'll Cry If I Want To*, that provided the inspiration for di Rienzo's cover.

371

elle était si jolie  RCA VICTOR, 
86.618 M
sélectionnée par la R.T.F. au Grand Prix Eurovision de la chanson 1963
le temps d'une valse · plus je t'entends · la route
**ALAIN BARRIERE**

Despite good publicity and high-profile concert appearances, Di Rienzo never made the jump to stardom, although she would remain a presence in the French pop market-place for many years[705].

Romantic balladeer Alain Barrière was an obvious choice for *Eurovision* and represented France in 1963 with the sweet 'Elle était si jolie'. He came joint fifth on the night,[706] but the EP featuring the song (which also included the far more interesting 'La route' and the dramatic 'Plus je t'entends') became a major hit. Despite overly lush arrangements, Barrière retained enough earthy appeal to span the radio spectrum, delivering a run of hits that peaked with 1964's 'Ma vie', a smash across both Europe and South America.[707] Amidst these successes, he also scored a host of lesser triumphs, ranging from 1963's rhythmic 'Longtemps' to the pop fluff of 'Un été' the following year, although it was the singalong 'La Marie Joconde' that best illustrated his appeal to an audience left behind by the changes in popular music.

Away from *Eurovision*, Georges Blaness made a name for himself at the Barcelona-based *Festival de la Canción Mediterránea*. Despite a recording career stretching back to the late fifties,[708] Blaness was just another struggling singer when he represented France at the festival in 1962 with 'Je t'aime, je t'aime'. He didn't win, but he recorded the song in both French and Spanish for a moderate hit of sorts, and he had a second go the following year[709] with 'Chérie madame', with much the same result. He continued recording for some years, although he eventually found more fame as a film actor.

Romantic songs also formed the main stock-in-trade of Henri Markarian, a French singer and songwriter whose 1961 debut, 'FLAndre 24-56 (Je t'appelle, mon amour)', was roundly ignored. This prompted him to change his name to Marc Aryan, set up his own Markal label and decamp to Belgium, where audiences proved more receptive. His soothing vocal style was matched by his compositional skills, and his 1963 Belgian debut, 'Doudou', marked the start of a long career. The gentle 'Ballade' showed he had the talent to make it and his popularity grew steadily until 1964, when he established himself as a major draw in Belgium and in the Netherlands – though not in France – with the party rhythms of 'Si j'étais le fils d'un roi'.

---

[705] Her subsequent success as a member of Les Troubadours will be covered in Volume 2.

[706] Sharing fifth place was Monaco's entry, 'L'amour s'en va' by Françoise Hardy. Barrière's song was promptly covered by former *Eurovision* laureate Jean-Claude Pascal.

[707] It was subsequently reworked in English by Kenny Damon as 'While I Live' and became something of a favourite on UK pirate radio.

[708] He initially recorded as Georges Blanès.

[709] Other 1963 competitors included Frida Boccara, who also represented France with 'Mediterranean Skies' and Katia Valère, another little-known singer, who represented Monaco with 'Je suis là'. Boccara and Blaness both also performed 'Qu'en a tu fait' at the festival.

Newcomer Pierre Perrin picked up one of the biggest hits of the decade in 1962 with the daft but catchy tango 'Un clair de lune à Maubeuge', its traditional music hall sound standing proud at the height of twist fever. The song was covered across the whole spectrum of French pop from Bourvil (in his usual lighthearted style) to Claude François.[710] Despite the record's success, Perrin never had another hit, though his hit song was later turned into a film.

Bourvil also enjoyed respectable sales with his version, subsequently staging a comeback in 1963 with the summer ballad 'La tendresse', one of the big hits of the year, but this proved to be a last hurrah. Neither 'J'suis papa et j'suis dans l'coup',[711] nor the sentimental 'Bonjour, monsieur le maître d'école' caught fire, and, despite continued cinematic success, by the middle of the decade Bourvil's time as a major-league singer was over.

Perrin's smash was also covered by Annie Cordy, who sang it with the same giggle in her voice that she applied to everything else. In 1963 and 1964, credible readings of Charles Aznavour's 'For me... formidable' and the George & Ira Gershwin classic, 'Oh, Lady Be Good'[712] ('Oh! Lady Bigoudi!') showed that, while sales were falling, her talent was far from exhausted. Comic knockabouts remained her calling card, from the *yé-yé* pastiche 'J'ai froid les pieds' to the exotica throwback 'Valentina', to the mock-C&W 'Tu m'as vou-lue'. The country fiddle returned for 'Je te félicite', but this time the effect was purely decorative.

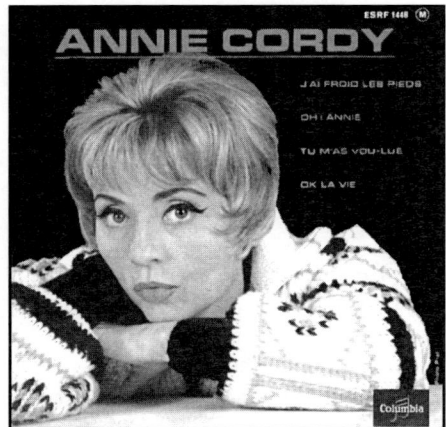

Cordy may have found record sales hard to come by, but comic veterans Pierre Dac et Francis Blanche enjoyed major success in 1964 with the classic sketch 'Le Sâr Rabin Dranath Duval'. This was, however, an anachronism and although such performers remained popular on television, by the middle of the decade straight comedy records were being

---

[710] On his EP, Bourvil's version was mistitled 'Le clair de lune à Maubeuge', but was corrected on subsequent album releases. François' version appeared on his debut EP, which was released under the pseudonym 'Kôkô'.

[711] This was a response to an innocuous, if vaguely rebellious song by Sheila, 'Papa, t'es plus dans l'coup'.

[712] First performed on Broadway by Walter Catlett, the song had been a hit in 1925 for Cliff Edwards, Carl Fenton and Paul Whiteman, although it was Ella Fitzgerald's 1947 scat rendition that inspired Cordy's release.

**ARMAND**
LA FEMME DU SERGENT — LES CACAHUÈTES GRILLÉES
J'AI L'HONNEUR
451.194 S
DECCA

**pierre vassiliu**
Orchestre dirigé par Eddie VARTAN

elbowed off the airwaves by more musical humorous outings.

Fernandel also played it for laughs on 1962's 'Ne frotte pas, François', before returning to his provincial roots for 'Le cul du berger', a highlight of his 1963 *Quelques airs de Provence* EP. A much-loved and much-laughed-at figure on stage and screen, his record sales were, however, significantly below those of the decade's leading pop singers.

The irreverent Pierre Vassiliu forged a career with hilarious, jazzy pastiches that pointed the finger at society in a knowing way. Commencing in 1963 with the drunken party atmosphere of 'Armand', he ran up a barrage of near-hits that offered more depth and insight than might have been expected. The martial yet anti-militarist 'La femme du sergent (J'étais dans les rizières)' was banned from radio for its subversive intent,[713] but it established him firmly on the border where music met satire, while the beat-heavy 'Charlotte' offered salacious lyrics set to the *schlager* sound that was popular across the Rhine. The *yé-yé idoles* bore the brunt of his coruscating wit on the wickedly accurate 'Twist anti-yé' (not that this prevented him from joining Sylvie Vartan on the bill at the Olympia Theatre in 1964[714]), while the daring 'Ma cousine' kept him in the spotlight as the decade ticked on.

Marcel Amont was not a songwriter and happily promoted the work of others, enjoying a major hit in 1962 with the Charles Aznavour-penned novelty, 'Le Mexicain',[715] as his easygoing style won him a huge audience via the rapidly growing medium of television. He recorded another Aznavour confection, 'Dans mon pays...', for the same EP and continued to champion the cause of Claude Nougaro via versions of 'Le jazz et la java' and the Latin-flavoured 'Le porte-plume'. Mixing smooth offerings like 'Ma petite symphonie' (adapted from the Ronnie Height/Rod Lauren/Michael Holliday flop, 'The One-Finger Symphony') with old-fashioned songs like 'Pigalle'[716] kept his career

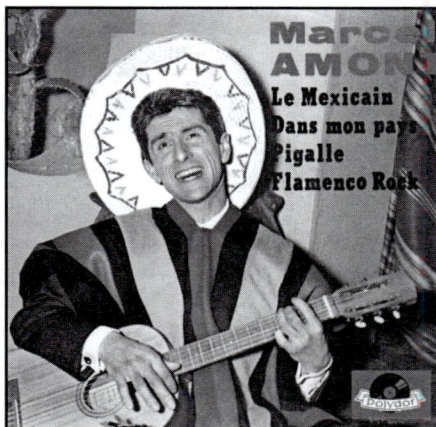

Marcel AMONT
Le Mexicain
Dans mon pays
Pigalle
Flamenco Rock

---

[713] Oddly enough, Vassiliu did get to perform it on television.

[714] Top of the bill was an up-and-coming British group just beginning to build a French audience: the Beatles.

[715] Some Amont albums list this as 'Un Mexicain'.

[716] Which harked back to the run of Paris-flavoured songs earlier in the century. Amont even slipped briefly into English in the manner of Maurice Chevalier to poke gentle fun at English and American tourists in the capital.

buoyant, but dalliances into less familiar territory, such as his 1962 cover of Milva's 'Flamenco rock', laid bare his limitations. In 1963, Amont smooched his way through 'Cœur à cœur' (Bobby Vinton's 'Blue On Blue') and turned in a decent cover of Kyu Sakamoto's jazz-pop hit 'Sukiyaki' ('Sukiyaki (Sous une pluie d'étoiles)'). Although his record sales started to wane by the` middle of the decade, his live popularity remained undiminished, with his one-man show at the Bobino Theatre in Paris running to over 100 performances.

LE PONT VERS LE SOLEIL . CHANTE ENCORE MON CŒUR ESRF 1342
LE TANGO DES ILLUSIONS          C'EST JOLI LA MER   (M)   Columbia

Jacqueline Boyer also tackled a wide variety of material, cutting a cover of Manos Hadjidakis' Greek ballad, 'Min ton rotas ton ourano' ('C'est joli la mer') and a dreadful version of Elvis Presley's 'Can't Help Falling In Love'[717] ('Chante encore mon cœur') in 1961. While the title of 1962's 'Excusez-moi si j'ai vingt ans' suggested she might be pandering to the *yé-yé* market, the sound of the record soon cleared up any misconceptions. Although Boyer's previous triumphs guaranteed her a presence on television, her records steadfastly refused to climb the charts.

Georges Guétary enjoyed a hit in 1962 with the sickly parent-and-child duet 'Dis Papa...', but a tacky tribute to the world's greatest footballer, 'Le roi Pelé', was not enough to keep him in the hit parade.

Fellow veteran André Claveau was also outward bound, his 'Le petit tramway' and 'Le petit train de l'amour' both failing to pick up many

passengers. By 1962, when 'Toi, mon amour' hit the buffers, even his record company had given up on him.

Maurice Chevalier followed his surprise 1962 collaboration with Les Chaussettes Noires, 'Le twist du canotier', with the soberly titled album *Maurice Chevalier*. This featured the hit alongside a version of Charles Aznavour's 'Mômes de mon quartier', revivals of old chart successes like 'Valentine' and 'Mimi', and a set of new songs in the style that he had spent forty years developing, of which the jolly 'Moi, avec

---

[717] Itself a reworking of the timeless 'Plaisir d'amour'.

une chanson' was the pick of the bunch.

For Tino Rossi, hit records were increasingly a distant memory, even though 1962's 'La paloma' (a reworking of Bing Crosby's 'Amor'[718]) and the following year's 'J'avais vingt ans' were sublime easy listening experiences. His 1963 mini-operetta *Le temps des guitares* was a crass attempt to ride the *yé-yé* bandwagon, but the EP was a major hit, its electric guitars, rock'n'roll rhythm and teen-pop backing vocals sending the title track soaring up the charts. However, this excursion into the teenage market turned out to be a one-off, and Rossi instead went on to release a stream of albums offering old hits, Corsican folk songs, tangos, waltzes and other varieties of pre-rock'n'roll pop, all of which sold by the trailerload right through to the end of the decade.

Charles Trenet also remained a popular concert draw, though he gradually cut down his performing commitments as the decade progressed. 1962's 'Jardin du mois de mai' proved perfect for mid-afternoon tea dances, while the following year's 'La famille musicien'[719] was a late blossom that ranked among his finest work, some twenty-five years after his recording debut.

Line Renaud also maintained a hectic concert schedule while keeping her recording career alive with the likes of 'En vacances en Italie' and 'La môme whisky'. Occasional forays into *yé-yé* territory, such as her 1962 cover of Johnny Burnette's 'Little Boy Sad' ('C'est toi baby'), were less well received, but she picked up a sizeable hit in 1963 with 'Un jour tu me reviendras'.

Zizi Jeanmaire maintained her position as the leading nightclub draw in the country, despite seeing her recording career wither on the vine, and although 1962's 'Les bras d'Antoine'[720] kept up the quality, the record-buying public had moved on. LPs were a better medium for a singer whose exhuberance could not be contained within the grooves of a 45, and thematic works like 1961's *Zizi Paris*, featuring favourites like the Lucienne Delyle/Jean Sablon classic 'Sur les quais du vieux Paris' and Jacques Brel's 'Les prénoms de Paris', were perfect purchases for tourists seeking a souvenir of a visit to the city.

---

[718] Probably inspired by Ben E. King's revival of the song a year earlier.
[719] Swiftly covered by Sacha Distel.
[720] A Guy Béart original that Jeanmaire transformed into a typically dynamic performance

Colette Rivat swerved erratically from 1963's mature 'Garde moi' to a teen-pop cover of Brenda Lee's 'The Grass Is Greener' ('L'herbe est plus verte') in 1964 without satisfying any audience, while Maria Vincent tried to build a following with ballads drawn from American sources (e.g. her 1963 take on Wayne Newton's 'Danke Schoen') to equally minimal reward.

GRAND PRIX
du DISQUE
1962
Académie
Charles Cros

ON SE REVERRA
REVIENDRA-T-IL LE TEMPS
VIVRE
J'AI BESOIN DE CROIRE

Colette
Deréal

Colette Deréal fared slightly better, despite a somewhat less-than-stellar reading of Brenda Lee's 'Dum Dum' in 1961. Her syrupy rendition of the Danyel Gérard-penned ballad 'Reviendra-t-il le temps' sold poorly, but the soaring 'On se reverra' gifted her a sizeable hit in 1962. She revealed a more rhythmic side to her character on 'J'ai besoin de croire', and hit the commercial jackpot in 1963 with the best of many vocal versions of the Tornados' 'Telstar'.[721] The more traditional 'À la gare Saint-Lazare' on the same EP gave her a further hit, but neither preserved her star status for very long. Despite cutting a fine interpretation of Connie Francis's 'Your Other Love' ('Je serai là') in 1964, she never came near the charts again.

Israeli singer Rika Zaraï made a few ripples in 1962 with the trite 'Une pâquerette' and a cover of Bobby Vinton's 'Roses Are Red (My Love)' ('Je reviendrai, my love'), while a 1963 take on Kai Winding's 'More' ('Où êtes-vous?') demonstrated her feel for swinging rhythms. She switched styles at will, laying back on 'L'écho', returning to a Mediterranean pop sound on 'L'olivier', and picking up minor hits with 'Tournez manèges' and a cover of Alain Barrière's 'Elle était si jolie'.

More substantial was the work of balladeer Leny Escudero, who found crossover success on *Salut les copains*. After an opening salvo of hits in 1962, including the shimmering 'Ballade à Sylvie', the complex 5/4 ballad 'Rupture à cinq temps'[722] and the Spanish-influenced 'Pour une amourette', he soared high in the charts with the gentle 'À Malypense' before a withdrawal from the limelight prefigured a slump in sales. After 1963's accordion-decked

LENY
ESCUDERO
accompagné par
PAUL MAURIAT
et son orchestre

BALLADE A SYLVIE
POUR UNE AMOURETTE
PARCE QUE TU LUI RESSEMBLES
VINGT ANS APRÈS

---

[721] With the honourable exception of Les Compagnons de la Chanson, most of the competition was dire to say the least. Ditto the English-language version, 'Magic Star', by American country singer Margie Singleton. A version sung in English by the otherwise dependable Burt Blanca was a particular disappointment. On some reissues, Deréal's recording was subtitled 'Une étoile en plein jour'.

[722] Swiftly – and expertly – covered as an instrumental by Les Champions.

'La malvenue', he lost his audience, and worthy subsequent releases like 1964's 'Stéphanie' and 1965's 'Si tu étais reine' failed. His public had already moved on.

Algerian-born Enrico Macias was even more successful, delivering simple melodies in an emotive voice filtered through an accent that sounded exotic to most, but perfectly normal to the thousands of French North Africans – the so-called *pieds noirs* who had arrived in France during and after the end of the Algerian War (1954-62). Blending Arabic sounds with Spanish and Jewish influences, he was an instant sensation and the striking 'L'oriental', opening with a guitar flourish before swinging into a gently rolling rhythm already familiar from a thousand other songs, established a signature style that served him well. After hitting the top in 1963 with 'Vagabonds sans rivage' (Augusto Algueró's 'Nubes de colores') and the corny 'Enfants de tous pays', he embarked on a run of hits, all of them suffused with nostalgia for the past and dreams of a better future.

Early efforts like the reflective 'Ma maison, ma maison', the acoustic guitar workout 'Adieu, mon pays', and the heartfelt 'Mon ami, mon frère' tapped into the concerns of the *pieds noirs*, while the six-string flurries on 1963's 'Au cœur de la Camargue' and 1964's 'L'amour, c'est pour rien' accentuated his Mediterranean roots. However, ballads like the 1964 smash, 'Paris, tu m'a pris dans les bras', sold equally strongly to both the new arrivals and a home audience seduced by his gentle easy listening arrangements.

**The last rites for exotica**

In one sense, Macias' blend of Mediterranean sounds was simply the latest development in the now-fading exotica craze, though his sentimental lyrics and heartfelt performances offered more substance than the escapist fluff of the fifties. Other singers, however, continued to peddle the successful formulae of the past – with ever-diminishing success.

Moroccan-born Maya Casabianca was launched in 1960 in a blatant attempt by the Philips label to find their very own Dalida, but the likes of 1961's 'Reviens à Sorrente' (based on the Neapolitan classic 'Torna a Surriento')[723] and 'Tango gitano' were doomed attempts to reignite a fire that had long gone out, although her 'Guitare-tango' went on to be a huge international hit in instrumental form for the Shadows as 'Guitar Tango'.

---

[723] Composed in 1902, this dramatic song has since been performed by countless singers. It was adapted into English for Charles Kullman as 'Come Back To Sorrento' in 1934, in which guise it was later covered by Josef Locke (1947), Dean Martin (1952), and many others. It was later given a fresh set of lyrics by Doc Pomus and Mort Shuman and became an international smash for Elvis Presley in 1961 as 'Surrender'. Casabianca's vocal had none of Presley's power.

MAYA CASABIANCA

MEDIUM 432.590 BE

GUITARE TANGO

du film : La goût de la violence
PROTÈGEZ-MOI SEIGNEUR

COMME UNE SYMPHONIE

CHAMPS-ÉLYSÉES

PHILIPS

Efforts to update Casabianca's style likewise came to nought, her covers of Perry Como's 'Caterina' and the Cascades' 'Rhythm Of The Rain' ('En écoutant la pluie') being squashed by hit versions by Sacha Distel and Sylvie Vartan respectively.[724] By 1964, her shot at stardom was over.

Les Compagnons de la Chanson briefly kept the flame of exotica alive with 'Amour brésilien' (Breno Ferreira's 'Andorinha preta'), though they adopted a more contemporary sound for their 1962 hit, 'Cheveux fous et lèvres roses'[725] and a cover of Ruby & The Romantics' US chart-topper, 'Our Day Will Come' ('Ce jour viendra'). Such efforts were less well received by their older fans, who preferred the orchestrated 'De ville en ville' or the imitation western theme 'Là où finit le ciel', both of which were more in keeping with their massed-vocal style. Never ones to miss a commercial opportunity, the Compagnons covered Alain Barrière's 'La Marie Joconde'[726] in 1964, but their biggest successes came when they returned to the Charles Aznavour songbook for precise readings of 'La mamma' and another mock-western effort, 'Les aventuriers'.

The going proved harder still for the stalwarts of the exotica boom. Luis Mariano said farewell to the charts in 1962 with a cover of Ramón Cabrera's 'Esperanza', although he remained a popular operetta and TV performer. André Dassary failed to reignite his career with 'Gloire au "France" ', a tribute to the great ocean-going liner S.S. *France*, although he retained enough credibility for Barclay to attempt an abortive relaunch in 1963. Maria Candido's latter-day releases, such as 1963's 'Le soleil', saw her modernising her sound, but it was a case of too little, too late, and within a year she was out of contract and effectively out of business.

EGF 667 (M)

WATERMELON MAN     AH ! QUELLE MERVEILLE
SCARLETT O'HARA    T'EN VA PAS COMME ÇA

GLORIA LASSO

Photo Marcilly

Even the great Gloria Lasso found herself in trouble. A Petula Clark-style makeover of Jet Harris & Tony Meehan's 'Scarlett O'Hara' produced another miss for her,[727] and a cover of Dionne

---

[724] Richard Anthony also charted with 'En écoutant la pluie'.
[725] A cover of Conny Froboess' *Eurovision* entry, 'Zwei kleiner Italiener', also a hit for Colette Deréal. The Compagnons' version featured an attractive electric guitar part buried in the mix.
[726] The song title was listed without 'La' on the EP sleeve.
[727] Largely because it lacked the commercial clout that Clark had brought to her earlier Shadows adaptations.

Warwick's 'Don't Make Me Over' ('T'en vas pas comme ça') ate dust behind Nancy Holloway's more inspired reading. Her take on the Herbie Hancock/ Mongo Santamaria Latin-jazz hit, 'Watermelon Man' – sung in Spanish – was absolutely on the button, but the game was up. She relocated to Mexico, where her star still burned brightly.

Dario Moreno did what he did best on 1962's 'Moi Dario' and the following year's 'Limbo bossa'[728] before retreating to the concert circuit. In 1963, he milked the now-moribund exotica craze for every last drop with the LP *Tropical Dario*. Built around classics like Don Azpiazú's 'El manisero',[729] Xavier Cugat's 'Perfidia' and Caterina Valente's 'Malagueña', it was a steady seller to an audience hankering after the familiar sounds of their youth.

Los Machucambos enjoyed strong sales in 1962 with both 'Chico cha cha cha' and yet another version of 'Perfidia', following on later that year with a cover of Los Hermanos Rigual's 'Cuando calienta el sol'[730] and a rare original, 'Non monsieur', which again utilised the cha-cha-cha rhythm. As the exotica boom faded, they hit the dance floor with a rendition of Ray Barretto's 'El Watusi', then dabbled in the *chanson* market with a cover of Charles Aznavour's 'La mamma' as their popularity began to ebb away.

John William impressed in 1961 with 'Le voyageur sans étoile', a stylish effort that won top prize at the 1961 *Coq d'Or de la chanson française* festival, and a classy revival of the Gershwin classic, 'Summertime'[731] ('C'est l'été'). However, his usual diet was film music: his 1962 recording of Paul Anka's theme from *The Longest Day* ('Le jour le plus long') was deservedly a major hit, and he scored again in 1963 with Elmer Bernstein's theme from *The Great Escape*, 'La grande évasion'. On record, these were often issued alongside pop efforts like

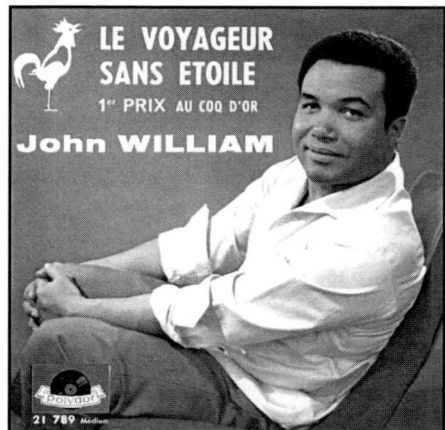

---

[728] The original of this appears to be a Billy Strange song entitled 'Limbo Bossa Nova', although the only recorded version under that title was released by New Zealand's Fowler-Buchanan Quintet in 1962.
[729] Best known to anglophone audiences as Louis Armstrong's 'Peanut Vendor'.
[730] Also covered (as 'Quand le soleil était là') by Gloria Lasso, John William and fading pop singer Orlando, this song is known to American audiences as the Ray Charles Singers' 'Love Me With All Your Heart'.
[731] First sung by Abbie Mitchell in the 1935 stage show *Porgy and Bess*.

'Un oiseau blanc' or 'Comme une symphonie' (Pino Donaggio's Italian smash, 'Come sinfonia') that were slightly at odds with his deep voice, but in the right setting his talent shone through. His 1963 live album, *Negro spirituals*, offered a mixture of powerful performances like 'Merci Dieu, merci' ('I'm So Glad Jesus Lifted Me'[732]) and revivals of classic spirituals like Paul Robeson's 'Deep River' ('Va mon cœur'). Both the LP and a spin-off EP sold steadily throughout the decade.

### Jazz old and new

Showcasing a different African-American sound were Les Haricots Rouges, a New Orleans-styled jazz band who were all first-class musicians but played around as often as they played it straight. Similar in style to the UK's Temperance Seven, whose blend of humour and jazz paralleled their own, they cut a string of best-selling EPs and albums, covering both jazz standards and pop hits in the same game-for-a-laugh way. After establishing their name in 1964 with a revival of the Original Dixieland Jazz Band's 'At The Jazz Band Ball', they recorded a version of Georges Brassens' 'Les copains d'abord' on their way to a long and successful career.

Covering similar ground were Les Parisiennes, a group of female jazz singers including Nicole Croisille assembled by Claude Bolling to revive the heady days of the twenties. They delivered a sound directly descended from the Boswell Sisters, kick-starting their career in 1964 with the jazzy 'Il fait trop beau pour travailler'. However, when the record charted, the singers refused to give up their day jobs and Bolling was forced to recruit another line-up to carry on the group name.

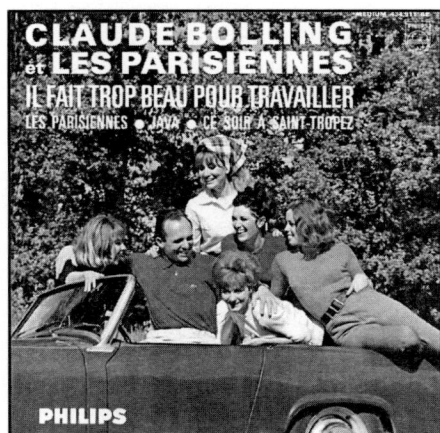

Their debut album, *Claude Bolling et les Parisiennes*, hit the heights in 1964 with the high-stepping 'On a déjà retenu pour le mois d'août', the showgirl-styled 'Ce soir à Saint-Tropez' (a cover of the Dixiebelles' 'Southtown, U.S.A.') and a vocal arrangement of Al Hirt's 'Java'. Thanks to release on EP, the frantic 'C'est tout de même malheureux... qu'on ne puisse pas se promener tranquillement dans les rues après neuf heures du soir' (whose title

---

[732] As recorded by the Voices of Victory in 1958.

was almost as long as the song) and 'L'oiseau rare', a living example of the music hall pap that was supposed to have been eradicated by the *yé-yé* explosion, both enjoyed good radio play.

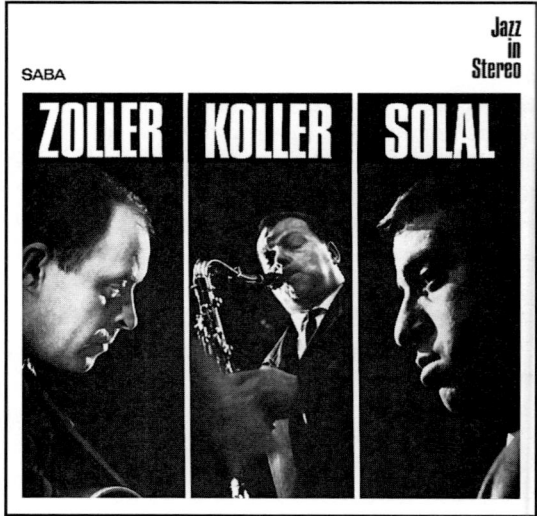

While Bolling (and to a lesser extent, Les Parisiennes) represented the traditional end of the jazz market, pianist Martial Solal offered a more modern variant. Having spent most of the fifties recording in small trios and quartets, he had ended the decade scoring Jean-Luc Godard's cinematic classic, *À bout de souffle*, which brought him to the attention of the American jazz audience. The 1963 live album *À Newport* provided a perfect entrée to his world, with improvisations on Harry James's 'Stella By Starlight', Cole Porter's 'What Is This Thing Called Love?'[733] and Thelonius Monk's 'Round Midnight' rubbing shoulders with a lengthy original composition, 'Suite pour une frise'. Solal went on to become a giant of the European jazz world, cutting a string of albums including 1965's acclaimed *Zo Ko So* with guitarist Attila Zoller and tenorman Hans Koller, and scoring over twenty films during his career.

The cinema also opened its doors to Michel Legrand, who won plaudits around the world for his 1964 filmed operetta, *Les parapluies de Cherbourg*.[734] Acclaimed for the fact that every line of dialogue was sung *recitativo*, rather than spoken, the score was picked up around the world, its main theme resurfacing in English as 'I Will Wait For You' in recordings by Jack Jones, Frank Sinatra and many others. Legrand also had a brief stab at a singing career[735] before the film's success gave

---

[733] Originally performed by Elsie Carlisle in the 1929 Broadway show *Wake Up and Dream*. The first hit versions were by Ben Bernie, Leo Reisman and Fred Rich in 1930.

[734] The film starred the young Catherine Deneuve, although her singing parts were overdubbed by seasoned performer Danièle Licari.

[735] Only the light, *yé-yé*-tinged '1964' made any real impact.

him the chance to work in Hollywood, where he became one of the most sought-after film composers of the decade.

One of the more remarkable jazz outfits of the decade were Les Swingle Singers, formed in 1962 by former Les Double Six members Lamar Ward Swingle and Christiane Legrand. Their *Jazz Sébastien Bach* LP containing wordless vocal arrangements of classical melodies by Johann Sebastian Bach was the surprise hit of 1963 – not only in France, but across the globe. With minimal instrumentation to carry the rhythm, the group sang their way through complex arrangements, giving the impression of a choir scatting *en masse*. Sold-out tours around the world ensued, with further albums (the Grammy Award-winning *De Bach aux baroques* (issued internationally as *Going Baroque*) and *Swinging Mozart* (aka *Anyone For Mozart?*), keeping cash registers ringing until the novelty began to wear off.

Not going quite as far back in time, Les Bretell's presented themselves as a rejuvenated barbershop quartet, but under the influence of mentor Henri Salvador they combined comedy, doo-wop, pop songs and even surf music on a run of EPs from 1963. Although they debuted strongly with a cover of Jan & Dean's 'Honolulu Lulu' ('Lulu d'Honolulu'), the rest of their debut EP, which included vocal renditions of 'Watermelon Man' ('Marchand de melons') and Glenn Miller's 'Fools Rush In' ('Ne dis pas'),[736] revealed their true colours.

They subsequently played on their comic talents on the dire 'Chou-chou chérie' before returning to the sounds of California with the passable 'Les filles du soleil' (the Beach Boys' 'The Girls On The Beach') in an attempt to find a hit that never came.

Salvador himself released a stream of pastiches, parodies, jazz and ballads that delivered hits with the beautiful 'Syracuse' and the jazzy tribute 'Count Basie' (adapted from Basie's 'Li'l Darlin' '). Although comic knockabouts like 'Minnie, petite souris' (Lou Monte's 'Pepino The Italian Mouse')

---

[736] Possibly inspired by Rick Nelson's recent revival of the song.

grabbed the most airplay, it was ballads like 'Dis-moi que tu m'aimes', 'Va-t'en vit', mon amour' (Steve Lawrence's 'Go Away Little Girl') and 'Tu es entrée dans mon âme' that proved more enduring. A natural entertainer, Salvador was ideal for television, and as the decade ticked on he wound down his interests in his stable of stars to produce a series of TV specials (*Salves d'or*) designed to showcase his latest records.

## Bossa nova

One of Henri Salvador's many releases was a late 1962 EP aimed at children, but reflecting the biggest commercial development in jazz for many years. *Bossa nova pour les tout petits* offered a range of pre-teen favourites, yet musically the record tapped a fusion between samba and jazz that had been developed in Brazil during the late fifties and had first come to international attention with Luiz Bonfá's popular 'Manhã de Carnaval'. The theme from the 1959 film, *Orfeu negro*,[737] this had been reworked into French for Maria Candido as 'La chanson d'Orfeu', but her version languished behind far superior efforts by Dalida and Gloria Lasso.[738]

Other French singers also had a stab at the bossa nova sound over the next two years. Among the better attempts were Jacqueline Boyer's 1961 interpretation of João Gilberto's 'Chega de saudade' ('Il fait gris dans mon cœur'), Audrey Arno's 'La bosse à nova', and Sacha Distel's early 1962 cover of Antônio Carlos Jobim's 'Samba de uma nota só'[739] ('Chanson sur une seule note'), although none of them came near to dislodging rock'n'roll from the top of the charts.

Thereafter, the style slowly seeped into public consciousness around the globe before exploding on a 1962 US album by saxophonist Stan Getz and guitarist Charlie Byrd, *Jazz Samba*. The big hit from the LP was a reworking of Antonio Carlos Jobim's 'Desafinado', and before 1962 was out the song was on the French record charts, not only in the original instrumental version by Getz and Byrd, but also a vocal adaptation by Ella Fitzgerald.[740] It was also recorded in French as 'Faits pour s'aimer' by Richard Anthony, Sacha Distel, Laura Villa and Gloria Lasso, the latter under its original Brazilian title. Distel's spot-on interpretation was released alongside 'Ting-toung (Viens danser le bossa nova)'[741] on the appropriately titled *Sacha bossa nova* EP and became

---

[737] Known to British and American audiences as *Black Orpheus*.
[738] Dalida's and Lasso's versions were retitled 'La chanson d'Orphée'. American singer Jack Jones recorded it in English in 1966 as 'A Day In The Life Of A Fool'.
[739] The song introduced to anglophone audiences by Stan Getz & Charlie Byrd as 'One-Note Samba'. Distel's recording was covered by both Jean-Claude Pascal and Michèle Arnaud.
[740] Subtitled 'Nicely Out Of Tune'.
[741] An original composition partially derived from João Gilberto's 'Bim-bom', the song was also covered by Annie Cordy.

a sizeable hit. Along with Anthony's poppier rendition, it opened French ears to the new wave in Brazilian jazz, and, almost overnight, the bossa nova rhythm permeated every corner of the music industry.

Belgium's Les Chakachas weighed in early with 'Bossa de moda', as did Los Machucambos with 'Dona Rosa' and Les Trois Ménestrels with yet another version of 'Desafinado' ('Faits pour s'aimer'). The Ménestrels subsequently charted their own course, making modest waves with 1963's 'Le bide' and 'Suliram' while continuing to pack them in at their ever-popular live shows.

Jacqueline François had recently undertaken a jazzy makeover of Dave Brubeck's 'Take Five' ('Ne boude pas'), but in 1963 she took a punt on the new Brazilian sound as well with 'Nossa samba (Notre samba)', before tackling Astrud Gilberto's 'The Girl From Ipanema' ('La fille d'Ipanema') in 1964. Eventually, she conceded defeat and bowed out, reverting to type in 1965, when her 1960 recording of 'I Could Have Danced All Night' ('J'aurais voulu danser') was reissued to coincide with the release of the film version of *My Fair Lady* starring Audrey Hepburn.

Nana Mouskouri also had a go at 'La fille d'Ipanema' in 1964, a year after she failed to win *Eurovision* for Luxembourg with the ballad 'À force de prier'. Although she was one of the biggest stars on the circuit in Spain, West Germany and her native Greece, not even a gift from Serge Gainsbourg, 'Les yeux pour pleurer', succeeded in lifting her into the French charts. Covers of Joey Dee & The Starlighters' 'I Lost My Baby' ('Laissez-moi pleurer') and Dionne Warwick's 'This Empty Place' ('La place vide') likewise went nowhere, and her reworkings of the Jaynetts' 'Sally, Go 'round The Roses' ('Rose (parmi les roses)') and Dionne Warwick's 'Don't Make Me Over' ('T'en vas pas comme ça') lost out to Richard Anthony and Nancy Holloway respectively. French audiences proved resistant to Mouskouri's charms, but as her international fame grew, the market began to warm to her crystal-clear voice.

While the sum total of pure bossa nova hits was small, they had started a trend, and the number of records that cast a nod in the direction of South America would continue to grow inexorably over the next decade and a half. In the meantime, Sacha Distel, who probably did more than

385

anyone to popularise the bossa nova in France, had transited effortlessly out of the teenage market with excellent covers of Tony Bennett's 'I Wanna Be Around' ('J'aimerais être là') and 'The Good Life' ('La belle vie'), the latter having started life as 'Marina', an instrumental he had penned for the 1961 film *Les 7 péchés capitaux*.

A natural for television, Distel was offered his own show in 1963, going on to host the family-favourite *Sacha Show*, a shop window that gave him the opportunity to sing all styles of pop for eight years. Covers of Paul Anka's 'A Steel Guitar And A Glass Of Wine' ('Guitare et copains') and Bobby Rydell's 'I Wanna Thank You' ('J'ai un rendez-vous') kept him connected with the youth market, but he generally leant towards love songs like 'C'est fait pour durer toujours' or Perry Como's 'Caterina', determined to become an international cabaret draw. American tunes provided easy pickings, but Distel also cut material by songsmiths from his own country – notably 'Le myosotis', a gift from Georges Brassens, which was included on his 1963 live album, *Sacha Distel à l'Olympia*.

## Singing actresses and a singing nun

With cinema still providing a gateway to a huge audience, actresses who had found fame on celluloid continued to aspire to parallel singing careers. Jeanne Moreau stunned audiences with her performance in François Truffaut's 1962 classic, *Jules et Jim*, which also gave her a hit with the ersatz folk song that served as the film's theme, 'Le tourbillon'. This led a year later to the LP *Jeanne Moreau*, containing a set of songs crafted specifically for her by Cyrus Bassiak. And indeed, the *grande dame* of the silver screen impressed with personalised treatments of the *chansons* on offer, transforming 'La vie de cocagne' into a Sinatra-esque swinger, and showing real feeling for smoky, late-night jazz on 'Le blues indolent'. The album also generated a radio hit with 'J'ai la mémoire qui flanche', encouraging Moreau to dabble in music for the rest of the decade.

Another actress with musical aspirations, Brigitte Bardot, released her second album, *B.B.*, at the end of 1963. Flirting with the sounds of *yé-yé*, the infectious 'Moi je joue'[742] and the humorous 'Ça pourrait changer' duly became the first of her hits to cross over into the teenage market. The LP itself was a mixed bag, but nevertheless generated further chart successes with

---

[742] Revived nearly forty years later for a Renault commercial.

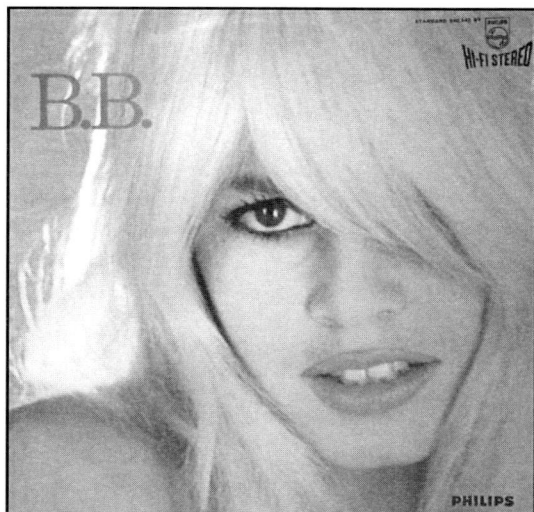

the poppy 'Je danse donc je suis' and a cover of *yé-yé* girl Peggy's 'Ne me laisse pas l'aimer', while Bardot made plain her love for Latin American music with the charming 'Ciel de lit'.[743]

Lost in Bardot's shadow, fellow actress Françoise Deldick offered her own sex-kitten style of pop on 1963's wonderful 'Tout' nue, les mains dans les poches', a wickedly salacious effort that (predictably) flopped in the conservative pop marketplace, as did the more conventional girl group outing 'Le garçon de l'été', a year later.

While sex was the main selling point on the records of Bardot and Deldick, it had absolutely nothing to do with the success of the biggest surprise star of the decade: Sœur Sourire. A Belgian nun who had made some records to raise money for charity, she sang sweetly to her own guitar accompaniment in a style redolent of the contemporary American folk revival, though there seemed little chance of religious songs like 'Entre les étoiles' and 'Résurrection' ever reaching a wide audience. Nevertheless, these and others were pressed up by Philips on a pair of albums[744] and made their way across the Atlantic, where an imaginative record mogul decided they might be worth a punt.

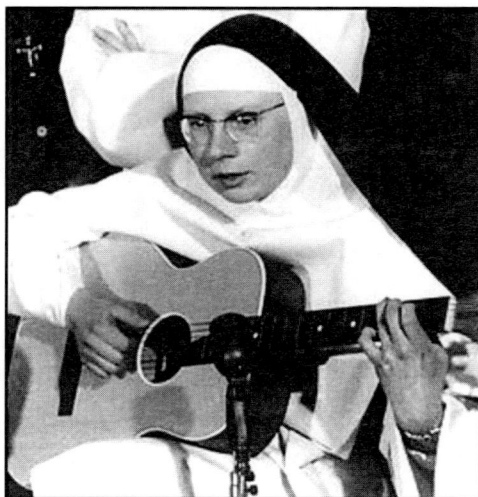

Rebranded as 'The Singing Nun' for international audiences, the good sister subsequently enjoyed a smash hit all around the world with 'Dominique', a song dedicated to the founder of the Dominican order, which rocketed up the US charts in the weeks following the assassination of President John F. Kennedy on 22 November 1963. The single topped the *Billboard* charts at the end of the year, with the album *The Singing Nun* following suit.[745] Sadly, however, this transatlantic triumph

*Sœur Sourire.*

---

[743] It was duly covered by Los Machucambos in much the same style.
[744] Both untitled.
[745] In Britain, the single reached No. 7 on the *Record Retailer* chart. It had already made the Top 10 in Belgium before it was released in the US.

did not bring Sœur Sourire happiness. Her follow-up single, 'Tous les chemins', all but flopped, while jealousy within the walls of the convent eventually drove her to resume a life outside the order.

## The death of Édith Piaf

Sœur Sourire may have been the biggest-selling francophone artist worldwide, but back in France there was still nobody to touch Édith Piaf, whose success continued uninterrupted from the fifties into the sixties, with best-sellers like 1961's banjo-toting 'Mon vieux Lucien' and accordion-laden 'Les mots d'amour'. While the offbeat orchestration of 'Jérusalem' and the big band bash of 'Le billard électrique' showed Piaf to be open to new musical ideas, her live shows were more traditional affairs – as illustrated by her *Récital 1961* album, which presented listeners with an extraordinary new song, 'Les blouses blanches', a horrifying account of incarceration in a mental asylum.

Piaf's ongoing musical partnership with Charles Dumont resulted in the 1961 four-song 10" LP *Quatre chansons de Charles Dumont*, with the sweet 'Faut pas qu'il se figure' and the late-night ambience of 'Qu'il était triste cet Anglais' keeping the quality high. Thereafter, Piaf poured her energies into launching the career of her latest protégé and husband, Théo Sarapo, with whom she recorded the hit duet 'À quoi ça sert l'amour' in 1962, and delivered some exceptional live shows that were captured on the album *Récital 1962*.

Piaf also contributed two songs to Sarapo's first solo EP, including the intriguing 'Chez Sabine' (which dipped from *chanson* into jazz with just a hint of *yé-yé*), while 'Pour qui tu t'prends' utilised the jaunty piano style she had favoured during the mid-fifties. Alas, Sarapo failed to find any success on his own and was routinely dismissed as an imposter trying to ride his wife's skirts to the top – a harsh, if unsurprising verdict. His second EP, graced by the enticing 'Garce de vie', certainly deserved a wider audience than it reached.

While Sarapo struggled to get his career off the ground, Piaf continued working despite persistent health problems that threatened to stop her in her tracks. Her 1962 LP, *Les amants de Teruel*, was not her best, although the strident 'Fallait-il' and 'Toi, tu l'entends pas', and the lush 'Ça fait drôle' showed her interpretative talent to be undiminished. The show-stopping 'Le droit d'aimer' (on which she defended her decision to marry Sarapo, a man twenty years her junior) was a sizeable hit in 1963, although it paled in comparison to the rendition included on the previous year's live album.

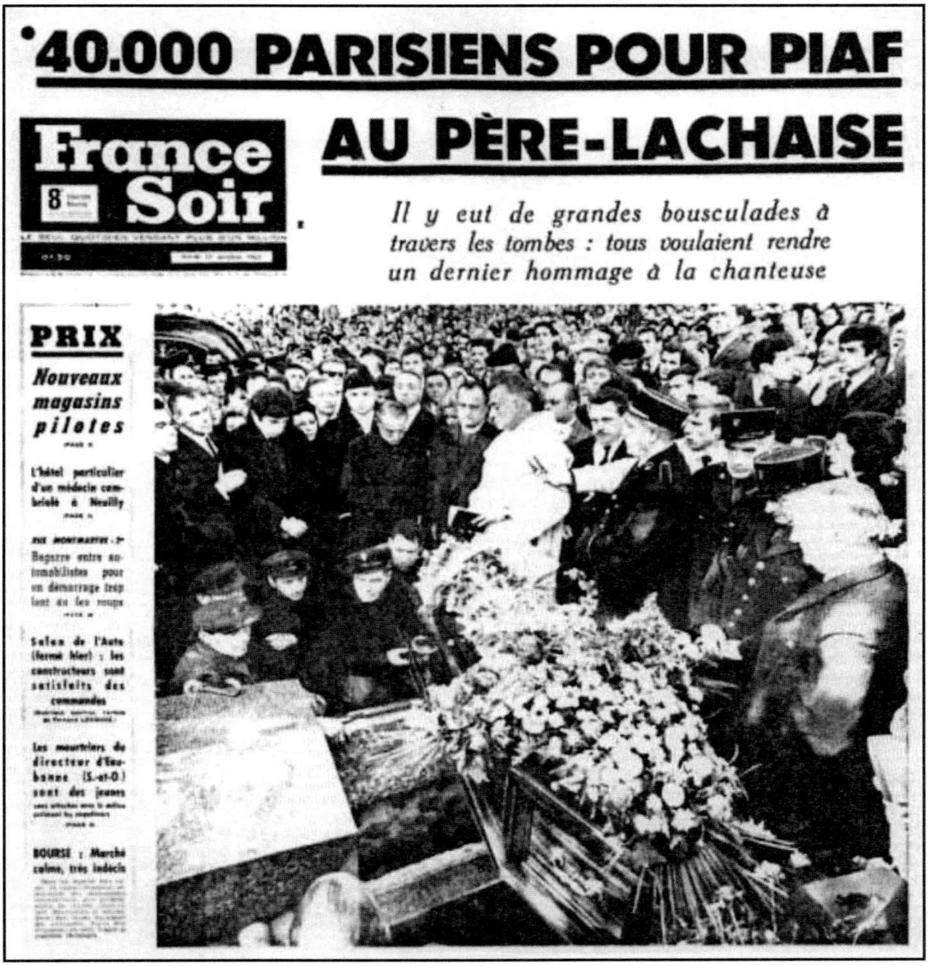

# 40.000 PARISIENS POUR PIAF AU PÈRE-LACHAISE

France Soir

*Il y eut de grandes bousculades à travers les tombes : tous voulaient rendre un dernier hommage à la chanteuse*

**PRIX**

*Nouveaux magasins pilotes*

L'hôtel particulier d'un médecin cambriolé à Neuilly

Salon de l'Auto (fermé hier) : les constructeurs sont satisfaits des commandes

Les meurtriers du directeur d'Eaubonne (S.-et-O.) sont des jeunes

BOURSE : Marché calme, très indécis

Piaf was soon back on stage for another series of shows, captured on the remarkable concert set *Récital Bobino 1963*, on which she unveiled the harrowing 'C'était pas moi', a tale of a man wrongly accused of murder. Although her heart remained as defiant as ever, her body was fast giving up the fight. On 11 October 1963, after a lifetime of hard living, emotional trauma, and drug and alcohol abuse, she died, aged just 47.

Piaf's passing brought down the curtain on the golden era of *la chanson française*, although this was not immediately apparent. Sales of her records soared as the country reeled in shock from the loss of its favourite *chanteuse*, and 40,000 people turned up to her burial at the Père Lachaise Cemetery in Paris.[746] She left behind a huge hole in the heart of French popular music, and for the next few years the industry expended maximum effort trying to find a 'new Piaf' who could similarly touch the hearts of the same vast audience,

[746] A short distance from where the Doors' Jim Morrison would be interred eight years later.

without ever finding one.

Her final departure from the stage also marked a symbolic turning point for French pop. Although the *chansonniers* and *chanteurs réalistes* would always remain a part of French musical culture (indeed, some of the greatest *chansons* ever written would appear in the next few years), Piaf's exit allowed for a symbolic passing of the baton to the young Johnny Hallyday. From now on, it was rock'n'roll and *yé-yé* that would rule the marketplace.

Yet *yé-yé* too was soon to change in unforeseen ways, developing from the simplistic teenage pop froth of the early sixties into a vibrant, creative and utterly unique form of music pushed along, as ever, by the latest wind blowing in from across the sea. A few days before Piaf's passing, the chart in *Salut les copains* had included for the first time the name of a new musical act that would forever change the way that France, and the world, thought about pop music: the Beatles.

# Appendix I

## FRENCH POP
## AROUND THE WORLD

The years since the end of the Second World War have gradually seen English becoming the dominant language of international pop culture, but this trend was by no means as pronounced during the period covered by this book. Although the advent of rock'n'roll served as a springboard for the use of English in pop music around the world, up until the 1980s it had to battle hard against local languages, and English was by no means the only 'foreign' language able to find its way onto the international airwaves and into the charts. While the UK and US markets were largely (albeit not entirely) closed to foreign-language recordings, the European, Asian and South American markets were far less insistent on hearing songs sung only in English.

Although few French artists managed to achieve the global appeal enjoyed by Elvis Presley, it is nonetheless true that, for many of the country's leading singers of the fifties and early sixties, international sales counted for as much as, or more than, domestic sales. The far-flung outposts of the former French Empire remained predominantly francophone and French pop was widely popular in such disparate places as Lebanon, Quebec and Madagascar, while the leading French stars were also guaranteed a fair hearing closer to home in the French-speaking parts of Belgium and Switzerland.

Even more remarkably from the perspective of today's English-dominated market, many French singers and groups enjoyed huge sales across Europe, both in the 'free' Western half of the continent and behind the Iron Curtain. Françoise Hardy found tremendous success in Italy, Johnny Hallyday topped the charts in the Netherlands, and Sacha Distel picked up major sales in West Germany. Even minor-league artists could enjoy international success, with Orlando becoming a major star in Czechoslovakia and Georgie Dann proving more successful in Spain than he had ever been at home. Travelling even further afield, Édith Piaf enjoyed enormous success in Australia, Richard Anthony was accorded superstar status in South America, and Yvette Giraud enjoyed massive sales in Japan. Moreover, these were not isolated cases: Françoise Hardy would, in 1963, be ranked among the top ten best-selling artists in the world. The fifties and sixties were a profitable time for French pop on the international market.

While the number of French recording acts to make the record charts in

the UK and US was relatively small compared to the number who charted elsewhere across the globe, many of the big French hits of the day were adapted into English. Some became hits, while many others found their way onto big-selling albums by the leading pop and easy listening stars of the era, bringing further success to composers like Francis Lemarque, Gilbert Bécaud and Charles Aznavour.

The two lists that follow examine in detail the success of French singers and songwriters in the international market. In the interests of completeness, theme songs from French (and international) films which enjoyed commercial success as records are also included, even though such recordings to a large extent fall outside the scope of this volume. Film soundtracks were hugely popular during the sixties, particularly in Japan, and many French composers found themselves high in the international charts with spin-off single and EP releases.

*Part A* seeks to identify all recordings by French, Belgian or Swiss artists dating from the years covered by this book that made the charts somewhere other than France.

A number of foreign artists who chose to base themselves in France (for example Petula Clark, Mickey Baker and Vince Taylor) had previously enjoyed some chart success in their native lands. Those hits are excluded from this list, although any international hits they enjoyed after moving to France are included.

*Part B* lists international hits which began life as recordings by French artists before being covered or adapted for foreign audiences.

For reasons of space, I have reluctantly had to omit Belgian, Swiss and Canadian hits by the artists covered in this book, along with domestic and international covers of French songs that charted in those markets. As these are all, in part, francophone countries, it would take far too many pages to list them all.

French hits after 1963 are excluded, as are covers of such songs. For the sake of completeness, however, post-1963 covers of French hits created before this date are included.

This does not pretend to be a complete list. It is likely, particularly for the earlier years and for those countries for which no record chart books are available, that there remain many songs of French origin yet to be identified. Readers who spot omissions in either list are invited to contact the author, who will endeavour to include the missing information in any subsequent editions. Contact details may be found in the *Author's Note and Acknowledgements* at the front of this book.

## Sources

There was no official national chart in the UK until the end of the sixties, and even then, its accuracy has been disputed for decades. During the period covered by this volume, music fans had a variety of charts from which to choose. For the purposes of this appendix, a 'hit' constitutes a record or a song which appeared in charts published by any of the following: *Disc*, *Melody Maker* (sheet music sales – to 1965 only), *Melody Maker* (record sales), *Mersey Beat*, *Music Echo*, *New Musical Express*, Capital Radio (not all charts currently available), Radio 270 (not all charts currently available), Radio Caroline (not all charts currently available), Radio City (not all charts currently available), Radio London (not all charts currently available), *Record Mirror/New Record Mirror* (singles chart, EP chart, and the individual record outlet charts published between 1954 and 1961) and *Record Retailer* (singles chart, EP chart, and the short-lived 'Breakers' chart that tracked climbers below the Top 50). For the period prior to 1953, I have also taken into consideration the retrospective sales charts from 1940-52 compiled by the late Colin Brown, edited by Steve Waters and published by Rock History Ltd. in 2014 (see *Appendix III* for details).

Although *Billboard* is generally considered to be the 'official' chart for the United States, its mix of sales and airplay when calculating chart places during this period means that some fans (and artists) preferred to follow the charts in *Cash Box* or *Music Vendor* (later *Record World*). I have therefore referred to the following sources: *Billboard* Adult Contemporary Chart, *Billboard* Country Chart, *Billboard* Dance Chart, *Billboard* Disco Chart, *Billboard* Easy Listening Chart, *Billboard* Pop Chart (including the 'Bubbling Under' and Christmas charts), *Billboard* Rhythm & Blues Chart, *Billboard* Soul Chart, *Cash Box* Pop Chart, *Cash Box* Rhythm & Blues chart, *Cash Box* Soul Chart, *Music Vendor/Record World* Pop Chart (including the variously-titled 'Bubbling Under' charts). For the period prior to 1955, I have also used Joel Whitburn's *Pop Memories* book, which provides a synthesis of information from a variety of sources. I have not included songs that only appeared on charting albums – such a task is beyond me!

For other countries, I have been reliant on the international sections of *Billboard* and *Cash Box*, or data published in books (see *Appendix III*) or provided online (*Appendix IV*) by seasoned chart enthusiasts whose commitment, dedication and passion for the truth makes them reliable sources. Foremost among these is Eric Stazzu, whose collection of charts from France and beyond is truly mind-blowing.

Eagle-eyed readers will note that some of the charts mentioned above post-date the period covered by this volume. I have only researched these charts for revivals of songs that were originally created during this period.

# *Part A*

## International Hits by French, Belgian and Swiss Artists

The column headers are indicated by diagonal lines pointing to: Artist, Title, Release year, Country, Foreign title (if any)

### ADAMO

| Title | Release year | Country | Foreign title (if any) |
|---|---|---|---|
| Cara bambina | 1965 | Japan | |
| Sans toi ma mie | 1963 | Italy | Sei qui non me |
| | 1963 | Netherlands | |
| | 1965 | Japan | |
| En blue jeans et blouson de cuir | 1965 | Japan | |
| Amour perdu | 1963 | Netherlands | |
| | 1965 | Turkey | Sen sevme beni |
| N'est-ce pas merveilleux? | 1963 | Netherlands | |
| Crier ton nom | 1963 | Netherlands | |
| | 1964 | Italy | Gridare il tuo nome |
| Tombe la neige | 1964 | Italy | Cada la neve |
| | 1964 | Netherlands | |
| | 1964 | Spain | |
| | 1965 | Turkey | Her yerde kar var |
| | 1969 | Japan | |
| | 1971 | Japan | Yuki ga furu |
| Car je veux | 1965 | Italy | Non voglio nascondermi |
| Vous permettez, Monsieur? | 1964 | Netherlands | |
| | 1964 | West Germany | |
| | 1964 | West Germany | Gestatten Sie, Monsieur? |

### AIMABLE, SON ACCORDÉON ET SON ORGUE

| Title | Release year | Country | Foreign title (if any) |
|---|---|---|---|
| Hernando's Hideaway[747] | 1955 | UK | |
| Alte Kameraden | 1961 | West Germany | |
| Grüß an Kiel | 1961 | West Germany | |
| Beer Barrel Polka (Modranska Polka) | 1962 | West Germany | |
| Alo-Ahé | 1962 | West Germany | |

### THE ALLEGRETTES

| Title | Release year | Country | Foreign title (if any) |
|---|---|---|---|
| When | 1959 | Italy | |

### MARCEL AMONT

| Title | Release year | Country | Foreign title (if any) |
|---|---|---|---|
| La chanson du grillon (The Cricket Song) | 1961 | Spain | |
| Dans le cœur de ma blonde (Wheels) | 1962 | Italy | |
| | 1962 | Malta | |

---

[747] Aimable's accordion instrumental of 'Hernando's Hideaway' (issued in France as 'Amour, castagnettes et tango') was one of many versions available at the time in the UK and is listed in the sheet music charts. It did not make the Top 20 best-selling records lists.

## RICHARD ANTHONY[748]

| | | | |
|---|---|---|---|
| *Let's Twist Again* | 1962 | Argentina | |
| *La leçon de twist (Twistin' The Twist)* | 1962 | Japan | |
| *J'entends siffler le train (Five Hundred Miles)* | 1962 | Austria | |
| | 1962 | Israel | |
| | 1962 | Italy | |
| | 1963 | Italy | *E il treno va* |
| | 1963 | Spain | |
| | 1964 | UK | |
| | 1964 | UK | *Five Hundred Miles* |
| *J'irai pleurer sous la pluie (Crying In The Rain)* | 1965 | UK | *Crying In The Rain* |
| *Faits pour s'aimer (Desafinado)* | 1962 | Italy | |
| *Loin (Greensleeves)* | 1963 | Italy | |
| *Tout ça pour la bossa nova (Blame It On The Bossa Nova)* | 1963 | Argentina | |
| *Donne-moi ma chance (Too Late To Worry)* | 1963 | Italy | |
| | 1963 | Italy | *Per questa volta* |
| | 1963 | Netherlands | |
| | 1963 | Sweden | |
| | 1964 | UK | |
| | 1964 | UK | *Too Late To Worry* |
| | 1965 | Brazil | *Per questa volta* |
| *En écoutant la pluie (Rhythm Of The Rain)* | 1964 | UK | |
| *Sur le toit (Up On The Roof)* | 1964 | UK | |
| *C'est ma fête (It's My Party)* | 1964 | Brazil | |
| | 1964 | Italy | *La mia festa* |
| | 1965 | Argentina | |
| | 1965 | Brazil | *La mia festa* |
| *Tchin tchin* | 1964 | Argentina | |
| | 1964 | Brazil | *Cin cin* |
| | 1964 | Chile | |
| | 1964 | Italy | *Cin cin* |
| | 1964 | Spain | |
| | 1964 | West Germany | *Cin Cin* |
| *Walking Alone (À malypense)* | 1963 | UK | |
| | 1964 | UK | |

## AUDREY ARNO AND THE HAZY OSTERWALD SEXTET

| | | | |
|---|---|---|---|
| *La Pachanga* | 1961 | US | |
| | 1961 | West Germany | *Paschanga* |

## JACK ARY

| | | | |
|---|---|---|---|
| *Toi, ma petite poupée* | 1961 | Italy | *Yo tengo una muñeca* |
| *Midi midinette* | 1961 | Italy | |

---

[748] Richard Anthony's UK hits came on two EPs. *Richard Anthony* included 'Donne moi ma chance (Too Late To Worry)', 'En écoutant la pluie (Rhythm Of The Rain)', 'J'entends siffler le train (500 Miles)' and 'Sur le toit (Up On The Roof)'; *Walking Alone* included 'Five Hundred Miles', 'If I Loved You', 'Too Late To Worry' and 'Walking Alone'. 'Walking Alone' also charted as a single. 'If I Loved You' was not recorded until 1964 and so does not feature in the list above; details of this recording will appear in Volume 2.

## LYS ASSIA[749]

| Mademoiselle de Paris | 1951 | UK | |
|---|---|---|---|
| Ba-Loom Ba-La | 1953 | UK | |
| O Mein Papa | 1953 | UK | Oh! My Pa-Pa[750] |
| | 1954 | Netherlands | |
| Arrivederci Darling | 1955 | UK | Arrivederci Darling (Arrivederci Roma)[751] |
| | 1956 | West Germany | |
| Was kann schöner sein? | 1956 | West Germany | |
| Refrain | 1957 | Italy | |
| Deine Liebe | 1957 | West Germany | |
| Mi casa, su casa | 1957 | West Germany | |
| Mélodie d'amour | 1958 | West Germany | Melodie d'amour |
| Wenn die Glocken hell erklingen (Les trois cloches) | 1959 | West Germany | |
| La golondrina | 1960 | West Germany | |
| Ein Schiff wird kommen (Ta pedia tou Piréa) | 1960 | West Germany | |
| Signore | 1960 | Denmark | |
| Ein Mann wie du | 1960 | Denmark | |
| Wenn die Sonne scheint in Portugal | 1960 | Denmark | |
| Caballero | 1960 | Denmark | |
| Johnny, nimm das Heimweh mit | 1961 | West Germany | |
| Die Sterne von Syrakus | 1962 | West Germany | |

## ISABELLE AUBRET

| Un premier amour | 1962 | Finland | |
|---|---|---|---|
| | 1962 | Italy | |

## CHARLES AZNAVOUR

| Tu t'laisses aller | 1962 | West Germany | Du lässt dich geh'n |
|---|---|---|---|
| L'amour et la guerre | 1962 | Italy | |
| | 1962 | Italy | L'amore e la guerra |
| Je m'voyais déjà | 1962 | Italy | |
| Il faut savoir | 1962 | Israel | |
| | 1962 | Italy | |
| | 1962 | Italy | Devi sapere |
| | 1963 | Spain | |
| Esperanza | 1962 | Italy | |
| | 1963 | Netherlands | |
| Alléluia | 1963 | Spain | |
| Les comédiens | 1963 | Netherlands | |
| | 1963 | Spain | |
| Je t'attends | 1963 | Uruguay | |
| For me... formidable | 1963 | Netherlands | |
| Bon anniversaire[752] | 1971 | Italy | Buon anniversario |

---

[749] Lys Assia's 1960 Danish hits were on the EP *Lys Assia*.

[750] Assia's 'Oh! My Pa-Pa' was one of many versions available at the time in the UK and is listed in the sheet music charts. It did not make the Top 20 best-selling records lists.

[751] 'Arrivederci Darling' is credited to Lys Assia & The Johnston Brothers, a British vocal outfit who backed her on the recording. It was one of many versions available at the time in the UK and is listed in the sheet music charts and was also listed as a regional hit in *Record Mirror*. It did not make the Top 20 best-selling records lists.

[752] Aznavour's orginal French version, 'Bon anniversaire', was released in 1963 on the album *Qui?* He did not record it in Italian until the 1970s.

## CHARLES AZNAVOUR *(continued)*

| | | | |
|---|---|---|---|
| *Donne tes 16 ans* | 1963 | Italy | |
| *La mamma* | 1964 | Brazil | |
| | 1964 | Greece | |
| | 1964 | Italy | |
| | 1964 | Netherlands | |
| | 1964 | Spain | |
| | 1964 | Uruguay | |
| | 1966 | Brazil | |
| *Et pourtant* | 1964 | Greece | |
| | 1964 | Italy | *Ma perchè* |
| | 1964 | Spain | |
| | 1965 | Argentina | |
| | 1966 | Mexico | |

## BOB AZZAM ET SON ORCHESTRE

| | | | |
|---|---|---|---|
| *Mustapha* | 1960 | Brazil | |
| | 1960 | Italy | |
| | 1960 | Netherlands | |
| | 1960 | Spain | |
| | 1960 | Sweden | |
| | 1960 | UK | |
| | 1960 | West Germany | |
| | 1961 | India | |
| *T'aimer follement (Makin' Love)* | 1960 | Spain | |
| *Marina* | 1960 | Spain | |
| *Manuela* | 1960 | Spain | |
| *Tintarella di luna* | 1960 | West Germany | |
| *C'est écrit dans le ciel* | 1961 | Italy | |

## EDDIE BARCLAY ET SON ORCHESTRE

| | | | |
|---|---|---|---|
| *La goualante du pauvre Jean* | 1956 | UK[753] | |
| *O Cangaceiro* | 1955 | US | *The Bandit* |
| *C'est à Hambourg* | 1956 | US | |
| *Gelsomina* | 1956 | US | *(Love Theme From) La Strada* |

## BRIGITTE BARDOT

| | | | |
|---|---|---|---|
| *Sidonie* | 1962 | Japan | |

## ALAIN BARRIÈRE

| | | | |
|---|---|---|---|
| *Elle était si jolie* | 1964 | Chile | |
| | 1964 | Spain | |
| *Plus je t'entends* | 1964 | Italy | *E più ti amo* |
| | 1965 | Uruguay | |
| | 1966 | Brazil | *E più ti amo* |

## RIA BARTOK

| | | | |
|---|---|---|---|
| *Cœur (Heart (I Hear You Beating))* | 1964 | Spain | |

---

[753] Barclay's orchestral treatment of 'La goualante du pauvre Jean' was one of many versions available at the time in the UK and is listed in the sheet music charts alongside those which bore the English title, 'The Poor People Of Paris'. It did not make the Top 20 best-selling records lists.

## FRANCIS BAY ET SON ORCHESTRE

| Tequila | 1958 | Netherlands | |
|---|---|---|---|
| Manhattan Spiritual | 1961 | Denmark | |
| | 1961 | Sweden | |
| Por dos besos | 1960 | Italy | |
| In The Mood | 1962 | Sweden | |

## GUY BÉART

| L'eau vive | 1958 | Japan | |
|---|---|---|---|

## GILBERT BÉCAUD

| Le pianiste de Varsovie | 1963 | Spain | |
|---|---|---|---|
| Le jour où la pluie viendra | 1958 | UK | The Day The Rains Came[754] |
| | 1959 | Italy | |
| | 1960 | Spain | |
| Le mur | 1959 | Italy | |
| Marie, Marie | 1960 | Italy | |
| Quand l'amour est mort | 1962 | Italy | |
| Et maintenant | 1962 | Brazil | |
| | 1962 | Italy | |
| | 1962 | Spain | |
| | 1963 | Argentina | |
| | 1963 | Netherlands | |
| | 1963 | Uruguay | |
| Le bateau blanc | 1962 | Italy | La vela blanca |
| Je t'attends | 1963 | Italy | |
| Au revoir | 1964 | Brazil | |
| | 1964 | Chile | |

## SIDNEY BECHET

| Theme From 'The Threepenny Opera' | 1956 | UK | |
|---|---|---|---|
| Petite fleur | 1959 | Italy | |
| | 1959 | Spain | |
| | 1959 | UK[755] | |
| Si tu vois ma mère | 1959 | Netherlands | |

## JOSÉ BERGHMANS ET SON ORCHESTRE

| La guerre des boutons | 1963 | Japan | |
|---|---|---|---|

## LES BLUE STARS

| La légende du pays des oiseaux (Lola) (Lullaby Of Birdland) | 1955 | US | |
|---|---|---|---|
| Tout bas (Speak Low) | 1956 | US | |
| Broadway At Basin Street | 1956 | US | |
| The Kissing Dance | 1956 | US | |
| Jumpin' At The Woodside | 1956 | US | |
| Amour, castagnettes et tango (Hernando's Hideaway) | 1956 | US | |

---

[754] Bécaud's 'The Day The Rains Came' is an English-language version of his 'Le jour où la pluie viendra'. It was one of many versions available at the time in the UK and is listed in the sheet music charts. It did not make the Top 20 best-selling records lists.

[755] Bechet's original recording of 'Petite fleur' was reissued in the UK following the success of Chris Barber's cover. It was one of many versions available at the time in the UK and is listed in the sheet music charts. It did not make the Top 20 best-selling records lists.

## GIORGIO BOYER ET SON ORCHESTRE

| Le doulos | 1963 | Japan | |
|---|---|---|---|

## JACQUELINE BOYER

| Tom Pillibi | 1960 | Denmark | |
|---|---|---|---|
| | 1960 | Italy | |
| | 1960 | Netherlands | |
| | 1960 | Spain | |
| | 1960 | Sweden | |
| | 1960 | UK | |
| | 1960 | West Germany | |
| Si tu rencontres l'amour | 1960 | West Germany | Grüß mir die Liebe |
| Mitsou | 1963 | West Germany | |

## LUCIENNE BOYER

| Hands Across The Table | 1934 | US | |
|---|---|---|---|
| Parlez-moi d'amour | 1934 | US | |

## JACQUES BREL

| Les bourgeois | 1962 | Spain | |
|---|---|---|---|

## THE BRUSSELS NEW CONCERT ORCHESTRA

| Hawaiian Calypso | 1963 | Australia | |
|---|---|---|---|

## GÉRARD CALVI ET SON ORCHESTRE

| Premier bal | 1960 | US | Our First Dance |
|---|---|---|---|
| La belle Américaine | 1962 | West Germany | Twist Music |

## CAMILLO

| Sag warum (Oh Why) | 1960 | West Germany | |
|---|---|---|---|
| | 1961 | Italy | |
| | 1963 | Spain | |

## PATRICIA CARLI

| Je ne voudrais pas pleurer | 1965 | Turkey | |
|---|---|---|---|
| Virginia | 1965 | Turkey | |

## LESLIE CARON

| Hi-Lilli, Hi-Lo[756] | 1953 | UK | |
|---|---|---|---|
| | 1953 | US | |
| | 1954 | Netherlands | |

## LES CHAKACHAS

| Eso es el amor | 1959 | Italy | |
|---|---|---|---|
| | 1959 | UK | |
| Vénus | 1959 | Italy | |
| Les enfants du Pirée | 1960 | Italy | |
| (Ta pedia tou Piréa) | 1961 | Argentina | |
| La pachanga | 1961 | Italy | |
| Brigitte Bardot | 1961 | Italy | |
| Twist, twist | 1962 | Italy | |
| | 1962 | UK | |
| | 1962 | West Germany | |

---

[756] Leslie Caron's 'Hi-Lili, Hi-Lo' is a duet with American actor Mel Ferrer.

## LES CHAKACHAS *(continued)*

| Madison 62 | 1962 | West Germany | |
|---|---|---|---|
| | 1963 | Austria | |

## LES CHAMPIONS
*See* Danyel Gérard avec Les Champions

## LES CHATS SAUVAGES

| Twist à Saint-Tropez | 1962 | Denmark | |
|---|---|---|---|
| | 1962 | Sweden | |
| | 1963 | Finland | |

## LES CHAUSSETTES NOIRES

| Daniela | 1961 | Spain | |
|---|---|---|---|

## ROBERT CHAUVIGNY ET SON ORCHESTRE

| French Rockin' Waltz | 1959 | US | |
|---|---|---|---|
| The Bottle Hymn | 1959 | US | |

## MAURICE CHEVALIER[757]

| Louise | 1929 | US | |
|---|---|---|---|
| Wait Till You See My Chérie | 1929 | US | |
| My Love Parade | 1930 | US | |
| You Brought A New Kind Of Love To Me | 1930 | US | |
| My Ideal | 1931 | US | |
| Mama Inez | 1931 | US | |
| Mimi | 1932 | US | |
| On A Slow Boat To China | 1949 | UK | |
| I Love Paris | 1961 | West Germany | |
| Jessica | 1962 | Japan | |
| Enjoy It | 1963 | UK | |
| Let's Climb (Grimpons) | 1963 | UK | |

## LÉO CLARENS ET SON ORCHESTRE

| Le danseur de Charleston | 1956 | US | Charleston Parisien |
|---|---|---|---|

## PETULA CLARK[758]

| Adonis | 1959 | UK | |
|---|---|---|---|
| Cinderella Jones | 1960 | UK | |
| Sailor (Seemann)[759] | 1961 | Australia | |
| | 1961 | Denmark | |
| | 1961 | Ireland | |
| | 1961 | Israel | |
| | 1961 | Netherlands | |

---

[757] Maurice Chevalier's 1961 West German hit was a duet with Frank Sinatra taken from the soundtrack album of *Can-Can*, although it did not feature in the film itself. Chevalier's two 1963 UK hits were on the soundtrack EP from the 1962 film *In Search Of The Castaways*, in which he starred alongside UK actress Hayley Mills. 'Enjoy It' was a duet with Mills.

[758] Petula Clark had several hits in the UK (and elsewhere) before she relocated to France at the end of the fifties. They were therefore not French pop hits, strictly speaking, and are not included in this list. However, some of them were covers of French hits (see *Part B* for details).

[759] Clark recorded 'Sailor' in both English and French versions. The French version was entitled 'Marin'. Both versions were adapted from Lolita's big German hit, 'Seemann'.

## PETULA CLARK *(continued)*

| | | | |
|---|---|---|---|
| *Sailor (Seemann)* continued | 1961 | New Zealand | |
| | 1961 | Spain | |
| | 1961 | UK | |
| | 1968 | South Africa | |
| *Something Missing (L'absent)*[760] | 1961 | UK | |
| *Romeo (Salome)*[761] | 1961 | Australia | |
| | 1961 | Denmark | |
| | 1961 | Ireland | |
| | 1961 | Netherlands | |
| | 1961 | New Zealand | |
| | 1961 | Norway | |
| | 1961 | UK | |
| | 1962 | Italy | *Roméo* |
| *My Favourite Things*[762] | 1961 | UK | |
| *My Friend The Sea* | 1961 | Australia | |
| | 1961 | UK | |
| | 1962 | Ireland | |
| *Ya ya twist (Ya Ya)* | 1962 | Ireland | |
| | 1962 | Italy | |
| | 1962 | Spain | |
| | 1962 | Sweden | |
| | 1962 | UK | |
| *I'm Counting On You* | 1962 | UK | |
| *Whistlin' For The Moon* | 1962 | Australia | |
| | 1962 | UK | |
| *My Heart (Amor)* | 1962 | Italy | |
| *Chariot* | 1962 | Italy | |
| | 1963 | Brazil | |
| | 1963 | Denmark | |
| | 1963 | Denmark | *I Will Follow Him* |
| | 1963 | Israel | |
| | 1963 | Italy | *Sul mio carro* |
| | 1963 | Singapore | *I Will Follow Him* |
| | 1963 | Spain | |
| | 1963 | UK | |
| | 1963 | West Germany | *Cheerio* |
| *Jumble Sale* | 1962 | UK | |
| *Monsieur*[763] | 1962 | Netherlands | |
| | 1962 | West Germany | |
| | 1963 | Austria | |
| | 1963 | Denmark | |
| | 1963 | Italy | |
| *Je chante doucement* | 1964 | Spain | *Cantando al caminar* |
| *Cœur blessé (Torture)* | 1963 | Netherlands | |
| | 1964 | Italy | *Pagherai* |
| *L'enfant do (Cottonfields)* | 1963 | Singapore | |
| *Casanova baciami*[764] | 1963 | Denmark | |
| | 1963 | Netherlands | |

---

[760] 'Something Missing' is an English-language cover of Gilbert Bécaud's 'L'absent'.
[761] Clark also recorded 'Romeo' in French, with the slightly modified title 'Roméo'.
[762] 'My Favourite Things' appeared on a Pye Various Artists EP, *The Sound Of Music*, which made the UK EP charts.
[763] Despite its French title, 'Monsieur' was sung in German.
[764] Despite its Italian title, 'Casanova baciami' was sung in German. Although the recording was identical, the title was shortened to 'Casanova' for the UK release.

## PETULA CLARK (continued)

| Casanova baciami  continued | 1963 | UK | Casanova |
|---|---|---|---|
| | 1963 | West Germany | |
| | 1964 | Japan | |
| Mille mille grazie[765] | 1963 | Denmark | |
| | 1963 | West Germany | |
| Baby It's Me[766] | 1965 | UK | |
| Elle est finie (La belle histoire) | 1963 | Italy | La nostra storia |
| Je me sens bien (auprès de toi) (Dance On) | 1964 | Italy | Sto volentieri con te |
| Warum muß man auseinandergeh'n (Mit weißen Perlen) | 1964 | West Germany | |

## ANDRÉ CLAVEAU

| La petite diligence | 1951 | Netherlands | |
|---|---|---|---|
| Mademoiselle de Paris | 1951 | UK | |
| La ronde de l'amour | 1952 | Netherlands | |
| Dors mon amour | 1958 | Italy | |

## LES COMPAGNONS DE LA CHANSON[767]

| The Three Bells (Les trois cloches) | 1950 | UK | |
|---|---|---|---|
| | 1952 | Australia | |
| | 1952 | US | |
| | 1959 | UK[768] | |
| Mélodie perdue (Armen's Theme) | 1959 | US | Lost Melody |
| Les Gitans | 1959 | US | The Gypsies |
| Fais ta prière (Tom Dooley) | 1959 | Spain | |
| Le marchand de bonheur | 1960 | Japan | |
| Qu'il fait bon vivre (Down By The Riverside) | 1960 | US | Down By The Riverside |
| Un Mexicain | 1962 | Netherlands | |
| Les comédiens | 1963 | Israel | |
| | 1963 | Netherlands | |

See also Édith Piaf et Les Compagnons de la Chanson

## EDDIE CONSTANTINE

| Ich wünsch' dir einen schlaflosen Abend | 1956 | West Germany | |
|---|---|---|---|
| L'homme et l'enfant | 1956 | US | |
| | 1956 | West Germany | Der Vagabund und das Kind[769] |
| Et bâiller et dormir | 1957 | West Germany | Jeder macht mal eine Pause |
| Carina | 1959 | West Germany | |
| Beim Flüstertango[770] | 1963 | West Germany | |

---

[765] Despite its Italian title, 'Mille mille grazie' was sung in German.

[766] Petula Clark's 'Baby It's Me' flopped on its original 1963 UK release, but charted two years later as part of the Downtown EP.

[767] Aside from 'The Three Bells', the group's US hits were all sung in French, even though they were listed in English on the labels.

[768] Les Compagnons de la Chanson's 'The Three Bells' is an English-language version of their 1946 hit recording with Édith Piaf, 'Les trois cloches'. They recorded it twice in English, with the first rendition charting in the UK in 1950 and in the US in 1952, and the second scoring in the UK seven years later.

[769] Like the original French version, 'Der Vagabund und das Kind' (sung in German) was a duet by Constantine and his daughter Tania.

[770] 'Beim Flüstertango' was a duet with German actress and singer Elga Andersen.

## HÉLÈNE CORDET

| | | | |
|---|---|---|---|
| *Ki Ri* | 1954 | UK | |

## LOUISE CORDET

| | | | |
|---|---|---|---|
| *I'm Just A Baby* | 1962 | Sweden | |
| | 1962 | UK | |

## ANNIE CORDY

| | | | |
|---|---|---|---|
| *Le petit cordonnier*[771] | 1954 | UK | *The Little Shoemaker* |

## THE COUSINS

| | | | |
|---|---|---|---|
| *Kili Watch* | 1961 | Chile | |
| | 1961 | Netherlands | |
| | 1961 | West Germany | |
| | 1968 | Japan | |
| *Dang Dang* | 1962 | New Zealand | |
| *Relax* | 1962 | Netherlands | |
| *The Robot* | 1963 | Netherlands | |
| *Limbo Rock* | 1963 | Argentina | |

## DALIDA

| | | | |
|---|---|---|---|
| *Histoire d'un amour (Historia de un amor)* | 1959 | Italy | |
| *Gondolier (With All My Heart)* | 1959 | Italy | |
| *Le jour où la pluie viendra* | 1959 | Austria | *Am Tag als Regen kam* |
| | 1959 | Italy | |
| | 1959 | Spain | |
| | 1959 | West Germany | *Am Tag als Regen kam* |
| *Les Gitans* | 1959 | Italy | |
| | 1959 | Italy | *Gli Zingari* |
| | 1959 | Spain | |
| *Come prima* | 1959 | Spain | |
| *Tu m'étais destiné (You Are My Destiny)* | 1959 | Spain | |
| *Du moment qu'on s'aime (Piccolissima serenata)* | 1959 | Spain | |
| *Amstramgram (The Children's Marching Song)* | 1959 | Spain | |
| *Ciao, ciao bambina (Piove)* | 1959 | Spain | |
| *Tout l'amour (Passion Flower)* | 1959 | Spain | |
| *La chanson d'Orphée (Manha da carnaval)* | 1959 | Italy | *La canzone di Orfeo* |
| | 1960 | Spain | |
| *Love In Portofino* | 1959 | Italy | |
| *Marina* | 1960 | Spain | |
| *Adonis* | 1960 | Italy | |
| *T'aimer follement (Makin' Love)* | 1960 | Italy | *T'amerò dolcemente* |
| | 1960 | Spain | |
| *Milord*[772] | 1960 | Austria | |
| | 1960 | Italy | |
| | 1960 | West Germany | |
| *Romantica* | 1960 | Spain | |

---

[771] Annie Cordy's 'The Little Shoemaker' is an English-language cover of Francis Lemarque's 'Le petit cordonnier'. It was one of many versions available at the time in the UK and is listed in the sheet music charts. It did not make the Top 20 best-selling records lists.

[772] Dalida recorded versions of Édith Piaf's 'Milord' in both German and Italian, but not in French.

## DALIDA *(continued)*

| | | | |
|---|---|---|---|
| Le petit clair de lune (Tintarella di luna) | 1960 | Spain | |
| Dans les rues de Bahia (Too Much Tequila) | 1960 | Spain | |
| Les enfants du Pirée | 1960 | Italy | |
| (Ta pedia tou Piréa) | 1960 | Italy | Uno a te, uno a me (I ragazzi del Pireo) |
| | 1960 | Mexico | |
| | 1960 | Netherlands | |
| | 1960 | Spain | |
| | 1960 | Spain | Los niños del Pireo |
| | 1960 | UK | Never On Sunday |
| | 1960 | West Germany | Ein Schiff wird kommen |
| Itsy bitsy petit bikini | 1960 | Italy | Pezzettini di bikini |
| (Itsy Bitsy Teenie Weenie Yellow Polka Dot Bikini) | 1960 | Spain | |
| O sole mio | 1960 | Spain | |
| Garde-moi la dernière danse (Save the Last Dance For Me) | 1960 | Italy | Chiudi il ballo con me |
| Pépé | 1961 | Austria | Pepe |
| | 1961 | Netherlands | |
| | 1961 | Spain | Pepe |
| | 1961 | West Germany | Pepe |
| 24 000 baisers (24 000 baci) | 1961 | Austria | |
| | 1961 | Spain | |
| Et maintenant | 1962 | Italy | |
| Le petit Gonzalès (Speedy Gonzales) | 1963 | Spain | |
| Le jour le plus long (The Longest Day) | 1963 | Spain | |
| Sois heureux | 1965 | Argentina | |
| Eux | 1965 | Argentina | |
| | 1965 | Argentina | Dos |

## DANY DAUBERSON

| | | | |
|---|---|---|---|
| Be My Love | 1951 | UK | |
| Ma'moiselle de Paris | 1951 | UK | |
| La ronde de l'amour | 1951 | UK | Love's Roundabout |

## GEORGES DELERUE ET SON ORCHESTRE

| | | | |
|---|---|---|---|
| Classés tous risques | 1960 | Japan | |
| Jusqu'au bout du monde | 1964 | Japan | |

## LUCIENNE DELYLE

| | | | |
|---|---|---|---|
| Montagnes bleues | 1955 | Netherlands | |
| C'est magnifique | 1955 | Netherlands | |

## JACK DIÉVAL ET SON ORCHESTRE

| | | | |
|---|---|---|---|
| Be My Love | 1951 | UK | |

## SACHA DISTEL

| | | | |
|---|---|---|---|
| Scoubidou (Pommes et poires) (Apples, Peaches And Cherries) | 1959 | Spain | |
| Oui, oui, oui, oui | 1959 | Spain | |
| Personnalités ((You've Got) Personality) | 1959 | Spain | |

## SACHA DISTEL *(continued)*

| | | | |
|---|---|---|---|
| *Mon beau chapeau* | 1960 | Spain | |
| *Oui devant Dieu (La novia)* | 1961 | Spain | |
| *Caterina* | 1963 | Spain | |
| *Adios Amigo* | 1962 | Austria | |
| | 1962 | West Germany | |
| *Loin de toi (Recado)* | 1963 | Spain | |
| *Wir könnten Freunde sein (Zwei Glas Rum)* | 1963 | West Germany | |
| *Ein paar Tränen* | 1963 | West Germany | |

## ÉVELYNE DORAT

| | | | |
|---|---|---|---|
| *L' âme des poètes*[773] | 1952 | UK | |

## LENY ESCUDERO

| | | | |
|---|---|---|---|
| *Ballade à Sylvie* | 1963 | Spain | |

## LÉO FERRÉ

| | | | |
|---|---|---|---|
| *Paris canaille* | 1955 | Netherlands | |

## NINO FERRER[774]

| | | | |
|---|---|---|---|
| *C'est irréparable* | 1965 | Turkey | |

## LES FLASH

| | | | |
|---|---|---|---|
| *Twistarella* | 1967 | Japan | |

## ROGER FRANCE ET SON ORCHESTRE

| | | | |
|---|---|---|---|
| *Vivre sa vie* | 1964 | Japan | |

## CLAUDE FRANÇOIS

| | | | |
|---|---|---|---|
| *Dis lui (Tell Him)* | 1964 | Spain | |
| *Si j'avais un marteau (If I Had A Hammer)* | 1964 | Spain | |

## JACQUELINE FRANÇOIS

| | | | |
|---|---|---|---|
| *Mademoiselle de Paris* | 1955 | Japan | |
| *Les lavandières du Portugal* | 1956 | US | |
| *My One And Only Love* | 1957 | US | |
| *Le gondolier (With All My Heart)* | 1959 | Japan | |

## THE FRENCH ARMY BAND

| | | | |
|---|---|---|---|
| *Marche Lorraine* | 1919 | US | |

## SERGE GAINSBOURG

| | | | |
|---|---|---|---|
| *L'eau à la bouche* | 1962 | Italy | |

## GENEVIÈVE[775]

| | | | |
|---|---|---|---|
| *Cherie, Cherie* | 1958 | US | |

---

[773] Evelyne Dorat's version of Charles Trenet's 'L'âme des poètes (Longtemps, longtemps)' was issued in the UK along with the multiple English versions listed in *Part B*. It is listed in the sheet music charts along with Trenet's own version, but did not make the Top 20 best-selling records lists

[774] Nino Ferrer's career is covered in Volume 2.

[775] Geneviève made a handful of records in France during the mid-fifties, but was better known as an actress. Her US hit was not issued in France.

## DANYEL GÉRARD AVEC LES CHAMPIONS

| | | | |
|---|---|---|---|
| *Elle est trop loin* | 1964 | Italy | |
| *America* | 1964 | Spain | |

## ANDRÉ GIRARD ET SON ORCHESTRE

| | | | |
|---|---|---|---|
| *Thème de 'Ballon'* | 1961 | Japan | |

## YVETTE GIRAUD

| | | | |
|---|---|---|---|
| *Le marchand de bonheur* | 1960 | Japan | |
| *Papa aime maman* | 1960 | Japan | |

## ALAIN GORAGUER ET SON ORCHESTRE

| | | | |
|---|---|---|---|
| *Blues de Memphis* | 1960 | Japan | |

## ROCCO GRANATA

| | | | |
|---|---|---|---|
| *Marina* | 1959 | Netherlands | |
| | 1959 | US | |
| | 1959 | West Germany | |
| | 1960 | Denmark | |
| | 1960 | Finland | |
| | 1960 | Italy | |
| | 1960 | Japan | |
| | 1960 | Norway | |
| | 1960 | Spain | |
| | 1960 | Sweden | |
| *Oh, oh, Rosi* | 1960 | Italy | |
| | 1960 | West Germany | |
| *La bella* | 1960 | Netherlands | |
| | 1960 | West Germany | |
| *En italiano* | 1960 | West Germany | |
| *Rocco cha cha* | 1961 | West Germany | |
| *Carolina dai* | 1961 | Italy | |
| | 1961 | Netherlands | |
| *Irena* | 1961 | Netherlands | |
| | 1961 | West Germany | |
| *Signorina bella* | 1961 | West Germany | |
| *Tango d'amore* | 1962 | Finland | |
| *Buona notte bambino* | 1963 | Netherlands | |
| | 1963 | West Germany | |
| | 1964 | Austria | |
| *Plum plum serenata* | 1963 | Netherlands | |

## ONÉSIME GROSBOIS ET SON PIANO D'OCCASION

| | | | |
|---|---|---|---|
| *C'est à Hambourg* | 1956 | US | *The Left Bank* |

## GEORGES GUÉTARY

| | | | |
|---|---|---|---|
| *Ma belle Marguérite* | 1947 | UK | |
| *This Is My Lovely Day* | 1947 | UK | |
| *No Orchids For My Lady* | 1948 | UK | |
| *Clopin-clopant* | 1949 | UK | |
| *Boléro* | 1950 | UK | |
| *I'll Build A Stairway To Paradise* | 1952 | Australia | |
| *Papa aime maman* | 1960 | Japan | |

## LES GUITARES DU DIABLE

| | | | |
|---|---|---|---|
| *Twistin' U.S.A.* | 1962 | Argentina | |

407

## JOHNNY HALLYDAY

| | | | |
|---|---|---|---|
| *Souvenirs, souvenirs* *(Souvenirs)* | 1961 | Spain | |
| *Kili watch* | 1961 | Chile | |
| *Viens danser le twist* *(Let's Twist Again)* | 1962 | Israel | |
| | 1962 | Italy | |
| | 1962 | Spain | |
| *Douce violence* | 1962 | Italy | |
| | 1963 | Japan | |
| *Retiens la nuit* | 1962 | Italy | |
| | 1962 | Spain | |
| *Shake The Hand Of A Fool* | 1962 | US | |
| *Be-Bop-A-Lula* | 1962 | US | |
| *Madison twist* *(Meet Me At The Twistin' Place)* | 1962 | Spain | |
| *Pas cette chanson* *(Don't Play That Song (You Lied))* | 1962 | Spain | |
| *Hey Baby* | 1962 | Italy | |
| | 1962 | Spain | |
| *L'idole des jeunes* *(Teen Age Idol)* | 1963 | Spain | |
| *Tout bas, tout bas, tout bas* *(Apron Strings)* | 1963 | Denmark | |
| *Tes tendres années* *(Tender Years)* | 1963 | Netherlands | |
| | 1963 | Spain | |
| *Les bras en croix* | 1963 | Spain | |
| *Da dou ron ron* *(Da Doo Ron Ron)* | 1963 | West Germany | |
| | 1964 | Spain | |
| *Pour moi la vie va commencer* | 1963 | Netherlands | |
| | 1964 | Spain | |
| | 1965 | Japan | |
| *Ma guitare* | 1964 | Italy | *La mia chitarra* |
| | 1964 | Netherlands | |
| | 1964 | Spain | |

## JACK HAMMER

| | | | |
|---|---|---|---|
| *Kissin' Twist* | 1962 | Israel | |
| | 1962 | Sweden | |
| | 1962 | West Germany | |
| *Boogie Woogie Twist* | 1962 | Italy | |

## FRANÇOISE HARDY[776]

| | | | |
|---|---|---|---|
| *Tous les garçons et les filles* | 1963 | Denmark | |
| | 1963 | Israel | |
| | 1963 | Italy | *Quelli della mia età* |
| | 1963 | Netherlands | |
| | 1963 | Spain | |
| | 1963 | West Germany | |
| | 1963 | West Germany | *Peter und Lou* |
| | 1964 | Brazil | |
| | 1964 | UK[777] | |

---

[776] Several of Françoise Hardy's UK hits appeared the 1964 EP *C'est Fab,* which included 'L'amour s'en va', 'C'est à l'amour auquel je pense', 'Ton meilleur ami' and 'Tous les garçons et les filles'. The last of these also charted as a single. Another four ('J'aurais voulu', 'Avant de t'en aller' , 'Le premier bonheur du jour' and 'L'amour d'un garon') were on the 1964 EP *C'est Françoise,*

## FRANÇOISE HARDY (continued)

| J'suis d'accord | 1963 | Italy | |
|---|---|---|---|
| Oh oh chéri | 1963 | Italy | |
| C'est à l'amour auquel je pense | 1963 | Italy | E' all'amore che penso |
| | 1963 | Spain | |
| | 1964 | UK | |
| Le temps de l'amour | 1963 | Italy | L'età dell'amore |
| (Fort Chabrol) | 1963 | Spain | |
| L'amour s'en va | 1963 | Netherlands | |
| | 1963 | Sweden | |
| | 1964 | Italy | L'amore va |
| | 1964 | UK | |
| L'amour d'un garcon | 1964 | UK | |
| Ich steig dir auf's Dach | 1963 | West Germany | |
| Ton meilleur ami | 1964 | Netherlands | Only Friends |
| | 1964 | Singapore | Only Friends |
| | 1964 | UK | |
| | 1965 | Malaysia | Only Friends |
| Le premier bonheur du jour | 1964 | Italy | Il saluto del mattino |
| | 1964 | Spain | |
| | 1964 | UK | |
| | 1965 | Brazil | |
| J'aurais voulu | 1964 | UK | |
| Avant de t'en aller (Think About It) | 1964 | UK | |

## IRÈNE HILDA

| I Love Paris | 1954 | UK | |
|---|---|---|---|
| C'est Magnifique[778] | 1954 | UK | |

## ANDRÉ HOSSEIN ET SON ORCHESTRE

| Blues de la séduction | 1960 | Japan | |
|---|---|---|---|

## MAURICE JARRE ET SON ORCHESTRE

| La femme idéale | 1959 | Japan | |
|---|---|---|---|
| Theme From 'Lawrence Of Arabia' | 1963 | Italy | |

## ROBERT JEANTAL

| Dans le creux de ta main | 1961 | Spain | |
|---|---|---|---|

## GEORGES JOUVIN, SA TROMPETTE ET SON ENSEMBLE

| Le jour où la pluie viendra[779] | 1958 | UK | The Day The Rains Came |
|---|---|---|---|
| Histoire d'un amour (Historia de un amor) | 1959 | Finland | |
| La leçon de twist | 1962 | Japan | |
| (Twistin' The Twist) | 1962 | Spain | |

---

[777] Hardy did record 'Tous les garçons et les filles' in English (as 'Find Me A Boy'), but UK record buyers opted for the French-language original.

[778] Irène Hilda starred in the London run of the musical Can-Can and her two hits came from that show. Her version of 'C'est Magnifique' was a duet with English singer Edmund Hockridge.

[779] Jouvin's cover of Gilbert Bécaud's 'Le jour où la pluie viendra' was one of several versions available at the time in the UK. It made the sheet music charts, however only Jane Morgan's English-language version (see below) made the best-selling singles charts.

## GEORGES JOUVIN, SA TROMPETTE ET SON ENSEMBLE *(continued)*

| | | | |
|---|---|---|---|
| *Ballade pour une trompette* | 1962 | Peru | |
| | 1963 | Spain | |
| *Mea culpa* | 1963 | Japan | |

## THE KESSLER SISTERS[780]

| | | | |
|---|---|---|---|
| *Honey-Moon* | 1959 | West Germany | |
| *Mondschein und Liebe (Sweet Love)* | 1960 | West Germany | |
| *Hallo Blondie* | 1960 | West Germany | |
| *Pollo e champagne* | 1961 | Italy | |
| *Da da um pa* | 1961 | Italy | *Da-da-um-pa* |
| *Champagne twist* | 1962 | Italy | |

## RINA KETTY

| | | | |
|---|---|---|---|
| *J'attendrai (Tornerai)* | 1939 | Netherlands | |
| *Chante encore dans la nuit* | 1950 | Netherlands | |
| *Montevideo* | 1950 | Netherlands | |

## KORAFAS

| | | | |
|---|---|---|---|
| *C'est écrit dans le ciel* | 1961 | Japan | |

## MARIE LAFORÊT

| | | | |
|---|---|---|---|
| *Saint-Tropez Blues* | 1961 | Japan | |
| *Les vendanges de l'amour* | 1964 | Italy | *La vendemmia dell'amore* |
| | 1964 | Mexico | |
| | 1964 | Mexico | *Y volvamos al amor* |
| | 1964 | Spain | *Y volvamos al amor* |

## GLORIA LASSO

| | | | |
|---|---|---|---|
| *Ave Maria no morro* | 1955 | Netherlands | |
| *Corazón de melon* | 1959 | Spain | |
| | 1960 | Japan | |
| *Eso es el amor* | 1959 | Spain | |
| *Luna de miel* | 1959 | Spain | |
| *Vénus* | 1959 | Spain | |
| *La canción de Orfeo (Manha da carnaval)* | 1959 | Spain | |
| *Scoubidou (Pommes et poires) (Apples, Peaches And Cherries)* | 1959 | Spain | |
| *Adiós, Tristeza (À felicidade)* | 1959 | Spain | |
| *Les enfants du Pirée (Ta pedia tou Piréa)* | 1960 | Italy | |
| | 1961 | Mexico | *Los niños del Pireo* |
| | 1961 | Spain | *Los niños del Pireo* |
| *La novia* | 1961 | Spain | |
| *Plus je t'entends* | 1965 | Argentina | *Tu voz* |

## GLORIA LASSO ET LUIS MARIANO

| | | | |
|---|---|---|---|
| *Canastos* | 1959 | Spain | |
| *Amor, no me quieras tanto* | 1959 | Spain | |

---

[780] The Kessler Sisters' records were released under a variety of names internationally. In West Germany they were known as both Die Kessler-Zwillinge and Alice und Ellen Kessler; in Italy they were known as Le Gemelle Kessler; in Canada as Les Sœurs Kessler; and in Australia as the Kessler Twins. Their three West German hits were credited to Alice, Ellen und Peter, 'Peter' being German singer Peter Kraus, who performed with them on these releases.

## RAYMOND LE SÉNÉCHAL ET SON ORCHESTRE

| Château en Suède | 1964 | Japan | |
|---|---|---|---|

## HENRI LECA ET SON ORCHESTRE

| O Cangaceiro | 1954 | UK | The Bandit |
|---|---|---|---|

## RAYMOND LEFÈVRE ET SON ORCHESTRE

| The Day The Rains Came | 1958 | UK | |
|---|---|---|---|
| (Le jour où la pluie viendra)[781] | 1958 | US | |
| Les enfants du Pirée (Ta pedia tou Piréa) | 1961 | Mexico | |
| Exodus | 1961 | Netherlands | |

## MICHEL LEGRAND ET SON ORCHESTRE

| Gelsomina | 1956 | US | Love Theme From 'La Strada' (The Road) |
|---|---|---|---|
| Bonjour Paris | 1959 | Japan | |
| Terrain vague | 1961 | Japan | |
| Cool And Cool | 1962 | Italy | |

## CLAUDE LUTER ET SON ORCHESTRE

| La goualante du pauvre Jean[782] | 1956 | UK | |
|---|---|---|---|
| Le jour où la pluie viendra[783] | 1958 | UK | The Day The Rains Came |

## LOS MACHUCAMBOS

| Pepito | 1961 | Denmark | |
|---|---|---|---|
| | 1961 | Finland | |
| | 1961 | Israel | |
| | 1961 | Italy | |
| | 1961 | Netherlands | |
| | 1961 | Spain | |
| | 1961 | UK | |
| | 1961 | West Germany | |
| | 1962 | Austria | |
| | 1962 | South Africa | |
| Dimelo en septiembre | 1961 | Spain | |
| Luna de Benidorm | 1961 | Spain | |
| La cucaracha | 1961 | Spain | |
| Contigo en la distancia | 1961 | Spain | |
| Otorrino laringologo | 1961 | Spain | |
| | 1962 | Italy | |
| Cuando calienta el sol | 1963 | Netherlands | |
| La mamma | 1964 | Spain | |
| América | 1964 | Spain | |

---

[781] Raymond Lefèvre's recording of 'The Day The Rains Came' was an instrumental version of Gilbert Bécaud's 'Le jour où la pluie viendra'. It was one of many versions available at the time in the UK and is listed in the sheet music charts. It did not make the UK Top 20 best-selling records lists, however it did chart in the US.

[782] Claude Luter's instrumental treatment of 'La goualante de pauvre Jean' was one of many versions available at the time in the UK and is listed in the sheet music charts alongside those which bore the English title, 'The Poor People Of Paris'. It did not make the Top 20 best-selling records lists.

[783] Claude Luter's 'The Day The Rains Came' is an instrumental version of Gilbert Bécaud's 'Le jour où la pluie viendra' issued in the UK under the English title. It was one of many versions available at the time in the UK and is listed in the sheet music charts. It did not make the Top 20 best-selling records lists.

## ENRICO MACIAS

| Adieu mon pays | 1966 | Italy | Il paese del mio cuore |
|---|---|---|---|

## LUIS MARIANO
See Gloria Lasso et Luis Mariano

## TEDDY MARTIN & HIS LAS VEGAS TWISTERS

| Twistin' The Twist | 1962 | Italy | |
|---|---|---|---|

See also Jerry Mengo

## LOS MAYAS

| La playa | 1965 | Japan | |
|---|---|---|---|

## JERRY MENGO ET SON ORCHESTRE

| Il bidone | 1958 | Japan | |
|---|---|---|---|

See also Teddy Martin

## ROBERT MONOT ET SON ORCHESTRE

| Les grands chemins | 1963 | Japan | |
|---|---|---|---|

## YVES MONTAND

| Les feuilles mortes | 1950 | Netherlands | |
|---|---|---|---|
| | 1958 | Japan | |
| | 1962 | Japan | |
| Les grands boulevards | 1952 | Netherlands | |

## JEANNE MOREAU

| Le tourbillon | 1964 | Japan | |
|---|---|---|---|

## DARIO MORENO

| Si tu vas à Rio | 1959 | Spain | |
|---|---|---|---|
| Eso es el amor | 1959 | Spain | |

## JANE MORGAN

| April In Portugal | 1953 | UK | |
|---|---|---|---|
| Say You're Mine Again | 1953 | UK | |
| Why (Are There Things We Can't Explain) | 1954 | US | |
| Two Different Worlds[784] | 1956 | US | |
| Midnight Blues | 1956 | US | |
| Let's Go Steady[785] | 1956 | US | |
| From The First Hello To The Last Goodbye | 1957 | US | |
| Come Home, Come Home | 1957 | US | |
| Around The World | 1957 | UK, US | |
| Fascination | 1957 | Australia | |
| | 1957 | New Zealand | |
| | 1957 | UK | |
| | 1957 | US | |
| I'm New At The Game Of Romance | 1957 | US | |

---

[784] Jane Morgan's 'Two Different Worlds' is jointly credited to Morgan and American pianist Roger Williams, who accompanied her on the recording.

[785] Jane Morgan's 'Let's Go Steady' was credited to Jane Morgan & The Jones Boys.

## JANE MORGAN *(continued)*

| | | | |
|---|---|---|---|
| It's Been A Long, Long Time | 1957 | US | |
| I've Got Bells In My Heart | 1958 | US | |
| Only One Love | 1958 | US | |
| Enchanted Island | 1958 | US | |
| To Love And Be Loved | 1958 | US | |
| Le jour où la pluie viendra | 1958 | US | |
| The Day The Rains Came | 1958 | Australia | |
| (Le jour où la pluie viendra)[786] | 1958 | UK | |
| | 1958 | US | |
| | 1959 | Ireland | |
| | 1959 | Italy | |
| | 1959 | New Zealand | |
| | 1959 | Norway | |
| If Only I Could Live My Life | 1959 | UK | |
| Again (Si je pouvais un jour revivre ma vie)[787] | 1959 | US | |
| With Open Arms | 1959 | US | |
| I Can't Begin To Tell You | 1959 | UK | |
| | 1959 | US | |
| Happy Anniversary | 1959 | Australia | |
| | 1959 | US | |
| Romantica[788] | 1960 | UK | |
| Lord And Master | 1960 | UK | |
| In Jerusalem | 1961 | US | |
| Love Makes The World Go 'round | 1961 | US | |
| Moon River | 1962 | Hong Kong | |
| What Now My Love (Et maintenant)[789] | 1962 | US | |
| In Other Words | 1962 | Philippines | |
| Bless 'em All | 1963 | US | |

## NANA MOUSKOURI

| | | | |
|---|---|---|---|
| Xypna, agapi mou | 1960 | Spain | |
| Weiße Rosen aus Athen[790] | 1961 | Austria | |
| | 1961 | West Germany | |
| | 1962 | US | The White Rose Of Athens |
| | 1963 | Italy | Rosa d'Atene |
| Ich schau' den weißen Wolken nach | 1962 | Austria | |
| | 1962 | West Germany | |
| Einmal weht der Südwind wieder | 1962 | Austria | |
| | 1962 | West Germany | |
| Am Horizont irgendwo | 1962 | West Germany | |
| Heimweh nach Wind und Meer | 1962 | West Germany | |

---

[786] 'The Day The Rains Came' is an English-language cover of Gilbert Bécaud's 'Le jour où la pluie viendra'. Morgan's French-language version was on the flip side.

[787] 'If I Could Live My Life Again' is an English-language cover of Gilbert Bécaud's 'Si je pouvais un jour revivre ma vie'.

[788] 'Romantica' is an English-language cover of Dalida's hit of the same name. Although Dalida's version was itself a cover of the Italian original ('Romantica' by Renato Rascel), it is likely, given Morgan's French connection, that she took the song from Dalida. It was also a US hit for Gordon Jenkins.

[789] 'What Now My Love' is an English-language cover of Gilbert Bécaud's 'Et maintenant'.

[790] Nana Mouskouri also recorded 'Weiße Rosen aus Athen' in French as 'Roses blanches de Corfou', but this version did not chart internationally.

## NANA MOUSKOURI *(continued)*

| Was in Athen geschah | 1962 | West Germany | |
|---|---|---|---|
| *À force de prier* | 1963 | Italy | *Notte non lo sa* |
| *Rote Korallen* | 1963 | West Germany | |
| | 1964 | Austria | |
| | 1965 | Italy | *Rosso corallo* |

## GEORGES MOUSTAKI

| Mon Île de France | 1970 | Italy | |
|---|---|---|---|

## JO MOUTET ET SON ORCHESTRE

| Gelsomina | 1956 | US | *Love Theme From 'La Strada'* |
|---|---|---|---|

## HAROLD NICHOLAS

| Las secretarias | 1962 | Brazil | |
|---|---|---|---|
| *Le Madison* | 1963 | Spain | |

## JACKY NOGUEZ, SON ACCORDÈON, SES CHŒURS ET SON ENSEMBLE

| Ciao, ciao bambina (Piove)[791] | 1959 | Australia | |
|---|---|---|---|
| | 1959 | US | |
| *Marina*[792] | 1959 | US | |
| | 1960 | Australia | |
| *Amapola* | 1960 | Australia | |
| | 1960 | US | |
| *C'est écrit dans le ciel* | 1961 | Japan | |
| *Les enfants du Pirée (Ta pedia tou Piréa)* | 1961 | Mexico | |

## HAZY OSTERWALD SEXTET

| Kriminal-Tango | 1959 | West Germany | |
|---|---|---|---|
| | 1960 | Italy | |
| | 1960 | Netherlands | |
| *Panoptikum* | 1960 | West Germany | |
| *Konjunktur-Cha-Cha* | 1961 | West Germany | |
| *Trout In Blue* | 1962 | Italy | |

*See also* Audrey Arno and the Hazy Osterwald Sextet

## MICHEL PAJE

| J'avais juré | 1964 | West Germany | *Ich schwöre dir* |
|---|---|---|---|

## MILKO PAPAYAKI ET SON ORCHESTRE

| Les enfants du Pirée (Ta pedia tou Piréa) | 1960 | UK | Never On Sunday |
|---|---|---|---|

## JEAN-CLAUDE PASCAL

| Nous les amoureux | 1961 | Italy | |
|---|---|---|---|
| | 1961 | Spain | |

## PATACHOU

| Paris canaille | 1954 | Netherlands | |
|---|---|---|---|
| *J'ai rendez-vous avec vous* | 1955 | Netherlands | |

---

[791] 'Ciao, ciao bambina' is an instrumental version of Dalida's hit of the same name. Although Dalida's own version was itself a cover of the Italian original ('Piove' by Domenico Modugno), the use of the French title indicates that Noguez took the song from Dalida.

[792] 'Marina' is an instrumental version of Rocco Granata's hit of the same name.

## MICHEL PHILIPPE-GÉRARD

| Bébert et l'omnibus | 1964 | Japan | |
|---|---|---|---|

## ÉDITH PIAF

| La vie en rose[793] | 1948 | Netherlands | |
|---|---|---|---|
| | 1948 | UK | |
| | 1950 | USA | |
| Hymne à l'amour | 1951 | Netherlands | |
| | 1953 | UK | |
| | 1958 | Italy | |
| | 1961 | Italy | |
| Si tu partirais | 1951 | UK | |
| Padam... padam | 1952 | Australia | |
| | 1952 | Netherlands | |
| Milord | 1960 | Austria | |
| | 1960 | Denmark | |
| | 1960 | Finland | |
| | 1960 | Italy | |
| | 1960 | Netherlands | |
| | 1960 | Norway | |
| | 1960 | Spain | |
| | 1960 | Sweden | |
| | 1960 | UK | |
| | 1960 | West Germany | |
| | 1961 | Australia | |
| | 1961 | New Zealand | |
| | 1961 | US | |
| Non, je ne regrette rien | 1961 | Austria | |
| | 1961 | Italy | |
| | 1961 | Netherlands | |
| | 1961 | Spain | |
| | 1961 | UK | |
| | 1961 | West Germany | |
| | 1963 | Netherlands | |
| Exodus | 1961 | Finland | |
| | 1961 | Israel | |
| | 1961 | Italy | |
| | 1961 | Netherlands | |
| | 1961 | Spain | |
| | 1961 | US | |

## ÉDITH PIAF ET LES COMPAGNONS DE LA CHANSON

| Les trois cloches | 1946 | Netherlands | |
|---|---|---|---|
| | 1949 | Netherlands | |

See also Les Compagnons de la Chanson

## LES PLAYERS

| Le ciel est si beau ce soir (A Song For Young Love) | 1964 | Japan | |
|---|---|---|---|

[793] Despite its title, the version of Édith Piaf's 'La vie en rose' that charted in the US was sung in English and was recorded four years after she cut the original French version. Her other international hits were all sung in French.

## FRANCK POURCEL ET SON ORCHESTRE

| | | | |
|---|---|---|---|
| *Kisses* | 1958 | US | |
| *Only You (And You Alone)* | 1959 | Australia | |
| | 1959 | US | |
| *Tango militaire* | 1959 | US | |
| *Anytime* | 1960 | US | |
| *Milord*[794] | 1961 | US | |
| *Il faut savoir* | 1962 | Italy | |
| *Chariot* | 1962 | Italy | |
| | 1963 | Argentina | |
| | 1963 | Brazil | |
| | 1963 | Uruguay | |
| *L'arlequin de Tolède* | 1963 | Uruguay | |
| *Et maintenant* | 1963 | Brazil | |
| | 1963 | Venezuela | |
| *Faits pour s'aimer (Desafinado)* | 1963 | Italy | |
| *Héléna* | 1963 | Italy | |
| *Si j'avais un marteau (If I Had A Hammer)* | 1964 | Argentina | |

## LE QUINTETTE DU HOT CLUB DE FRANCE

| | | | |
|---|---|---|---|
| *After You've Gone* | 1937 | US | |

## KEMAL RACHID ET SES OTTOMANS

| | | | |
|---|---|---|---|
| *Mustapha* | 1960 | UK | |

## COLETTE RENARD

| | | | |
|---|---|---|---|
| *Irma la Douce* | 1959 | Italy | |

## LINE RENAUD

| | | | |
|---|---|---|---|
| *The Love Of My Life* | 1953 | UK | |
| *Le soir* | 1953 | UK | *I'd Love To Fall Asleep* |
| | 1957 | US | *I'd Love To Fall Asleep* |
| *Moulin Rouge* | 1953 | UK | *The Song From Moulin Rouge*[795] |
| *April In Portgual* | 1953 | UK | |
| *Relax-Ay-Voo*[796] | 1955 | UK | |
| | 1956 | Australia | |

## ROCKY ROBERTS & THE AIREDALES

| | | | |
|---|---|---|---|
| *T. Bird (Thunderbird Twist)* | 1966 | Italy | |

## CLAUDE ROBIN

| | | | |
|---|---|---|---|
| *Ave Maria no morro* | 1955 | Netherlands | |

## BENNY ROCK *(Benny Couroyer)*

| | | | |
|---|---|---|---|
| *Bang-Bang-Boogie* | 1957 | Italy | |

---

[794] Pourcel's 'Milord' is an instrumental version of Édith Piaf's hit of the same name. It was issued on the flip side of Piaf's US single.

[795] Renaud's 'The Song From Moulin Rouge' was one of many versions available at the time in the UK and is listed in the sheet music charts. It did not make the Top 20 best-selling records lists.

[796] 'Relax-Ay-Vous' is a duet with American singer Dean Martin.

## ROGER ROGER ET SON ORCHESTRE

| | | | |
|---|---|---|---|
| Dalilia | 1962 | Australia | |
| | 1967 | Australia | |

## JAN ROSOL

| | | | |
|---|---|---|---|
| I Love Paris[797] | 1954 | UK | |

## TINO ROSSI

| | | | |
|---|---|---|---|
| Petit Papa Noël | 1945 | Netherlands | |
| Poème | 1947 | Netherlands | |
| Catari, Catari | 1949 | Netherlands | |
| Santa Lucia | 1949 | Netherlands | |
| Cerisier rose et pommier blanc | 1951 | Netherlands | |
| Luna rossa (Prière à la lune) | 1952 | Netherlands | |
| Johnny Guitare | 1955 | Netherlands | |

## JEAN SABLON

| | | | |
|---|---|---|---|
| Sur le pont d'Avignon | 1939 | Netherlands | |
| Symphonie | 1946 | UK | Symphony |
| My Foolish Heart | 1950 | UK | |
| C'est si bon | 1950 | UK | |
| Moulin Rouge | 1953 | UK | The Song From Moulin Rouge (Where Is Your Heart)[798] |

## HENRI SALVADOR

| | | | |
|---|---|---|---|
| Maladie d'amour | 1958 | Netherlands | |
| Le loup, la biche et le chevalier | 1952 | Italy | |
| L'abeille et le papillon | 1954 | Netherlands | |
| Rose | 1959 | Italy | |
| Dans mon île | 1959 | Italy | |
| Le lion est mort ce soir | 1962 | Austria | Der Löwe schläft heut' Nacht |
| (Wimoweh)[799] | 1962 | West Germany | Der Löwe schläft heut' Nacht |
| La mia bambina | 1962 | Italy | |
| Roma | 1962 | Italy | |

## CATHERINE SAUVAGE

| | | | |
|---|---|---|---|
| Paris canaille | 1955 | Netherlands | |

## DANY SAVAL

| | | | |
|---|---|---|---|
| C'est bien mieux comme ça | 1962 | Japan | |

## LES SCARLET

| | | | |
|---|---|---|---|
| Chariot | 1963 | Italy | |

## PIERRE SELLIN ET SON ORCHESTRE

| | | | |
|---|---|---|---|
| Verte campagne (Green Fields) | 1961 | Argentina | |
| Notre concerto (Il nostro concerto) | 1961 | Argentina | |

---

[797] Jan Rosol's version of 'I Love Paris' was a duet with British singer Gwen Campbell.

[798] Sablon's 'The Song From Moulin Rouge' was one of many versions available at the time in the UK and is listed in the sheet music charts. It did not make the Top 20 best-selling records lists.

[799] 'Wimoweh' is a South African song (originally known as 'Mbube' and recorded by Solomon Linda). 'Wimoweh' was the title of the 1951 version by American folk outfit the Weavers, however the titles of both the French and German versions indicate that Henri Salvador got the song via the Tokens' 1961 US hit, 'The Lion Sleeps Tonight'.

417

## SHEILA

| L'école est finie | 1963 | Spain | |
|---|---|---|---|
| | 1964 | Greece | |
| Pendant les vacances (All I Have To Do Is Dream) | 1963 | Israel | |
| Première surprise-partie | 1963 | Israel | |
| Le sifflet des copains | 1963 | Israel | |
| Chante, chante, chante (Sing (And Tell The Blues So Long)) | 1963 | Israel | |

## SŒUR SOURIRE[800]

| Dominique | 1963 | Australia | |
|---|---|---|---|
| | 1963 | Denmark | |
| | 1963 | Japan | |
| | 1963 | New Zealand | |
| | 1963 | UK | |
| | 1963 | US | |
| | 1964 | Argentina | |
| | 1964 | Austria | |
| | 1964 | Brazil | |
| | 1964 | Finland | |
| | 1964 | Ireland | |
| | 1964 | Mexico | |
| | 1964 | Netherlands | |
| | 1964 | Norway | |
| | 1964 | Peru | |
| | 1964 | South Africa | |
| | 1964 | Spain | |
| | 1964 | Sweden | |
| | 1964 | Uruguay | |
| | 1964 | West Germany | |
| Entre les étoiles | 1964 | Austria | |
| Tous les chemins | 1964 | Austria | |
| | 1964 | US | |

## LES SŒURS ÉTIENNE

| C'est si bon | 1950 | Netherlands | |
|---|---|---|---|

## STAÏFFI ET SES MUSTAFA'S

| Mustafa (Mustapha) | 1960 | Italy | |
|---|---|---|---|
| | 1960 | UK | |

## LES SURFS

| Reviens vite et oublie (Be My Baby) | 1964 | Mexico | Tu seras mi baby |
|---|---|---|---|
| | 1964 | Spain | Tu seras mi baby |
| Ne t'en vas comme ça (Don't Make Me Over) | 1964 | Spain | No, no te vayas |
| Écoute cet air-là (Crossfire) | 1964 | Spain | El crossfire |
| Si j'avais un marteau (If I Had A Hammer) | 1964 | Italy | Datemi un martello |
| | 1964 | Spain | |

## LES SWINGLE SINGERS[801]

| Fugue en ré mineur | 1964 | Netherlands | |
|---|---|---|---|
| | 1964 | UK | |

---

[800] Many of Sœur Sourire's international releases were credited to 'The Singing Nun'.
[801] The Swingle Singers' UK hits were on the EPs *Jazz Sebastien Bach, Volumes 1 and 2*.

## LES SWINGLE SINGERS *(continued)*

| | | | |
|---|---|---|---|
| Prélude pour chorale d'orgue No. 1 | 1964 | UK | |
| Prélude en fa majeur | 1964 | UK | |
| Bourrée | 1964 | UK | |
| Fugue en do mineur | 1965 | UK | |
| Fugue en ré majeur | 1965 | UK | |
| Prélude No. 9 | 1965 | UK | |
| Sinfonia | 1965 | UK | |
| Prélude en do majeur | 1965 | UK | |

## CHARLES TRENET

| | | | |
|---|---|---|---|
| Je chante | 1939 | Netherlands | |
| Ménilmontant | 1939 | Netherlands | |
| Que reste-t-il de nos amours? | 1945 | Netherlands | |
| Douce France | 1950 | Netherlands | |
| La mer | 1951 | Australia | |
| | 1952 | Netherlands | |
| L'âme des poètes (Longtemps, longtemps)[802] | 1952 | Netherlands | |
| | 1952 | UK | |

## TRUMPET BOY ET SA TROMPETTE-SUCCÉS[803]

| | | | |
|---|---|---|---|
| Oh! Quelle nuit | 1960 | Denmark | |
| (Oh Lonesome Me) | 1960 | Sweden | |
| Reveille rock | 1960 | Denmark | |
| T'aimer follement (Makin' Love) | 1960 | Denmark | |
| Luna Caprese | 1960 | Denmark | |
| Voulez-vous danser avec moi | 1960 | Denmark | |
| Afrikaan Beat | 1962 | Argentina | |

## SYLVIE VARTAN

| | | | |
|---|---|---|---|
| Est-ce que tu le sais? (What'd I Say) | 1963 | Spain | |
| Dansons (Let's Dance) | 1963 | Spain | |
| | 1965 | Turkey | |
| En écoutant la pluie (Rhythm Of The Rain) | 1963 | Spain | |
| Twiste et chante (Twist And Shout) | 1964 | Argentina | |
| | 1964 | Spain | |
| Si je chante (My Whole World Is Falling Down) | 1964 | Argentina | |
| | 1964 | Spain | |
| | 1965 | Uruguay | |

## CORA VAUCAIRE

| | | | |
|---|---|---|---|
| La complainte de la Butte | 1955 | Japan | |
| Trois petites notes de musique | 1962 | West Germany | |

## RAY VENTURA ET SES COLLÉGIENS

| | | | |
|---|---|---|---|
| It's A Pity To Say Goodnight | 1947 | UK | |
| Méfiez-vous fillettes | 1958 | Japan | |

[802] Charles Trenet's 'L'âme des poètes (Longtemps, longtemps)' is the original version of the popular hit 'At Last, At Last' (see *Part B* for details). It was one of many versions available at the time in the UK (albeit as an import) and is listed in the sheet music charts. It did not make the Top 20 best-selling records lists.

[803] Apart from 'Oh! Quelle nuit', Trumpet Boy's Danish hits were on the EP *Trumpet Boy og hans succes-trompet.*

## LES WAIKIKI'S

| | | | |
|---|---|---|---|
| *Hawaii Tattoo* | 1961 | Netherlands | |
| | 1962 | Australia | |
| | 1962 | Austria | |
| | 1962 | Denmark | |
| | 1962 | New Zealand | |
| | 1962 | West Germany | |
| | 1964 | US | |
| | 1965 | UK | |
| *Hilo Kiss* | 1962 | West Germany | |
| *Honolulu Rag* | 1962 | West Germany | |
| *Hula-Hochzeit* | 1963 | West Germany | |
| *Hawaiian Honeymoon* | 1965 | US | |

## RIKA ZARAÏ

| | | | |
|---|---|---|---|
| *Exodus* | 1961 | Netherlands | |
| *Hava naguila* | 1964 | Phillippines | |
| *Elle était si jolie* | 1963 | Israel | |

# Part B

## International Hit Covers of French Songs by Foreign Artists

Title

Original by

Covered by    Release year    Country

Foreign title
(if any)

### À MALYPENSE (Leny Escudero, 1963)

| Covered by | Release year | Country | Foreign title |
|------------|--------------|---------|---------------|
| Roger Williams | 1963 | US | Walking Alone[804] |

### À MOI DE PAYER (Sidney Bechet, 1955)

| Covered by | Release year | Country | Foreign title |
|------------|--------------|---------|---------------|
| Kenny Ball & His Jazzmen | 1962 | Ireland, UK | The Pay-Off |
| The Ray Price Quartet | 1962 | Australia | |

### À QUOI ÇA SERT L'AMOUR? (Édith Piaf & Théo Sarapo, 1962)

| Covered by | Release year | Country | Foreign title |
|------------|--------------|---------|---------------|
| Conny Vandenbos & Wim Rijken | 1988 | Netherlands | Wie weet wat liefde is? |

### À T'REGARDER (Charles Aznavour, 1954)

| Covered by | Release year | Country | Foreign title |
|------------|--------------|---------|---------------|
| The Lassies | 1956 | US | I Look At You |
| Jimmy Young | 1956 | US | I Look At You |

### L'ABEILLE ET LE PAPILLON (Henri Salvador, 1954)

| Covered by | Release year | Country | Foreign title |
|------------|--------------|---------|---------------|
| Lawrence Welk & His Champagne Music | 1957 | US | The Bridge Of Saint Lo |

### ACCORDÉON (Jacques Hélian, 1946)

| Covered by | Release year | Country | Foreign title |
|------------|--------------|---------|---------------|
| Jimmy Leach & His New Organolians | 1947 | UK | Accordion |
| Joe Loss & His Orchestra | 1947 | UK | Accordion |
| Jack Simpson & His Sextet | 1947 | UK | Accordion |

### AH! QUEL BONHEUR (Luis Mariano, 1955)

| Covered by | Release year | Country | Foreign title |
|------------|--------------|---------|---------------|
| Nelson Riddle & His Orchestra | 1956 | US | The Love Of Genevieve |

### ALLÉLUIA (Charles Aznavour, 1962)

| Covered by | Release year | Country | Foreign title |
|------------|--------------|---------|---------------|
| Rudy Ventura y su Conjunto | 1962 | Spain | Aleluya |

### ALOUETTE (Charles Lebel, 1906)

| Covered by | Release year | Country | Foreign title |
|------------|--------------|---------|---------------|
| Frank Fontaine | 1964 | US | Alouette, Pretty Alouette (I Will Get You Yet) |

---

[804] 'Walking Alone' was the English title used for Richard Anthony's UK hit version of Escudero's song (see *Part A* for details).

## LES AMANTS D'UN JOUR *(Édith Piaf, 1955)*

| Herbert Pagani | 1969 | Italy | *Albergo a ore* |
|---|---|---|---|
| Gino Paoli | 1969 | Italy | *Albergo a ore* |

## LES AMANTS MERVEILLEUX *(Édith Piaf, 1960)*

| Cory Brokken | 1961 | West Germany | *Er sah aus wie ein Lord* |
|---|---|---|---|

## L'ÂME DES POÈTES (LONGTEMPS, LONGTEMPS) *(Charles Trenet, 1951)*

| Kurt Burling & His Rococo Orchestra | 1952 | UK | *At Last! At Last!* |
|---|---|---|---|
| Bing Crosby | 1952 | UK | *At Last! At Last!* |
| David Hughes | 1952 | UK | *At Last! At Last!* |
| Bill Hurley | 1952 | UK | *Long, Long Ago* |
| Roberto Inglez & His Orchestra | 1952 | UK | *At Last! At Last!* |
| Lee Lawrence | 1952 | UK | *At Last! At Last!* |
| Guy Lombardo & His Royal Canadians | 1952 | UK | *At Last! At Last!* |
| Ray Martin & His Concert Orchestra | 1952 | UK | *At Last! At Last!* |
| Tony Martin | 1952 | UK | *At Last! At Last!* |
| Norrie Paramor & His Orchestra | 1952 | UK | *At Last! At Last!* |
| Ted Straeter & His Orchestra | 1952 | UK | *At Last! At Last!* |

## AMOUR PERDU *(Adamo, 1963)*

| Jukka Kuoppamäki | 1961 | Finland | *El milloinkaan i* |
|---|---|---|---|

## L'ARLEQUIN DE TOLÈDE *(Jocelyne Jocya, 1960)*[805]

| Milva | 1961 | Italy | *Arlecchino gitano* |
|---|---|---|---|
| Angela Maria | 1962 | Brazil | *O trovador de Toledo* |
| Gilda Lopes | 1962 | Brazil | *O trovador de Toledo* |
| Agnaldo Timóteo | 1962 | Brazil | *O trovador de Toledo* |

## AU CLAIR DE LA LUNE[806] *(Yvonne Printemps, 1931)*

| The Springfields | 1963 | UK | *Say I Won't Be There* |
|---|---|---|---|

## AVES LES ANGES *(Colette Renard, 1956)*

| Diana Trask | 1961 | Australia | *Our Language of Love* |
|---|---|---|---|

## LE BAL AUX BALÉARES *(Line Renaud, 1953)*

| Ronald Chesney | 1955 | UK | *Majorca* |
|---|---|---|---|
| Petula Clark | 1955 | UK | *Majorca* |
| The Johnston Brothers | 1955 | UK | *Majorca* |
| Monte Kelly & His Orchestra | 1955 | UK | *Majorca* |
| Joe Loss & His Orchestra | 1955 | UK | *Majorca* |
| Bob Manning | 1955 | UK, US | *Majorca (Isle Of Love)* |

---

[805] Jocya performed 'L'arlequin de Tolède' at the *Coq d'Or de la chanson française* song festival, and also recorded it, although Dalida enjoyed the bigger hit.

[806] 'Au clair de la lune' is actually an old folk song. It is not known which version inspired the Springfields' cover, however Yvonne Printemps' recording was one of the earliest and the most famous at that time.

## LE BAL AUX BALÉARES *(continued)*

| Norrie Paramor & His Orchestra | 1955 | UK | *Majorca* |
|---|---|---|---|
| Sidney Torch & His Orchestra | 1955 | UK | *Majorca* |

## LA BALLADE DE MADAME DE MORTEMOUILLE *(Gérard Calvi, 1959)*

| Joe 'Mr. Piano' Henderson | 1960 | UK | *Ooh La La* |
|---|---|---|---|
| Jimmy Durante | 1966 | US | *One Of Those Songs* |
| The Fluegel Knights | 1969 | US | *One Of Those Songs* |

## BOLÉRO *(Georges Guétary, 1949)*

| Bing Crosby | 1950 | UK, US | *All My Love* |
|---|---|---|---|
| Xavier Cugat & His Orchestra | 1950 | UK | *All My Love* |
| Dennis Day | 1950 | UK | *All My Love* |
| Denny Dennis | 1950 | UK | *Bolero* |
| Percy Faith & His Orchestra | 1950 | UK, US | *All My Love* |
| Lester Ferguson | 1950 | UK | *All My Love* |
| Allan Jones | 1950 | UK | *All My Love* |
| Guy Lombardo & His Royal Canadians | 1950 | US | *All My Love* |
| Joe Loss & His Orchestra | 1950 | UK | *All My Love* |
| Patti Page | 1950 | US | *All My Love* |
| Cyril Stapleton & His Orchestra | 1950 | UK | *All My Love* |
| Bing Crosby | 1951 | Australia | *All My Love* |
| Percy Faith & His Orchestra | 1951 | Australia | *All My Love* |
| Geraldo & His Orchestra | 1951 | UK | *All My Love* |
| Eddie Grant | 1951 | UK | *All My Love* |
| Roberto Inglez & His Orchestra | 1951 | UK | *All My Love – Bolero* |
| Guy Lombardo & His Royal Canadians | 1951 | UK | *All My Love* |
| Caterina Valente | 1958 | US | *All My Love* |
| Joe Damiano | 1960 | Italy | *Bolero* |

## BOLÉRO GAUCHO *(Patrice et Mario, 1951)*

| Mitch Miller & His Orchestra | 1956 | US | |
|---|---|---|---|

## BONJOUR TRISTESSE *(Juliette Gréco, 1958)*

| Angèle Durand | 1958 | West Germany | |
|---|---|---|---|
| Gogi Grant | 1958 | US | |
| Lucille Starr | 1968 | South Africa | Hello Sadness |

## BOUM!!.. *(Charles Trenet, 1938)*

| Turner Layton | 1940 | UK | *Boom!* |
|---|---|---|---|
| Sydney Lipton & His Grosvenor House Orchestra | 1940 | UK | *Boom* |

## LES BRAS EN CROIX *(Johnny Hallyday, 1963)*

| Mike Riós y los Relámpagos | 1964 | Spain | *Los brazos en cruz* |
|---|---|---|---|

## BRAVE MARGOT *(Georges Brassens, 1953)*

| Ray Bloch & His Orchestra | 1956 | US | |
|---|---|---|---|

## BRUXELLES *(Jacques Brel, 1962)*

| Liesbeth List | 1970 | Netherlands | *Brussel* |
|---|---|---|---|

## C'EST À HAMBOURG *(Édith Piaf, 1955)*

| Winifred Atwell | 1956 | UK | *The Left Bank* |
|---|---|---|---|
| Les Elgart & His Orchestra | 1956 | US | *The Left Bank* |

## C'EST BIEN JOLI D'ÊTRE COPAINS *(Le Petit Prince, 1963)*

| Suzanne Doucet | 1964 | West Germany | *Das geht doch keinen etwas an* |
|---|---|---|---|

## C'EST BIEN MIEUX COMME ÇA *(Les Chaussettes Noires & Gillian Hills, 1962)*

| Kirsti Sparboe | 1967 | Sweden | *Livet er herlig* |
|---|---|---|---|

## C'EST ÉCRIT DANS LE CIEL *(Bob Azzam, 1960)*

| Marino Marini ed il suo Quartetto | 1960 | Italy | *Era scritto nel cielo* |
|---|---|---|---|
| Duke Aces | 1961 | Japan | |
| Baby Bell | 1961 | Argentina | *Esta escrito en el cielo* |
| Vieno Kekkonen | 1961 | Finland | *Tähtien kertomaa* |
| Patricia Montes | 1961 | Argentina | *Esta escrito en el cielo* |
| Rauni Pekkala ja Neloset | 1961 | Finland | *Tähtien kertomaa* |
| Bill Ramsey | 1961 | West Germany | *Café orientale* |
| Vico Torriani | 1961 | West Germany | *Café orientale* |

## C'EST IRRÉPARABLE *(Nino Ferrer, 1963)*

| Mina | 1965 | Italy, Japan, Turkey | *Un anno d'amore* |
|---|---|---|---|
| Mina | 1965 | Japan | *Wakare* |
| Sachiko Wada | 1965 | Japan | *Wakare* |
| Hoki Yokuta | 1965 | Japan | *Wakare* |

## C'EST L'AMOUR *(Édith Piaf, 1959)*

| Hugo & Luigi | 1959 | US | *Just Come Home* |
|---|---|---|---|
| Hugo & Luigi | 1960 | Australia | *Just Come Home* |

## C'EST SI BON *(Yves Montand, 1948)*

| Louis Armstrong & His Orchestra | 1950 | Netherlands | *C'est Si Bon (It's So Good)* |
|---|---|---|---|
| Johnny Desmond | 1950 | US | *C'est Si Bon (It's So Good)* |
| Danny Kaye | 1950 | Netherlands, US | *C'est Si Bon (It's So Good)* |
| Eartha Kitt | 1953 | Netherlands, US | *C'est Si Bon (It's So Good)* |
| Stan Freberg | 1954 | US | *C'est Si Bon (It's So Good)* |
| Eartha Kitt | 1954 | Australia | *C'est Si Bon (It's So Good)* |
| Johnny Desmond | 1958 | US | *C'est Si Bon Cha Cha* |
| Conway Twitty | 1960 | US | *C'est Si Bon (It's So Good)* |
| Conway Twitty | 1961 | Australia, Italy New Zealand, UK | *C'est Si Bon (It's So Good)* |
| Dr. Buzzard's Original Savannah Band[807] | 1976 | US | *Se Si Bon* |

---

[807] The version of 'C'est si bon' by Dr. Buzzard's Original Savannah Band was part of a three-song medley with 'Whispering' and 'Cherchez la femme'. The other two songs are not of French origin.

## C'EST SI BON *(continued)*

| | | | |
|---|---|---|---|
| Dr. Buzzard's Original Savannah Band | 1977 | Australia, Netherlands | *Se Si Bon* |

## C'EST UN HOMME TERRIBLE *(Édith Piaf, 1959)*

| | | | |
|---|---|---|---|
| Al Saxon | 1960 | UK | *Blue Eyed Boy* |

## ÇA, C'EST PARIS *(Mistinguett, 1926)*

| | | | |
|---|---|---|---|
| The International Novelty Orchestra | 1927 | US | *Paree (Ça C'est Paris)* |

## LE CARILLON DE VENDÔME *(Traditional folk song, fifteenth century)*

| | | | |
|---|---|---|---|
| David Crosby | 1971 | US | *Orleans* |

## CASANOVA BACIAMI *(Petula Clark, 1963)*

| | | | |
|---|---|---|---|
| Cocky Mazzetti | 1963 | Italy | |
| Cocky Mazzetti | 1964 | Japan | |

## CÉCILE *(Georges Auric, 1958)*

| | | | |
|---|---|---|---|
| George Cates | 1958 | US | *Dance From Bonjour Tristesse* |
| David Seville | 1958 | US | *Dance From Bonjour Tristesse* |

## CERISIER ROSE ET POMMIER BLANC *(André Claveau, 1950)*

| | | | |
|---|---|---|---|
| Les Baxter & His Orchestra & Chorus | 1955 | Australia, UK | *Cherry Pink And Apple Blossom White* |
| Eddie Calvert | 1955 | Netherlands, UK | *Cherry Pink And Apple Blossom White* |
| Xavier Cugat & His Orchestra | 1955 | UK | *Cherry Pink And Apple Blossom White* |
| Alan Dale | 1955 | Netherlands, UK, US | *Cherry Pink And Apple Blossom White* |
| Georgia Gibbs | 1955 | UK | *Cherry Pink And Apple Blossom White* |
| Guy Lombardo & His Royal Canadians | 1955 | UK | *Cherry Pink And Apple Blossom White* |
| Vera Lynn[808] | 1955 | UK | *Cherry Pink And Apple Blossom White* |
| Pérez Prado & His Orchestra | 1955 | Australia, Japan, Netherlands, UK, US, W. Germany | *Cherry Pink And Apple Blossom White* |
| Edmundo Ros & His Orchestra | 1955 | UK | *Cherry Pink And Apple Blossom White* |
| Victor Young & His Singing Strings | 1955 | UK | *Cherry Pink And Apple Blossom White* |
| Jerry Murad's Harmonicats | 1960 | Australia, US | *Cherry Pink And Apple Blossom White* |
| Jerry Murad's Harmonicats | 1961 | UK | *Cherry Pink And Apple Blossom White* |
| Pat Boone | 1961 | Philippines | *Cherry Pink And Apple Blossom White* |
| Modern Romance | 1982 | Ireland, UK | *Cherry Pink And Apple Blossom White* |

---

[808] Vera Lynn's version of 'Cherry Pink And Apple Blossom White' was a part of 'Popular Medley No. 4', the remainder of which consisted of songs with no connection to French pop.

## CHANSON DE GERVAISE *(Juliette Gréco, 1956)*

| Felicia Sanders | 1958 | US | Song Of Gervaise (To Have And To Hold) |
|---|---|---|---|

## CHANSON POUR L'AUVERGNAT *(Georges Brassens, 1954)*

| Lawrence Welk & His Champagne Music | 1957 | US | Ten Little Trees |
|---|---|---|---|

## CHARIOT *(Franck Pourcel et son Orchestre, 1961)*[809]

| Lara Bittencourt | 1963 | Brazil | |
|---|---|---|---|
| Joe Borsani | 1963 | Argentina | La tierra |
| Los Cinco Latinos | 1963 | Argentina | La tierra |
| Rosemary Clooney | 1963 | Japan | I Will Follow You |
| Fran Cooper | 1963 | Israel | I Will Follow Him |
| Los Cuatro del Embers | 1963 | Argentina | La tierra |
| Betty Curtis | 1963 | Italy, Japan, Uruguay | |
| Dyno | 1963 | Argentina | La tierra |
| Poky Evans | 1963 | Argentina | La tierra |
| Percy Faith & His Orchestra | 1963 | Argentina | I Will Follow Him |
| George Freedman | 1963 | Brazil | Eu hei de seguir |
| Georgia Gibbs | 1963 | Japan | I Will Follow You |
| José Guardiola | 1963 | Spain | |
| Little Peggy March | 1963 | Argentina, Australia, Brazil, Chile, Denmark, Finland, Hong Kong, Israel, Italy, Japan, New Zealand, Peru, Philippines, South Africa, Sweden, Uruguay, US, West Germany | I Will Follow Him |
| Juan Ramón | 1963 | Argentina | La tierra |
| Violeta Rivas | 1963 | Argentina | La tierra |
| Ennio Sangiusto | 1963 | Argentina, Spain | La tierra |
| Joe Sentieri | 1963 | Argentina, US | |
| Dee Dee Sharp | 1963 | Hong Kong | I Will Follow Him |
| Los Top-Son | 1963 | Spain | |
| Claudja Barry | 1982 | US | I Will Follow Him |
| José | 1982 | Netherlands | I Will Follow Him |

## LA CHASSE AUX PAPILLONS *(Georges Brassens, 1954)*

| Lu Ann Simms | 1957 | US | Matchin' Kisses |
|---|---|---|---|

## CHÉRIE, MADAME *(Georges Blaness, 1963)*

| Franciska | 1963 | Spain | Cherrie Madame |
|---|---|---|---|
| Los Mustang | 1963 | Spain | Cherrie Madame |
| Los T.N.T. | 1963 | Spain | Cherrie Madame |

---

[809] 'Chariot' was a smash hit for Petula Clark, and almost all of the covers that followed took her version as the template, although the song actually began life as an instrumental recorded by Franck Pourcel.

## LE CHEVALIER DE PARIS *(Édith Piaf, 1950)*

| | | | |
|---|---|---|---|
| Eartha Kitt | 1965 | US | *When The World Was Young* |

## LA CHNOUF *(Marc Lanjean et Michel Legrand, 1955)*

| | | | |
|---|---|---|---|
| Les Elgart & His Orchestra | 1956 | US | |

## CIAO, CIAO MON AMOUR *(Dalida, 1959)*

| | | | |
|---|---|---|---|
| Gene Rockwell | 1965 | South Africa | *Ciao* |

## UN CLAIR DE LUNE À MAUBEUGE *(Pierre Perrin, 1962)*

| | | | |
|---|---|---|---|
| Mr. Acker Bilk | 1963 | UK | *Midnight Tango* |

## CLOPIN-CLOPANT *(Henri Salvador, 1948)*

| | | | |
|---|---|---|---|
| Ambrose & His Orchestra | 1949 | UK | |
| Jean Cavall | 1949 | UK | |
| Joe Loss & His Orchestra | 1949 | UK | |
| Victor Silvester & His Ballroom Orchestra | 1949 | UK | |

## CŒUR DE MON CŒUR *(Yves Montand, 1954)*

| | | | |
|---|---|---|---|
| Mantovani & His Orchestra | 1956 | US | *Heart Of My Heart* |

## CŒUR DE NEIGE *(Georges Guétary, 1962)*

| | | | |
|---|---|---|---|
| Johnny Hoes | 1962 | Netherlands | *Vader, waar is Moder gebleven?* |

## LES COMÉDIENS *(Charles Aznavour, 1962)*

| | | | |
|---|---|---|---|
| José Guardiola | 1963 | Spain | *Los comediantes* |

## COMME ÇA *(Yves Montand, 1954)*

| | | | |
|---|---|---|---|
| Dick Roman | 1956 | US | |

## CONNAIS-TU? *(Tino Rossi, 1961)*

| | | | |
|---|---|---|---|
| Brenda Lee | 1963 | Australia, Hong Kong, Israel, Japan, New Zealand, UK, US | *Losing You* |
| Doris Day | 1964 | Philippines | *Losing You* |
| Lynne Fletcher | 1967 | Australia | *Losing You* |
| D.J. Curtis & the Kerry Blues | 1974 | Ireland | *Losing You* |

## CREOLE JAZZ *(Claude Luter et son Orchestre, 1960)*

| | | | |
|---|---|---|---|
| Mr. Acker Bilk & His Paramount Jazz Band | 1961 | UK | |

## DANIELA *(Les Chaussettes Noires, 1961)*

| | | | |
|---|---|---|---|
| Los Pantalones Azules | 1961 | Spain | |
| Adriano | 1962 | Argentina | |
| Peppino di Capri | 1962 | Argentina, Italy | |
| Jackie | 1962 | Argentina | |
| Fredy Luciano | 1962 | Argentina | |
| Juan Ramón | 1962 | Argentina | |

## DANS LE CREUX DE TA MAIN *(Robert Jeantal, 1961)*

| Los Pájaros Locos | 1961 | Spain | *En la cruz de tu mano* |
|---|---|---|---|
| José Guardiola | 1962 | Spain | *En la cruz de tu mano* |

## LE DANSEUR DE CHARLESTON *(Philippe Clay, 1955)*

| Guy Lombardo & His Royal Canadians | 1956 | US | *Charleston Parisien* |
|---|---|---|---|

## DARLING, JE VOUS AIME BEAUCOUP *(Patrick et son Orchestre de Danse, 1935)*[810]

| Hildegarde | 1943 | US | |
|---|---|---|---|
| Nat 'King' Cole | 1955 | Australia, Netherlands, US | |

## DÉJÀ *(Jean-Claude Pascal, 1955)*

| Shirley Bassey[811] | 1961 | UK | *All At Once* |
|---|---|---|---|

## DIS-MOI D'OÙ VIENT LE VENT *(Christian Sarrel, 1963)*

| Rick Nelson | 1964 | Australia, US | *There's Nothing I Can Say* |
|---|---|---|---|

## DIS, PAPA *(Hélène et Georges Guétary, 1962)*[812]

| José Guardiola y Rosa Mary | 1962 | Argentina, Spain | *Di Papa* |
|---|---|---|---|
| Luis Ordoñez | 1962 | Argentina | *Di Papa* |
| Siro San Roman con Margelita | 1962 | Argentina | *Di Papa* |
| Raúl Lavié | 1963 | Argentina | *Di Papa* |

## DOMINIQUE *(Sœur Sourire, 1962)*

| Los Alegres Cantores | 1964 | Argentina | |
|---|---|---|---|
| Chuck Anderson | 1964 | Mexico | |
| Angélica Maria | 1964 | Argentina, Chile, Mexico, Peru | |
| Stirling Brandy | 1964 | Argentine, Uruguay | |
| Raquel Castaño | 1964 | Uruguay | |
| Las Dominicas | 1964 | Argentina, Mexico | |
| Los Dominicos | 1964 | Uruguay, Venezuela | |
| Queta Garay | 1964 | Mexico | |
| Gelu y los Mustang | 1964 | Spain | |
| Giane | 1964 | Brazil | |
| Las Hermanas Alegría | 1964 | Argentina, Mexico, Uruguay | |
| Los Hermanos Záizar | 1964 | Mexico | |
| The Lennon Sisters | 1964 | Philippines | |
| Luis Pérez Meza | 1964 | Mexico | |
| Connie Philip | 1964 | Peru | |
| Poly | 1964 | Brazil | |

---

[810] 'Darling, je vous aime beaucoup' was best known in the version by Jean Sablon, but bandleader Patrick recorded it first.

[811] Shirley Bassey's adaptation of Jean-Claude Pascal's 'Déjà' ('All At Once') made the chart thanks its inclusion on the hit EP *Shirley No. 2*. The other tracks on the EP had no connection to French pop.

[812] Hélène was Georges Guétary's young daughter.

## DOMINIQUE *(continued)*

| | | | |
|---|---|---|---|
| Juan Ramón | 1964 | Argentina | |
| Daisy Somons | 1964 | Uruguay | |
| Sonia | 1964 | Argentina | |
| Trio Esperança | 1964 | Brazil | |
| Tony Sandler & Ralph Young | 1966 | US | |
| Sœur Plus | 1995 | Netherlands | |

## DOMINO *(André Claveau, 1950)*

| | | | |
|---|---|---|---|
| Bing Crosby | 1951 | US | |
| Doris Day | 1951 | UK, US | |
| Tony Martin | 1951 | US | |
| Bing Crosby | 1952 | UK | |
| Doris Day | 1952 | Netherlands | |
| Lester Ferguson | 1952 | UK | |
| Teddy Johnson | 1952 | UK | |
| Charlie Kunz & His Music | 1952 | UK | |
| Tony Martin | 1952 | Australia, Netherlands, UK | |
| Mary Mayo | 1952 | UK | |
| The Melachrino Strings | 1952 | UK | |
| Betty Paul | 1952 | UK | |
| Victor Silvester & His Ballroom Orchestra | 1952 | UK | |
| Mary Small | 1952 | UK | |
| Ethel Smith | 1952 | UK | |
| Sidney Torch & His Orch. | 1952 | UK | |
| Doris Day | 1963 | Philippines | |

## DONNEZ-MOI TOUT ÇA *(Les Sœurs Étienne, 1956)*

| | | | |
|---|---|---|---|
| Don Cherry | 1956 | US | *Give Me More* |

## DOUCE VIOLENCE *(Johnny Hallyday, 1961)*

| | | | |
|---|---|---|---|
| Masaaki Hirao | 1963 | Japan | *Amai bōryoku* |

## L'ÉCOLE EST FINIE *(Sheila, 1963)*

| | | | |
|---|---|---|---|
| Billie Davis | 1964 | Denmark | *School Is Over* |

## ELLE ÉTAIT SI JOLIE *(Alain Barrière, 1963)*

| | | | |
|---|---|---|---|
| Gelu y los Mustang | 1963 | Spain | *Élla es muy bonita* |
| Tito Mora | 1963 | Spain | *Élla es muy bonita* |
| George Maharis | 1964 | US | *Sara Darling* |

## EMBRASSE-MOI... OH MON AMOUR *(Gilbert Bécaud, 1957)*

| | | | |
|---|---|---|---|
| Toni Arden | 1958 | US | *Desire Me* |

## EN ÉCOUTANT MON CŒUR CHANTER *(Charles Trenet, 1946)*

| | | | |
|---|---|---|---|
| Johnnie Johnston | 1945 | US | *(All Of A Sudden) My Heart Sings* |
| Martha Stewart | 1945 | US | *(All Of A Sudden) My Heart Sings* |
| Roy Hamilton | 1957 | US | *(All Of A Sudden) My Heart Sings* |
| Paul Anka | 1958 | US | *(All Of A Sudden) My Heart Sings* |
| Paul Anka | 1959 | Australia, Italy, Spain, UK, West Germany | *(All Of A Sudden) My Heart Sings* |

## EN ÉCOUTANT MON CŒUR CHANTER *(continued)*

| Paul Anka | 1961 | Argentina | *(All Of A Sudden) My Heart Sings* |
|---|---|---|---|
| Enrique Guzmán | 1961 | Argentina, Mexico, Venezuela | *Mi corazón canta* |
| Mel Carter | 1965 | Australia, US | *(All Of A Sudden) My Heart Sings* |

## UNE ENFANT *(Édith Piaf, 1951)*[813]

| Boudewijn de Groot | 1965 | Netherlands | *Een meisje van 16* |
|---|---|---|---|
| Noël Harrison | 1965 | US | *A Young Girl (Of Sixteen)* |
| Noël Harrison | 1966 | Australia, UK | *A Young Girl (Of Sixteen)* |

## ENTRE LES ÉTOILES *(Sœur Sourire, 1962)*

| Frankie Laine | 1964 | Malaysia | *Among The Stars* |
|---|---|---|---|

## ET MAINTENANT *(Gilbert Bécaud, 1961)*

| Shirley Bassey | 1962 | Italy, UK | *What Now My Love* |
|---|---|---|---|
| Monna Bell | 1962 | Spain | *¿Porque me dejas?* |
| Los Cinco Latinos | 1962 | Spain | *¿Porque me dejas?* |
| Gelu | 1962 | Spain | *¿Porque me dejas?* |
| José Guardiola | 1962 | Spain | *¿Porque me dejas?* |
| Alda Perdigão | 1962 | Brazil | *E agora* |
| Rudy Ventura | 1962 | Spain | *¿Porque me dejas?* |
| Anibal Abeena | 1963 | Venezuela | *Y ahora qué* |
| Los Abriles | 1963 | Argentina | *¿Porque me dejas?* |
| Monna Bell | 1963 | Peru | *¿Porque me dejas?* |
| Los Cinco Latinos | 1963 | Argentina, Uruguay | *¿Porque me dejas?* |
| Coro e Conjunto Gold Star | 1963 | Brazil | *E agora* |
| Lucho Gatica | 1963 | Argentina, Spain, Uruguay, Venezuela | *Y ahora qué* |
| Gelu | 1963 | Argentina | *¿Porque me dejas?* |
| Raúl Lavié | 1963 | Argentina | *¿Porque me dejas?* |
| Wilson Miranda | 1963 | Brazil | *E agora* |
| Agnaldo Rayol | 1963 | Brazil | *E agora* |
| Pery Ribeiro | 1963 | Brazil | *E agora* |
| Ben E. King | 1964 | US | *What Now My Love* |
| Marianne Faithfull[814] | 1965 | UK | *What Now My Love* |
| Herb Alpert & The Tijuana Brass | 1966 | Australia, US | *What Now My Love* |
| Vic Dana | 1966 | Hong Kong | *What Now My Love* |
| 'Groove' Holmes | 1966 | US | *What Now My Love* |
| Sonny & Cher | 1966 | Australia, Sweden, UK, US | *What Now My Love* |
| Jan Malmsjö | 1967 | Sweden | *Den gamla vanliga visan* |
| Mitch Ryder | 1967 | US | *What Now My Love* |
| Frank Sinatra | 1967 | Spain | *What Now My Love* |

[813] Charles Aznavour wrote 'Une enfant' for Édith Piaf and later recorded it himself. It was in fact Aznavour's version that was the source for Noël Harrison's cover, which in turn inspired De Groot's version.

[814] Marianne Faithfull's hit version of Gilbert Bécaud's 'Et maintenant' ('What Now My Love') was on her EP *Go Away From My World*. None of the other songs had any connection to French pop.

## ET POURTANT *(Charles Aznavour, 1963)*

| José Guardiola | 1964 | Spain | *Y por tanto* |
|---|---|---|---|
| Steve Lawrence | 1964 | Australia, Hong Kong, US | *Yet I Know* |
| Los Tamara | 1964 | Spain | *Y por tanto* |
| Los Tres de Castilla | 1964 | Spain | *Y por tanto* |
| Los Cinco Latinos | 1965 | Argentina | *Y por tanto* |
| Lucio Milena | 1965 | Argentina | *Y por tanto* |
| Jimmy Frey[815] | 1980 | Netherlands | *Yet I Know* |

## FASCINATION *(Jane Morgan, 1957)*

| Nat 'King' Cole | 1957 | Australia, Italy | |
|---|---|---|---|
| Robert Earl | 1957 | UK | |
| Ray Ellis & His Gypsies | 1957 | US | |
| Dick Jacobs & His Orchestra & Chorus | 1957 | Australia | |
| The Troubadours | 1957 | US | |

## LES FEUILLES MORTES *(Cora Vaucaire, 1948)*[816]

| Ray Anthony & His Orchestra | 1950 | UK | *Autumn Leaves* |
|---|---|---|---|
| Steve Conway | 1950 | UK | *Autumn Leaves* |
| Bing Crosby | 1950 | UK | *Autumn Leaves* |
| Alan Dean | 1950 | UK | *Autumn Leaves* |
| Fred Hartley & His Music | 1950 | UK | *Autumn Leaves* |
| Melachrino Strings | 1950 | UK | *Autumn Leaves* |
| Mitch Miller & His Orchestra & Chorus | 1950 | UK | *Autumn Leaves* |
| Victor Silvester & His Ballroom Orchestra | 1950 | UK | *Autumn Leaves* |
| Jo Stafford | 1950 | UK | *Autumn Leaves* |
| Paul Weston & His Orchestra | 1950 | UK | *Autumn Leaves* |
| Bing Crosby | 1951 | Australia | *Autumn Leaves* |
| Roberto Inglez & His Orchestra | 1951 | UK | *Autumn Leaves* |
| Mitch Miller & His Orchestra & Chorus | 1951 | Australia | *Autumn Leaves* |
| Jack Pleis & His Orchestra | 1951 | UK | *Autumn Leaves* |
| Artie Shaw & His Orchestra | 1951 | UK | *Autumn Leaves* |
| Steve Allen & George Cates | 1955 | US | *Autumn Leaves* |
| The Ray Charles Singers | 1955 | US | *Autumn Leaves* |
| Jackie Gleason & His Orchestra | 1955 | US | *Autumn Leaves* |
| Mitch Miller & His Orchestra & Chorus | 1955 | US | *Autumn Leaves* |
| Roger Williams[817] | 1955 | US | *Autumn Leaves* |

---

[815] Jimmy Frey was a Belgian singer who made a minor impact in France during the sixties. By the time of his revival of "Et pourtant', he had, however, long since ceased singing in French in favour of a largely Flemish (and occasionally English) repertoire, hence its inclusion here.

[816] 'Les feuilles mortes' was made famous by Yves Montand, but the first commercially available recording was by Cora Vauciaire.

[817] American pianist Roger Williams recorded two versions of 'Autumn Leaves' ('Les feuilles mortes'), charting in 1955 and 1965 respectively.

## LES FEUILLES MORTES *(continued)*

| | | | |
|---|---|---|---|
| Victor Young & His Singing Strings | 1955 | US | *Autumn Leaves* |
| Nat 'King' Cole | 1956 | Australia | *Autumn Leaves* |
| Jackie Gleason & His Orchestra | 1957 | Italy | *Autumn Leaves* |
| Betty McLaurin | 1957 | US | *Autumn Leaves* |
| Frank Sinatra | 1957 | US | *Autumn Leaves* |
| Keely Smith | 1957 | US | *Autumn Leaves* |
| Los Cinco Latinos | 1959 | Spain | *Las hojas muertas* |
| Nat 'King' Cole | 1960 | Japan | *Autumn Leaves* |
| Enrique Guzmán | 1963 | Spain | *Las hojas muertas* |
| Roger Williams | 1965 | US | *Autumn Leaves – 1965* |
| Carl-Erik Thörn | 1966 | Sweden | *En stjärna föll* |
| Steve Lawrence & Eydie Gormé[818] | 1971 | US | *Autumn Leaves* |

## LE FIACRE *(Jean Sablon, 1939)*

| | | | |
|---|---|---|---|
| Gisele MacKenzie | 1952 | US | |

## FORT CHABROL *(Les Fantômes, 1962)*

| | | | |
|---|---|---|---|
| Wanderléa | 1966 | Brazil | *É tempo do amor*[819] |

## UN GARÇON DES ÎLES *(Henri Salvador, 1962)*

| | | | |
|---|---|---|---|
| Tony Bennett | 1964 | US | *I Will Live My Life For You* |

## LE GARS DE ROCHECHOUART *(Anny Gould, 1957)*

| | | | |
|---|---|---|---|
| Edmundo Ros & His Orchestra | 1958 | US | *Saunabad* |

## GINA *(Eddie Constantine, 1955)*

| | | | |
|---|---|---|---|
| Leroy Holmes & His Orchestra | 1957 | US | |

## LES GITANS *(Dalida, 1959)*

| | | | |
|---|---|---|---|
| Gelu | 1960 | Spain | *Los Gitanos* |

## LA GOUALANTE DU PAUVRE JEAN *(Édith Piaf, 1954)*

| | | | |
|---|---|---|---|
| Chet Atkins | 1956 | Netherlands, US | *The Poor People Of Paris (Jean's Song)* |
| Winifred Atwell | 1956 | UK | *The Poor People Of Paris* |
| Les Baxter & His Orchestra & Chorus | 1956 | Australia, UK, US | *The Poor People Of Paris*[820] |
| Geraldo & His Orchestra | 1956 | UK | *The Poor People Of Paris* |
| Joe Loss & His Orchestra | 1956 | UK | *The Poor People Of Paris* |

[818] Steve Lawrence & Eydie Gorme's version of 'Autumn Leaves' was recorded as a medley with 'Love Is Blue'. The latter is also a French song, from 1967 (for details see Volume 2).

[819] The title for the Brazilian hit version of Les Fantômes' 'Fort Chabrol' indicates that Wanderléa actually picked up the song via the vocal version, 'Le temps de l'amour' by Françoise Hardy (or possibly from the earlier recording by José Salcy, although, as Hardy was better known in Brazil, the former is more likely).

[820] The UK pressing of Les Baxter's version of 'La goualante du pauvre Jean' was titled 'Poor John', although when it was issued on EP it carried the usual English title, 'The Poor People Of Paris'.

## LA GOUALANTE DU PAUVRE JEAN *(continued)*

| Russ Morgan & His Orchestra | 1956 | UK, US | *The Poor People Of Paris* |
|---|---|---|---|
| Norrie Paramor & His Orchestra | 1956 | UK | *The Poor People Of Paris* |
| Primo Scala & His Accordion Band | 1956 | UK | *The Poor People Of Paris* |
| Victor Silvester & His Ballroom Orchestra | 1956 | UK | *The Poor People Of Paris* |
| Lawrence Welk & His Champagne Music | 1956 | UK, US | *The Poor People Of Paris* |
| Les Baxter & His Orchestra & Chorus | 1957 | Italy | *The Poor People Of Paris* |

## LA GRENOUILLE *(Francis Lemarque, 1954)*

| Frankie Laine | 1956 | UK, US | *Ticky Ticky Tick (I'm Gonna Tell On You)* |
|---|---|---|---|

## LE GRISBI *(Jean Wetzel, 1954)*

| The Three Suns | 1954 | US | *The Touch* |
|---|---|---|---|
| Larry Adler | 1955 | Japan | |
| The Three Suns | 1962 | Japan | *The Touch* |

## GUITARE-TANGO *(Maya Casabianca, 1961)*

| The Shadows | 1962 | Australia, Ireland, Netherlands, New Zealand, Norway, South Africa, Sweden, UK, West Germany | *Guitar Tango* |
|---|---|---|---|
| Los Estudiantes | 1963 | Spain | *Guitar Tango* |
| The Shadows | 1963 | Spain, UK[821] | *Guitar Tango* |

## HANDS ACROSS THE TABLE *(Lucienne Boyer, 1934)*

| Hal Kemp | 1934 | US | |
|---|---|---|---|
| Fats Domino | 1962 | US | |

## HAWAII TATTOO *(The Waikiki's, 1962)*

| The Exotic Sounds of Martin Denny | 1964 | Australia, US | |
|---|---|---|---|
| Rob E.G. | 1964 | Australia | |
| Rob E.G. | 1965 | New Zealand | |

## HI-LILI, HI-LO *(Leslie Caron and Mel Ferrer, 1953)*

| Jean Cerchi | 1953 | Australia | |
|---|---|---|---|
| Dinah Shore | 1953 | Australia | |
| Les Welch & His Orchestra | 1953 | Australia | |
| The Dick Hyman Trio | 1956 | US | |
| Roger Williams | 1956 | US | |
| Richard Chamberlain | 1963 | US | |
| Manfred Mann | 1965 | Australia | |
| The Moonlighters | 1966 | Sweden | |

---

[821] The Shadows' version of 'Guitar Tango' charted twice in the UK, firstly as a single in 1962 and then in 1963 as a track on the hit EP *Dance On*.

## HI-LILI, HI-LO *(continued)*

| | | | |
|---|---|---|---|
| The Alan Price Set | 1966 | Australia, Netherlands, Spain, Sweden, UK, US, West Germany | |
| The Shanes | 1966 | Sweden | |
| Katri Helena | 1967 | Finland | |
| Peter Kraus | 1979 | West Germany | |

## L'HOMME ET L'ENFANT *(Tania et Eddie Constantine, 1955)*

| | | | |
|---|---|---|---|
| Eddie Albert & Sondra Lee | 1956 | US | *Little Child* |
| Lael & Cab Calloway | 1956 | US | *Little Child* |
| Danny Kaye & Dena Kaye | 1956 | UK, US | *Little Child (Daddy Dear)* |
| Frankie Laine & Jimmy Boyd | 1956 | US | *Little Child* |
| Gisele MacKenzie & Billy Quinn | 1956 | US | *The Little Child* |

## HYMNE À L'AMOUR *(Édith Piaf, 1950)*

| | | | |
|---|---|---|---|
| Eve Boswell | 1953 | UK | *If You Love Me (I Won't Care)* |
| Rose Brennan | 1953 | UK | *If You Love Me (I Won't Care)* |
| Ray Burns | 1953 | UK | *If You Love Me (I Won't Care)* |
| Robert Earl | 1953 | UK | *If You Love Me (I Won't Care)* |
| Vera Lynn | 1953 | UK | *If You Love Me (Really Love Me)* |
| Dorothy Squires | 1953 | UK | *If You Love Me (I Won't Care)* |
| Maurice Winnick & His Sweet Music | 1953 | UK | *While We Love* |
| Vera Lynn | 1954 | Australia, US | *If You Love Me (Really Love Me)* |
| Kay Starr | 1954 | Australia, UK, US | *If You Love Me (Really Love Me)* |
| LaVern Baker | 1959 | UK, US | *If You Love Me (I Won't Care)* |
| Shirley Bassey | 1959 | UK | *If You Love Me* |
| Wilma Bentivegna | 1959 | Brazil | *Hino ao amor* |
| Shirley Bassey | 1961 | UK | *If You Love Me*[822] |
| Brenda Lee | 1964 | Japan | *If You Love Me (Really Love Me)* |
| Jackie Trent | 1964 | UK, US | *If You Love Me (Really Love Me)* |
| Mary Hopkin | 1976 | Netherlands, Rhodesia, UK | *If You Love Me (I Won't Care)* |
| Elaine Paige | 1995 | UK | *If You Love Me (I Won't Care)* |

## I'M WATCHING YOU *(Sylvie Vartan, 1963)*

| | | | |
|---|---|---|---|
| Little Peggy March | 1964 | Australia, Israel, Japan, US | *(I'm Watching) Every Little Move You Make* |

## ICH SCHAU' DEN WEIßEN WOLKEN NACH *(Nana Mouskouri, 1962)*

| | | | |
|---|---|---|---|
| Ann-Louise Hanson | 1963 | Sweden | *Vita sommarmoln* |

## IL FAUT SAVOIR *(Charles Aznavour, 1961)*

| | | | |
|---|---|---|---|
| Diane Ferraz & Nicky Scott | 1966 | UK | *You've Got To Learn* |
| Kamahl | 1969 | Australia | *You've Got To Learn* |

## IRMA LA DOUCE *(Colette Renard, 1958)*

| | | | |
|---|---|---|---|
| Mantovani & His Orchestra | 1960 | US | |

---

[822] Shirley Bassey's version of 'Hymne à l'amour' ('If You Love Me') was a regional hit in *Record Mirror* and also made the UK sheet music chart in 1959, then charted again in 1961 as part of the EP *As Long As He Needs Me*.

## J'AI DEUX AMOURS *(Joséphine Baker, 1930)*

| | | | |
|---|---|---|---|
| Phylicia Allen[823] | 1978 | US | *Two Loves Have I* |

## LA JARDINÈRE DU ROI *(Lys Assia, 1949)*

| | | | |
|---|---|---|---|
| Gene Autry & Jo Stafford | 1951 | UK | *My Heart Cries For You* |
| The Beverley Sisters | 1951 | UK | *My Heart Cries For You* |
| Eve Boswell | 1951 | UK | *My Heart Cries For You* |
| Billy Cotton & His Band | 1951 | UK | *My Heart Cries For You* |
| Vic Damone | 1951 | US | *My Heart Cries For You* |
| Billy Farrell | 1951 | UK, US | *My Heart Cries For You* |
| The Johnston Brothers | 1951 | UK | *My Heart Cries For You* |
| Evelyn Knight & Red Foley | 1951 | UK, US | *My Heart Cries For You* |
| Joe Loss & His Orchestra | 1951 | UK | *My Heart Cries For You* |
| Guy Mitchell | 1951 | UK, US | *My Heart Cries For You* |
| Al Morgan with the Keynotes | 1951 | UK, US | *My Heart Cries For You* |
| Donald Peers with the Merry Macs | 1951 | UK | *My Heart Cries For You* |
| Dinah Shore | 1951 | UK, US | *My Heart Cries For You* |
| Billy Thorburn's The Organ, The Dance Band & Me | 1951 | UK | *My Heart Cries For You* |
| Jimmy Wakely | 1951 | UK, US | *My Heart Cries For You* |
| Victor Young & His Orchestra | 1951 | UK, US | *My Heart Cries For You* |
| Ray Stevens | 1959 | US | *My Heart Cries For You* |
| Ray Charles | 1964 | Australia, US | *My Heart Cries For You* |
| Connie Francis | 1967 | US | *My Heart Cries For You* |
| Jimmy Roselli | 1969 | US | *My Heart Cries For You* |

## JE ME SENS SI BIEN *(Lucienne Delyle, 1955)*

| | | | |
|---|---|---|---|
| Tony Bennett | 1956 | US | *Capri In May* |

## JE N'EN CONNAIS PAS LA FIN *(Édith Piaf, 1939)*

| | | | |
|---|---|---|---|
| Kitty Kallen | 1956 | US | *Ah, Ah, Ah, Ah (The Song That Haunts My Heart)* |

## JE NE CROIS PLUS AU PÈRE NOËL *(Lucienne Boyer, 1945)*

| | | | |
|---|---|---|---|
| Nina & Frederik[824] | 1961 | UK | |

## JE NE SAIS PAS *(Line Renaud, 1954)*

| | | | |
|---|---|---|---|
| Betty Madigan | 1956 | US | *To You My Love* |
| Nick Noble | 1956 | US | *To You My Love* |
| Georgie Shaw | 1956 | US | *To You My Love* |

## JE SUIS COMME JE SUIS *(Juliette Gréco, 1951)*

| | | | |
|---|---|---|---|
| Tamara Lund | 1963 | Finland | *Olen mikä olen* |

---

[823] Phylicia Allen was an American singer and actress who later found fame on *The Cosby Show*. Her cover of Joséphine Baker's 'J'ai deux amours' ('Two Loves Have I') was part of a concept album dedicated to Baker, produced by Jacques Morali (Village People, Ritchie Family, etc.).

[824] Nina & Frederik's revival of Lucienne Boyer's 'Je ne crois plus au Père Noël' was on their hit EP *Christmas At Home with Nina & Frederik*. The other tracks on the EP had no connection to French pop.

## JE SUIS LÀ *(Katia Valère, 1963)*

| | | | |
|---|---|---|---|
| Elisio del Toro | 1963 | Spain | *Junto a tí* |

## JE T'AIME, JE T'AIME *(Georges Blaness, 1962)*

| | | | |
|---|---|---|---|
| Santy | 1962 | Spain | *Te amo, te amo* |

## JE T'APPARTIENS *(Gilbert Bécaud, 1955)*

| | | | |
|---|---|---|---|
| Jill Corey | 1957 | US | *Let It Be Me* |
| The Blue Diamonds | 1960 | Netherlands, Spain | *Let It Be Me* |
| Detlef Engel | 1960 | West Germany | *Zeig mir bei Nacht die Sterne* |
| The Everly Brothers | 1960 | Australia, Netherlands, UK, US | *Let It Be Me* |
| The Everly Brothers | 1962 | UK | *Let It Be Me*[825] |
| Betty Everett & Jerry Butler | 1964 | Australia, New Zealand, Singapore, US | *Let It Be Me* |
| Arthur Prysock | 1966 | US | *Let It Be Me* |
| Johnny Young & Kompany | 1966 | Australia | *Let It Be Me* |
| The Sweet Inspirations | 1967 | US | *Let It Be Me* |
| Mick Tinsley | 1967 | UK | *Let It Be Me* |
| The Hep Stars | 1968 | Finland, Netherlands, Sweden | *Let It Be Me* |
| Jarkko ja Laura | 1968 | Finland | *Se oli silloin* |
| Nino Tempo & April Stevens | 1968 | US | *Let It Be Me* |
| Glen Campbell & Bobbie Gentry | 1969 | US | *Let It Be Me* |
| Magnus | 1969 | Sweden | *Låt det bli vi* |
| Kees van Kooten & Wim de Bie | 1969 | Netherlands | *Kom bij me terug* |
| Percy Sledge | 1970 | South Africa | *Let It Be Me* |
| The Buffoons | 1973 | Netherlands | *Let It Be Me* |
| Willie Nelson | 1982 | US | *Let It Be Me* |

## JE T'ATTENDS *(Gilbert Bécaud, 1963)*

| | | | |
|---|---|---|---|
| Pasi Kaunisto | 1970 | Finland | *Maa muuttukoon* |

## JO LE ROUGE *(Henri Serre, 1962)*

| | | | |
|---|---|---|---|
| Al Caiola | 1967 | US | *Sailor From Gibraltar* |

## LE JOUR OÙ LA PLUIE VIENDRA *(Gilbert Bécaud, 1957)*

| | | | |
|---|---|---|---|
| Ronnie Hilton | 1958 | UK | *The Day The Rains Came* |
| The Jones Boys | 1958 | UK | *The Day The Rains Came* |
| Al Saxon | 1958 | UK | *The Day The Rains Came* |
| Betty Curtis | 1959 | Italy | *La pioggia cadrà* |
| Vera Lynn[826] | 1959 | UK | *The Day The Rains Came* |
| Heinz Schachtner | 1959 | West Germany | *Am Tag als Regen kam* |

---

[825] The Everly Brothers' version of Gilbert Bécaud's 'Je t'appartiens' ('Let It Be Me') was a UK hit in 1960, and again in 1962 on the EP *The Everly Brothers No. 6*. The other tracks on the EP had no connection to French pop.

[826] Vera Lynn's hit version of 'The Day The Rains Came' was part of a medley, 'Vera Sings Today's Pop Hits', the remainder of which had no connection to French pop.

## KILI WATCH *(The Cousins, 1960)*

| Bobbejaan | 1960 | West Germany | |
|---|---|---|---|
| The Carr Twins | 1961 | Chile | |

## 'LASTIC *(Sidney Bechet, 1950)*

| Mr. Acker Bilk & His Paramount Jazz Band[827] | 1959 | UK | |
|---|---|---|---|
| Mr. Acker Bilk & His Paramount Jazz Band | 1960 | UK | |

## LES LAVANDIÈRES DU PORTUGAL *(Jacqueline François, 1955)*

| Joe 'Fingers' Carr | 1956 | Australia, UK, US | *The Portuguese Washerwoman* |
|---|---|---|---|
| Joe Sherman & His Orchestra & Chorus | 1956 | US | *The Portuguese Washerwoman* |
| The Baja Marimba Band | 1966 | US | *The Portuguese Washerwoman* |

## LE LOUP, LA BICHE ET LE CHEVALIER *(Henri Salvador, 1951)*

| Tony Brent | 1953 | UK | *Make It Soon* |
|---|---|---|---|
| The Stargazers | 1953 | UK | *Make It Soon* |
| The Tanner Sisters | 1953 | UK | *Make It Soon* |

## LOUISE *(Maurice Chevalier, 1929)*

| Paul Whiteman's Rhythm Boys | 1929 | US | |
|---|---|---|---|

## MALADIE D'AMOUR *(Henri Salvador, 1948)*

| The Ames Brothers | 1957 | UK, US | *Melodie d'Amour (Melody Of Love)* |
|---|---|---|---|
| Marty Gold & His Orchestra | 1957 | US | *Melodie d'Amour (Melody Of Love)* |
| Edmundo Ros & His Orchestra | 1957 | US | *Melodie d'Amour (Melody Of Love)* |
| The Ames Brothers | 1958 | Australia, Netherlands, New Zealand, West Germany | *Melodie d'Amour (Melody Of Love)* |
| Angèle Durand | 1958 | West Germany | *Melodie d'Amour* |
| Edmundo Ros & His Orchestra | 1958 | Netherlands, West Germany | *Melodie d'Amour (Melody Of Love)* |
| Nina & Frederick | 1959 | Spain | |
| Nina & Frederik[828] | 1960 | UK | |
| Paul Anka | 1961 | Peru | *Melodie d'Amour (Melody Of Love)* |

## LA MAMMA *(Charles Aznavour, 1963)*

| Rosamel Araya | 1964 | Argentina, Uruguay | *La mama* |
|---|---|---|---|
| | | | |
| Cory Brokken | 1964 | Netherlands | |
| La Cava Bengal | 1964 | Argentina | *La mama* |
| Alberto Cortéz | 1964 | Spain | *La mama* |
| Danielo | 1964 | Argentina | *La mama* |

---

[827] Mr. Acker Bilk's cover of Sidney Bechet's ''Lastic' was on the hit EP *Acker's Away*, which charted in 1959 and then again in 1960. The other tracks on the EP had no connection to French pop.

[828] Nina & Frederik's cover of Henri Salvador's 'Maladie d'amour' was on the hit EP *Nina & Frederik (Volume 2)*. The other tracks on the EP had no connection to French pop.

## LA MAMMA (continued)

| Enrique Dumas | 1964 | Argentina | La mama |
|---|---|---|---|
| Margot Eskens | 1964 | Austria | Mama |
| Connie Francis | 1964 | US | For Mama |
| José Guardiola | 1964 | Spain | La mama |
| Luis Lucena | 1964 | Spain | La mama |
| Matt Monro[829] | 1964 | UK | For Mama |
| Antonio Prieto | 1964 | Argentina, Uruguay | La mama |
| Ramuncho | 1964 | Argentina | La mama |
| Eduardo Rodrigo | 1964 | Argentina | La mama |
| Fulvio Salamanca | 1964 | Argentina | La mama |
| Los Tamara | 1964 | Spain | La mama |
| Lita Torelló | 1964 | Spain | La mama |
| Cory Brokken | 1965 | West Germany | |
| Connie Francis | 1965 | Japan, Philippines | For Mama |
| Matt Monro | 1965 | Hong Kong, UK, US | For Mama |
| Jerry Vale | 1965 | Philippines, US | For Mama |
| Agnaldo Rayol | 1966 | Brazil | Mamae |
| Agnaldo Timotéo | 1966 | Brazil | Mamae |

## LE MARCHAND DE POISSONS (Sidney Bechet, 1952)

| Ian Menzies & His Clyde Valley Stompers | 1960 | UK | The Fish Man |
|---|---|---|---|

## MARIE, MARIE (Gilbert Bécaud, 1959)

| Roger Williams | 1959 | US | |
|---|---|---|---|
| Serino | 1961 | US | |
| Kris Ryan | 1965 | UK | |

## MARINA (Rocco Granata, 1959)

| Willy Alberti | 1959 | Australia, Netherlands, Norway, US | |
|---|---|---|---|
| Will Brandes | 1959 | West Germany | |
| Bueno de Mesquita | 1959 | Netherlands | |
| The Dutch Swing College Band | 1959 | Netherlands | |
| Marino Marini ed il suo Quartetto | 1959 | Italy | |
| Tony Martin | 1959 | US | |
| Max van Praag | 1959 | Netherlands | |
| Willy Alberti | 1960 | Italy | |
| Peppino di Capri | 1960 | Italy | |
| Leny Eversong | 1960 | Brazil | |
| Piero Giorgetti | 1960 | Italy | |
| Eino Grün | 1960 | Finland | |
| Laila Kinnunen | 1960 | Finland | |
| Little Gerhard | 1960 | Sweden | |
| Raquel Rastenni | 1960 | Denmark, Sweden | |

---

[829]  Matt Monro's version of Charles Aznavour's 'La mamma' ('For Mama') was a UK hit in 1964, and again in 1965 on the EP Somewhere. The other tracks on the EP had no connection to French pop.

## MARINA *(continued)*

| | | | |
|---|---|---|---|
| Al Saxon | 1960 | Sweden | |
| Jack Terry | 1960 | West Germany | |
| Caternia Valente | 1960 | Italy | |
| Claudio Villa | 1960 | Italy | |
| Joe Vina | 1960 | New Zealand | |
| Peter und John | 1973 | West Germany | |
| Chico & The Gypsies | 1996 | Netherlands | |

## MARINA *(Sacha Distel, 1961)*

| | | | |
|---|---|---|---|
| Tony Bennett | 1963 | Australia, New Zealand, UK, US | *The Good Life* |
| Sergio Franchi | 1963 | US | *The Good Life* |
| Kathy Keegan | 1963 | US | *The Good Life* |
| Tony Bennett | 1964 | Philippines | *The Good Life* |
| Mr. Acker Bilk | 1964 | US | *The Good Life* |

## MARJOLAINE *(Francis Lemarque, 1957)*

| | | | |
|---|---|---|---|
| Gogi Grant | 1958 | US | *Marjolaina* |
| Jimmy James & the Candy Kanes | 1958 | US | |
| Gogi Grant | 1959 | Italy | *Marjolaina* |

## MÉLODIE EN SOUS-SOL *(Michel Magne, 1963)*

| | | | |
|---|---|---|---|
| Hubert Bianco & His Orchestra | 1963 | Japan | |
| Jimmy Smith | 1963 | US | *Theme From 'Any Number Can Win'* |

## MÉLODIE PERDUE *(Dalida, 1958)*

| | | | |
|---|---|---|---|
| Al Alberts | 1958 | US | *Willingly* |
| Monte Kelly & His Orchestra | 1958 | US | *Willingly* |
| Al Alberts | 1959 | UK | *Willingly* |
| Johnny Desmond | 1959 | UK | *Willingly* |
| Monte Kelly | 1959 | UK | *Willingly* |
| Joe Loss & His Orchestra | 1959 | UK | *Willingly* |
| Mal Perry | 1959 | UK | *Willingly* |
| Malcolm Vaughan | 1959 | UK | *Willingly* |
| David Whitfield | 1959 | UK | *Willingly* |

## LA MER *(Roland Gerbeau, 1946)*[830]

| | | | |
|---|---|---|---|
| Benny Goodman & His Orchestra | 1948 | US | *Beyond The Sea* |
| Roger Williams | 1956 | US | *La Mer (Beyond The Sea)* |
| Trade Martin | 1959 | US | |
| Bobby Darin | 1960 | Australia. Ireland, Spain, UK, US | *Beyond The Sea* |
| Ray Conniff & His Orchestra & Chorus | 1962 | Mexico | *Beyond The Sea* |
| Die Gitarros | 1962 | West Germany | *La Mer d'Hawaii* |
| Enrique Guzmán | 1963 | Spain | *El mar* |

---

[830] 'La mer' was written and recorded by Charles Trenet, whose version is the most famous of the French language interpretations. However, Gerbeau actually recorded it before Trenet.

## LA MER *(continued)*

| The Reveres | 1964 | US | *Beyond The Sea* |
|---|---|---|---|
| Smith | 1966 | UK | |
| The Scandinavian Five | 1967 | Sweden | *Blå hav* |

## MES MAINS *(Gilbert Bécaud, 1953)*

| Tony Brent | 1956 | UK | *With Your Love* |
|---|---|---|---|
| Petula Clark | 1956 | UK | *With Your Love* |
| Robert Earl | 1956 | UK | *With Your Love* |
| Vera Lynn | 1956 | UK | *With Your Love* |
| Malcolm Vaughan | 1956 | UK | *With Your Love* |

## METS DEUX THUNES DANS L'BASTRINGUE *(Catherine Sauvage, 1954)*

| Lou Busch & His Orchestra | 1956 | US | *The Charming Mademoiselle From Paris* |
|---|---|---|---|

## MEXICO *(Luis Mariano, 1955)*

| André van Duin | 1987 | Netherlands | *Eskimo* |
|---|---|---|---|

## MILORD *(Édith Piaf, 1959)*

| Lily Broberg | 1960 | Denmark | |
|---|---|---|---|
| Cory Brokken | 1960 | Netherlands, West Germany | |
| The Dutch Swing College Band | 1960 | Netherlands, West Germany | |
| Ritva Kinnunen | 1960 | Finland | |
| Anita Lindblom | 1960 | Italy | |
| Lore Lorenz | 1960 | West Germany | |
| Die Melody-Stars | 1960 | West Germany | |
| Milva | 1960 | Italy | |
| Frankie Vaughan | 1960 | UK, West Germany | |
| Teresa Brewer | 1961 | US | |
| Gaynor Bunning | 1961 | Australia, New Zealand | |
| Dubé y su Conjunto | 1961 | Spain | |
| Billy Longstreet's Jazz Band | 1961 | Australia | |
| Jørgen Ingmann | 1962 | Spain | |
| Bobby Darin | 1964 | Australia, US | |
| King Richard's Fluegel Knights | 1966 | US | |

## MON BEAU CHAPEAU *(Sacha Distel, 1960)*

| Peter Kraus | 1961 | Peter Kraus | *Mein neuer Hut* |
|---|---|---|---|

## MON CŒUR EST UN VIOLON *(Lucienne Boyer, 1945)*

| Ken Dodd | 1960 | UK | *Love Is Like A Violin* |
|---|---|---|---|

## MON HOMME *(Mistinguett, 1916)*

| Aileen Stanley | 1921 | US | *My Man* |
|---|---|---|---|
| Paul Whiteman & His Orchestra | 1921 | US | *My Man* |
| Fanny Brice | 1922 | US | *My Man* |
| Belle Baker | 1928 | US | *My Man* |
| Fanny Brice | 1928 | US | *My Man* |

## MON HOMME *(continued)*

| | | | |
|---|---|---|---|
| Teddy Wilson & His Orchestra (Vocal: Billie Holiday) | 1938 | US | *My Man* |
| Wayne King & His Orchestra | 1939 | US | *My Man* |
| Dinah Shore | 1941 | US | *My Man* |
| Dick Contino | 1957 | US | *My Man* |
| Peggy Lee | 1959 | US | *My Man* |
| Walter Gates | 1964 | US | *My Man* |
| Barbra Streisand[831] | 1965 | UK | *My Man* |
| Barbra Streisand | 1965 | UK | *My Man* |
| Ernestine Anderson | 1968 | US | *My Man* |

## MON ONCLE *(Jacqueline François, 1959)*

| | | | |
|---|---|---|---|
| Conjunto Farroupilha | 1959 | Brazil | *Meu tio* |

## MON PETIT MONDE À MOI *(André Claveau, 1952)*

| | | | |
|---|---|---|---|
| The Bon Bons | 1955 | US | *That's The Way Love Goes* |

## LE MORIBOND *(Jacques Brel, 1960)*

| | | | |
|---|---|---|---|
| The Kingston Trio | 1964 | US | *Seasons In The Sun* |
| The Fortunes | 1969 | Netherlands | *Seasons In The Sun* |
| Tommy Sands | 1969 | Australia | *Seasons In The Sun* |
| Terry Jacks | 1974 | Australia, Austria, Brazil, Denmark, Finland, Greece, Ireland, Israel, Netherlands, New Zealand Norway, Rhodesia, South Africa, Spain, Sweden, UK, US, West Germany | *Seasons In The Sun* |
| Arto Sotavaita | 1974 | Finland | *Pâivâit kuin unta* |
| Bobby Wright | 1974 | Australia, South Africa, US | *Seasons In The Sun* |
| Terry Jacks | 1984 | Iceland | *Seasons In The Sun* |
| Westlife | 1999 | Australia, Germany, Ireland, New Zealand Norway, Sweden, UK | *Seasons In The Sun* |

## MOULIN À CAFÉ *(Sidney Bechet et l'Orchestre de Claude Luter, 1950)*

| | | | |
|---|---|---|---|
| Humphrey Lyttleton & His Band | 1955 | UK | *Coffee Grinder* |

---

[831] Barbra Streisand's recording of Mistinguett's 'Mon homme' ('My Man') was a hit single in the UK, and also appeared on the hit EP, *My Man*. The other tracks on the EP had no connection to French pop.

## MOULIN ROUGE *(Line Renaud, 1952)*

| Buddy de Franco | 1953 | UK | *The Song From Moulin Rouge* |
|---|---|---|---|
| Percy Faith & His Orchestra | 1953 | Australia, Netherlands UK, US | *The Song From Moulin Rouge* |
| Ron Goodwin & His Concert Orchestra | 1953 | UK | *The Song From Moulin Rouge* |
| Hutch | 1953 | UK | *The Song From Moulin Rouge* |
| June Hutton | 1953 | UK | *The Song From Moulin Rouge* |
| Mantovani & His Orchestra | 1953 | Netherlands, UK, US | *The Song From The Moulin Rouge (Where Is Your Heart)* [832] |
| Norrie Paramor & His Orchestra | 1953 | UK | *The Song From Moulin Rouge* |
| Henri René & His Orchestra | 1953 | UK, US | *The Song From Moulin Rouge* |
| Felice Sanders | 1953 | Australia | *The Song From Moulin Rouge* |
| Victor Silvester & His Ballroom Orchestra | 1953 | UK | *The Song From Moulin Rouge* |
| Ethel Smith | 1953 | UK | *The Song From Moulin Rouge* |
| Victor Young & His Singing Strings | 1953 | UK | *The Song From Moulin Rouge* |
| Mantovani & His Orchestra | 1960 | UK | *The Song From The Moulin Rouge (Where Is Your Heart)* |
| Connie Francis | 1962 | Philippines | *The Song From Moulin Rouge* |
| Peters & Lee | 1977 | Netherlands | *The Song From Moulin Rouge* |

## MUSTAPHA *(Bob Azzam et son Orchestre, 1960)*

| Archie Bleyer & His Musikyoun | 1960 | US | *Mustafa* |
|---|---|---|---|
| Los Españoles | 1960 | Japan | |
| Clinton Ford | 1960 | UK | |
| The Four Lads | 1960 | Japan | *Mustafa* |
| José Guardiola | 1960 | Spain | |
| Brita Koivunen | 1960 | Finland | |
| Leo Leandros | 1960 | West Germany | *Mustafa* |
| José Solá y su Orquestra | 1960 | Spain | *Mustafà català* |

## MY IDEAL *(Maurice Chevalier, 1930)*

| Billy Butterfield & His Orchestra | 1943 | US | |
|---|---|---|---|
| Maxine Sullivan | 1943 | US | |
| Jimmy Dorsey & His Orchestra | 1944 | US | |

## NE ME QUITTE PAS *(Jacques Brel, 1959)*

| Damita Jo | 1966 | US | *If You Go Away* |
|---|---|---|---|
| Shirley Bassey | 1967 | UK | *If You Go Away* |
| Anki | 1968 | Finland | *Jos nyt menet pois* |
| Dusty Springfield | 1968 | Japan | *If You Go Away* |
| Ray Barrett | 1969 | UK | *If You Go Away* |
| Mari Trini | 1969 | Spain | |
| Scott Walker | 1969 | Japan | *If You Go Away* |
| Patty Pravo | 1970 | Italy | *Non andare via* |

---

[832] Mantovani's recording of 'The Song From The Moulin Rouge' charted in 1953, and again in 1960 on the EP *Mantovani's Big Four*. The other tracks on the EP had no connection to French pop.

## NE ME QUITTE PAS *(continued)*

| Terry Jacks | 1974 | Australia, Austria, Denmark, Israel, Netherlands, Norway, Sweden, UK, US, West Germany | *If You Go Away* |
|---|---|---|---|

## NON, JE NE REGRETTE RIEN *(Édith Piaf, 1961)*

| Milva | 1961 | Italy | *Nulla rimpiangerò* |
|---|---|---|---|
| Kay Starr | 1963 | US | *No Regrets* |
| Shirley Bassey | 1965 | UK,US | *No Regrets* |
| Gun Sjöberg | 1967 | Sweden | *Nej jag ångrar ingenting* |
| Samantha Jones | 1971 | Netherlands | *No Regrets* |

## NOUS LES AMOUREUX *(Jean-Claude Pascal, 1961)*

| Dubé y su Conjunto | 1961 | Spain | *Sol de nuestro amor* |
|---|---|---|---|
| Gelu | 1961 | Spain | *Sol de nuestro amor* |
| José Guardiola | 1961 | Spain | *Sol de nuestro amor* |

## O MEIN PAPA *(Lys Assia, 1953)*[833]

| Ray Anthony & His Orchestra | 1953 | US | *O Mein Papa (Oh! My Papa)* |
|---|---|---|---|
| The Brasshats | 1953 | UK | *Oh, Mein Papa* |
| Eddie Calvert | 1953 | Netherlands, UK, US | *Oh, Mein Papa* |
| Eddie Fisher | 1953 | Netherlands UK, US | *Oh! My Pa-Pa (O Mein Papa)* |
| Marty | 1953 | Netherlands | *Oh mijn papa* |
| The Radio Revellers | 1953 | UK | *Oh My Papa* |
| Ray Anthony & His Orchestra | 1954 | UK | *Oh! My Pa-Pa* |
| The Beverley Sisters | 1954 | UK | *Oh! My Pa-Pa (O Mein Papa)* |
| Billy Cotton & His Band | 1954 | UK | *Oh! My Papa* |
| Diana Decker | 1954 | UK | *Oh My Papa (Oh, Mein Papa)* |
| Eddie Fisher | 1954 | Australia | *Oh! My Papa (O! Mein Papa)* |
| Annette Klooger | 1954 | UK | *Oh! My Papa (O Mein Papa)* |
| Ken Mackintosh & His Orchestra | 1954 | UK | *Oh! My Papa* |
| Russ Morgan & His Orchestra | 1954 | UK | *Oh! My Papa* |
| Muriel Smith | 1954 | UK | *Oh! My Pa-Pa (O Mein Papa)* |
| Dick Lee | 1961 | US | *Oh Mein Papa* |
| Arne Lamberth | 1970 | Sweden | |
| Marty | 1973 | Netherlands | *Oh mijn papa* |

## OH, OH, ROSI *(Rocco Granata, 1960)*

| Marino Marini ed il suo Quartetto | 1960 | Italy | |
|---|---|---|---|

## ON DIT DE LUI *(Françoise Hardy, 1963)*

| Ornella Vanoni | 1963 | Italy | *Coccodrillo* |
|---|---|---|---|

[833] Lys Assia's 'O mein Papa' was not, strictly speaking, a French pop hit as it was recorded in German (although she did also record a French version, 'Oh! Mon papa'). Although more popular in Germany, the Swiss singer was nevertheless a regular fixture on the French pop scene during the fifties and thus the song is included here.

## OTORRINO LARINGOLOGO *(Los Machucambos, 1961)*

| Los Tamara | 1961 | Spain | |
|---|---|---|---|

## OUI, OUI, OUI, OUI *(Jean Philippe, 1959)*

| Los Tamara | 1960 | Spain | *Si, si, si, si* |
|---|---|---|---|

## PADAM... PADAM *(Édith Piaf, 1952)*

| Vera Lynn | 1953 | Australia | *Padam Padam (How It Echoes The Beat of My Heart)* |
|---|---|---|---|

## PADRE DON JOSÉ *(Gloria Lasso, 1957)*

| Toni Arden | 1958 | Australia, US | *Padre* |
|---|---|---|---|
| Valerie Carr | 1958 | US | *Padre* |
| Kay Starr | 1958 | US | *Help Me* |
| Sarah Vaughan | 1958 | US | *Padre* |

## PAPA AIME MAMAN *(Tino Rossi, 1960)*

| José Guardiola | 1960 | Spain | *Papá quiere a Mamá* |
|---|---|---|---|
| Donald Peers | 1960 | UK | *Papa Loves Mama* |
| Joan Regan | 1960 | UK | *Papa Loves Mama* |
| Caterina Valente | 1960 | Japan | |
| Jean Michel | 1961 | Japan | |

## PARIS CANAILLE *(Léo Ferré, 1953)*

| Angèle Durand | 1956 | West Germany | *So ist Paris* |
|---|---|---|---|

## PARLEZ-MOI D'AMOUR *(Lucienne Boyer, 1930)*

| Ulla Sallert | 1968 | Sweden | *Kärlekens ord* |
|---|---|---|---|

## PASSE TON CHEMIN *(Gilbert Bécaud, 1954)*

| Sammy Davis Jr. | 1956 | UK | *Back Track* |
|---|---|---|---|

## PEPITO *(Los Machucambos, 1961)*

| Yvonne Carre | 1961 | West Germany | |
|---|---|---|---|
| Cocky Mazzetti | 1961 | Italy | |
| Maria Zamora | 1961 | West Germany | |
| Tuula ja Paula | 1962 | Finland | |

## LE PETIT CORDONNIER *(Francis Lemarque, 1954)*

| Eve Boswell | 1954 | UK | *The Little Shoemaker* |
|---|---|---|---|
| Petula Clark | 1954 | Australia, UK | *The Little Shoemaker* |
| Alma Cogan | 1954 | UK | *The Little Shoemaker* |
| The Gaylords | 1954 | Australia, Netherlands, UK, US | *The Little Shoemaker* |
| The Regent Ballroom Orchestra | 1954 | UK | *The Little Shoemaker* |
| Frank Weir, His Saxophone & His Orchestra | 1954 | Australia, UK | *The Little Shoemaker* |
| Hugo Winterhalter & His Orchestra | 1954 | US | *The Little Shoemaker* |

## LE PETIT TRAIN *(André Claveau, 1952)*

| Doris Day | 1953 | US | *Choo Choo Train (Ch-Ch-Foo)* |
|---|---|---|---|

## LA PETITE DILIGENCE *(André Claveau, 1951)*

| David McKersie | 1951 | Netherlands | |
|---|---|---|---|
| Bob Scholte | 1951 | Netherlands | *De kleine diligence* |

## PETITE FLEUR *(Sidney Bechet, 1952)*

| Chris Barber's Jazz Band | 1959 | Australia, Denmark, Finland, Ireland, Italy, Japan, Netherlands, New Zealand, Norway, Sweden, UK, US, West Germany | |
|---|---|---|---|
| Bob Crosby & The Bob Cats | 1959 | Japan, UK | |
| Wilbur de Paris & His New Oreleans Band | 1959 | UK | |
| The Wally Fawkes & Sandy Brown Quintet | 1959 | UK | |
| Teddy Johnson and Pearl Carr | 1959 | UK | |
| Laila Kinnunen | 1959 | Finland | *Pieni kukkanen* |
| The Gene Krupa Quartet | 1959 | UK | |
| Werner Müller und sein Orchester | 1959 | Brazil | |
| The Roman New Orleans Jazz Band | 1959 | Italy | |
| Ricardo Santos und sein Orchester | 1959 | Japan | |
| The Scamps | 1959 | UK | |
| Peter Schilperoort & His Quartet | 1959 | Netherlands | |
| Victor Silvester & His Ballroom Orchestra | 1959 | UK | |
| Bert Weedon & His Music For dancing | 1959 | UK | |
| Los Cinco Latinos | 1960 | Spain | *Pequeña flor* |
| José Guardiola | 1960 | Spain | *Pequeña flor* |
| Britt Hagen | 1961 | West Germany | *Sag adieu* |
| Kormendy & His Band | 1963 | Hungary | |
| Don Powell | 1964 | Italy | *Un tempo per amare, un tempo per piangere* |
| Lou Johnson | 1965 | US | *A Time To Love, A Time To Cry* |

## LA PETITE TONKINOISE *(Polin, 1906)*

| Gisele MacKenzie | 1956 | US | *It's Delightful To Be Married* |
|---|---|---|---|

## LA PETITE VALSE *(Jo Heyne, 1950)*

| Guy Lombardo & His Royal Canadians | 1950 | US | *The Petite Waltz* |
|---|---|---|---|

## PIANISSIMO *(Jacqueline Boyer, 1961)*

| Ken Dodd | 1962 | UK | |
|---|---|---|---|

## LE PIANO DU PAUVRE *(Léo Ferré, 1950)*

| Les Elgart & His Orchestra | 1956 | US | *The Poor Pianist Of Paris* |
|---|---|---|---|

445

## PILOU... PILOU... HÉ *(Gilbert Bécaud, 1959)*

| Christa Williams | 1960 | West Germany | *Pilou Pilou* |
|---|---|---|---|

## PLAISIR D'AMOUR *(Yvonne Printemps, 1931)*[834]

| The Four Esquires | 1961 | US | *Can't Help Falling In Love* |
|---|---|---|---|
| Elvis Presley | 1961 | Australia, US | *Can't Help Falling In Love* |
| Keely Smith | 1961 | Hong Kong | *Can't Help Falling In Love* |
| Elvis Presley | 1962 | Denmark, Iceland, Ireland, Israel, Italy, Netherlands, New Zealand, Norway, South Africa, UK, West Germany | *Can't Help Falling In Love* |
| Los Sonor | 1964 | Spain | *Can't Help Falling In Love* |
| Joan Baez[835] | 1965 | UK | |
| Donald Height | 1965 | US | *Can't Help Falling In Love* |
| Anna-Lena Löfgren | 1967 | Sweden | |
| The Dixies | 1969 | Ireland | *The Joys Of Love* |
| Al Martino | 1970 | Australia, US | *Can't Help Falling In Love* |
| Andy Williams | 1970 | Australia, Ireland, Netherlands, South Africa, US | *Can't Help Falling In Love* |
| The Soft Tones | 1973 | US | *Can't Help Falling In Love* |
| The Stylistics | 1976 | Ireland, UK, US | *Can't Help Falling In Love* |
| Engelbert Humperdinck | 1979 | US | *Can't Help Falling In Love* |
| Jimmy Castor | 1980 | US | *Can't Help Falling In Love With You* |
| Corey Hart | 1986 | US | *Can't Help Falling In Love* |
| UB40 | 1993 | Australia, Austria, Germany, Ireland, Italy, New Zealand, Norway, Spain, Sweden, Switzerland, UK, US, Zimbabwe | *(I Can't Help) Falling In Love With You* |
| The A*Teens | 2002 | Argentina, Australia, Sweden | *Can't Help Falling In Love* |
| Christina Grimmie | 2014 | US | *Can't Help Falling In Love* |

## LE PLAT PAYS *(Jacques Brel, 1962)*

| Emili Vendrell | 1964 | Spain | *El clar pais* |
|---|---|---|---|

---

[834] Yvonne Printemps was probably not the first singer to record 'Plaisir d'amour', which is one of the oldest documented French compositions (see *Chapter 1*), although she did enjoy a hit with it and her version is one of the more famous. It is not strictly true that 'Can't Help Falling In Love' was a cover of 'Plaisir d'amour', although the tune bears on obvious debt to its French predecessor. It is unclear where Elvis Presley first encountered the song, although he may have heard it while on military service in Europe. With the exception of the recordings by Joan Baez, the Dixies and Anna-Lena Löfgren, all of the other charting versions were clearly inspired by Presley's treatment of the song, although many singers have also tackled the original French version over the years.

[835] Joan Baez's version of 'Plaisir d'amour' was on the hit EP *Silver Dagger and Other Songs*. The other tracks on the EP had no connection to French pop.

## LA PLAYA[836] *(Los Mayas, 1963)*

| Graeme Bartlett | 1965 | Japan | |
|---|---|---|---|
| Nancy Li | 1965 | Argentina | |
| Lucio Luciano y su Conjunto | 1965 | Argentina | |
| Lucio Milena | 1965 | Argentina | |
| Dany Montano | 1965 | Argentina | |
| Aldo Perricone | 1965 | Argentina | |

## PLUS JE T'ENTENDS *(Alain Barrière, 1963)*

| Enrique Guzmán | 1964 | Mexico | *Tu voz* |
|---|---|---|---|
| Agnaldo Rayol | 1964 | Brazil | *A tua voz* |
| Enrique Guzmán | 1965 | Argentina, Uruguay | *Tu voz* |
| Agnaldo Rayol | 1966 | Brazil | *A tua voz* |

## PODEROSO SEÑOR *(André Hossein, 1961)*[837]

| Los Pekenikes | 1969 | Spain | |
|---|---|---|---|

## POUR TOI *(Tino Rossi, 1957)*

| Morris Albert | 1975 | Australia, Brazil, Ireland, Italy, Netherlands, New Zealand, South Africa, Spain, UK, US, West Germany | *Feelings*[838] |
|---|---|---|---|
| John Daniels | 1975 | Italy | *Feelings* |
| Leisha | 1975 | Australia | *Feelings* |
| Andy Williams | 1975 | US | *Feelings* |
| Morris Albert | 1976 | Finland | |
| Walter Jackson | 1976 | US | *Feelings* |
| André van Duin | 1976 | Netherlands | *File* |

## PREMIER BAL *(Gérard Calvi, 1960)*

| Buck Clayton | 1961 | Japan | |
|---|---|---|---|

## PRIÈRE PÉRUVIENNE *(Luis Mariano, 1955)*

| Percy Faith & His Orchestra | 1955 | US | *Valley Valparaiso* |
|---|---|---|---|

## QUAND MARIA CHANTAIT *(Tino Rossi, 1954)*

| Vic Damone | 1956 | US | *We All Need Love* |
|---|---|---|---|
| Percy Faith & His Orchestra | 1956 | US | *We All Need Love* |
| Liberace | 1956 | US | *We All Need Love* |

---

[836] The most famous version of 'La playa' was by Claude Ciari, former guitarist with Les Champions. That recording dates from 1964 and will be featured in Volume 2, so Ciari's version is excluded from this list.

[837] 'Poderoso Señor' was the theme from the film *Le gout de la violence*, for which Hossein wrote the music. A vocal version by Dalida ('Protégez-moi Seigneur') was the bigger hit.

[838] Morris Albert's 'Feelings' was not initially credited as a cover of 'Pour toi', but it is clearly the same melody. The composer of Rossi's hit, Louis Gasté, sued the publishers of the new version and ultimately emerged victorious after an eight-year court battle, winning a huge fortune in damages. In the meantime, the song was adapted back into French for a chart-topping hit for seventies' teen idol Mike Brant as 'Dis-lui'.

## QUAND ON N'A QUE L'AMOUR *(Jacques Brel, 1956)*

| Dion | 1969 | US | *If We Only Have Love* |
|---|---|---|---|
| Dionne Warwick | 1972 | US | *If We Only Have Love* |

## QUAND TU DORS PRÈS DE MOI *(Yves Montand, 1961)*

| Ferrante & Teicher | 1961 | Italy, US | *Theme From The Motion Picture 'Goodbye Again'* |
|---|---|---|---|
| Ornella Vanoni | 1961 | Italy | *Le piace Brahms* |
| Pino Calvi | 1962 | Italy | *Aimez-vous Brahms?* |

## QUE RESTE-T-IL DE NOS AMOURS? *(Lucienne Boyer, 1942)*[839]

| Danny Kaye | 1950 | US | *I Wish You Love* |
|---|---|---|---|
| Monica Lewis | 1956 | US | *I Wish You Love* |
| Keely Smith | 1956 | US | *I Wish You Love* |
| Keely Smith | 1958 | US | *I Wish You Love* |
| Robert Goulet | 1964 | Philippines | *I Wish You Love* |
| Gloria Lynne | 1964 | Australia, US | *I Wish You Love* |
| The Bachelors | 1966 | Mexico | *I Wish You Love* |
| Rondallo di Santillo | 1969 | Mexico | *Te deseo amor* |

## RELAX-AY-VOO *(Dean Martin and Line Renaud, 1955)*

| The Keynotes | 1955 | US | *Relax-Ay-Vous* |
|---|---|---|---|

## RETIENS LA NUIT *(Johnny Hallyday, 1962)*

| Mike Riós | 1963 | Spain | *Detens la noche* |
|---|---|---|---|

## RIEN NE POURRA CHANGER *(Pierre Dorsey, son Piano et son Orchestre, 1956)*

| Vic Damone | 1956 | US | *When My Love Smiles* |
|---|---|---|---|

## LE RIFIFI *(Magali Noël, 1955)*

| Larry Adler & His Harmonica | 1956 | US | |
|---|---|---|---|

## RIVIERA *(Georges Moustaki, 1961)*

| Umberto Bindi | 1961 | Italy | |
|---|---|---|---|

## LA RONDE DE L'AMOUR *(André Claveau, 1951)*

| John Cameron | 1951 | UK | *Love's Roundabout* |
|---|---|---|---|
| Teddy Johnson | 1951 | UK | *Love's Roundabout* |
| Peter Kreuder & His Rhythms | 1951 | UK | *Love's Roundabout* |
| Gisele MacKenzie | 1951 | UK | *Love's Roundabout* |
| Mantovani & His Orchestra | 1951 | UK | *Love's Roundabout* |
| The Melachrino Orchestra | 1951 | UK | *Love's Roundabout* |
| Lou Preager & His Charm of the Waltz Orchestra | 1951 | UK | *Love's Roundabout* |
| Jan Rosol | 1951 | UK | |
| Anton Wallbrook | 1951 | UK | *Love's Roundabout* |
| David McKersie | 1952 | Netherlands | |
| Lou Preager & His Charm of the Waltz Orchestra | 1952 | Australia | *Love's Roundabout* |
| Anton Wallbrook | 1952 | Australia, Netherlands | *Love's Roundabout* |

[839] Boyer was the first to record 'Que reste-t-il de nos amours?'. Roland Gerbeau was the second. The song is, however, best known in the version by Charles Trenet, who also composed it.

## ROSE-MARIE POLKA *(Tohama, 1952)*

| Ronnie Tober | 1977 | Netherlands | *Rosemarie* |
|---|---|---|---|

## ROSINA *(Adamo, 1961)*

| Rex Gildo | 1961 | West Germany | |
|---|---|---|---|

## LA SAINT AMOUR *(Félix Marten, 1955)*

| Joe 'Fingers' Carr | 1956 | US | *Lucky Pierre* |
|---|---|---|---|

## SAM'DI SOIR *(Johnny Hallyday, 1962)*

| Los Mustang | 1963 | Spain | *La noche del sábado* |
|---|---|---|---|

## SANS TOI MA MIE *(Adamo, 1963)*

| Toshiji Fubuki | 1965 | Japan | *Aishiteru no mi* |
|---|---|---|---|
| Goto Maki | 2003 | Japan | *Aishiteru no mi* |

## SARAH *(Aïda Aznavour, 1957)*

| The Mary Kaye Trio | 1958 | US | *Belong To Me* |
|---|---|---|---|

## LA SEINE *(Jacqueline François, 1948)*

| Doris Day | 1950 | Australia | *The River Seine* |
|---|---|---|---|
| Guy Lombardo & His Royal Canadians | 1950 | Australia | *The River Seine* |

## SEUL UN HOMME PEUT FAIRE ÇA *(Francis Lemarque, 1956)*

| The Four Aces | 1956 | US | *Someone To Love* |
|---|---|---|---|

## SI TU PARTAIS *(Édith Piaf, 1947)*

| Alan Dean | 1951 | UK | *If You Go* |
|---|---|---|---|
| Lester Ferguson | 1951 | UK | *If You Go* |
| Vera Lynn | 1951 | UK | *If You Go* |
| The Melachrino Orchestra | 1951 | UK | *If You Go* |
| Victor Silvester & His Ballroom Orchestra | 1952 | UK | *If You Go* |
| Roger Williams | 1968 | US | *If You Go* |

## SI TU REVIENS UN JOUR *(Gloria Lasso, 1960)*

| Marilyn Maye | 1968 | US | *Till You Come Back* |
|---|---|---|---|

## SI TU VAS À RIO *(Dario Moreno, 1959)*

| Torrebruno | 1959 | Spain | |
|---|---|---|---|

## SI TU VOIS MA MÈRE *(Sidney Bechet, 1952)*

| Chris Barber's Jazz Band | 1959 | Netherlands, UK | *Lonesome* |
|---|---|---|---|
| Peter Schilperoort & His Quartet | 1959 | Netherlands | *Lonesome* |

## LE SOIR *(Line Renaud, 1952)*

| Shirley Abicair | 1953 | UK | *I'd Love to Fall Asleep* |
|---|---|---|---|
| Derrick Francis with the Coronets | 1953 | UK | *I'd Love to Fall Asleep* |
| Penny Nicholls | 1953 | UK | *I'd Love to Fall Asleep* |
| Muriel Smith | 1953 | UK | *I'd Love to Fall Asleep* |
| Beryl Templeman with the Wondertones | 1953 | UK | *I'd Love to Fall Asleep* |

**LE SOIR** *(continued)*

| Billy Thorburn's The Organ, The Dance Band & Me | 1953 | UK | *I'd Love to Fall Asleep* |
|---|---|---|---|

**SOUS LE CIEL DE PARIS** *(Jean Bretonnière, 1951)*

| Mitch Miller & His Orchestra & Chorus | 1953 | US | *Under Paris Skies* |
|---|---|---|---|
| Chris Connor | 1958 | US | *Under Paris Skies* |
| Andy Williams | 1964 | US | *Under Paris Skies* |

**SOUS LES PONTS DE PARIS** *(Georgel, 1913)*

| Eartha Kitt | 1954 | Australia | *Under The Bridges of Paris* |
|---|---|---|---|
| Percy Faith & His Orchestra | 1955 | UK | *Under The Bridges of Paris* |
| Eartha Kitt | 1955 | UK | *Under The Bridges of Paris* |
| Dean Martin | 1955 | Australia, UK, US | *Under The Bridges of Paris* |
| Victor Silvester & His Ballroom Orchestra | 1955 | UK | *Under The Bridges of Paris* |

**SUR LE PONT D'AVIGNON** *(Jean Sablon, 1939)*

| Billy Cotton & His Band | 1944 | UK | *On The Bridge At Avignon* |
|---|---|---|---|

**SUR MA VIE** *(Charles Aznavour, 1955)*

| Robert Earl | 1956 | UK | *Believe In Me* |
|---|---|---|---|
| Alan Kent | 1956 | UK | *Believe In Me* |
| Dawn Lake | 1956 | UK | *Believe In Me* |

**SYMPHONIE** *(Fred Adison et son Orchestre, 1945)*

| Adriano Celentano | 1965 | Italy | *Non mi dir* |
|---|---|---|---|

**LA TAMISE ET MON JARDIN** *(Tino Rossi, 1955)*

| Kim Bennett | 1955 | UK | *Softly, Softly* |
|---|---|---|---|
| Alma Cogan | 1955 | UK | *Softly, Softly* |
| Guy Lombardo & His Royal Canadians | 1955 | UK | *Softly, Softly* |
| Joe Loss & His Orchestra | 1955 | UK | *Softly, Softly* |
| Mantovani & His Orchestra & Chorus | 1955 | UK | *Softly, Softly* |
| Jaye P. Morgan | 1955 | US | *Softly, Softly* |
| Ruby Murray | 1955 | UK | *Softly, Softly* |
| The Regent Ballroom Orchestra | 1955 | UK | *Softly, Softly* |
| The Roland Shaw Orchestra | 1955 | UK | *Softly, Softly* |
| Victor Silvester & His Ballroom Orchestra | 1955 | UK | *Softly, Softly* |

**TANGO D'AMORE** *(Rocco Granata, 1963)*

| Eino Grön | 1963 | Finland | |
|---|---|---|---|

**LE TANGO MAGIQUE** *(Tino Rossi, 1954)*

| Tony Brent | 1954 | UK | *The Magic Tango* |
|---|---|---|---|
| Hugo Winterhalter & His Orchestra | 1954 | US | *The Magic Tango* |

## TCHIN TCHIN *(Richard Anthony, 1963)*

| | | | |
|---|---|---|---|
| Carlos Amador | 1964 | Chile | *Cin cin* |
| Bick Ford | 1964 | Argentina | *Cin cin* |
| Franco | 1964 | Argentina | *Cin cin* |
| Heiko Henss & The Comets | 1964 | West Germany | *Cin-Cin* |
| Los Jets | 1964 | Argentina | *Cin cin* |
| Anita Martínez | 1964 | Peru | *Chin chin* |
| Tito Mora | 1964 | Spain | *Cin cin* |
| Ricardo Rey | 1964 | Argentina | *Cin cin* |
| Violetta Rivas | 1964 | Argentina | *Mentiras, mentiras* |
| Sandro | 1964 | Argentina | *Cin cin* |
| Jimmy Santi | 1964 | Peru | *Chin chin* |
| Los Santos | 1964 | Argentina | *Cin cin* |
| Los Tamara | 1964 | Spain | *Chin chin* |

## TE DEUM[840] *(Guy Lambert et son Orchestre, 1953)*

| | | | |
|---|---|---|---|
| Drafi | 1971 | Netherlands | *United* |

## TÉLÉPHONEZ-MOI, CHÉRIE *(André Dassary, 1954)*

| | | | |
|---|---|---|---|
| Peggy King | 1956 | US | *Kiss And Run* |
| Jeri Southern | 1956 | US | *Kiss And Run* |
| Nan Wynn | 1956 | US | *Kiss And Run* |

## LE TEMPS DE L'AMOUR *(José Salcy, 1962)*
*See* FORT CHABROL

## LA TERRE *(Georges Guétary, 1961)*

| | | | |
|---|---|---|---|
| Gitte | 1962 | Finland | *Tämä maa* |

## THANK HEAVEN FOR LITTLE GIRLS *(Maurice Chevalier, 1958)*

| | | | |
|---|---|---|---|
| Andy Griffith | 1958 | US | |
| King Brothers | 1959 | UK | |
| Victor Silvester and His Ballroom Orchestra | 1959 | UK | |

## THEME FROM 'LAWRENCE OF ARABIA'
*(London Philharmonic Orchestra cond. Maurice Jarre, 1962)*

| | | | |
|---|---|---|---|
| Percy Faith & His Orchestra | 1963 | Italy | |
| Ferrante & Teicher | 1963 | US | |
| Percy Faith & His Orchestra | 1964 | US | |

## TOM PILLIBI *(Jacqueline Boyer, 1960)*

| | | | |
|---|---|---|---|
| José Guardiola | 1960 | Spain | |
| Los Pájaros Locos | 1960 | Spain | |
| Raquel Rastenni | 1960 | Denmark | |
| Torrebruno | 1960 | Spain | |

---

[840] 'Te Deum' is a seventeenth-century classical piece composed by Marc-Antoine Charpentier. Lambert's 1953 arrangement was used for many years as the theme music for *Eurovision*. Drafi's hit was inspired by that recording.

## TOMBE LA NEIGE *(Adamo, 1963)*

| Los Catinos | 1964 | Spain | *Cae la nieve* |
|---|---|---|---|
| Franciska | 1964 | Spain | *Cae la nieve* |
| Lita Torelló | 1964 | Spain | *Cae la nieve* |
| Danny | 1969 | Finland | *Vain lunta kaikkialla* |

## TOUS LES GARÇONS ET LES FILLES *(Françoise Hardy, 1962)*

| Los Catinos | 1963 | Spain | *Todos los chicos y chicas* |
|---|---|---|---|
| Los Pájaros Locos | 1963 | Spain | *Todos los chicos y chicas* |
| Catherine Spaak | 1963 | Italy | *Quelli della mia età* |

## TOUS MES RÊVES PASSÉS *(Jacques Pills, 1952)*

| Patti Page | 1957 | US | *I'll Remember Today* |
|---|---|---|---|

## TOUT ÇA *(Henri Salvador, 1948)*

| Ray Anthony & His Orchestra | 1950 | UK, US | *Count Every Star* |
|---|---|---|---|
| Dick Haymes with Artie Shaw & His Strings & Woodwind | 1950 | UK, US | *Count Every Star* |
| Herb Jeffries | 1950 | UK | *Count Every Star* |
| Kathryn Oldfield | 1950 | UK | *Count Every Star* |
| Hugo Winterhalter & His Orchestra & Mixed Chorus | 1950 | UK, US | *Count Every Star* |
| Hugo Winterhalter & His Orchestra & Mixed Chorus | 1951 | Australia | *Count Every Star* |
| The Rivieras | 1958 | US | *Count Every Star* |
| Donnie & The Dreamers | 1961 | US | *Count Every Star* |
| Linda Scott | 1962 | US | *Count Every Star* |
| Linda Scott | 1963 | Australia | *Count Every Star* |

## TRISTESSE *(Tino Rossi, 1939)*

| Ken Dodd | 1964 | UK | *So Deep Is The Night* |
|---|---|---|---|

## LES TROIS CLOCHES *(Édith Piaf et les Compagnons de la Chanson, 1946)*

| Tommy Dorsey & His Orchestra | 1949 | UK | *While The Angelus Was Ringing* |
|---|---|---|---|
| Dick Haymes with the Jeffrey Alexander Chorus | 1949 | UK | *While The Angelus Was Ringing* |
| Allan Jones with the Lyrian Singers | 1949 | UK | *While The Angelus Was Ringing* |
| Archie Lewis with the Luton Girls' Choir | 1949 | UK | *While The Angelus Was Ringing* |
| Josef Locke | 1949 | UK | *While The Angelus Was Ringing* |
| Guy Lombardo & His Royal Canadians | 1949 | UK | *While The Angelus Was Ringing* |
| Anne Shelton with the Wardour Singers | 1949 | UK | *While The Angelus Was Ringing* |
| Frank Sinatra | 1949 | Netherlands, UK | *While The Angelus Was Ringing* |
| Margaret Whiting | 1949 | UK | *While The Angelus Was Ringing* |
| June Valli | 1952 | Australia | *The Three Bells (The Jim Brown Song)* |
| Ralf Bendix | 1959 | West Germany | *Wenn die Glocken hell erklingen* |

## LES TROIS CLOCHES *(continued)*

| The Browns | 1959 | Australia, Italy, Japan, Netherlands, New Zealand, Norway, Sweden, UK, US, West Germany | *The Three Bells* |
|---|---|---|---|
| Dick Flood | 1959 | UK, US | *The Three Bells (The Jimmy Brown Story)* |
| Shane Rimmer with the Spinners | 1959 | UK | *The Three Bells* |
| Wolfgang Sauer | 1959 | West Germany | *Wenn die Glocken hell erklingen* |
| The Browns | 1960 | Denmark | *The Three Bells* |
| Towa Carson | 1960 | Sweden | *De tre klockorna* |
| Dick Flood | 1960 | Netherlands | *The Three Bells (The Jimmy Brown Story)* |
| Shane Rimmer with the Spinners | 1960 | Netherlands | *The Three Bells* |
| Mieke Telkamp | 1960 | Netherlands | *De drie klokken* |
| Ernest Klein | 1962 | Japan | *Wenn die Glocken hell erklingen* |
| Brian Poole & The Tremeloes | 1964 | Australia, UK | *The Three Bells* |
| The Tokens | 1965 | US | *The Three Bells (The Jimmy Brown Song)* |
| Julie Rogers | 1966 | UK | *While The Angelus Was Ringing* |
| Tony Angel | 1975 | New Zealand | *The Three Bells* |
| André van Duin | 1982 | Netherlands | *Bim bam* |
| Daniel O'Donnell | 1993 | UK | *The Three Bells* |

## TROIS FOIS LA FRANCE *(Sacha Distel, 1961)*

| Ken Dodd | 1961 | UK | *Once In Every Lifetime* |
|---|---|---|---|

## TU AS BEAU SOURIRE *(Franca di Rienzo, 1963)*

| Ed Ames | 1967 | US | *Time, Time* |
|---|---|---|---|

## TU T'LAISSES ALLER *(Charles Aznavour, 1960)*

| Friedel Hensch und die Cyprys | 1962 | West Germany | *Mein Ideal* |
|---|---|---|---|
| Caterina Valente | 1962 | West Germany | *Mein Ideal* |
| Cory Brokken | 1963 | Netherlands | *Mijn ideaal* |

## TWIST À SAINT-TROPEZ *(Les Chats Sauvages, 1961)*

| Mike Riós | 1962 | Spain | *Twist de Saint-Tropez* |
|---|---|---|---|
| Timo Jämsen | 1963 | Finland | *Yterin twist* |

## TWISTIN' THE TWIST *(Teddy Martin, 1961)*

| Jo Fedeli | 1962 | Italy | |
|---|---|---|---|
| Mieko Hirota | 1962 | Japan | *Twist And Twist* |
| Caterina Valente und Silvio Francesco | 1962 | Italy | |
| Caterina Valente und Silvio Francesco | 1962 | West Germany | *Popocatepetl Twist* |
| Jackie y los Ciclones | 1963 | Uruguay | *Leccion de twist* |
| Los Redcaps | 1963 | Uruguay | *Leccion de twist* |
| Caterina Valente | 1963 | Uruguay | *Leccion de twist* |
| Marta Zaraï | 1963 | Hungary | *Popocatepetl twist* |

## TWO DIFFERENT WORLDS *(Jane Morgan, 1956)*

| | | | |
|---|---|---|---|
| Dick Haymes | 1956 | US | |
| Ronnie Hilton | 1956 | UK | |
| Don Rondo | 1956 | US | |
| David Hughes | 1957 | UK | |
| Robert Goulet | 1962 | US | |
| Lenny Welch | 1965 | US | |
| The Duprees | 1969 | US | |

## VALENCIA *Mistinguett, 1926)*

| | | | |
|---|---|---|---|
| Jesse Crawford | 1926 | US | *Valencia (A Song Of Spain)* |
| Ross Gorman & His Earl Carroll Orchestra | 1926 | US | *Valencia (A Song Of Spain)* |
| The Revelers | 1926 | US | *Valencia (A Song Of Spain)* |
| Ben Selvin & His Orchestra | 1926 | US | *Valencia (A Song Of Spain)* |
| The Paul Whiteman Orchestra | 1926 | US | *Valencia (A Song Of Spain)* |
| Tony Martin | 1950 | US | *Valencia (A Song Of Spain)* |

## LES VENDANGES DE L'AMOUR *(Marie Laforêt, 1963)*

| | | | |
|---|---|---|---|
| Ginette Acevedo | 1964 | Chile | *Y volvamos al amor* |
| Los T.N.T. | 1964 | Spain | *Y volvamos al amor* |
| Los Mustang | 1965 | Spain | *Y volvamos al amor* |

## LA VIE EN ROSE *(Édith Piaf, 1948)*

| | | | |
|---|---|---|---|
| Jean Cavall | 1948 | UK | |
| Frederick Ferrari | 1948 | UK | *Take Me To Your Heart Again* |
| Gracie Fields | 1948 | UK | |
| Geraldo & His Orchestra | 1948 | UK | *Take Me To Your Heart Again* |
| Greta Keller | 1948 | Netherlands | |
| The London Piano Acordion Band | 1948 | UK | *Take Me To Your Heart Again* |
| The Melachrino Strings | 1948 | UK | |
| Victor Silvester & His Ballroom Orchestra | 1948 | UK | *Take Me To Your Heart Again* |
| Rita Williams | 1948 | UK | *Take Me To Your Heart Again* |
| Geraldo & His Orchestra | 1949 | Australia | *Take Me To Your Heart Again* |
| Rita Williams | 1949 | Australia | *Take Me To Your Heart Again* |
| Louis Armstrong & His Orchestra | 1950 | US | |
| Bing Crosby | 1950 | US | |
| Ralph Flanagan & His Orchestra | 1950 | US | |
| Tony Martin | 1950 | US | |
| Paul Weston & His Orchestra | 1950 | US | |
| Victor Young & His Singing Strings | 1950 | US | |
| Louis Armstrong | 1951 | Netherlands | |
| Vince Hill | 1966 | UK | *Take Me To Your Heart Again* |
| Carl-Erik Thörn | 1966 | Sweden | *I rosenrött jag drömmer* |
| Anita Lindblom | 1973 | Sweden | *Mitt liv har fått ett skimmer* |
| Grace Jones[841] | 1977 | Italy, Netherlands, US | |

---

[841] Grace Jones actually began her singing career in France, The story behind this, and her other early recordings, will be covered in a later volume.

## LA VIE EN ROSE *(continued)*

| Grace Jones | 1978 | Portugal, Spain, Turkey, West Germany | |
| --- | --- | --- | --- |
| Grace Jones | 1983 | Netherlands | |

## VIENI, VIENI *(Tino Rossi, 1934)*

| Rudy Vallee & His Connecticut Yankees | 1937 | US | |
| --- | --- | --- | --- |

## WEIßE ROSEN AUS ATHEN[842] *(Nana Mouskouri, 1962)*

| David Carroll | 1962 | Australia, Netherlands, US | *The White Rose Of Athens* |
| --- | --- | --- | --- |
| The Chordettes | 1962 | Australia | *The White Rose Of Athens* |
| Ann-Louise Hanson | 1962 | Sweden | *Vita rosor från Aten* |
| Albert Vosser | 1962 | West Germany | |
| Ivanka Kraševec | 1964 | Yugoslavia | *Bele rože iz Aten* |

## XYPNA, AGAPI MOU *(Nana Mouskouri, 1960)*

| José Guardiola | 1960 | Spain | *Despierta, mi amor* |
| --- | --- | --- | --- |

## YOU BROUGHT A NEW KIND OF LOVE TO ME *(Maurice Chevalier, 1930)*

| The High Hatters | 1930 | US | |
| --- | --- | --- | --- |
| Helen Ward | 1930 | US | |
| Paul Whiteman & His Orchestra | 1930 | US | |
| Joe Williams | 1959 | US | |
| Frank Sinatra | 1963 | US | |

Also note:

## L'AMOUR EST CE QU'IL EST

Written by Mort Shuman and Michèle Vendôme for Édith Piaf, but never recorded by her. Recorded as 'Love's Just A Broken Heart' by Cilla Black, a hit in Australia, Ireland, New Zealand and the UK in 1966.

## LE DERNIER TRAIN DE L'ESPACE

Written by Albert Raisner
Recorded as 'The Last Space Train' by Swedish instrumental group the Spotnicks, a hit in the UK in 1963 (EP *The Spotnicks In Paris*) and in Japan in 1966.

## HOMMAGE EN ÉDITH PIAF

A medley of songs originally recorded by Édith Piaf.
Recorded by Conny Vandenbos, a hit in the Netherlands in 1978.

## T'EN VAS PAS

Written by Émile Gardaz and Géo Voumard.
Recorded by Israeli singer Esther Ofarim as the 1963 Swiss entry for *Eurovision*. The German-language version, *Melodie einer Nacht*, was a hit in West Germany in 1963.

---

[842] Nana Mouskouri's 'Weiße Rosen aus Athen' was a German-language song that topped the charts in West Germany in 1962. Although Mouskouri also recorded it in French (as 'Roses blanches de Corfou'), it is not, strictly speaking, a French-pop original. However, given that Mouskouri was based in France at the time and has superstar status in the French pop industry, it has been included in this list.

The following songs all have tunes written by French songwriters. The author has been unable to trace the original French versions, if any ever existed:

## AROUND THE CORNER FROM THE BLUES
Written by Alain Romans.
Recorded by Al Hibbler (US, 1957).

## BACK IN MY ARMS
Written by Roger Roger.
Recorded by Nat 'King' Cole (US, 1958).

## EVERYDAY
Written by Margeurite Monnot.
Recorded by Della Reese (US, 1960).

## THE GIRL I LEFT IN ROME
Written by Alex Demoulin.
Recorded by Al Martino (US, 1956).

## HURRA HURRA VAD DET ÄR ROLIGT I MOSKVA
Written by Charles Trenet.
Recorded by Michael Dee (Sweden, 1983).

## NIE KNIEZE, NIE ZEURE
Written by Émile Prud'homme.
Recorded by John en de Hofzangers en zangeressen (Netherlands, 1980).

## OO-LA-LA, OUI-OUI!
Written by Guy Morgan and Mick Micheyl.
Recorded by Bob Sharples & His Orchestra (US, 1957).

# Appendix II

## RECOMMENDED LISTENING

To compile a definitive listening guide to French pop from the fifties and early sixties would be a gargantuan task well beyond the scope of this book. Given the limitations of space, what follows is at best an introduction to some of the highlights of the era's music. Readers wishing to access particular songs or albums, or seeking more detailed discographies, will readily be able to find many of them on the Internet. Most of the big hits have been reissued on CD over the past four decades, though many overlooked gems are sadly still only available on the collectors' market (or, increasingly, on mp3 or YouTube).

For ease of use, this guide has been arranged by chapter, with a selection of useful compilations (both single-artist and multi-artist sets) spanning several chapters or eras listed separately at the end. While not every performer mentioned in this book will be found in this section, I have endeavoured to ensure that all major releases of interest are included. In the final analysis, however, the selection will inevitably be subjective, and I apologise in advance to any reader unable to locate a recommended release. As astute collectors of any style of music will know, reissues tend to come and go at sometimes frightening speed, so I have not hesitated to refer to original vinyl releases where appropriate: the growth in Internet selling makes these far more available across the world today than was the case when I began work on this book. Unless otherwise specified, all the releases mentioned below are from France.

### 1   PLAISIR D'AMOUR
**French pop at the start of the twentieth century**
Maurice Chevalier - *Vol. 1: Anthologie 1919-1930* (Frémeaux, 1999) 2-CD
Harry Fragson - *Succès et raretés 1903-1912* (Chansonophone, 1994) CD
Georgel - *Le roi du caf' conc'* (Marianne Mélodie, 1995) CD
Georgius - *L'amuseur surréaliste 1924-1943* (Frémeaux, 1998) 2-CD
Mistinguett - *Mon homme* (Milan, 2001) 2-CD

### 2   J'AI L'CAFARD
**The *chanson* tradition in French music (1880-1940)**
Aristide Bruant - *Aristide Bruant* (Pathé, 1997) 2-CD
Damia - *50 succès essentiels* (Mariam, 2013) 2-CD
Lucienne Delyle - *Anthologie 1936-1946* (Frémeaux, 1998) 2-CD

Marie Dubas - *Intégrale 1927-1945* (Frémaux, 1996) 2-CD
Fréhel - *Anthologie 1930-1939* (Frémaux, 1999) 2-CD
Lys Gauty - *Anthologie 1932-1944* (Frémaux, 2003) 2-CD
Rina Ketty - *La madone de la chanson* (Forlane, 2003) CD
Édith Piaf - *Vol. 1: 1935-1947* (Frémaux, 1998) 2-CD
Berthe Sylva - *1929-1937* (Frémaux, 2002) 2-CD

## 3    JE SUIS SWING
### The arrival of jazz (1920-40)
Alibert - *1932-1945* (Frémaux, 2002) 2-CD
Joséphine Baker - *J'ai deux amours* (Milan, 2006) CD
Lucienne Boyer - *Parlez-moi d'amour* (Naxos (UK), 2001) CD
Danielle Darrieux - *Intégrale 1931-1951* (Frémaux, 2002) 2-CD
Fernandel - *Anthologie 1931-1948* (Frémaux, 1999) 2-CD
Django Reinhardt - *Accords parfaits* (Vogue, 2000) CD
Tino Rossi - *Anthologie 1932-1950* (Frémaux, 2003) 2-CD
Jean Sablon - *Le siècle d'or* (Chant du Monde, 2011) 2-CD
Suzy Solidor - *Anthologie 1933-1952* (Frémaux, 2005) 2-CD
Charles Trenet - *Chante la joie* (Milan, 2005) CD
Ray Ventura - *Ray Ventura et ses Collégiens 1928-1956* (Frémaux, 2013) 3-CD

## 4    DOUCE FRANCE
### War and liberation (1940-50)
Bourvil - *1946-1953* (Frémaux, 2006) 2-CD
Les Compagnons de la Chanson - *Anthologie 1946-1958* (Frémaux) 2-CD
Georges Guétary - *1937-1960* (Frémaux, 2011) 2-CD
Jacques Hélian - *20 succès inoubliables* (Marianne Mélodie, 1999) CD
Yves Montand - *À Paris* (Marianne Mélodie, 2001) 2-CD
Patrice et Mario - *Montagnes d'Italie* (Marianne Mélodie, 2001) CD
Édith Piaf - *Vol. 2: 1948-1958* (Frémaux, 2009) 2-CD
Tino Rossi - *Mes 40 titres d'or* (EMI, 2003) 2-CD
Henri Salvador - *Maladie d'amour 1942-1948* (Frémaux, 2000) 2-CD
Charles Trenet - *The Extraordinary Garden* (EMI (UK), 1990) CD

## 5    MOI, J'AIME LE MUSIC-HALL
### A return to normality (1948-59)
Lys Assia - *Lys Assia* (Disky (Netherlands), 2011) CD
Charles Aznavour - *Je t'aime comme ça* (Not Now Music (UK), 2009) 3-CD
Gilbert Bécaud - *Mes mains* (Chant du Monde, 2009) 2-CD
André Claveau - *Complainte de la Butte* (Chansonophone, 2005) CD
Jacqueline François - *Mademoiselle de Paris* (Marianne Mélodie, 1989) CD
Zizi Jeanmaire - *Mon truc en plumes* (Phonogram, 1989) CD
Francis Lemarque - *Le siècle d'or* (Chant du Monde, 2010) 2-CD
Luis Mariano - *The Best Of Luis Mariano* (Wagram, 2014) 3-CD
Édith Piaf - *L'hymne à l'amour* (Warner, 2002) 2-CD
Line Renaud - *Le meilleur de Line Renaud* (Pathé, 1999) 2-CD

## 6    JE SUIS COMME JE SUIS
### Existentialism and a new type of *chanson* (1950-58)
Charles Aznavour - *Charles Aznavour Chante (Vol. 3)* (EMI, 1992) CD
Georges Brassens - *La mauvaise réputation* (Philips, 1988) CD
Jacques Brel - *C'est comme ça* (Not Now Music (UK) 2008) 2-CD

Les Compagnons de la Chanson -
*Le meilleur des Compagnons de la Chanson* (EMI, 1999) 2-CD
Léo Ferré - *Les chansons de Léo Ferré* (Chant du Monde, 1998) 2-CD
Les Frères Jacques - *Le siècle d'or* (Chant du Monde, 2010) 2-CD
Juliette Gréco - *Muse de Saint-Germain* (Frémaux, 2009) 2-CD
Félix Leclerc - *Moi mes souliers: La siècle d'or* (Chant du Monde, 2009) 2-CD
Mouloudji - *Un jour tu verras: Le siècle d'or* (Chant du Monde, 2009) 2-CD
Patachou - *1950-1961* (Frémaux, 2014) 2-CD
Catherine Sauvage - *Toi qui disait: Le siècle d'or* (Chant du Monde, 2009) 2-CD

## 7   AMOUR, CASTAGNETTES ET TANGO
### The exotica boom (1954-58)
Maria Candido - *Torrent* (Marianne Mélodie, 2005) CD
Eddie Constantine - *Ah! Les femmes* (Marianne Mélodie, 2005) CD
Annie Cordy - *Annie Cordy* (EMI, 1999) 2-CD
Dalida - *Bambino* (Barclay, 1991) CD
Gloria Lasso - *25 succès inoubliables* (Marianne Mélodie) CD
Dario Moreno - *Oh! Qué Dario* (Polygram, 2007) CD

## 8   À SAINT-GERMAIN-DES-PRÉS
### Post-war jazz (1945-58)
Sidney Bechet - *Petite fleur* (Chant du Monde, 2014) 3-CD
Claude Bolling - *Original Ragtime* (Mercury, 1998) CD
Sacha Distel - *Jazz Guitarist* (Emarcy, 2003) CD
Claude Luter - *À Saint-Germain-des-Prés* (Vogue 1988) CD
Jane Morgan - *An American Songbird In Paris* (Sepia (UK), 2008) 2-CD
Henri Salvador - *Le petit Indien* (Frémaux, 2009) 2-CD
Boris Vian - *Le déserteur* (Mercury, 1997) CD

## 9   SALUT LES COPAINS
### A new generation finds its feet (1952-58)
Gilbert Bécaud - *Salut les copains* (EMI, 2003) CD
Dalida - *Come prima* (Barclay, 1991) CD
Lionel Hampton - *Lionel Hampton à l'Olympia* (Versailles, 1956) 2-LP
Marie-Josée Neuville - *La collégienne de la chanson* (Marianne Mélodie, 2010) CD
Georges Ulmer - *Georges Ulmer à l'Alhambra* (Véga, 1958) LP

## 10  GEORGES, VIENS DANSER LE ROCK N' ROLL!
### The early movers and shakers (1954-58)
Earl Cadillac - *King Of Rock And Roll* (Vogue, 1956) LP
Annie Cordy - *Jazz-party chez Annie Cordy* (Columbia, 1956) EP
François Deguelt - *Mes premières chansons* (RDM, 2012) CD
Christian Garros - *Sois pas cruelle* (Columbia, 1957) EP
Gloria Lasso - *Diana* (Pathé, 1958) EP
Michel Legrand - *Rock And Roll* (Philips, 1956) EP
Mac-Kac - *Mac-Kac et son rock'n'roll* (Versailles, 1956) LP
Moustache - *Moustache* (Barclay, 2004) CD
Magali Noël - *Rock And Roll* (Philips, 2002) CD
Albert Raisner - *Voici le rock'n'roll* (Festival, 1957) EP
Henri Salvador - *Alias Henry Cording* (Mercury, 2002) CD

## 11 ROCK, C'EST UN ROCK
### Rock'n'roll, French style (1958-59)
The Allegrettes - *Stagger Lee* (Pacific, 1959) EP
Richard Anthony - *Nouvelle vague* (Magic, 1999) CD
Petula Clark - *Anthologie (Vol. 6)* (Anthology's, 2001) CD
Annie Cordy - *Docteur miracle* (Columbia, 1958) EP
Gabriel Dalar - *Twistin' The Rock (Vol. 1)* (Universal, 2002) CD
Dalida - *J'ai rêvé* (Barclay, 1959) EP
Sacha Distel - *The Very Best of* (Union Square Music (UK), 2015) CD
Danyel Gérard - *1958-59* (Magic, 2010) CD)
Claude Piron - *Intégrale 1958-1960* (EMI, 1994) CD

## 12 UNE BOUM CHEZ JOHN
### The first rock'n'roll stars (1960-61)
Richard Anthony - *EP rare et inédit* (Magic, 2000) CD
Dany Fischer - *Twistin' The Rock (Vol. 18)* (Universal, 2002) CD
Johnny Hallyday - *Hello Johnny* (Vogue, 2003) CD
Frankie Jordan - *Tu parles trop* (Decca, 1960) EP
Rocky Volcano - *Twistin' The Rock (Vol. 15)* (Universal, 2002) CD

## 13 QUAND LES CHATS SONT LÀ
### The groups: The first wave (1960-62)
Les Blousons Noirs - *Les Blousons Noirs* (Born Bad, 2007) CD
Les Champions - *L'intégrale chanté* (Magic, 2005) 2-CD
Les Chats Sauvages - *Twist à Saint-Tropez* (Magic, 2012) CD
Les Chaussettes Noires - *100% Rock* (Barclay, 2006) CD
Claude et ses Tribuns - *Rock! Twist! Madison!* (LCD, 1999) CD
Les Copains - *La collection sixties des EP's français* (Magic, 1998) CD
Danny Boy et ses Pénitents - *Best of* (Intense Music, 2010) CD
Les Pirates - *Salut les amis* (Magic, 2010) CD
Les Vautours - *L'intégrale* (Magic, 1999) CD

## 14 DIEU MERCI, ELLE M'AIME AUSSI
### The early girl singers (1960-62)
Petula Clark - *Anthologie (Vol. 1)* (Anthology's, 1998) CD
Nicole Croisille - *Nicole Croisille* (Fontana, 2003) CD
Dalida - *Les enfants du Pirée* (Barclay, 1991) CD
Gélou - *Rockin'n'twistin'* (LCD, 2005) CD
Hédika / Nicole Paquin - *Twistin' The Rock (Vol. 4)* (Universal, 2002) CD
Gillian Hills - *Twistin' The Rock (Vol. 9)* (Universal, 2002) CD
Sylvie Vartan - *Sylvie* (Ariola, 1991) CD

## 15 NOUS LES GARS, NOUS LES FILLES
### The growth of French rock'n'roll (1961-62)
Lucky Blondo - *Twistin' The Rock (Vol. 17)* (Philips, 2002) CD
Jean-Jacques Debout - *Les feux rouges* (Vogue, 1963) EP
Danyel Gérard - *1961-62* (Magic, 2010) CD
Johnny Hallyday - *Nous les gars, nous les filles* (Vogue, 1992) CD
Les Pingouins - *Les Pingouins* (Big Beat, 1996) CD
Henri Salvador - *Monsieur Boum-Boum* (Magic, 2000) CD
Vince Taylor - *Le rock c'est ça* (Barclay, 2003) CD
El Toro et les Cyclones - *El Toro et les Cyclones* (Magic, 1995) CD

## 16  C'EST BEAU LA VIE
### Holding hard to old traditions (1958-62)
Marcel Amont - *Dans le cœur de ma blonde* (Magic, 2013) CD
Charles Aznavour - *C'est ça* (EMI, 1992) CD
Guy Béart - *Chansons intemporelles* (EPM, 2015) CD
Gilbert Bécaud - *Tête de bois* (EMI, 1993) CD
Georges Brassens - *Le pornographe* (Philips, 1988) CD
Jacques Brel - *La valse à mille temps* (Barclay, 1988) CD
Philippe Clay - *Philippe Clay* (Forlane, 2008) CD
Dalida - *Ciao, ciao bambina* (Barclay, 1991) CD
Léo Ferré - *Paname* (Barclay, 2005) CD
Serge Gainsbourg - *Du chant à la une!...* (Philips, 2002) CD
Juliette Gréco - *Jolie môme* (Philips, 1991) CD
Édith Piaf - *Face à son public* (EMI, 2000) 3-CD

## 17  VIENS DANSER LE TWIST
### Rock'n'roll takes over (1961-63)
Richard Anthony - *Let's Twist Again* (Magic, 1998) CD
Burt Blanca - *Burt Blanca et ses Guitares Magiques* (Magic, 1996) 2-CD
Billy Bridge - *L'intégrale sixties* (Magic, 2000) 2-CD
Les Chats Sauvages - *Sa grande passion* (Magic, 2012) CD
Les Chaussettes Noires - *Rock'n twist* (Barclay, 2007) CD
Dalida - *Le petit Gonzalès* (Barclay, 1991) CD
Danny Boy - *Twist* (Ricordi, 1962) EP
Gary 'L'Ange Noir' - *Twistin' The Rock (Vol. 2)* (Universal, 2002) CD
Danyel Gérard - *1962* (Magic, 2010) CD
Johnny Hallyday - *Salut les copains* (Philips, 1993) CD
Harold Nicholas - *Hully Gully Firehouse* (Barclay, 1963) EP
Les Pirates - *Milk Shake Party* (Magic, 2010) CD
Henri Salvador - *Le lion est mort ce soir* (Magic, 2013) CD
Vince Taylor - *There's A Lot Of Twistin Goin' On* (Barclay, 1962) EP
Sylvie Vartan - *Le loco-motion* (RCA Victor,1962) EP

## 18  COMME UNE OMBRE
### The groups: The second wave (1961-64)
Les Aiglons - *Stalactite* (Magic, 2008) CD
Les Bourgeois de Calais - *French 60's EP Collection* (Magic, 1995) CD
Les Champions - *Complete 60's Instrumental* (Magic, 2004) CD
Les Chats Sauvages - *Derniers baisers* (Pathé, 1992) CD
Les Chaussettes Noires - *Comment réussir en amour* (Barclay, 2003) CD
The Cousins - *Complete 60's Instrumentals* (Magic, 2005) CD
Les Fantômes - *L'intégrale sixties* (Magic, 2000) CD
Les Fingers - *L'intégrale instrumental (Vol. 1)* (Magic, 1995) CD
Les Fingers - *L'intégrale instrumental (Vol. 2)* (Magic, 1995) CD
Les Fingers - *L'intégrale instrumental (Vol. 3)* (Magic, 1996) CD
The Four Dreamers - *French 60's EP Collection* (Magic, 1995) 2-CD
Les Guitares du Diable - *L'intégrale* (Magic, 2000) 2-CD
Les Playboys - *Les Playboys* (Magic, 2007) CD
Les Schtroumpfs - *Complete 60's Instrumentals* (Magic, 2002) CD
The Sunlights - *French 60's EP Collection* (Magic, 1996) CD

## 19 TOUS LES GARÇONS ET LES FILLES
### The *yé-yé* explosion (1962-64)

Adamo - *Tombe la neige* (Magic, 1999) CD
Frank Alamo - *Frank Alamo* (Barclay, 2003) CD
Richard Anthony - *J'entends siffler le train* (Magic, 1998) CD
Ria Bartok - *French EP Collection* (Magic, 1999) 2-CD
Patricia Carli - *Tendres années 60* (Universal, 2003) CD
Petula Clark - *Anthologie (Vol. 3)* (Anthology's, 1999) CD
Alice Dona - *L'intégrale 1963-1966* (Magic, 2001) 2-CD
Claude François - *Belles! Belles! Belles!* (Magic, 2014) CD
Johnny Hallyday - *L'idole des jeunes* (Philips, 1993) CD
Françoise Hardy - *Françoise Hardy* (Cherry Red, 2013) CD
Nancy Holloway - *La collection sixties des EP's français* (Magic, 1996) 2-CD
Marie Laforêt - *Marie Laforêt (Vol. 1)* (Magic, 1998) CD
Dick Rivers - *Baby John* (Magic, 1998) CD
Sheila - *Sheila* (Warner Bros., 2006) CD
Sophie - *L'intégrale* (Magic, 1999) CD
Sylvie Vartan - *En écoutant la pluie* (Magic, 2014) CD
Tiny Yong - *L'intégrale 1961/1964* (Magic, 1997) CD

## 20 L'IDOLE DES JEUNES
### The triumph of *yé-yé* (1963-64)

Frank Alamo - *Tendres années 60* (Universal, 2014) 2-CD
Richard Anthony - *En écoutant la pluie* (Magic, 1998) CD
Brigitte Bardot - *Brigitte Bardot* (Philips, 2002) CD
Petula Clark - *Anthologie (Vol. 4)* (Anthology's, 1999) CD
Danny Boy - *Le twist à Danny* (LCD, 2006) CD
Jean-Jacques Debout - *Anthologie 1959-1999* (Magic, 1999) 2-CD
Les Faux-Frères - *1963-1993* (Evasion, 1993) CD
Claude François - *Si j'avais un marteau* (Magic, 2014) CD
France Gall - *N'écoute pas les idoles* (Philips, 1963) EP
Les Gam's - *Twistin' The Rock (Vol. 13)* (Universal, 2002) CD
Danyel Gérard - *Danyel Gérard et les Champions* (Magic, 2010) CD
Larry Gréco - *Surprise-partie* (Musidisc, 1991) CD
Johnny Hallyday - *Les bras en croix* (Philips, 1993) CD
Françoise Hardy - *Le premier bonheur du jour* (RDM, 2014) CD
Jocelyne - *Twistin' The Rock (Vol. 19)* (Universal, 2002) 2-CD
Vic Laurens - *Le rock c'est ça* (Polygram, 1990) CD
Eddy Mitchell - *Eddy in London* (Barclay, 2006) CD
Jacky Moulière - *La collection sixties des EP's français* (Magic, 1996) 2-CD
Claude Nougaro - *Le cinéma* (Philips, 2007) CD
Dick Rivers - *Tu n'es plus là* (Magic, 1998) CD
Sheila - *Écoute ce disque* (Warner Bros., 2010) CD
Les Surfs - *Les Surfs (Vol. 1)* (Magic, 1998) CD
Sylvie Vartan - *Sylvie à Nashville* (RCA Japan, 1999) EP

## 21 NON, JE NE REGRETTE RIEN
### Evolution and counter-revolution (1961-64)

Marcel Amont - *Récital 1962* (Polydor, 1962) LP
Isabelle Aubret - *Chanson française* (Universal, 2010) CD
Charles Aznavour - *Qui?* (EMI, 1992) CD
Barbara - *Dis, quand reviendras-tu?* (Sony, 2004) CD

Brigitte Bardot - *B.B.* (Philips, 2003) CD
Alain Barrière - *Collection (Vol. 1)* (RCA, 1992) CD
Gilbert Bécaud - *Bécaud à l'Olympia* (La Voix de son Maître, 1963) LP
Georges Brassens - *Les copains d'abord* (Philips, 1988) CD
Jacques Brel - *Le plat pays* (Barclay, 1988) CD
Dalida - *Le jour le plus long* (Barclay, 1991) CD
Sacha Distel - *Sacha Distel à l'Olympia* (RCA Victor, 1963) LP
Leny Escudero - *French 60's EP Collection* (Magic, 1995) CD
Jean Ferrat - *Nuit et brouillard* (Barclay, 1997) CD
Léo Ferré - *Les chansons interdites et autres* (Barclay, 2005) CD
Serge Gainsbourg - *Couleur café* (Philips, 1996) CD
Juliette Gréco - *Juliette Gréco à Bobino* (Philips, 1964) LP
Les Parisiennes - *Les Parisiennes et Claude Bolling* (Mercury, 2007) CD
Les Swingle Singers - *Jazz Sebastien Bach* (Philips, 2000) CD
Los Machucambos - *Tendres années 60* (Universal, 2007) CD
Enrico Macias - *L'oriental* (EMI, 2001) CD
Yves Montand - *Montand chante Prévert* (Universal, 1992) CD
Pierre Perret - *Les plus grands succès de Pierre Perret* (Vogue, 1994) CD
Édith Piaf - *Bobino 1963* (EMI, 2003) LP
Sœur Sourire - *Intégrale* (FGI Productions, 2009) CD


## Single-artist compilations

The following list offers a selection of one-stop career retrospectives for artists whose work is otherwise scattered throughout the listening guide above. It is by no means exhaustive: many of the big names contained herein have had their entire back catalogues compiled into massive box sets running to 10, 20 or even 50 CDs in length. These are not for the casual listener, but may well prove necessary for readers who get 'hooked'. I have excluded such releases from this discography in favour of single, double or triple sets that are (or have been) on sale at more reasonable prices. Some of the items that follow include material outside the scope of this volume.

Adamo - *Platinum Collection* (EMI, 2005) 3-CD
Richard Anthony - *Nouvelle vague* (EMI, 1993) 2-CD
Charles Aznavour - *Best of 40 chansons* (Barclay, 2013) 2-CD
Gilbert Bécaud - *BecOlympia* (EMI, 1997) 2-CD
Lucky Blondo - *Salut les copains* (Universal, 2015) 2-CD
Georges Brassens - *La mauvaise réputation* (Philips, 2001) 3-CD
Jacques Brel - *Quand on n'a que l'amour* (Barclay, 1996) 3-CD
Les Chats Sauvages - *Laissez-nous chanter* (EMI, 2000) 3-CD
Les Chaussettes Noires - *Intégrale 1960-1964* (Polydor, 1999) 3-CD
Petula Clark - *Une baladine: Best of Petula Clark* (BMG, 2010) 3-CD
Dalida - *Les années Barclay* (Barclay, 1997) 2-CD
Sacha Distel - *Profession chanteur* (EMI, 2005) 4-CD
Jean Ferrat - *C'est toujours la première fois* (Barclay, 2010) 3-CD
Léo Ferré - *Thank You Ferré* (Barclay, 1998) 3-CD box set
Claude François - *Le jouet extraordinaire* (Philips, 1998) 3-CD
Serge Gainsbourg - *Initials S.G.* (Mercury, 2002) CD
France Gall - *Poupée de son* (Philips, 1992) 4-CD
Juliette Gréco - *Parlez-moi d'amour* (Universal, 2008) 3-CD
Johnny Hallyday - *Anthologie 1960-63* (Universal, 1998) CD

Françoise Hardy - *The Vogue Years* (Camden Deluxe/BMG, 2001) 2-CD
Marie Laforêt - *Les vendanges de l'amour* (Universal, 2002) 3-CD
Long Chris - *Twistin' The Rock (Vol. 12)* (Philips, 2002) 2-CD
Eddy Mitchell - *Et s'il n'en reste qu'un* (Polydor, 2008) 3-CD
Nana Mouskouri - *Chanter la vie* (Philips, 2008) 3-CD
Claude Nougaro - *Jazz et java* (Mercury, 1998) 3-CD
Édith Piaf - *30ᵉ Anniversaire* (EMI, 1993) 2-CD
Les Pirates - *L'intégrale* (Magic, 1998) 2-CD
Dick Rivers - *Les titres d'or* (Magic, 1999) CD
Henri Salvador - *Ses plus grandes chansons* (Universal, 2001) 2-CD
Sheila - *Les années yé-yé* (East West, 1999) CD
Vince Taylor - *Jet Black Leather Machine* (Ace (UK), 2009) CD
Sylvie Vartan - *Les années RCA* (BMG, 2010) 5-CD


## Various Artists compilations

*Les années yé-yé (Vol. 1)* (Universal, 1999) CD
*Les années yé-yé (Vol. 2)* (Universal, 1999) CD
   **Mercury, Polydor, Philips and Barclay-label *yé-yé* singers.**
*Aznavour et ses premiers interprètes* (Frémaux, 2008) 2-CD
   **Early Aznavour songs by a range of music hall singers.**
*Belles! Belles! Belles! (Vol. 1)* (LCD, 1997) CD
*Belles! Belles! Belles! (Vol. 2)* (LCD, 1998) CD
   **Yé-yé girl singers.**
*Café de Paris* (Not Now Music, 2010) CD
   ***Chanson* and music hall singers.**
*Elvis Made In France* (Universal, 2002) 10-CD
   **Box set rounding up hundreds of covers from the Presley songbook, across the whole spectrum of pop.**
*Instrumental Guitars (Vol. 1)* (Magic, 2000) CD
*Instrumental Guitars (Vol. 2)* (Magic, 2005) CD
*Instrumental Guitars (Vol. 3)* (Magic, 2005) CD
*Instrumental Guitars (Vol. 4)* (Magic, 2006) CD
   **Original EPs by instrumental groups.**
*La légende du Golf Drouot* (Polygram, 1994) 3-CD
   **Yé-yé singers and groups.**
*Nice, Côte d'Azur 1930-1951* (Frémaux, 2004) 2-CD
   **Pre-war *chanson* and music hall singers.**
*Paris 1919-1950* (Frémaux, 2003) 2-CD
   **Pre-war *chanson* and music hall singers.**
*Les plus belles chansons françaises* (Wagram, 2012) 4-CD
   ***Chanson* and music hall singers.**
*Les plus grands titres des guinguettes* (Wagram, 2012) 4-CD
   ***Chanson* and music hall singers.**
*Le printemps de Vogue* (Vogue, 1993) 2-CD
   **Vogue-label *yé-yé* singers.**
*Rock and roll à la française* (Saphyr, 2010) 6-CD with 236-page book
   **Mammoth selection of fifties' French attempts at rock'n'roll.**
*Rock en France (Vol. 1)* (LCD, 1995) CD
   **Lesser-known *yé-yé* singers and groups.**
*Saint-Germain – Rive Gauche, 1926-1954* (Frémaux, 2007) 2-CD
   **Early *chanson* singers and jazz.**
*Toutes mes années 60/70 (Vol. 1)* (Marianne Mélodie, 2008) 2-CD
*Toutes mes années 60/70 (Vol. 2)* (Marianne Mélodie, 2008) 2-CD
*Toutes mes années 60/70 (Vol. 3)* (Marianne Mélodie, 2009) 2-CD
   **Mainly lesser-known pop and *yé-yé* singers.**

*Trésors des années 60* (Vogue, 1999) 4-CD
    **Vogue-label *yé-yé* singers.**
*Les Zazous: Swing obsession* (Frémaux, 2005) 2-CD
    **Wartime French jazz.**

# Appendix III

## RECOMMENDED READING

Although there is a huge amount of reading material available on the subject of French pop, not much of it is in English (hence my decision to write *this* book). Those with minimal knowledge of the French language may find many of the following titles of little use, although those with a working knowledge may find many to be of interest. Fortunately, there has been a steady trickle of publications in English in recent years, and I have highlighted those books and magazines below.

### BIOGRAPHIES AND AUTOBIOGRAPHIES

**Adamo**
Coljon, Thierry - *C'est sa vie* (Le Félin, Paris) 2003
**Frank Alamo**
Alamo, Frank - *Mes sixties: D'hier à aujourd'hui* (Michel Lafon, Paris) 2006
**Richard Anthony**
Anthony, Richard - *Il faut croire aux étoiles* (Michel Lafon, Paris) 1994
**Hugues Aufray**
Delhasse, Guy – *Hugues Aufray* (L'Arbre, Brussels) 2008
**Charles Aznavour**
Aznavour, Charles - *À voix basse* (Don Quichotte, Paris)2009
Réval, Annie & Bernard - *Aznavour: Le roi de cœur* (France-Empire, Paris) 2000
**Joséphine Baker**
Bonini, Emmanuel - *La véritable Joséphine Baker* (Pygmalion, Paris) 2000
**Barbara**
Barbara - *Il était un piano noir... Mémoirs interrompus* (Fayard, Paris) 1998
Lehoux, Valérie – *Barbara* (Pluriel, Paris), 2017
**Brigitte Bardot**
Bardot, Brigitte - *Initiales B.B.: Mémoirs* (Grasset et Fasquelle, Paris) 1996
**Guy Béart**
Vignol, Baptiste – *Guy Béart: Il n'y a plus d'après* (L'Archipel, Paris) 2016
**Gilbert Bécaud**
Réval, Annie & Bernard - *Gilbert Bécaud: Jardins secrets*
    (France-Empire, Paris) 2001
**Georges Brassens**
Calvet, Jean-Louis – *Georges Brassens* (Payot, Paris) 1993
Louki, Pierre - *Georges Brassens* (Christian Pirot, Paris) 1999
**Jacques Brel**
Clayson, Alan - *Jacques Brel* (Sanctuary, Chessington, Surrey) 1996 *In English*
Todd, Olivier - *Jacques Brel: Une vie* (Robert Laffont, Paris) 1998

**Les Chats Sauvages**
  Liesenfeld, Thierry - *Quand les Chats sont là*
    (Éditions Saphyr / Kalohé Production, Zimmerbach) 2011
**Les Chaussettes Noires**
  Achard, Maurice - *Dactylo rock* (Flammarion, Paris) 1994
  Liesenfeld, Thierry - *Ceci est leur histoire*
    (Éditions Saphyr / Kalohé Production, Zimmerbach) 2003
**Maurice Chevalier**
  Berruer, Pierre, & François Vals - *Maurice Chevalier* (Plon, Paris) 1988
**Dalida**
  Bonini, Emmanuel - *La véritable Dalida* (Pygmalion, Paris) 2004
  Lelait-Helo, David - *Dalida: D'une rive à l'autre* (Payot et Rivages, Paris) 2004
**Danny Boy**
  Messé, Yves - *Ce normand pionnier du rock français* (Bertout, Luneray) 2003
**Jean Ferrat**
  Brierre, Jean-Dominique - *Jean Ferrat: Une vie* (L'Archipel, Paris) 2010
**Léo Ferré**
  Perrin, Jean-Éric - *Léo Ferré: Poète et rebelle* (Alphée, Paris) 2008
**Daniel Filipacchi**
  Madjar, Robert - *Daniel Filipacchi* (Michel Lafon, Paris) 1997
**Claude François**
  Duforest, Dominique - *Claude François: 20 ans déjà* (Hors Collection, Paris) 1998
**Serge Gainsbourg**
  Clayson, Alan - *Serge Gainsbourg: View from the Exterior*
    (Sanctuary, Chessington, Surrey) 1998  *In English*
  Simmons, Sylvie - *Serge Gainsbourg: A Fistful of Gitanes*
    (Helter Skelter, London) 2001  *In English*
  Verlant, Gilles - *Gainsbourg* (Albin Michel, Paris) 2000
**Juliette Gréco**
  Dicale, Bertrand - *Juliette Gréco, une vie en liberté*
    (Éditions Jean-Claude Lattès, Paris) 2001
**Johnny Hallyday**
  Hallyday, Johnny - *Destroy: Autobiographie* (Michel Lafon, Paris)1997, 1998
**Françoise Hardy**
  Hardy, Françoise - *Le désespoir des singes... et autres bagatelles*
    (Robert Laffont, Paris) 2008
**Boby Lapointe**
  Pericot, Jacques - *Boby Lapointe* (Éditions Denoël Paris) 1997
**Eddy Mitchell**
  Bernett, Sam - *Eddy Mitchell* (Albin Michel, Paris) 2004
**Yves Montand**
  Amiel, Carole - *Montand: Tout simplement* (NiL, Paris) 1997
**Nana Mouskouri**
  Mouskouri, Nana - *Memoirs* (Phoenix, London) 2007
    *In English, translated by Jeremy Leggatt*
**Claude Nougaro**
  Deschamps, Stéphane - *Claude Nougaro: À fleur de mots*
    (Hors Collection, Paris) 2001
**Édith Piaf**
  Bret, David – *The Piaf Legend* (Robson, London) 1988 *In English*
  Piaf, Édith - *My Life* (Peter Owen Modern Classics, London) 2000
    *In English, translated by Margaret Crosland*

**Dick Rivers**
> Rivers, Dick - *Very Dick* (Michel Lafon, Paris) 1996
> Rivers, Dick – *Rock 'n' roll* (Le Pré aux Clercs, Paris) 2006

**Henri Salvador**
> Miquel, Olivier – *Henri Salvador: L'enchanteur* (Editions du Moment, Paris) 2014

**Sheila**
> Quinonero, Frédéric - *Sheila: Biographie d'une idole*
>    (Éditions de Tournon, Paris) 2007
> Sheila - *Danse avec ta vie* (Éditions Archipoche, Paris) 2013

**Vince Taylor**
> Liesenfeld, Thierry - *Vince Taylor: Le perdant magnifique*
>    (Éditions Saphyr / Kalohé Production, Zimmerbach) 2015
> Taylor, Vince - *Alias Vince Taylor: Le survivant* (Delville, Paris) 1976

**Charles Trenet**
> Balen, Noël - *Charles Trenet* (Éditions de Rocher, Paris) 2001).

**Sylvie Vartan**
> Vartan, Sylvie - *Entre l'Ombre et la Lumière* (XO Éditions, Paris) 2004

## GENERAL HISTORIES AND GUIDES

Barsamian, Jacques, & François Jouffa - *Génération Johnny* (Gründ, Paris) 2010
**Well-written history of the yé-yé phenomenon with lots of photographs.**

Brierre, Jean-Dominique - *Jazz français* (Hors collection, Paris) 2000
**Good account of French jazz.**

Brillé, Michel, & Christian Gauffre - *L'aventure Salut les copains*
(Éditions du Layeur, Paris) 2009
**Coffee table-sized book with superb account of the history of the radio show.**

Brunschwig, Chantal, Louis-Jean Calvet & Jean-Claude Klein -
*Cent ans de chanson française* (Éditions du Seuil, Paris) 1981
**Pocket-sized encyclopaedia of French pop from 1880 to 1980.**

Calon, Olivier - *Chanson: Les années 50* (L'Archipel, Paris) 2004
**The story of *chanson* during the fifties.**

Chalvidant, Jean, & Hervé Mouvet -
*La plus belle histoire des groupes de rock français des années 60*
(Fernand Lanore, Paris) 2001
**Brief encyclopedia covering around 30 French groups.**

Dawson, Jim - *The Twist* (Faber & Faber, Boston, MA) 1995 *In English*
**The story of the twist dance craze.**

Deluxe, Jean-Emmanuel – *Yé-Yé Girls Of 60's French Pop*
(Feral House, Port Townsend, WA) 2013 *In English*
**Glossy overview of the yé-yé girl singers**

Dicale, Bertrand – *Ces chansons qui font l'histoire* (Textuel, Paris) 2010
**Brief stories about selected (mainly) French songs and their impact on history/society**

Gambaccini, Paul, Jonathan Rice and Tony Brown -
*The Complete Eurovision Song Contest Companion 1999*
(Pavilion, London) 1999 *In English*
**The story of a never-ending success story.**

Gosselin, Michel - *Twist Again* (Alternatives, Paris) 1999
**History of dance crazes in France from the sixties through to the nineties.**

Gourbin, Bernard - *Stars des sixties* (Ouest-France, Rennes) 1997
**A brief look at the usual big names.**

Fabien Lecœuvre – *Le petit Lecœuvre illustré* (Rocher, Paris) 2012
**Potted histories of more than 500 French songs, from 1792 to the new millenium**

Leproux, Henri - *Le temple du rock* (Robert Laffont, Paris) 1982
**The story of the famous Parisian rock'n'roll club, the Golf Drouot.**

Liesenfeld, Thierry - *Rock and roll à la française*
(Éditions Saphyr/Kalohé Production, Zimmerbach) 2010
**Fascinating account of the birth of rock'n'roll in fifties' France, published with 6-CD box set.**

Loosely, David L. -
*Popular Music In Contemporary France (Authenticity, Politics, Debate)*
(Berg, Oxford) 2003  *In English*
**Although rather academic in tone and focused on contemporary pop, this provides a decent background look at the fifties, sixties and seventies.**

Picaud, Loïc - *L'odyssée du rock français* (Fetjaine, Paris) 2009
**Short history of rock in France.**

Quillen, Christophe - *Nos années Salut les copains 1959-76* (Flammarion, Paris) 2009
**History of the magazine and the radio show with lots of illustrations.**

Rioux, Lucien - *50 ans de chanson française* (L'Archipel, Paris) 1992
**A solid history of French pop and *chanson* since the forties.**

Sabatier, Benoît - *Nous sommes jeunes, nous sommes fiers* (Hachette, Paris) 2007
**Excellent history of popular culture in post-war France.**

Saka, Pierre - *Les années twist* (Édition No. 1, Paris) 1996
**Released to tie in with a TV series, this book charts the course of the sixties in France.**

Saka, Pierre - *La chanson française: À travers ses succès* (Larousse, Paris) 1999
**Attractive coffee-table book covering the history of French popular song.**

Saka, Pierre, & Yann Plougastel - *La chanson française et francophone*
(Larousse, Paris) 1999
**Straightforward and easy-to-use encyclopedia of French rock, pop and *chanson*.**

Sweeney, Philip - *Virgin Directory Of World Music* (Virgin, London) 1991  *In English*
**Small but useful guide to the indigenous styles of music played around the world, including France.**

Verlant, Gilles (ed.) - *L'encyclopédie de la chanson française*
(Hors Collection, Paris) 1997
**Excellent, large-format encyclopaedia of French pop throughout the twentieth century.**

Verlant, Gilles (ed.) - *L'encyclopédie du rock français* (Hors Collection, Paris) 2000
**A companion volume to the above title, this time focusing exclusively on French rock music.**

Vian, Boris - *Manual Of Saint-Germain-des-Prés* (Rizzoli, New York) 2005
*In English, translated by Paul Knobloch*
**Vian's famous 1951 treatise on the bohemian quarter of Paris.**

Wangermée, Robert (ed.) - *Dictionnaire de la chanson en Wallonie et à Bruxelles*
(Mardaga, Brussels, Belgium) 1995
**Concise encyclopedia of French-language pop and *chanson* in Belgium.**

## DISCOGRAPHIES

Bouderlique, Pierre, & Jacques Leblanc (eds.) -
*Jukebox magazine: L'argus du disque – Les 33 tours 25 & 30 cm français*
(Jacques Leblanc Éditions, Paris) 1999 *(2 volumes)*
**Indispensable guides to the original 10" and 12" LPs of the era.**
**Volume 1: A-K; Volume 2: L-Z.**

Leblanc, Jacques (ed.) -
*Jukebox magazine: L'argus du disque – Les Super 45 tours français années 50/60*
(Jacques Leblanc Éditions, Paris) 1998, 1999, 2002, 2003, 2004 *(five volumes)*
**Equally indispensible guides to EP releases.**
**Volume 1: A-C; Volume 2: D-G; Volume 3: H-M; Volume 4: N-R; Volume 5: S-Z.**

Lesueur, Daniel - *Johnny Hallyday: Discographie complète et cotations*
(Alternatives, Paris) 1999
**Complete discography and price guide to the work of Johnny Hallyday.**

Vinci, José - *45 Révolutions par minute: Discographie rock français depuis 1954*
(Self-published, Fontenay) 2002
**A selective listing of French rock (and some pop) single and EP releases covering a period of more than thirty years.**


## FRENCH HIT PARADES AND OTHER CHART LISTINGS

Ferment, Fabrice - *40 ans de tubes 1960-2000* (Larivière, Clichy) 2001
Lesueur, Daniel - *Hit parades 1950-1998* (Alternatives/Parallèles, Paris) 1999
Suiveng, Yannick - *Dictionnaire des tubes en France*
(Carrefour du Net, Domptin) 2010

Various issues of the now-defunct *Platine* magazine featured reprints of some charts (*La Bourse des chansons*, *Music-Hall* and *Salut les copains*).

Various issues of the now-defunct *Jukebox magazine* featured reprints of the charts from *Disco revue*.


## INTERNATIONAL HIT PARADES AND OTHER CHART LISTINGS
*In English if published in an English-speaking country, otherwise in the local language.*

### Australia
Barnes, Jim & Stephen Scanes - *The Book: Top 40 Research* (9th ed.)
(Top 40 Research, Riverstone, NSW) 2015
Kent, David - *Australian Chart Book 1940-1969*
(Australian Chart Book Pty. Ltd., Turramurra, NSW) 2005
Kent, David - *Australian Chart Book 1970-1992*
(Australian Chart Book Pty. Ltd., St. Ives, NSW) 1993
Ryan, Gavin - *Adelaide Chart Book 1959-2002*
(Moonlight Publishing, Golden Square, VIC) 2003
Ryan, Gavin - *Brisbane Chart Book 1956-2002*
(Moonlight Publishing, Golden Square, VIC) 2003
Ryan, Gavin - *Melbourne Chart Book 1956-2002*
(Moonlight Publishing, Golden Square, VIC) 2003
Ryan, Gavin - *Perth Music Charts 1989-2006*
(Moonlight Publishing, Golden Square, VIC) 2007
Ryan, Gavin - *Sydney Pop Music Charts 1953-2003*
(Moonlight Publishing, Golden Square, VIC) 2004

**Belgium**
Collin, Robert - *Het Belgisch Hitboek* (Uitgwverij CODA, Antwerp) 1994

**Canada**
Kennedy, Ted - *Charts Canada* (Canadian Chart Research, Canada) 1994
Tarling, Brian – *CHUM's Charted Songs* (Self-published, Vancouver) 2019

**Germany**
*See* West Germany

**Ireland**
Gogan, Larry - *The Larry Gogan Book Of Irish Chart Hits*
  (Maxwell Publications, Dublin) 1987

**Italy**
Racca, Guido - *50 Anni di Superclassifica Singoli, Sorrisi e Canzoni TV* (2nd ed.)
  (Self-published through Lulu Press, Morrisville, NC) 2013
Racca, Guido - *Hiiiiit Parade: Tutto Sulla Hit Parade RAI dai 1967 al 1994*
  (Self-published through Lulu Press, Morrisville, NC) 2012
Racca, Guido – *Musica e Dischi Classifiche Mensili Singoli 1959-2019*
  (Self-published through Lulu Press, Morrisville, NC) 2019
Salvatori, Dario - *Storia Dell'Hit Parade*
  (Gremese Editore, Rome) 1989
Spinetoli, John Joseph - *Artisti in Classifica (Singoli) 1960-1999*
  (Musica e Dischi, Milan) 2000

**Netherlands**
Van Slooten, Johan - *Hit Dossier 1939 tot 1998* (7th ed.)
  (Becht Haarlem, Bloemendaal) 1998

**New Zealand**
Freeman, Warwick - *New Zealand Top 20 Singles* (2nd ed.)
  (Top Pop Books, Auckland) 1993
Freeman, Warwick - *New Zealand Top 20 Singles Of The Sixties (Compiled)*
  (Self-published, Auckland) 2017
Scapolo, Dean - *The Complete New Zealand Music Charts 1966-2006*
  (Transpress, Wellington) 2007

**Norway**
Gilde, Tore - *Den Store Norske Hitboka* (Exlex Forlag, Oslo) 1994

**Spain**
Salaverri, Fernando - *Sóló Éxitos Año à Año 1959-2002*
  (Iberautor Promociones Culturales, Madrid) 2005

**Sweden**
Gurell, Lars – *Svensktoppen i våra hjärtan*
  (Premium Publishing, Stockholm) 1996
Hallberg, Eric & Ulf Henningsson - *Tio i Topp med de Utslagna på Försök 1961-1974*
  (Premium Publishing. Stockholm) 2012
Högen, Heta - *Poporama 1974-84*
  (Premium Publishing, Stockholm) 1992
Wendt, Wille - *Topplistan: The Official Swedish Single & Album Charts* (1st ed.)
  (Premium Publishing, Stockholm) 1993

## UK

Driscoll, Colin – *Hits That Missed: The UK Bubbling Under Chart 1954-1961*
  (Music Mentor Books, York) 2019
Henson, Brian & Colin Morgan - *First Hits: The Book of Sheet Music 1946-1959*
  (Boxtree, London) 1989
Jasper, Tony (ed.) - *20 Years Of British Record Charts 1955-1975*
  (Queen Anne Press, London) 1976
Readioff, Lonnie – *The Chart Book – The Decade Series*
  *The Albums Volume 1 1956-1969*
  (E-book, self-published via **www.TheChartBook.co.uk**), 2017
Readioff, Lonnie – *The Chart Book – The Decade Series*
  *Volume 1: The 1950's Singles*
  (E-book, self-published via **www.TheChartBook.co.uk**), 2017
Readioff, Lonnie – *The Chart Book – The Decade Series*
  *Volume 2: The 1960's Singles*
  (E-book, self-published via **www.TheChartBook.co.uk**), 2017
Readioff, Lonnie – *The Chart Book – The Decade Series*
  *Volume 3: The 1970's Singles*
  (E-book, self-published via **www.TheChartBook.co.uk**), 2018
Readioff, Lonnie – *The Chart Book – The Specials*
  *The Disc Single and Album Charts 1958-1967*
  (E-book, self-published via **www.TheChartBook.co.uk**), 2017
Readioff, Lonnie – *The Chart Book – The Specials*
  *The Melody Maker EP Charts 1959-1963*
  (E-book, self-published via **www.TheChartBook.co.uk**), 2017
Readioff, Lonnie – *The Chart Book – The Specials*
  *The Melody Maker Singles Charts 1956-1969*
  (E-book, self-published via **www.TheChartBook.co.uk**), 2018
Readioff, Lonnie – *The Chart Book – The Specials*
  *Record Mirror Singles 1955-1962*
  (E-book, self-published via **www.TheChartBook.co.uk**), 2017
Rees, Dafydd, *et al.* - *40 Years Of NME Charts*
  (Boxtree, London) 1992
Roberts, David (ed.) - *British Hit Singles & Albums* (17th ed.)
  (Guinness, London) 2004
Waters, Steve - *The British Hit Singles January 1940–October 1952*
  (RockHistory Ltd., London) 2014
White, George R. - *British Hit EPs 1955-1989* (2nd ed.)
  (Music Mentor Books, York) 2014

## US

Albert, George & Frank Hoffmann -
  *The Cash Box Black Contemporary Singles Charts 1960-1984*
  (Scarecrow, Meutchen, NJ) 1986
Whitburn, Joel - *Bubbling Under: Singles And Albums*
  (Record Research, Menomonee Falls, WI) 1998
Whitburn, Joel - *Cash Box Looking Ahead Pop Hits 101-150: 1959-1993*
  (Record Research, Menomonee Falls, WI) 2014
Whitburn, Joel - *Cash Box Pop Hits 1952-1996*
  (Record Research, Menomonee Falls, WI) 2014
Whitburn, Joel - *Cash Box Regional Hits 1956*
  (Record Research, Menomonee Falls, WI) 2018
Whitburn, Joel - *Cash Box Regional Hits 1957*
  (Record Research, Menomonee Falls, WI) 2018

Whitburn, Joel - *Cash Box Regional Hits 1958*
  (Record Research, Menomonee Falls, WI) 2019
Whitburn, Joel - *Hit Country Records: Music Vendor/Record World 1954-1982*
  (Record Research, Menomonee Falls, WI) 2015
Whitburn, Joel - *Hit Records: Music Vendor/Record World 1954-1982*
  (Record Research, Menomonee Falls, WI) 2012
Whitburn, Joel - *Hit Records 101-150: Music Vendor/Record World 1959-1982*
  (Record Research, Menomonee Falls, WI) 2012
Whitburn, Joel - *Hot Dance / Disco 1974-2003*
  (Record Research, Menomonee Falls, WI) 2003
Whitburn, Joel - *Pop Hits Singles And Albums 1940-1954*
  (Record Research, Menomonee Falls, WI) 2002
Whitburn, Joel - *Pop Memories 1890-1954*
  (Record Research, Menomonee Falls, WI) 1986
Whitburn, Joel – *Radio & Records: Top Pop Hits 1973-2009*
  (Record Research, Menomonee Falls, WI) 2019
Whitburn, Joel - *Top Adult Songs 1961-2006*
  (Record Research, Menomonee Falls, WI) 2007
Whitburn, Joel - *Top Country Singles 1944-1993*
  (Record Research, Menomonee Falls, WI) 1993
Whitburn, Joel - *Top Pop Singles 1955-2014*
  (Record Research, Menomonee Falls, WI) 2015
Whitburn, Joel - *Top R&B Singles 1942-1988*
  (Record Research, Menomonee Falls, WI) 1988

**West Germany**
Ehnert, Günter - *Hit Bilanz: Deutsche Chart Singles 1956-1980*
  (Taurus Press, Hamburg) 1990
Ehnert, Günter - *Hit Bilanz: Deutsche Chart Singles 1981-1990*
  (Taurus Press, Hamburg) 1991


## PHOTO BOOKS

Périer, Jean-Marie - *Mes années 60* (Filipacchi, Paris) 1999
Périer, Jean-Marie - *Mes années 60 (Tome 2)* (Filipacchi, Paris) 2000
Perry, Georges (ed.) - *Paris dans les années 60* (La Martinière, Paris) 2001
Thomas, Marcel & Éric Zimmermann: *Chanson française – 200 portraits inédits*
  (Didier Carpentier, Paris) 1997


## MAGAZINES

*Club des Années 60* (Collectif – Club des Années 60, La Picaudière)
  **Fanzine issued three times a year since 1986 to members of the club of the same name.
  For details of how to join the club and how to buy back issues, contact the magazine at:
  Club des Années 60, Route de la Gare, F-42310 La Picaudière, France.**

*Je chante* (Panorama de la Chanson, Chelles)
  **Quarterly magazine dedicated to *la chanson française* in all its forms. For details of how
  to subscribe and a full list of back issues, see www.jechantemagazine.com**

*Jukebox magazine* (Jacques Leblanc Éditions, Paris)
  **The absolute bible for fans of sixties' French pop, now no longer in business. Back
  issues can be picked up online at Rakuten, eBay, and elsewhere.**

*Mojo* (EMAP, London) *In English*
> **Monthly magazine covering music across the spectrum, including occasional articles of French pop For details of how to subscribe and other information, see www.mojo4music.com.**

*Platine* (Platine, Boulogne)
> **Monthly magazine devoted to French popular song in all its forms, sadly now defunct. For details of how to purchase back issues, contact the magazine at: 6 rue Damiens, F-92100 Boulogne, France.**

*Record Collector* (Diamond Publishing, London) *In English*
> **Monthly magazine covering music across the spectrum, including occasional articles of French pop. For details of how to subscribe and a full list of back issues, see www.recordcollectormag.com.**

*Shindig!* (Silverback Publishing, Sutton) *In English*
> **Monthly magazine covering a range of music from the sixties to the present day, including occasional articles (some by the author of this book) on French pop. For details of how to subscribe and a full list of back issues, see www.shindig-magazine.com.**

# Appendix IV

## RECOMMENDED WEBSITES

The amount of information available on the Web seems to grow daily, and by the time this book is in print the sites listed below will have been joined by many others of variable quality, while some, sadly, will have disappeared. Not all the sites listed here are 'official' websites, but all offer sufficient interest to make them worthy of inclusion. Most are in French, although some are in English and others offer bilingual (or even multi-lingual) versions.

The online radio stations listed are the ones which to my mind feature the best selection of French sixties' pop and *chanson* (as well as more recent material), although sadly not French rock. I have not included 'blog' sites that make such material available, legally or otherwise.

Finally, the shops listed here all carry a decent range of *yé-yé*, *chanson* and French rock and pop material, and are readily accessible online. There are likely to be stores in the UK and US where such material is available, but I have confined myself here to listing French stores/marketplaces that offer a range unlikely to be available abroad. Sadly, in the years I have been writing, many great shops have gone to the wall, so please support those that remain.

### General Sites

| | |
|---|---|
| Belgian pop music | www.houbi.com/belpop |
| | www.memoire60-70.be |
| Discographies | www.45cat.com |
| | www.discogs.com |
| | www.encyclopedisque.fr |
| | discographypagebelgium.blogspot.com |
| French rock'n'roll | www.amourdurocknroll.fr |
| French singers | www.rfimusic.com |
| Girl singers | www.readysteadygirls.eu |
| Scopitones | www.stim.com/Stim-x/9.4/scopitone/scopitone-09.4.html |
| *Yé-yé* singers | www.retrojeunesse60.com |

### Artist Websites

| | |
|---|---|
| Adamo | www.adamosalvatore.com |
| Richard Anthony | richard-anthony.fr.gd |

| | |
|---|---|
| Isabelle Aubret | www.isabelle-aubret.com |
| Charles Aznavour | www.charlesaznavour.com |
| Barbara | www.passion-barbara.net |
| Brigitte Bardot | www.fondationbrigittebardot.fr |
| Guy Béart | jack200.free.fr/beart |
| Georges Brassens | www.lesamisdegeorges.com |
| Jacques Brel | www.jacquesbrel.be |
| Petula Clark | www.petulaclark.net |
| Annie Cordy | www.anniecordy.com |
| Dalida | www.dalida.com |
| Sacha Distel | www.sachadistel.com |
| Léo Ferré | www.leo-ferre.com |
| Serge Gainsbourg | www.sergegainsbourg.com |
| Johnny Hallyday | www.johnnyhallyday.com |
| Françoise Hardy | www.francoise-hardy.com |
| | www.geroki.de |
| Gillian Hills | www.gillianhills.com |
| Nancy Holloway | www.nancyholloway.com |
| Enrico Macias | www.enricomacias.net |
| Eddy Mitchell | www.eddymitchell.net |
| Nana Mouskouri | www.nana-mouskouri.net |
| Claude Nougaro | www.nougaro.com |
| Édith Piaf | www.little-sparrow.co.uk |
| Django Reinhardt | papabecker.com/All_About_Django_Reinhardt.htm |
| Line Renaud | www.linerenaud.com |
| Dick Rivers | www.dick-rivers.com |
| Jean Sablon | www.jeansablon.com |
| Henri Salvador | www.henrisalvador-discographie.com |
| Sheila | ondit.unblog.fr |
| Sœur Sourire | deckers66.homestead.com |
| Vince Taylor | www.rockabilly.nl/artists/vtaylor.htm |
| Charles Trenet | www.charles-trenet.net |
| Sylvie Vartan | www.sylvissima.com |
| | www.sylvie-vartan.com |

## French Charts/Hit Parades

| | |
|---|---|
| *La Bourse des chansons* | www.ukmix.org/forums/viewtopic.php?f=5&t=10225&sid=d3472a9854ee4a03ba1aa99048542b2f |
| *Disco revue* | www.ukmix.org/forums/viewtopic.php?f=5&t=94938&sid=d3472a9854ee4a03ba1aa99048542b2f |
| *France disques* | www.ukmix.org/forums/viewtopic.php?f=5&t=102090&sid=d3472a9854ee4a03ba1aa99048542b2f |
| *Music-Hall* | https://www.ukmix.org/forums/viewtopic.php?t=109971&f=5 |

| | |
|---|---|
| *Salut les copains* | www.ukmix.org/forums/viewtopic.php?f=5&t=107733 &sid=d3472a9854ee4a03ba1aa99048542b2f www.ukmix.org/forums/viewtopic.php?f=5&t=126753 &p=6544960 http://cicatrice.hautetfort.com/archives/category/ hit-parades-slc/index-8.html |
| French charts (synthesis) | www.infodisc.fr www.top-france.fr |

## International Charts/Hit Parades

| | |
|---|---|
| *Billboard Hits of the World* | www.billboard.com |
| *Cash Box International* | https://archive.org/details/cashbox |
| International charts (general and selected) | http://artisteschartsventes.blogspot.co.uk |
| Austria | www.austriancharts.at |
| Canada (Quebec) | www.banq.qc.ca/collections/collections_patrimoniales/ musique/collection_numerique/bd_specialisee/palmares/ |
| Denmark | https://web.archive.org/web/20181209082040/ http://danskehitlister.dk |
| Finland | suomensinglelistat.blogspot.co.uk wiki.pomus.net/wiki/Etusivu |
| Ireland | www.irishcharts.ie www.ukmix.org/showthread.php?31291 |
| Israel | www.ukmix.org/forums/viewtopic.php?f=5&t=126486 www.ukmix.org/forums/viewtopic.php?t=47636&f=5 |
| Japan | www.ukmix.org/forums/viewtopic.php?f=5&t= 15869&start=1900 www.ukmix.org/forums/viewtopic.php?f=5&t= 117075&hilit=japan www.ukmix.org/forums/viewtopic.php?f=5&t= 119356&hilit=japan www.ukmix.org/forums/viewtopic.php?f=5&t= 126543&p=6539321 |
| Netherlands (radio) | www.radiotrefpunt.nl |
| New Zealand | |
|    General | www.charts.nz- |
|    *Lever Hit Parade* | www.flavourofnz.co.nz/index.php?qpageID=Lever %20hit%20parades#n_view_location |
|    *Playdate* | www.flavourofnz.co.nz/index.php?qpageID=Playdat e%20charts#n_view_location |
| South Africa | https://sacharts.wordpress.com |
| Spain | |
|    *Superventas* | http://listadesuperventas.blogspot.co.uk |
| Sweden | |
|    *Kvällstoppen* (1962-75) | www.kvallstoppen.se |
| UK | |
|    Pirate radio | www.offshoreradio.co.uk |
|    Radio London | www.radiolondon.co.uk |

US
    *Your Hit Parade*            https://archive.org/details/YourHitParadeCharts19351940/page/n1

## Radio Stations / Video Clips

| | |
|---|---|
| Bide et Musique | www.bide-et-musique.com |
| Nostalgie | www.nostalgie.fr |
| YouTube | www.youtube.com |

## Record Labels:

| | |
|---|---|
| Frémaux | www.fremeaux.com |
| Magic Records | www.magic-records.com |
| Marianne Mélodie | www.mariannemelodie.fr |

## Shops

| | |
|---|---|
| Amazon | www.amazon.fr |
| Arlequin (Brussels) | www.arlequin.net |
| Balades Sonores (Paris/Brussels) | www.baladessonores.com |
| Bouldingue (Lyon) | www.bouldingue.fr |
| La Bourse (Lyon) | www.librairielabourse.com |
| CD and LP | www.cdandlp.com |
| The Collector (Brussels) | www.the-collector.be |
| Crocodisc (Paris) | www.crocodisc.com |
| Les Enfants de Bohème (Rennes) | www.lesenfantsdeboheme.fr |
| FNAC | www.fnac.com |
| Gibert Joseph | www.gibert.com |
| Lucky Records (Paris) | www.lucky-records.com |
| Monster Melodies (Paris) | www.monstermelodies.fr |
| Paralleles (Paris) | www.librairie-paralleles.com |
| Rakuten | www.rakuten.fr |

# GLOSSARY OF TERMS

*bal-musette* — Venue at which *musette* was performed.

*café-concert, caf' conc'* — Café featuring entertainment by professional or semi-professional singers.

*chanson (française)* — A traditional form of lyric-driven song unique to France. It can be distinguished from the rest of French 'pop' music in that it follows the rhythms of the French language, rather than those of English, and aspires to a higher lyrical standard.

*chanson fantaisiste* — A song designed purely for entertainment, often comic in intent and delivery. Antonym of *chanson réaliste*.

*chanson paillarde* — A type of singalong music, often erotic or scatalogical, occasionally political, and usually derived from old folk songs.

*chanson réaliste* — A song with a focus on real life, typically about the lives of Paris' poor working class inhabitants. Antonym of *chanson fantaisiste*.

*chansonnier/chansonnière* — A writer or singer of *chansons*.

*chanteur/chanteuse réaliste* — A writer or singer, most often female, of *chansons réalistes* (see above).

*guinguette* — Popular drinking establishment including a restaurant and/or dancing. A lively style of accordion-based dance music performed at these venues.

*musette* — A sensual, polka-styled, accordion-driven form of dance music that first became popular in Paris in the 1880s.

*variétés* — Name by which the music performed in music halls was known. The term correlates roughly to the Anglo-American 'popular song' and is still in use today for what British and American audiences would term 'pop' (as opposed to 'rock') music.

# INDEX OF PEOPLE'S NAMES

1    Groups whose names were prefixed by 'Les', 'Los', etc, are listed with the appropriate definite article. Those whose names began with 'The' (i.e. most US and UK groups, many Belgian and a few French) are listed without.

2    Many French group names included a grammatically incorrect 'greengrocer's apostrophe' (for example, Les Beaver's, Les Gam's). For accuracy and authenticity, the original spellings have been preserved throughout this book.

# INDEX OF SONGS AND MUSICAL WORKS

1   French, Belgian and most other foreign releases only have the first word capitalised, in accordance ith the convention in those countries. Song titles which are capitalised throughout were either US or UK releases.

2   Alternative titles and alternative spellings of titles are shown in square brackets. For example, where 'Le' appears in square brackets, the song appeared both with and without this word.

# INDEX OF VENUES

# INDEX OF FILMS AND SHOWS

For operas and operettas see Index of Songs and Musical Works.

# ILLUSTRATIONS & PHOTO CREDITS

All illustrations are from the Music Mentor Books archive unless otherwise stated.
All photos except those by Rancurel Photothèque and Michel Rigot are public domain.
Record company logos appear by kind permission of the respective copyright holders.

Ads on pages 38, 98, 129, 163, 174, 175, 194, 198, 225, 316 and 329 from Author's collection;

Chart on page 26 courtesy *Disco Revue*, from Author's collection; chart on page 27 courtesy *Salut les copains*, from Author's collection.

EP sleeves on pages 185, 197 (top), 212 (top), 214 (top), 215 (bottom), 218, 283, 289, 313, 324 (top), 328, 330, 345 and 353 from Author's collection; EP sleeves on pages 256, 312, 331 and 339 courtesy Terry Kay.

LP sleeve on page 212 (bottom) from Author's collection.

Magazine covers on pages 25, 241 and 245 from Author's collection.

Photo of Édith Piaf on the back cover courtesy of Disques Columbia; photo of Maurice Chevalier on the back cover courtesy Paramout Pictures; photo of Johnny Hallyday on the back cover courtesy of Disques Vogue; photos on pages 210, 323 and 355 © and by Michel Rigot, courtesy Christian Nauwelaers; photos on pages 30, 37, 39, 45, 50, 51, 53, 54, 64 (top), 65, 68, 70, 71, 77, 81, 82, 86, 91, 101, 103, 142, 251 and 387 by unknown photographer/studio; photos on pages 31, 48, 74 and 237 by unknown photographer/studio, from Author's collection; photos on pages 34 and 40 courtesy Paramount Pictures; photos on pages 41, 42 and 47 by Studio Piaz (Teddy Piaz); photos on pages 43, 64 (bottom), 115 and 132 by Studio Harcourt; photos on pages 55 and 56 courtesy Gray-Film; photo on page 130 courtesy Disques Vogue; photo on page 137 courtesy Les Films Impéria, Productions Georges de Beauregard and SNC; photo on page 192 © and by Rancurel Photothèque, courtesy Christian Nauwelaers; photos on pages 278 and 351 by unknown photographer, courtesy Christian Nauwelaers.

Poster on page 33 courtesy Pathé, from Author's collection; poster on page 36 from Author's collection; posters on page 46 and 79 courtesy Columbia, from Author's collection; poster on page 110 courtesy La Voix de son Maître.

Record company logos: Columbia logo on page 19, Odéon and Palette logos on page 21, and Teppaz logo on page 23 from Author's collection.

Sheet music on page 313 from Author's collection; sheet music on page 363 courtesy Christian Nauwelaers.

# OTHER TITLES FROM MUSIC MENTOR BOOKS

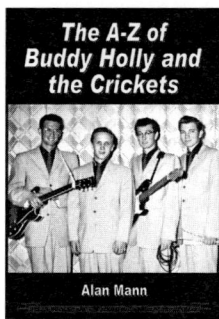

### The A-Z of Buddy Holly and the Crickets
**Alan Mann**
ISBN-13: 978-0-9547068-0-7 *(paperback, 320 pages)*

*The A-Z of Buddy Holly and the Crickets* draws together a mass of Holly facts and info from a variety of published sources, as well as the author's own original research, and presents them in an easy-to-use encyclopaedic format. Now in its third edition, it has proved to be a popular and valuable reference work on this seminal rock'n'roller. It is a book that every Holly fan will want to keep at their fingertips. It is a book about a musical genius who will never be forgotten.

### American Rock'n'Roll: The UK Tours 1956-72
**Ian Wallis**
ISBN-13: 978-0-9519888-6-2 *(paperback, 424 pages)*

The first-ever detailed overview of every visit to these shores by American (and Canadian!) rock'n'rollers. It's all here: over 400 pages of tour itineraries, support acts, show reports, TV appearances and other items of interest. Illustrated with dozens of original tour programmes, ads, ticket stubs and great live shots, many rare or previously unpublished.

### The Big Beat Scene
**Royston Ellis**
ISBN-13: 978-0-9562679-1-7 *(paperback, 184 pages)*

Originally published in 1961, *The Big Beat Scene* was the first contemporary account of the teenage music scene in Britain. Written before the emergence of the Beatles, and without the benefit of hindsight, this fascinating document provides a unique, first-hand insight into the popularity and relevance of jazz, skiffle and rock'n'roll at a time when Cliff Richard & The Shadows were at the cutting edge of pop, and the social attitudes prevailing at the time.

### British Hit EPs 1955-1989
**George R. White**
ISBN-13: 978-0-9562679-6-2 *(paperback, 320 pages)*

Fully revised and expanded second edition of the only chart book dedicated to British Hit EPs. Includes a history of the format, an artist-by-artist listing of every 7-inch hit EP from 1955 to 1989 (with full track details for each record), a trivia section, the official UK EP charts week by week, and much more. Profusely illustrated with over 600 sleeve shots.

### Brook Benton: There Goes That Song Again
### Herwig Gradischnig & Hans Maitner
**ISBN-13: 978-0-9562679-8-6** *(paperback, 434 pages)*

This first ever in-depth study of this magnificent singer's life and career is the result of a collaboration between two Austrian music experts and long-time Benton fans. The biographical part is based on an album of newspaper cuttings personally compiled by Benton and contains the singer's views on a wide variety of topics, as well as reviews of his work. The exhaustive discography by Hans Maitner identifies over 660 known recordings by Brook. Profusely illustrated with many rare photographs, vintage ads, record sleeves etc.

### The Chuck Berry International Directory (Volume 1)
### Morten Reff
**ISBN-13: 978-0-9547068-6-9** *(paperback, 486 pages)*

For the heavyweight Berry fan. Everything you ever wanted to know about Chuck Berry, in four enormous volumes compiled by the world-renowned Norwegian Berry collector and authority, Morten Reff. This volume contains discographies for over 40 countries, plus over 700 rare label and sleeve illustrations.

### The Chuck Berry International Directory (Volume 2)
### Morten Reff
**ISBN-13: 978-0-9547068-7-6** *(paperback, 532 pages)*

The second of four volumes in this extensive reference work dedicated to rock'n'roll's most influential guitarist and composer. Contains details of bootlegs; radio albums; movies; TV shows; video and DVD releases; international tour itineraries; hits, achievements and awards; Berry's songs, roots, and influence on other artists; tributes; Chuck Berry in print; fan clubs and websites; plus annotated discographies of pianist Johnnie Johnson (post-Berry) and the ultimate Berry copyist, Eddy Clearwater.

### The Chuck Berry International Directory (Volume 3)
### Morten Reff
**ISBN-13: 978-0-9547068-8-3** *(paperback, 608 pages)*

The third volume in this award-winning reference work dedicated to rock'n'roll's most influential guitarist and composer. Contains details of over 4,500 cover versions of Chuck Berry songs including many rarities from around the world. Alphabetical listing by artist (brief biography, comprehensive details of recordings and relevant releases, illuminating commentary and critiques), plus dozens of label and sleeve illustrations.

### The Chuck Berry International Directory (Volume 4)
### Morten Reff
ISBN-13: 978-0-9547068-9-0 *(paperback, 546 pages)*

The fourth and final volume of this groundbreaking work contains an A-Z of cover versions of Chuck Berry songs, details of hit cover versions, cover versions in the movies and on TV, over 900 Berry soundalikes, a 'No Chuck' section (non-Berry songs with similar titles), games, and even a brief chapter on Chuck Berry karaoke! Also over 100 pages of additions and updates to *Volumes 1, 2* and *3*, plus useful indices of Berry's releases by title and by label.

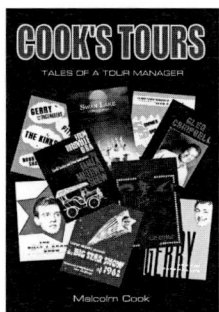

### Cook's Tours: Tales of a Tour Manager
### Malcolm Cook
ISBN-13: 978-0-9562679-4-8 *(paperback, 324 pages)*

Throughout his 44 years in the entertainment industry, Malcolm Cook met and worked with some of the biggest names in show business. In this humorous, fast-paced biographical account, Cook lifts the lid on what it takes to keep a show on the road and artists and audiences happy. It's all here: transport problems, unscrupulous promoters, run-ins with East German police, hassles with the Mafia, tea with the Duke of Norfolk, the wind-ups, the laughter, the heartbreak and the tears. A unique insight into what really goes on behind the scenes.

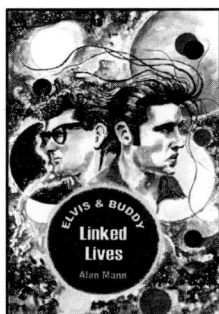

### Elvis & Buddy – Linked Lives
### Alan Mann
ISBN-13: 978-0-9519888-5-5 *(paperback, 160 pages)*

The achievements of Elvis Presley and Buddy Holly have been extensively documented, but until now little if anything has been known about the many ways in which their lives were interconnected. The author examines each artist's early years, comparing their backgrounds and influences, chronicling all their meetings and examining the many amazing parallels in their lives, careers and tragic deaths. Over 50 photos, including many rare/previously unpublished.

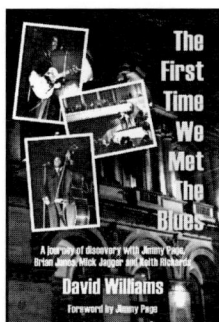

### The First Time We Met The Blues – A journey of discovery with Jimmy Page, Brian Jones, Mick Jagger and Keith Richards
### David Williams
ISBN-13: 978-0-9547068-1-4 *(paperback, 130 pages)*

David Williams was a childhood friend of Led Zeppelin guitar legend, Jimmy Page. The author describes how they discovered the blues together, along with future members of the Rolling Stones. The climax of the book is a detailed account of a momentous journey by van from London to Manchester to see the 1962 *American Folk-Blues Festival*, where they got their first chance to see their heroes in action.

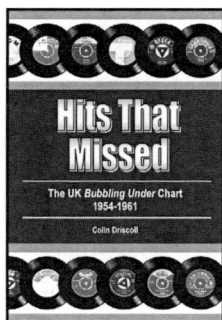

### Hits That Missed – The UK Bubbling Under Chart 1954-61
**Colin Driscoll**
**ISBN-13: 978-0-9562679-9-3** *(paperback, 428 pages)*

*Hits That Missed* presents – for the first time anywhere – a comprehensive listing of all the singles, EPs and LPs that 'bubbled under' the UK hit parade between June 1954 and March 1961. Compiled from dealers' returns, the UK Bubbling Under Chart documents the pre-chart history of records which went on to become hits, as well as details of all those 'also rans' that never made it. A goldmine of information, it is sure to be an invaluable resource for music fans and researchers alike.

### Jet Harris – In Spite of Everything
**Dave Nicolson**
**ISBN-13: 978-0-9562679-2-4** *(paperback, 208 pages)*

As a founder member of the Shadows, and a chart-topper in his own right, bassist Jet Harris scaled the heights of superstardom in the 1960s. A helpless alcoholic for most of his adult life, he also sank to unimaginable depths of despair, leaving a string of broken hearts and shattered lives in his wake. In this unauthorised biography author Dave Nicolson examines his eventful life and career, and how he eventually overcame his addiction to the bottle.

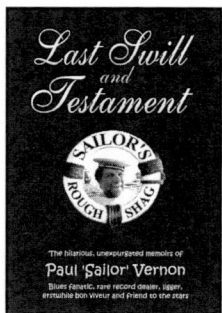

### Last Swill and Testament
#### – The hilarious, unexpurgated memoirs of
**Paul 'Sailor' Vernon**
**ISBN-13: 978-0-9547068-4-5** *(paperback, 228 pages)*

Born in London shortly after the end of World War II, Paul 'Sailor' Vernon came into his own during the 1960s when spotty teenage herberts with bad haircuts began discovering The Blues. For the Sailor it became a lifelong obsession that led him into a whirlwind of activity as a rare record dealer, magazine proprietor/editor, video bootlegger and record company director. It's all here in this one-of-a-kind life history that will leave you reaching for an enamel bucket and a fresh bottle of disinfectant!

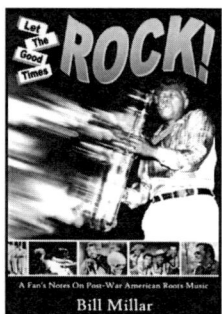

### Let The Good Times Rock!
#### – A Fan's Notes On Post-War American Roots Music
**Bill Millar**
**ISBN-13: 978-0-9519888-8-6** *(paperback, 362 pages)*

For almost four decades, the name 'Bill Millar' has been synonymous with the very best in British music writing. This fabulous book collects together 49 of his best pieces – some previously unpublished – in a thematic compilation covering hillbilly, rockabilly, R&B, rock'n'roll, doo-wop, swamp pop and soul. Includes essays on acappella, doo-wop and blue-eyed soul, as well as detailed profiles of some of the most fascinating and influential personalities of each era.

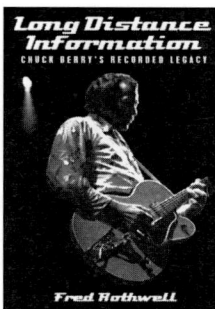

## Long Distance Information
### – Chuck Berry's Recorded Legacy
**Fred Rothwell**
ISBN-13: 978-0-9519888-2-4 *(paperback, 352 pages)*

The lowdown on every recording Chuck Berry has ever made. Includes an overview of his life and career, his influences, the stories behind his most famous compositions, full session details, listings of all his key US/UK vinyl and CD releases (including track details), TV and film appearances, and much, much more. Over 100 illustrations including label shots, vintage ads and previously unpublished photos.

## Mike Sanchez: Big Town Playboy
**Michael Madden (Foreword by Robert Plant)**
ISBN-13: 978-0-9562679-7-9 *(paperback, 314 pages)*

The compelling story of one of the foremost exponents of authentic rhythm & blues and rock'n'roll in the world today. Author Michael Madden has been given full access to a vast archive of material charting Mike Sanchez's journey from his Spanish roots through an eventful 35-year musical career that has seen him progress through the ranks of the Rockets, the Big Town Playboys and Bill Wyman's Rhythm Kings to fronting his own band and performing with some of the biggest names of the rock world including Robert Plant, Eric Clapton, Mick Fleetwood and Jeff Beck.

## More American Rock'n'Roll: The UK Tours 1973-84
**Ian Wallis**
ISBN-13: 978-0-9562679-3-1 *(paperback, 380 pages)*

The long-awaited follow-up to *American Rock'n'Roll: The UK Tours 1956-72*. Like its predecessor, it's crammed full of information about every American or Canadian rock'n'roller who visited Britain during the period covered. If you love rock'n'roll, you will wish to relive memories of all those nights spent in hot, sweaty clubs amongst the honking saxes, pounding pianos and twanging guitars. It is 'the greatest music in the world', and all those wonderful memories can be found again within these pages.

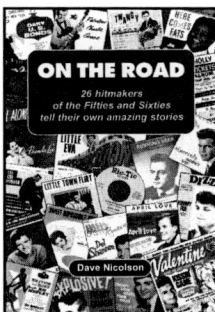

## On The Road
**Dave Nicolson**
ISBN-13: 978-0-9519888-4-8 *(paperback, 256 pages)*

Gary 'US' Bonds, Pat Boone, Freddy Cannon, Crickets Jerry Allison, Sonny Curtis and Joe B. Mauldin, Bo Diddley, Dion, Fats Domino, Duane Eddy, Frankie Ford, Charlie Gracie, Brian Hyland, Marv Johnson, Ben E. King, Brenda Lee, Little Eva, Chris Montez, Johnny Moore (Drifters), Gene Pitney, Johnny Preston, Tommy Roe, Del Shannon, Edwin Starr, Johnny Tillotson and Bobby Vee tell their own fascinating stories. Over 150 illustrations including vintage ads, record sleeves, label shots, sheet music covers, etc

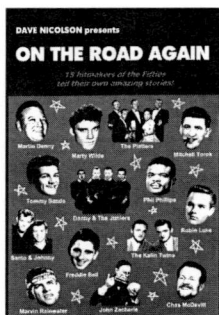

### On The Road Again
### Dave Nicolson
**ISBN-13: 978-0-9519888-9-3** *(paperback, 206 pages)*

Second volume of interviews with the stars of pop and rock'n'roll including Freddie Bell, Martin Denny, Johnny Farina (Santo & Johnny), the Kalin Twins, Robin Luke, Chas McDevitt, Phil Phillips, Marvin Rainwater, Herb Reed (Platters), Tommy Sands, Joe Terranova (Danny & The Juniors), Mitchell Torok, Marty Wilde and the 'Cool Ghoul' himself, John Zacherle.

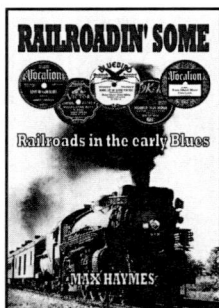

### Railroadin' Some: Railroads In The Early Blues
### Max Haymes
**ISBN-13: 978-0-9547068-3-8** *(paperback, 390 pages)*

This groundbreaking book, written by one of the foremost blues historians in the UK, is based on over 30 years research, exploration and absolute passion for early blues music. It is the first ever comprehensive study of the enormous impact of the railroads on 19th and early 20th Century African American society and the many and varied references to this new phenomenon in early blues lyrics. Includes ballin' the jack, smokestack lightning, hot shots, the bottoms, chain gangs, barrelhouses, hobo jungles and more.

**Music Mentor books are available from all good bookshops, online booksellers, or by mail order from:**

**Music Mentor Books**
**69 Station Road**
**Upper Poppleton**
**YORK YO26 6PZ**
**England**

*Telephone:* **+44 (0)1904 330308**
*Email:* **music.mentor@ntlworld.com**
*Website:* **http://musicmentor0.tripod.com**